Iolanda Perrone

EXPERIMENTAL PSYCHOLOGY

Research Tactics and Their Applications

EXPERIMENTAL PSYCHOLOGY

Research Tactics and Their Applications

D. Chris Anderson
University of Notre Dame

John G. Borkowski
University of Notre Dame

Scott, Foresman and Company   Glenview, Illinois
Dallas, Tex.   Oakland, N. J.   Palo Alto, Cal.   Tucker, Ga.   London, England

To Judson Brown,
and John, Mary, Matt, Kara, Greg

Library of Congress Cataloging in Publication Data

Anderson, David Chris, 1934-
   Experimental psychology.

   Bibliography: p.
   Includes index.
   1. Psychology, Experimental. I. Borkowski,
John G., 1938-   joint author. II. Title.
BF181.B64 1978   150'.7'24   77-25102
ISBN 0-673-07866-3

12345678910-RRC-858483828180797877

ACKNOWLEDGMENTS

Table 1.1. W. F. Hill, *Learning: A Survey of Psychological Interpretations*. New York, Chandler Publishing Company, 1963. Reprinted by permission.   Figure 1.2. From *Behavior Theory and Conditioning* by K. W. Spence. Yale University Press, 1956. Reprinted by permission.   Figure 1.3. From "Human Memory: A Proposed System and Its Control Processes" by R. C. Atkinson and R. M. Shiffrin in K. W. Spence and J. T. Spence (Eds.), *The Psychology of Learning and Motivation: Advances in Research and Theory* (Vol. 2). Academic Press, 1968. Reprinted by permission of the authors and publisher.

Figure 2.1. From "Transfer of Mediational Strategies in Children: The Role of Activity and Awareness During Strategy Acquisition" by J. G. Borkowski, S. Levers, and T. M. Gruenenfelder, *Child Development,* 1976, pp. 779–786, Vol. 47. University of Chicago Press. Reprinted by permission.   Figure 2.2. Figure 1 (p. 21) and excerpt from pp. 21–22 in *Psychology: The Science of Mental Life* by George A. Miller. Copyright © 1962 by George A. Miller. Reprinted by permission of Harper & Row, Publishers, Inc., and Hutchinson Publishing Group, Ltd.

Table 3.2. From "Relearning and the Measurement of Retention" by H. P. Bahrick in *Verbal Learning and Verbal Behavior,* 1967, 6, 79–84. Academic Press, 1967. Reprinted by permission of the author and publisher.

Figure 4.5. Benton J. Underwood, *Experimental Psychology,* © 1949. Reproduced by permission of Prentice-Hall, Inc., Englewood Cliffs, New Jersey.

Quote on p. 207. Ernest Eliel quoted by Jean Horiszny in "The Importance of Being Ernest," *Notre Dame Magazine,* Vol. 1, No. 2, April 1972, pp. 41–45. Reprinted by permission.   Material on pp. 219–230. From "Effects of Anxiety and Interference on Short-Term Memory" by John G. Borkowski and Thomas Mann in *Journal of Experimental Psychology,* 1968, Vol. 78, No. 2, pp. 352–354. Copyright © 1968 by the American Psychological Association. Reprinted by permission.

Preface

This book is about the tools of experimental psychology and their applications in selected content areas. Its purpose is twofold: to provide students with practical and organized guidelines on how to conduct psychological research, and to show how others have successfully used these guidelines to advance the knowledge base of psychology.

The dominant methodological concerns we discuss are placed within broad philosophical and historical perspectives, shedding light on the many ways in which psychology, as a scientific discipline, can add to our storehouse of knowledge. We take a strong stand on the importance of the manipulative research strategy. Our emphasis is on *the experiment* as a way of uncovering the causes of behavioral relationships. We do not ignore correlational and observational strategies, although we primarily consider their potential strengths to initiate research programs and to explore new research domains, as well as their more limited ability to produce information on causal relations among variables and concepts as these relations (or laws) contribute to theory construction.

Our organization and coverage is straightforward. In Part I we cover general methodology and design principles, while in Part II we apply these principles to four content areas. We discuss in Chapter 1 the framework and philosophy of experimental psychology as rooted in the quest for laws, theories, and explanations. In Chapter 2, we focus on the experimental-manipulative strategy, presenting its historical evolution to better understand the experiment as one method for accumulating knowledge. In Chapter 3 we discuss the experimental model and the issues surrounding the development of hypotheses, sample construction, and variable selection. Confounding and how to control it is taken up in detail in Chapter 4. The development and implementation of experimental designs, and data-gathering techniques are discussed in Chapter 5. In Chapter 6, we examine scientific communication skills in general and the techniques of writing experimental research reports in particular.

Chapters 7 to 10 cover methodology and content in the areas of perception and psychophysics, basic learning processes, memory and cognition, and social psychology. Our concern in these latter chapters is not so much that students be exposed to a comprehensive overview of content in each area, but rather that they attain a clear understanding of the interplay between method and experimentation, between experimentation and theory development, and between method and theory as major factors in advancing psychological knowledge. Nonetheless, we can assure the student that a thorough mastery of Chapters 7 through 10 provides a well-balanced familiarization with major themes in perception, learning, memory, and social psychology. Although our text presupposes some minimal acquaintance with elementary statistical methods, we do not introduce statistics in great depth except as they relate to hypothesis formation, sampling, and design.

Anyone who has recently taught an experimental psychology course has most likely encountered problems in maintaining student interest. Tactical material can, at times, seem dull in comparison with the exciting research and theory found in many of the content areas of our discipline. At a time when the sensational, the novel, and the faddish are emphasized in pedagogy, it is especially difficult to convince beginning students of the importance of acquiring basic methodological skills and design techniques. Nonetheless, a solid case still can be made for rigorous grounding in the methodologies of our discipline, not only because of their integral contribution to sound research and theory construction, but more generally because exposure to tactical issues can assist all of us in making everyday discriminations, separating knowledge derived from logical, data-based procedures from statements steeped in subjectivism and rhetoric. William Bevan (1976) states our position succinctly: "The experimental attitude that comes with an understanding of science is essential if we are going to make it in our technologically oriented world. . . . Science must be taught, on the one hand, as a way of finding out about nature and, on the other, as a particular conceptualization of nature acquired through this empirical approach. As a world view, it must be set beside other world views, not to provoke confrontation, but to illuminate the broad experience of man" (pp. 486, 488).

Every discipline is supported by its methodology; there is no substitute for a careful, thorough exposure to tactics and tools and to their diverse applications. In science, this means a commitment to the process of repeating observations and verifying relationships among antecedent and consequent events in a wide variety of contexts and circumstances. The tactics that underlie observation and verification constitute the essence of experimental psychology. Without the proper tactics and tools there can be no laws, and without laws and the theories they stimulate there can be no science. We hope that this text makes both the difficult task of learning methodology and understanding its applications more rewarding for undergraduates, the job of teaching research tactics easier and more focused for instructors.

We want to thank W. Tom Bourbon of Stephen F. Austin State University for contributing Chapter 7 on Psychophysics and Perception and Richard J. Sebastian of the University of Notre Dame for contributing Chapter 10 on Research Tactics in Social Psychology. Part II was enhanced by their expertise in these areas. We owe a special debt of thanks to our consulting editor, Judson Brown, who gave the manuscript very careful, critical, and constructive reading. We profited greatly from his keen insights. We want to thank Professors John Belmont, William Botzum, Vaughn McKim, and Paul Messbarger for commenting on various chapters in Part I, and Charles Crowell and Chris Cunningham for their help with sections of Part II. James Romig and John Nolan of Scott, Foresman made important organizational and editorial suggestions. We acknowledge the work of John Cavanaugh in developing the glossary and discussion questions of Part I. Without the patient efforts of Kay Davis, Peggy Hogan, Kitty Nifong, Mary Smith, and Pat Daily, who typed various drafts of this text, our endeavors would have been tedious and slowed. Finally, we thank our colleagues at Notre Dame, including both faculty and many undergraduate and graduate students, for hearing us out on our biases and perspectives as to what experimental psychology is all about.

D. Chris Anderson
John G. Borkowski

Contents

PART TWO   APPLICATIONS OF RESEARCH TACTICS

9
Chapter

Research Tactics in Complex Learning, Memory, and Cognition by John G. Borkowski   387

List of Boxes

Part One

Research Tactics and Methodology

The Framework of Experimental Psychology

1
Chapter

The game of science is, in principle, without end. He who decides one day that scientific statements do not call for any further tests, and that they can be regarded as verified, retires from the game.

(Popper, 1959, p. 53)

Science is the attempt to explain the existing picture of the world, but this attempt is not based on the adoption of this picture; rather it leads to changes of that picture.

(Agassi, 1966, p. 24)

The search for an understanding of human behavior is as ancient and varied as human history itself. As this search has acquired direction and form, as it has become more systematic, it has qualified for a position in a select company of bodies of knowledge. The scientist and the artist, the theologian and the historian, all engage in scholarly inquiry; their activities, together with the activities of those in other disciplines, contribute to the sum total of human knowledge. Each scholar searches for knowledge and truth, but each limits the pursuit to a particular range of inquiry. Each employs a particular method in order to secure knowledge. Each presents findings and interpretations with a logic appropriate to his or her specific discipline.

Science is but one approach to the discovery and ordering of knowledge. Some of the features that distinguish science from other approaches include the development and use of a special vocabulary marked by precision and clarity; a set of rules for gathering and organizing observations, the primary source of scientific insight; and a process of logical inference that guides decision making.

Although the stereotyped image of the scientist is that of an isolated researcher working in the confines of a remote laboratory, science

1

in the fullest sense is a truly social enterprise (Agassi, 1966). Its observations and methodologies are public, precise, and repeatable in that all sciences rest on the verification of their findings by others. Its explanations are aimed at increasing knowledge of self, others, and the world around us. Its more pragmatic achievements enhance our social welfare.

For science—including psychology, the science of behavior—the primary source of information is controlled observation. Psychology, like the other sciences, has its unique research tactics and established ways of using them, its methodology, to obtain knowledge. _Experimental psychology_ embraces all knowledge obtained through an appropriate application of controlled observations of behavioral phenomena. This is simply another way of saying that experimental psychology is a collection of methods, procedures, and tools that psychologists employ under controlled conditions plus the information that is gathered through the application of these tactics. The information collected by experimental psychologists typically is designed to further our understanding of developmental, motivational, social, perceptual, physiological, and abnormal components of behavior, to name but a few of the content areas of the discipline.

The tactics and tools of experimental psychology are powerful assets for advancing our knowledge of behavior. In brief, the tactics and tools relate to *(a)* the formulation of scientific questions; *(b)* the translations of these questions into the procedures and design of an experiment; *(c)* the careful and controlled execution of the experiment; *(d)* the resulting observations upon which judgments are made about the presence, reliability, and meaning of some behavioral phenomenon; and *(e)* the incorporation of these judgments into a theoretical network.

In the present chapter we will set the stage for the rest of the book by presenting a framework and a philosophy for experimental psychology. We will discuss the origins of scientific knowledge; the job of the scientist in formulating laws, theories, and explanations; and the concept of science as a revolutionary enterprise. Initially, we will locate experimental psychology within the various systems of knowledge and present a rationale for experimentation as the central method for understanding and explaining behavioral events.

ORIGINS OF SCIENTIFIC KNOWLEDGE

Scientific innovations such as moon shots and nuclear-powered, hydroelectric plants are not the achievements of a single generation. All human history provides the background out of which our present knowledge has evolved. To understand better the subject of this book, experimental psychology, we will take a brief but considered journey through a few major systems of thought, each characteristic of certain periods in our intellectual history. Perhaps the most prominent and persistent philosophical approach to knowledge is rationalism, the intellectual fountainhead not only of modern scientific thought but of Western civilization itself (cf. Thonnard, 1956).

Rationalism

Obvious as it appears today, the fundamental assertion of rational philosophy is that every effect has a cause and that all causal sequences are located within the realm of nature. A further assertion is that causal sequences can be grasped by a particular human faculty—reason. An attendant and no less significant claim of the rationalist is that this power to know, and thereby to control the world, is the faculty that distinguishes human beings from other organisms and that gives them their favored position in the universe of created being.

In contrast to practitioners of irrationality and superstition, the rationalist searches for the meaning of phenomena not in myth or folklore, but in the orderliness of nature, permanent and incontrovertible. This initial assumption that the universe is orderly and that humans can discover this orderliness through systematic study is the basis for all subsequent philosophical and scientific thought. From this starting point rationalists fashioned an elaborate system of logical analysis and demonstration. In the hands of men such as Aristotle and Thomas Aquinas, rationalism illuminated vast areas of human experience, developed an orderly inventory of phenomena, and organized this inventory into comprehensive accounts of known reality.

Rationalists begin their analysis with an assumption which is virtually undemonstrable. By following exact rules of logic, rationalists examine the assumption in order to extend to the furthest possible limits all the implicit bits of information that can be inferred from it. Sometimes the source of these critical assumptions is the observation of specific events. Aristotle, for example, formulated his definition of tragedy from reading and viewing numerous Greek plays. But just as frequently assumptions were thought to spring from the mind itself or from the habitual and commonsensical beliefs of a particular culture or society. Thomas Jefferson rested his entire justification for political revolution on the assumption that a premise could be ''self-evident.'' Herein lies the principal difficulty of rationalism.

While as a method of inquiry rationalism offers the virtues of clarity and orderliness, it is incapable of bringing the same rigor to the evaluation of its assumptions. Rationalism can thus become a religion. An assumption in a rational system of thought carries a kind of authority that makes it as invulnerable to critical analysis as an article of faith, for there is no provision in either system by which to determine the validity of an assumption. With its determination to establish inflexible laws of nature and human behavior, rationalism leans toward dogmatism and thereby undermines the value of its own authentic discoveries. Consider, for example, British criminology during the so-called "glorious era of the Enlightenment," a period when rationalism was the dominant philosophic attitude of the lawmakers. Assuming that the leading social classes best epitomized the natural law of native worth and ability and that the common citizen could be deterred from criminal behavior only by harsh and punitive laws, English lawmakers reacted to an increase in petty thievery by making the crime of picking pockets punishable by death. The subsequent discovery that the incidence of picking pockets greatly increased during times of public executions did not force a change of the initial assumption, and the law remained in effect for half a century. This one example, of course, does not undercut the value and the accomplishments of rational philosophy over the centuries. It does indicate, however, certain weaknesses that can result from the exclusive application of the rational method.

There are certain similarities and differences between the methods of the traditional rationalist and those of the contemporary scientist. Like the scientist, the rationalist can make every step of the reasoning process explicit and available for critical public scrutiny and evaluation. However, a major problem for the rationalist is the internal consistency and validity of propositions. For instance, to the question "Why did so-and-so behave in the manner he did?" the rationalist would most likely reply because so-and-so wished or willed or wanted to behave in that way. Will, volition, and reason are the rationalist's springboards for behavior. In order to make man sufficiently transcendent over infrahumans, his will or rational processes are by their very nature asserted to be inaccessible to examination. It therefore is not uncommon to encounter in the writings of rational philosophers statements suggesting that the mind, the house of intellect and reason, has attributes and laws unto itself. For the rationalist, the human mind is by definition free of some of the restraints, contingencies, and forces which account for nonrational behavior in lower animals. The rationalist often resorts to authority or to consensus to form definitions, theorems, and explanations. In certain respects then, the rationalist is much more subjective than the scientist in the search for knowledge.

Empiricism

In the latter part of the seventeenth century, a time of rapid social change particularly in Western Europe, the philosopher John Locke developed a theory of knowledge and a method of analysis that undermined rational philosophy. His contribution is known as empiricism. For Locke, the central object of the inquiring mind was sensory experience itself; the fundamental data for the person who attempted to know reality were obtained through observation. Since the source of sense-data can be specified through measurement and can be reproduced under controlled circumstances, the inquirer was provided with a way of authenticating or checking premises and conclusions. The effect of these empirical claims on the intellectual life of Locke's contemporaries was rapid and enormous; empiricism provided a respectable go-ahead for the experimental movement of the eighteenth century. Modern experimental science thus finds one of its earliest ancestors in John Locke. Eventually, Locke's empiricism developed into the philosophy of logical positivism proposed by Auguste Comte. Comte's objective theory of reality, although stridently materialistic, provided further stimulus to scientific investigation by removing questions of value and ultimate purpose from the active concern of the investigator.

Philosophical movements sometimes seem to follow a rhythmic pattern, and the ascendance of one method or approach over another nearly always produces a countermovement. For some philosophers the methodological notions of Locke, Comte, and their followers were overly restrictive in the kinds of events and phenomena that could be meaningfully studied, especially with regard to the realm of human experience. The rigid objectivity of empiricism eliminated as a valid source of study the more subjective experiential world. If valid analysis and inquiry were to be limited to only that which could be objectively grasped and publicly verified as specified by logical positivism, then what was to become of that most vital but presumably unobservable human quality, conscious experience? For many people the functional significance of human experience in understanding why people do what they do is self-evident. To opt for a method of inquiry (empiricism) that seemingly could not or would not address itself to experiential phenomena was the equivalent of admitting that man was little more than a passive organism whose mentality was primarily composed of mechanical linkages. The major issues in this debate were: (a) whether conscious experience qualifies as usable information in the same way as the information obtained from publicly observable phenomena, and (b) whether the information obtained by analyzing private experience is needed in order to understand human behavior.

Phenomenology

Phenomenalism emerged in reaction to strict empiricism and challenged the primacy of sense-data (Thonnard, 1956). The phenomenalists argued that impressions and experiences produced by impinging stimuli from the world outside the mind can produce private, and unique, idiosyncratic effects. For example, the experience implied by the statement, "I have a headachy feeling," might be different qualitatively and quantitatively for any two people. Obviously the phenomenalist position imposes severe limitations on the scientific enterprise. Since impressions produce uniquely private reactions totally unavailable for public survey, there would be little objective data to report; and it would not be possible to verify the observations of others who simultaneously were exposed to similar physical stimulation. Precise communication between the parties to or the investigators of a given experience may not be possible.

Because it affirms the possibility of individuation, phenomenalism has received strong support from its beginning. Its modern advocates hold that the breadth and richness of the human condition is represented most completely in unabridged experience. The pure phenomenological position is that any encroachment or confinement of experience can partially deprive a human being of that which conveys his or her fullest being (cf. Brody & Oppenheim, 1966). Accordingly, those that would study man should not ignore such an important source of knowledge as phenomenal experience. The phenomenological position poses a dilemma for those who define psychology as the science of behavior. Since private experience alone, by common agreement, cannot be the subject matter of an objective scientific analysis—an analysis which relies on the measurement of overt events to ensure repeatability—the phrase "phenomenological psychology" appears to be a contradiction in terms. In this vein, Weimer (1974) draws an important distinction between knowledge by description (empiricism) and knowledge by acquaintance (phenomenology):

> We are acquainted with phenomenal experience: the sights, sounds, smells, tastes, and touches of our sensory systems, our feelings and emotions, etc. We know these things personally, experientially; we are literally acquainted with them. But this is not the sort of knowledge that science discloses. Scientific knowledge is knowledge by description, of the structural characteristics of the nonmental realm. Scientific knowledge of the nonmental realm is *never* of the intrinsic or first-order properties of objects: We don't *experience* the objects that science discloses, and yet we *know* them as well as, if not better than, we know our own "raw feels.". . . Now if all the mystic were saying is that knowledge by description is not knowledge by acquaintance, his claim would be but a tautology, coupled perhaps to a lament. But apparently he wants to claim more: that experience (of the appropriate sort) can deliver knowledge of reality that is incomprehensible to science. Now this claim is simply nonsense. Knowledge

by description can "capture" or, better *represent* anything we can know. If the mystic *knows* anything, it can be formulated, propositionally, in terms of knowledge by description. If the "ineffable" experience is truly that, it is not a knowledge *claim* (it is nothing more, nor less, than an experience). We may not have had the mystic's experience, to be sure, but we can know it if he can describe it. If he can't describe it, he can't know it descriptively either; he can just endure it. (p. 435)

It follows that if psychology is a science, then psychology must adhere to the rules of science with its emphasis on objective methodology. Since most contemporary phenomenologists contend that an objective methodology is antithetical to their approach—Bridgman (1959) claims that objectification diminishes the human condition—phenomenology may well constitute a nonscientific branch of philosophy dedicated to the derivation of a particular kind of knowledge about our essence and nature. Like those using other approaches to knowledge, phenomenologists must carefully define their method of approach to minimize ambiguity and maximize the pace and richness of their theoretical contributions.

In summary, there have been three major approaches to the development of knowledge. The first, the rational approach, deemphasizes the importance of sense-data and develops elaborate logical strategies to reach conclusions about people and nature. The second, the empirical approach, includes the use of rational strategies but emphasizes the assumption that fundamental information is primarily obtained through sensory contact with the physical world. The third, the phenomenological approach, holds that while sense-data are valid their impact on the organism produces uniquely private, unobservable reactions which are more important than those that are obtained under controlled observation. Phenomenologists believe that these unique covert reactions constitute the individual human quality of each person.

A number of objections can be leveled at each of these three approaches; science, as one approach to knowledge, simply constitutes a choice as to which of the approaches is most useful for achieving certain kinds of explanations. Science rests upon a foundation of sense-data combined with logical, rational analysis. A major contribution of the scientist has been to refine, modify, and adapt the empirical and rational approaches in order to minimize ambiguity in our understanding of events. One extremely significant refinement has been that of the *experiment* which, simply put, is *a set of rules that guide the arrangement and occurrence of certain events in a logical way so that sense-data can be used to formulate lawful relationships among these events.*

THE JOB DESCRIPTION OF THE SCIENTIST: EXPERIMENTATION AND DISCOVERY

When a person is hired by a firm, he or she is expected to perform certain duties. Most positions are accompanied by at least a vague description of duties and responsibilities. Obviously, there are many aspects of the job that are not clearly specified at the time of hiring but emerge as the new employee goes about learning the ropes. Although this vagueness is common to both the business and scientific worlds, it is possible to provide a few specific statements about what scientists are supposed to do. As you will discover, however, many of the specifics of the job emerge as practical expedients as scientists go about their work.

The Starting Point of Science

All sciences have the same point of departure—the immediate conscious experience of the scientist. The scientific enterprise begins when two or more persons report the same experience in the presence of the same events. Experience, as we have already pointed out, is the starting point of both the empirical and the phenomenological enterprises. The major distinction between the two is in how valid experience is defined. Whereas phenomenological experience is valid in its raw, individualized form, unanalyzed and uncommunicated, objective, scientific experience is valid only to the degree that it gives rise to equivalent communications or reports by two or more persons under equivalent circumstances.

From this common starting point sciences have been divided into separate domains, somewhat arbitrarily, on the basis of the kinds of events that are selected for observation and study. The geologist studies rock formations, the physicist examines falling bodies, and the economist observes price fluctuations. The fact that disciplines merge at the fringes of their domains (e.g., psychobiology, geophysics, biochemistry) does not alter the main point. All scientific disciplines have the same point of departure—the observing scientist's immediate experience of and concomitant report on an event that occurs under specifiable and controlled circumstances. Sciences then are differentiated in terms of the events chosen for observation and little else.

The Complex Nature of Observations

Scientific discovery rests on observations that are based on conscious experiences and that produce facts. A fact in its most general sense is little more than a stated observation that conveys some sort of empirical knowledge about the world. While not every kind of fact that is uncovered through the act of observation is worth knowing, facts certainly serve as the springboards for theory construction and explanation.

A major difficulty arises about facts because an observation is always the sum of one's immediate experiences *and* the various mental operations that follow closely upon those experiences to provide identification and interpretation. As Agassi (1966) asserts, "There are no hard and fast facts." What is implied in Agassi's statement is that observational facts contain the ideological views and theoretical biases of the scientist as well as pure sensations. Accordingly, the meaning of any observation under whatever conditions it is made is determined in part by the theories and world views with which it is connected (Feyerabend, 1970). This notion is given support by current research on memory which shows that mental schema or frames of reference representing our conceptions of the world may determine how we report our perceptions. The influence of our frames of reference on what we observe leads us to reconstruct the meaning of events in light of our unique world view (Bransford & McCarrell, 1974).

The notion of bias in simple observation undermines the premise that immediate experience is the inviolate rock bottom of a hierarchical structure which progresses from sense observations to regularities among events and then on to theory. This is why recent critics of scientific methodology such as Weimer (1974) have concluded: "Theories determine facts, not vice versa. Indeed, there would be no data at all without prior theoretical speculation of what, in the flux of experience, constitutes significant observation. Facts, far from being the data base upon which theory rests, are the end products of theory" (p. 419).

The goal of science is the development of theory in order to achieve explanation and to permit prediction. While observation is the starting point in fulfilling science's goal, observation is itself influenced by that goal, namely, theory. As Popper (1959) states:

> The empirical basis of objective science has thus nothing "absolute" about it. Science does not rest upon rock-bottom. The bold structure of its theories rises, as it were, above a swamp. It is like a building erected on piles. The piles are driven down from above into the swamp, but not down to any natural or "given" base; and when we cease our attempts to drive our piles into a deeper layer, it is not because we have reached firm ground. We simply stop when we are satisfied that they are firm enough to carry the structure, at least for the time being. (p. 111)

The Discovery of Relationships

Having observed a phenomenon, the scientist's next steps are to determine (a) whether the finding is stable and repeatable and (b) what events or conditions do and do not affect it. For example, preliminary experimentation may suggest that infants require physical contact with warm and soft objects for healthy personality development. First, the scientist would observe infants who do and do not have early contact with warm, soft objects and their subsequent personality patterns to verify the original observation. Next, the scientist might conduct systematic experiments in which the number and duration of contacts, the temperature and texture of the material, and the extent of the skin area touched are systematically manipulated to determine the circumstances under which the original finding remains consistent.

The above example epitomizes the job description of the scientist—an initial stage of controlled observation and classification followed by a search for and discovery of conditions under which certain phenomena reliably occur. The discovery stage involves a systematic attempt to identify specific events which, when varied, bring about orderly or regular changes in the phenomenon chosen for observation. The scientist's task can be conceptualized in terms of a formula in which the phenomenon to be understood constitutes the left-hand side of an equation which reads $X = f(Y_1, Y_2, \ldots Y_n)$. The event X (in the above example X is whatever behaviors define the personality development of the child) is assumed to be a function of some factor (Y_1) or set of factors $(Y_1, Y_2, \ldots Y_n)$. In our illustration Y_1 might be the number of physical contacts with warm, soft objects, Y_2 their duration, and Y_3 the type of objects used. In short, a relationship is established between X and Y. If $X = f(Y_1)$, a causal chain existing between X and Y has been discovered and specified by the scientist. The Ys in the equation constitute the antecedent events that determine or influence some consequent event, X.

The job description of the scientist in any discipline is always the same—to discover the factors (the Ys in the equation) that affect the phenomenon under study (the X in the equation). The scientist works in a manner such that his or her research procedures are specifiable and therefore repeatable by others. The public process of discovery means that several scientists working independently under controlled conditions can report basically the same data, i.e., similar changes in X as a function of similar changes in one or more Ys. At the risk of overstatement, we can summarize the major ingredients of the job of the scientist as (a) to identify a reliable phenomenon, (b) to discover and specify antecedent events, and (c) to state a functional relationship between the phenomenon and the antecedent events.

The designation of a discipline as scientific or nonscientific seems to hinge on differences in methodologies. What this means is that the methods and procedures chosen and the manner in which they are applied determine whether the knowledge of a given area qualifies as scientific or as something else, for example, literary, esthetic, or religious. Is the information gathered by the physicist more scientific than that reported by the economist? Or the psychologist? Or the biologist? The answers to these questions rest on an analysis of the job descriptions of those that work in these respective areas. If each obtains information through an application of the scientific method, then it would seem that the question amounts to how well the method is applied and not to whether the materials studied and conclusions derived are inherently scientific.

If the psychologist manipulates and observes the effects of variables under highly controlled circumstances and specifies the nature of procedures in such a manner that they can be replicated by competent persons, then his or her activity is no less scientific than that of the physicist, economist, or biologist. All are scientists who study relations among events for purposes of making quantitative statements about them. Sciences can be distinguished from one another by what events they study and not by how they study them.

THE LANGUAGE OF SCIENCE

Often scientists encounter problems when they attempt to clearly communicate their observations and discoveries. Unless they can phrase their observational statements in unambiguous and clear terms, there is little value in making them at all. Since language is an agreed upon convention to use terms in specified ways—usually as symbols to label something else—scientists are obligated to report their observations of phenomena in ways that conform to these conventions. Some words and concepts are more suitable for this aspect of the game of science than others. What is necessary is that scientists use words to depict their observations in such a manner that anyone who has the proper training and appropriate instruments can know what it is that they saw and duplicate it.

The Observation Language

Some words are easily understood by almost everyone. Most such words describe common objects, events, or attributes and refer to familiar experiences. Hempel (1952) has referred to the class of words used to depict observable events as the *observation language*. The vocabulary that makes up the observation language consists of terms that *(a)* specify and, hence, identify physical objects (dog, word, etc.); or *(b)* indicate their properties (eight-year-old, two-syllable, etc.); or *(c)* describe their relations to one another (before, below, etc.). The vocabulary of the observation language is the foundation of scientific communication because statements in this language can be evaluated as true or false by reference to sense-data that result from direct observation. The major benefit of the observation language is that there is widespread public acceptance regarding the use of its concepts. People always agree about whether or not there is an instance of the concept at a given moment in time. In short, concepts in the observation language are highly reliable.

The role of the observation language in science has been extended by Brodbeck (1963) who has noted that at least two kinds of features of the world can be distinguished. First, there are those that _stand out_ "almost begging for names" (Brodbeck, 1963). Examples include animals, plants, various colors and tastes. Each "differentiated slice of reality" seems to impinge upon the senses and literally courts a label. Each is a source of sensory experience that repeatedly impinges upon all of us. Indeed, the consistency and obtrusiveness of sensory experiences makes it possible to come to a consensual agreement in labeling stand-out features of reality. Much of the language of common sense consists of names for objects of direct experience. These objects need no special definitional treatment aside from that of listing the observable (experienced) attributes which characterize them. If, for example, one were asked to specify what sort of observations gave rise to the report that "I saw a dog," one would proceed by listing the observable, stand-out attributes of dogs. *Dog* entails having four legs, being covered with hair, having a tail, and possessing a collection of equally specifiable behavioral qualities. In essence, the term *dog* is shorthand for a combination of other words that denote the attributes of a specific kind of mammal. Thus, certain kinds of words used in reports for many observations are relatively easy to define simply by pointing to the stand-out features of those observations.

A second kind of feature of the world is that which requires special conditions for its observation. Special conditions serve the function of *cutting out* the feature so that it can be observed (Brodbeck, 1963). Although some stand-out features are of interest to scientists, the events that occupy most of their time are those that are abstract and require specific conditions for their observation. Such events are not objects in the sense of such stand-out features as dog and child. Instead, cut-out features represent things and events that are not conspicuously observable such as intelligence, anxiety, aggression, love, and fear.

We can now introduce what is meant by definition and show how it relates to the use of language and observation. A *definition* is a statement about the use of words and takes the logical form "A if and only if B, C, etc." For example, let A stand for "dog," let B stand for "having four legs," and let C stand for "being covered with hair," etc. Then the term *dog* is used correctly if and only if the observed object has four legs, is covered with hair, and so forth. The value of a definition is that it gives the scientist a shorthand way of communicating without restricting the scientific vocabulary to the observation language. Even simple communication between scientists would be cumbersome if they were required to specify what they observed in fundamental terms. The definition provides a way of communicating so that unequivocal meaning is preserved while excessive verbiage is minimized. Thus, in order to speed up communication a scientist may adopt a term or symbol as a substitute for a lengthy set of descriptive phrases.

Cut-out features of the world require a different kind of definition from that used to specify stand-out features. This is because unlike *dog*, such terms as *IQ, aggression,* and *need achievement* are not accompanied by distinct sensory qualities that are subject to pointing and listing operations. If asked what one means by the observation that "individual X is aggressive," there is no easily listed set of enduring and distinctive attributes for the term *aggressive* as there is for the term *dog*. Clearly, cut-out words in themselves do not *mean*; their meanings are determined by their usage. In the case of the more abstract concepts of science, we stipulate what we mean by *operational definition*.

Operational Definitions

There is a sense in which scientific concepts are more abstract than the concepts of everyday life. Scientific concepts are often complicated because they specify features of the world that can be known only under specific conditions. These conditions, in turn, become part of the concept. In other words, such conditions supply the meaning of the concept and therefore become part of its defining properties (Brodbeck, 1963).

Generally, *operational definitions* take the form of conditional or "if-then" sentences. The "if" clause states the specific conditions or the requirements for making certain observations or measurements. The "then" clause states the outcome which will be observed or measured after the test conditions have been imposed. An operational definition is complete when the defining words are all part of the basic vocabulary of the science and hence are understood without ambiguity. The longer the chain of defining words needed before the basic vocabulary is reached, the more abstract the concept being defined (Brodbeck, 1963).

Operationism refers to the fact that a concept is defined by the operations used in measuring it. For instance, the physicist's observation that a particular object has the property of elasticity can be understood in terms of what is done in order to make that observation and what happens as a result of what is done. An object behaves elastically *if* after stretching it in such and such a manner, it *then* measurably contracts back to or near its original dimensions. Note that the property of behaving elastically was defined in terms of a before and an after. The before or antecedent condition is the act of stretching an object in such and such a manner. The after or consequent condition is the actual contraction that occurs upon release. A description in terms of the observation language of exactly what is done and of what happens thereby defines the meaning of the observation that a given object possesses the property of elasticity. Operationally defined concepts are called *dispositional* since they refer to the tendency or disposition of things or people to react in regular ways or exhibit regular characteristics under specified conditions. See the discussion in Box 1.1 for an operational definition of a key psychological concept.

The Significance of Concepts

Abstract concepts are given meaning by operational specification. But not all meaningful concepts are significant from a scientific point of view. A concept is *significant* only if it appears in a statement of a relationship that links separate facts or events together. Such statements are called laws. As scientists, we search for laws because without them theory construction, explanation, and prediction are impossible. Hence, a scientific concept is hardly worth having if it does not appear in a law connecting it with other concepts or facts. As Brodbeck (1963) puts it:

> A good concept has both meaning and significance. In other words, a good concept has a reliably identifiable referent (meaning) about which we know one or more laws. The more laws into which a concept enters, the more significant it is, because the more we then know about how it is connected with other things. (p. 58)

LAWS AND THEORIES

The term *law* is used so frequently that it usually comes as a surprise to students that a large section of a chapter can be devoted to a discussion of something so obvious. As very young children some

Box 1.1 Operational Definitions of Conflict

In psychology, concepts such as conflict, anxiety, intelligence, achievement motivation, and many others require operational definitions. For
example, let us define *conflict* as it might refer to the approach and
avoidance tendencies of an organism placed in a choice situation. If
animal X has been fed in a white goal box when hungry, then X will
tend to *approach* the white goal box when deprived of food. Further,
if at another time X has been shocked when entering the white goal
box, X will have a tendency to *avoid* the white goal box. It is assumed
that X's tendencies to approach and to avoid the white goal box are
aroused simultaneously when X is hungry and near the goal box.
Therefore, because the tendencies to approach and avoid are aroused
at the same time, X will show vacillatory behavior and will be in
a state of conflict. The *antecedent* components of this definition of
conflict are feeding and shocking X in the white goal box; the *consequent* component is the measured vacillatory behavior when X is returned to this same situation.

Figure 1.1 depicts the approach-avoidance conflict as well as ap-
proach-approach and avoidance-avoidance conflicts. In the latter situations, X is either attracted to or repelled by two goals. The term *conflict* is thus given enriched meaning by examining its operations in
three experimental contexts.

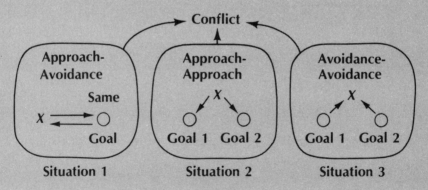

Figure 1.1 Schematic representation of the concept of conflict.

of us were told that God transmitted messages through his prophets in the form of laws for us to use in guiding our thoughts and behavior. Then, as schoolchildren, we learned that governments often performed similar acts. These actions were made acceptable to some on the grounds that God could not have been as explicit as we might wish regarding laws governing a complex society. Thus, supplementary laws or rules of conduct were needed to govern corporations, taxation, personal rights, and so forth. The term *civil law* refers to a rule of conduct and the attendant punishment for its breach. Civil laws, necessitated by practical social considerations, protect society and allow human beings to live together reasonably free from interpersonal conflict. Law, in this sense, is usually derived out of necessity, a solution through the establishment of rules and the consequences for their violation.

As with many other terms that serve multiple duties in our language, law means something quite different with reference to science than it does in connection with religion and government. In contrast to arbitration out of necessity, as in the case of the evolution of religious or governmental laws, the term *law* in science refers to the process of discovery—the discovery of relations between concepts and events.

Laws Defined

It is sometimes argued that psychology has spent much of its history fighting over terminology rather than analyzing behavioral phenomena. Although precise terminology is essential, the real contribution of any science is determined by its ability to specify precise, empirical relationships among concepts that designate phenomena in its domain of study. By a *scientific law* we mean that one instance of a concept is always related to the occurrence of an instance of another concept. For example, the sentence "if X is a dog, X is carnivorous" represents a universal or general statement connecting individual facts. Such connecting or relational statements are called laws. In a more restricted sense, if the set of operations that is used to define Y is accompanied by orderly changes in those that are used to describe X, then the functional relationship $X = f(Y)$ is said to hold.

Box 1.2 illustrates a psychological law—a law relating frustration to aggression. There are many ways in which the terms *frustration* and *aggression* could be defined. Subjects can be thwarted by being told that they failed an important test, shown attractive objects that are just out of their reach, given a strong unexpected criticism for making a slight error, and so forth. The antecedent manipulations and behavioral measures taken under each of these conditions would be viewed as particular instances of the more general concept of frustra-

Box 1.2   Law in Psychology: Frustration-Aggression

The statement that "frustration produces aggression" can be used to illustrate the meaning of a psychological law. Explicitly, this law states that when a given individual X is frustrated, then X will likely behave aggressively. However, to meet strict scientific criteria, the statement presumes that we know the precise conditions and events to observe when individual X is both frustrated and aggressive. Operational definitions of both concepts are required in order for the scientist to make the necessary observations showing that the one concept (frustration) is related to the other (aggression). Since laws, much like operational definitions, can take the form of if-then-statements, a more formal application of the scientific law on frustration and aggression might be: If individual X is thwarted from attaining a prized goal, X will show increased activity; moreover if a target object Y, the possible source of the frustration, is nearby, then X will bite, punch, or kick Y more often than under nonthwarting conditions.

tion. Further, there are many ways to define aggression, including hostile remarks made to an abusive superior, scores on a paper-and-pencil test of aggressiveness, the number of times and the intensity with which a subject delivered electric shocks to a thwarting confederate, and so forth. Again, each of these measures are but particular instances of the more general concept of aggression. All that a scientist can do in any single situation is to observe instances of more general terms. Hence, for any given experiment, frustration and aggression of necessity are very narrowly defined in terms of specific instances of the terms. If the presence of one instance, e.g., failing an important test and showing concomitant increased restlessness, is related to the presence of the other, e.g., the delivery of more electric shocks to the presumed test grader when given the chance, and the absence of one is related to the absence of the other, then two specific facts or concepts are combined into what is termed a *general law*. The more connections that can be found between both concepts in a law, the more confidence one can place in the generalized form of that law.

Experimental psychologists have produced many well-documented, general laws. In the area of animal learning, psychologists have discovered that if partial or periodic reinforcement is used during conditioning (e.g., rewards are given on 50 percent of the trials), then the rate of extinction will be slower than if 100 percent reinforcement had been used during conditioning. In the field of human learning and memory, psychologists have found that high meaningful material will be learned more rapidly than low meaningful material but that high meaningful material will be forgotten more rapidly than low meaningful material, provided the extent of original learning is the same and there is no intervening rehearsal (Young, Saegert, & Linsley, 1968).

Types of Laws

For psychologists, a lawful statement describes a relationship between concepts or variables. Variables are observable events that can take on more than one value. As Spence (1956) has pointed out, the variables studied by psychologists fall into three classes: (1) response events (R-events), exemplified by the behavior of living organisms; (2) stimulus events (S-events), the measurable features of the physical and social environments that surround living organisms; and (3) organismic events (O-events), the measurable neurological and/or physiological properties of organisms.

Simply stated, the job of the psychologist is to discover and refine the knowledge of relations that exist among these three classes of events. Attempts to formulate laws fall into three general types: $R=f(R)$, $R=f(S)$, and $R=f(O)$ (Spence, 1956). In these three types of laws, the behavior, R, of the organism is the dependent or consequent variable. The independent or antecedent variable on the right side of the equations can be either a response, a stimulus, or an organismic event. The observed connection between the independent and dependent variables constitutes the lawful statement. In a lawful statement the dependent and independent variables require operational definitions and/or must be part of the observation language. We will now briefly consider some examples of each type of law.

In an R-R law the association between two or more response measures is assessed, generally by means of a statistic called the *correlation coefficient*. The correlation coefficient shows the degree of relationship between the two events under study. An example of an R-R law would be provided by a high correlation between college board scores and grade point averages. The first R-event could be a summary of scores from student responses to standardized test questions; the second R-event could be the representative responses of the same students obtained at the end of the freshman year of college. Torgerson (1958) has argued that R-R relationships represent the lowest level of laws in science and are more characteristic of new or developing disciplines than of mature sciences. Historically, much of psychology seems to have passed through the stage of extensive concern with the formulation of R-R laws.

Most contemporary psychologists search for laws of the S-R type. Response measures, the dependent variable, are related to environmental manipulations, the independent variable. Our example of a law in Box 1.2 relating frustration by thwarting (S-event) to the presence and magnitude of aggressive behavior (R-event) is an illustration of an S-R law. Many of the contemporary laws of learning, motivation, perception, memory, and social psychology are of the S-R type. These laws describe behavioral changes that result from variations in the stimulus environment.

The past twenty years have witnessed an ever increasing amount of O-R research. Rapid advances in technology now permit more precise manipulation and measurement of organic events. Furthermore, improved behavioral assessment devices, like Skinner's (1938) operant conditioning chamber, have added greater precision to measurement and evaluation techniques. Such factors have been responsible for the dramatic proliferation of knowledge in the area of physiological psychology, where O-R laws abound. In O-R research precisely specified chemical and electrical events or tissue-removal techniques are experimentally introduced and related to observable behavioral changes.

Although the three types of psychological laws discussed above are useful categories, they are not mutually exclusive. There is much overlap among the three types of laws. For instance, the development

of precise S-R laws in classical conditioning has invited O-R speculation and research on the underlying organic nature of the whole conditioning process (cf. Thompson, 1976). One mark of a competent scientist is his or her ability to discern meaningful interrelationships among
different laws and to suggest original scientific hypotheses to explain
those interrelationships.

Theory in Science

The goal of a sophisticated scientific discipline is not merely the collection of a multitude of simple laws. The distinctive characteristic of
more advanced scientific disciplines is the search for commonalities
or similarities among laws. When such commonalities and similarities
are discovered, the scientist can then formulate general principles
which are not simply specific to the highly restricted conditions that
characterize single, isolated experiments. The distinction we are making here is between simple laws based on the results of single experiments and more general statements that serve to combine and integrate
more elementary lawful regularities. General statements are arrived
at by extrapolating or combining features shared by a variety of empirically derived laws. Abstract principles help unite otherwise separate
laws and are essential building blocks in theory formation.

A *scientific theory* is a systematically related set of laws that provides a unified account of some limited range of phenomena. A good
theory serves two major functions: (1) by integrating a large amount
of information contained in the form of isolated laws, a theory contributes to the comprehensiveness of our scientific knowledge and en-
hances our understanding, and (2) a theory is typically productive in
that it suggests new avenues of research and can be used to generate
new empirical hypotheses. We should point out that conclusions drawn
from testing new hypotheses can, in turn, be used to substantiate,
modify, or refute elements of the original theory.

Thus, theory is never static; it is always dynamic, ever changing.
In one sense, this leads us to the somewhat ironic conclusion that,
to be good or useful, a theory must be disprovable. A theory can
be said to be potentially disprovable by its capacity to generate testable
predictions which, if not confirmed, require its modification.

Theory without laws?   The degree to which theorizing is useful in
science depends directly upon how clearly the existing lawful statements and the complexity of the phenomena under study are specified.
Unfortunately, some psychologists have constructed low-level
theories which include many abstract concepts but few lawful statements. A good deal of the theorizing of Sigmund Freud and Carl Jung

in the area of personality, for example, can be shown to contain a plethora of abstract concepts but very few lawful relationships. Many personality theories are characterized both by the absence of and/or the capacity to produce scientific data in support of major propositions. For instance, there are few data to indicate the importance of the Oedipus complex as marking a developmental crisis in the emergence of the male personality. The basic problem stems in part from the lack of an operational specification of how the terms *Oedipus complex* and *personality* are to be used and how they relate to other operationally specified terms. Since Freudian and neo-Freudian personality theories have a tendency to avoid operationalism, their impact on contemporary psychological research is minimal.

Higher-order theory.   If a phenomenon under study *(a)* involves a large number of simple laws and their associated variables and *(b)* if these laws and variables can be systematically integrated by the use of abstract concepts, processes, or principles, then we have the ingredients for a higher-order theory. One of the best known examples of higher-order theory in psychology is that of Hull (1943) and Spence (1956). The Hull-Spence model attempted to reconcile a number of the otherwise isolated laws of classical and instrumental conditioning through the introduction of postulates and summary statements. Box 1.3 sketches some of the more elementary relationships among independent variables, operationally specified concepts, and behavioral events in the Hull-Spence model. Also shown is the integration of separate laws by way of combination statements.

Our example serves to illustrate the dual usefulness of theory: (1) Theoretical statements serve to unify knowledge by interrelating what otherwise appear to be independent lawful statements. (2) Theoretical statements, because they are generalizations of particular observations, can suggest new hypotheses which can, in turn, test the precision and scope of the theory. For instance, do the functional-theoretical relationships in the Hull-Spence theory hold for other learning situations with animals? Furthermore, do they hold for experiments involving the verbal responses of human subjects such as those obtained in paired-associate or serial learning tasks?

We should point out that the Hull-Spence model is an example of deductive theorizing. Movement is from the general level of theory formulation to the level of experimentation. The logical process behind this form of theory construction proceeds from the general to the particular and then back to the general if a modification of the theory is suggested by the experimental findings. Rationally based hypotheses derived from primitive theoretical speculations stimulate specific experiments which, in turn, yield data upon which the specifics of the theory are reconstructed.

Box 1.3 The Hull-Spence Model: A Higher-Order Theory of Learning

The terms *habit strength* (H), *drive* (D), *incentive motivation* (K), and *inhibition* (I) represent scientific concepts which are anchored in the observation language by means of operational specifications. For example, the associative or learning variable, H, was defined by Spence (1956) in terms of the number of trials an organism was given in a particular learning task. The motivational variable, D, was specified in terms of the amount of food deprivation or in terms of the intensity of an electric shock on an alleyway floor.

Initially, Hull noted that running speed was related both to the number of rewarded trials and to the number of hours since the animals had been given food. These observations were used to formulate tentative statements relating the operationally specified events and provided a basis on which concepts could be introduced to symbolize and interrelate these observations. For example, a systematic relationship between the operationally defined concept, H, and behavior (running speed) was established—i.e., $R=f(H^n)$—where R is the speed of running and n the number of rewarded trials given the subject. This simple law paved the way for the next step.

Since some of the operations that were used to specify H and D were overlapping—namely, they had the similar consequence of increasing running speed—a statement integrating the two concepts seemed feasible. By concurrently manipulating the antecedent operations that had been used to define H and D (number of trials and hours of food deprivation respectively) and by using the common measure of alleyway running speed to assess the consequent behavior, the relations between H, D, and R were given empirical significance. The results of an experiment by Ramond (1954) suggested that H and D operated together in a multiplicative fashion ($R = H \times D$) since as trials progressed the differences in performance for groups of animals with low D (4 hrs. of food deprivation) and high D (22 hrs. of food deprivation) increased dramatically. These results are shown in the graph in Figure 1.2. This graph relates running speed in an alleyway to levels of D (high or low) across a series of trials. Note that the difference on the terminal block of trials between high and low D groups is much greater than on early trials; this was the basis for postulating a multiplicative relationship between H and D. An additive relationship would have resulted had the differences between the two D groups on early and late trials been equivalent.

Other laws that resulted from assessing the effects of different variables on running speed were integrated into the theory by means of additional summary statements. In the simplified portion of the Hull-Spence theory presented in Table 1.1, four isolated laws relating running speed in a straight alley to intervening constructs are themselves interrelated by way of the functional statement $R = f[H \times (D + K) - I]$. All mathematical relationships in this last statement (i.e., $\times$, $+$, and $-$) were based on the results of experimental observations (Spence, 1956).

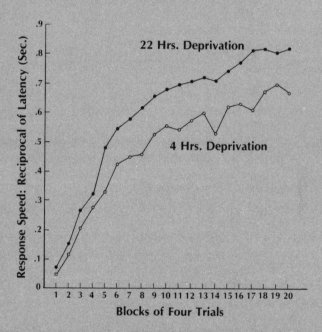

Figure 1.2 Speed curves of acquisition of an instrumental bar-touching response at two levels of hunger. The increasing difference between the motivational groups with training trials suggests that D and H combine **multiplicatively** to determine the performance level. After Spence (1956).

Table 1.1 Diagrammatic illustration of a portion of the Hull-Spence learning theory (adapted from Hill, 1963).

Antecedent Events (Independent Variables)	Operationally Defined Concepts	Consequent Events (Dependent Variables)	Isolated Laws	Higher-Order Lawful Statement
Number of Reinforced Trials	Habit Strength (H)	Running Speed (R)	$R = f(H)$	
Food Deprivation	Drive (D)	Running Speed (R)	$R = f(D)$	$S^E R = f[H \times (D + K) - I]$, Where $S^E R$ is Response Probability
Noxious Stimulation				
Magnitude of Reward	Incentive Motivation (K)	Running Speed (R)	$R = f(K)$	
Delay of Reward	Inhibition (I)	Running Speed (R)	$R = f(I)$	

A more recent example of higher-order theory is provided by the Atkinson-Shiffrin (1968) model of human memory. Basically, this model distinguishes between two aspects of memory: permanent structural features and transient control processes, the latter being governed by the subject and/or the experimenter. Structurally the memory system is divided into three stores: the sensory register (SR), the short-term store (STS), and the long-term store (LTS). Information in SR decays or fades out in a matter of milliseconds, while information is lost in STS in 10 to 30 seconds if not rehearsed or repeated. The more permanent store, LTS, holds information for long periods of time and is affected more by interference from other materials than by decay. Control processes serve to transfer information from one store to the next. For instance, control processes such as mediational strategies aid in the transfer of material from STS to LTS. Other examples of control processing would be chunking or organizing items into more manageable units or using mnemonic devices such as interacting imagery to store material in a more permanent fashion. Control processes operate in each structural store and bring about the shifting of information among stores. Box 1.4 contains a more detailed discussion of the multistore memory model of Atkinson and Shiffrin (1968).

A study of the Hull-Spence and Atkinson-Shiffrin theories reveals several similarities and one major difference. (1) Both theories make use of a wide range of data from many different experiments. (2) Both theories integrate data by introducing new constructs which provide a unifying scheme for incorporating otherwise isolated bits of information. (3) The Hull-Spence theory contains combination statements phrased in terms of how separate concepts, defined operationally, are best joined either by multiplicative or additive signs. In contrast, the Atkinson-Shiffrin model uses control processing to describe how information is transferred in a functional sense from one stage to another. The combining operations uniting the three stages are defined by processes that keep information moving in or out of the memory system. (4) Finally, both theories have generated considerable research, testing the limits under which the model holds or extending it to incorporate new domains of interest.

Contemporary theoretical trends. Although the Hull-Spence theory stimulated a great deal of research between 1945 and 1965, interest in such ambitious theorizing has diminished in recent years. One reason is the powerful impact of the semiatheoretical ideology of B. F. Skinner (1938). Skinner has pointed out that premature theorizing in the absence of substantial data can be misleading and can result in an endless series of experiments which ultimately are of little or no use in producing a storehouse of meaningful knowledge (Skinner, 1950). The best strategy, according to Skinner, is to establish an ample

Box 1.4   The Atkinson-Shiffrin Memory Model

The three memory stores proposed by Atkinson and Shiffrin (1968) preserve information for different durations, have different anatomical bases, function for different purposes, and lose information in different ways. Figure 1.3 should help explain some of the differences in the SR, STS, and LTS systems.

In 1968 Atkinson and Shiffrin tied the sensory register to visual input although they left open the possibility of other sources of sensory input, such as auditory input. Subsequent research has shown that the auditory system also provides input to the sensory register. The sensory register accepts all sensory input and preserves it long enough for some information to be selectively transferred to the short-term store. Material either decays in the sensory register or is erased by incoming information.

Information attended to in the sensory register enters a rehearsal buffer in the short-term store. This store is anatomically based in the auditory, verbal, and linguistic systems. It not only receives information from the sensory register but also from the long-term store. Conscious mental processing occurs in the rehearsal buffer of the short-term store. Once information is in the buffer, it can be maintained indefinitely if continuously attended to; if information is not attended to, it begins to decay and is likely to be gone in less than 30 seconds. Since the buffer has a limited capacity, the learner must eliminate unwanted items. If unwanted items are not eliminated, the oldest, weakest items are lost from the short-term store through disuse and decay.

Information in the short-term store that is actively studied and analyzed by means of some control process, such as imagery, is likely to be transferred to the long-term store. As far as we know, the information capacity of this system is unlimited; its anatomical base is varied and losses occur generally through disruption (interference). The purpose of the long-term store is to enable the learner to retain selected information for long periods of time.

Figure 1.3

Structure of the memory system. From Atkinson & Shiffrin (1968).

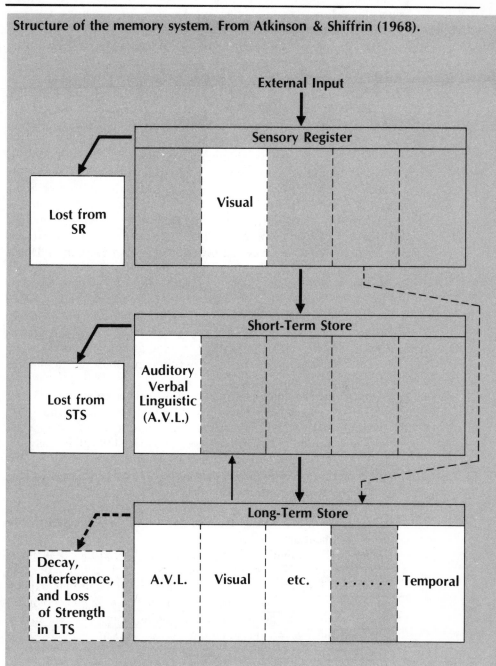

foundation of empirically based laws before any elaborate theorizing takes place. From the semiatheoretical viewpoint, experimentation is the master of theory.

The Skinnerian approach to research seemingly proceeds in an inductive fashion. The process of induction moves from the specific experiment to a more general statement. However, as Popper (1959) has pointed out, the method of science rarely travels the inductive route. Pretheoretical ideas—in the form of anticipations, loose hypotheses, or rather intricate theoretical networks—almost always are preliminary to experimentation. Conclusions are then reached following experimentation by means of logical deduction. The induction-from-particulars model does not square well with what we believe is the connection between observation and theory, with the former being inescapably linked to the latter.

There has been increasing interest in functional, miniature theories in the last decade (Marx, 1963). Miniature theories represent a possible compromise between higher-order theories such as Hull's and the semiatheoretical position of Skinner. Miniature theories are small-scale theories characterized by close adherence to data, minimal use of abstract concepts, and a tendency to restrict explanations to relatively circumscribed problem areas. They are functional in the sense that their concepts often are tied closely to the psychological processes they describe and explain. In general, if any type of theory construction characterizes modern psychology, it is the miniature, functional type.

Finally, we should emphasize a current concern about theory and variability—a connection often neglected in constructing psychological theories. Underwood (1975) has recognized that a sound theory must account for the individual differences, or variability, almost always present in the behavior of the group of people towards whom the theory is directed. Variability in processing and performing is so fundamental to humans and animals alike (cf. Battig, 1975) that every psychological theory must account for this important characteristic of behavior. Unless it passes the individual differences test, a theory requires modification.

What is this individual differences test of a good theory? Underwood's (1975) procedure is rather simple. First an observation of some event is needed, together with a theory which might be used to explain that event. Second, two independent measures of a psychological process contained in the theory are required. Third, the test of the theory's adequacy is in terms of whether differences among individuals on one measure are closely parallel or related to differences on the second measure. In essence, the individual differences test assesses whether two independent measures of some theoretically important psychological process are in agreement that the process varies in an orderly way among people (cf. Butterfield and Dickerson, 1976). A theory requires further development if it fails to account for the variability among individuals.

EXPLANATION IN SCIENCE

When asking someone to explain an event, most of us want to know *why* it happened, *why* it worked, or *why* it was that way. As philosophers have long pointed out, a final answer to *why* questions ultimately requires resort to some sort of preeminent force or final cause that is usually not available as a specifiable, observable entity. As it turns out, however, there is a way of arriving at a scientific explanation which avoids the dilemma posed by *why* questions.

The minimum requirements for the scientific explanation of a phenomenon are: *(a)* the prior establishment of some general principle or law known to hold for events of the type in question—i.e., $X=f(Y)$; *(b)* the fact that event Y was present when X occurred; and *(c)* the fact that no other potentially precipitating factor Z was present when X occurred (Hempel, 1966). As we proceed to explain a phenomenon scientifically, we will focus on an account of how the event came about—what factors, usually historical, were a sufficiently significant part of the situation to invoke a principle related to the event—and not on why the factors worked as they did.

Let us apply the principles of scientific explanation to the somewhat unusual phenomenon of a ghetto child who cries whenever he sees his teddy bear. The child's crying might be understood in terms of the occurrence of certain antecedent conditions—for example, the child could have been bitten by a rat and, because of that experience, could have learned to fear rodents. In addition, the child's crying might be understood in terms of the law of stimulus generalization—we respond to stimuli that are similar to those which were present during an original learning experience. Since a teddy bear is similar to a rat in that it is furry, small, and animallike, the principle of stimulus generalization might be reasonably invoked and would satisfy the first requirement of scientific explanation. The explanation for this unusual phenomenon would then be that the teddy bear elicited crying behavior (thereby fulfilling the second requirement of scientific explanation), since the crying behavior could be reasonably traced to and linked with the presence of the rat. Moreover, if there were no other precipitating factors that might have caused the crying behavior—no other related stimuli were present besides the teddy bear when the behavior occurred—the third and final requirement of scientific explanation would be met. In this instance then, the specification of antecedent conditions and the statement of an appropriate principle permit a reasonable explanation for our unusual phenomenon. The answer to the question, "Why does the child cry in the presence of his teddy bear?" thus boils down to an exposition of the crucial factors that triggered the reaction and the invocation of a previously established law which suggests how these factors may have worked together.

In some respects the scientific explanation of an event and the definition of an abstract scientific term have much in common. Both explanation and definition should be unambiguous and precise. However, an explanation also must enrich our understanding of the event in question by isolating the factors responsible for its occurrence and excluding alternate accounts. A good theoretically based explanation in psychology should have the following characteristics: *(a)* operational precision, *(b)* noncircularity (its ingredients should not rely upon the behavior to be explained for their definition), and *(c)* testability through contrast with alternate explanations. Another way of stating this last condition is to say that an explanation is testable only when we know what facts would falsify it. If we cannot conceive of any way in which it could be refuted, then it is merely a pseudoexplanation. It would make no empirical claim and hence could be compatible with any other account of the phenomenon that might logically be advanced. Meaningful testability would be impossible.

Thus, explanation in science refers to the use of concepts, laws, and theories to account for an experimental outcome or for a naturally occurring event. An explanation takes on added usefulness if, through extrapolation, it provides the basis for accurate prediction or control of future events.

SCIENCE AND REVOLUTION

How does scientific knowledge accumulate? Most general textbooks in any science say that there is an orderly, cumulative development of laws and theories. They portray science as a game of construction in which each question solved or theory discovered adds another "brick" into the "total building." Textbooks focus on the continuity of scientific knowledge and obscure the discontinuity or crises which are an inevitable aspect of the science game. This is why scientific revolutions are often "invisible" (Kuhn, 1970).

Crisis is a normal, expected part of science (Kuhn, 1970). A prevailing scientific paradigm fails to resolve a pressing issue and is replaced by a new paradigm. It is difficult for scientists operating in the old paradigm to accept the new and, sometimes, even to recognize the inadequacy of the old paradigm. The new paradigm succeeds and becomes dominant because it works; it resolves crises and anomalies, yielding new perspectives on our knowledge of the world. Yet the new paradigm will last only until it encounters its own crises and gives way, slowly, to a new paradigm.

A scientific paradigm is a broad umbrella which captures a scientific discipline's unique research conventions. These conventions include metascientific or ideological assumptions about the phenomena of interest, specific subject matter, unique research methodologies, types of concepts used in constructing laws and theories, and the metaphoric orientation of theories.

The two dominant scientific paradigms in contemporary experimental psychology are associationism and information processing. They differ in their answers to the following important questions: *(a)* Is behavior learned or innate? Can the mind reconstruct reality? *(b)* Should research focus on models of memory and thought or on reinforcement theories in classical and operant conditioning? *(c)* Should concepts like storage-retrieval or habit strength be used? *(d)* Should theories employ analogies with computer programming and simulation or be based on S-R mechanistic models? These and other important questions divide the associationistic and information-processing paradigms. We will return to a discussion of these two contemporary research orientations in the last section of Chapter 2.

SUMMARY

Science rests on a foundation of empiricism and rationalism. The experiment is simply one way to use sense-data in a logical way in order to form statements of relationship among events under study. The job of the scientist is to determine, for the purposes of explanation and prediction, the lawful relationships which hold among observable events. The chief difference among the various sciences lies in the choice of events to be studied. Psychology has chosen to deal with the systematic changes in the behavior of living organisms. Its goals are to develop laws and theories of behavior. Laws are statements of functional relationships between concepts. Theories are statements of interrelations between laws using abstract concepts and combination statements.

Research psychologists employ three major strategies in the formulation of lawful statements: $R=f(R)$; $R=f(S)$; and $R=f(O)$. In each an independent variable (an R-, S-, or O-event) is manipulated and consequent changes in a response, the dependent variable, are assessed. In developing laws and theories, the psychologist employs a unique vocabulary consisting of two types of terms: (1) those of the observation language which is composed of words referring to point-at-able phenomena about which there is high inter- and intra-subject agreement, and (2) more abstract, operationally defined concepts which are specified by words in the observation language and which have the potential for entering into meaningful laws.

The primary functions of theory in psychology are to integrate existing laws and to generate new research. If theory is to be used to explain an event, then it should be characterized by precision of specification, noncircularity, and testability in contrast to alternate explanations. The utility of explanatory constructs and theories is often reflected by their capacity to accurately predict and/or control behavior in a variety of situations.

Finally, the developmental course of science follows a revolutionary pattern. When the prevalent scientific paradigm fails to advance knowledge at a satisfactory pace or to clarify anomalies, a crisis results, spawning a scientific revolution. The conventions of the new paradigm—such as its metascientific ideas about the nature of events under study, specific subject matter, methodology, acceptable lawful concepts and types of analogies and theories—supersede those of the old paradigm. This pattern of scientific revolution should be accepted rather than feared by the scientific community.

QUESTIONS

1. What is the starting point for all scientific disciplines? What is paradoxical about this starting point? What are the goals of science?
2. Why are cut-out features of reality of more interest to scientists than stand-out features? How are cut-out features and operational definitions related? What are the two criteria for using abstract concepts in the scientific vocabulary?
3. What is a law? What are the three types of psychological laws?
4. Why is theory important in psychology? What is the process by which a scientist modifies a theory? Why is it necessary for a theory to be testable?
5. Using either the Hull-Spence or Atkinson-Shiffrin model, show how a theory can incorporate the various topics of this chapter (e.g., experiment, observation language, definition, law, etc.).
6. Why is the deductive method used more often in psychology than the inductive method? What would you consider to be a good example of an inductive theory?
7. Compare and contrast higher-order theory, the semiatheoretical approach, and miniature theories. What are the advantages and disadvantages of each? What historical factors caused the first two approaches to combine and form the third approach?
8. Why is it necessary to have some means by which individual differences can be accounted for in psychological theory?

Experimentation: The Science of Psychology

2

The theoretician puts certain definite questions to the experimenter, and the latter, by his experiments, tries to elicit a decisive answer to these questions, and to no other. All other questions he tries hard to exclude.

(Weyl, 1949, p. 116)

What compels the theorist to search for a better theory is almost always the *falsification* of a theory, so far accepted and corroborated: it is, again, the outcome of tests guided by theory. . . . Accidental discoveries occur too, of course, but they are comparatively rare.

(Popper, 1959, p. 108)

Experimental psychologists study a wide range of behaviors common to individuals of different species, ages, sexes, and races. Some choose to study the perceptual world of infants while others concern themselves with attentional processes in the elderly. Some study aggression in rats while others develop theories of creativity and problem solving. Still others conduct research on schizophrenia, classroom management, criminal rehabilitation, propaganda, and a host of other interesting topics.

All experimental psychologists are committed to the analysis of behavior through the rigorous application of the principles of scientific methodology. Whether interested in theoretical laboratory-based problems such as memory, or applied problems such as hyperactivity in a special education classroom, all experimentalists strive to use appropriate observational strategies, judiciously choose independent variables, make accurate measurements, employ sound experimental designs, use reasonable procedures, control for extraneous or undesirable side effects, provide sensitive data analyses, and formulate legitimate interpretations and explanations.

In this chapter we will explore the research strategies used by experimental psychologists to gather knowledge and develop theory. We will then discuss in detail the essential ingredients of an experiment; this section is particularly important since Chapters 3, 4, and 5 will focus on how the experimental psychologist goes about conducting a sound experiment. We will conclude the chapter by presenting a historical overview of experimental psychology, focusing on the evolution of research strategies and research interests.

RESEARCH STRATEGIES

In our everyday life we frequently use the essentials of the scientific method to solve problems. We form hypotheses about events important to us, test them through observations, and reach conclusions about the world around us. In many respects the scientific method is nothing more than a refinement of what we do in attaining both self-understanding and knowledge about why other people act as they do. By attempting to escape from the dogmatic influences of others and from our own subjectivism, we try to be true to ourselves. We repeat our tests over and over again in order to confirm our opinions. Finally, we communicate our views to others in order to check their accuracy and, usually, to exert influence and control. At times, we do this in the hope of helping others, changing their prejudices, or achieving a more equitable society.

The scientific method, then, does not differ from the ordinary pattern of gathering knowledge used by a thoughtful, critical, non-scientific observer nor does it necessarily have different objectives. It is instead a rigorous refinement and an explicitly public elaboration of that ordinary pattern of gathering knowledge. By bringing their methodology to a more conscious level, scientists can better control undesirable influences on their observations. The minimum requirement for a scientist is the ability to discriminate between one and zero—between the occurrence and nonoccurrence of some events. The scientific method also requires the scientist to be as accurate as possible in making observations; to repeat procedures and measurements to ensure their consistency and accuracy; and to make public findings for others to judge their merit.

There are three basic research strategies used in science to test ideas and to gather new or substantiate old information. These strategies are the descriptive, the correlational, and the manipulative. The manipulative strategy is the strategy most closely identified with experimentation in psychology because it is more likely to yield a cause-effect relationship. Before outlining in some detail the manipulative strategy, let us briefly consider the descriptive and correlational approaches.

Description

The descriptive research strategy involves the acts of observing and recording behaviors as they occur in the real world. Underwood and Shaughnessy (1975) cite four main functions of the descriptive strategy: *(a)* it helps identify important behavioral phenomena; *(b)* it may suggest key independent variables for further study; *(c)* it may point to certain behaviors that should be recorded as well as specific dependent measures; and *(d)* it can sometimes be used to study issues that cannot be addressed by the correlational or manipulative strategies.

Enumeration. The most elementary descriptive strategy is that of simple enumeration. Counting or measuring the frequency of an available object, event, or characteristic often provides a sufficient, although usually tentative, answer to a scientific hypothesis. An example of the practical use of enumeration would be that of a sociologist who was asked to predict the amount of garbage in New York City that would require disposal in the year 1984. One possible way to answer this question would be to calculate the amount of garbage per person for the present year, add a constant to represent increased individual garbage needs for each succeeding year (derived from past information on yearly increments in disposal requirements), and then multiply that sum by the number of people who are estimated to be living in New York in 1984. Given rigorous and accurate methods of measurement, specified precisely so that they could be verified by any appropriately trained person, enumerative description and projection is no less scientific than any laboratory investigation. This type of descriptive research is the most primitive form of inquiry in any science.

Naturalistic observation. Naturalistic observation is a descriptive strategy that entails the observation and measurement of behavior as it occurs in its natural or normal state. An example of naturalistic observation is provided by an ethologist interested in the general issue of territorial boundaries of selected species who conceals herself in a dense thicket and meticulously records her observations on the reactions of one animal to another when imaginary boundary lines are crossed (cf. Eibl-Eibesfeldt, 1975). By labeling behavior, categorizing observations, and tallying frequency distributions, she may discover important information regarding such a topic as mating behavior as it relates to territorial intrusions. Sensitive, precise, and repeatable observations and measurements are the cornerstones of the descriptive research strategy used in naturalistic observations.

Among ethologists it is a common view that animals quarrel when one male member of the same species enters an area resided in by another male. Such behavior might give rise to the general concept of spatial or territorial boundaries. Thus, quarreling (X) between males is functionally connected with intraspecies transgression of a particular spatial area (Y): $X=f(Y)$. To verify this lawful connection one might employ controlled observations under more restricted conditions. These restricted conditions might include the use of a more refined behavior-recording method, for example, noting whether quarreling is related to the age or the social status of the involved males. The aim is to define the concept of territoriality in terms of its limiting conditions.

The ethologist might also alter the environment in some way in order to verify the concept of territorial boundaries. However, such an intrusion would constitute a manipulation of conditions which goes beyond pure descriptive strategy and naturalistic observation. By manipulating the situation, of course, the environment is no longer natural. Nonetheless, introducing the manipulative strategy might aid the ethologist in clarifying the concept of territoriality.

Case histories. Still another strategy in describing behavior and searching for new information is to survey records or case histories. For instance, if a clinical psychologist analyzes records collected over the past decade and discovers that during the last five years the percentage of neurotic male patients expressing feelings of sexual impotency has increased 500 percent over the preceding five years, the case history technique would provide important descriptive information. This rather startling finding would likely invite speculation as well as research on possible sociopsychological factors responsible for the increase in reports of male impotency.

Correlation

The study of case histories sometimes yields a hypothesis about the relations between events. If a therapist observes that extraverted, hostile patients diagnosed as neurotic seem to show more rapid remission of symptoms than introverted, nonhostile neurotic patients, then the therapist moves beyond the stage of simple counting, recording, and describing events into a higher level of knowledge. This higher level of knowledge implies the beginning of a law—the specification of a relationship between events. Statements of relationship can result from using the correlational research strategy.

In Chapter 1 we pointed out that the correlational approach involved the collection of two or more observations or behavioral measures from each of a number of individuals. The degree of relationship between these observations and measures would then be statistically determined by means of a correlation coefficient. While the correlational approach has sometimes come under attack as a research strategy, it has nevertheless been a valuable tool in the history of psychological research, especially in the area of personality and intellectual assessment (cf. Cattell, 1968). The most frequent use of this strategy is where manipulation would be either impractical or impossible, or in a relatively unresearched area where there is need for a preliminary specification of possibly important variables.

As one illustration of the use of the correlational approach, suppose we wished to evaluate the effects of poverty on racial prejudice. For humane reasons, it would be impossible to systematically manipulate the amount of poverty for given individuals. Hence, an alternative might be to relate possible indices of prejudice (ratings of attitudes toward school integration, job training, and open housing) to various income levels. However, there are certain problems with the correlational approach as used in this example. For instance, the existence of a strong statistical relation between poverty and prejudice would not justify the conclusion that poverty was responsible for prejudice or that prejudice produced poverty. Both factors might be related to a third causal factor, such as quality or amount of education. Correlational results often provide important clues to the appropriateness of the experimental question as well as tentative hypotheses for approaching the problem in greater depth and with greater precision, but rarely do correlational results provide definitive support for conclusions involving causal statements.

Deese (1972), however, has argued that causal statements based on the correlational strategy are possible if the temporal relations between events A and B are carefully and systematically evaluated. That is, if one can demonstrate a substantial correlation between A and B only when A precedes B temporally, but not when B precedes A, then there are grounds on which to develop a causal statement linking B to A in that the occurrence of A reliably leads to B.

A second possible use of the correlational strategy is as a tool to explore new, unresearched areas. Indeed, the multiple correlation or factor analytic technique in which many variables are interrelated has frequently been employed to determine the presence and importance of relevant clusters of common factors (Guilford, 1954; Thurstone, 1947). The correlational approach has proved to be effective in psychometric research where characteristics or traits common to a particular personality style or type of intellectual processing are determined.

The third and perhaps the most frequent way in which the correlational strategy has been employed is to determine the *validity* (accuracy) and *reliability* (consistency) of response-defined tests such as standard IQ tests, rating questionnaires, and personality inventories. For example, if we were to conduct a study calling for the judgments of different raters regarding the behavior of subjects, it would be essential to determine the reliability of these judgments. An interobserver correlation—that is, a comparison of the ratings of several judges—would determine the consistency of the judgments. If the interobserver ratings were similar, a subsequent experiment could then proceed on a more solid basis with greater confidence in the reliability of the dependent variable.

One criticism of the correlational strategy cannot be overemphasized; namely, that in the final analysis it can only provide tentative conclusions regarding the causal relations at issue. Consider again our first illustration of the correlational approach in which we tried to relate poverty to prejudice. There are at least two issues of concern that we must make clear: *(a)* since a variety of other variables can be correlated with poverty, we can never be sure whether poverty or one or more of these correlated variables is the primary cause of prejudice; *(b)* since there is no sure way of knowing which condition developed first, one cannot know whether poverty or the factors contributing to it caused prejudice or whether prejudice in some way leads to poverty.

Another frequent criticism of the correlational strategy is that it often has been used in situations that involve response measures of questionable reliability and validity. As previously noted, reliability refers to the questions of consistent measurement and validity to the question of accuracy. For example, an investigator may be interested in the relationship between ego strength, as defined by performance on a scale of a clinical-diagnostic test like the Minnesota Multiphasic Personality Inventory (MMPI), and dogmatism, as measured by a test developed by Rokeach (1960). Unless both tests have been sufficiently validated against the actual behaviors they represent and shown to be consistent in their measurement, any resultant correlation between ego strength and dogmatism could not be meaningfully interpreted. Problems concerning the reliability and validity of response-defined tests have plagued the correlational research strategy and often have made interpretations based on this approach tenuous.

Manipulation

The third and most powerful research strategy is the manipulation of one or more independent variables. This strategy, which has been previously identified with S-R and O-R laws, is most applicable when a causal statement is sought as the answer to a hypothesis. As Hume (1739) first pointed out, the best evidence in support of *causation* is that two events invariably occur together, one precedes the other always in the same order, and neither occurs alone. The postulation of causation is always an inference that goes beyond existing evidence and acts of observation. The manipulative strategy simply makes the inference of causation more plausible. If a scientist can demonstrate a consistent change in a dependent variable through the systematic manipulation of one or more independent variables, all other things being held constant, then confidence is increased with regard to the possibility of causation. In addition, the reproduction of findings based upon the manipulation of events under controlled conditions traditionally has been viewed as providing supportive evidence of causation.

In its broadest sense, an experiment is the application of a set of manipulations, procedures, and controlling operations in such a manner so as to provide unambiguous information about a phenomenon. The experiment is one way of providing reliable, repeatable, and communicable data as a test for a rationally derived hypothesis. Essentially, it represents a unique integration of rational processes, logic, and sense-data. Initially, the formulation of a testable hypothesis is dependent upon analytic and creative thought processes. The data-gathering phase of the experiment, with its reliance on the measurement of behavior change due to changes in the manipulated variable, can then proceed in an orderly and meaningful fashion. This process consisting of (a) an original insight or hunch; (b) a logical analysis of the orderly, connected events in the original speculation leading to an experimental hypothesis; (c) more precise, controlled manipulations and observations made in the context of a formal experiment; (d) further logical analysis of the reasons for the outcome; and (e) additional experimentation and interpretation typifies the sequence of the experiment in science. In psychology, the result of this sequence is the continuous refinement and advancement of our knowledge about behavioral events.

As with the descriptive and correlational approaches, the manipulative approach has its unique hazards. Problems such as obscuring the effects of the independent variable on the dependent variable because of the presence of undesirable extraexperimental factors, inadequate control of actual experimental procedures, and a host of others we shall encounter in succeeding chapters require special attention. Moreover, because the experimental-manipulative approach requires precise control of the conditions surrounding an experiment, this approach has sometimes been labeled "artificial" and/or "trivial." Information derived from the manipulative approach has been challenged for being unrepresentative of events that occur outside the laboratory.

It may be possible for experimentalists who use the manipulative strategy to avoid the criticism of artificiality by systematically introducing into the laboratory characterizations of real life situations and observing their effects in precise and controlled ways, as Darley and Latané did in their study (1968) of bystander apathy toward people in need of help. Eventually, experimental psychologists should be able to study events in the real world with the same precision and control they now exercise in certain laboratory contexts. For the time being, we should realize that research criticized as trivial by some can be the stepping-stone for a major scientific advance by others.

THE EXPERIMENTAL MODEL

How do scientists use the experimental-manipulative strategy? While there is no simple answer to this question, there are a number of standard concerns that we as scientists must face in conducting experiments.

1. Our first concern is that the experiment be justified. Is the purpose of the experiment to advance a theory? To gather information that might help solve a problem? To extend the generality of some finding to different areas, to other types of people, or to new independent variables? In other words, before we perform an experiment or read the results of another, we must know something about the issues under consideration and why information regarding these issues is being sought.
2. Our second concern is that specific independent and dependent variables be designated as well as a specific hypothesis relating them to each other. We must know what event is being varied (the independent variable) and what behavior is to be assessed (the dependent variable). Even though we may have good reason to suspect that the variable to be manipulated is a major determinant of the phenomenon under study, the proper way to express our hypothesis is in the form of a *null hypothesis*—a statement expressing the absence of any effect of the independent variable on the dependent variable. That is, the only kind of hypothesis that can be answered scientifically is one that holds that the variables in question will *not* affect the behavior being studied.
3. Our third concern is for the subjects of our experiment. How many subjects should be chosen and from which population? How should they be chosen? What roles should they play in the experiment? Can too few or too many subjects be chosen? Should the subjects be chosen at random from the general population or should they be members of a specific subgroup?
4. Given that our concerns regarding sample size and method of selection are resolved, our fourth concern is a specification of the risks involved in rejecting the null hypothesis given that it is actually true or rejecting a false null hypothesis. In short, how powerful an experimental effect do we wish to observe before we call it a significant or nonchance effect? How do we decide if a statistically significant outcome is scientifically significant?

5. Our fifth concern is how to avoid confounding—contamination of the results by the presence of unwanted and potentially influential factors. What safeguards should we employ? Should subjects be matched so that they are in some way equivalent to one another at the outset of the experiment? Should counterbalancing, that is, arranging orders and sequences of experimental conditions so that possible undesirable side effects are spread evenly across the conditions representing the independent variable, be employed as an equating procedure? Should subjects be used as their own controls so as to minimize confounding?

6. Our sixth concern is for the design of the experiment—its precision, efficiency, and comprehensiveness. Should subjects serve in one condition, several conditions, or all conditions of the experiment? What are the advantages and disadvantages of each design possibility?

7. Our final concern is handling, reducing and analyzing the data in order to lead us to legitimate conclusions, interpretations, and explanations.

We pose these standard experimental concerns not to bewilder or confuse, but simply to illustrate the pattern, style, and complexities of the experimental-manipulative research strategy. Each of the seven concerns will be taken up in some detail in succeeding chapters. In total, the seven concerns represent the essential ingredients of an experiment in psychology. We will devote the rest of this section to an illustration of a recent experiment in order to highlight some of the questions which investigators must face in carrying out their research.

Borkowski, Levers, and Gruenenfelder (1976) were interested in whether young children who had been taught a mediational strategy would spontaneously use it in a learning situation two weeks later. The study centered on the factors leading to the successful transfer of the mediational strategy by very young children, thereby improving their learning abilities. A sketch of the design, procedures, and results of this study is presented in Box 2.1.

Why was the study run? Basically, because past research indicated only inconsequential benefits from mediational strategy training on a follow-up or transfer task. Stated another way, experimenter-trained strategic behavior is easily lost. Borkowski, Levers, and Gruenenfelder attempted to produce sizable and durable strategy transfer by providing mediational training with precise and consistent instructions and procedures. In addition, they studied how the degree of activity during mediational training might influence the size of the transfer effect. This variable was chosen because previous studies had suggested the importance of actively involving the learner in strategy training (Wanschura and Borkowski, 1974, 1975). An additional component of the

Box 2.1 Transfer of Mediational Strategies in Young Children: The Role of Activity During Strategy Acquisition

Borkowski and his colleagues trained children to use a mediational strategy. The question was whether the strategy would then assist them in learning a series of object pairs (e.g., a flag and a whistle). Each child was asked to associate the members of each pair so that when the first member was shown, its mate could be accurately reported. This is called paired-associate learning (cf. Jung, 1968). The _mediational strategy_ consisted of teaching some of the children that the word pairs could be easily learned if joined by a preposition (e.g., the flag _under_ the whistle).

All children learned nine-item paired-associate lists during five sessions, separated by one- or two-week intervals. First, there was a pretest session designed to obtain estimates of each child's learning ability. These measures were used to assign children so that the groups were matched in learning ability at the outset of the study. Then, three strategy training sessions were held. Finally, a posttest session, in which no training occurred, served as a test of how well the children _transferred_ their strategies to a new task. The pretest and posttest were similar in that no mediational prompts or special instructions were given.

The independent (manipulated) variable was the degree of activity required of the child during the training sessions. In the first experiment, forty nursery-school children were assigned to one of four conditions, each one of which represented a different level of activity during strategy training. In the _passive_ condition, the experimenter supplied the prepositions to the child. In the _active_ condition, the child was instructed to place the objects in the relationship prescribed by the experimenter. In the _active-film_ condition, the child saw a two-minute movie, immediately after the pretest, in which a model child _actively_ learned the pretest list using prepositions. The purpose of the film was to increase the child's awareness of a more efficient strategy for learning. In all other respects, the active-film and active conditions were identical. In the _control_ condition, the paired objects were linked by the conjunction _and_; no prepositional mediators were provided.

The dependent variable was the number of correct word associations on each trial. Only performance on the first three trials of each session was used because many children learned the nine-pair lists very quickly. The results of this experiment are plotted in Figure 2.1. The percentage of correct responses is shown for each session and activity level. Statistical analyses confirmed that all experimental conditions were superior to the control condition during training. Of greater interest were differences in performance levels on the posttest list (Session 5). It is here the durability of the strategies was measured. Both the active and active-film conditions were superior to the passive and control conditions, which were not different from one another. Children in the two active conditions retained the prepositional strategy over the two-week interval and then spontaneously utilized this strategy on the transfer list.

In summary, this study showed both sizable and durable strategy transfer provided that active manipulation of object pairs occurred during the training sessions. A second experiment in this project, with first-graders, suggested that an awareness of a strategy's effectiveness (i.e., the active-film condition) prior to the onset of strategy training can be an additional inducement leading to successful strategy transfer.

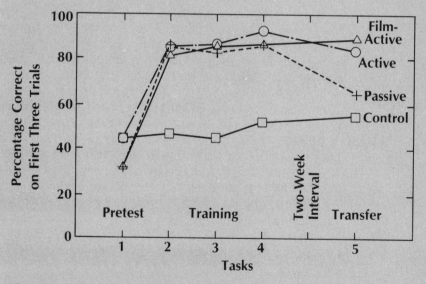

Figure 2.1 Percentage of correct answers on the first three trials of the Borkowski, Levers, and Gruenenfelder experiment.

design, a sensitization-oriented, awareness-inducing film, was included to maximize strategy transfer. This component was included because a recent study by Kennedy and Miller (1976) suggested that information about the merit or utility of a strategy might enhance its durability. The experimenters decided to use four- and five-year-old boys and girls in a nursery school, since previous research had been unsuccessful in demonstrating strategy transfer in this age group.

The design of the experiment involved a pretest followed by three training sessions and then a posttest. Each child served in one and only one of the four treatments. The pretest familiarized the children with the experimenter and with the paired-associate task, as well as supplied information for assigning children to conditions and groups on the basis of their learning abilities. The pretest equating-procedure increased the probability that the results obtained during training and transfer would be attributable to the treatment conditions rather than to random factors, such as those related to pre-experimental differences in learning abilities.

The experimental procedures were carried out under carefully specified conditions. For instance, the study time for each pair was 3 seconds; 5 seconds was provided for each test trial (when a stimulus was shown and a response requested). These exposure times were the same from list to list for all children. All responses were recorded, including the number of correct responses on each trial. Statistics were chosen to help decide when group differences during training and transfer were sufficiently large to label significant. The statistics assessed whether the null hypothesis, stating that the groups were not different from one another, was tenable or untenable. Finally, a conclusion was reached about the importance of the learner's active involvement during strategy training in order for the strategy to be spontaneously transferred to a new task at some future time.

Of course, the decisions described above were only a few of those made during the course of this experiment. Some were based on logic and sound reasoning, others were only best guesses. Indeed, no one study can raise all the issues that experimenters must face in conducting their research. It is the purpose of the remaining chapters of this book to discuss the major issues and choices which research psychologists invariably encounter in conducting an experiment.

BASIC AND APPLIED RESEARCH

Today more than ever before, psychology is under pressure to assist society in coping with its many serious problems. There is a growing recognition in the profession that more attention must be directed to the immediate and staggering problems of education, mental health, crime prevention, the aged, and environmental control; we must not confine our attention solely to the effects of concurrent reinforcement schedules on bar pressing, learned helplessness in nonhuman subjects, short-term memory in college students, and similar basic research issues. Wherever reasonable we must extend our laboratory-based findings and direct our own research energies to the solution of applied problems. This theme was sounded as early as 1969 by George Miller in his Presidential Address to the American Psychological Association:

> The most urgent problems of our world today are the problems we have made for ourselves. They are human problems whose solutions will require us to change our behavior and social institutions. As a science directly concerned with behavior and social processes, psychology might be expected to provide intellectual leadership in the search for new and better social arrangements. . . . This is the social challenge that psychologists face. In the years immediately ahead we must not only extend ourselves and deepen our understanding of mental and behavioral phenomena, but we must somehow incorporate our hard-won knowledge more effectively into the vast social changes we all know are coming.

The precipitous increase in publications dealing with applied research is partial testimony that experimental psychologists are becoming more conscious of the social implications of their work (cf. *Journal of Applied Behavior Analysis*). Social concern is visibly demonstrated as researchers delve into the problems of children, the elderly, minorities, criminals, the environmentally deprived, and the organically impaired. Most psychologists believe that our success in applying psychology to social problems will be directly related to the ingenuity, skill, and sophistication of behavioral researchers. We contend that psychology, conceived of and practiced as a science, will continue to contribute to the betterment of people everywhere in the decades ahead.

It would not be at all unusual for a beginning student to view experimental psychology with some ambivalence. On the one hand, one may stand in awe of the precision and detail of experimental psychology while, on the other, one may question the relevance of much of the research on the grounds that it appears trivial. Although both observations may have some degree of truth, we should introduce a distinction here. Any discipline that claims possession of a special body of knowledge, whether scientific in nature or not, is composed not only of that content knowledge that distinguishes it from other disciplines but also of tools or tactics by which its information was acquired.

When a critic decides that experimental psychology is trivial or artificial, this decision refers more to the information or theories derived from experimentation rather than to the experimental process itself. Since negative judgments often seem to be made concerning research directions or experimental outcomes and not usually concerning the research tools employed, the interesting question arises as to what kinds of research efforts most often receive negative evaluations. One possible answer may be linked to the preferred status of applied over basic research in the minds of governmental leaders as well as many beginning psychology students. Negative evaluations are generally connected with the outcomes of basic research projects. The questions asked in and the answers obtained from basic research often seem remote if not totally divorced from contemporary social problems.

A criticism of experimental psychology on the grounds that it is trivial or irrelevant thus seems more a matter of what problems psychologists should study rather than how they should proceed with their study. Our view is that the discipline of psychology probably will profit from the efforts of researchers with both concerns—basic and applied—as long as these efforts are grounded in solid experimental tactics and procedures. In fact, the two approaches are so closely interrelated that it is rare to find an important applied discovery in psychology that cannot be traced to laboratory-oriented, basic research.

We have no easy remedy for increasing an appreciation of basic research activities. It may be of help to point out that the tools and knowledge developed in the context of basic research can sometimes be used to resolve applied problems. Experimental psychologists have long realized and appreciated this possibility. As B. F. Skinner and his students have demonstrated, content knowledge once considered basic often turns out to play a key role in solving an applied problem. Perhaps the best example of this type is the extension of operant learning principles, based on a functional analysis of the behavior of pigeons and rats in restricted learning environments, to the fields of clinical and educational psychology in the form of behavior modification techniques.

Obviously each psychologist must decide whether to apply his or her particular experimental skills to traditional or novel, to pure or applied research problems. Both types of research are essential for the advancement of psychological knowledge; they should be viewed as complementary and interdependent rather than as antithetical and antagonistic. In the long run, the impact of psychology on society will be linked to the boldness, imagination, and creativity that is employed in the generation of both basic and applied knowledge about behavior.

EXPERIMENTATION AND THE HISTORY OF PSYCHOLOGY

The rate of growth for any science is closely linked to its development of sophisticated experimental strategies. It is worthwhile to consider some of the basic shifts in concerns, orientations, and research strategies that have taken place in experimental psychology since its beginning in 1879. These shifts were often paralleled by changes in specific subject matter or revolts against prevailing doctrines concerning the nature of both science and humanity. In the remainder of this chapter, we will focus discussion on three distinguishing features of experimentation in tracing the evolution of the major historical schools in psychology: *(a)* definitions of the task of psychology, *(b)* paramount research interests, and *(c)* preferences for particular types of lawful statements and experimental strategies.

Structuralism

The marriage of German experimental physiology with the subject matter of British associationism was accomplished by the father of modern psychology, Wilhelm Wundt. In his psychological laboratory at Leipzig, Wundt began his analysis of the content of mental life by using a technique resembling the experimental method called *introspection*. Introspection required trained subjects to look into themselves, to reflect on changes in their conscious experiences, and to report these changes in accordance with controlled environmental stimulation. The psychologist's task was the analysis of consciousness into more basic or elementary states. The introspective report was the passport by which the psychologist could gain entrance into the subject's mental life. From verbal reports the experimenter determined the most basic components of conscious experience for a given sensation (Marx and Hillix, 1973).

In his attempt to reduce consciousness to its constituent parts, Wundt followed a direction already characteristic of the biological investigations of his day, in part because he was trained by the nineteenth-century physiologist Johannes Müller. The biological model, a reductionist approach based on developments in physics and chemistry, provided a framework in which all sciences could make rapid advances. The key to rapid advancement was invariably the invention of sophisticated research instruments. The biologist engaged in molecular analysis needed a tool that would make available to the senses the characteristics of cellular phenomena. That tool was the microscope. Wundt directed his own efforts toward discovering a similar instrument for studying the psyche, a subject matter that science had generally ignored in favor of material properties.

Having no mechanical instrument equivalent to the microscope, Wundt used introspection as its functional equivalent in his study of the mind. Wundt argued that introspection could make available to the senses the elements which constituted the consciousness and mental life of the human organism. For Wundt, psychology's primary subject matter was mental life—a point of view he shared with the British associationists as well as with many older philosophical schools. The uniqueness of Wundt's work on sensation and feeling was his insistence on the experimental method as the means of gaining access to consciousness. Examples of Wundt's research provided by George Miller (1962) help clarify the use of introspection as an experimental tool. One research project used a metronome that produced clicks at regular intervals for gathering introspective reports on the conscious experience of feeling. The description of that project in Box 2.2, provided by Miller (1962), helps clarify the use of introspection in the experimental analysis of feeling.

Many characteristics of the experimental method were present in Wundt's introspective technique. For instance, the observer (i.e., the subject) and the experimenter were highly trained, procedures were carefully programmed, and data were systematically recorded. Wundt demonstrated conclusively that a combination of detailed instructions and training can produce high consistency in the subject's verbal reports to various visual and auditory stimuli. Of course, little or nothing can be said of the accuracy of those reports.

Whenever a verbal report indicated to the experimenter that the observer was attending to the details of the stimulus display at the expense of his or her sensations, a stimulus error was recorded. The presence of a stimulus error meant that the observer was not attending to the processing of information, ideas, or feelings taking place in his or her mind. A series of stimulus errors on the part of a student did nothing to enhance the prospects of obtaining a doctoral degree from Wundt!

Since Wundt and his followers, called *structuralists*, attempted to develop laws about the combination of mental events, the type of lawful statement resulting from their research might be loosely classified as R-R. One element of conscious experience, defined by the verbal response of a trained judge, was related to another element, also revealed by a verbal report, until a pattern for that particular sensation was described. In the tridimensional theory of feeling (see Figure 2.2), the interaction of the elementary states of excitement and pleasure combined to produce a feeling of positive affect. It should be clear that the responses of the observer were translated into more elementary mental states only with great difficulty and imprecision. The point we wish to make, however, is that the search for laws about mental events was an inherent part of Wundt's attempt to develop an empirical science of psychology.

Box 2.2 Wundt's Method of Introspection

Wundt reported from his own introspections that at the end of a rhythmic row of beats he had the impression of an agreeable whole. That is, some rhythmic patterns are more pleasant, more agreeable than others. He concluded from this self-observation that part of the experience of any pattern of beats is a subjective feeling of pleasure or displeasure, a feeling that can be located somewhere along a continuum ranging from the agreeable to the disagreeable. While he listened to the clicks, however, he detected another kind of feeling about them. As he expectantly awaited each successive click he felt a slight tension; after the anticipated click occurred he felt relief. This alternation between tension and relief was clearest when the clicks came at a slow rate. In addition to a pleasure-displeasure continuum, therefore, his feelings seemed to have a tension-relief dimension. But that was not all. When the rate of the clicks was increased, he said he felt mildly excited; when the rate slowed, he had a quieting feeling. In this way, by patiently varying the speed of the metronome and carefully noting his subjective experience—his sensations and feelings—Wundt teased out three distinct and independent dimensions: agreeableness-disagreeableness, strain-relaxation, and excitement-calm (see Figure 2.2). Every conscious feeling, he said, can be located somewhere in three-dimensional space. (Miller, 1962)

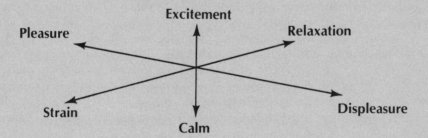

Figure 2.2   Wundt's tridimensional theory of feeling. Every
              feeling is supposed to be located somewhere in
              this space. From Miller (1962).

The transition from structural to behavioral psychology was accomplished simply by directing attention to the operations involved, namely, the presentation of a visual or auditory stimulus and the consequent record of elapsed time between the stimulus onset and the subject's response. Although the structuralist focused on the presumed intervening event of consciousness to explain differences in reaction times, the behavioral fact of these differences has proved quite useful to contemporary psychologists with very dissimilar interests. For instance, psychologists working in the fields of perception, motor learning, mental retardation, aging, and psychopathology have all, at times, been interested in reaction-time phenomena. Over the years, considerable controversy has persisted over the value of treating consciousness and mental life as events that can be investigated by means of introspection versus the value of focusing exclusively upon overt behavior to the exclusion of consciousness. That this controversy remains with us today can be seen from the title and contents of a relatively recent article published in the *Psychological Bulletin*, "Concerning introspective 'knowledge' " (Natsoulas, 1970).

Wundt's structuralist school trained large numbers of European and American scientists who were later to play influential roles in developing behavioral trends in psychology. Brief mention should be made of two such scientists, James McKeen Cattell and Hermann Ebbinghaus, who were precursors of the first native American movement, functionalism. James McKeen Cattell, a personal student of Wundt's, became interested in the study of how and why individuals differ in their reaction times. The importance of this study is that it was in many respects unrelated to the analysis of mind and conscious experience; rather, it was concerned with the systematic study of individual differences associated with an isolated segment of behavior—speed of reactions. Cattell's study is one of the first attempts in the history of psychology to utilize the S-R research strategy. In his experiment, the R was a public and quantifiable variable, speed of reaction, while the S was the stimulus display which produced orderly changes in R.

A similar departure from the structural tradition of Wundt can be seen in the work of Hermann Ebbinghaus. Although Ebbinghaus received no formal training in psychology, his research on memory has become a classic study in experimental psychology. Ebbinghaus, using himself as a subject, examined the systematic decline in recall that occurred at different time intervals ranging up to 48 hours after original learning. The importance of Ebbinghaus's research for experimental psychology is threefold: (1) it marks a departure from Wundt in the type of lawful relationship studied (i.e., from R-R to S-R); (2) it represents an expansion in research interest from simple sensation to the areas of learning and memory; (3) it signals the development of an original research strategy, namely, the manipulation of variables. In the case of Ebbinghaus's memory research, the independent variable was the time between the original learning and its recall.

Two other early pioneers are worthy of mention here because their scientific approaches significantly departed from Wundt's in terms of experimental strategy, research interest, and type of organism to be studied. E. L. Thorndike (1898) and Ivan Pavlov (1903) had embarked quite independently of each other and of Wundt upon what broadly can be called an analysis of learning processes. Both men employed animals, abandoned the use of unanchored inferences regarding the mind or consciousness, and were operationally specific in their use of techniques, variables, and constructs. While Pavlov declared an interest in the "reflexes of the mind," his entire theoretical framework was logical and empirical. Pavlov was not interested in mental life and attempted to separate himself from psychologists who defined their subject in that fashion by categorizing his work as physiological rather than psychological. Thorndike likewise employed objective techniques to define his constructs, and his lawful statements about learning processes were built on research with a wide variety of organisms. One of Thorndike's classic studies in learning involved an analysis of the trial-and-error behavior of cats in a puzzle box.

Würzburg School

Shortly after the beginning of the structuralist school at Leipzig, a second German system of psychology emerged at Würzburg. The foremost figure of this school was Oswald Külpe who was originally trained in Wundt's laboratory (cf. Boring, 1950). Külpe focused his studies on the act rather than the content of conscious experience. Act was an irreducible element and thought was the most important aspect of the mental act.

It is useful in understanding Külpe's approach to psychology to divide consciousness into its contents and the processes by which those contents emerge. According to this division, the acts of feeling, thinking, or reasoning presumably underlie and produce the end-product—the sensation, mental image, or ideation. Külpe argued that Wundt focused too intently on the passive aspects or contents of consciousness and not upon the activity by which they were produced. However, Külpe's approach was, in principle, not different from Wundt's in that introspection remained the research strategy and private mental events remained the objects of analysis.

As Gustav Bergmann, a philosopher of science, has pointed out, the Würzburg school can be viewed as a transition between structuralism and functionalism, which was soon to become the first native American school of psychology. In the first place, Külpe and his associates, in contrast to the structuralists, were more interested in molar or global than in molecular or miniscule aspects of mental life. In the second place, their interests gradually shifted from the study of mind to the analysis of problem-solving behavior. This shift in research interests made their studies more practical and related to real life situations than the studies of the structuralists. Much of the research at Würzburg dealt with the effects of "sets" or predispositions on problem-solving abilities. Finally, the style of research at Würzburg represented a preview of the utility of the S-R manipulative strategy that was soon to become a trademark of functionalism.

Gestalt Psychology

The Würzburg school was antecedent to the Gestalt school (Marx & Hillix, 1973). The main figures of this school—Wertheimer, Köhler, and Koffka—criticized the structuralists' attempts to analyze or reduce the mind into more basic elements. They maintained that the sum of the elements of mind would not be equivalent to the whole mind, that the whole was greater than the sum of its individual parts. The task adopted by the Gestalt psychologists was the study of the immediate experience of the whole organism (Köhler, 1947).

The Gestaltists, like the structuralists, used the method of introspection as a component of their research strategy. However, unlike the structuralists whose research on sensation had minimal impact on the field, the research of Gestalt psychologists resulted in major, long-lasting contributions to the field of perception. In part, their impact was great because their research was based on the manipulative strategy and reflected an increased concern for control in the application of the experimental method. For example, they placed much greater emphasis upon specification of the physical stimuli that produced specific perceptual phenomena. In Wertheimer's classic exposition of the *phi phenomena* (i.e., the demonstration that the successive illumination of two stationary lights separated by a short distance can produce the sensation of apparent movement), great care was taken to quantify stimulus parameters such as the duration the lights remained on and the distance between them. Similar care was exerted in the construction of stimulus materials giving rise to such perceptual phenomena as *closure* (i.e., the tendency to see as continuous a disconnected but semiorganized line or figure) and *good figure* (i.e., the tendency to report as complete, a semicomplete figure) and *prägnanz* (a term proposed by Wertheimer to denote the most characteristic shape a form can assume and toward which, according to Köhler, every form or structure tends). Gestalt psychology thus represented a significant methodological advance in that greater emphasis was placed on the specification of the physical world that gave rise to a perceptual response. The Gestalt principles of perception and the laws of perceptual organization generally correspond to the S-R or the S-O-R research models (Woodworth & Schlosberg, 1954), and many of the conclusions of the Gestalt school are based on accurate scientific observations.

On the other hand, the Gestalt system was characterized more by physiological speculation than by specific, quantifiable relationships. In fact, Gestalt psychologists paid little attention to quantifying response measures. For instance, the key doctrine of *isomorphism*— that is, subjective experiences and the physiological processes which underlie them have the same structure (Köhler, 1947)—is acceptable at a commonsense level, but in terms of actual organic and behavioral events does not hold up. Viewed from a historical perspective, unsupported principles such as isomorphism did serious damage to the effectiveness and credibility of the Gestalt system of psychology.

Another serious criticism of Gestalt theories was the vagueness and lack of operational specification of certain key constructs and postulates. Take, for example, the classic phrase, "The whole is greater than the sum of its parts." If this phrase means that at any moment a given behavior is dependent upon the interaction or combination of all relevant variables operating contiguously and historically upon a behavior, then the position is perfectly correct. However, if this phrase means that the discovery of higher-order laws (i.e., combination or interaction laws) and theory is impossible, then this position stifles experimentation especially on those complex psychological processes that can be analyzed only in terms of their interacting, component parts (Madden, 1952). The former position is acceptable to all; the latter position is totally unacceptable to most contemporary experimental psychologists.

Just as the Gestaltists emerged in reaction to the sterility and elementalism of the structuralists, so the behaviorists eventually emerged in reaction to the wholism of the Gestaltists. Before turning to behaviorism, however, we will consider the development of the first native American school of psychology—functionalism.

Functionalism

The feature that distinguished functionalists such as John Dewey, William James, and James Rowland Angell from the structuralists was their concern for the process of adaptation. Pragmatic, functional interests can in general be traced to the pervasive influence of Darwinism (1859) on American science, industry, and education. In contrast to the structuralists, the functionalists asked questions relating to the how and why of mental operations. More specifically, they wanted to know the purpose of a given mental event and why that event occurred only under special circumstances. This functional emphasis promoted the rapid development of new fields such as genetic psychology (G. Stanley Hall at Clark), comparative psychology (Harvey Carr at Chicago), learning psychology (Robert S. Woodworth at Columbia), and the study of individual differences (James McKeen Cattell at Columbia and L. L. Thurstone at Chicago).

Functional interests directed American psychologists toward applied research. Functionalists were rebels against the allegedly sterile research interests of Wundt and his most famous American disciple, E. B. Titchener. The unifying theme of functionalist research was the attempt to describe the relationship between events under study; for the most part, their research was based on the manipulative, S-R research strategy. The organism's adaptation (R) to changes in its environment (S) was the central focus of functionalism.

Functionalism rapidly expanded in the major American universities. It took many forms and developed new research horizons. Yet the emphasis on process (how something works) characterized virtually all varieties of functionalism. The question asked by the early functionalists, "How does consciousness work?" represents quite a different point of view from the kind of question posed by the structuralists, "Of what is consciousness composed?" The former, the process approach, implies a search for mechanisms which account for behavior, while the latter, the content approach, results in a description of behavior. The process orientation precluded the use of large-scale theorizing and tended to keep the researcher closer to the data. Today major figures such as Arthur Melton, Leo Postman, and Benton Underwood reflect the style and attitude of the early functionalist school. In some respects the tradition represented by this school is more characteristic of contemporary experimental psychology, especially in human learning and memory, than any other school or system.

Most functionalists retained an interest in the operations of mind. The subject matter of mind and the teleological flavor of the early functionalists forced John B. Watson, a student of James Rowland Angell, to reject the functionalist position. Teleological explanations of behavior ascribe purposes to acts. These purposes represent future rather than past causes of behavior. A teleological explanation of why a rat runs rapidly down an alleyway to obtain food in a goal box, for instance, might be cast in terms of the rat's expectations or anticipations of the future consequences of its running behavior. In contrast, a nonteleological account of the rat's goal-oriented behavior would rely more upon particulars in the rat's history, such as prior exposure to food in the goal area, as a way of explaining its present performance. Since teleological explanations invariably rest upon the assumption of reason and volition, they are in their purest form similar to the explanations of traditional rationalism. They are nonscientific in the sense that they preclude empirical specification. The elements of teleology in functionalism prompted the rebellion of John Watson.

Behaviorism

In "Psychology as the Behaviorist Views It," Watson (1913) made his final break with the structuralists and the functionalists because of their preoccupation with the contents and operations of mind.

> Human psychology has failed to make good its claim as a natural science. Due to a mistaken notion that its fields of facts are conscious phenomena and that introspection is the only direct method of ascertaining these facts, it has enmeshed itself in a series of speculative questions which, while fundamental to its present tenets, are not open to experimental treatment. In the pursuit of answers to these questions, it has become further and further divorced from contact with problems which vitally concern human interest. . . . The Behaviorist, in his efforts to get a unitary scheme of animal response, recognizes no dividing line between man and brute. The behavior of man, with all of its refinement and complexity, forms only a part of the behaviorist's total scheme of investigation. (Watson, 1913)

Watson's classic paper dramatically emphasized his contention that psychology is a natural science whose basic data are of the same general nature as those of other sciences—public, verifiable observations. For Watson, the specific purpose of psychology was to analyze the behavior of living organisms. His preference was to focus on environmental manipulations as they related to the adaptation of organisms. In most of his research on learning, he employed the experimental-manipulative strategy, and the resulting lawful relations were of the S-R variety.

Watson's primary contribution was his insistence on objectivity in the study of the observable aspects of behavior. His research approach and research philosophy are lasting contributions to experimental psychology. As Kenneth Spence (1963) has concluded, "So far as I know there are no proponents today of the original Watsonian Behaviorism. . . . However, many of the basic postulates of his formulation are to be found in the present-day varieties of behaviorism and, what is more important, probably, in the underlying working assumptions of the great majority of present-day American psychologists.'' Indeed, the tenets of behaviorism have been successfully integrated into most contemporary research activities. It is probably accurate to conclude that most experimental psychologists can be classified as methodological behaviorists.

We should not be distracted from the basic message of Watson because of the many polemics and controversies that surround his contribution. For example, Watson denied neither the existence nor the utility of consciousness. For Watson, consciousness formed the basic data of all sciences since each and every scientist, whether physicist or psychologist, must rely upon his or her own conscious sensations to report measurements. We can credit Watson (1913) with the important insight that behavior constitutes the most important source of information that psychologists possess regarding human nature.

Ultimately, whether one's interpretive biases are humanistic, psychoanalytic, behavioral, or phenomenalistic in origin, we have one thing in common—to account for the behavior of organisms. Problems arise when one's interpretive frame of reference, especially if founded upon anecdotally derived or nonempirical grounds, directs one's observations. For example, if a person engaged in the treatment of mental illness speaks in terms of clashes between the warring forces of the patient's id, superego, and ego, that person is obviously using constructs symbolic of or correlated with certain behaviors exhibited by the patient. To evaluate the meaning and usefulness of this diagnosis, all we need to know are the behavioral referents and conditions of observation that define id, superego, and ego and the empirically derived relationships between these terms and other behaviors necessary for the satisfactory adjustment of the patient. The degree to which these ingredients are absent is the degree to which we are dealing more with literary than with scientific constructs.

The basic point in this discussion is that contemporary methodological behaviorism is a framework, an approach, and a subject matter more than a theory of behavior or a philosophy of human nature. It contains the basic assertion that, to be a legitimate scientific enterprise, psychology must deal with events that are public and observable—events capable of being verified.

Contemporary Paradigms:
Associationism and Information Processing

We concluded our first chapter with a discussion of scientific revolutions. We shall now briefly follow up on that discussion because today we are witnessing a revolution against *associationism*—the preeminent behavioristic paradigm of the 1940s and 1950s. The new, revolutionary paradigm is called *information processing.*

The revolution is not in terms of experimental strategies because both paradigms rely heavily on the experimental-manipulative approach. Rather, it is in terms of dominant research interests, types of concepts and analogies used, and assumptions made about human nature. The key differences between the two contemporary paradigms are the following:

1. An interest in the adaptation of the organism (associationism) versus an interest in the thinking mind (information processing).
2. A prevailing assumption that people are the products of their environments (associationism) versus a view of people as possessing innate predispositions and potentialities (information processing).
3. The use of concepts such as reinforcement, habit, drive, and extinction (associationism) versus the use of concepts such as encoding, rehearsal, storage, and retrieval (information processing).
4. Theories built on mechanistic S-R models (associationism) versus theories based on information-feedback, computer-simulation models (information processing).

These key differences suggest a shift in research philosophy and orientation—a return to the philosophical framework of structuralism and functionalism. The information-processing paradigm stands in sharp contrast to the associationistic, neobehavioristic paradigm that for so long dominated the direction of psychological research. Whereas the neobehavioristic approach focused almost exclusively on learning principles and theories, psychology's newest research orientation emphasizes the structure and function of mental life as reflected through language, memory, and thought. Information processing is a revolution not only in terms of subject matter but also in terms of beliefs, concepts, analogies, and methodology. It may well become the dominant research paradigm in psychology during the next decade.

SUMMARY

Of the three major research strategies—the descriptive, the correlational, and the manipulative—the most useful has been the manipulative. This strategy makes the inference of causation plausible because it enables the scientist to demonstrate systematic changes in behavior as a result of variations in antecedent events. Descriptive and correlational strategies are more characteristic of immature sciences and often lead to equivocal conclusions. However, the correlational approach has been valuable in researching new domains of study, in validating test instruments, and in instances where manipulation would be impossible or undesirable.

The scientific experiment is a way of arranging, manipulating, and controlling events so as to demonstrate relations between independent and dependent variables. An experiment occurs when the effects of two or more treatments are assessed in terms of their behavioral impact. A good experiment is one where all extraneous and/or undesirable factors are eliminated or minimized so as to avoid confounding and obscuring the relationship between the independent and dependent variables. The experimental model serves equally well when attempting to solve problems of either a basic-theoretical or an applied-practical nature.

The major schools of psychology—structural, Würzburg, Gestalt, functional, and behavioral—can be distinguished from one another in terms of their research interests and unique methodologies. The history of experimental psychology can be viewed in terms of the evolution of the three major experimental strategies; research psychologists first employed the descriptive strategy, then they turned to the correlational strategy, and today they express a distinct bias in favor of the manipulative strategy. Psychology's newest paradigm, information processing, represents a combination of the research interests of both structuralism and functionalism. Interest in the structure and function of mind puts information processing in direct contrast with associationism—a contemporary paradigm traceable to Watsonian behaviorism.

QUESTIONS

1. In what ways does everyday experience reflect the use of the scientific method?
2. Compare and contrast the descriptive, correlational, and manipulative research strategies. What are their strengths and weaknesses? Give examples of three situations in which each might be used most effectively.
3. Why has manipulation emerged as the most important method in science? What advantages does it have over description and correlation?
4. Why are both basic and applied research needed in contemporary psychology? Relate basic and applied research and illustrate with an example from the work of B. F. Skinner and his colleagues.
5. What seven concerns must an experimenter almost always face when using the manipulative research strategy?
6. How was the experimental method incorporated by the struc-

turalists? What are the major features of the structuralists' methodological and theoretical positions?

7. What is the relationship among the research of Wundt, Cattell, and Ebbinghaus? What type of lawful relationship did each investigate? How did Thorndike and Pavlov differ from Wundt and from each other?

8. Compare and contrast the major schools of psychology with regard to their research interests and methodologies.

9. How are structuralism and functionalism related to information processing?

10. What are the major points of agreement and disagreement between information processing and associationism? How and why do these two contemporary paradigms reflect an apparent regression to earlier psychological schools in terms of research philosophy and orientation?

The Anatomy of Psychological Experiments: Hypotheses, Samples, and Variables

A hypothesis anticipates nature and proposes certain conditions that might be found to exist, but that do not now exist as far as we know. It is a guess that needs to be explored. It must be demonstrated that the conceptual aspects of the hypothesis are supported by empirically derived facts. We set up an investigation to test the implications of the hypothesis and thus to collect evidence concerning these conceptual aspects.

(Brown & Ghiselli, 1955, p. 157)

In designing an experiment, we must devise the data-collecting procedures in a way that will provide a basis for estimating the importance of chance factors. This is accomplished when all factors except the experimental variable are forced to operate in an unsystematic way. . . . We must be able to detect in the subject all of the changes that are pertinent to the stimulus conditions we present to him.

(Brown & Ghiselli, 1955, p. 191)

An experiment consists of all that a scientist does in searching for regularities among interesting events, while controlling all other events. Typically, the experiment begins with a scientist's curiosity about the cause of an anomaly in nature. While few restraints are placed upon the origin of the scientist's experimental question, progress toward its resolution depends upon how the question is expressed.

The formal statement of a research question represents a critical step in an experiment. It dictates the selection of the subjects, the events to be manipulated, a set of procedures and a design, and an appropriate measurement technique. The origin and formulation of scientific hypotheses is the initial topic of this chapter. In discussing this initial topic, we will consider three types of scientific questions, the reasons why the to-be-tested hypothesis is most properly phrased in null form, the conditions that lead to the confirmation or rejection of the null hypothesis, and the two types of error that can be made in the confirmation/rejection decision.

We will then turn our attention to the selection of subjects. It is the task of the experimenter to clearly indicate which population of subjects is involved in the experiment and to select subjects for experimentation in a way that ensures they are representative of the parent population. Subjects should be selected so as to maximize the generality of scientific observations. Some of the techniques that can increase the breadth of generalizations from samples to populations are random sampling, large samples, stratified samples, and special experimental designs.

The term *variable* threads its way throughout the sequence of an experiment—from the formulation of the scientific question to the designation of the manipulated event to the measurement of behavioral change. The concepts that are used in formulating scientific questions are usually defined by observable features of the world that vary in specified ways. The essence of an experiment is the question of whether variations in one feature of the world will be accompanied by systematic variations in others. But what does *variation* mean in these contexts? How do features vary? Must some features vary before or after others? These and other questions will be taken up in our discussion of variables in psychological research.

In the final section of this chapter we will focus on one particular class of variables called the *dependent* or *response variable.* Of primary concern will be the issues of response consistency, sensitivity, and validity; the conditions under which more than a single response can be recorded; and the problems that surround the setting of a criterion for responding and the averaging of responses across repeated measurements in an experiment.

THE ORIGIN AND FORMULATION OF SCIENTIFIC HYPOTHESES

Scientific questions arise from a variety of sources. An analysis of a theory for purposes of extending a generalization may call for new observations. Perhaps, alternative theories force a critical experiment. Equally often, the scientist develops a researchable question rather informally, sometimes responding to little more than the anecdotal observations of others or to personal experience. It is at this early stage that phenomenological experiences are useful in science. Both approaches—the theoretical and the personal—can stimulate questions, phrased as scientific hypotheses, about regularities in the world.

Hypotheses as Declarative Statements

Because the science of psychology is in its adolescence, relatively few formal, elaborate theories are available for purposes of deductive analysis and subsequent hypothesis formation. Instead, many current scientific questions about behavior have their origins in the insights, experiences, and anecdotal observations of curious scientists. The so-called frustration-aggression hypothesis, for example, emerged from discussions, anecdotal observations, and analyses of recorded clinical materials by a group of social scientists who met regularly at Yale University in the late 1930s. The material they sifted through consisted of a wealth of observations regarding aggressive behavior. From a logical analysis of alleged aggression-provoking incidents, the Yale scientists concluded that each aggressive incident was in some way preceded by a frustrating event. They postulated that all antecedent, aggression-provoking incidents could be classified as frustrating be-cause each, in some sense, thwarted or blocked the attainment of a desired goal (Dollard, Doob, Miller, Mowrer, & Sears, 1939). Further consideration suggested that aggressive behavior generally occurred following exposure to frustrating incidents but did not often occur in other contexts. These observations then led to a tentative hypothesis, stating that frustrating events, F, produced aggressive behavior, A. The presumption here was "If F, then A." An additional presumption was that, in general, one did not occur without the other—"If not F, then not A."

   The frustration-aggression hypothesis was originally a tentative formulation based on collective analyses of the readings and observa-tions of several prominent social scientists. It represented only a speculative answer to the question, "What factors are related to the occurrence of aggressive behaviors?" The tentative formulation, ag-gression is produced by frustration, nicely illustrates the declarative status of a scientific hypothesis. Scientific hypotheses are not phrased in the form of the questions that mirror the original curiosity or concern of the scientist; instead, they are phrased as positive relationships, as tentative answers.

   Scientists must pose questions in the form of declarative answers because science is an undertaking that combines the rules of logic with the rules of controlled observation. Logically speaking, the declarative sentence is the only kind of sentence that can be confirmed or rejected through observation. To ask whether a sentence expressed in the form of a question or an imperative is empirically confirmable is a non sequitur. Only a declarative statement can be supported or rejected.

General and Explicit Hypotheses

The introductory section of most research papers usually contains both a general and an explicit statement of the problem to be addressed by the experiment. The more general statement sets the stage for the explicit formulation of the hypothesis with its emphasis on well-defined concepts, procedures, and design. The general statement, phrased in global terms, can be stated either in the form of an interrogative or a declarative sentence without creating problems because only the more explicit, experimental hypothesis constitutes the declarative statement to be judged acceptable or unacceptable in terms of the controlled observations. Box 3.1 contains a number of general statements from recent research articles.

There are at least three good reasons for beginning an experimental report with the broadest possible presentation of the scientific question. A general statement of the question (a) sets the stage for a better understanding of the purposes of the study by showing how the study fits into contemporary psychological thought, (b) provides for a more considered and careful formulation of the specific hypotheses that follow, and (c) anticipates some of the generalizations that the experimenter may later make about the results.

In contrast, the explicit statement of the problem is a careful restatement in terms of the study's specific conditions, operations, and procedures. Thus, the *experimental hypothesis* is an explicit reformulation of the original research question that clarifies (a) the presumed relationship between the variables that will be manipulated, (b) the type of subjects to be tested, (c) the procedures and materials to be used, and (d) the response measures that will serve as the dependent variables.

A social psychologist concerned with the effects of frustration on aggression would need to restate the broad hypothesis—frustration produces aggression—in terms of the specific operations that define instances of frustration and instances of aggression. Frustration might be defined, for example, as a prearrangement in which a confederate of the experimenter interrupts and annoys a subject who is engaged in the solution of an anagram task (cf. Konečni, 1975). A subsequent test situation would allow frustrated and nonfrustrated subjects to display aggression toward the confederate. An instance of aggressive behavior might be defined by the number or duration of electric shocks delivered to the confederate by each subject. While the subject is led to believe the shocks to be of feedback value to the confederate who is performing a creative task, the experimenter uses the number or the duration of shocks as an index of aggression. Explicitly stated, the experimental hypothesis might read, "Students who are interrupted by a confederate while solving anagram problems will deliver more

Box 3.1   Broad Statements of Scientific Hypotheses

Almost all research articles in psychological journals contain examples of the various ways in which general problem statements are phrased. Consider these illustrations:

The present study deals with one of the apparent consequences of some of these differences (between men and women), namely, the fact that so few women enter scientific fields and even fewer achieve "eminence." (Walberg, 1969)

The present investigation was an attempt to determine whether humans have the ability to discriminate light from darkness with their hands and arms. (Steinberg, 1966)

This paper is concerned with the problem of attainment of conversation. (Wallach & Sprott, 1964)

The experiments reported in the present paper were carried out to gain further insights into the processes involved in good memory performance. (Craik & Tulving, 1975)

Does, in short, an infant hear the same pattern of phonetic identity and difference among parts of syllables that the adult hears? (Fodor, Garrett, & Brill, 1975) and longer electric shocks to the person who interrupts them than will students not so interrupted by the same confederate."

In summary, all research endeavors are ways of obtaining answers through controlled observations to questions that arise from the lack of information regarding a theory, set of anecdotal observations, or some personal experience. The need for the scientist to satisfy curiosity leads to a logical analysis of the available information, whether anecdotal or scientific, in order to evolve tentative speculations in the form of general hypotheses. In turn, the general statement is used as an outline from which a more precisely formulated hypothesis is evolved. The more precise statement is the experimental hypothesis; it is expressed in terms of an assumed relationship between the variables that comprise the experiment for a particular group of subjects. The experimental hypothesis forces decisions on the type of subjects, procedures, and materials that ultimately give meaning to concepts that are to be related. Finally, both the general and experimental hypotheses provide the conceptual structure from which conclusions assume significance.

Types of Scientific Questions

The quest for description.   There are two kinds of questions, one more basic than the other, that can be asked by the scientist. The more basic question concerns the description of some aspect of the population of subjects about whom the scientist is concerned. This type of question takes the form, "How much?" or "How many?"; the answer to which is usually expressed in terms of a percentage. "What percentage of American men and women entered psychology graduate school in the last decade?" or "What percentage of couples in Indiana adopted children in each of the past twenty years?" are examples of descriptive questions. This kind of question presumes the existence in a given population of target characteristics that can by quantified. It is a fundamental type of question in science, requiring little more than counting or tallying an event. Generally, the information derived from descriptive questions is not directly used in the formulation of laws.

The quest for difference.   The second type of scientific question seeks information on a difference between characteristics or behaviors in a population. This second kind of question takes the general form, "Is there a difference between characteristics, conditions, or events?" For example, a researcher may wish to know if having a high-school diploma is related to job security or to community leadership or to divorce. The comparison implied by a difference question is between two populations of subjects (e.g., between the populations of people who have and those who do not have a high-school diploma) and deals with a determination of whether one has more or less of a given feature (e.g., job durability, community status, or divorces).

The prevalence of the difference type of question in a science is an indication of its sophistication and importance. It represents a search for laws and requires more than the simple operation of counting. Difference questions are concerned with the discovery of new relationships among events in the world. Because of the importance of this type of question for the development of psychological laws and theories, the greater part of the remainder of this text is devoted to an exposition of the ways of maximizing the chances of obtaining clear answers to questions of difference.

The Null Hypothesis as a Test for Differences

Satisfaction of scientific curiosity usually requires that the broad hypothesis be rephrased into a declarative statement—the explicit experimental hypothesis stating a relationship between events. This relationship usually implies the prediction of a difference in performance as a function of the presence versus the absence of some characteristic or feature in a population. That is, people who have or receive the particular characteristic or event are hypothesized to perform differently, often in a specified direction, than those who have or receive either less or none of the characteristic or event. This prediction of a difference in performance is the experimental hypothesis. However, a final step in hypothesis formation must be taken before the scientist can make appropriate observations and correctly interpret them. This step is the formation of the *null hypothesis*, so called because it can be "nullified" or rendered untenable. The formation of the null hypothesis is necessary to determine whether a performance difference obtained through experimentation is important or simply results from factors other than those intentionally investigated as part of the study.

Assume for the moment that you have discovered that the experimental subjects (Y_E) in our earlier example who were interrupted while working anagram problems gave more electric shocks to the interrupting confederate than did the control subjects (Y_C) who had not been interrupted. Before claiming that the experimental hypothesis had been confirmed, it must first be shown that the observed difference in aggressive shocks given by the experimental and control subjects was not due to chance or accidental factors. Such accidental factors might include the placement of more aggressive, more active, or more anxious subjects in the experimental condition than in the control condition. Concerns such as these are important even if the obtained difference is quite large, and in the predicted direction. Even large differences can occur on occasion by chance alone, and it is just as likely that such differences might be in the predicted as in the nonpredicted direction. Put succinctly, how can it be determined whether a performance difference is an important one, attributable to Y_E, or not?

To assert the existence of a performance difference requires by implication a demonstration of inequality. Support for an experimental hypothesis asserting a performance difference ($\overline{Y}_E > \overline{Y}_C$) due to some characteristic or condition (Y_E) is obtained when it has been convincingly demonstrated that it is unreasonable to argue that $\overline{Y}_E$ is equal to $\overline{Y}_C$. Note that when $\overline{Y}_E$ and $\overline{Y}_C$ are used, we are referring to a performance index (mean); when Y_E and Y_C are used, we are referring to the experimental (treatment) and control conditions, respectively.

The test of an explicit experimental hypothesis is indirect. Its support depends upon the outcome of the test of a null hypothesis—namely, the test that the presence of Y_E was irrelevant to the observed difference. This form of the hypothesis, expressed as H_O: $\overline{Y}_E = \overline{Y}_C$, may seem paradoxical since it represents a statement opposite to the very relationship that the scientist wishes to demonstrate, namely, $\overline{Y}_E > \overline{Y}_C$.

To show that an observed difference between groups $\overline{Y}_E$ and $\overline{Y}_C$ is real, it must first be shown that the difference could not have occurred by chance. This is done both by testing the null hypothesis which states that the factor of interest (Y_E) had no effect (i.e., that the presence or absence of Y_E was unrelated to the performance difference) and then by showing this position to be untenable. If the null hypothesis is untenable, then one of two alternatives must be acceptable—either $\overline{Y}_E > \overline{Y}_C$ or $\overline{Y}_E < \overline{Y}_C$. The direction of observed performance difference then dictates which of the two alternative hypotheses is the more reasonable.

A null statement of no difference implies a specific value, zero, against which an observed difference between conditions $\overline{Y}_E$ and $\overline{Y}_C$ can be compared. To conclude that an experimental hypothesis is tenable—that the observed difference in performance due to Y_E versus Y_C is real—is tantamount to saying that the null hypothesis ($\overline{Y}_E = \overline{Y}_C$ or $\overline{Y}_E - \overline{Y}_C = 0$) is untenable. If the null hypothesis is untenable, how much greater than zero must the difference between Y_E and Y_C be? To answer this question, we must first briefly discuss sampling theory.

Departures from the null. Consider the possible outcomes of an experiment when the null hypothesis is actually true. The experiment in question measures the effects of the presence (Y_E) and absence (Y_C) of prior frustrations on aggressive behavior, defined by the number of shocks given to an interrupting confederate. Because of chance factors, it is unlikely that the performance averages for $\overline{Y}_E$ and $\overline{Y}_C$

would be identical in any one experiment. However, if the experiment were done precisely the same way a very large number of times, it would be possible to plot a frequency distribution of mean differences for $\overline{Y}_E$ and $\overline{Y}_C$. A frequency distribution of mean differences ($\overline{Y}_E - \overline{Y}_C$) obtained from a large number of replications of the same basic experiment, is termed a *sampling distribution of mean differences.* Each pair of means is computed, and the differences, $\overline{Y}_E - \overline{Y}_C$, are included in the sampling distribution of mean differences. The sampling distribution in most cases is hypothetical because it consists of an infinite number of mean differences. The average value of a sampling distribution of mean differences is zero. In addition, statisticians have shown that a frequency distribution of mean differences is normal in form.

It is possible to conceive of a difference between two means obtained from a single experiment as but a randomly drawn statistic from a theoretical sampling distribution of such differences, each coming from one of an infinite number of similar experiments, with the sampling distribution of mean differences having its own mean of zero and a normal form. Due to chance, it is unlikely that any one difference between means from a given experiment will itself equal zero, the mean of the sampling distribution. Given that the null hypothesis (H_O: $\overline{Y}_E = \overline{Y}_C$) is correct, any observed difference in an experiment would be a departure from zero and, to the extent of that deviation, an error. In a sense, all values of the sampling distribution of mean differences except the mean value itself (zero) are in error. The size of the error is the extent of their deviations from the sampling mean. The standard deviation of the variations among mean differences in a sampling distribution is known as the *standard error* of the difference between means.[1] Box 3.2 is an example of a hypothetical frequency distribution of differences between means as it relates to decisions about a true null hypothesis.

Searching for significant differences.   Now that we have briefly discussed the concept of a sampling distribution of mean differences, we can return to the question of how large the difference between means must be before the null hypothesis is rejected as untenable. If the value of the standard error and the form of the hypothetical sampling distribution are known, the researcher can determine how often a difference would occur by chance given that the null hypothesis is true. As can be seen in Figure 3.1, a relatively small deviation of an observed mean difference from the average of the sampling distribu-

---

1. The size of the standard error of a sampling distribution of differences between means depends on both the sample size and an estimate of the population variances. Specifically, the standard error of the difference between means is equal to the square root of the sum of estimated population variances ($\sqrt{\sigma_1^2 + \sigma_2^2}$), where each σ^2 is calculated from the formula $\frac{S^2}{n-1}$; S is the standard deviation in the sample $S = \sqrt{\dfrac{\Sigma(X-M)^2}{n}}$ and n is the sample size (cf. Blommers & Lindquist, 1960).

Box 3.2 Sampling Distributions: When the Null Is True

Figure 3.1 depicts a sampling distribution of an infinite number of instances of differences between means obtained from the conditions Y_E and Y_C when the null hypothesis is true. For any given experiment, a difference in performance means $(\overline{Y}_E - \overline{Y}_C)$ is quite likely even though, on the average, the mean difference is zero. Thus, any observed difference for a particular experiment would represent a sampling error, small differences being more likely to occur by chance than large ones. This is due to the fact that a majority of possible mean differences lie in close proximity to the mean of the sampling distribution, zero. In addition positive and negative differences would be equally likely due to the symmetry of the normal curve.

By chance, relatively large positive or negative differences from the null hypothesis occur only rarely. However, such deviations can happen even when the null is true. When a specific mean difference is large enough to fall at least two standard error units away from the mean in the so-called areas of rejection, it might be incorrectly concluded that the particular observed difference was too great to have occurred by chance alone. Fortunately, such errors in rejecting true null hypotheses occur only rarely, and the probability of such errors occurring at all is known in advance of an experiment.

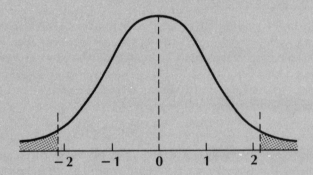

Area of Rejection   **Area of Rejection**

$(Y_E - Y_C < 0)$ $(Y_E - Y_C = 0)$ $(Y_E - Y_C > 0)$

Figure 3.1   **A sampling distribution of mean differences between sample means Y_E and Y_C with a mean of zero and a standard deviation of one.**

tion is very likely to occur by chance. This can be inferred from the proportionately large number of small positive and small negative deviations that are clustered around the mean. Therefore, a small performance difference obtained for any given experiment would not be taken by a scientist as justification for rejecting the null hypothesis.

From Figure 3.1 you can see that as mean differences increase in distance from the sampling average (in terms of standard error units), they also decrease in frequency. What this indicates is that a relatively large deviation is much less likely to occur by chance than a small deviation. Indeed, if a deviation exceeds a given magnitude, established arbitrarily by generally accepted statistical conventions in excess of approximately ± 2 standard error units, it is no longer conceded to be due to chance but to more systematic factors. In our frustration-aggression example, this would mean a relatively large difference, expressed in standard error units, in the mean number of shocks delivered by Y_E versus Y_C. The greater the deviation of an observed mean difference from the mean of the theoretical sampling distribution of differences, the more likely this performance difference will be judged as statistically significant. In this sense, *significance* refers to *nonchance occurrences*.

Several levels of improbability, measured by the number of standard error units from the null value, have been used by scientists to define whether an observed statistic is significant. These levels are commonly the 5%, 1%, and the 0.1% levels of significance. A standard error deviation of a sampling distribution is said to be at the 5% level if only 5 times out of 100 a deviation as large or larger than the observed value would occur by chance. The choice of a level of significance depends upon a number of factors such as the exactness of measurement, the importance of the decision that is based upon the results, the sample size, and accepted conventions.

The procedure for determining whether an observed statistic is significantly different from the hypothesized mean of the sampling distribution of mean differences is called a *test of significance*. If a test of a null hypothesis is conducted, such as in our frustration-aggression example, and the result turns out to be significant, then the null hypothesis can be rejected. Since the process of hypothesis testing involves means, standard errors, and sampling distributions, the null hypothesis has sometimes been called the statistical hypothesis.

The experimental hypotheses ($\overline{Y}_E > \overline{Y}_C$ and $\overline{Y}_E < \overline{Y}_C$) that are the alternatives to the null hypothesis cannot be tested directly. An experimental hypothesis differs from the null hypothesis in that it does not state exactly what the mean of the sampling distribution will be but merely states a departure from the null in a given direction. There is no way of directly rejecting or accepting the experimental hypothesis on other than speculative grounds. However, if the null hypothesis is rejected because a significant result occurred in the direction predicted by the experimental hypothesis, the latter hypothesis is supported. The experimental hypothesis is tested indirectly in the sense that it is evaluated only after a direct assessment of the null hypothesis has been completed.

In most experiments the scientist is interested primarily in the experimental hypothesis and may not even mention the null or exact hypothesis in analyzing the data or writing the research report. This custom is solely a matter of convention aimed at enhancing communication. Nevertheless, the null hypothesis is clearly the most important part of the logic underlying an experiment. Unless an experiment is designed so that the null can be directly evaluated, it is of no value because the experimental and general hypotheses will remain untested.

The absolute size of an observed difference between means, in and of itself, has little bearing upon the acceptance or rejection of the null hypothesis. What is important is the size of a mean difference relative to the size of the standard error of the relevant sampling distribution of mean differences. If the standard error is large, then a large difference between observed means would not necessarily invalidate the null hypothesis. However, if the standard error is small, relative to the observed difference between means, the null hypothesis will very probably be untenable.

Small standard errors result, in part, from research efforts that minimize performance differences among subjects. Figure 3.2 presents the results for a learning experiment in terms of individual performance curves across trials for three experimental conditions (E_1, E_2, and E_3) and a control condition (C). The standard error of the mean in E_1 will be larger than in E_2 because of the greater variability in the performance curves in the former.[2] In addition, the standard error in E_3 will be smaller than E_2 because there are twice as many subjects in E_3, though the variations in performance for E_2 and E_3 are very similar. It is likely that a statistical comparison of the means for Groups E_1, E_2, and E_3 with the mean for Group C would show that only the comparison between Group E_3 and Group C was significant because there was less variability in E_3 than E_1 and there were more subjects in E_3 than in both E_1 and E_2, thereby reducing the standard error in E_3.

We have discussed only one type of null hypothesis, namely, the test of a possible difference between two sample means. The reason we have focused on this type of null hypothesis is that it underlies most psychological research. There are, however, other types of null comparisons—the test that a sample mean is equal to a specified value, a constrast of two proportions, or the test that a correlation coefficient

2. The standard error of the mean is calculated from the formula $\sigma = \dfrac{S}{\sqrt{n-1}}$, where S is the standard deviation of scores in the sample and n is the number of subjects.

Figure 3.2

Individual subject variations in performance in three experimental conditions and a control condition. The mean of each group for all trials is signified by $\overline{Y}$. The null hypotheses are $\overline{Y}_C = \overline{Y}_{E_1}$, $\overline{Y}_C = \overline{Y}_{E_2}$, and $\overline{Y}_C = \overline{Y}_{E_3}$.

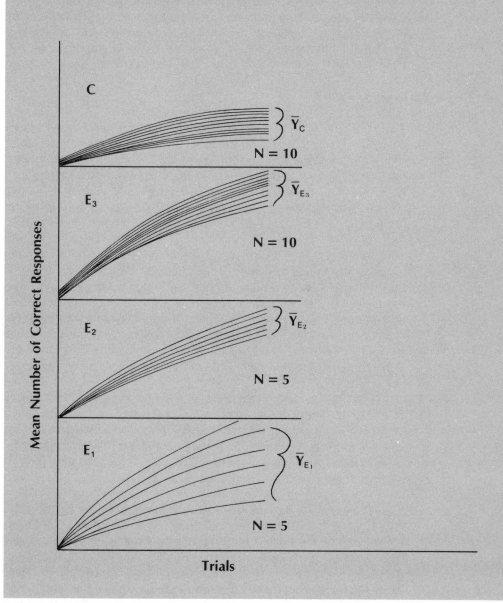

is zero, to name only a few. However, by and large, the most useful comparison index is provided by the declarative statement that there will be no difference between the performance measures taken for two groups, often experimental and control groups. The null hypothesis provides an explicit standard by which to compare an observed difference in an experiment and to decide whether an outcome is significantly greater than might be expected on the basis of chance. Finally, if the null is untenable, a decision is made as to which alternative experimental hypothesis ($\overline{Y}_E > \overline{Y}_C$ or $\overline{Y}_E < \overline{Y}_C$) is more reasonable.

Types of Error

Two types of error can occur when testing the null hypothesis. A decision to reject the null on the basis of sample data would be incorrect if the hypothesis of no difference was actually true. A decision to accept would also be incorrect if the null hypothesis was actually false. Fortunately, scientists can state the risks of making these two types of errors in confirming or rejecting a null hypothesis at the outset of an experiment.

Type I errors.   As we have seen, large observed deviations from the mean of a sampling distribution can occur by chance alone. If a true null hypothesis is rejected—implying that a significant departure from the expected null value had occurred—while in fact the difference was due solely to chance, a *Type I error* would have been committed. If a 5% level had been chosen to define nonchance occurrences, the so-called level of significance, then the probability of committing a Type I error (α) would be .05. In other words, 5% of the time the null would be rejected when true.

Alpha (α) per se is not a Type I error, but merely the probability of such an error occurring when the null hypothesis is true. The likelihood of the acceptance of the null hypothesis when it is true is $1-\alpha$ and is appropriately termed the *area of acceptance*. The area of acceptance includes all of the sampling distribution associated with the test of the null hypothesis except α, the *area of rejection* (see Figure 3.1).

Type II errors.   If the null hypothesis is accepted when it is actually false, a *Type II error* has been committed. The risk of making a Type II error (β) is determined by a number of experimental factors: the number of subjects used, sample variability, the level of α chosen, the choice of a one- or two-tailed test of significance, and the true nature of the distribution of mean differences. In general, the greater the number of subjects, the smaller the group variability, the larger the α level (e.g., .05 rather than .01), the choice of a one-tailed rather than a two-tailed test of significance, and the greater the true difference between means, the less will be the risk of committing a Type II error. One highly desirable way to reduce the possibility of a Type II error is to employ procedures that reduce the variability of the sampling distribution. A reduction in variability can be accomplished by *(a)* careful measurement procedures so as to reduce recording errors, *(b)* control of ambient background conditions in order to avoid contaminating factors, and *(c)* an increase in sample sizes.

While β is the probability of committing a Type II error, 1-β represents the *power* of the statistical test. Power is the probability of rejecting a false null hypothesis, thus detecting a significant departure from the null. One test of significance is said to be more powerful than another if it is more likely to result in the rejection of a false null hypothesis. The more powerful test is more likely to detect a difference between two means.

On Accepting and Rejecting the Null Hypothesis

We have analyzed the null hypothesis in terms of its tenability (acceptance) or untenability (rejection) rather than in terms of its proof or disproof. There is good reason for our choice of terms since there is no logical way to prove or disprove the null hypothesis. The strategy of testing the null hypothesis is simply a way to establish a quantitative standard by which to indirectly evaluate an experimental hypothesis.

The null hypothesis permits the designation of exact limits beyond which, were an observed difference to occur, a decision to reject the null would follow. Rejection does not mean disproof, since there is always the possibility that the observed deviation, while large enough to be judged as nonchance, was nevertheless due to chance factors, resulting in a Type I error. In addition, the null hypothesis cannot be proved anymore than it can be disproved since there remains the possibility of a Type II error, namely, accepting the null when it is false. It is for these reasons that the terms tenable and untenable are appropriate when discussing the null hypothesis.

THE SELECTION OF SUBJECTS

Experimentation is a controlled observational procedure that, hopefully, provides the basis for a generalized conclusion. The validity of the generalization based on the outcome of an experiment is related, in part, to the degree that the subjects are representative of the larger population to which the generalization refers. In the following section we will take up the problems relevant to subject selection and representativeness.

The Concept of a Sample

The general hypothesis in an experiment is presumed to have broad applicability, even though the test that follows is composed of highly specific features and events. Consider one possible test of the general hypothesis that frustration produces aggression. The test might be made in terms of the well-defined operations of "insulting and interrupting" students engaged in anagram problems as an instance of frustration and number of shocks delivered to the annoyer as an instance of aggression. The specific operations are assumed to be representative instances of more general concepts.

Just as experimentation necessitates the particularization of concepts in terms of specific operations since it is generally impossible to examine all instances, it is also necessary to particularize the subjects chosen for an experiment since usually all of the subjects at whom the generalization is aimed cannot be tested. Thus, the frustration-aggression hypothesis is intended to apply to all instances of frustration and of aggression as well as to all humans and, perhaps, nonhumans—past, present, and future. Since it is obviously impossible for all individuals in the population to serve as subjects for an aggression experiment, the scientist is forced to select but a few subjects from the total population to which the general hypothesis has relevance.

The concept of *population*, as used in its broadest sense, refers to a frequency distribution of all of the members of a particular class having one or more qualities in common. A population can refer to anything from a binomial collection of scores, to the six possible values of a die, to all high-school seniors, to individuals with different IQs, ages, scores on a personality test, and so forth. In psychology, the concept of a population is usually applied to all of the members of a particular class who are capable of behaving similarly. When all members of a population are measured, scores such as the mean and standard deviation can be derived. These scores, applicable to the entire population, are known as *population parameters*.

Seldom is it feasible to obtain a measure of some quality for an entire population. Usually, the scientist must be content to select a subgroup of the parent population, called a *sample*, and measure a particular behavior for the members of that subgroup. Scores based on sample data are called *statistics*. From the scores in the sample it is possible to estimate or infer the parameters of the parent population.

The Random Sample

Since sample statistics are used to infer population parameters, a major concern of the behavioral scientist is to ensure that the sample itself is a good representative of the population. The degree to which a sample accurately represents the population in question is the degree to which sample statistics mirror population parameters. The central problem in achieving this correspondence is the proper selection and assignment of subjects to the samples in an experiment so that each sample is a good reflection of the parent population. Actually, there are several ways in which samples can be constructed so as to ensure their representativeness. Perhaps the most useful is that of random selection. If each and every member of the parent population is equally likely of being included in the sample, the sampling is said to be random, and the sample is a *random sample*.

A *random sample* ensures that a subgroup of subjects is selected from the population so that their probability of selection was the same as the probability of selecting any other set of subjects from the same population. In the case of the frustration-aggression example, random samples for the conditions of "interruption" and "noninterruption" would ensure that individuals of all ages, sexes, educational backgrounds, geographical locations, socioeconomic levels, religious interests, etc., had an equal chance of selection. This does not mean that all of the many different kinds of subjects in the parent population necessarily would be represented in the sample. For instance, a person with twenty years of education would be far less likely to appear in a random sample than would a person with twelve years of education. It does mean that each and every subject of concern to the general hypothesis has an equal probability of selection from the population to which the hypothesis applies. Virtually every parametric test of significance is based on the assumption of random selection at some point in its application. For example, a decision with regard to the statistical rejection of the null hypothesis for the difference between means is linked to the procedures of random sampling.

Unbiased and Biased Samples

When no restrictions are placed on the possible inclusion of each subject of a population in a given sample or when the restrictions that are placed on each subject do not prevent the sample from being truly representative of the population, it is said to be an *unbiased sample*. The reason for this designation can be understood in terms of the nature of a theoretical sampling distribution of a statistic (e.g., mean) based on an infinite number of such samples. If an infinite number of unbiased samples of equal size were taken independently from a parent population and their means plotted in a relative frequency distribution (the sampling distribution of the means), the arithmetic average of that distribution would equal the population mean. This rather complicated statement is just another way of saying that a sample is unbiased if a statistic calculated from that sample is, *on the average*, equal to the population parameter that it represents. If the mean IQ of a sample belonged in a sampling distribution of IQ means, the mean of that distribution being 100, then the sample is an unbiased estimate of the population mean regardless of the particular value of its sample mean.

It follows that a *biased sample* belongs in a theoretical sampling distribution whose mean is not the population parameter in question. Any restriction on the possible inclusion in the sample of an individual in the parent population biases the sample. It renders the sample as nonrepresentative of the parent population to which a generalization is intended. For example, a scientist may hypothesize that a given treatment will elevate IQ in contrast to a control condition. In choosing subjects for the samples to test this hypothesis, any restriction that precludes the chances of selecting a subject, or set of subjects, from the parent population will bias these samples, making them unrepresentative of the population to which the conclusion is to apply.

Bias, by definition, means that a sample is not representative due to a fatal restriction that occurred as part of the subject selection procedure, thus introducing systematic error. By *systematic error* is meant that, over an infinite number of sample repetitions, a sampling distribution would be generated whose mean was not the population mean. This is why the pairs of terms *unbiased* and *representative*, and *biased* and *unrepresentative* are treated as synonyms in regards to sampling theory. Each set of terms applies to samples that are formed so that the mean of their respective sampling distributions is or is not the same as their population mean.

While random sampling often is the best procedure to achieve the goal of representativeness, it sometimes happens by chance that this method produces a subgroup of subjects who do not possess all of the characteristics of the parent population judged to be important for testing the hypothesis. A moment's reflection will undoubtedly suggest the near impossibility of a sample being exactly like the population it is presumed to mirror, even if it is truly randomly selected. This is especially true of very small samples that contain only a few members of the parent population.

Clearly, the only type of sample exactly like the population is the population itself. As the size of a sample is increased, including more and more of the members who make up the population, the more likely it will incorporate most of those features that characterize the parent group in important ways. This line of reasoning would suggest that large sample sizes are desirable because they lead to greater representativeness. However, you will soon learn that there are good reasons for selecting relatively small samples in psychological research.

Sampling Error

If randomly chosen small samples have little likelihood of duplicating on a miniature basis the characteristics of the parent population, why are they nonetheless designated as unbiased and representative? The answer to this question requires an examination of the theoretical sampling distribution of which the statistic for each random sample is a part. Recall the main characteristics of a hypothetical sampling distribution of sample means: (1) Most of the sample means cluster around the mean of the sampling distribution. (2) A few sample means are discrepant from the sampling distribution mean by either very large or very small values. (3) The mean of an infinitely large number of random sample means would equal the population mean.

The degree to which each sample mean deviates from the population mean is its degree of error. However, this degree of error is entirely accidental in that the random selection procedure used to form each sample prevents the systematic occurrence of similar deviations. This accidental, nonsystematic kind of error is termed sampling error. *Sampling error* is simply the difference between the value of a population parameter and that of its corresponding sample statistic. It is the deviation that can occur from sample to sample due to misrepresentations of population characteristics in the samples.

Even though the mean of a random sample differs from the population mean because of the presence of sampling error does not alter the fact that it is an unbiased estimate of the population mean. What qualifies the sample mean, or any statistic, as an unbiased estimate of a population parameter is that it belongs to a sampling distribution whose mean is the population mean or other appropriate parameter. The sample mean belongs there by virtue of the sampling procedure that was used to form it. In the case of a random procedure, any error due to sampling is nonsystematic or acccidental. The random sample is representative because its statistic falls in a sampling distribution whose grand mean is the mean of the population, even though it is unlikely that a single sample will have as its mean a value that is equal to the population mean.

Types of Sampling Error

Random sampling procedures are valuable since they represent the framework from which generalizations are extended to populations. It follows that a scientist must learn the skills involved in the formation of random samples so as to justify to the scientific community that his or her experimental outcomes can be generalized to relevant populations. Nonetheless, a random sampling procedure can introduce accidental error that forces an incorrect decision about the null hypothesis. One index of the magnitude of accidental error is the standard error of the sampling distribution. A relatively large standard error, due to the presence of considerable error variation from sample to sample or to small sample size, would require a very large difference between the means in order to reject the null hypothesis. Not only do the requirements of a good experiment demand that samples be representative of the parent population but also that samples be free from sampling error so as to acheive a relatively small standard error (Linquist, 1953). We will now turn to a brief discussion of the kinds of sampling errors and various ways to reduce them.

Type S errors.   By accident, a sample may consist of a disproportionate number of peculiar subjects who are, for example, of superior intelligence, less introverted, or more democratic than individuals in the population. These and many other accidents of sampling that result in unrepresentative individuals being included in a sample are called *Type S sampling errors.* Type S errors can result in an ambiguous interpretation of the experimental outcome. Consider our frustration-aggression example in this regard. Although randomly chosen, a disproportionate number of anxious subjects might be picked for inclusion in the interrupted group as opposed to the noninterrupted group. The accidental presence of anxiety could affect the experimental outcome; for instance, the interrupted subjects might give more shocks to the confederate than the noninterrupted subjects. It would not be clear then whether the incidence of more shocks was due to the presence or absence of interruption, to the differential presence of anxiety, or to both factors. The presence of Type S errors can increase the chances of mistakenly rejecting or mistakenly accepting a null hypothesis, depending upon which of the samples in an experiment is affected by the sampling error. Good research minimizes the likelihood that Type S errors due to unwanted individual differences will influence experimental results (Lindquist, 1953).

Type G errors.   Even when Type S errors have been largely eliminated and the samples are close to the parent population in all important respects, incidental changes in the physical or social environment of the experiment might still disturb the performance of an entire subgroup. The accidental occurrence of some environmental feature that inadvertently influences the performance of an entire sample of subjects is called a *Type G sampling error.*

Consider an experiment testing the following general hypothesis: the nature of pre-experimental instructions will affect the outcome of a study. Assume that randomly selected groups are chosen and that each is given different information about the purpose of the study.

The experiment is conducted in a group setting and each subject's task is to report words that are briefly flashed on a screen. Some of the words are relatively neutral, such as *dog* and *green*, and some are emotionally charged, such as *Kotex* or *penis*. Group A is informed that the experiment is a simple word-recognition task, while Group B is told it is a study of anxiety tolerance. Assume that an unusually vocal and suspicious subject in Group A loudly proclaims in the presence of the entire group that he has strong reservations about the truth of the pre-experimental information. His social-environmental intrusion increases overall skepticism about the study for many of the individuals in Group A and, consequently affects their word-recognition performance. This intrusion would qualify as a Type G sampling error, even though the sample was random, unbiased, and representative. It would not be possible to determine whether the outcomes of the word-recognition test for Groups A and B were due to different sets of pre-experimental instructions, to the pervasive effects of one subject's skeptical comments, or both. Type G sampling errors are caused by environmental or social factors *extrinsic* to a sample of subjects (Lindquist, 1953).

Type R errors.   Even if Type S and G sampling errors were minimized or eliminated, it would still be possible for an unbiased sample, by chance alone, to contain still another source of sampling error. Assume that a researcher wished to examine the effects of shock intensities on the escape times of rats from an electrified alley into a nonelectrified goal area. Four groups were formed. Experimental groups were given low, intermediate, and high shock intensities in the alleyway; the control condition received no shock. In selecting subjects for these conditions, the experimenter chose rats from each of four large cage racks, Group 1 from Rack A, Group 2 from Rack B, and so forth. The logic in this selection procedure appears sound since the rats had originally been randomly assigned to racks. However, once the rats had been assigned cage racks, the members of a given rack may become targets for conditions that do not otherwise uniformly prevail throughout the animal quarter. For example, lighting, sound, temperature, and other environmental factors may differ from location to location in a colony, thereby systematically affecting subjects in one rack but not in others. The colony caretaker might use a cleaning routine that involves movement of some but not other racks, again introducing possible systematic error. While the subjects of each group were chosen from randomly selected racks, it is possible by chance that one or more of the racks that supplied these groups had been located in an unusually cold or unusually warm portion of the colony, had been moved a great deal or very little by the caretaker, and so forth. Note that these differential conditions could influence the entire collection of rats housed in a single rack. In turn, this differential influence could indirectly affect the shock-escape performance of the subjects due, perhaps, to differences in physical health, lethargy, or nervousness. The occurrence of such an error would be accidental in that each rack was carefully selected on a random basis, and subjects within each rack were randomly assigned to a condition. This type of sampling error represents a part of the makeup of an entire group and, as such, appropriately might be labeled as an intrinsic error. *Intrinsic* refers to the presence of some relatively permanent or enduring feature that distinguishes a subpopulation from its parent population. The selection of a subpopulation containing an intrinsic, idiosyncratic characteristic defines a *Type R sampling error.*

A Type R sampling error obscures a clear interpretation of the experimental outcome in much the same way as Type S and G errors. Type S, G, and R errors can produce an entirely incorrect interpretation of an experimental finding—no matter how accidental their presence. Every precaution that minimizes or eliminates the presence of sampling errors should be incorporated into experimental procedures and designs.

Reducing Sampling Error

There are several methods to minimize accidental sampling errors, thereby reducing the chances of either rejecting a true null hypothesis or confirming a false hypothesis. Each of these methods has its own strengths and weaknesses. When considering these methods in this section, we will be careful to designate their legitimate uses. The first two procedures, the large sample technique and stratification, are used to combat Type S errors. The third procedure, the use of special experimental design, is used primarily to handle the problems of Type G and Type R sampling errors.

The large sample.   The selection of a large number (N) of subjects for a sample generally minimizes the occurrence of Type S sampling errors. As the sample size increases, it becomes more like the population as a whole. A large sample decreases the likelihood that important features of the parent population will be either disproportionately represented or omitted altogether. Statisticians have noted the reduction that occurs in the variability of a sampling distribution as a function of increased sample size. Intuitively, we can understand their finding by realizing that the mean of a large sample is more likely to be similar to the population mean than the mean of a small sample. Hence, the mean of a large sample would deviate less, on the average, from the mean of the sampling distribution. This is tantamount to saying that the mean of a large sample is more stable than the means of smaller samples. In the extreme case where the sample size is the same as the population size, the sample mean would be the population mean, and there could be no sampling error. Thus, as the sample size increases, thereby increasing the chances that all features of a population will have proportionate representation, the chances of a Type S error occurring decrease.

However, we must exercise considerable caution when using very large samples. For instance, sample sizes of 100 for the interrupted and noninterrupted groups in our frustration-aggression example would almost automatically produce a significant difference. But what would *statistical significance* mean? If the difference in means were very small—but significant—due to the use of large samples, would the result be *scientifically significant?* Would the result contribute to the development of meaningful laws and theory? The answer would probably be no. Clearly, statistical significance, gained merely through the use of large Ns, is not equated with scientific significance. See Box 3.3 for a discussion of statistical and scientific significance.

The effect of large samples is to increase the probability of rejecting the null hypothesis when in fact the treatment had no meaningful effect on the performance measures of the experiment. A statistically reliable difference is perhaps more impressive when the sample is relatively modest in size—15 to 25 subjects per group in human experiments or 5 to 10 subjects in most animal learning studies. The logic for selecting modest samples is that if an arithmetic difference is large enough to be statistically reliable when the standard error is relatively large, due to a small N, this difference may stand a better chance of proving scientifically important. We discuss a statistic for assessing the scientific importance of an experimental effect in Box 3.4.

The stratified sample. A *stratified sample* is formed, first, by dividing the population of concern into categories that are related to the outcome of the experiment and, second, by selecting a proportionate number of subjects from each category on a random basis to form the samples. Some characteristics of a population may be more important than others in the sense of being relevant to the experimental outcome. For example, an accurate representation of all age levels of a population in the samples may be judged important as far as evaluating the treatment condition on the experimental outcome. The population might then be stratified into categories that bridge 5-year spans—0–4.9 yrs., 5–9.9 yrs., 10–14.9 yrs., and so on.

Stratification of a population can be along as many dimensions as is necessary. In our example, in addition to stratification by age, stratification of the population in terms of sex could also be achieved by ascertaining the proportion of males and females at each age range

Box 3.3   Significance: Statistical and Scientific

Statistical significance is specified rather arbitrarily in terms of a significance level that establishes the limits beyond which obtaining a particular experimental outcome by chance is unlikely, assuming the null hypothesis to be true. The arithmetic magnitude of an obtained difference between sample means is not as important as the size of the difference relative to the standard error of the sampling distribution. Since the outcome of almost any experiment can be statistically significant if the samples are sufficiently large, the problem is how to discriminate between meaningful and nonmeaningful results when almost any result might meet the statistical criterion of significance because of large sample size. In other words, statistical significance (i.e., rejection of the null hypothesis) does not necessarily imply scientific significance.

Essentially, scientists are interested in how much of the variability in performance is due to the manipulated variable; they are not interested in variability in performance due to factors such as sampling errors. If most of the variability in performance measures is due to the experimental treatment, then not only will the outcome be statistically significant but also scientifically important. The demonstration of a statistically significant effect is definitely not the only important goal of research. Consistent performance for all of the subjects in a treatment condition is equally important for establishing scientific significance.

Box 3.4   A Measure of Scientific Significance: Omega^2

Every scientific experiment must be designed so that it can detect an important outcome without introducing procedures that render the experiment overly sensitive to trivial effects. There is a statistical technique that scientists can employ to assist in the determination of the scientific significance of an experimental outcome called *omega^2*. Omega^2 can be used to indicate the portion of variability in performance that actually is accounted for by the treatment condition under experimental scrutiny (Hays, 1973; Dodd & Schultz, 1973). Omega^2 is an arithmetic expression of the potency of the experimental manipulation and a quantitative index of the amount of control over the subjects' behavior exerted by the experimental condition. Since a major goal of psychology is the control of behavior, the more control exerted by an experimental condition, the more scientifically important is that condition.

In a certain sense, statistical significance and scientific significance go hand in hand. Both are determined by a comparison of the variability in individual performance scores with the variability in group performance means. However, statistical significance can be achieved even in the presence of considerable variability in individual performances. All that statistical significance requires is that the group means be more variable than the averaged individual performances within each group, even though both indices of variability may be relatively large. On the other hand, scientific significance is expressed in terms of a reduction in individual performance variations due to a treatment relative to overall variations in performance.

Omega^2 was applied to 112 randomly selected studies appearing in research journals published by the American Psychological Association (Dunnette, 1966). Although statistical significance was obtained in all cases, only a small portion of the total variability in performance measures (less than 30%) was associated with the experimental manipulations in about one-third of the studies (Dunnette, 1966). While there are no pre-established criteria for deciding on how much performance variability should be due to an experimental condition in order to achieve scientific importance, less than 30% is not overly impressive for those scientists who view regularity, precision, and generality as the criteria for meaningful scientific discovery. The use of omega^2 informs the psychological community about the scientific significance of statistically significant experimental outcomes.

and then reflecting this information proportionately in the selection of subjects for the samples of the experiment. *Stratification,* then, is a way to ensure representativeness through imposition of certain restrictions on the composition of a sample. The restrictions promote a closer match between relevant features in the parent population and corresponding features in the sample. It should be clear that the likelihood of a large overall Type S error due to the stratification factor is reduced by this technique as opposed to random sampling. Proper sample stratification ensures a representative and balanced proportion of subjects at each level of a relevant dimension.

Of pivotal importance in the stratification technique is the existence of prior knowledge that the stratified feature (e.g., age, IQ, anxiety) is relevant to the outcome of the experiment. If, for example, a division of the population into age levels had little to do with the outcome, the stratification of the sample according to age level would exert minimal influence on reducing Type S sampling errors. The stratification procedure would be unnecessary and would probably reduce the efficiency of the experiment. Great care must be exerted to determine that the stratified dimension is a relevant one; it should be highly correlated with performance measures.

There are both practical and logical reasons that limit the usefulness of the stratification procedure. Stratification may not be practical for those population characteristics about which there is little prior information regarding the relationship between the to-be-stratified feature and the performance measure under study. In addition, requirements of expense, time, and energy almost always are greater with the stratification procedure than with the random sampling procedure. Further, even if the relevance of a given population characteristic to the outcome is known, little information may be available regarding exactly how it should be handled. In spite of these difficulties, the use of a modest stratification procedure is often wise.

Special Experimental Designs

Neither the large sample nor the stratified sample can eliminate chance fluctuations that selectively affect one group but not others in an experiment (Type G and R sampling errors). In order to understand the methods that can be used to combat Type G and R errors, a slight readjustment in perspective is needed. Recall that one way to reduce the chances of large Type S errors is to add more subjects to each experimental group, thereby reducing sample-to-sample fluctuations with regard to relevant population characteristics. In a sense, increased sample size balances out unwanted fluctuations in group constituency. Similar logic can be applied to the control of Type G and R errors.

The only difference is that, instead of increasing the number of individuals in a given sample in order to reduce group-to-group fluctuations, the number of groups exposed to the treatments of the experiment is increased. Basically, groups are conceived of as collections of samples that can themselves be randomly assigned. Since there are two major ways to assemble sample groups in an experiment in order to combat Type G and R errors, we will consider them separately.

Groups-within-treatments.   Carefully chosen experimental designs can be of great assistance in nullifying the effects of Type S, R, and G sampling errors. The *groups-within-treatments* design is one in which multiple samples from the same population are drawn at random and each sample is given only one of several possible treatment conditions (Lindquist, 1953). For instance, if a school district contained 100 elementary schools, an investigator might *randomly* pick 30 schools. He would then *randomly* assign 10 of the 30 schools to each of three treatment conditions. Within each school, students from the same grade would be *randomly* selected and presented one of the treatment conditions since each school was assigned to one and only one treatment. There is little reason why the kind of extrinsic and intrinsic features (Type G and R errors) that differentiate subpopulations (i.e., individual schools) from one another should be greater for one treatment than for another when the treatment effects are averaged over several subgroups.

The key features of the groups-within-treatments design are that a number of different groups receive each treatment condition and that the overall treatment effect consists of finding the average performance of all groups within a treatment condition. In other words, the effect of a given treatment, X, given to groups 1 through 10, is found by summing the weighted treatment means for each of these groups ($\Sigma n_i \overline{X}_i$) and dividing by the number of subjects $\frac{(n_1\overline{X}_1 + n_2\overline{X}_2 + \ldots n_{10}\overline{X}_{10})}{n_1 + n_2 + \ldots n_{10}}$. Obviously, the effect of X on the various groups making up a condition should be relatively consistent. Nevertheless, any one of these groups may perform differently due to the influence of all three sampling errors—Type S, G, and R. However, by randomly assigning the groups to treatment conditions, Type S, G, and R should be evenly distributed across conditions and their influence should be relatively uniform for each treatment.

We should point out that one problem with the groups-within-treatments design is that there remains the possibility of an uneven distribution of sampling errors across conditions unless a large number of groups are employed. The fewer the number of groups, the more likely the chance for accidents of random assignment. With only six groups, for example, of which one exhibited a large Type S error and another fell victim to a Type G error, it is possible that both types of errors might end up in the same treatment condition and adversely affect the outcome simply through random assignment to one of two conditions. The larger the number of groups, the less likely this will happen. However, more groups represent additional investments in expense, time, and energy. An experimental design that increases the likelihood of an even distribution of all three types of errors across treatment conditions is the random replications design (Lindquist, 1953).

Random replications design.   Perhaps the surest way to accomplish a distribution of Type S, G, and R errors across treatment conditions is to repeat the entire experiment within each of several groups. This procedure is referred to as the *random replications design.* In our preceding example we randomly selected 30 of 100 schools, assigning 10 schools to each of three treatments. In the random replications design, *each* of 10 randomly selected sample schools is divided into three *subgroups.* Treatments are then randomly assigned to the subgroups of each school. In a sense, each school provides a miniature experiment; the more randomly chosen schools employed, the more replications of the experiment. All assignments—from the choice of schools, to their division into subgroups, to the assignment of treatments to subgroups—are made on a random basis. Thus, there is an effective distribution of sampling errors across the various treatment conditions. The major advantage of the random replications design is that the means ($\overline{X}_I$, $\overline{X}_{II}$, $\overline{X}_{III}$) would contain approximately equal amounts of Type S, G, and R sampling errors. A schematic representation of the random replications design is presented in Box 3.5.

The advantage of the random replications design over the group-within-treatments is that it requires fewer groups (e.g., 10 as opposed to 30 schools). In addition, more types of sampling errors (especially Type G and R errors) are eliminated from a comparison of the treatment means ($\overline{X}_I$, $\overline{X}_{II}$, and $\overline{X}_{III}$). The random replications design is built on a general rule applicable to all research in psychology: Experiments should contain several replications in order to ensure that the original causal relationship is reliable.

THE CONCEPT OF THE VARIABLE IN PSYCHOLOGICAL RESEARCH

The word *variable* is one of the more frequently used words in science. It generally refers to the conditions that are manipulated in an experiment and is used in conjunction with the concept of experimental treatment. Strictly speaking, experimental treatments correspond to various levels of some variable.

There are other contexts in which the concept of a variable is used. Our discussion of sampling errors dealt with variables although they were not designated as such. For example, a Type S error refers to accidents in the selection of peculiar subject characteristics that conceivably might influence the outcome of the experiment. What this means is that, by chance, a disproportionately large or small number of subjects in possession of some dispositional feature (e.g., intelligence or anxiety or age) occurred in a particular sample. These characteristics could just as easily be designated as the variables of intelligence, anxiety, or age. The presence of a large Type S error, then, is the same as the chance occurrence of a disproportionate representation of some variable in the sample relative to the parent population. The same logic applies to an analysis of Type G and R errors in terms of the disproportionate representation of variables common to the members of a sample.

Finally, performance measures collected from the subjects of the samples reflect the effects of the experimental conditions and represent another class of variable. Performance measures vary with changes in the experimental treatments, time, or trials. Indeed, it is proper to refer to the results of an experiment in terms of the performance variable as its outcome.

Definition of Variable

The term *variable* refers to some feature of the world that can be specified by at least two or more scale values. Designations such as red, green, and blue belong to the variable of color. The physical manipulation of electromagnetic wavelength, itself a physical variable, produces changes in the verbal reports of color sensations. Two variables are part of this example because they represent distinct features of the world, the electromagnetic spectrum and the reported experiences of different colors. Each is specifiable in terms of two or more scale values. Actually, it would be equally proper to designate these two variables as *dimensions* or as *continua* since there is a large number of orderly gradations from one scale value to another in each case. Parenthetically, this illustration of the concept of variable describes a correlation between systematic changes in one variable, different values on the electromagnetic spectrum, and corresponding changes in another, reports that accompany the perception of colors. The statistical demonstration of this relationship by means of a correlation coefficient is a *psychophysical function*, relating changes in a physical variable to changes in a psychological variable.

Box 3.5 An Example of a Random Replications Design

Each horizontal row of Table 3.1 represents one of the 10 randomly selected samples. The subsamples (x) within a given row represent the performance means for one-third of each sample as a function of the three treatments in the experiment (I, II, and III). Since all samples are similarly subdivided and exposed to the identical three experimental conditions, the overall performance average for each row (e.g., Group A, Group B, etc.) should not differ from sample to sample unless there are differences in the amounts of the sampling errors associated with each group. Any variation between the overall row means, shown in the last column of the table, is due to replication variability because of differences in the amounts of overall sampling error (especially Type G and R errors).

The mean values in any one of the columns (e.g., $\bar{x}_a$ or $\bar{x}_d$ for Treatment I) represent mean performances for subsamples presented the same experimental condition. These means are averaged at the bottom of each column to express the overall mean for each experimental condition. It is possible to argue that the three overall treatment means contain the same amount of sampling error; for any given sample, whatever error was present for one-third of that group would likely be present for the other two-thirds and, hence, would be constant over the three experimental conditions.

In essence, the amount of sampling error that was present for one experimental condition, averaged over the 10 respective subsamples, should be the same for any other condition. Sampling error takes on the status of a constant value in that its presence and magnitude should be approximately the same for each of the three treatments. It follows that any differences that may occur in the overall means ($\bar{X}_I$, $\bar{X}_{II}$, and $\bar{X}_{III}$) should be due to the effects of the treatments themselves and not to the differential presence of sampling errors.

Table 3.1   Random replications design.

Schools	Treatments			
	I	II	III	
A	$\bar{x}_a$	$\bar{x}_a$	$\bar{x}_a$	$\bar{X}_A$
B	$\bar{x}_b$	$\bar{x}_b$	$\bar{x}_b$	$\bar{X}_B$
C	$\bar{x}_c$	$\bar{x}_c$	$\bar{x}_c$	$\bar{X}_C$
D	$\bar{x}_d$	$\bar{x}_d$	$\bar{x}_d$	$\bar{X}_D$
E	$\bar{x}_e$	$\bar{x}_e$	$\bar{x}_e$	$\bar{X}_E$
F	$\bar{x}_f$	$\bar{x}_f$	$\bar{x}_f$	$\bar{X}_F$
G	$\bar{x}_g$	$\bar{x}_g$	$\bar{x}_g$	$\bar{X}_G$
H	$\bar{x}_h$	$\bar{x}_h$	$\bar{x}_h$	$\bar{X}_H$
I	$\bar{s}_i$	$\bar{x}_i$	$\bar{x}_i$	$\bar{X}_I$
J	$\bar{x}_j$	$\bar{x}_j$	$\bar{x}_j$	$\bar{X}_J$
$\sum\limits_{i=a}^{J} \bar{X}_i = \bar{X}_i$	$\bar{X}_I$	$\bar{X}_{II}$	$\bar{X}_{III}$	$\sum\limits_{i=a}^{J} \bar{X}_i = \dot{X}$

A major element in the definition of a variable is that it represents a collection of different, mutually exclusive scale values. For instance, it is possible to specify intelligence as an operationally defined variable in terms of different IQ values obtained by different subjects on a test of intelligence such as the Stanford-Binet. These different values indicate differences in how much of the variable characterizes each individual. The same logic applies to every important concept in psychology that serves as a variable. By arranging the conditions of measurement so that different values can be obtained either from the same subjects under different circumstances or from different subjects under the same situation, concepts such as aggression, dependency, need achievement, anxiety, altruism, etc., all fulfill the basic definitional requirements that designate them as variables. In each case, the measurements associated with these concepts are used to specify differences in magnitude and/or direction.

It is difficult to define the term *variable* without simultaneously using such terms as *magnitude, direction* or *how much*. These terms are all related to the concept of scales. Before proceeding further with our discussion of variables, we will examine the concept of a scale, the different kinds of scales used in psychological research, and the relationship of scales to variables.

Definition of Scale

Every variable is specified in part by the type of scale along which its different values are located. The variables intelligence and loudness involve different scales; these different scales in part highlight the meaning of each concept. *Scales* assign discriminably different designations, in terms of a prescribed set of rules, to the various objects or features of the world to which they refer. This assignment of different designations, usually numbers, can be done rather primitively, such as simply indicating that one object or feature is different from another. Or, it can involve a much more complicated designation procedure in which the assignment of numbers implies order, direction, and distance among characteristics of events and people around us.

Kinds of Scales

Nominal. A *nominal scale* is one in which numbers, or other symbols, are used to designate a class of objects from another. No attempt is made to determine whether one object is larger than or smaller than another with respect to some attribute they have in common. The numbering of basketball players is an example of a nominal scale. A large or small number is not used to designate degree of competence, weight, or position on the team; a number simply identifies a player. Numbers on a nominal scale identify or label discriminably different objects, events, people, or attributes.

Ordinal. A scientist constructs an *ordinal scale* by assigning numbers to events to indicate differences in magnitude. For example, if numbers are assigned ordinally to a hardness scale, the object assigned the numeral 10 is harder than the object assigned the numeral 9; object 10 scratches object 9; but object 9 does not scratch object 10. Objects, events, people, or attributes characterized by statements of greater than or less than are scaled ordinally.

Interval. If an increase between consecutively numbered objects on a scale is the same as between any other two consecutively numbered objects on that scale (e.g., the increase in hardness between objects 3 and 4 is the same as between objects 9 and 10), then that scale is an *interval scale.* An interval scale not only provides for statements of greater than and less than, but also specifies how many equal intervals greater than or less than. An interval scale has the properties of order (i.e., direction and magnitude) and additivity of numbers. Additivity results from an equality of differences between sets of numbers on a scale.

Ratio. It is rare, except possibly in the psychology of sensation and psychophysics, that more than ordinal or interval status is assigned to scales underlying variables that are employed in psychological investigations. However, to complete our discussion of scales, we should point out that there is a more advanced type of measurement sometimes used by psychologists. *Ratio scales* not only provide information as to the equality of differences between two items on a scale in comparison with two other items, as in the interval scale, but also have a true zero point. Familiar examples of ratio scales are those that designate inches and pounds. In either instance, the designation of a zero point on the scale has meaning. In sensory psychology, ratio scales have been developed for loudness, the Sone Scale, and for pitch, the Mel Scale (Stevens & Davis, 1938; Stevens, Volkman, & Newman, 1937).

Types of Variables

Most scales used in psychological research are of the ordinal or interval variety. They form the basis for specifying and defining variables that have reference to the manipulations of the experimenter, some inadvertent alteration of conditions, or the responses of subjects at various times in an experiment. Our next task will be to identify these different kinds of variables in terms of their source.

The independent variable.   Whenever a variable is manipulated by an experimenter such as through the presentation of treatments to different groups of subjects at the same time or to the same group at different times, it is defined as the *independent variable* of that study. In the case of our frustration-aggression experiment, the manipulated variable conforms to the difference in the amount of frustration that was delivered to each group. The interrupted subjects presumably received more frustration than the noninterrupted subjects. Obviously, we could have varied the degree of the frustration variable. A strongly annoyed and interrupted group, given more frequent and intense insults and distractions while working anagrams than a mildly annoyed and interrupted group, could have been included in addition to the group given no insults or distractions. These three values of the variable of frustration, defined in terms of the operations of differential interruption and annoyance, conform to what is meant by different levels or treatments of the independent variable; they have been referred to in previous sections as experimental manipulations, conditions, or treatments. Since no effort was made in our frustration-aggression example to specify how many units of frustration were involved in each treatment, the three levels of the frustration variable conform to an ordinal scale rather than to an interval scale.

Independent variables are categorized in terms of the origin of the manipulated conditions. There are three types of independent variables: situational, subject, and organismic.

Situational.   A number of experiments in psychology involve *situational manipulations* in which some aspect of the physical environment, the task presented to the subject, or the social situation is varied in order to examine changes in performance measures. The different levels of frustration that were employed in our frustration-aggression experiment constitute an environmental independent variable. The manipulation of any feature of the external environment, such as varying a tone or a light or a shock intensity, qualifies as an example of a situational independent variable.

The systematic manipulation of a task qualifies as a task independent variable. Examples include: (1) the rate at which task materials are presented; (2) the interval between trials, as in studies of the effects of massed versus distributed practice on learning; (3) the type of material, such as concrete and abstract words or high-meaningful and low-meaningful items; (4) the instructions on how to perform a learning task, such as using prepositions as mediating links in associating pairs of words or pictures.

Finally, social influences can be manipulated in a number of ways, including varying the social milieu in which the subjects perform a task. Variations in the social makeup of a group (e.g., its size) or in the social conditions (e.g., type of group pressure exerted on an individual to conform) produced before or during the time when performance is measured qualify as social independent variables.

Subject. Sometimes the direct manipulation of a variable is not possible due to the fact that it is possessed in different amounts by a group of individuals. Presumably such differences, called *subject variables*, result from experiences that transpired earlier in the life history of the organism. Evaluation of the influence of subject variables on performance may be desired, even though their occurrence must be arranged rather than manipulated. Different levels of an arranged variable qualify as a variable in an experiment in much the same way as do systematically manipulated variables.

There are a large number of variables that are of concern to psychologists that have arisen due to historical factors—age, need for achievement, anxiety, dogmatism, to name but a few. These variables are ready-made in the sense that they exist in varying amounts as part of the existing makeup of the individuals who are available for selection at the time of an experiment. Generally, subject variables are not amenable to direct manipulation. Rather, psychological tests and direct assessment procedures have been devised to measure the subject characteristics of a population. The results of these assessment procedures are then grouped according to different levels of the subject variable. For instance, the amount of anxiety, assessed by scores on a test such as the Taylor Manifest Anxiety Scale (1959), has been varied by grouping subjects with high scores into a high anxious condition, those with intermediate scores into a mildly anxious condition, and those with extremely low scores into a low anxious condition. The anxiety is presumably present in the subjects prior to the study and is simply assessed, not manipulated, by the experimenter.

Problems can arise when using subject variables as a way of forming the conditions of a study. They can pose serious difficulties in the interpretation of outcomes because, in selecting subjects in terms of the amount of one ready-made variable, it is possible that another ready-made variable may interfere. Consider, for example, an experiment in which sensory changes are investigated as a function of differences in age. While age is the main variable in this study, it cannot be directly varied through a manipulation procedure in the same sense that, for example, the amount of interruption can be varied in a frustration-aggression study. Instead, different age groups must be formed by a selection procedure. But in selecting subjects of widely disparate ages in order to examine sensory impairment, it is conceivable that different amounts of some other, correlated variable also might have been selected, such as differences in general health or education. Since differences in general health or education can influence performance, it is difficult to decide whether the performances of the several age groups reflected age-related, health-related, or education-related sensory changes. Clearly, correlated factors must be eliminated either logically (by making a reasoned decision that a related variable could have no effect on the outcome) or methodologically (e.g., by only choosing subjects in good health and with 12 or more years of education) before using subject variables in psychological research.

Organismic.   It is possible to manipulate certain internal events of living organisms. For example, research interest may center on the functions of a specific brain structure in producing a specific behavior. For one group of subjects the specific brain structure might be removed by surgical ablation, while for another group of subjects all aspects of the surgical procedure would be followed except for the actual ablation. The manipulation of an organic structure is called an *organismic variable*. Other examples of organismic variables that have been manipulated by psychologists include alteration of endocrine functioning by such means as the removal of an endocrine gland or through the inhibition of pituitary gland activity; electrical or chemical stimulation of various brain structures; and the introduction of chemical substances, such as drugs, directly into the circulatory system. The manipulation of organismic variables is the general province of physiological psychologists.

The dependent variable.   Important variables in any science are those chosen by an experimenter to reflect the effects of the independent variable. Since changes in performance depend upon an experimental manipulation, either situational or organismic, these variables have been termed *dependent variables*. The dependent measures of an experiment can take a wide variety of forms, as can be seen from an appraisal of any recent psychological research journal. In our frustration-aggression experiment, the dependent measure was the number of shocks given to a confederate. More common examples of dependent measures in psychology include the number of correct responses per trial, reaction or decision times, frequency of responses per unit of time, and magnitude of responses.

Of prime importance in selecting a dependent variable are its *reliability, sensitivity,* and *validity.* Researchers must ask themselves the following questions: Does the variable show the property of consistency in the sense that the same value could be obtained under identical repetitions of the procedure? (Is the measure reliable?) Will the variable reflect an effect of the independent variable if there really is one? (Is the measure a sensitive one?) Finally, does the variable measure what it is intended to measure? (Is the measure valid?) These questions will be discussed in greater detail in the last part of this chapter.

Often, more than one dependent measure is used in a single experiment because (a) different measures may reflect different processes or different aspects of the same process, (b) the most sensitive measures may be unknown in a virgin research area, or (c) there may be a priori theoretical reasons to do so. For example, in our frustration-aggression experiment the duration of each shock might have been recorded together with its frequency. Either measure might be more sensitive in reflecting the effects of interruptions and annoyance. Multiple response recording can pose problems, however, in that an experimental outcome may be reflected differently for each measure and may make the interpretation of the results extremely perplexing.

Confounding variables.   The results reflected in the dependent variable of an experiment require interpretation. The basis for this interpretation is the independent-dependent variable relationship. Ideally, changes in the dependent variable should clearly and unequivocally reflect the effects of the independent variable. Unfortunately, there are numerous instances where this has not been the case. In these instances factors other than those intended as part of the experiment have been introduced, usually inadvertently, and have confounded the interpretation of the experimental outcome. It cannot be determined which factors affected the dependent measure. These factors, expressed as variables since they also can assume more than a single value along a scale, are appropriately termed *confounding variables*.

We already have noted one kind of variable that can confound the interpretation of an experiment, namely, sampling error. The differential presence of any one of the three types of sampling error, Types S, G, and R, in two or more treatment groups may influence the dependent measures. It would be impossible to determine the extent to which the dependent variable reflected the effects of sampling error, the independent variable, or both. Confounding can also result from the inadvertent manipulation of an antecedent variable other than the independent variable. Recall the experiment on the effects of age on sensory functioning in our discussion of subject variables; if the level of general health and education varied along with the different age levels of our subjects, then these unwanted variables would be confounded with the independent variable (age).

In a sense, a confounding variable competes with the independent variable for interpretative priority. We cannot know whether the variable that was manipulated, the unintended variables, or both produced the experimental outcome. Moreover, a confounding variable may work either to diminish or to enhance the effects of the manipulated variable. Unwanted, confounding variables render an experimental result less valuable, perhaps worthless. Confounding factors must be eliminated or minimized in psychological research.

One might suspect that more experienced and knowledgeable investigators would have no problem avoiding the pitfall of confounded variables in their research. Unfortunately, even the best scientists sometimes employ inappropriate subject-selection techniques, inadvisable procedures to manipulate and control variables, and/or deficient experimental designs. The net result of these flaws is an uninterpretable experimental outcome. In Chapter 4 we will discuss confounding more extensively. Whether confounding is present in an experiment depends upon how the research question is phrased, the sophistication of the researcher in terms of background knowledge of issues and methodology, and the precision involved in the choice and execution of procedures used to test the hypothesis.

Research strategy and the designation of variables.   When psychologists employ the correlational or R-R research strategy, there is no clearcut basis for designating the variables of interest as independent or dependent. An R-R strategy does not involve a clear manipulation of variables—generally a necessary operation if a causal conclusion is sought. Correlational research is often exploratory in nature, ideal for a preliminary search for relationships, especially between subject variables. For example, one might investigate whether anxiety, specified by one set of responses to a questionnaire, is related to self-complacency, defined by a second set of responses from the same subjects. Both R-type variables may be indexed in terms of performances on tests, self-report questionnaires, or behavioral rating tasks. Neither the anxiety nor the self-complacency variable is antecedent to the other, even though a strong relationship may exist between them. That is, the R-R strategy usually cannot make clear which of the variables involved is required for the appearance of the other. Moreover, there is the possibility that a third variable may underlie the other two and thereby cause the observed R-R relationship.

There are several precautions that help forestall interpretive dilemmas in correlational research. First, if the research is guided by a theory which predicts that two and only two responses should be related, there is basis upon which to logically eliminate alternative variables in accounting for an R-R relationship. Second, if past research has shown it unlikely that a third factor (R_3) contributed to the relationship between R_1 and R_2, then the correlational research strategy is on firmer interpretive ground. Third, a correlational statistic, the partial correlation, is available to mathematically assess the R_1-R_2 relationship, independent of the effects of R_3. If, for example, R_3 is age, the partial correlation coefficient represents an estimate of what the R_1-R_2 correlation would be if age were held constant or eliminated. For instance, if age was related positively to both R_1 and R_2, then the R_1-R_2 correlation would be lowered when age was partialled out. A comparison of the simple and partial R_1-R_2 correlations tells us how much of the R_1-R_2 relationship can be accounted for by the presence of the third factor (McNemar, 1962). Finally, if R_1 correlates with R_2 when it precedes R_2 but no such correlation exists when R_1 follows R_2, there is logical support for the conclusion that R_1 was causally related to R_2 (cf. Deese, 1972.).

SELECTION AND USE OF RESPONSE MEASURES

The payoff for conceptualizing and executing an experiment depends in large part on the adequacy of the measurement that reflects the effects of the independent variable. The remainder of this chapter is devoted both to a discussion of the factors that influence the selection of a response measure in an experiment and an analysis of some of the safeguards that can be taken to ensure that response measures possess consistency, sensitivity, and validity. All of our discussion centers around the correct choice of a dependent variable—one that consistently measures what it has been chosen to measure as a result of variations in the independent variable.

Definition of Response

The term *response* means different things to different types of experimental psychologists. Its meanings are determined by such factors as the focus and area of the psychologist's investigation, the psychologist's theoretical orientation, and the physical scales the psychologist chooses to give numerical significance to behavioral events. For example, a physiological psychologist is likely to define a response in terms of biochemical or electrical changes in an organism. These might include changes in heart activity, electroencephalographic displays (brain waves), the secretions of various glands, or alterations in the delicate chemical balance of specific areas of the brain. In one respect, these physiological definitions of dependent variables correspond to a molecular analysis of behavior.

In contrast, other types of psychologists have been more global or molar in their definition and measurement of *responses.* Examples of molar responses include a bar press, running speed, a verbal response, or aggressive behavior in the form of shocks to a confederate. Social, personality, experimental-clinical, and cognitive psychologists are more likely to choose the molar type of dependent variable, while researchers in classical conditioning are more likely to be interested in the molecular type of dependent variable. Still other types of psychologists use both molar and molecular responses to compare changes in behavior. Thus, there are many ways in which *response* can be conceptualized, all of them dependent upon the scientist's empirical and theoretical orientation.

Response Reliability

The concept of response reliability refers to the consistency with which a behavior is detected. The detection of a performance change is a function of the type and the precision of the rules which guide the measurement of a behavior. Rules specify the conditions of observation necessary to obtain a quantitative measure of a response. These rules take a variety of forms, ranging from the use of automated devices that convert the movements of given organisms into numbers to the use of human observation procedures in which raters are trained to record behaviors in a prescribed, systematic manner. The key point is that rules of measurement are useful to the degree that their application results in the consistent detection of a response. Rules should be sufficiently clear so that properly trained independent researchers with the same equipment or scoring system can produce the same behavioral outcome.

Automated scoring. Often, it is possible for a psychologist to use electronic and mechanical devices to obtain precise response measurements. Such devices include photobeams that can be broken as the subject crosses an invisible plane, relays that can be activated by vocalizations, and switches that are activated by the manipulation of keys or levers. Each of these electromechanical devices is used to operate elapsed-time indicators or counters that convert behavior into numbers. The degree to which an electronic or mechanical apparatus is integrated successfully into the response-recording system is the degree to which that response measure is likely to exhibit high reliability; generally, a switch displacement or the interruption of a photobeam represent far more impartial methods for detecting a response than a human scorer. This is just another way of saying that machine detection is often a more objective measurement procedure than human judgment.

Behavioral ratings and test consistency. There are a number of experiments in which human judgment is the only feasible way to record the performances of subjects. This is especially true for cases where the subject's response requires an assessment of content, such as with hyperactivity, cooperative behavior, or self-help skills. These cases require that human scorers, usually well trained and reliable in their judgments, observe and record the responses of interest. The rules that define the occurrence and nonoccurrence of the target response are carefully formulated in advance so that they can be applied in another laboratory by a different researcher with the same results.

When human judgments form the basis of the scoring system, their reliability must be demonstrated prior to the experiment. A standard procedure is to train several raters in the use of the scoring procedure and then require them to demonstrate their skills in scoring the behavior of practice or pilot subjects. Typically, each rater is required to score the behavior of a single subject, independently of the others. Generally, judgments must show at least 90% agreement in order for the scoring procedures (the rules of measurement) to be judged reliable.

An issue of considerable importance when using questionnaires, rating scales, or item inventories to define a response is whether they supply consistent measurements. Assessment of test reliability can be accomplished in several different ways, but the essential feature is that the same individual receives the same relative score upon retaking the original or a similar test. Test reliability is little more than a demonstration of the test's consistency.

Measurement of response attributes.   While the breadth and variety of responses recorded by psychologists are substantial, every dependent variable will reflect at least one of four attributes: response *latency*, response *duration*, response *magnitude*, or response *frequency*. Once any response has been specified by its rules of measurement, the actual recordings will assess one or a combination of these four response attributes. Whether the response is a bar press, eyelid movement, word, yes-no response, or hostile comment, its recording will be in terms of the time it takes to occur, its duration, its size, or its frequency.

It is not the bar press itself that is of experimental concern in operant research, but the number of bar presses per unit of time. It is not the fact that a rabbit exhibits an eyeblink response, but rather the frequency or amplitude of blinks per block of conditioning trials which is the dependent variable in classical conditioning. It is not that a business executive has success following exposure to sensitivity training sessions, but rather how much success and how permanent that concerns an industrial psychologist. The emphasis is on the consistency of the response attribute—its latency, duration, magnitude, or frequency. Response attributes are measured by a timer, recording apparatus, or observer.

What are the consequences of using an unreliable response measure? This is a simple question to answer. To acknowledge response inconsistency is tantamount to admitting that the results of an experiment could be due to variability in the measurement procedure rather than to the manipulated conditions. An unreliable response measure has the same effect as any other confounding variable. Its presence can obscure a clear interpretation of the experimental outcome. This underscores the importance of ensuring that the response measure is reliable prior to starting research. Without this information, the scientist can never be certain whether the outcome was due to response inconsistency, the manipulation of the independent variable, or both.

Response Sensitivity

Once a response measure has been shown to be reliable, there remains the issue of its sensitivity in mirroring the effects of the independent variable. A response measure can be either too sensitive or too insensitive to the effects of the independent variable. For example, a response might be so sensitive as to fluctuate almost capriciously in the presence of incidental stimuli that are unrelated to the experimental manipulation. Such a measure is said to have *noise*—that amount of variability in the measurement index that is unrelated to the manipulation of the independent variable. A good response, of course, is not plagued by excessive noise.

How does a novice researcher choose a sensitive response measure? The first step is to look through the research journals and survey the variety of responses used with similar research questions; this first step will help the novice to limit the range of choices and, perhaps, to come up with an educated guess as to the most sensitive and reliable measure. Regardless of its similarities to well-documented, time-tested response measures, the response measure should always undergo preliminary experimentation in order to give the researcher a chance to correct any problems that might develop as the procedure unfolds in front of a subject. Pilot work can show whether the response is insensitive, showing no change in behavior, or overly sensitive, showing a 100% level of responding. The researcher's rule of thumb is that if you first do not succeed, keep trying until a suitable response measure is discovered through pilot testing. The response measure must only be sensitive to behavior changes stemming from changes in the independent variable.

Response Validity

The final consideration in the choice of a response measure, along with its reliability and sensitivity, is that the measure represents what it purports to represent—its *validity*. Whether it be number of shocks delivered to a presumed tormentor by college sophomores or the number of bar presses emitted by rats in an operant chamber, a major consideration is whether the dependent variable is a reasonable instance of the more general concept that it defines.

Psychologists often choose a dependent variable on purely rational or historical grounds and frequently pay little attention to additional demonstrations that their measure is a valid indicator of the concept that it represents. To illustrate this problem, consider the several measurement indices that have been used to represent the concept of aggression. Having hypothesized that an experiment deals with the influence of an independent variable on aggression, various researchers have chosen as their dependent measures such diverse variables as the number and duration of shocks administered to a confederate, number of street assaults, frequency of brutalized children, number of bites on a rubber hose by a restrained monkey, number of times that a Bobo doll is struck, and a host of others. These measures indicate the diversity of task situations and measurements that have been chosen as instances of aggression primarily on rational or consensual grounds.

How do we know a response is valid? To answer this question we must demonstrate that our response measure correlates highly with other, documented response measures that have been employed successfully in past research and have entered into psychological laws. If, for example, aggression is defined in terms of the number of shocks delivered to a tormentor by annoyed and interrupted college students in a large number of past studies, then any new measure should correlate with this shock delivery behavior in order to obtain empirical justification that it is a valid representation of the same concept.

Problems arise in connection with how a relationship between response measures might be demonstrated. One difficulty is that different subjects usually supply the measures to be related in order to validate a dependent variable. Also, different experimental contexts often provide the two sets of measures, even though each context is thought to evoke the same phenomenon. How, then, is it possible to determine response validity by showing the relationship of one measure to another?

The concept of relationship as used to demonstrate response validity refers to the degree to which different response measures are similarly affected by the same independent variable in the same or in different studies. To illustrate, we will use our frustration-aggression example. The variable of thwarting is defined as the disruption of goal-directed behavior. It has been shown that various definitions of thwarting all result in increased frequency with which college students will shock a confederate. Now, assume that hose biting is chosen by an animal researcher as the response measure of aggression. One way to empirically demonstrate that hose biting is a valid indicator of aggression is to show that it increases in frequency following thwarting. The degree to which both hose biting by nonhuman subjects and shock frequency by college students are increased by a manipulation of the same independent variable—thwarting—would be the degree to which both dependent measures can be said to correlate, in a nonstatistical sense, with one another. The stronger the relationship as documented by relative changes in both indices in reaction to similar changes in amounts of thwarting, the more valid is the new response measure. Another way to demonstrate response validity is to interrelate dependent variables used in the same study. Box 3.6 describes an experiment by Berkowitz (1965) in which two dependent measures were recorded for each subject.

Operant psychologists have long pursued a similar strategy in showing that their major dependent variables, frequency of bar pressing and key pecking responses in nonhuman subjects, can be used as suitable measures for the general concept of learning. Having compiled an extensive literature during the last three decades on the relationship of independent variables with these two response measures, a number of operant reseachers have proceeded to extend their learning laws to humans. They have shown that the same independent variables operative in their animal laboratories have much the same effect when manipulated in natural settings such as state hospitals for the mentally ill and mentally retarded, elementary school classrooms, and prisons. However, in these natural settings quite different response measures, such as the frequency of self-help skills, cooperative behaviors, and hyperactivity, were developed. Similarities in behavioral outcomes in the laboratory and in natural settings as a result of changes in reward and punishment contingencies document the validity of the new response measures used in behavior modification research with humans.

Multiple Response Measures

Some response measures may be better than others for assessing the effect of an independent variable. But in advance of an experiment it is difficult to know which measure is the most sensitive, reliable, and valid. One alternative is to record multiple dependent measures.

Multiple measurements can be used in two possible ways. Sometimes the same attribute from different behaviors provides more than one measure in a study. An example from the field of behavior modification is where the researcher records both the frequency of hostile outbursts and the frequency of positive social exchanges in hyperac-

Box 3.6 A Demonstration of Response Validation

It is not always the case that different subjects are involved in assessing response validity. For example, Berkowitz (1965) showed that college students, following exposure to an arousing segment of the movie, *The Champion*, and then to a hostile verbal interchange with a confederate, produced similar increments in two separate response measures of aggression. The students produced higher scores on a paper-and-pencil test (the first measure of aggression) and delivered more electric shocks to a colleague (the second measure) following the movie and the annoying episode than did a nonannoyed group. The similarity in results increased our confidence in the validity of both measures. In terms of our view of response validity, if these two dependent variables had yielded different results from the same manipulation, then one or the other or both would not be valid measures of the concept of aggression.

tive, aggressive children who are receiving a reward-punishment treatment procedure. In contrast, multiple measures may be taken on different aspects of a single response. Box 3.7 describes two examples, one from human and the other from animal learning, in which different aspects of a single response are assessed.

In the final analysis, the main consideration in the choice of either a single response measure or multiple response measures is that the influence of the independent variable be visible when such effects are scientifically important. Furthermore, a good response measure does not show capricious results in the absence of a genuine effect attributable to the independent variable. Historical precedent primarily determines whether a dependent measure is likely to be fruitful. Has the variable been successful in producing cause-effect statements in the past? If the answer is yes, then the adoption of that response measure is quite likely the best choice until research results, logical considerations, or theory dictates new measures.

Precautions in Using Response Measures

As experimental psychology increases in age and sophistication, new issues arise in the choice and utilization of response measures. The net effect is a gradual improvement in our understanding of the complexities that underlie the selection of appropriate dependent variables. In closing, we will consider two of many recent methodological advances in using response measures.

Response averaging. It is a standard procedure in most learning experiments to average data across trials. For instance, if response averaging is used, the comparison of Conditions A and B in Figure 3.3. would be made on data collapsed over the 10 trials of the experiment. This would be the most general comparison of Conditions A and B and would appear to be legitimate since nearly identical differences between A and B existed on each of the 10 trials. Undoubtedly, a statistical contrast of the mean number of correct responses for Condition A would be significantly greater than for Condition B, provided, of course, that there was minimal variability among the subjects in each condition. The test of significance would be based on response averaging for A and for B.

Is response averaging a legitimate procedure? Not always. When subjects are using the same method or strategy from trial to trial, then an averaging procedure is defensible. But what if the task in our example involved paired-associate learning and some subjects used a passive learning strategy on Trials 1, 2, and 3, and an active learning strategy (e.g., vivid images as mediating links between stimu-

Box 3.7 Multiple Measures from a Single Response

Most responses used in psychological research have various attributes, any of which can serve as the dependent variable. Consider the possible measures of a verbal response collected in a paired-associate learning study. A series of stimulus-response pairs is presented to a subject, the task being to learn to associate each response with a particular stimulus. One way to measure paired-associate learning is by means of the anticipation method. First, a stimulus is presented to a subject for a fixed duration, generally about 2 sec. The subject then attempts to recall the response unit that is associated with the stimulus; this is the test period. Whether or not the subject recalls the response correctly, he or she is then presented both the stimulus and response; this is the study period. This procedure is repeated for each stimulus-response pair until the entire series is shown. At this point, a single trial has elapsed. Repeated trials are given until the subject can accurately recall all of the response terms. One measure of learning proficiency in a paired-associate task is the *number of correct responses* on each trial. Another measure is the *number of trials needed to reach a specified criterion of performance*, such as one perfect recitation of the list. Yet another measure is the *elapsed time* from stimulus onset to the verbalization of the response on test trials. These multiple measures are all taken from a single response.

Consider another way of analyzing a response into its components. There are many measurement tasks in psychology that call for the timing of continuous behavior, such as running. Such behavior can be subdivided in various ways. For instance, a subdivision of a continuous response into its component parts can easily be made with alleyway running time, a response collected by researchers in instrumental conditioning. One measure is the total time taken by a subject to traverse the alley. Total time can then be subdivided into the time taken to run respective thirds or halves of the runway. This subdivision is done in order to evaluate whether total running time and the component time measures are interrelated and, more importantly, to test whether certain motivational variables, such as the magnitude of the food reward in the goal box, have differential influences on the various running speeds. Learning theorists such as Spence (1956) and Logan (1960) have used early, middle, and terminal running times in straight alleyways to develop rather elaborate theories of instrumental conditioning.

Figure 3.3

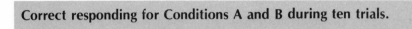

Correct responding for Conditions A and B during ten trials.

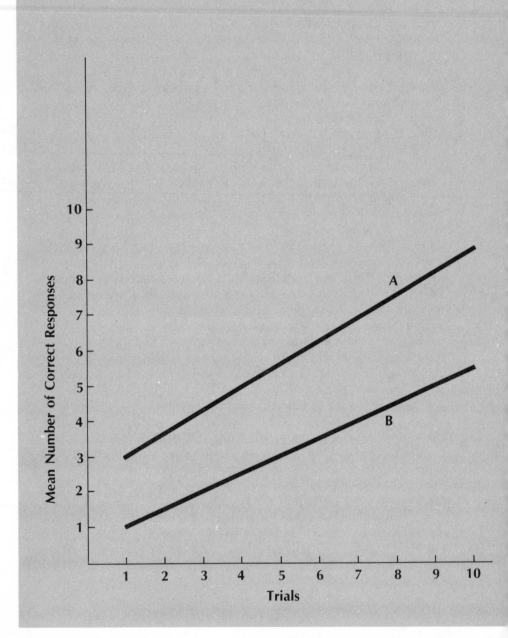

lus and response units) on all other trials? Or what if different subjects used different learning strategies? In these instances, response averaging is inappropriate because it incorrectly forces a single score (e.g., a mean) to reflect diverse psychological processes. Newell (1973) has provided experimental psychologists with a useful rule regarding response averaging: Never average over response measures if they reflect different learning methods, strategies, or processes. We can detect the consistency of a strategy or process by *directly* measuring it, independent of our measurement of the behavior under study.

On selecting the best response attribute.   There are instances in the history of psychology where an experimental outcome did not prove statistically significant, but where a later revision in the response measure produced a different effect. For example, Bahrick (1967) was concerned with the specific methodological question of which response measure best reflects the retention of learned materials, but his research has general implications for us. Bahrick presented each of thirty subjects with a list of sixteen nonsense syllables in serial order. A subject was required to learn the syllables in their correct order and to anticipate each unit immediately before it appeared. The number of trials required for the correct anticipation of each of the sixteen syllables was the dependent variable. Bahrick (1967) presented the same list to his subjects 24 hrs. after original learning and counted the number of trials needed to relearn the entire serial list again to the level of one perfect recitation. His procedure was designed to measure how much effort in original learning was saved during relearning.

Bahrick (1967) employed as his index of retention a ratio measure that essentially involved the number of trials required to relearn the list relative to the number of original learning trials. Since relearning typically took fewer trials than original training, the ratio was in terms of the number of trials saved the second time around. The savings measure was determined by subtracting the number of trials required during relearning from the number of trials during original learning. This difference was then divided by the number of trials during original learning, and the quotient multiplied by 100 to obtain a percentage score, e.g., savings $= \dfrac{OL - RL}{OL} \times 100\%$ where OL and RL refer to the number of original learning and relearning trials, respectively.

Bahrick (1967) noted that a traditional method for measuring memory, trials required to reach a 100% criterion, had proved unreliable and insensitive to the manipulation of a number of variables in verbal learning research. He argued that a 100% criterion for learning placed too much emphasis on the trials needed to learn the last one or two syllables not previously reported correctly. Because of the extreme difficulty in learning the last few items, the number of trials required to complete the original and the relearning tasks to 100% criteria is likely inflated. Bahrick concluded that, by requiring a criterion of perfect recitation of the responses, the true learning rates for items responded to correctly prior to the final learning trial are obscured by the problems encountered in learning the final item(s).

To test his hypothesis, Bahrick (1967) tabulated the number of trials needed to correctly anticipate each of the sixteen items in the serial list during original learning and relearning. Savings scores were then computed. For example, the savings score for anticipating three correct items during relearning was the number of trials required for the original learning of three items minus those needed for relearning three items correctly, divided by the number of original learning trials. This quotient was then multiplied by 100% to reflect the percentage saved. Bahrick's (1967) data are reported in Table 3.2.

One important feature of these data is that the savings scores were obviously larger when calculated for the retention of an intermediate number of items (e.g., nine correct) than for a few or for many correctly retained items. For instance, mean savings scores were poorest for either a few (one or two items) or for many (sixteen items)— 58% for one correct, 62% for two correct, and 66% for 16 items correct. Another striking feature of the data was the variability for the savings scores at the sixteen different criteria. Clearly, variability was

Table 3.2   Statistical analysis of successive savings criteria as reported by Bahrick, 1967.

Criteria (Number of Correct Syllables)	Mean Percent Saved	Standard Deviation	Frequency of 100% Savings Scores	Median r with Other Criteria
1	58	38	10	.27
2	62	34	8	.37
3	67	39	8	.56
4	76	35	7	.54
5	82	19	6	.63
6	86	10	5	.49
7	85	9	4	.61
8	85	9	2	.66
9	87	7	1	.65
10	85	11	1	.63
11	80	11	0	.60
12	81	11	0	.59
13	80	12	0	.56
14	77	14	0	.66
15	72	15	0	.60
16	66	21	0	.30

substantially lower for intermediate criteria (see Column 3 of Table 3.2).

The most important implication of the data in Table 3.2 can be found in the correlations reported in the last column. The savings scores for each of the sixteen criteria were correlated with savings scores for all other criteria. The median correlation coefficient (r) for all intercorrelations at each criterion level is reported in the last column. Lowest median intercorrelations were reported for one, two, or sixteen items correct. These criterion levels were also the most variable. Of special interest is the median correlation for the criterion of sixteen correct anticipations—the commonly used measure of learning and retention. Whereas the median intercorrelation for the criterion of fifteen correct items was .60, it was only .30 for the criterion of sixteen correct items. According to Bahrick's hypothesis, this result is likely due to the greater difficulty encountered in mastering the last, most difficult item each subject learned in the list.

Thus, the increased number of trials required to achieve the 100% level of learning obscured the effort needed to learn most other items. Even though trials to reach a perfect criterion is apparently the least representative response measure, it has nevertheless been the measure of choice in many verbal learning experiments. In other words, the most popular measure of the retention of serially presented materials has proved to be the least sensitive.

An implication of Bahrick's study is that the selection of a performance measure can sometimes obscure the real meaning of the data or can mislead the experimenter as to the possible independent-dependent variable relationships. Fortunately, in this illustration an alternative method for selecting more appropriate response criteria was available. Unfortunately, the solutions to other subtle problems of response measurement are not always as obvious. Clearly, the judicious choice of response variables is a critical step in the experimental process.

SUMMARY

We began this chapter with the promise that it would launch you directly into the important and exciting arena of experimentation. To accomplish this goal we introduced the issues involved in the conception and execution of an experiment and the subsequent interpretation of its outcome. The first step in the process of scientific inquiry involves the formulation of a problem in broad perspective. The problem is a product of the life experiences of the scientist; it may be arrived at through armchair speculation, anecdotal reports, perusal of historical materials, or theoretical perplexity. The general formulation of the problem enables both the experimenter and the scientific community at large to evaluate more clearly whether the experiment is a meaningful one. The actual conduct of the study requires a reformulation of the broad question into a tightly worded, operationally defined declarative statement called the *experimental hypothesis*. In fact, the experimental hypothesis stands in contrast to the often implicit hypothesis which is to be tested, the null hypothesis. The null hypothesis, a convenient way of phrasing anticipated results in terms of a zero difference so that statistical procedures can be used to evaluate the significance of the outcome, states that no behavioral effects will result from the experimental manipulation.

There are two kinds of error that can result when making a decision about a null hypothesis. The null hypothesis can be rejected when it is actually true (Type I error) or accepted when it is false (Type II error). These errors can be minimized by such factors as sample size, confidence levels, and experimental control of variability. Statistical significance, which involves a rejection of the null hypothesis, does not necessarily imply scientific significance. For instance, if the sample size is exceptionally large, statistical significance will almost automatically result. A statistical technique, omega^2, was discussed as a way of establishing scientific significance. Omega^2 represents a measure of the proportion of the total variation in performances that can be accounted for by the experimental manipulation. The goal of good psychological research is to state hypotheses clearly, concisely, and with operational specification in the hope of achieving statistically significant relationships that have scientific importance and usefulness.

The sampling process for an experiment constitutes the first and most fundamental step in psychological research. The degree to which generalizations from sample results to the parent population are legitimate is the degree to which the sample is representative of the population. Representativeness is defined in terms of whether the sample was drawn from the population in accord with the principles of random selection. If random procedures were not used, the sample statistic is a biased estimate of the population parameter it represents. However, even if random selection is used, a sample statistic is unlikely to coincide exactly with its corresponding population parameter. Such discrepancies are termed sampling errors. A sampling error due to fluctuations in subject characteristics is called a *Type S error*. A *Type G error* occurs when a sample systematically differs from other samples because of the accidental influence of extraneous factors. A *Type R error* results from attributes or peculiarities intrinsic to a particular subpopulation. Techniques designed to minimize or eliminate sampling errors include the use of large samples, sample stratification, and special experimental designs. Perhaps the most powerful design in minimizing sampling error is the random replications design in which Type S, G, and R errors are distributed evenly across treatment conditions.

Laws are established when a manipulated variable, the independent variable, is shown to produce changes in performance as assessed by the dependent variable. Independent variables may be classified as situational, organismic, or subject depending upon whether their origin is rooted in environmental manipulations or personal characteristics. Confounding variables vary along with the independent variable and compete with it for interpretive priority in an experimental outcome. If the relationship between the independent and dependent variables is to be clearly specified, confounding variables must be eliminated.

Care must be taken to specify in operationally defined terms what behavior to record, when to record it, and how to record it. A dependent measure is selected in terms of pragmatic considerations—reliability, validity, and sensitivity. Once a response class has been selected, it is possible to use various response attributes such as its latency, duration, frequency, or amplitude to reflect different aspects of the same response. One good rule of thumb is to choose multiple response measures whenever theoretically meaningful and experimentally feasible. Multiple response measures help to assure sensitivity and reliability, and often uncover unexpected relationships between independent and dependent variables.

QUESTIONS

1. What is the relationship between the general statement of the research problem and the more specific experimental hypothesis? Using the general statements in Box 3.1, formulate experimental hypotheses for each problem.
2. How does an investigator go about formulating an experimental hypothesis? What sources of information can the investigator use?
3. Which type of scientific question is used in the actual formulation of a lawful statement? What are the differences between the experimental hypothesis and the null hypothesis? Why are both important? Would it be possible for both to be true at the same time? Why or why not?
4. What are Type I and Type II errors? How are they related? How might one reduce the chances of these errors occurring (be careful to consider what happens to one type of error when the other is altered)?
5. What are the differences between statistical significance and scientific significance? Which is the more important? Why?
6. What is sampling error? What methods are available to reduce each type of sampling error? What are the advantages and disadvantages of these methods and how might they be interrelated?
7. What is an independent variable? How many different types of independent variables are there? Why are they important for psy-

chological research? What is a dependent variable? How does it relate to the independent variable?

8. What is a confounding variable? How is confounding related to sampling error and the use of independent variables?

9. Why is it important to clearly specify, in operationally defined terms, what behavior is to be examined in an experiment? What factors should be considered when choosing a response measure? What problems must be avoided? Give some examples of properly chosen and well-defined response measures.

The Anatomy of Psychological Experiments: Confounding and Strategies of Control

Our aim in doing an experiment is to identify an agent of change explicitly. To do this, we must avoid a confounding of our independent variable by some other (independent) variable. Two variables are confounded when the variation in the magnitude of our intended independent variable is accompanied by a variation in the magnitude of another known or potential independent variable. . . . The consequence is that we cannot identify the cause of the behavioral change; it might be due to one or the other independent variable, or to some combination of both.

(Underwood & Shaughnessy, 1975, p. 29)

It is possible to achieve control over extraneous situational variables by varying them systematically. For example, the usual way of controlling the order in which experimental stimuli are presented is by *counterbalancing*; half the subjects may receive them in order AB and the other half in order BA.

(Scott & Wertheimer, 1962, p. 87)

We must arrange the conditions of interest so that the effects of progressive error will be distributed equally over the measurements taken under Condition A and Condition B. . . . More generally, we say that we must be alert to the possibilities of differential transfer. If in going from Condition A to Condition B, the carry-over of skills or habits or sets or expectations is different from the carry-over from B to A, we have differential transfer.

(Underwood & Shaughnessy, 1975, pp. 77, 82)

How do we know that a manipulated variable actually produced an observed effect? The causal link between the independent and dependent variables cannot always hold up because conditions not directly relevant to the experiment sometimes change simultaneously with the manipulated variable. We must face an unfortunate dilemma: Which of the several factors in an experiment, the manipulated or contaminating events, influenced the dependent measure? In this chapter we will discuss more fully both the nature of the variables that can contaminate the interpretation of an experimental outcome and the use of procedures that eliminate such unwanted variables. These unwanted variables were designated *confounding variables* in Chapter 3, and we refer to the procedures used to eliminate them as *strategies of control*.

The effect of any manipulated variable is assessed in terms of the concurrent changes that occur in some performance measure. The concept of *control* refers to procedures that ensure that the manipulated variable (not some other condition) exclusively produced the performance change. Control refers to methods and procedures that allow an investigator to conclude unambiguously that the manipulated variable did or did not have an effect on some dependent variable.

THE PROBLEMS OF CONFOUNDING

The problems that result from a confounded experiment are far-reaching. If the outcome of a critical experiment involves undetected confounding, the subsequent empirical, logical, and theoretical analyses may be misdirected. The problem is compounded because confounding variables are often so difficult to discern that a confounded experimental outcome may be accepted by the scientific community for a prolonged period of time. These possible consequences of confounding can be illustrated by looking at a study by Collier and Marx (1959).

Collier and Marx focused on the issue of how prior exposure to a given amount of reward might affect subjects' subsequent performance. Since the same subjects were exposed at different times to two amounts of the reward, this research represents an examination of reward contrast effects. Collier and Marx attempted to make three groups of rats as equivalent as possible at the outset of their study by balancing each group with respect to weight and age. Their experiment involved two phases. In Phase 1 three groups were given different concentrations of a sucrose solution—one a 4% concentration, a second an 11.3% concentration, and a third a 32% concentration. Following repeated drinking sessions, Phase 2 was begun; it involved training each subject to make bar-press responses to earn minute quantities of the 11.3% concentration of sucrose reward. Esssentially, Phase

2 included shifting two of the groups from either a higher or a lower concentration of sucrose during pre-bar-press training to the intermediate concentration; the third group had the same 11.3% concentration for both phases of the study. With the exception of prior exposure to different concentrations of sucrose (the manipulated variable), Collier and Marx made every effort to ensure otherwise identical procedures for the three groups. The results showed that over the 10 days of bar-press training during which the 11.3% sucrose concentration was used for all groups, the rate of bar pressing differed substantially—the 4% group showed a higher and the 32% group a lower rate of bar pressing than the nonshifted, 11.3% control group.

The results of the Collier and Marx (1959) experiment were widely interpreted as follows: The rewarding effect of a given event can be modified by prior experience with a different amount of the same rewarding event. Moreover, these and several related findings by Marx and his colleagues were accepted for over a decade as persuasive support for this conclusion. In 1969, Dunham and Kilps showed that the findings of Collier and Marx (1959) may have been unrelated to the influence of their manipulated variable—shifts in amount of reward —and instead, perhaps, were due to the presence of an unrelated, confounded variable. Dunham and Kilps (1969) discovered that differences in average body weights for the three groups may have developed during the period of initial exposure to the different amounts of reward, with the 32% group showing a relative increase in mean body weight and the 4% group the greatest relative loss compared to the unchanging weight of the 11.3% control group. Moreover, these weight differences may have persisted throughout bar-press training even though all groups had been shifted to the same 11.3% concentration of reward. The development of differences in relative body weight and their persistence throughout the two phases are shown in Figure 4.1. Differences between groups in mean body weight thus covaried with the different treatment conditions, thereby qualifying as a potential confounding variable.

Was the experimental outcome of Collier and Marx (1959) attributable to exposure to the different sucrose concentrations during pretraining, to the group differences in body weights that may have developed in Phase 1, or to both? Dunham and Kilps (1969) showed that when body weights were kept equal, differential rates of bar pressing between the shifted and control groups during Phase 2 did not develop. They concluded that the variable that Collier and Marx (1959) had explicitly manipulated in Phase 1 of their experiment actually was not the effective agent in producing changes in bar-pressing performance during Phase 2. Instead, the confounded variable of different body weights was the functional variable.

Figure 4.1

Percentage of ad libitum weight during magazine and bar-pressing sessions for upshift (US), downshift (DS), and control (C) groups.
After Dunham and Kilps (1969).

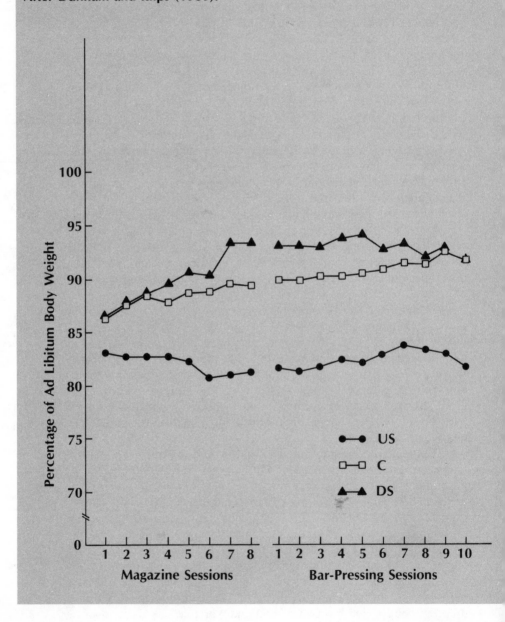

The Collier and Marx (1959) experiment is instructive in understanding the deleterious effects of confounding. The presence and influence of a confounded variable often is difficult to detect and may go undiscovered for a long period of time, exerting a misleading influence on the course and development of further research in a given area. The experimental design of Collier and Marx's (1959) study appeared sound (equating weights at the outset of the study), and most scientists viewed their group-equating procedures as acceptable. Nonetheless, the possible confounding uncovered by Dunham and Kilps (1969) went undiscovered for almost a decade; in the interim the findings of Collier and Marx (1959) had considerable impact in the area of reinforcement contrast effects.

The point we wish to make is that a good experiment requires the location and elimination of confounding. Even then features may be overlooked that can result in gross misinterpretations of the data. Notwithstanding this hazard, the problem of locating sources of confounding can be made somewhat easier by learning *where* confounding factors are most likely to occur and *how* to identify them. Various classification schemes designed to locate sources of confounding have been proposed by different authors (D'Amato, 1970; Underwood, 1957). We will consider portions of these classification schemes for purposes of specifying the sources of confounding that most often arise in psychological experiments. By specifying the various types of confounded variables we will be in a better position to consider procedures that can nullify or minimize their influence.

SOURCES OF CONFOUNDING

The way in which a variable can confound the interpretation of an experiment depends, in part, upon its source. The major sources of confounding include inadvertent variations in aspects of the *situation* in which the experiment is conducted; inadvertent variations in the *subjects* who participate in the experiment; and inadvertent variations in the spatial and temporal *arrangement* of conditions, events, and responses that are part of the experimental procedure. Although these classes of variables are not as clearly defined as they may appear at first glance, they are useful in organizing our discussion of the kinds of factors that can and frequently do confound the interpretation of an experiment. Table 4.1 summarizes the three preceding sources of confounding and the types of problems that can occur with each.

Situational Confounding Variables

Situational variables refer to the spatial and temporal aspects of the environment, the experimental task, the instructions, and the experi-

Table 4.1 Confounding variables. The left-hand column lists major sources of confounding. The right-hand column indicates some of the events or conditions that can occur as confounded variables within each category.

Source	Nature of Confounding
	Coincident with different levels of the independent variable . . .
Situational Confounding Variables	1. Environmental conditions may differ, such as temperature, noise level, etc. 2. Aspects of the task may vary, such as materials, arrangement of materials, etc. 3. Instructional materials may be different, such as wording, etc. 4. Biases of experimenter also may differ, such as predispositions about the outcome for each treatment, etc.
Subject Confounding Variables	Characteristics of the subjects can vary, this being especially prevalent in the ex post facto research strategy.
Arrangement Confounding Variables	1. The spatial and temporal order of stimulus presentations can vary. 2. Residual effects of prior treatment stimulation can be present. 3. Repetitious stimulus and/or response effects can develop, resulting in changes in performance due to practice, habituation or fatigue.

menter that may vary along with the independent variable and influence the experimental outcome.

Environmental variables. Aspects of the environmental setting that, through covariation with the experimental manipulation, can produce unwanted performance changes include alterations in lighting, changes in temperature and humidity, noise level, etc. Each of these features, if uncontrolled, can alter the performance of subjects by affecting motivational level or serving as distractors. Box 4.1 contains examples of confounding in terms of environmental variables.

Task variables. Any feature of the task, including its construction and method of presentation, that is not an explicit part of the manipulated variable can exert unsuspected influence on the outcome of the experiment and thus qualifies as a task-confounding variable. For example, unwanted performance changes can arise from the improper use of stimulus testing materials or from the presentation of materials in ways that emphasize subject biases (see Box 4.2).

Consider, for example, a study in which one wished to discover whether speed of discrimination learning in children is related to the attentional value of the employed stimuli. Two different sets of stimuli—differing in attention value—might represent the manipulated condition of the experiment. The basic comparison would be the speed with which a discrimination is learned with the low versus with the high attention-getting materials. An immediate problem would be to define *attention-getting* both in order to select appropriate stimuli for the study and to ensure that the concept is compatible with current usage. One possible definition might be in terms of degree of stimulus complexity, complexity being specified in terms of the number of angles of 60° or greater depicted as part of each of the figures. In collecting materials, the experimenter must be careful that the two sets of material differ from each other only in terms of those aspects that define *attention-getting*—number of 60° angles; hence the stimuli within each set must not differ in any other respect. Once the to-be-manipulated dimension has been specified, great care must be taken to ensure that other possible dimensional aspects of the materials, such as color, meaningfulness of the configuration, and size, are not inadvertently manipulated.

Numerous instances can be cited where inadvertent task confounding can easily occur in psychological research. For example, in studies of pitch discrimination where two physically different frequency values are chosen for exposure to the subject, care must be taken to ensure that the intensity of the stimuli does not differ. A similar problem exists in studies of visual pattern discrimination. Different visual patterns must be of equivalent brightness to avoid confounding these two stimulus attributes. When choosing stimulus materials that should differ in only one respect, great care must be taken to ensure that they also do not differ in other ways.

A problem that is related to choice of task materials is how these materials are presented. Various methods of presentation can inadvertently introduce unwanted but systematic variations in ready-made response tendencies. One such tendency is that of position preference. By position preference is meant that the subject may react to location, either spatial or temporal, rather than to the specific stimulus features that are manipulated. If stimuli A and B always occur in a set so that A is on the right and B on the left of the display and B is always the rewarded event, will a subject learn to differentially respond to the rewarded and nonrewarded stimuli because of location, because of the distinguishing features of each stimulus display, or both? Although we will discuss ways to combat this source of confounding in a subsequent section, suffice it to say here that a trial-by-trial stimulus arrangement procedure that eliminates spatial and/or temporal location as a systematic variable is required.

Box 4.1 Examples of Environmental Confounding

As an example of concomitant variation in an independent variable and an environmental confounding variable, consider a series of studies by Tolman and his colleagues (1946a, 1946b, 1947a, 1947b; Ritchie, 1947) dealing with the so-called place-learning controversy. The investigators were interested in determining whether learning was a matter of acquiring knowledge about the places where rewards and punishers were located or whether it was a matter of acquiring specific sequences of responses that led to or from these events. Tolman's theory was that the specific responses that subjects emit in reaching a given place are irrelevant; rather, subjects acquire a "cognitive map" of their environment and may take any of a number of paths to the goal.

As one procedure to test his view, Tolman used a radiating pathway maze in which rats first were trained to run from an elevated platform down a pathway to a goal box, usually identified with a light. Following this initial training, he placed the same subjects on the starting platform, in the center of which was a series of new paths arranged as radiating pathways much like the spokes of a wheel. The original training pathway that led from the platform to the goal box was blocked. However, one of the new pathways did lead directly to the goal box. The dependent variable was the percentage of rats that took the path that led directly toward the goal box. In their first study, 36% of the rats chose the most direct pathway while the remaining 64% chose the remaining 11 pathways. Tolman interpreted this result as favorable to his theory.

Unfortunately, both the nature of Tolman's theory and the procedures that he adopted to evaluate it almost inevitably introduced the possibility of uncontrolled situational-environmental confounding. Kimble (1961) has noted that Tolman's result might simply be understood as the outcome of situational-environmental confounding rather than in terms of choice of response alternatives leading to different places. The concept of *place*, presumably manipulated by presenting the subject with multiple pathways, was confounded with the different environmental cues associated with each path. The question that Kimble (1961) legitimately raised is whether Tolman's rats learned to go to a specific place or whether they learned to approach distinctive environmental locations, one of which signaled the presence of reward.

A proper experimental test of this issue is to eliminate all cues that might be associated with the different places in the maze. A number of subsequent studies (Blodgett & McCutchan, 1948; Hill & Thune,

1952; Waddell, Gans, Kempner, & Williams, 1955) attempted to do just that. They reduced the effects of these potentially confounding situational-environmental cues by placing the maze in a visually homogeneous environment—underneath a dome made of muslin or in a room with low illumination so as to minimize cue differences. When this was done, the response-learning groups almost always were superior to the place-learning groups.

In spite of the lesson on environmental confounding to be learned from this series of studies, psychologists continue to be plagued with analogous problems. For example, McHose and his colleagues (McHose, Jacoby, & Meyer, 1967; McHose & Ludvigson, 1966) have reported that odors which originate on nonrewarded trials and are present on reward trials can provide an unwanted source of learning in studies where other independent variables are of focal concern. Whereas the manipulated variable in many of these studies has involved interspersing nonrewarded with rewarded trials (studies of partial reinforcement), McHose discovered that this manipulation could result in the concurrent emergence of distinctive odors for each kind of trial—odors that could themselves alter the performance of the subjects. That is, variations in the schedule of reinforcement were confounded by inadvertent but systematic variations in the situational-environmental stimulus of odor. By controlling for the differential presence of distinctive odors on rewarded and nonrewarded trials, McHose was able to show that this source of confounding could indeed be an important determinant of performance.

Box 4.2   Task Confounding: Fixed Order in a Paired-Associate Task

Great care must be given to the arrangement and presentation of stimulus materials. Consider a paired-associate learning experiment in which the subject must learn associations between pairs of items. The paired-associate task involves memorizing a list of paired words using the study-test method described in Chapter 3. Assume that the list involves 10 paired-associates and is to be presented for a maximum of 10 trials or two perfect recitations.

Now, consider the possibilities of confounding if the 10 paired-associate items always are presented in the same order on each trial. Each stimulus-response pair in a study sequence would consistently precede and follow another pair. This arrangement of materials would provide the subject with two important pieces of information that could be used to facilitate learning of the pairs. The subject indeed might learn the connections between pairs of syllables, which is the goal of the experiment. But, the subject also might learn a serial connection between the response terms of successive pairs during the study trials, which is not the goal of the study. While performance might be a function of the strength of the associations between a given stimulus and its response term, it is possible it could also be a function of the serial associations between successive response units. To avoid the possible confounding between paired-associate and serial learning in this task, the sequencing of the materials should be different for each successive trial.

Instruction variables.   Many tasks depend upon the subject's use of instructions for their implementation. Unfortunately, instructions can be a potent source of confounding. For instance, they can be so poorly worded that the subject is misled or is given unintentional assistance or the hypothesis is revealed. The major problem in formulating instructions is to word them so that they provide the subject with the information needed to perform appropriately on a given task while not giving away the actual purpose of the experiment. In general, instructions should assist in implementing an examination of the effects of the independent variable on task performance but should not themselves exert an influence.

Sometimes, however, instructions are explicitly designed to be part of the independent variable. As an example, consider a hypothetical experiment where instructions are used to manipulate perceptual set. Assume that the stimulus material in this study is the reversible face-vase configuration that often is depicted in the perception chapter of general psychology texts (see Figure 4.2). In this experiment, perceptual set might be manipulated by instructing one group to expect to see a face in the stimulus pattern, while giving no orienting instructions to a second group. Presumably, the effect of these different instructions would be to produce a different perceptual orientation—to prepare or set the subject in the experimental group to see and respond in a given way to the pattern within the stimulus complex. The question here that relates to the issue of confounding is what actually is the independent variable? Is it the different instructions, is it the internal set established by the instructions, or is it both?

Some researchers assume that different sets induced by different instructions constitute the real manipulated variable. However, our suggestion is that the independent variable in instructional research actually consists of two components: (1) the physically specifiable instructions and (2) whatever internal set is induced. These two components combine in some manner to influence each subject's verbal report. The assumption in using instructions in such a manner is that they are simply a way of inducing a hypothetical internal response that, in turn, causes the performance in question. According to this analysis, what begins as a manipulation-type experimental strategy (the use of different instructions) becomes, in essence, an observational-correlational strategy in which the presumed internal response that makes up the induced set is correlated with changes in another response, namely, the verbal report.

Instructions can be viewed in much the same way as any other set of stimulus materials that might be employed as part of the manipulated conditions of an experiment. Sentences in a set of instructions are themselves composed of verbal stimuli, and great care must be taken when varying these stimuli to ensure that only the intended

Figure 4.2

Reversible figure and ground. Reversible face-vase is a favorite pattern for a figure-ground reversal. Note that either the light portion or the dark portion can be perceived as a figure against a background.

aspect of the instructional content and nothing else has been altered. Unfortunately, changing words in sentences is, in many respects, different from varying the complexity of a visual stimulus or the frequency of an auditory stimulus. Often the same sentence is understood in different ways by each subject. Moreover, an alteration of even one or two words may change the entire meaning or sense of a phrase as it may be interpreted by various listeners. This is not to say that this research strategy should be avoided altogether, but rather to suggest that particular caution must be taken when instructions are part of the manipulated variable.

Certain safeguards can be used to ensure that the influence of instructions is restricted to the purposes of the experiment. These include: (1) repeated presentation of the instructional material, (2) restatement by the subject in his or her own words as to what is asked in the instructions, (3) use of pretraining or practice trials as a test of the subject's comprehension of the instructions, and finally (4) actual manipulation of the instructions to determine if their influence is as intended.

Experimenter variables.   A researcher unintentionally may emit cues that can be detected by subjects and can influence their performance (Rosenthal, 1967). These cues can bias the outcome of an experiment and have been appropriately labeled *experimenter-bias effects*. Rather surprisingly, the attitude of the experimenter toward his or her study and its participants may be as influential in determining the results of the experiment as the manipulated variable itself. Several aspects of experimenter bias have been investigated, one of the more prominent being how information is transmitted from the experimenter to the subject (Rosenthal & Rosnow, 1969). Some of the factors that have been implicated as promoting unwanted communication have included the occurrence of well-timed body gestures and verbalizations by the experimenter in the presence of subjects. Once detected, this overt communication may increase the likelihood of one experimental outcome over others because of the tendencies by subjects to comply with authority and status.

There are other ways in which bias may influence the results of an experiment. For instance, the experimenter may observe only what he or she is disposed to see. Thus, even though other aspects of performance might suggest quite a different interpretation, the experimenter may measure only those aspects of a subject's behavior that conform to pre-experimental expectations.

Fortunately, there are safeguards to protect against experimenter bias. For example, research assistants can be recruited who are uninformed of the purpose or design of the study. These experimenters are *blinded*, so to speak, as to the hypotheses and essential variables

Box 4.3 Experimenter Bias

To more fully appreciate the significance of experimenter-bias effects, consider a study in which the behavior of two groups of rats was evaluated by different groups of college students. In one group of rats specific brain tissue was removed (an organisimic-type independent variable). The other group of rats simply was exposed to a sham operation in which the surgical procedures were performed but no tissue was destroyed. One group of students was instructed that the sham-operated animals were brain-lesioned; another group of students was told the actually lesioned animals were not brain damaged. Still other groups of students were essentially uninstructed as to the surgical history of the animals. Although independent observers could not discern behavioral differences for the instructed or uninstructed students during the course of the experiment, the performance of the sham-operated rats as recorded by the misinstructed students was similar to performance recorded by the uninstructed students for the animals that had real brain lesions. The effect of misinstruction thus appears to have influenced the outcome of the experiment as much as did the actual removal of brain tissue.

Rosenthal and Rosnow (1969) have described multiple instances in which experimental outcomes were the result of experimenter bias rather than, or along with, the influence of a manipulated variable. They also have provided evidence that a major way in which these biases are communicated is through covert, incidental interactions between the subject and the experimenter. The data of Rosenthal and his colleagues suggest that the careless psychologist stands a good chance of disturbing the phenomenon being studied through unintended communications to subjects about the purpose of the experiment.

of the experiment. In this manner, there are no predispositions or biases about the experiment to be communicated to the subjects.

There always is the possibility that a research assistant may discover the purpose of the study even though effort has been made to prevent such knowledge. Assistants are curious and can be quite clever in finding out the purpose of the experiment. Once the study's purpose is uncovered, the assistant qualifies as an agent of potential bias and confounding. One way to combat this problem is to employ several assistants. Each assistant conducts the equivalent of a complete miniexperiment or replication. By averaging the results of several replications, the bias effect attributable to a single informed assistant would have only limited influence on the overall outcome.

Finally, experimenter bias may influence the observation procedures and data collection. One way to circumvent this problem is through the use of automated recording techniques whenever possible. However, many studies involve dependent variables that are not subject to automation—assessment of personality characteristics or behavioral ratings in natural settings. These variables depend heavily upon observer judgments and the major check on bias effects in these kinds of experiments is multiple rating or recording procedures by several blinded raters so that reliability measures can be obtained. If multiple observers produce similar behavioral records, then one can relax somewhat about the possible presence of bias effects on measurements.

Subject Confounding Variables

We already have touched upon subject confounding variables in our discussion of position preference. Subject variables refer to the many individual differences that can characterize any given person and which can obscure the effect of the independent variable. Certain potentially confounding features can be part of the relatively permanent psychological or physical makeup of the subject, such as age, sex, personality, and measured intellectual ability (Type S errors). These features represent subject dimensions that can serve as sources of confounding when they covary with changes in the manipulated variable. Other confounding characteristics are not so enduring and may include such factors as whether the subject is a volunteer or a paid participant or whether he or she previously participated in psychological research. For example, subjects who volunteer for psychological studies may differ from those who do not with regard to variables that can affect the experimental outcome. Compared to nonvolunteers, volunteer subjects have been shown to have higher educational level, occupational aspirations, need for social approval, and measured intelligence scores (Rosenthal & Rosnow, 1969; Rosnow & Rosenthal, 1970). A volunteer's greater need for social approval could lead him or her to be more concerned with helping the experimenter validate the hypothesis. In short, volunteer subjects show greater cooperation than nonvolunteer subjects (Adair, 1973), a factor that could influence the outcome of a study and thereby confound any interpretation that otherwise would be attributed to the manipulated variable.

Generally, confounding by subject variables must be considered whenever an ex post facto experimental strategy is employed. An ex post facto strategy differs from the usual experimental approach involving direct manipulation in that the experimental variable is introduced after the fact (Underwood, 1957). Instead of exposing subjects to different values of a given independent variable, subjects are formed into groups according to the amount of a variable that they already possess. We discussed this research method in Chapter 3 in connection with subject independent variables. The example that we used there was a hypothetical study in which various age levels were selected as the experimental variable. Since age is a condition that subjects possess at the time of experimentation, an examination of its effects upon some performance measure qualifies as an ex post facto research strategy.

Typically, when a variable is manipulated, it is exposed in different degrees or amounts to different groups at the same time or to a single group at different times. It is possible in the former instance to equate groups before each treatment is given. But the very nature of ex post facto research makes it difficult to use a pre-experimental, group-equating procedure due to the fact that subjects are chosen because they differ on some index that is presumed to influence performance. It would be difficult to argue that they are equivalent to one another at the outset of the experiment. The major issue of methodological concern in this design is not whether the groups are fully equivalent at the beginning of the experiment, but whether they are equivalent on all but the subject variable being studied at the outset of experimentation. If they are not, then any experimental outcome may be confounded because the groups may differ systematically on both the possessed variable and on some other factor.

In the age-level study described in Chapter 3, a number of subject characteristics might vary concomitantly with variations in age level. Physical health, sex, socioeconomic, geographical, and so-called generational differences are likely to covary with age (cf. Schaie, 1968). For example, it is well known that females live longer on the average than males, that older persons tend to settle in warmer climates, live on pensions, and are exposed early in life to cultural experiences that undoubtedly are different from those of younger subjects. Differences in these variables are no less possessed by different age groups than is age itself. Unless some provision is made to eliminate or minimize their contribution, unwanted variables can be as influential on an experimental outcome as differences in age.

There can be no question that certain content areas, such as personality and social psychology, rely heavily on the existence of subject variables. These variables are not easily manipulated in that their presence is dependent upon prior cultural and experiential factors. Attributes such as latent homosexuality, chronic anxiety, dogmatism, political conservatism, leadership potential, etc., all depend for their occurrence upon historical factors. They appear in individuals in varying degrees. An additional problem is that their presence often is inconstant. A dogmatic person does not always exhibit inflexible behavior, and even a chronically anxious person often does not manifest anxiety except under stress.

Several methods for measuring subject variables are questionnaires, self-rating scales, and batteries of test items. Using one of these instruments, test scores can be obtained from subjects that possess varying amounts of the variable under study. For example, one popular ex post facto research strategy has been to administer the Taylor Manifest Anxiety Scale (MAS) to subjects in order to separate individuals that score at the extreme ends of the scale. Extreme scorers are labeled as either high- or low-anxious subjects. Each group is then exposed to a task, such as classical eyelid conditioning, to determine if a relationship exists between anxiety level, as defined by the MAS test scores, and task performance (see Box 4.4). Scores on the MAS have been shown to correlate highly with performance on a number of classical, instrumental, and verbal learning tasks (Spence, 1956).

Arrangement Confounding Variables

Three sources of confounding related to the arrangement and sequencing of events are: (1) spatial and temporal arrangement, (2) treatment carry-over, and (3) stimulus or response repetition.

Spatial and temporal arrangement.   When stimuli or treatment conditions are presented in an invariant temporal or spatial arrangement, whether for the same or for different groups, confounding may occur. Assume that three levels of a given variable are chosen as the treatments in an experiment: A_1, A_2, and A_3. Furthermore, assume that Treatment A_1 is given on Day 1, Treatment A_2 on Day 2, and Treatment A_3 on Day 3 to the same group of subjects. Note that two features have been manipulated simultaneously—different treatments were

Box 4.4   An Alternative to the Ex Post Facto Design

What could be concluded from ex post facto research if scores on the Taylor MAS were highly correlated with other subject variables besides that of anxiety? For example, degree of cooperativeness or amount of extraversion-introversion represent other possible dimensions of personality that could covary with scores on the MAS. If high-MAS subjects also were more cooperative than low-MAS subjects, the interpretation of any performance difference on an experimental task would be confounded by the presence of this other subject characteristic. This problem arises because the ex post facto method is essentially an observational rather than a manipulated-variable experimental approach. That is, it represents an R-R rather than an S-R research strategy. It is difficult to conclude a cause-effect sequence from an R-R relationship because it is, perhaps, more susceptible to the undetected presence of subject confounding variables.

One obvious alternative to the ex post facto research strategy using subject variables is to attempt to convert the entire procedure into an S-R manipulated-variable study. This might be accomplished through the experimental production of different amounts of the subject variable by some sort of training or instructional procedure. This approach would have the advantage of equating subject characteristics at the outset of the study, prior to the training procedures. Some progress has been made with the instructional approach; there is now evidence for the successful application of instructional procedures to manipulate anxiety levels, degree of cooperativeness, and amount of aggressiveness (cf. Janis, 1958, 1968; Berkowitz, 1975).

given at different temporal locations. In essence, Days 1 through 3 constitute three levels of a variable much in the same way as treatment levels A_1 through A_3. Since variations occur together, an interpretation of the experimental outcome is confounded. The question we must ask is whether the outcome is due to the Treatments or the Days effect? Spatial and temporal location or placement of stimulus materials or treatments represent sources of confounding if these features inadvertently covary with the independent variable.

The mere temporal or spatial ordinal location of an event can be an important factor when it covaries with the event itself. If this covariation occurs, it is impossible to determine whether the experimental manipulation, location, or both influenced the outcome of the experiment. Moreover, confounding due to arrangement can occur whether different groups receive different stimulus conditions or whether all stimulus conditions are given at different times or in different places to the same group.

Order. The order in which a set of materials is presented can also influence the experimental outcome. This happens primarily when (a) the same subjects receive all of the conditions and (b) some of the conditions have residual carry-over effects that can influence performance under the subsequent conditions. The key to understanding order-of-presentation effects depends upon the notion of treatment-produced, carry-over (or residual) influences. If treatment effects persist over time, then there may be a residual effect from the first treatment which might influence the subsequent treatment. The actual effect of the second treatment on performance could be obscured by the presence of a residual, carry-over influence from the prior treatment simply because its presentation occurred in a fixed order.

Consider a hypothetical study in which the same group of students is exposed to two different teaching styles, one autocratic and the other democratic; the effects of each teaching style are assessed by achievement test scores collected at the end of the day. Assume that the autocratic approach is used in the morning session and is followed by the democratic approach in the afternoon. There is evidence to suggest that exposure to the autocratic style may produce a considerable amount of emotional arousal due to the frustration and conflict produced by the arbitrariness that usually characterizes this procedure. Moreover, it is a reasonable assumption that strong emotional states dissipate slowly over time. Thus, the emotional arousal produced by the autocratic approach during the morning session might carry over to the more permissive democratic class in the afternoon session and thereby influence student responsiveness and performance. Although achievement scores for the autocratic approach may be an accurate measure of the effectiveness of that teaching method, a similar performance measure obtained for the democratic approach would likely reflect both the carry-over emotional influence of the autocratic method together with whatever effect the democratic approach might exert. Thus, the fixed order of the treatments given to a particular group is confounded with the effects of the treatments themselves. Confounding due to order arises when residual effects from one treatment obscure the influence of subsequent treatments because of the fixed sequence of their presentation.

The nature of carry-over confounding can differ depending upon both the kind of treatments administered and the way in which they are administered. For example, the magnitude of any residual effect might be relatively constant from one treatment to the next—the increment in going from A_1 to A_2 is the same as from A_2 to A_3. An unchanging residual carry-over produced by each treatment would constitute a linear carry-over effect. On the other hand, one treatment may contribute a sizable carry-over effect while others may contribute none at all or minimal carry-over effect. In this case, the magnitude of the order effect as distributed over all treatments is nonlinear.

Another way to analyze the treatment residual is to determine whether the carry-over is the same or different when going from Treatment A_1 to A_2 as opposed to going from A_2 to A_1. If the residual influences of A_1 to A_2 are the same for the reverse order, the carry-over effects are reciprocally equal. Residual effects are reciprocally unequal if the consequence of going from A_1 to A_2 is different than from A_2 to A_1. The techniques for minimizing confounding due to linear and reciprocally equal arrangement or sequencing effects are presented in the next section.

Repeated responding. Repeated stimulation frequently is accompanied by repeated responding. Even though it may be possible temporally to stagger repeated stimulation in order to reduce some of the effects associated with a long session of responding, some changes in behavior will still result simply as a function of repeated reactions within any experimental session. Since performance changes can be due to sheer response repetition alone, the amount of prior responding can serve to confound the interpretation of an experimental outcome.

Repeated responding can affect experimental performances in two ways. First, it can improve performance because of such factors as increased familiarization with the materials and the demands of the task, the development of a set to respond or to learn, and increased confidence due to earlier successes in the task. These improvements in performance have been labeled practice effects. Practice effects are interpreted in terms of both transitory improvement in performance due to warm-up and a more permanent component called learning-to-learn (Thune, 1950). Second, relatively prolonged responding can result in performance deterioration because of such factors as excessive fatigue, habituation, and adaptation; a deterioration in performance due to response repetition is called a *fatigue effect*. Control procedures must be employed to minimize the degree to which practice and fatigue effects confound the independent-dependent variable relationship.

No brief survey of confounding can fully cover all of the problems and pitfalls that can occur in any experiment. Nonetheless, we have identified some of the more obvious sources of confounding including: (1) the situation in which the experiment is conducted, embracing the actual environmental context, the experimental task, the instructions that are used, and the biases of the experimenter; (2) the features and characteristics of the subjects that compose the groups, with special problems existing in ex post facto research where subject variables often constitute the conditions under study; and (3) the various ways in which the arrangement of treatment conditions, stimulus materials, and repeated responses constitute confounding variables. In the next section we take up procedures that are designed either to minimize or eliminate sources of confounding.

STRATEGIES OF CONTROL

So far we have presented two basic kinds of experimental design as if they were equivalent ways of resolving scientific questions. In one design, the levels or treatment conditions of a manipulated variable are presented to different groups of subjects—the *between-subjects* or *separate-groups* experimental design. In the other design, the same group of subjects is used for all of the treatment conditions—the *within-subjects* or *single-group design*. The confounding that can occur when employing these two basic design strategies is quite different, and separate control procedures are required.[1]

Each of the two basic experimental designs has its distinctive risks and advantages. Consider an example that resulted in two different outcomes when the same variable was investigated by means of two experimental designs. Grice (1966) used between- and within-subjects designs to evaluate the effects of moderate and strong stimulus intensities on performance. In the separate-groups approach, Grice exposed different groups to a tone of either moderate or strong intensity. The subjects were instructed to react to the tone as quickly as possible by depressing a telegraph key which in turn terminated a

---

1. Actually, there is a third design, the *single-subject design*, that is quite similar to the single-group approach, except that only a few subjects are used. This research method will be discussed in the last portion of the chapter.

clock that was activated at tone onset. The mean difference in reaction times between groups was only slight and not statistically significant. However, when Grice used an otherwise identical procedure in which both moderate and strong tone intensities were given to a single group, a large performance difference for the two experimental conditions resulted. Shorter reaction times were associated with the stronger tone. Apparently, the experimental design that is used can determine whether a difference in performance will result from the manipulation of a variable and how large that difference will be. The results reported by Grice (1966) indicate that the choice of experimental design and strategy can influence conclusions about the nature of empirical laws. The choice of an experimental design, then, is an extremely important decision in psychological research.

Control procedures used for any experiment also depend on whether a between-subjects or within-subjects design is chosen to evaluate the effects of a manipulated variable. The group differences usually present at the outset of an experiment in which a between-subjects design is used are one of the most important sources of confounding. The presence of a pre-experimental difference between groups can prevent an accurate evaluation of any effect that might be attributed to the independent variable. Much of the subsequent discussion of control procedures for between-subjects designs deals with pre-experimental group differences. These control procedures are used to answer the question, "How do I know, or how confident can I be, that the groups were not different in the first place?" Separate-groups control procedures are designed to ensure equivalent groups prior to the introduction of treatment conditions.

Control in between-subjects (separate-groups) designs is further complicated by the fact that, once equated, the groups may not remain equivalent during the actual conduct of the experiment because of the appearance of nontreatment factors. Recall the study of Collier and Marx (1959) in which the groups that received different concentrations of sucrose weighed the same at the outset of the study but in which weight differences developed once the treatments were initiated, producing changes in the dependent measure. Some of the discussion that follows will take up control procedures that can be used to correct this sort of problem.

Although they can generate problems that are similar to those of separate-groups experiments, the goal of control in single-group (within-subjects) experiments focuses on ensuring that the group remains unchanged from its original pretreatment condition at the beginning of each consecutive new treatment. This can be a major problem for the single-group design since exposure to one treatment can change the group in some important way so that the subjects are no longer the same when the next treatment is given. In other words, the experimenter must incorporate procedures so that the consecutive performances of the same group can be meaningfully evaluated even though there is the possibility that the effect of each treatment may carry over to influence the effects of subsequent treatment(s). Conditions must be put into effect so that whatever outcome is produced by a given treatment does not differentially influence the effects of subsequent treatments. Control procedures for within-subjects designs employ special operations that deal with the order in which multiple treatments are presented and with the spatial and temporal distribution of those treatments. If it can be assumed that there are no carry-over influences due to exposure to prior treatments, then the experimenter can rest easy. A single-group design should incorporate control procedures that preserve as much as possible the subjects' naiveté—naive being the state that characterizes them prior to the presentation of the initial experimental treatment.

Since the initial treatment in an experiment often alters the naiveté of the subjects, many of the control procedures that are used in within-subjects experiments are designed to distribute carry-over effects equally across all subsequent treatment conditions. When the influence of any confounding variable is distributed equally across all treatments, any group mean represents a composite of the effects of a particular treatment plus a proportion of the distributed arrangement effects.

The major similarity in the control procedures for separate- and single-group designs is that both are concerned with achieving equivalent baseline or beginning performances with respect to the dependent measure prior to the administration of treatment conditions. These procedures differ, however, in terms of *how* this is accomplished and in *what* is to be made equivalent. The separate-groups design demands control procedures that ensure that all groups will be approximately equal with respect to the dependent variable at the beginning of the experiment. The single-group design requires control procedures that either eliminate carry-over effects from treatment to treatment or, if that is not possible, produce an equal distribution of sequencing effects across all treatments.

Sometimes control procedures appropriate to either design can be invoked in the same experiment because many studies combine both separate- and single-group research approaches at the same time. The phrase *mixed designs* has been used to designate these types of experiments (cf. Lindquist, 1953); mixed designs will be taken up in detail in Chapter 5. To simplify matters, we will discuss the control procedures that are applicable to the between- and within-subjects designs separately.

(between subjects)

METHODS OF CONTROL IN SEPARATE-GROUP EXPERIMENTS

The most basic, properly controlled, separate-groups experimental design is one in which one group is given an amount of a variable and another group is given none. All other conditions are the same for both groups. Table 4.2 shows a schematic of the separate-groups design in which an experimental group is given a treatment while a control group is given no treatment. Following exposure to these two conditions, both groups are tested for performance differences on a criterion task.

The separate-groups design enables the researcher to decide on the presence or absence of some phenomenon—on whether the treatment had an effect on the behavior of the experimental group relative to the behavior of the control group. A variation on this use of a control strategy in the separate-groups design is illustrated in Table 4.3. In this variation, the control group also receives the treatment, but its value is much less than that given to the experimental group. There are some circumstances in which this control strategy can be quite useful in psychology. Note that in the treatment versus nontreatment control procedure of Table 4.2 and the more versus less treatment procedure of Table 4.3, any difference between the experimental and control groups can be interpreted as evidence for an effect due to the presence of a specified amount of the independent treatment variable. The major advantage for the approach shown in Table 4.3 is that both the experimental and control groups receive some of the

Table 4.2   The traditional use of control in a between-subjects, separate-groups design.

	Treatment	All Other Influences	Test for Effects of Treatment
Experimental Group	Yes	Yes	Yes
Control Group	No	Yes	Yes

Table 4.3   Variation on the traditional use of control in a separate-groups design.

	Treatment	All Other Influences	Test for Effects of Treatment
Experimental Group	Yes	Yes	Yes
Control Group	Yes, But Much Less	Yes	Yes

treatment condition, thereby suggesting an even greater likelihood that the two groups are equivalent in all but the actual amount of the treatment.

Both control strategies can be combined (see Table 4.4) to yield an even more powerful design. Here, two control groups are employed so that (1) it is possible to assess whether a phenomenon or experimental effect has or has not occurred (Experimental Group vs. Control Group 2), and (2) to determine whether the complete absence of the treatment in the zero-level condition exerted some unwanted effect on the dependent measure (Control Group 1 vs. Control Group 2). The rule of thumb is that the more the control and experimental conditions are alike, except for the presence of the manipulated variable, the less ambiguous is the interpretation of the experimental outcome.

Table 4.4   A control strategy in which two types of control are used.

	Treatment	All Other Influences	Test for Effects of Treatment
Experimental Group	Yes	Yes	Yes
Control Group 1	Yes, But Much Less	Yes	Yes
Control Group 2	No	Yes	Yes

A major problem for these three designs is whether or not the control and experimental groups are equivalent with regard to the dependent variable at the outset of the study, before the treatments are given. Clearly, if the control and experimental groups are different, then it makes little difference if the conditions of Tables 4.2, 4.3, or 4.4 are met; the outcome of the study cannot be clearly interpreted. In the following section we will discuss some of the more common methods that have been used by psychologists to achieve pretreatment equality between experimental and control groups.

Randomization as an Equating Procedure

A *random sample* was defined in Chapter 3 as a sample in which each and every member of the parent population is equally likely of being included. Randomization can also be used to equate groups at the outset of an experiment. By selecting subjects so that each and every individual in a given population has the same probability as any other of (*a*) being chosen and (*b*) being assigned to any group, it can be assumed that, in the long run, all groups will be equivalent in terms of their subject characteristics. Randomization works best as an equating procedure when sample sizes are large. Problems can arise with randomization as a group-equating procedure when sample sizes are small. Small samples are not likely to mirror all of the important characteristics of the members of the population. When using small samples, it is probably not sound to trust the long run condition to prevail in a particular instance. Thus, the replication of the experimental finding, when either small or large samples are used, is a desirable procedure—only after replication can the experimental outcome be viewed with confidence.

A procedure for random selection. There are a number of ways in which subjects can be randomly chosen. Most random selection techniques are based on a table of random numbers (see Box 4.5). This table is constructed so that numbers can be chosen by proceeding in any direction, i.e., horizontally, vertically, or obliquely. The obtained numbers will occur in an unsystematic fashion. The probability of obtaining any number in the table is the same as the probability of obtaining any other no matter what direction is followed. If, for example, the first page of the table is entered at the top of Column 2 and values are chosen by proceeding downward in a horizontal fashion so as to obtain a set of 20 values from 0 to 99, this set would have the same probability of occurrence as any other possible combination of numbers.

Suppose that one wanted to determine whether college students showed the same basic form of learning to escape painful shock as do many species of nonhuman subjects. As a substitute for the alleyway escape situation that often has been used with animals, especially rats, the college students are instead required to depress a telegraph key at the beginning of each electric shock, and to continue pressing until the shock is discontinued. The dependent measure is the time that it takes to make 50 presses, the number that has been chosen as sufficient to terminate the shock. Three groups of subjects are formed, each being given a different shock intensity, designated as high, intermediate, and low (the use of a zero shock level would make little sense since no performance could be expected for this condition).

The important issue here concerns the formation of student groups in such a way that they do not differ with respect to the dependent measure at the outset of the experiment. This is the same as requiring that their mean escape times to make 50 presses would be identical if each group were given the same shock level. There are a number of ways in which these groups might differ at the beginning of the study that could cause initial group differences. For example, differences in age level, overall physical health, sensitivity to shock,

Box 4.5   Table of Random Numbers

	Columns				
	1	2	3	4	5
1	19038	59491	29248	24511	66803
	73498	33560	44437	33816	39253
	84373	95964	21006	09152	78501
	89018	82703	51191	63587	76081
	95357	47087	56365	87091	49209
	76852	19969	92158	70922	35266
	24001	00065	99383	07439	99053
	28472	85723	68994	79955	30719
	66062	72269	93101	25418	21687
	62636	82021	29585	41093	28884
	35615	94260	56103	18086	04844
	75323	16060	55240	48640	59824
	73306	40241	17779	51910	83806
	44362	85247	35700	88268	68052
	31032	10662	04011	95984	04932
	95355	25745	21110	66026	75578
	27490	61298	12006	90509	21595
	18866	58477	67356	25058	37753
	23958	31981	79009	52148	15169
	00541	72150	79649	51787	46093
	56066	70534	87173	14763	47460
	80522	39519	69704	33075	84380
	65185	26803	17758	99409	92589
	02428	91660	23020	17089	63070
	71203	24263	56538	08495	87919
	17774	16048	54319	64289	20535
	34417	19036	28350	76331	48208
	12255	96244	68979	74971	48336
	43548	52311	67764	83086	11749
	43024	77244	34682	66136	30444
	80498	62321	22579	14642	94812
	89198	99850	87970	20298	13074
	60108	66833	21040	51784	04988
	85333	13959	13233	50167	61227
	16017	31084	14118	24723	73656
	44260	09343	91949	65811	70299
	44889	41005	48561	64998	79006
	08739	38585	73968	29849	62570
	27813	76618	59459	18356	11527
	90217	85809	94851	84283	17578
	09061	57149	62468	17819	47032
	01482	82747	10144	10420	46017
	58165	11502	27753	09205	21109
	70983	40317	06435	87658	62646
	65628	41445	38464	44813	62233
	74927	05730	34146	70694	25021
	59009	25187	72744	56601	14141
	08418	85631	82426	89860	80601
	14873	05054	54193	58108	14604
50	42289	97984	80167	06338	07612

Rows

or sophistication as experimental subjects might occur by chance alone (Type S errors). These subject characteristics could themselves contribute to different experimental performances. Care must be taken to ensure that these influential subject characteristics are equally represented in each group at the outset of the study.

In using a random selection procedure to equate the groups, assume that a large general psychology class of 500 students is chosen from which to obtain subjects. One way to implement the random selection procedure would be to arbitrarily (randomly) assign each student a number from 001 through 500. Turning to the random table (Box 4.5) and using three digit numbers, one could begin at any point and systematically trace in one of the three given directions, i.e., horizontally, vertically, or obliquely. Twenty subjects per group will be used, making a total of 60 in all. The first 60 values that occur from those numbers that range from 001 to 500 represent the subjects that will be chosen. Adherence to this procedure would result in a properly constituted set of subjects with whom to begin the study. However, there is the added problem of assigning subjects to each of the three groups. This assignment must also be accomplished by a random procedure similar to the one employed in selecting the sample of 60 subjects.

Advantages of random selection.   As noted, random selection is the very best procedure to employ if the goal is to achieve equivalence between groups over the long run. The use of a truly random selection procedure is necessary for the application of statistical techniques to assess the meaning of the collected data. Furthermore, random selection techniques probably are the most economical of the several equating procedures available. It is relatively easy to assign numbers to subjects and to consult a random table to constitute groups. Almost any other equating procedure is more time consuming and costly.

Limitations of random selection.   There are many circumstances that call for very small samples. But the smaller the sample size, the more likely that Type S errors will occur so that the groups nonetheless may differ on critical subject characteristics at the outset of experimentation—characteristics that may confound the outcome. As an extreme example, consider an experiment that involves two groups of two subjects. The IQ of subject A is 120, B is 90, C is 130, and D is 100. Assume further that unequal mean IQs for the two groups will confound the interpretation of the results since IQ is known to affect the behavior being studied. What are the chances that the mean IQ for the two groups will be equal as a result of randomization? Since there are six ways in which to form two groups of two subjects each and only one of these combinations (S_{90} and S_{130} vs. S_{100} and

S_{120}) will equalize IQ, the probability is one-in-six that a desirable form of randomization would occur. It is obvious from this example that increasing the sample size increases the probability of obtaining group equivalence when a random selection procedure is used.

In addition to the problems posed because of small sample size, there are many situations that prevent random selection altogether. Some subjects, although randomly chosen, may refuse to participate in experiments. Other factors that can preclude actual participation by randomly chosen subjects include unexpected illnesses or simple forgetfulness. Often, at the last minute, investigators may find it necessary to insert substitute participants for randomly chosen subjects. This substitution sometimes contaminates the true random character of the assignment procedure.

On discarding subjects. A word of caution is necessary regarding the problems that can arise from discarding subjects. In most instances, loss of a very few randomly chosen subjects is not a serious problem and can be remedied by the random selection of substitute subjects from the original population. When such replacement is not possible or when a large number of subjects needs to be replaced, undesirable consequences can occur: (1) The representativeness of the samples may be affected—they may no longer be unbiased samples from the original population. (2) The comparability of groups can be changed in terms of their pretreatment equality.

To illustrate these undesirable consequences, assume that an experimenter is interested in the hormonal basis of sexual behavior and wishes to assess whether the presence or the absence of a particular testicular hormone at an early age affects the sexual response of the adult male rat. As part of the experimental design, some subjects are castrated at birth and, through surgical manipulation, have their testicular material restored through implantation of a hormone-producing gland 30 days later. A second group is *sham-operated.* By a sham operation is meant that all of the surgical procedures are performed as on the experimental animals with the single exception that the control animals do not receive the crucial aspect of surgery—actual castration is not performed. Assuming that the experimenter has taken precautions to ensure that the two groups were randomly formed, the only difference between them should be the presence vs. the absence of testicular material during the first 30 days of life. Of course, the experimenter must choose some aspect of sexual activity during adulthood to serve as a sensitive, reliable, and valid dependent variable, such as various aspects of copulatory behavior in the presence of a receptive female rat. The basic test might be to individually place the male rats of each group in an environment with a receptive female for a specified period of time. The number of approaches, mountings, and intromissions would then be tallied.

Assume that the experimenter is alert to the possible presence of confounding influences due to the early sugically manipulated testicular change. For example, the hormone manipulation may create differences in activity levels between the two groups. If this is the case, group differences in adult sexual behavior might be related either to the hormone manipulation during infancy or to activity changes. To circumvent this possible confounding, activity measures might be collected on each subject following the castration treatment or sham operation and prior to testing. Unless it can be shown that the two groups were comparable in activity levels prior to testing, no firm conclusion regarding the effects of castration on adult sexual behavior would be possible.

What if the experimenter discovered that the experimental group contained fewer active animals than the sham-operated group? It might be reasoned that inactive animals could be replaced with freshly operated subjects in the treatment condition, measuring their activity, again replacing those that still do not perform appropriately in the activity test until both groups contain an equivalent number of equally active rats. Would such a procedure maintain the random quality that characterized the original formation of the treated group? The answer is no. Most likely, the experimenter would end up with a randomly constituted sham-treatment group and a biased experimental group. It is rarely possible to achieve the requirement of equally probable subject selection under conditions such as described for the surgery condition. The replacement animals would likely be a very select set of animals, with favorable subject characteristics.

Any time a subject is discarded following manipulation of an experimental variable, it is possible that the essential randomness of that group will be disturbed. More explicitly, if differential subject discard (one group loses more subjects than another) is part of the procedure and systematic subject replacement is used, the result may be a confounding that obscures a clear interpretation of the outcome. Furthermore, the random character of such a sample may be violated with the consequence that parametric statistical tests of the data cannot legitimately be carried out.

Pretreatment Matching as an Equating Procedure

It is sometimes possible prior to the experimental treatment to obtain measurement information on subjects that can be used to form the groups of the study. Groups can, in other words, be systematically equated in advance of the experiment on those measures that, if different in mean value from group to group, would confound the study.

Pretreatment matching has the advantage of removing the chance factor that is present in the random assignment method by explicitly eliminating the possibility of a particular subject characteristic from affecting the results.

There are two ways that pretreatment measures can be used to equate groups. One method eliminates possible confounding by a Type S error by ascertaining its value for each subject prior to introduction of the treatment conditions and making its mean value the same for all groups. This approach has been called the *matching-elimination* procedure by D'Amato (1970) since the groups are explicitly equated on the confounding variable and since, by virture of this matching, its effect is eliminated because it cannot make a differential contribution to the outcome. A second pretreatment method is to concomitantly manipulate the potentially confounding variable for purposes of assessing its influence along with the effect of the treatment variable. This second technique is called the *matching-evaluation* procedure (D'Amato, 1970).

Matching to Eliminate Confounding Variables

The matching-elimination procedure is an explicit attempt to ensure that experimental and control groups are quantitatively similar on one or more measures at the outset of the experiment. The rationale for matching is clear. If the groups are identical at the outset, then any posttreatment difference is more likely to be due to the treatment itself rather than to chance factors. We should underscore that matching will be of little value unless the measure used to equate groups is related to the performance variable of the study. For instance, if changes in bar-pressing rates were to be used as the dependent variable, then it would be most desirable if the groups could be equated on rate of bar pressing prior to the introduction of the treatment by allocating an equivalent number of high, low, and intermediate bar-pressing subjects to each group. Matching the dependent measure is a highly desirable way to eliminate the influence of a potentially confounding variable since the measure used to assess the effects of the treatment is also the one on which the groups have been matched at the outset of the study (see Box 4.6).

Unfortunately, it is not always advisable or even possible to obtain pretreatment matching with respect to the dependent variable. The next best procedure is to match groups on a measure that is highly correlated with the dependent variable. For example, in a study in which the acquisition of an instrumental response, alleyway locomotion, is the object of experimental interest, it is sometimes not possible to expose the subjects to alley running prior to acquisition training to effect matching for fear of disturbing an accurate assessment of the dependent measure. The groups must be equated on a measure other than the dependent variable, but one that is nonetheless highly related to it. If the variable upon which the groups are equated is unrelated to the dependent variable, of course, the purpose of matching would be undermined. The groups still could differ on the dependent measure at the outset of the study. The more perfectly correlated the equating variable with the performance measure, the more effective will be the matching at the outset of the study.

There are numerous instances in psychological research where a matching-through-elimination procedure is the easiest and most desirable way to equate groups. Usually there is advance information that a particular variable, if present in different amounts across groups prior to the treatment manipulation, can confound an interpretation of the treatment effects. Sometimes advance information is readily available from a careful consideration of the literature. For example, if an investigator was interested in the effect of a training procedure designed to increase the vocabulary comprehension ability in preschool children, it is relatively obvious from a reading of the available research that precautions should be taken to ensure that the groups have equivalent IQs, especially verbal IQs, at the outset of the study. If one group possessed higher IQs than the other, this intellectual advantage would probably combine with the treatment procedure to accelerate vocabulary comprehension training for that group. While accelerated comprehension on a test is the desired outcome, it nonetheless would not be possible to determine whether the treatments or the different intellectual abilities caused such a finding.

Matching serves to eliminate the influence of the contaminating variable altogether. In the case of the preschool vocabulary comprehension study, an accepted measure of intellectual performance, such as scores on the Binet IQ test, could be obtained from the subjects prior to group formation. The groups could then be equated by assigning subjects in such a manner that each group exhibited the same variance and mean IQ. Intelligence would be eliminated as a potential influence on the experimental outcome since its contribution to the results of the study would be the same for all groups. Any difference between groups would have to be attributed to the differential presence of some other factor—hopefully, the manipulated variable.

Matching on pretest scores.   Matching more often than not requires that the correlated measures be obtained from subjects prior to the introduction of the experimental treatment. These measures are sometimes available from sources such as case histories or admissions records, making a specific collection procedure unnecessary before experimentation. As in the example in Box 4.6, these measures can

Box 4.6 An Example of Matching to Eliminate Confounding: The Use of Pretest Scores

A good example of matching with respect to the dependent variable is a study by Anderson, Plant, and Paden (1967). The purpose of this study was to evaluate the effect of punishment on running behavior by means of a buzzer stimulus that had been paired with painful electric shock. The assumption was that the buzzer, because of its association with shock, could serve as a substitute for shock in suppressing a well-established alleyway locomotor response.

Initially, 40 hungry rats were each given multiple trials in running down a 6-ft. alleyway for a food reward. Once these running times reached relatively stable levels, 4 groups were formed. The 40 rats were ranked from fastest to slowest in terms of their median alleyway running times on the last 5 training trials. The first 4 fastest animals were randomly assigned so that one rat went to each of the 4 groups. The next 4 fastest subjects similarly were assigned so that one rat went to each of the 4 groups. The next 4 fastest subjects were similarly assigned, and so on. This particular assignment procedure has been termed a *randomized-block assignment method* (cf. D'Amato, 1970) because the subjects are grouped into sets or blocks of 4 each (a number that is equal to the number of groups) and then are equally represented within each group. The reason that different groups were used was to show conclusively that the buzzer was effective in suppressing performance because it had been paired with shock.

Each group was then subjected to the treatment conditions involving exposure to one of several combinations of the buzzer and/or shock. These respective treatments were given on each of the next 4 consecutive days. To determine whether the groups remained equivalent with respect to the dependent measure at the end of these different treatments, all subjects were returned to the alley on the day following the last treatment session and were given 3 additional alleyway running trials. Group means were then computed and were shown to be unchanged from pretreatment mean running times.

Testing consisted of the removal of the food from the goal area and substitution of the buzzer in the goal area. The buzzer was activated in the goal box at the onset of each trial for each subject. Alleyway running times were collected and converted into speed scores. Since this measure was also used to equate the groups, it could be assumed that differences in the performances of the groups following the various treatments could be attributed to the differences in the treatments and not to the presence of extraneous factors.

also be collected as part of an initial preparatory procedure. In addition, there are other instances in which correlated measures must explicitly be collected through administration of a pretreatment test. Often pretesting occurs when naive human subjects are used and there is a lack of available background information on them. Because subjects have widely diverse personal and social backgrounds, information on correlated variables is sometimes collected through pre-experimental testing for purposes of matching. This pretest approach to matching is outlined in Table 4.5. The pretests and posttests may be identical or may be equivalent forms of the same test. Both the control and experimental groups receive a pretest, but the control group does not receive the treatment. The scores on the pretest can be used to form or, if already formed, to rearrange the subjects so each group exhibits equivalent means test scores at the outset of the study. Posttest differences are then more likely due to the treatment than to the pretest differences.

Pretesting is not without its hazards. For example, the pretest might sensitize subjects to aspects of a treatment that otherwise might be ignored. In effect, a pretest can serve to direct or guide the subject's attention to critical aspects of the treatment that otherwise might have been overlooked. It is conceivable that certain treatments might be ineffective unless preparatory or orienting information about them is given through the pretest procedure. A treatment simply might not exert its maximum effect if administered in the absence of the instructions that are implicit in the pretest. Thus, one result of pretesting is to maximize the possibility of a treatment effect, the pretest in effect becoming part of the independent variable. In this circumstance, the two-group pretest design illustrated in Table 4.5 would not be suitable since it would not detect this sensitizing treatment-related effect of pretesting.

The sensitization problem can be handled through the introduction of two groups in addition to those listed in Table 4.5. The four-group pretest, posttest design is shown in Table 4.6. Two experimental groups are given the same treatment, one following pretreatment test-

Table 4.5   A pretreatment test matching approach in which two groups are tested before and after the treatment or nontreatment conditions.

	Pretreatment Test	Treatment	Posttreatment Test (Same)
Experimental Group	Yes	Yes	Yes
Control Group	Yes	No	Yes

Table 4.6   A four-group pretest experimental design in which treatment vs. nontreatment conditions are combined with pretest vs. nonpretest.

	Pretreatment Test	Treatment	Posttreatment Assessment
Experimental Group 1	Yes	Yes	Yes
Experimental Group 2	No	Yes	Yes
Control Group 3	Yes	No	Yes
Control Group 4	No	No	Yes

ing and the other in the absence of the pretest. Two control groups are untreated, but only one is pretested. A comparison of the two untreated control groups allows for an assessment of the effects of the pretreatment testing procedure variable. If these two groups are different, then the pretesting had an effect that was independent of the treatment in itself. Any difference between the two experimental groups, assuming all else is held constant. can be used to determine the sensitizing effect of pretesting on the treatment condition. Finally, both experimental groups can be compared with the two control groups in order to assess the extent to which the treatment was effective in combination with and independent of the administration of the pretest.

The major limitation of this 4-group design is that it does not solve all the problems associated with pretesting. Since some of the groups depicted in Table 4.6 are not pretested, it is necessary to rely solely upon random assignment to constitute two of the groups in this design; only the two pretested groups can be matched. We must assume that the control and experimental groups that are not pretested are nonetheless equivalent to one another and to the pretested subjects. But it remains entirely possible that the two randomly constituted groups might be different from the pretested groups at the outset of the experiment.

Matching through yoking.   Sometimes, certain features of the experimental situation that must be controlled are not directly under the control of the experimenter. This sort of problem often arises when the performance of the experimental subject determines the amount of a given treatment that he or she is to receive. Individual differences in responding between subjects means that each subject will receive different amounts of the treatment. The problem requires a procedure that dispenses equivalent amounts of the treatment to control subjects.

The *yoked control* procedure has proven useful in these cases. Yoked control exposes a control subject to those features of the treatment stimulation that have been previously determined by an experimental subject.

For example, assume that an experimenter wished to show that rats could learn to remain motionless to escape painful electric shock. The experimenter might shock the subject until it remained immobile for two consecutive seconds. Note that the subject's behavior determines the amount of shock stimulus that it receives. But, without a proper control procedure, it could be argued that immobility has little to do with any reduction in activity that might be observed. Simple exposure to the shock itself might promote behavioral freezing; thus, the observed immobility would have little to do with the shock-termination procedure under study. A yoking control procedure could be used in which a control rat is exposed to the same sequence of shock stimulation as determined by the immobility behavior of one of the experimental rats. The behavior of the control subject would have no effect on the shock duration presented. Since both experimental and control subjects receive the same amount of treatment stimulation, is the shock-control behavior of the experimental subject important in producing immobility? It should be noted that the yoked subject may not have any characteristics in common with its experimental counterpart other than the same sequence of events minus the crucial variable of the experiment. Church (1964) has indicated that lack of commonality between subjects can itself be a problem for the yoking procedure.

Matching Through Evaluation

An evaluation-matching procedure is very much like running two experiments at the same time. Consider a hypothetical study in which a drug's effectiveness on physical stamina is to be determined. Should males, females, or both be used? Since there is reason to believe that the drug would have a quite different effect on men and women, one investigator decides not to use a randomization procedure for the sex factor; only females are selected for the two samples. From another perspective, an experimenter may feel it overly restrictive to limit the study to females since both males and females could use the drug. A more representative study would include both sexes. This could be accomplished by explicitly adding the sex variable to the design of the study. A comparison of the matching-elimination procedure (where only one sex is included in the experimental and control groups) with the matching-evaluation procedure (where sex is a variable in its own right) is illustrated in Table 4.7.

Table 4.7   A comparison of two matching techniques.*

Matching Elimination | Matching Evaluation

	Drug	Performance Means		Sex		Performance Means
Group 1 (Experimental)	Yes	$\bar{X}$ Treated	Yes	Treated Males	Treated Females	$\bar{X}$ Treated
		(Both groups composed of members of same sex)	No	Untreated Males	Untreated Females	$\bar{X}$ Untreated
				$\bar{X}$ Males	$\bar{X}$ Females	
Group 2 (Control)	No	$\bar{X}$ Untreated				

*The left-hand portion illustrates the matching-elimination procedure in which sex as a potential confounding variable is eliminated by randomly assigning subjects of the same sex to both the experimental and control groups. In this manner, the outcome of the study cannot be due to the differential effect of the drug on the gender of the subjects. The same condition prevails for the right-hand side of the table in that the same proportion of each sex is included in the control and in the experimental groups (compare the subject composition for the two row means). In addition, it is possible to evaluate the contribution of gender to performance by comparing the performances of the subjects in Column I with those in Column 2.

As can be seen from the left-hand portion of Table 4.7, the *matching-elimination* design does not allow for an evaluation of the role of the sex of the subject as far as the behavioral effects of the drug are concerned. The primary information is derived from a comparison of the means and the standard deviations of the drugged and undrugged groups for the samples of female subjects. In contrast, the matching-evaluation procedure, illustrated on the right-hand side of Table 4.7, provides much more information—data are available on the drugged and undrugged performances for each sex.

Perhaps the most important advantage of the matching-evaluation over the matching-elimination procedure is that a comparison can be made of the difference in performances of drugged and undrugged males with the performances of drugged and undrugged females to determine if the magnitude of these two differences is the same. This comparison is the *interaction effect* and will be considered at great length in Chapter 5. Briefly, an interaction occurs when the effects of one variable depend upon the levels of a second variable. In the present illustration, an interaction effect would have occurred

Figure 4.3

Hypothetical performance differences for males and females that were given either a drug or a control substance.

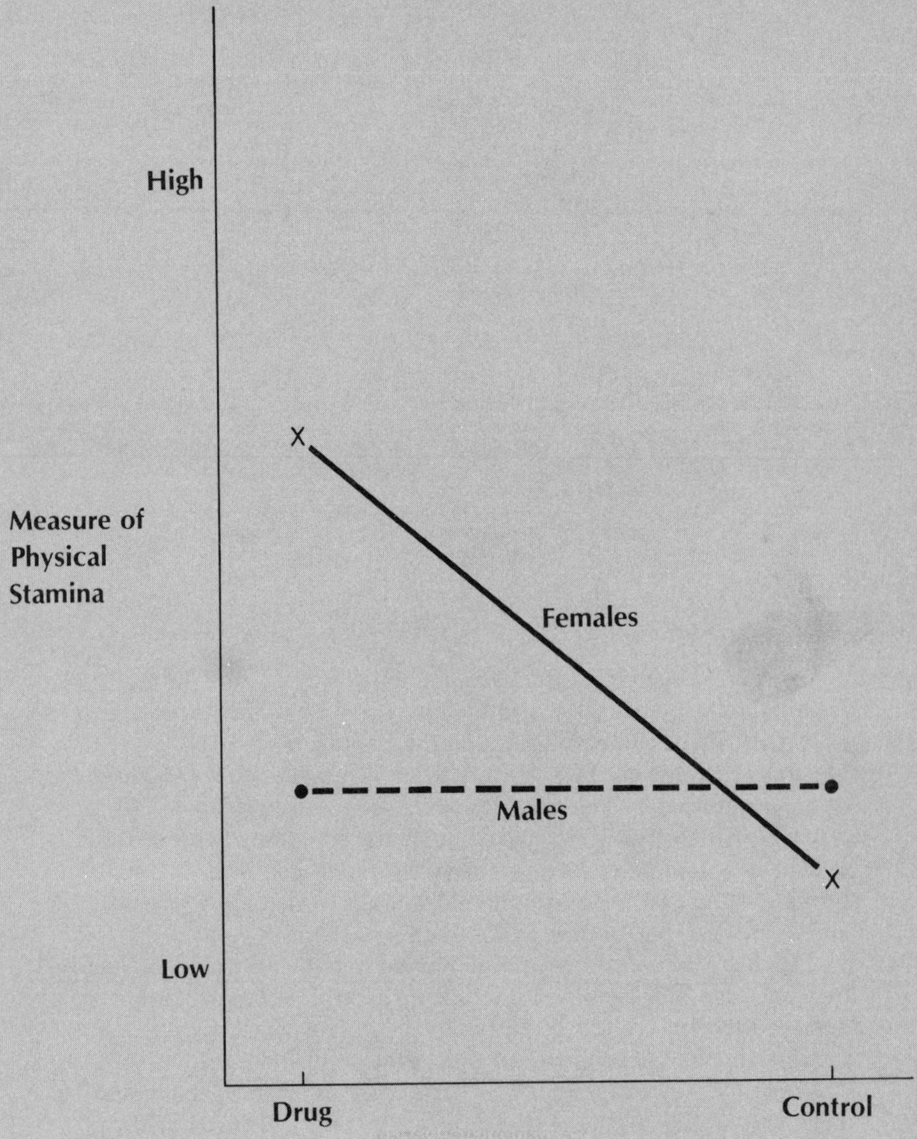

if the influence of the drug was different for males than for females. Conceivably, this might happen if the drug temporarily increased physical stamina for females but not for males. This hypothetical outcome is depicted in Figure 4.3. These data indicate not only that males generally perform less well, but that they exhibit little change from the drugged to the nondrugged conditions relative to the change that occurs for females. In short, the effects of the drug are dependent upon the sex of the user.

What if a potential confounding variable does not divide easily into categories as did the sex variable in our example? Sex can take only one of two values, male or female. How can a continuous variable—one in which there is an infinite number of gradations between extreme values—be handled in a matching-evaluation procedure? For example, family income level might be correlated with the effect of variations in preschool language training on verbal fluency. The experi-

Table 4.8   Hypothetical matching-evaluation study in which the effect of preschool training is studied in terms of measured changes in verbal fluency. Since socioeconomic background may be related to learning in children, it is controlled by distributing it equally for each level of preschool training.

Preschool Training
(The Independent Variable)

	Yes	No
Socioeconomic Level (The Matching Variable)		
High (Parent Income = $30-$50,000 Annually)	N = 30 Yes	N = 30 No
Middle (Parent Income = $10-$16,000 Annually)	N = 30 Yes	N = 30 No
Low (Parent Income = $4-$8,000 Annually)	N = 30 Yes	N = 30 No

(Verbal fluency is the dependent measure. Differences among row means reflect the influence of socioeconomic levels on verbal fluency.)

(A difference in column means reflects the effect of the manipulated variable on verbal facility for preschool children.)

menter might decide to control for this potential source of confounding. However, income level is a continuous rather than discontinuous or discrete variable: How can a matching-evaluation procedure be applied? The approach must be an arbitrary one: divide income level, a continuous variable, into as many levels as may be judicious for the experiment. Sometimes in a new area of research the extremes and a middle category are selected. Table 4.8 illustrates a design in which socioeconomic status is the matching variable; three income levels have been chosen.

The design illustrated in Table 4.8 can provide three types of information: namely, whether or not the preschool treatment procedure was effective; the influence of high, middle, and low socioeconomic levels on verbal fluency; and any possible interaction that may result from combining socioeconomic level with the preschool treatment. Note that within a single socioeconomic level, children are randomly assigned to the experimental and control groups.

METHODS OF CONTROL IN SINGLE-GROUP EXPERIMENTS

Suppose it were possible to give all of the treatments in an experiment to a single group. There are some advantages that accrue to this procedure over a separate-groups study in which each group receives but a single treatment. For example, by giving each of the different treatments on separate occasions to the same group, there is considerable savings in the number of subjects used. In addition, it is easier to select a single group that is representative of a population than to obtain a number of representative samples. The greatest potential advantage of the single- over the separate-groups design, however, is related to experimental precision

Single-group designs can result in a substantial increase in precision over separate-groups experiments that otherwise involve the same number of treatments. The fact that a single-group design can reveal reliable treatment effects even when the variability between treatment means is quite small is what is meant by increased precision. Increased precison is possible in the single-group design because the contribution to the dependent measure that individual differences normally produce within each treatment in the separate-groups design (occurring in different amounts due to Type S errors from treatment to treatment) can be eliminated. In a single-group design, individual differences are treated as a constant contribution to the total variability of each treatment and can be subtracted from each treatment in determining experimental effects.

Some of the sources of confounding that can affect a single-group experiment are the same as those already discussed in connection with separate-groups experiments. For example, environmental and task variables can confound either between-subjects or within-subjects experiments. To illustrate how situational variables might confound the outcome of a single-group experiment, consider the following: Treatment A is given to a group of subjects in the morning, Treatment B in the afternoon, and Treatment C in the evening. Since environmental conditions such as temperature, humidity, and level of fatigue may be different at each time of day, it is not possible to discern whether group performances were due to the treatments that were given, to the accompanying changes in environmental and subject conditions, or to both. This kind of confounding was referred to earlier in our discussion of temporal arrangement. Stimulus selection and arrangement as parts of the experimental task are no less important as potential sources of confounding for the single-group design than for the separate-groups design. Furthermore, the predispositions of the experimenter can bias the performances of subjects regardless of whether they appear in a single- or separate-groups experiment. All these sources of error must be controlled for the single-group approach just as for the separate-groups approach.

The Concept of Counterbalancing

There are certain sources of confounding that more often arise in single-group than in separate-groups designs. These sources originate from the very nature of the experimental approach—from the fact that each subject is exposed to more than a single treatment. The single-group strategy introduces the possibility that experiential factors may carry over to a subsequent treatment.

Clearly, the best way to control for the carry-over effects that can occur in single-group designs is through the use of a procedure that eliminates their contribution to the experimental outcome. One possible way to eliminate carry-over effects is through insertion of very long temporal intervals betweeen each treatment condition so that treatment aftereffects have a chance to dissipate. Use of long intervals between treatments might be especially valuable in eliminating carry-over effects due to habituation, fatigue, and adaptation since these factors are known to disappear over time. A major problem, however, is choosing an interval that allows for the maximum dissipation of aftereffects. Unfortunately, we have little information regarding the optimum intervals between treatments. Moreover, there are instances in which behavioral changes resulting from repetitious stimulation show little attenuation with the passage of time (cf. Thompson & Spencer, 1966). In addition, the insertion of long intervals between treatments can prolong the data-gathering phase and discourage participation by the subjects. An even more telling criticism of this procedure is that the use of long intertreatment intervals can invite the intrusion of other unwanted, extraexperimental variables.

In our discussion of separate-groups control strategies, the control procedures were designed to eliminate or evaluate the influence of potential confounding variables. In contrast, their elimination is rarely possible in single-group designs since carry-over effects are often an inseparable part of the design. Carry-over effects for most single-group experiments have prompted the use of control techniques that equalize undesirable effects across all of the treatment conditions of the study. That is, the control procedures of single-group designs are designed to evenly distribute the residual influences of the treatments and any effects due to repetitious responding over each treatment. Thus, carry-over effects cannot differentially influence outcomes, and comparisons between treatment effects are interpretable.

To illustrate the rationale underlying the control procedures that distribute carry-over effects across treatments, consider an experiment involving two treatments, A and B. If all subjects were initially exposed to Treatment A followed by Treatment B, it would not be possible to determine the direct influence of either A or B. While an experiment could obtain a relatively pure measure of performance due to A, there would be no way to determine whether performance on B was due to the carry-over effects of A, to the effects of B, or to both. Any performance under Treatment B could not be legitimately used in making a comparison with A. To correct the problems of carry-over effects from A to B, half of the subjects could be given first A then B, the other half could be given first B then A. Figure 4.4. illustrates how this procedure corrects for the problem of residual treatment influences on conditions A and B.

Note that the pure effect of Treatment A on performance was two units, as revealed by performance of the A → B subgroup, while the pure effect for B was one unit, as revealed by performance of the B → A subgroup. There was a carry-over effect due to an initial exposure; the subgroup that was initially exposed to A performed twice as well on B as the subgroup that was initially exposed to B. In contrast, the subgroup that was first exposed to B performed one unit better on A than the other subgroup also indicating a carry-over influence from B to A. Combining the performances of both subgroups on A [(2 + 3)/2 = 2.5] and on B [(1 + 2)/2 = 1.5], a relative index of the effects of both treatments can be obtained. Relative to each other, Treatment A is one unit more effective than B. This conclusion could have been reached by conducting a separate-groups comparison to determine the absolute effects of A and B. The important advantages of the single-group approach, however, are that fewer subjects are needed and a more precise comparison is possible.

Figure 4.4

Relative treatment effects due to the distribution of carry-over influences. Half of the group receives Treatment A and then B, the other half B and then A. Then the A and B groups are combined to obtain the average performances for both treatments. Subgroup A→B is given A and then B, subgroup B→A is given the treatments in reverse order.

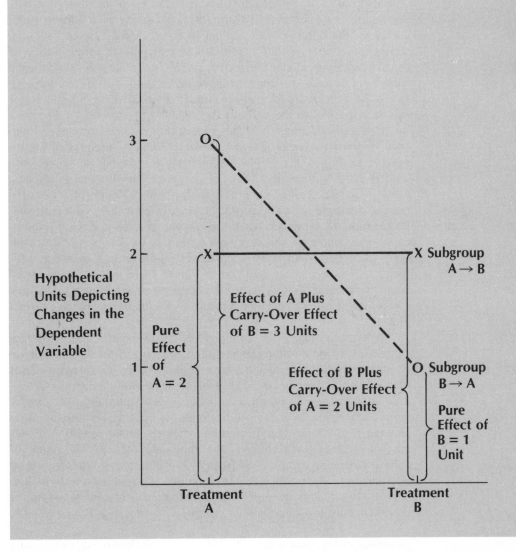

The control procedure used in our hypothetical illustration is an example of *counterbalancing*. The primary goal of a counterbalancing procedure is to evenly distribute carry-over effects across the conditions of an experiment. The reason that this control method is termed counterbalancing is that an attempt is made to "balance out" carry-over effects through an averaging procedure by altering the order of presentation so that all possible arrangements of the treatments are given an equal number of times. In the present illustration there were two possible arrangements of treatments A and B (A → B and B → A); these two arrangements occurred an equal number of times. Averaging the subgroup performances for a given condition (e.g., averaging the outcome for A when it is presented first and second) shows the effects of that specific treatment plus a representation of carry-over effects. Since carry-over effects are made constant for each treatment through the counterbalancing method, any differences between the averaged performances under the two treatment conditions can be attributed to the real effects of each.

Counterbalancing works best when the residual carry-over influence of the treatments is approximately equal or reciprocal. In our present example, this would mean that the influence of going from A to B is the same as the influence of going from B to A. Reciprocal carry-over effects offer no problems for interpretation of an experimental outcome when a counterbalancing procedure is employed. Problems arise, however, when the carry-over influence is not reciprocal. For example, if the carry-over from A to B was one unit, but carry-over from B to A was appreciably more or less than one unit, the distribution strategy outlined in Figure 4.4 would not produce an equal assignment of carry-over effects on the two treatments. Unequal carry-over effects can prohibit a meaningful comparison between treatments.

If the treatments are administered in the same order to every subject in a single-group design, then later performances in the sequence of treatments will be more influenced by carry-over effects than earlier performances. The goal of any counterbalancing procedure is to distribute potential sequencing effects equally over experimental conditions. The more treatments included in the counterbalancing, the more complicated becomes the implementation of this control strategy. Accordingly, the remainder of our discussion of counterbalancing will proceed from a consideration of *complete counterbalancing*, when only a few treatments are administered, to *incomplete counterbalancing* and *random counterbalancing*, when many treatments are given to a single group.

Complete counterbalancing.   Complete counterbalancing is typically the best counterbalancing procedure for distributing carry-over effects across the conditions of an experiment. One technique of complete counterbalancing has already been illustrated in Figure 4.4 for an experiment with two treatment conditions, A and B. The treatment conditions were completely counterbalanced since each of the two orders of presentation, A then B and B then A, were presented an equal number of times. This arrangement of treatments also resulted in each treatment following and preceding the other equally often.

Complete counterbalancing, however, can also be accomplished without subdividing the group and giving different sequences to each subgroup. When using this technique, the same subject is exposed to treatments A and B and then B and A in that order (ABBA). The number, order, and sequence of events are preserved for all subjects, thereby fulfilling the requirements of complete counterbalancing without dividing the group. However, each subject is given twice as many treatments and, hence, is engaged in twice as much responding.

The carry-over effects on the dependent measure are equalized if those effects exert a linear influence on performance as a function of the number of treatments (if the effect of carry-over is the same from A_1 to B_1 as from B_2 to A_2). This sort of carry-over distribution is depicted in Figure 4.5. Assume that there is a residual effect due to exposure to Treatment A that carries over to influence performance under Treatment B; also the carry-over effect from B to A is the same. In addition, these carry-over influences are cumulative in that they combine with one another as the number of treatment events increases.

To explain Figure 4.5, assume that the contribution of carry-over effects on performance under B from the initial exposure to A is one unit, and that B produces the same carry-over effect (one unit) on subsequent performance. Thus, one carry-over unit from A will influence the initial performance under B; this in turn will combine with the carry-over effect of the second treatment (B) so that two units will influence performance for the second presentation of B in the ABBA sequence; finally, these two units will combine with the residual influence of the second exposure to B to provide three units to affect the performance under A when given the second time. Adding these carry-over effects (CO) together for the two performances under A and B yields the following results: for A, $[(\overline{A}_1 + 0_{CO}) + (\overline{A}_2 + 3_{CO})]/2 = \overline{A} + 1.5\ CO$; and for B, $[(\overline{B}_1 + 1_{CO}) + (\overline{B}_2 + 2_{CO})]/2 = \overline{B} + 1.5\ CO$. The net amount of confounding due to carry-over effects is the same for both Treatments A and B.

There are many instances in psychological research where it is desirable to expose a single subject to more than two treatments. Consider how complete counterbalancing might be accomplished in these cases. Assume that only one variable is involved from which three values, A, B, and C, have been selected as treatment conditions. As-

Figure 4.5

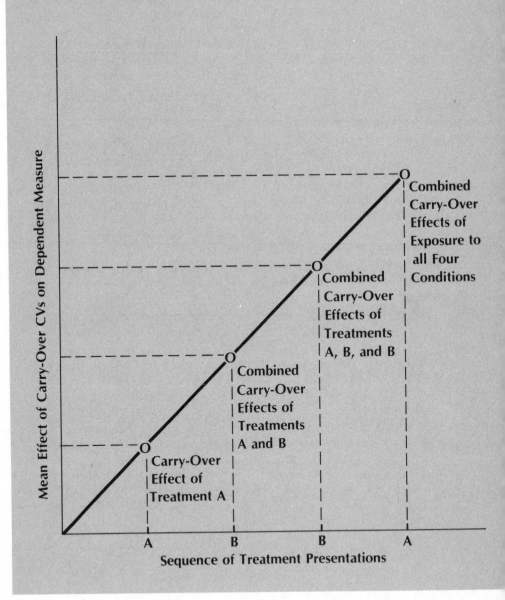

Cumulative carry-over effects from consecutive performances when the contributions are equal from treatment to treatment and the order of treatment presentations to each subject is ABBA. After Underwood (1949).

sume furthermore that it is feasible to give the three treatments to each subject during a single administration. This means that subjects will be needed for each of the ways that treatments A, B, and C can be combined if these conditions are to be completely counterbalanced.

The n-factorial (n!) formula indicates how many ways three or more events can be combined with one another. By n! is meant that each value implicit in the number, n, is multiplied by every other number. Thus, the values implicit in 3! are 1, 2, and 3. The three-factorial is computed: $3 \times 2 \times 1$, or 6. This means that there are six ways in which three things can combine. To ensure an equal number of exposures to each treatment in each ordinal position, preceding and following every other event an equal number of times, the number of subjects required must be an equal multiple of the number of such arrangements. Six or any multiple of six subjects are needed to implement the procedure of complete counterbalancing when three treatments are used. Thus:

Subject Assignment	Possible Treatment Combinations (n! = 3! = 6)
Subject 1	ABC
Subject 2	ACB
Subject 3	BCA
Subject 4	BAC
Subject 5	CAB
Subject 6	CBA

Note that each treatment occurs twice at each ordinal position and that each treatment precedes and follows every other treatment an equal number of times. Of course, subjects must be assigned randomly to these different treatment combinations. Any number of subjects other than an equal multiple of six will give rise to an imbalance in the distribution of progressive error.

As we have already noted, complete counterbalancing is the best strategy for controlling sequence or carry-over effects for single-group designs. Treatments are completely counterbalanced when each treatment occurs equally often at each ordinal position and each treatment follows and precedes the others an equal number of times. Complete counterbalancing does not eliminate carry-over effects but distributes them equally across treatments so that, through averaging, the relative effects of treatments can be accurately evaluated. However, if the influence of a sequencing effect is not linear—going from Treatment A_1 to B_1 is different than going from B_2 to A_2—no form of counterbalancing can distribute residual effects equally across conditions. The suspicion of asymmetrical carry-over effects should prompt the experimenter to reconsider the use of the single-group design in favor of a separate-groups design.

There are two major disadvantages to complete counterbalancing: (1) The number of combinations and permutations of the sequences required for more than four treatments is large, thereby requiring an excessively large sample size. (2) Numerous permutations can result in inefficient utilization of subjects. A factorial expansion of four treatments, i.e., $4 \times 3 \times 2 \times 1$, entails 24 possible combinations; five entails 120. Since the number of subjects must be an equal multiple of the number of sequences of treatment combinations for complete counterbalancing, a prohibitively large sample size is required for five or more treatments. The solution is incomplete counterbalancing.

Incomplete counterbalancing: The Latin square. There is a procedure, derived from the term *Latin square*, that can distribute linear carry-over effects equally when there is a large number of treatment conditions and only a few subjects available. This procedure allows for the use of fewer subjects than are required in complete counterbalancing. To illustrate the application of a Latin square counterbalancing technique, consider an experiment that involves four treatments (see Table 4.9).

All possible permutations of four events are shown in the first two columns of Table 4.9, and a selection of four of those permutations to be used for the partial counterbalancing of carry-over effects in the third column. The use of the Latin square technique requires selection, following certain rules, of only a few of the total number of possible treatment sequences. These sequences are chosen in such a way so as to be representative of all treatment combinations. By *representative* we mean that those sequences that are selected are more likely to contain and to equally distribute carry-over effects than any other partial combination of sequences.

One rule for selecting representative treatment sequences is that each treatment must occupy a different ordinal location from row to row (see the Latin square arrangement in Table 4.9). Each treatment occurs in each ordinal position only once. More generally, the rule is that each treatment should occur in each ordinal position an equal number of times. A second important rule evident in Table 4.9 is that each treatment precedes and follows every other treatment only once. Recall from our discussion of complete counterbalancing that each treatment should precede and follow every other treatment an equal number of times. This same condition must be followed in selecting treatment sequences for a Latin square design. Adherence to these two rules can reduce the total number of treatment combinations and permutations used in an experiment and, hence the total number of subjects needed. Since not all possible sequences are represented in a Latin square arrangement, there remains the possibility that this shorthand procedure of counterbalancing may inadvertently introduce or eliminate important sequencing effects. However, an attempt is

Table 4.9   A Latin square arrangement in which carry-over effects are distributed by a procedure that utilizes only a limited number of the total possible permutations for four treatments.

All Possible Permutations of Four Treatments (Complete Counterbalancing)			Latin Square Arrangement (Incomplete Counterbalancing)
1. ABCD	9. BDAC	17. CBAD	1. ABCD
2. ABDC	10. BDCA	18. CBDA	2. BDAC
3. ACBD	11. BADC	19. DABC	3. CADB
4. ACDB	12. BACD	20. DACB	4. DCBA
5. ADBC	13. CDAB	21. DBAC	
6. ADCB	14. CDBA	22. DBCA	
7. BCDA	15. CABD	23. DCAB	
8. BCAD	16. CADB	24. DCBA	

made to offset this problem through the equal and symmetrical representation of forward and backward treatment combinations (e.g., ABCD and DCBA) in the Latin square design.

Random assignment of subjects to treatment sequences must be adhered to in a Latin square design. A number of sources are available for a more complete discussion of random assignment and for elaboration on the construction of an appropriate set of treatment sequences in a Latin square design when the number of treatments either is odd or even (Edwards, 1972). The point we wish to make is that there are ways, applicable only for linear carry-over effects, in which the number of treatment sequences can be reduced and the number of subjects conserved even though multiple conditions are part of a within-subjects experimental design.

Randomized counterbalancing.   Randomized counterbalancing is perhaps the least desirable of the counterbalancing strategies since there is no assurance with this procedure that even linear carry-over effects will be adequately distributed. Nevertheless, by assigning numbers to each of the permutations resulting from an expanding n-factorial, one can use the random table to select fewer than the total number of combinations resulting from the expansion. Furthermore, each of the randomly selected sequences can then be randomly assigned to subjects.

An example of randomized counterbalancing is illustrated in Table 4.10. The left-hand portion of the table represents a complete listing of all the combinations or permutations of four treatments—A, B, C, and D. Note that each treatment combination has been numbered from 1 through 24. The right-hand portion of Table 4.10 contains numbers taken from a table of random numbers. Using only the second and third columns of the random table shown, the numbers with asterisks are those that conform to the numbered sequences of the left-hand portion of the table. Thus, sequences 22, 20, 02, and 06 randomly

Table 4.10   An example of randomized counterbalancing.

Combinations for Four Treatment Conditions			Numbers Taken from the Table of Random Numbers		
1. ABCD	9. BDCA	17. CABD	59491	*72269	(22)
2. ABDC	10. BDAC	18. CADB	33560	*82021	(20)
3. ACBD	11. BACD	19. DABC	95964	94260	
4. ACDB	12. BADC	20. DACB	82703	16060	
5. ADBC	13. CDAB	21. DBAC	47087	*40241	(02)
6. ADCB	14. CDBA	22. DBCA	19969	85247	
7. BCDA	15. CBAD	23. DCAB	00065	*10662	(06)
8. BCAD	16. CBDA	24. DCBA	85723		

are chosen to be represented in the experiment. These sequences are then randomly assigned to different randomly chosen subjects.

METHODS OF CONTROL IN SINGLE-SUBJECT EXPERIMENTS

Skinner (1938) and his colleagues have cogently argued that the focus of psychological research should be upon an analysis of the behavior of individual organisms. Group averages and related group statistics, they say, often obscure trends in individual performance. A group average may be highly misleading with regard to the performance characteristics of the individual subjects that comprise that group (Sidman, 1960). This consideration has prompted some behavioral scientists to focus their research efforts exclusively on the effect of treatments on individual organisms. Their experimental strategies and control procedures often parallel those used with the single-group design. The major difference is that a single organism rather than a group of subjects is repeatedly exposed to a single treatment or a series of treatments.

Single-subject research has long been a part of experimental psychology. Researchers in the area of psychophysics, where, for instance, interest may be in the construction of psychological scales or the determination of sensory thresholds, have found that most fruitful research requires repetitious stimulation and responding from a single organism. More recently, the single-subject approach has been the basis of research in operant conditioning and behavior modification.

Control and Causation in Single-Subject Designs

There are many instances in single-subject research where the issue is whether a treatment does or does not have an effect on behavior.

The experimental strategy entails hypothesis testing, and the presence of a treatment effect is used to refute the null hypothesis as untenable. How can one employ a single subject in hypothesis testing and, at the same time, employ proper control procedures so as to minimize the presence of possible confounding variables? A single-subject design, by definition, precludes the use of other subjects as a means of control. It is possible, however, to use segments of performance from a single subject as a control or base from which to evaluate yet other aspects of his or her performance. By collecting data from the subject before, during, and after the presence of the treatment, predictable behavioral changes that consistently parallel the introduction and removal of the treatment condition can be used as evidence for rejecting the null hypothesis—the hypothesis which holds that there is no treatment effect. In short, causal statements in single-subject research are formed by comparing the treated aspects of a subject's behavior to earlier and later untreated aspects. In this sense, control refers to the level of an individual's performance in its untreated state.

Baseline recording.   A major feature of the single-subject design is the recording of a behavior that doubles at one point in time as a baseline measurement and at another as an indicant of the presence or absence of the treatment effect. Typically, this is achieved by first promoting the stable occurrence of a response. In infrahuman research, this is accomplished, for example, by training a pigeon to consistently peck a key, a rat to steadily depress a lever, or a chimpanzee to regularly pull a chain. These behaviors can be established by dispensing food or water to the organism when hungry or thirsty for correct performance. Another way to obtain stable-state responding is to arrange conditions so that termination of an unpleasant stimulus is the outcome of the desired behavior. For instance, a stable and repetitious bar-pressing response can be produced by following each reaction with the termination of painful electric shock. Stable, steady behavior constitutes what is meant in single-subject research as *baseline behavior.*

In general, the measure of stable-state responding is rate. By *rate* is meant the number of responses per unit of time. Change in rate of responding from the values that characterize baseline performance coincident with treatment stimulation is the focus in single-subject research. In short, the rate of a specified response before treatment can be compared with the rate during the treatment to determine its effect. In this manner, the subject's own behavior serves as the control. Figure 4.6 represents a hypothetical illustration of a control strategy in a single-subject, operant conditioning experiment. The graph is based on a pen tracing on a slowly moving paper. Each time a response occurs, the pen changes in stepwise fashion diagonally across the paper, thereby producing a *cumulative record* of the subject's behavior. The actual rate of behavior is indicated on this sort of record in terms of the relative *steepness* of the tracing, the more perpendicular to the flow of the paper the higher the rate. Response stability is indicated by the relative *smoothness* of the tracing, with regular stepwise increments indicating more stability than highly irregular steps. Once performance is stabilized, producing the baseline record, introduction of a treatment can be indexed by a deviation in the angle of the pen tracing. In Figure 4.6, Point A indicates the introduction of a treatment that produces a corresponding acceleration in rate of responding. A deceleration would serve the same function—showing that the treatment exerted an effect.

Reversal control procedures.   A change from a stable-state baseline, associated in time with the introduction of a treatment, is not sufficient for concluding that the treatment caused the change. The change may have been accidental, perhaps caused by some other factor introduced at the same point as the treatment. To combat this problem, the treatment condition, once applied, can be removed so that the response rate has the opportunity to return to the original pretreatment baseline rate. An abrupt return to baseline rate that is correlated with removal of the treatment is more conclusive evidence that the treatment and not some accidental factor produced the initial treatment-related change in performance. Reintroduction of the treatment following a return to baseline rate can provide still further documentation of the treatment effect. If the individual again exhibits a change in performance parallel to that which occurred at the time of the initial treatment exposure, it is even more likely that the treatment and not some other variable produced the behavioral change. This research technique is called an ABAB *reversal control design* in which A refers to the baseline period and B to the introduction of the treatment. Clearly, the greater the number of AB reversals accompanied by orderly changes in behavior, the greater our confidence that the treatment variable effectively and reliably caused the alteration in performance.

Multiple baseline procedures.   A problem of interpretation can arise if, upon the removal of the treatment, the subject's performance does not return to baseline. Failure to return to baseline performance is clear cause for the suspicion that some other variable than the treatment condition produced the initial change. There is also the possibility that the treatment was so potent as to produce a lasting, durable influence on behavior. The research problem, of course, is to find a proper control condition to evaluate the event responsible for the behavior.

Figure 4.6

Hypothetical cumulative record of behavior for a rat that has learned to make a bar press response for a food reward. Steplike increments in the pen tracing indicate bar presses while the chart paper continuously advances at a slow pace. Rate of stepwise pen increases is indicated by the angle of pen tracing on the paper. The accelerated increment in stepwise pen movements, beginning at Point A, indicates introduction of a treatment stimulus. Removal of the event is accompanied by a return to the original rate of responding.

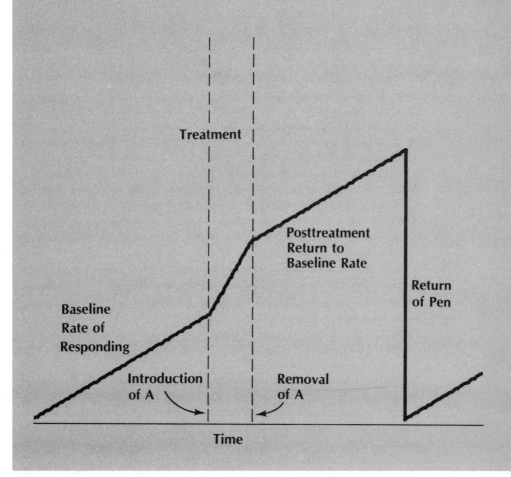

One possible solution is to employ multiple subjects, each receiving the same treatment but introduced at different times. If the observed changes in behavior are similar and invariably coincident with the introduction of the treatment for each individual, then the treatment can be implicated as the reason for the behavior. This design is called the *multiple baselines across subjects procedure.*

Another control technique is to establish *multiple baseline behaviors for different responses of the same subject.* We know that people can perform several different activities during the same temporal period; it is possible to teach a chimpanzee to depress a lever as well as pull a chain at the same time, each activity in response to a different kind of reinforcer. To assess whether a given treatment exerted a lasting residual effect, the treatment could initially be introduced for the lever press, then later for the chain pull. If the treatment produced similar changes in each behavior coincident with its introduction even though its removal did not result in a return to baseline in either case, it would be reasonable to conclude that the treatment exerted a relatively permanent change on the behavior. On the other hand, if the introduction of the treatment for one behavior produced concurrent changes in both behaviors, it would be impossible to know whether the treatment influenced the entire organism, whether some other overriding variable intruded simultaneously with the treatment presentation, or both. No causal conclusion is possible under this circumstance.

Finally, it is common in clinical research to obtain *multiple baselines on the same behavior in two or more settings.* For instance, if a mother in a clinic learns a treatment procedure to control her hyperactive child, will the procedure be equally effective when it is introduced in the home at a later date? The use of multiple baselines on the same and different behaviors in various settings provides useful information on the generalization of the treatment effect. Such single-subject designs have become extremely popular in research dealing with developmental, educational, and therapeutic problems.

SUMMARY

Control in psychological research refers to methods or procedures which allow the investigator to conclude whether or not the manipulated variable had an effect on behavior. Basically, the issue is whether a systematic relationship can be attributed to the causal influence of an independent variable or is due, in whole or in part, to some extraneous variable. Undesirable or extraneous factors are referred to as confounding variables because they prevent an unambiguous interpretation of an experimental outcome.

Confounding variables can be categorized according to their source or origin. These sources include: (1) uncontrolled aspects of the experimental *situation*, including features of the environment, task materials, and instructions, as well as predispositions of the experimenter regarding the outcome of the experiment; (2) uncontrolled features of the *subjects* that systematically vary from group to group prior to the actual conduct of the study; and (3) the *arrangement* of materials, treatments, and subjects. Special consideration must be given to how treatments are sequenced in terms of their presentation, as well as to their order.

There are two basic designs which can be employed to combat the problems of confounding. *Separate-groups designs* require control procedures which ensure that all groups are approximately equal with respect to the dependent variable at the onset of the experiment. *Single-group designs* require control procedures which ensure unchanged performance from treatment to treatment or result in the equal distribution of sequencing errors across all treatment conditions.

Separate-groups designs can take one of three forms: experimental group (receiving Treatment X) versus a control group (receiving a zero amount of X); experimental group versus a control group receiving a smaller amount of X; experimental group versus a zero control group versus a control group receiving a smaller amount of X. In separate-groups designs, pretreatment equivalence of groups can be achieved through randomization, matching-elimination, or matching-evaluation. Matching-elimination often occurs by testing subjects prior to the administration of the treatments and then balancing group means on the basis of pretest scores. However, pretest measures can sometimes sensitize subjects to treatments and, hence, pose problems in interpreting the experimental outcome. The pretest sensitization effect and the treatment effect can both be evaluated by employing a design in which there are two experimental and two control groups, one group in each set receives pretesting while the other group receives only the treatment (or control) condition followed by a posttest. The matching-evaluation technique allows the experimenter to investigate treatment effects, the matching variable, and the interaction between the two. An interaction occurs if the treatment effect occurs at one level of the matching variable but has no effect or a different effect at a second level of the matching variable.

Single-group designs require the minimization of confounding effects due to the sequencing of treatments by means of complete, incomplete, or random counterbalancing. The aim of counterbalancing strategy is to distribute unwanted order effects equally across treatments administered to the same subjects. Complete counterbalancing controls both order and sequence effects but is inefficient if more than four treatments are compared; a Latin square design or randomization procedure should be employed if more than four treatments are compared.

Single-subject designs are slight modifications of single-group designs. Experimental control in single-subject designs can be achieved through baseline recording, reversal designs, and multiple baseline recording. Single-subject designs are frequently used to study the modification of the behavior of individuals in terms of their development, education, or rehabilitation.

QUESTIONS

1. What is confounding? Why is it a central topic in psychology?
2. What are some sources of situational confounding variables? Give some examples and show how they might be interrelated at a conceptual level.
3. When is the problem of subject confounding variables most evident? Why is subject confounding difficult to control? What precautions are available to help avoid subject confounding?
4. Show that arrangement confounding variables are important by giving some examples. How might they be controlled?
5. What are the two basic experimental designs used in psychology? What are their respective advantages and disadvantages? Give some examples of the types of questions addressed by each.
6. What types of control procedures are best for between-groups designs? Compare and contrast each procedure.
7. What is the relationship between random samples and control procedures? When would an experimenter want to take advantage of this relationship? How would this be done?
8. What is matching? What procedures are involved in matching? When would matching be considered a better procedure than randomization? Give some examples.
9. What control procedures are best suited for within-subjects designs? What are the advantages and disadvantages of each. What is counterbalancing? What are the different types of counterbalancing? Why is counterbalancing best suited for within-subjects designs?
10. What types of control procedures are used in single-subject designs? Give some examples for each type, making sure to note their respective advantages and problems, as well as how they compare with one another with respect to the control of confounding variables.
11. Compare and contrast control procedures for between-subjects, within-subjects, and single-subject designs, pointing out the different types of problems best handled by each design.

The Anatomy of Psychological Experiments: Research Designs

 # test
F test is used
factorial designs
interaction data

There is no special merit in either a complicated experimental plan or a highly refined technique if equally accurate results can be secured with less effort in some other way. A good working rule is to use the simplest experimental design that meets the needs of the occasion.

(Cochran & Cox, 1957, p. 41)

Two independent variables may interact in their influence on behavior. By this is meant that the influence of one independent variable differs in magnitude as a function of the level at which another independent variable is set.

(Underwood & Shaughnessy, 1975, p. 13)

A good research design is an essential element in scientific inquiry. It enables the experimenter to evaluate his or her original hypothesis by providing the framework for determining the functional relation between events under study. A good design allows the experimenter to assess the systematic effects of the treatment conditions on a behavioral event by aiding in the control of extraneous or error variance.

A research design is the skeleton or framework of an experiment. Viewed in this way, a research design functions somewhat like a model that is to be filled in by procedural details. In other words, once the experimental question has been posed, both a general design and specific procedural details must be formulated in order to eventually arrive at a suitable answer. Depending upon the nature of the experimental question, there are a number of rules and guidelines that can be employed to determine which of several design models should be used.

WITHIN- VERSUS BETWEEN-SUBJECTS VARIABLES

After researchers have translated their hypotheses into explicitly defined independent and dependent variables, they must make a decision as to the manner in which their subjects are to be assigned to the various treatment conditions. That is, should they assign a subject to a single treatment or to more than one treatment? Earlier, we referred to this decision as the choice of a between-subjects versus a within-subjects design. When we use a between-subjects design, each subject is presented with only one experimental condition. In contrast, when we use a within-subjects design, several experimental conditions are presented to each subject. In this chapter we will consider a number of possible combinations of between- and within-subjects designs in terms of their advantages and disadvantages. The best design is the one which results in the highest possible degree of experimental precision for the least effort.

SIMPLE RANDOMIZED DESIGN

The simplest research design involves a comparison of two conditions, each administered to an independent group of subjects. Often in psychological research one of the conditions is a treatment condition and the other a control condition. For instance, if we were interested in the effects of a new drug on discrimination learning, we might assign one-half of our sample to a condition in which each subject received the drug prior to the discrimination task. The other half of our sample would receive a *placebo* or control drug (*see* Box 5.1) which would be administered in exactly the same manner as the experimental drug and with the same external features. By contrasting the performances of the control subjects with the performances of the treatment subjects with regard to the rate or accuracy of discrimination learning, we could reach a conclusion regarding the drug's effectiveness.

We would likely use a *double-blind* procedure in this drug study. Neither the subject nor the experimenter would have prior knowledge of the specific condition being administered at any given time during the experiment. The subjects would, of course, be randomly assigned to conditions so as to distribute effectively between the conditions as many of the extraneous sources of error as possible (i.e., Type S errors). Through random assignment, we would hope to achieve an equal distribution of individuals with different learning abilities and personality characteristics between the treatment and control groups.

We should point out that in the simple randomized design subject differences are only randomized—they are neither controlled nor eliminated. Researchers cannot eliminate variability due to accidental

Box 5.1   The Use of a Placebo in Experimental Design

The use of the term *placebo* is widespread in psychological research. In its broadest sense, a placebo refers to any condition that assesses the importance of suggestion on the experimental outcome. In a drug study, for example, a placebo may take the form of a solution or a tablet administered to the control subjects that contains all but the presumed key ingredient. At the close of the experiment, one might argue that both the control and treatment subjects were treated identically with the single exception that the latter received the to-be-assessed ingredient. The experimental outcome should be due to the treatment and not to the powerful side effects of suggestion.

An experimenter can actually measure the contribution of suggestion, perhaps resulting from the expectations of subjects based on their past experience with beneficial drugs, by adding a third group which receives neither the placebo nor the treatment conditions. Differences in performance scores between the placebo and nonplacebo, nontreatment groups would reflect the operation of suggestion factors. It is not uncommon to find that the suggestion variable will influence 20 to 30 percent of the subjects in an experiment. Clearly, the suggestion variable is a factor that requires experimental attention and control.

choice of idiosyncratic subjects (Type S errors) with the simple randomized design. Randomization simply ensures that each sample has the same chance of containing peculiar subject characteristics. As we discussed in Chapter 3, the larger a random sample the more likely it will reflect the characteristics of the population from which it has been drawn. Randomization is usually effective in equalizing subject variations across treatment conditions for research involving human subjects because psychologists frequently employ relatively large samples of from twenty to thirty people per group (cf. Lindquist, 1953). However, for research in behavior modification, psychophysics, and animal learning, psychologists often use small samples of five subjects or less per group; randomization is much less effective with small sample sizes.

Although our example of the effects of a new drug on discrimination learning only made use of two groups, the simple randomized design can be extended to include any number of treatment and control conditions. One difference between the simplest design (two groups) and more elaborate designs (three or more groups) has to do with the particular type of analysis used to examine the dependent measure. Generally, the two-group design is analyzed by a contrast statistic like the t test (Blommers & Lindquist, 1960). On the other hand, a simple randomized design containing more than two groups is usually analyzed by an analysis of variance (F test) which assesses overall differences among the treatment means. If the F test is significant, additional statistics (for example, t tests) are used to compare pairs of conditions to determine exactly where signficant differences occur. An example of the combined use of F and t tests to analyze differences between group means when two or more conditions make up the experimental design is given in Box 5.2. A valuable aid in analyzing data collected with the simple randomized design as well as with the other designs that we will discuss in this chapter is the *Computational Handbook of Statistics* by Bruning and Kintz (1977).

TREATMENTS-BY-LEVELS DESIGN

We encountered in Chapters 3 and 4 the possibility of Type S errors occurring when a simple randomized, between-subjects design is used. Even with large sample sizes there remains the distinct possibility of substantial error due to chance or sampling factors. We will now consider the circumstances which sometimes necessitate the construction of samples in such a way so as to minimize the chance of differences due to sampling error.

As noted in Chapter 3, it is possible through *stratification* (dividing population characteristics into levels or subsets) to achieve a greater

Box 5.2 The Use of *t* and *F* tests with the Simple Randomized Design

In Box 5.1 we discussed a study in which an investigator wanted to determine a certain drug's effectiveness on a discrimination learning task. If the experimenter had chosen a simple randomized design with two conditions (the drug and the placebo), he or she would have randomized the subjects in their assignment to one of the two groups, probably using a double-blind procedure. After collecting the data, a simple *t* test for independent measures would be used to assess whether the difference between the mean score of the drug condition and the mean score of the placebo condition was signficant. The following formula would be used for this comparison:

$$t = \frac{\bar{X}_1 - \bar{X}_2}{\sqrt{\left[\dfrac{\sum X_1{}^2 - \dfrac{(\sum X_1)^2}{N_1} + \sum X_2{}^2 - \dfrac{(\sum X_2)^2}{N_2}}{(N_1 + N_2) - 2}\right] \cdot \left[\dfrac{1}{N_1} + \dfrac{1}{N_2}\right]}}$$

where

$\bar{X}_1$ = the mean of the first group of scores
$\bar{X}_2$ = the mean of the second group of scores
$\sum X_1{}^2$ = the sum of the squared score values of the first group
$\sum X_2{}^2$ = the sum of the squared score values of the second group
$(\sum X_1)^2$ = the square of the sum of the scores in the first group
$(\sum X_2)^2$ = the square of the sum of the scores in the second group
N_1 = the number of scores in the first group
N_2 = the number of scores in the second group
$df = n_1 + n_2 - 2$

If the investigator had decided to measure the drug's as well as the placebo's effects on performance, he or she would have needed an additional condition—one in which the subjects would perform only the discrimination task without the drug or the placebo being given beforehand. The group means for the three conditions would then be compared with a one-way analysis of variance which would assess whether significant differences existed among the three means. If the *F* test proved significant, it is highly probable that at least one reliable difference could be found somewhere among the three means. The next step would be to find out exactly where the difference(s) was located. The drug mean would be compared to the placebo mean by using a *t* test to determine the drug's influence on performance. Next, the placebo mean would be contrasted to the nonplacebo, nondrug mean, again using a *t* test, to test for the suggestion effect. Of course, a comparison of the drug condition versus the nonplacebo, nondrug condition could be made, but this test would make little sense because the true effect of the drug could best be determined by comparing its effect with that of the placebo group.

degree of representation of certain population characteristics in the sample than might result from randomization. Furthermore, an experimenter might not only be interested in ensuring sample-to-population representativeness, but also in ensuring sample-to-sample equivalence. The treatments-by-levels design is a useful tool for achieving equivalence among several sample groups with respect to a particular subject characteristic. We will consider the sample-to-sample equivalence aspect of this design in some detail. We alluded to this design in Chapter 4 as the matching-through-evaluation technique.

In a treatments-by-levels design certain extraneous sources of variation due to accidents of sampling can be minimized by equating groups in terms of a matching variable. In Chapter 4 we defined a *matching variable* as one which is related to the dependent measure and which, if left uncontrolled, could influence the experimental outcome in some unknown and undesirable way. To illustrate the use of the treatments-by-levels design as a matching technique, let us return to our example involving the discrimination learning abilities of two groups—one receiving a drug and the other a placebo. If we had prior knowledge that the subjects in our population had various degrees of experience with certain drugs which might alter the behavioral effects associated with our treatment drug, it might be advantageous to match the subjects in the two conditions in terms of their prior drug experiences. For instance, we might formulate three degrees of drug usage: extensive, defined in terms of frequent (daily or weekly) drug usage; minimal, defined as the occasional (monthly) use of drugs; and none (no prior drug experience). Having formulated these three levels, we would then assign subjects from each level of drug usage to the control or the experimental conditions. The two samples would then be matched in terms of prior drug usage. Assuming that all other relevant subject variables were equally distributed across samples, any difference in our dependent measure of discrimination learning would likely be the result of the drug. In this case, the matching procedure was based on the assumption that different degrees of drug experience might have affected performance in the drug condition.

The major advantage of the treatments-by-levels design over the simple randomized design is that one source of individual differences is equalized in terms of its influence on the group means. As with randomization, matching does not eliminate the contributions of a given variable to the dependent measure. Instead, it distributes the effects of the matched variable equally among conditions. However, matching is advantageous *only* if the correlation between the matching variable (in our case, prior drug experience) and the dependent measure (for example, number of trials needed to perform the discrimination task successfully) is moderately large. Generally, the magnitude of this correlation should be greater than .30 (Feldt, 1958).

A second advantage of the treatments-by-levels design is that it permits an analysis of the interaction between the matching variable and the independent variable. An *interaction* occurs when the effects of one independent variable on some behavior are different for each level of a second independent variable. For instance, if discrimination learning for the drug condition *(a)* was superior to that of the placebo group when subjects had no prior drug experience, *(b)* was unaffected when subjects were minimally experienced, and *(c)* was poorer when subjects were frequent users, then an *interaction* between the matching variable (degree of drug experience) and the independent variable (treatment and control conditions) would have occurred.

Figure 5.1 illustrates several sets of data showing possible interactions, both nonsignificant (5.1a) and significant (5.1b and 5.1c), between the drug-placebo and degree-of-experience conditions. Note that the parallel lines in 5.1a indicate that the nonsignificant differences between the drug condition and the placebo condition were independent of the degree of prior drug usage, with an equal and small difference between drug and placebo conditions occurring at all three levels of prior experience. However, in both 5.1b and 5.1c the nonparallel lines indicate potentially significant interactions. The forms of the interactions in 5.1b and 5.1c are obviously not identical and lead to different interpretations. In 5.1b it appears that the interfering effects of the drug condition on discrimination learning occurred only for subjects who had frequent or minimal past drug experience. In contrast, 5.1c indicates that *(a)* frequent users required more trials to learn the discrimination tasks when given the drug condition, *(b)* drug-treatment subjects without prior experience learned faster, and *(c)* the drug had no effect on discrimination learning for minimal users. In short, the data in 5.1b and c suggest that the drug versus placebo contrasts would yield vastly different results at the various levels of prior drug experience. The significant interactions depicted in Figure 5.1 are only two of many possible significant interactions that could have occurred.

The matching procedure used in the treatments-by-levels design can be extended so that a single subject in one condition is identical in some designated way to another subject in a second condition. The two are identical in terms of the matching variable. This is an extreme case of the treatments-by-levels design and is called the *subject-by-subject matching procedure*. In this extension, a specific level exists for each degree or amount of the matching variable. Each level contains only one subject per condition. For instance, an investigator might wish to match the subjects in two (or more) conditions in terms of their intelligence, limiting the IQ range to scores between 100 and 120. Thus, there might be 20 levels of the matching variable, each characterized by two subjects, one assigned to the drug treatment

Figure 5.1

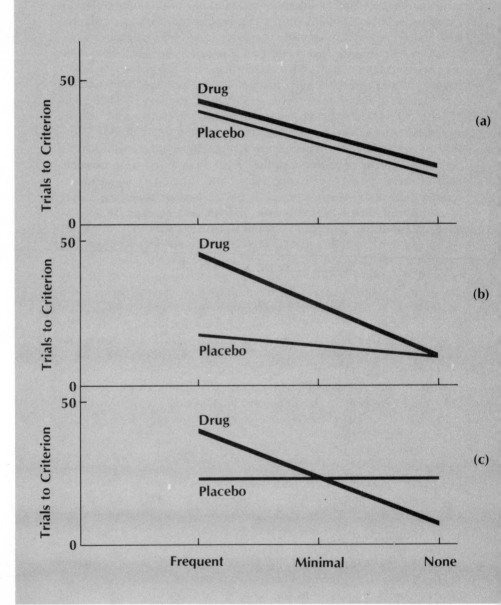

An illustration of significant (b and c) and nonsignificant (a) interactions between drug-placebo and degree-of-experience conditions.

and the other to the control condition. At each level, two subjects would have the same IQ value.

The subject-by-subject matching procedure eliminates the opportunity to assess the possible interaction between the matching variable and the treatment condition. In addition, it is at times difficult to achieve a subject-by-subject match because of practical considerations such as time and effort. Nevertheless, psychologists often use a measure of learning capacity or intelligence to match subjects—provided, of course, that there is a priori knowledge of a substantial correlation between the matching variable and the dependent measure. The implications of using a matching procedure when the correlation between the dependent and matching variables is low are considered in Box 5.3. If only two groups are being contrasted, the data of this design are analyzed by a *t* test for correlated measures (cf. Bruning and Kintz, 1977).

Up to this time, most of our discussion of research design has focused on the assignment of subjects to a single condition in any given experiment. We have referred to this procedure as the use of a between-subjects design. Now we shall consider experimental designs where subjects serve in more than one condition.

TREATMENTS-BY-SUBJECTS DESIGN

There are two major reasons why an experimenter might wish to assign a subject to more than one condition. The first is related to minimizing the influence of error variance on the treatment means. If a subject has served in all conditions of a given experiment, then it is unlikely that obtained differences between treatment means could be attributed to individual differences among subjects (Type S errors) because any extraneous subject variable, such as intelligence, would likely influence each treatment mean in the same way. For instance, requiring the subjects in our drug study to participate in both the experimental and control conditions would have eliminated intersubject differences in the comparison of the means of the two conditions. The drug and placebo group means would then be more likely to reflect the actual treatment effects.

A second reason for employing the treatments-by-subjects design is that of economy. Fewer subjects are required than in the simple randomized design. Hence, a within-subjects design, such as the treatments-by-subjects design, is more preferable if the size of the available sample is small or if it is desirable to use highly trained subjects.

A major difficulty of the treatments-by-subjects design is that the behavioral effects related to one treatment are sometimes greatly influenced by exposure to a prior treatment. The possible contamination

Box 5.3   Matching Designs and Correlation

Problems arise in using a matching design when the correlation between the matched variable and the dependent measure is low. For example, assume we suspected that IQ was an important factor in the outcome of our drug study. We hypothesized that the higher the IQ, the less would be the effect of the drug on discrimination learning. We decided to equate IQs in the drug and control conditions on a subject-by-subject basis. That is, for every person with a given IQ in the drug condition, there was a person with an identical IQ assigned to the control condition. Intelligence served as a matching variable and there were as many levels of the matching variable as there were different IQ pairs.

Now consider the formula for the t test for matched or correlated measures which would be used to analyze the discrimination learning scores:

$$t^* = \frac{\bar{X} - \bar{Y}}{\sqrt{\dfrac{S_x{}^2 + S_y{}^2 - 2rS_xS_y}{N-1}}}$$

where $\bar{X}$ = mean number of trials needed to reach the learning criterion in the drug condition

$\bar{Y}$ = mean number of trials needed to reach the learning criterion in the control condition

$S_x{}^2$ = variance of the X scores (drug condition)

$S_y{}^2$ = variance of the Y scores (control condition)

r = correlation between X and Y

N = number of pairs of scores

$df = N - 1$

A low correlation coefficient *(r)* between the X and Y scores would imply that they were unrelated—that is, that the IQ had *not* provided a link or relationship between the various paired members (the Xs and Ys) in terms of learning rates. If IQ was not related to the measure of performance, the low *r* between X and Y would result in a small reduction in the size of the denominator of the *t* test. However, since the degrees of freedom for the *t* test for correlated measures is one-half that for the *t* for independent measures (N-1 versus $N_1 + N_2 - 2$), considerable power or experimental precision is lost; and the risk of committing a Type II error is increased. One must weigh carefully the advantages of matching against the disadvantage of a substantial loss in degrees of freedom and the resulting loss of power in the experiment. Clearly, the deciding factor should be the magnitude of the correlation between the matched and the dependent variables. We emphasize the importance of a firm, logical, and empirically based rationale before deciding to control the effect of an extraneous factor with a matching design, such as the treatments-by-levels design.

*A more useful computational formula for the correlated measures t test is:

$$t = \frac{\bar{X} - \bar{Y}}{\sqrt{\dfrac{\Sigma D^2 - \dfrac{(\Sigma D)^2}{N}}{N(N-1)}}}$$

where D = the difference score between each X and Y pair
         N = the number of pairs of scores
         df = N − 1

of one treatment because of subjects' prior exposure to another treatment must be ruled out before using the treatments-by-subjects design or, for that matter, any other within-subjects design. In our drug example, for instance, if exposure to the experimental drug had an adverse emotional influence on our subjects, then their behavior under the placebo condition, following exposure to the actual drug, might be different than if they had no prior drug treatment. These circumstances might prompt us to use a counterbalancing procedure, giving half of the subjects the placebo followed by the drug and the other half the drug followed by the placebo. However, a between-subjects, randomized design would probably be much more desirable in this instance because counterbalancing, under these circumstances, would not distribute carry-over effects equally across treatments.

Another difficulty of the treatments-by-subjects design is related to the testing situation. In many learning tasks only a single treatment can be administered because of the high level of learning that occurs on the initial task; sometimes powerful effects from practice preclude the inclusion of a second task. It is not uncommon for cumulative practice effects on an initial task to be so pervasive as to require the use of between-subjects designs in many human and animal learning experiments. Prolonged practice may also cause fatigue or boredom, making performance on a second task impossible to interpret.

The field of perception, unlike human and animal learning, allows the experimenter great flexibility in the use of the treatments-by-subjects design. For instance, if reaction times as a function of the color of a visual stimulus (red, green, or white) were to be examined, several well-practiced subjects would be used, each presented with all experimental conditions in random sequence. The use of a within-subjects design eliminates individual differences in reaction time as a potential factor influencing the treatment means. In addition to its experimental precision, the treatments-by-subjects design requires only a relatively small number of subjects for reliable conclusions because the use of multiple measurements for each individual ensures highly stable performance estimates.

TREATMENTS-BY-TREATMENTS DESIGN

Psychology has advanced to the point where most current research efforts focus on an analysis of complex relations among behavioral events. A complex relation occurs when the effects of more than one independent variable are assessed in a given experiment. We have already discussed some aspects of more complex designs in our presentation of the treatments-by-levels model. There we observed that two variables, the treatment and the matched variable, could be simultaneously manipulated. The major difference between the treatments-by-levels and the treatments-by-treatments designs is the focus of our experimental interests. In the former design we were not concerned with the effects of the matching variable except perhaps as it interacted with the independent variable. Often, however, an experimenter might be equally interested in the effects of a second independent variable on the dependent measure. In the treatments-by-treatments design, subjects are not matched; instead, they are simply assigned randomly to conditions which contain a combination of two treatment levels, both of which are related to the experimental hypotheses. Both variables in the treatments-by-treatments design represent between-subjects dimensions; each subject is assigned to one and only one condition of the experiment.

Returning to our drug study, assume we predicted that the experimental drug would have a different effect on simple than on complex discrimination learning. Our experimental hypothesis was that the drug would facilitate discrimination learning with a simple, to-be-learned task but would inhibit learning on a complex task. The research design involved the assignment of subjects to one of four groups: drug-simple task, drug-complex task, placebo-simple task, and placebo-complex task. In other words, we simultaneously investigated discrimination learning as a function of task complexity and drug-nondrug conditions. In this instance, the theory predicted an interaction between the two independent variables; namely, the drug's effectiveness should be directly related to the difficulty of the discrimination task. The point we must make here is that we have advanced beyond the level of a simple functional relationship concerning the drug's effectiveness to an inquiry concerning its differential effectiveness on specific types of learning tasks. In this instance, the concept of interaction advances our research to a higher plateau of scientific inquiry. Interaction permits the formulation of a relatively complex lawful statement concerning the way two (or more) independent variables combine to affect performance.

The treatments-by-treatments design is often referred to as the 2 by 2 or 2×2 factorial experiment (Hays, 1973). It is one of the most common and useful designs employed by research psychologists. Basically, the factorial experiment is an extension of the simple randomized design that includes an additional independent variable. Because the factorial design permits a test for the interaction between two or more independent variables, it is said to yield more information than could be obtained from several isolated experiments investigating the variables separately.

In a 2×2 factorial design there are two main effects and an interaction effect. The main effects of the first variable are its mean values averaged over all levels of the second variable. The main effects of the second variable are its mean values averaged over the levels of the first variable. If the interaction is not significant, the main effects of each independent variable can be analyzed and clearly interpreted. In other words, a nonsignificant interaction implies that the influence of one variable is not dependent upon or related to the levels of the other variable. The absence of an interaction can be taken to mean that essentially two experiments have been run, each involving the manipulation of a single variable. The tests for the main effects of two variables reduce the 2 × 2 factorial to two simple randomized designs. The behavioral outcome due to one variable was not influenced by the second variable.

If the interaction is significant in a 2 × 2 factorial design, the effects of one independent variable are analyzed at each level of the second independent variable. Returning to our drug example, if the drug condition interacted with the task complexity condition, then we would likely contrast the drug versus the placebo treatment means separately in the simple and the complex discrimination tasks. Essentially, we would approach our data as if multiple experiments had been performed, the difference being that at least two comparisons are made between the drug-nondrug conditions for the simple as well as for the complex discrimination tasks when an interaction exists. That is, we would not average the drug-nondrug means over the dimension of task complexity as we did when there was no interaction. We refer to comparisons between means at one of the levels of another variable as the tests for *simple effects.*

Table 5.1 presents a schematic outline of the 2 × 2 factorial design with one main effect comparison (drug vs. placebo) and one simple effect comparison (drug vs. placebo with the complex task) highlighted. Note that we have emphasized the location of the main and simple effect comparisons in this table; the comparison of the main effect is averaged over subjects in both levels of task difficulty, while the simple effect comparison includes only those subjects who learned the complex task. We must remember that the simple effect comparison in the 2 × 2 factorial design is legitimate only if the interaction has been shown to be significant. In short, the dependency of one independent variable on the other must first be established before the analyses of simple effects are permissible.

Although the factorial design presented above had only two levels for each of two variables, one or both variables could have contained more than two levels. If such were the case, the conceptual as well as the statistical breakdown would be similar to that of the basic 2 × 2 design. That is, if the interaction was significant, we would proceed with the analysis of the simple effects for one variable at each level of the other. If the interaction was not significant, we would examine each main effect as if it were a simple randomized design with more than two levels (i.e., an F test followed by multiple t tests). Now we shall turn our attention to the addition of a third independent variable to the basic two-dimensional factorial design.

Table 5.1   Schematic diagram of a 2 × 2 factorial design with main and simple effect comparisons.

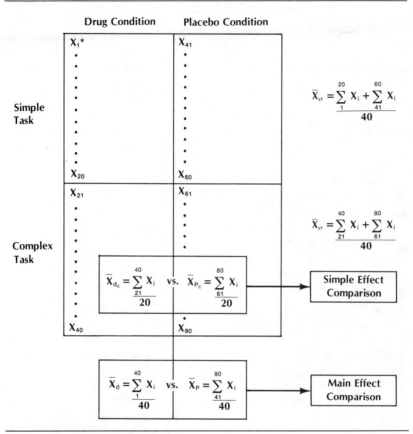

*X_1 represents the score of the first subject in the Drug Condition-Simple Task. This subject (X_1) is presented with one and only one of the four conditions.

THREE-FACTOR DESIGN

Statistics, especially analysis of variance, can prove to be a considerable aid in understanding experimental design. This is particularly true with respect to the conceptualization of interaction terms which are essential components in higher-order designs. These interaction terms hold the promise of yielding precise, complex lawful statements and represent the principal rationale for using a multidimensional design. To successfully employ higher-order designs, we should know how to proceed logically in analyzing complex interactions. In the long run, a detailed and thorough understanding of complex interactions should result in the formation of more comprehensive hypotheses in the initial stages of research.

All that the term *three-dimensional factorial design* means is that a third dimension has been added to the basic two-factor design. All three variables are between-subjects dimensions, and each subject is assigned to a single cell or condition. The basic outline of the three-factor design presented in Figure 5.2 shows variables A, B, and C with each variable having two levels. Note that subject S_1 is given only the condition associated with cell A_1, B_1, C_1 and none of the other conditions in the design. Since the three-factor design is important for many areas of psychological research, it requires our detailed consideration.

Let us assume we wanted to examine the effects of a certain drug (versus its appropriate placebo control) together with task complexity (easy or difficult) and level of intelligence (high, medium, and low) on discrimination learning. Conceptually, we would have a $2 \times 2 \times 3$ factorial design. A subject, classified at one level of intelligence, would receive either the easy or difficult task under the influence of the drug or the placebo condition. There would be twelve cells or conditions in the design, each containing an independent group of subjects. While randomization would be used in assigning subjects to the task complexity and drug-nondrug conditions, subjects could not be randomized across levels of the intelligence variable since assignment here would be set by their measured level of intelligence (high, medium, or low IQ).

The simultaneous manipulation of three variables naturally poses more problems than a design involving the manipulation of two variables. For example, the minimum number of interaction terms is increased fourfold. There can be an interaction between factors A and B, A and C, and B and C. Performance under any one of these variables (A, for instance) can be differentially influenced by the presence of the various levels of another of the variables (B and/or C). In addition, a potential fourth interaction in this design ($A \times B \times C$) implies that one or more two-factor interactions will likely be significant at one level of the third factor, whereas one or more two-factor interactions involving the same terms will not be significant at a different level of the same third factor. For instance, a triple-order interaction may result from the fact that AB is significant at C_1 but not at C_2 or that AC is significant at B_1 but not at B_2. The presence of a significant triple-order interaction in our previous example could have occurred if the levels of intelligence by type of drug interaction were significant when the task was complex but nonsignificant when the task was simple. A triple-order interaction is also implied if the forms

Figure 5.2

Basic outline of a three-dimensional design.

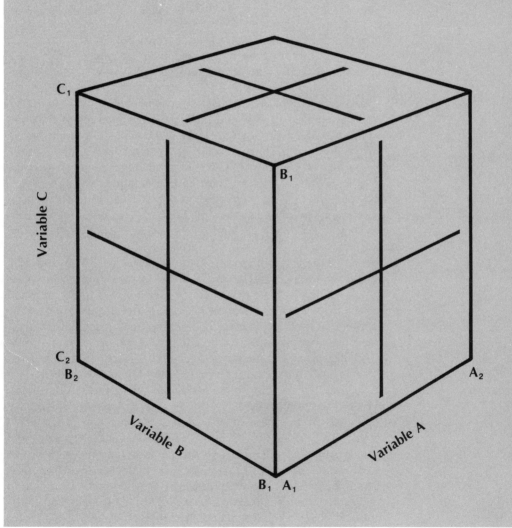

of significant two-factor interactions change radically across the levels of a third factor.

The first step in the conceptual analysis of the three-factor design is to examine the triple-order interaction (A × B × C). If the triple-order interaction is statistically significant, a subdivision into less complex two-factor interaction terms is required. Essentially, this means subdividing the experiment into a number of two-way factorial designs. If there were two levels of factor C, two separate analyses of the A × B interaction would be conducted at each level of C. One then would proceed to analyze each of these miniexperiments according to the procedures outlined in our preceding discussion of two-way factorial designs.

In psychological research triple-order interactions in the three-factor design often prove to be nonsignificant. Nevertheless, the possibility remains that any one of the three major two-way interactions may be statistically significant. For instance, if the B × C interaction were the only one that was statistically significant (A × B and A × C being nonsignificant), it would imply that the interaction does not change in character from level to level of Factor A. In other words, the effects of A are irrelevant with respect to the B × C interaction; hence, the analysis of the B × C interaction is carried out on data collapsed over Factor A. If none of the interaction terms in the three-factor design are significant, we can view the situation as three separate experiments involving the manipulation of three different independent variables. Factors A, B, and C would then be analyzed as main effects.

Figure 5.3 presents graphs of a set of hypothetical results in which the triple-order interaction (intelligence × drug condition × task complexity) is significant. Note that a triple-order interaction becomes apparent when both graphs in Figure 5.3 are carefully examined. The parallel functions in 5.3a (the easy task) suggest a nonsignificant intelligence × drug interaction; the nonparallel functions in 5.3b (the difficult task) depict a potentially significant two-factor interaction between intelligence and the drug-placebo conditions.

In Figure 5.3a the drug effects are independent of levels of IQ, and in 5.3b drug effects and IQ levels are interdependent. The appropriate analysis of the main effects of the drug-placebo condition in 5.3a would likely prove to be nonsignificant, whereas the expected effects of intelligence (i.e., better discrimination learning with higher IQ levels) would probably be statistically reliable in the easy task. With the difficult task, the breakdown of the two-factor interaction might reveal that the drug had no effect with low IQ subjects, although it would likely have a facilitating effect with average and high IQ subjects.

Figure 5.3

Discrimination learning as a function of drug condition, task complexity, and level of intelligence showing significant <u>triple-order interaction</u>.

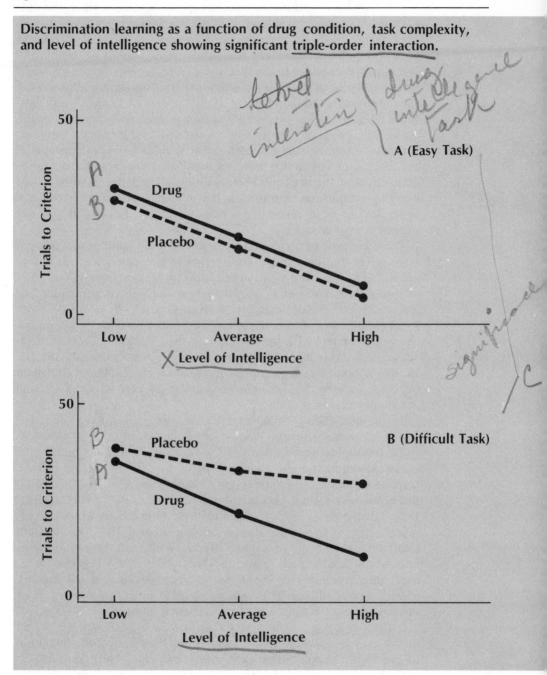

Let us suppose, again looking at our hypothetical experiment, that results indicate a nonsignificant triple-order interaction. The data presented in Figure 5.4 indicate that the two-factor interactions involving intelligence levels and drug conditions are identical at both levels of task complexity. Thus, the triple-order interaction is not significant. We would then want to analyze the two-factor interaction of major interest (intelligence × drug conditions) with the data averaged over the third factor, task complexity. If, as the data of Figure 5.4 suggest, the intelligence level × drug condition interaction were significant, we would analyze the simple effects of the drug dimension comparing the drug versus nondrug conditions at each level of intelligence. If the two-factor interaction were nonsignificant, we would analyze the main effect of the drug-placebo conditions. The latter analysis would proceed on the assumption that the influence of the drug was not dependent upon or related to specific levels of IQ or to the degree of task complexity.

We are now in a position to summarize the appropriate analytic steps, given that the triple-order interaction is nonsignificant as in Figure 5.4. The first step is to analyze the two-factor interactions (AB, AC, and BC). Each of these subanalyses can be conceptualized as a separate two-factor design. If a given term (A, B, or C) does not significantly enter into either of its two-factor interactions, then we can be concerned with the appropriate test for main effects. For instance if the AB and AC interactions were nonsignificant, and the BC interaction was significant, then we would analyze the overall main effect of A (here the data would be collapsed across B and C), and the simple effects of B and C.

The three-factor design examples we have cited have suggested only a fraction of the total number of possible analyses. For instance, if the triple-order interaction (ABC) were significant, one could look at the AB interaction at each level of C, the AC interaction at each level of B, and the BC interaction at each level of A. In Figure 5.3, there are seven such two-factor interactions (AB_{C1}, AB_{C2}, AB_{C3}, BC_{A1}, BC_{A2}, AC_{B1}, AC_{B2}). Each of these interactions would constitute a separate two-factor design and the subanalysis of each would focus on either main or simple effects. Which of these two-factor interactions are actually examined and interpreted when the triple-order interaction proves significant is directly related to the number of original hypotheses that were proposed. Generally, only a few of the possible interactions are of experimental interest.

The advantage of the three-factor design in particular and of all higher-dimensional designs in general is that they allow the formulation of precise and comprehensive lawful statements. More specifically, in the simple randomized design we can only say that A does or does not have an effect on some specified behavior. In contrast, with the

Figure 5.4

Discrimination learning as a function of drug condition, task complexity, and level of intelligence showing nonsignificant triple-order interaction. *(diverg) par (no int)*

A (Easy Task)

Placebo

Drug

Trials to Criterion

Low   Average   High

Level of Intelligence

B (Difficult Task)

Placebo

Drug

Trials to Criterion

Low   Average   High

Level of Intelligence

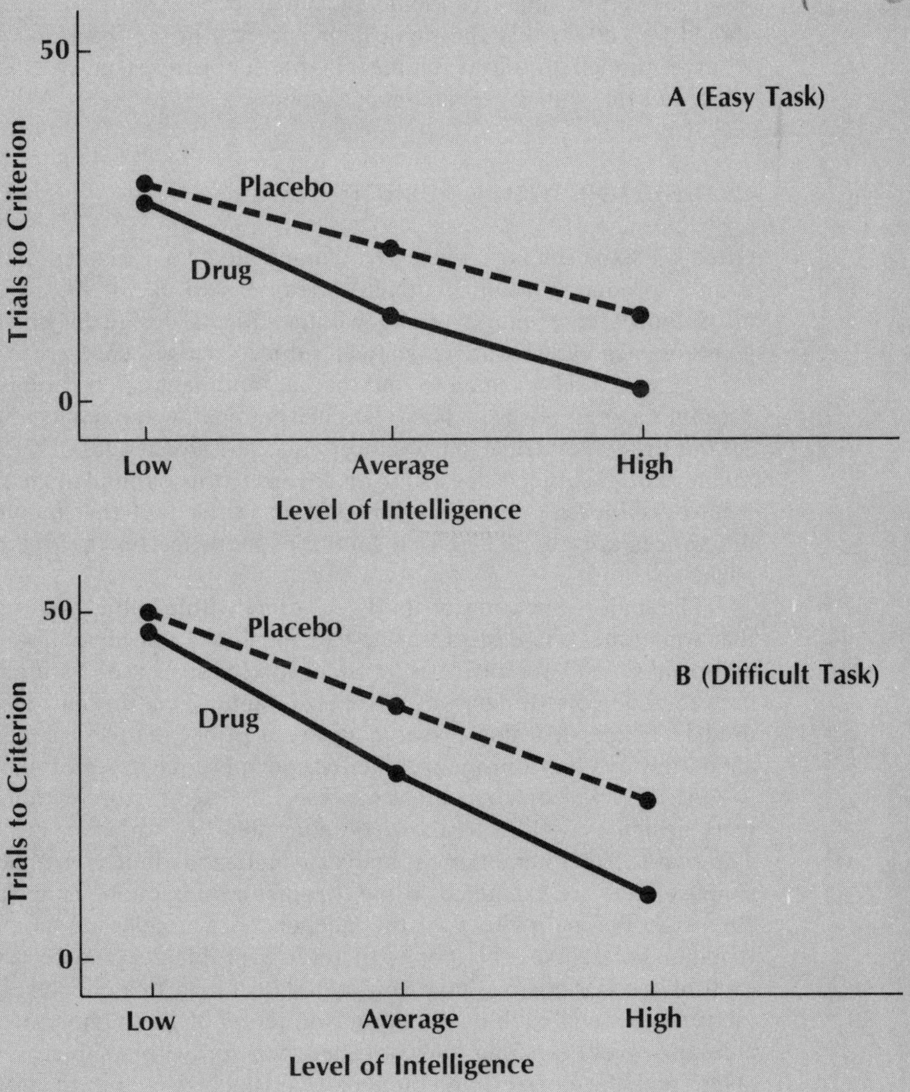

three-factor design we can say that A has an effect independent of conditions B and/or C, or that the effects of A are directly dependent upon given levels of B and/or C. These latter statements based on the use of the three-factor design represent higher-order laws.

Before researchers use a multidimensional design, they should identify those interactions which are of major interest in terms of relevance to their original hypotheses and should clearly understand how the eventual analyses should logically proceed. Furthermore, they should be certain that the number of subjects in the individual cells is large enough to allow for meaningful subanalyses given that the important interaction terms are significant.

TWO-FACTOR, WITHIN-SUBJECTS DESIGN

Often an experimenter wishes to manipulate two variables and yet is able to administer all treatment conditions to each subject. Such an instance represents a totally within-subjects design in which all levels of each variable are given to all subjects. In perceptual research, for example, it is common to find that all treatment combinations can be administered to each highly trained subject without introducing serious order, sequence, or fatigue effects. The advantages of the two-factor, within-subjects design are analogous to those found in the treatment-by-subjects design. Most important is the fact that individual differences are eliminated as a source of influence on the treatment means.

The major limitation of the two-factor, within-subjects design is that sometimes the effects of one treatment will not have dissipated before a second treatment is introduced. In this case, naturally, a between-subjects design would be preferable. This design rarely is used in animal learning research where a prior treatment condition almost always has a pronounced effect on subsequent performance.

At the level of conceptual analysis, the two-factor, within-subjects design is similar to the two-dimensional factorial experiment. The two-factor interaction is analyzed first; and, if it is significant, simple effects are examined. If the two-factor interaction is nonsignificant, then the main effects of the independent variables are assessed. It might be well, at this point, to refer to Table 5.2 and to review each of the designs we have considered so far in this chapter. Take the time to study each of the designs in terms of the number of variables involved, whether they are between- or within-subjects variables, and the possible interactions. Consider also how to proceed in the analyses of simple effects associated with significant interactions and main effects associated with nonsignificant interactions.

Table 5.2 Summary of basic experimental designs.

Design Type	Number of Variables	Type of Variable	Potential Interactions	Subanalyses
1. Simple Randomized	1 (A)	Between-S Variable (A)	None	Main Effects
2. Treatments X Level	2 (A, B)	Between-S Variable (A, B-Levels)	A X Levels	Main Effects or Simple Effects
3. Treatments X Subjects	1 (A)	Within-S Variable (A)	None	Main Effects
4. Treatments X Treatments	2 (A, B)	2 Between-S Variables (A, B)	AB	Main Effects or Simple Effects
5. Treatments X Treatments X Treatments	3 (A, B, C)	3 Between-S Variables (A, B, C)	ABC, AB, AC, or BC	Main Two-Factor Interactions* or Simple Two-Factor Interactions**, then Main Effects or Simple Effects
6. Treatments X Treatments X Subjects	2 (A, B)	2 Within-S Variables (A, B)	AB	Main Effects or Simple Effects

*For example, AB.
**For example, AB at C_1 and AB at C_2.

MIXED DESIGNS

The major purposes of a good experimental design are to control or minimize extraneous variability and, in turn, to provide sensitive conclusions related to experimental hypotheses. As we have seen, the control of extraneous variability, especially that associated with individual differences among subjects, is most effectively handled by using a within-subjects design. However, a within-subjects design is often impractical or impossible. For instance, if the number of treatment combinations is very large, it may be unwise to present all treatment combinations to each subject because of possible boredom or fatigue. Moreover, certain treatment conditions often alter the subjects' behavior or their expectations of future events such that any additional treatment would be contaminated by the first experience. These circumstances often force the experimenter to make a decision—either to choose a between-subjects design where factors such as confounding due to prior treatments or fatigue effects are usually nonexistent but where individual variability may be large, or to choose a within-subjects design where the desired control of individual variability may be offset by certain undesirable confounding factors. Fortunately, such decisions are made a bit less difficult because of the existence of mixed designs.

In a mixed design some treatments represent between-subjects variables and others represent within-subjects variables. A given subject might receive all the levels of one treatment but only one level of another treatment. Essentially, a mixed design implies some combination of the simple randomized design with the treatments-by-subjects design. That is, the variable corresponding to the simple randomized design would be between-subjects while the variable analogous to the treatments-by-subjects design would be within-subjects. We shall now discuss two of several possible mixed designs.

One-Within, One-Between Design

In our first illustration of a mixed design, suppose an experimenter wished to manipulate two independent variables. He decided to present all levels of one variable but only one level of the second variable to each subject. His aim was to contrast the effects of a certain experimental drug and a placebo control on a learning task. Since he was unable to present both conditions to each subject because of possible confounding or carry-over effects, he was forced to make the drug variable a between-subjects dimension. Moreover, he suspected possible changes in behavior from early trials to later trials so he decided to assess temporal changes in learning by making trials a within-subjects variable.

Figure 5.5 presents hypothetical learning data for the drug and placebo conditions across 10 blocks of 5 trials each. As we can see from the nonparallel functions, there is a strong suggestion of an interaction between the drug conditions and the trials dimension. The analysis of this interaction would indicate whether the main effects or the simple effects for the drug-placebo comparison should be analyzed. If the interaction proved to be significant, then the simple effects comparing the drug and placebo conditions would be examined at each trial block or, perhaps, during early (i.e., blocks 1 to 5) and during late trials (i.e., blocks 6 to 10).

In contrast, if the interaction were found to be nonsignificant, the main effects of the drug and placebo conditions would be assessed. This analysis is similar to that in a simple randomized design with two treatment conditions. The trials classification would be ignored and the data obtained during all fifty trials would be used to compare the drug to the placebo condition. If there were some interest in learning rates, then the trials dimension could be analyzed as a simple or main effect, again depending upon the outcome of the test for the interaction.

The usefulness of the one-within, one-between design for experiments which investigate temporal changes in behavior, in terms of trials or time, should be quite apparent. The trials variable is the within-subjects variable, and the variable of experimental interest is a between-subjects variable. It is probably the most common type of experimental design in contemporary psychological research, especially in learning research. To repeat, the distinctive feature of the one-within, one-between design is that each subject receives all levels of one variable at a specified level of a second variable.

One-Within, Two-Between Design

If the design just presented is extended to include a third variable and if this variable is a between-subjects variable, then each subject would receive all levels of one variable at only one level of each of the other two variables. As is true for most mixed designs, the one-within, two-between design is extremely useful in learning, personality, social, and clinical research. In these areas of research, the one within-subjects variable often represents behavioral assessments over time or trials, and the two between-subjects treatments represent the independent variables. An example of this design would be a contrast of the drug and placebo conditions using both simple and difficult tasks with trials as the within-subjects variable. If we were simply

Figure 5.5

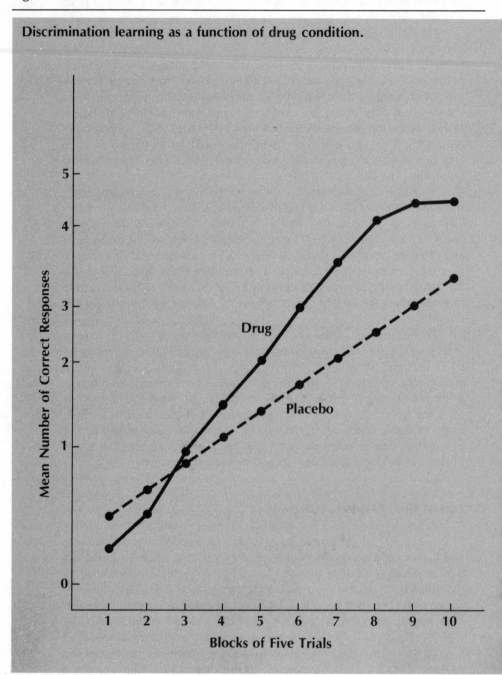

Discrimination learning as a function of drug condition.

to average the learning data over all trials and obtained a single estimate of performance or if we used a trials-to-criterion measure, then the design would be a 2×2 factorial.

On the other hand, if our interest centered on changes across trials, we would have a three-dimensional design with trials as a within-subjects effect and the drug and placebo conditions and task complexity as between-subjects effects. The sequential analyses of a three-factor, mixed design is presented in Table 5.3. We would begin the analyses at the level of the triple-order interaction, proceed to simple or main two-factor interactions, and then to the subanalyses of all interaction terms. A moderately good understanding of the information in Table 5.3 will ensure mastery of many of the important aspects of experimental and statistical design, especially with regard to the treatment of significant and nonsignificant interaction terms.

APPLICATIONS OF DESIGN PRINCIPLES

At this point in our discussion we could consider still more advanced designs with additional between- and within-subjects variables, but we think it more profitable to present a series of hypothetical cases with questions to test and reinforce the control and design principles that we have already introduced. The following three cases illustrate some of the uses and misuses of basic design techniques and their corresponding methods of analysis.

Case 1: Hallucinogenic Activity and Shock Therapy

A clinical psychologist wished to evaluate the effects of intensity of shock therapy on the degree of hallucinogenic behavior in a particular class of schizophrenic patients. She chose three levels of intensity and administered each level to an independent group of patients at systematic intervals over a two month period. At the end of the time period, she gave a reliable and valid test of hallucinogenic behavior and found that the intensity of the shock was related to the duration of hallucinogenic activity during the test phase. The linear function relating the independent and dependent variables is presented in Figure 5.6. The experimenter assessed the meaning of her data by means of a one-way analysis of variance (F test), associated with the use of a simple randomized design (See Box 5.2). Since the F test was significant, she concluded that a low amount of shock therapy reduced hallucinogenic activity more than medium or high levels of shock therapy. Furthermore, she concluded that low intensity shock therapy is an effective way to treat schizophrenic patients. Were her design and analysis sufficient to permit such conclusions?

Table 5.3   Analysis of a three-dimensional design where A and B are between-subjects variables and C a within-subjects variable.

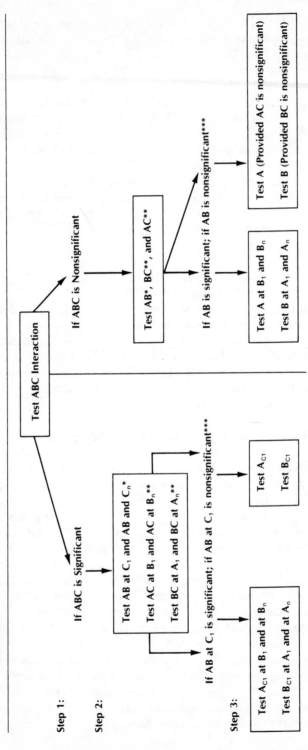

Step 1:

Step 2:

Step 3:

*This test is essentially the same as the analysis of a factorial design.

**This is essentially a one-within, one-between design.

***You would proceed in a similar manner in the breakdown of the other two-factor interaction terms (AC and BC) except that these analyses are one-within, one-between designs.

Figure 5.6

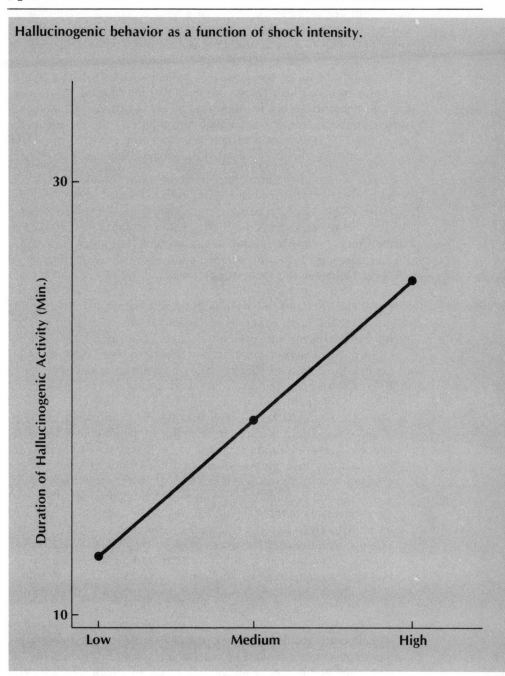

Hallucinogenic behavior as a function of shock intensity.

Comments on case 1. Let us first make the assumption that those details not discussed in the above case were either irrelevant or were taken into account by the experimenter. For instance, we should assume that such factors as the duration of hospitalization, the degree of schizophrenia, and the IQ levels of the patients were not responsible for any differences in the degree of hallucinogenic behavior among the three groups. Furthermore, we must assume that the prior literature on this problem has led the experimenter to choose a two month period of shock therapy rather than longer or shorter periods as the most effective treatment duration. We shall now consider the actual design and the statistical analysis of this experiment.

1. If you mastered the most important points in Chapter 4, you will have observed that a control group was not included in this study. More specifically, the experimenter should have included a group that was never shocked or, better yet, a group that was taken to the shock therapy room, prepared for shock, but given no therapy. The addition of control groups would allow the experimenter to decide whether the low intensity shock reduced or, perhaps, increased hallucinogenic behavior in contrast to a no-shock (placebo) condition. It is quite possible that the patients who were given the low level of shock experienced more hallucinogenic activity than no-shock control patients would have. The addition of control groups would permit more accurate and detailed conclusions regarding the effects of shock therapy on hallucinogenic behavior.

2. Even if the design and procedure were considered to be adequate, the analysis of the data would have been incomplete. The overall F test showed only that the three means were significantly different. It did not indicate the specific location of significant differences. Did the low-shock group experience significantly less hallucinogenic activity than both medium- and high-shock groups? Did the medium-shock group differ significantly from the high-shock group? These questions could only be answered by contrasting the treatments means with three separate tests (e.g., t tests for independent measures), given that the F test was significant.

3. The use of a between-subjects design in this instance was clearly more appropriate than a within-subjects design. This is due to the fact that an individual patient could serve in only one condition if the effects from one level of shock were to remain distinct from and unconfounded by the other levels of shock intensity.

4. Was the dependent variable a representative, accurate assessment of hallucinogenic behavior? Was a standardized test situation the most appropriate method of determining changes in the patients' emotional and cognitive states as a result of shock therapy? You can likely think of alternate ways in which to measure these behavioral changes, such as rating the patients' behavior in the wards.

Some of the alternatives would probably lead to more useful information than would come from the hallucinogenic measure used in this experiment.

Case 2: Expectancies in Problem Solving

A personality psychologist developed a theory concerning the effects of success-failure instructions on problem solving behavior. His study used a treatments-by-subjects design in which half of the subjects received the success-oriented instructions followed by a problem-solving task. Following a brief rest interval, the same half received the failure-oriented instructions followed by a second problem-solving task. The other half of the subjects received the conditions in the reverse order (i.e., failure then success instructions). The analysis of the data indicated that there was no difference in performance between the two groups. The success instructions did not lead to more rapid problem solving as the investigator had originally predicted.

Comments on case 2. A number of issues must be confronted when using a within-subjects design in any learning experiment. For instance, the tasks must not be so difficult as to produce boredom or fatigue during the test session. Moreover, the learning-to-learn factor must not reduce the final problem to an extremely simple learning task where a high level of performance would be insensitive to any real treatment differences. In addition to these general considerations, we offer the following specific criticisms.

1. The counterbalancing technique (i.e., half of the subjects being started with failure-oriented instructions and the other half being started with success-oriented instructions) used to balance the treatments in terms of possible practice effects was not a sound choice. The flaw was that differential transfer effects could have occurred for each group of subjects. In other words, after solving the relatively nonemotional, success-oriented problem, a subject then receiving the failure-oriented problem probably had minimal carry-over effects from the first task. In contrast, after a subject had first worked on the failure-oriented problem, he or she would be less likely to accept the credibility of the success instructions and might transfer the failure orientation from the first problem to the second problem. This carry-over phenomenon could produce differential transfer which would inflate the dependent variable (time to solve the problem) during the second problem, especially under success-oriented instructions. The resulting effect would then be to cancel the potentially facilitating effects of the success-oriented instructions for the group receiving the failure-oriented instructions first.

2. A more acceptable design would have been a simple randomized design with independent groups receiving the two conditions. Perhaps an even better alternative would have been to use a treatments-by-levels design with three or more levels of IQ. Of course, the choice of this latter design assumes that IQ would significantly influence the rate of problem solving and, hence, would be a desirable matching variable. Either of these between-subjects designs would have eliminated the possibility of differential transfer that might have occurred with the within-subjects design.

Case 3: Effects of Anxiety and Shock on Learning

The following paragraph contains the results and conclusions from a paper dealing with the effects of shock (low and high intensities) on the learning of a serial list presented for ten trials to groups of high anxious (HA) and low anxious (LA) subjects. The shocks were designed to induce stress and were given on the same aperiodic schedule to all subjects.

Since an examination of the mean number of correct responses across all conditions for males was approximately the same as for females, the effects due to sex differences were assumed negligible. The mean number of correct responses for LA and HA subjects under low intensity were 21.8 and 24.3 and under high intensity were 32.1 and 39.8, respectively. Since two *t* tests showed HA subjects to perform better than LA subjects under both shock intensities, it was concluded that "anxiety" facilitates this type of verbal learning and that the effect is not dependent upon shock intensity.

Comments on case 3.   We should mention that any experimental study subjecting humans to electric shock or any other traumatic agent must be designed with ethical and methodological foresight. In every human experiment the rights, welfare, protection, and the voluntary and informed consent of each subject must be given utmost consideration. The potential benefits must be compared to the potential risks. From this perspective, it is unlikely that our hypothetical experiment would ever be carried out. A consideration of these issues is *assumed* before the experimenter turns to problems of design and analysis.

1. The design of this shock experiment can be conceptualized as a $2 \times 2 \times 2$ factorial design with the three variables being degree of shock intensity, level of anxiety, and sex. However, a more careful reading of the statement of results indicates that a statistical

analysis based on a 2 × 2 × 2 factorial was probably not used. For instance, no mention was made of any of the possible interactions (three-factor as well as two-factor) that are associated with the three-dimensional factorial design. In fact, the sex dimension was apparently analyzed only as a main effect (i.e., averaged or collapsed over the other two conditions). This is inappropriate since we have some grounds on which to anticipate a sex-by-anxiety interaction with sex proving to be a relevant dimension only with HA subjects. In other words, HA males might be considerably different from HA females while male-female differences in learning might not be significant for LA subjects. Thus, the three-factor interaction and all two-factor interactions involving sex should have been initially examined and then the appropriate subanalyses carried out.

2. A second and similar criticism is related to the analysis of the effects of shock intensity level and anxiety. The investigator tested for the *simple effects* of anxiety at both high and low levels of shock intensity without first assessing the potential interaction between the two factors. Remember that tests for simple effects are legitimate only if the interaction has first been shown to be significant.

   The data indicate that the difference in the mean number of correct responses between the HA and LA subjects under low shock intensity was 2.5 and the difference under high intensity was 7.7. Such differences lead one to suspect a potential interaction, implying that the difference in performance between the anxiety groups would be significantly greater under high-intensity shock than under low-intensity shock. An intensity level by anxiety level interaction would lead to more precise, accurate, and detailed conclusions than were formulated by the investigator.

3. Essentially, the experimenter neglected to examine the interaction terms implicit in his design. He should have proceeded from an inspection of the three-factor interaction to the two-factor interactions and, finally, to simple or main effects. These steps in analysis, illustrated in Table 5.3, are absolutely necessary if the maximum amount of information is to be obtained from higher-order designs.

SUMMARY

Perhaps the most important task of the psychological researcher is translating a hypothesis into testable form. To do this the investigator must choose an appropriate, sound research design. The key issue confronting the investigator is whether a single subject should serve under one or several experimental conditions. A subject receives only one experimental condition in a between-subjects design; a subject receives all experimental conditions in a within-subjects design.

The simplest form of experimental design consists of a comparison of the performance of control subjects with experimental subjects. A simple randomized design is a between-subjects design, and a treatments-by-subjects design is a within-subjects design. The advantage of the treatments-by-subjects design is that it eliminates error variance due to individual subject differences (Type S errors). However, the treatments-by-subjects design can be used only if there are no differential transfer effects across successive conditions and if fatigue or boredom effects are not present.

The importance of the factorial design in which several dimensions are simultaneously investigated is related to the development of more comprehensive, lawful statements. These statements are based on the presence or absence of interaction terms. An interaction occurs when the effects of one independent variable on some behavior (i.e., on some dependent variable) are different for each level of a second independent variable. More specifically, if variable A has a significant behavioral effect at B_1 (e.g., the effects of A_1 are greater than A_2) but no effect (e.g., A_1 equal to A_2) or an opposing effect at B_2 (e.g., A_2 greater than A_1), then an interaction exists between the variables A and B. When a significant interaction is detected, simple effects are analyzed (e.g., A_1 vs. A_2 at B_1 and B_2); when the interaction is nonsignificant, main effects are analyzed (e.g., A_1 vs. A_2, with data averaged over B_1 and B_2). In a three-variable factorial design, the sequence of analyses is from the triple-order interaction (ABC) to main (e.g., AB) or simple (AB at C_1 and C_2) two-factor interactions, depending upon whether the ABC interaction is significant. Thereafter, the three-factor design reduces to a two-way factorial.

In a mixed design several independent variables are manipulated. However, at least one variable must be a within-subjects variable and at least one a between-subjects variable. For example, in learning research, trials might constitute the within-subjects variable and the manipulated variable (or variables) the between-subjects variable(s). Psychology has advanced to the point where higher-order mixed designs have become commonplace in most contemporary research.

QUESTIONS

1. What is the difference between within-subjects and between-subjects variables? What are the chief advantages of choosing a within-subjects variable? Under what conditions should one select a between-subjects variable?

2. When is an *F* test used prior to *t* tests? When an *F* test is used to compare the means of three conditions, does a significant result enable you to pinpoint which means are reliably different from one another? With what type of variable (and design) is the *t* test for independent measures used? With what type of variable (and design) is the *t* test for dependent or correlated measures used?

3. What is an interaction? How is the outcome of the test of the interaction related to subsequent analyses of main or simple effects? What is a triple-order interaction? Name two types of design in which a triple-order interaction might be present.

4. What are the similarities and differences between

   (a) the simple randomized and treatments-by-subjects designs?

   (b) the treatments-by-treatments design and one-within, one-between design and the two-factor, within-subjects design?

   (c) the three-factor design and the one-within, two-between design?

5. In a three-factor design, how do you proceed in examining the results if the ABC interaction is significant? If the ABC interaction is nonsignificant?

6. From what simple design is the two-factor, within-subjects design an outgrowth? At the level of conceptual analysis, the two-factor, within-subjects design is similar to what other design?

7. With what types of experiments are mixed designs most popular? What are the reasons for this popularity?

one case of experiment ej.
foctorial design.

IV = CPA
diff al task
Am. level
DV = Score on learning tasks

Scientific Communication: The Writing of the Research Report

6
Chapter

We do too little for science majors in the area of English. Probably 50 percent of my own success stems from an ability to express myself in writing. There are plenty of scientists who are better than I am, but my papers are readable, hence they are cited and read by other scientists.

(Eliel, 1972, p. 41)

To achieve clarity, good writing must be precise in its words, free of ambiguity, orderly in its presentation of ideas, economical in expression, smooth in flow, and considerate of its readers. A successful writer invites readers to read, encourages them to continue, and makes their task agreeable.

(APA Publication Manual, 1974, p. 25)

Science exists to serve society. To serve society means that scientists must not only communicate with one another but also with the public at large by sharing their data and ideas. During the last several years, the scientific community has begun to recognize its obligation to inform society. What this means is that each scientist—irrespective of discipline—has a duty to promote the common good. Obviously certain scientific disciplines and certain areas within certain disciplines are in a better position to more directly influence the needs and the attitudes of society. Within the field of psychology, clinical, child, and social psychologists are more likely to be directly relevant to the public welfare than are comparative, physiological, or mathematical psychologists. This, of course, in no way demeans the contribution of the latter but rather indicates a special obligation of the former to serve society because their findings are often more easily translatable to real life situations.

Learning to speak and to write so that a nonscientist can comprehend a scientific message is not an easy task. That effective communication to the lay public can be achieved is evidenced by the articles of those scientists who publish in periodicals such as *Scientific American* and *Psychology Today*. Some are testimony to the fact that highly technical and sometimes esoteric works can be translated into a relatively nontechnical language which permits widespread understanding.

Skills in communication, both oral and written, usually are not developed within the confines of a specific scientific discipline but are acquired during the early years of one's liberal education—in grade school, in high school, in college composition classes, or in journalism activities. We find it surprising that so many aspiring young psychologists are not informed about or do not avail themselves of opportunities to develop general writing skills.

SCIENTIFIC WRITING

You are by now well aware that the business of science is often conducted in the privacy of the laboratory. Knowledge, in terms of either facts or theory, can grow and mature only when individual scientists publish their data and ideas. To facilitate the promulgation of knowledge, scientists have developed customs of writing unique to each discipline. The skills required to perform well in English III or to develop an outstanding term paper in Medieval History do not guarantee that the young writer will be able to communicate well with the scientific community. Scientific writing is not equivalent in style and freedom to nontechnical, discursive writing aimed at the general community. In psychology we have our own methods and rules for developing scientific reports. The purpose of the present chapter is to assist you in learning how to prepare a journal article from the introduction section through your final comment in the discussion section to the summary of the entire project in the abstract.

In most experimental psychology courses, students are required to formulate, conduct, analyze, and write up one or more research projects. We know from past experience that you will undoubtedly experience some difficulty in learning the nuts and bolts of scientific communication. We also know that you will add to your research sophistication in the process of becoming a more proficient writer because scientific writing forces you to take prescribed steps which vividly bring to mind certain points that can be glossed over or neglected in the formulation of your first few research projects. In other words, the writing of a technical report or journal article will make you more attuned to logical and methodological problems, such as the interrelationship of your hypothesis with the relevant literature; the precise specification of subject, design, and procedural details that is necessary if your study is to be replicated; the large number of potential analyses which are available for each of your dependent variables; the interpretation of your data as it fits with and adds to existing facts and theories. The first few years in psychological research are a continuous learning experience, and scientific report writing is an important part of that experience.

We have found that in the long run, careful attention to your first adventure in scientific writing will be justly rewarded. Your second, fifth, and twentieth research paper will certainly be much easier to write and, probably, much easier to read as a result of your early efforts. Furthermore, if you decide to pursue a career in business or any other field, you will find the skills acquired in writing research manuscripts easily transferable to most technical writing assignments.

REQUIREMENTS OF GOOD SCIENTIFIC WRITING

Readability

A scientific report must enable the reader to comprehend and to evaluate research findings and interpretations. In order to understand a project, the reader must be directed through the initial comments on the broad hypothesis to the final conclusions. If you are concerned with making the task of reading your manuscript more manageable, you must *interest* and *motivate* the reader. Initially, a reader's attention is usually drawn to your study because of its title. Your reader may be doing similar research or, perhaps, may find your title intriguing although he or she may know absolutely nothing about its background literature or methodology.

The reader's job of comprehending your report must be made as easy as possible. You can make the reader's job easier by writing the paper for the person who is not terribly well informed about your topic rather than for the most knowledgeable person in your research area. You must lead the reader from a general statement of the problem, to the specific research hypothesis, to the design and procedure, and finally to the analyses and conclusions. Good English, an interesting style, and neither too much nor too little detail will likely result in a high level of readability. A readable paper will interest and attract your audience, while a dull or unintelligible paper might well result in no audience and no communication. A member of the National Academy of Science, one of the most published scientists in America, once said, "It's not so much that I'm a better scientist than the rest, it's just that I'm a better writer." Undoubtedly, Chemist Ernest Eliel understated his scientific abilities, but his point was well made. Scientific writing must be readable if the scientist is to attract and influence his or her audience.

Accuracy

A secondary purpose of a journal article is to allow another scientist with sufficient training, the necessary equipment, and a similar subject population to replicate the experiment. If another psychologist is unable to reconstruct the experiment and repeat the procedures, then the article is scientifically worthless even if it is highly readable. Psychology, like all other scientific disciplines, progresses only because research methods and procedures are shared, criticized, and improved. Psychologists share with their colleagues an accurate and complete description of their subjects' characteristics, the specific materials used, and their experimental procedures. Accuracy leads to repeatability, and repeatability leads to the growth of knowledge through a system of checks and balances. This system—based on the premise of repeatability—ensures the reliability of experimental results.

Accuracy is also important in reporting the findings, interpretations, and explanations of previous research. You must take the time to check the correctness of the statements you attribute to others. In addition, the analyses of your data and their presentation in the results section of your report must be totally accurate. This means that statistics must be properly chosen, correctly employed, and precisely reported.

Of course, accuracy must also occur in other sections of your report such as in the discussion section where conclusions must be concretely supported by prior results, the reference section where your citations must be correctly given, and the abstract section where you must faithfully summarize the procedures, major results, and conclusions. Accuracy is simply the most essential ingredient in scientific writing. Even a poorly written paper can have great value—but only if it is accurate.

Conciseness

Concise writing may seem a trivial requirement for good scientific communication. Nevertheless, many young psychologists fail to appreciate that a reader of research journals has a limited amount of time available to spend on any one article. Hence, a tight, concise report is more likely to be read and studied in its entirety than a lengthy, verbose report. The requirement of conciseness compels you to organize material logically, to prepare a detailed outline (at least in your mind), and to use short and carefully worded sentences to express each idea. *Tie* words together within a sentence as tightly as possible. *Tie* sentences together with minimum redundancy within a paragraph. *Tie* successive paragraphs together with clearly visible and meaningful transitional words, phrases, and thoughts. To reiterate: You must accurately report your procedures, design, and results; you should motivate and interest the reader by making your article as readable as possible. Readability and accuracy will be more likely to occur if you are logical in your organization and concise in your writing style.

Writing a good research article requires study, practice, and patience. Good scientific writers are not born, they are made—rather, they make themselves. Scientific writing is a skill that you can develop if you will follow the suggestions we have made above as carefully as possible. To further assist you in developing your communication skills, we will now consider each aspect of a scientific report in some detail, describing its major purposes: title, introduction, method, results, discussion, and abstract.

AN ANALYSIS OF THE RESEARCH REPORT

Title

The title of your research report should attract your reader's attention. From the title, a reader should be stimulated to compare your findings to his or her own, to develop new directions in thinking about a problem, to consider practical applications, or to develop new interests. Since so much depends on the title of your paper, we will consider its construction in some detail.

The problem with formulating a good title is that it must condense a great deal of information into just a few words. The following are the key elements of a good title: (1) a general indication of the problem area; (2) the general specification of the key independent variable(s); (3) brief mention of the major dependent variable or a global description of the behavior being measured (e.g., "reaction time" instead of "time between onset of stimulus and the response"); (4) a statement of the interrelationship of the independent (IV) and dependent variables (DV). Although it is at times unwieldy or impossible to include all of these elements in the title, you should nevertheless ensure that a title is indicative of the major purpose of your study. Frequently, titles of psychological research take one of three basic forms:

The Effects of IV on DV

Behavior "X" as a Function of IV

Behavior "X": Effects of IV on DV

Let us assume we have completed a discrimination learning study with five-year-old, moderately retarded, hyperactive children of two different IQ levels (a subject-type independent variable). Our purpose is to find the number of trials necessary to reach a criterion of seven consecutive errorless trials (the dependent variable) as a function of three dosages of a new drug (Dammital) designed to reduce hyperactivity in young children versus an appropriate placebo condition. One possible title might be: "The Effects of Dammital Dosage on Trials Necessary to Learn a Discrimination Task." However, the latter part of this title involving the statement of precise dependent measures is a bit cumbersome. Of more importance is the fact that the general problem area (reducing hyperactivity) was not specified, and no mention was made of the fact that retarded children were the population studied. In addition, the IQ dimension was omitted in the title. The omission of the IQ dimension would be particularly undesirable if it had an important effect on rate of discrimination learning or interacted with drug dosage.

A more accurate title might be: "Discrimination Learning by Hyperactive, Retarded Children as a Function of Dammital Dosage and Intelligence Level." In this title, all major features are included (independent variables, the basic task situation, and the important subject characteristics). The specific dependent variable was omitted because the title was already a bit lengthy. Still another appropriate title might be: "Discrimination Learning of Moderately Retarded Children: Effects of Dammital Dosage on Reducing Hyperactivity." This title omits the IQ variable which presumably was, in this instance, not a significant factor in the results. To summarize: Choose a title which reflects the problem under study and the important causal factors but don't make it too cumbersome.

Introduction

Your introductory statement should place your work in historical perspective. The introduction answers some, if not all, of the following questions: (1) What is your general problem area, and what are the specific aspects of past research related to your study? (2) What is the logic connecting your research to the relevant literature, and what are your specific hypotheses? (3) What are your independent and dependent variables, and what is the basic task situation? Often the answers to these questions will lead you to focus on the derivation of your hypothesis rather than on its formal explicit enunciation. In other words, your reader will probably be more interested in understanding the theoretical bases of your research than in reading about Hypotheses I, II, and III in a detailed manner. Novice writers often belabor their specific predictions at the expense of a more orderly, logical development of ideas and facts which state the rationale for their research.

Though many experimenters might not openly admit it, in truth it is unusual for an experimenter to have at his or her command all of the relevant data and theory related to a study prior to its commencement. However, as the project shifts to the communication phase, the researcher must complete a thorough, exhaustive search of the literature to learn of recent, relevant studies, to pick up older information which might have been missed, or to clarify some previously vague understanding of the key literature. A thorough literature review for a single piece of research is an enormous undertaking. It requires time, patience, and precision. Fortunately, the search is made easier by the existence of abstracts, review articles, and theoretical works. Box 6.1 contains a partial list of the major search aids available to the experimenter (Column A) as well as a partial listing of some of the more prominent research journals (Column B). Perhaps the most comprehensive aid that psychologists have at their disposal in researching topics is *Psychological Abstracts.*

Brief summaries of original research articles and summaries of theoretical and review articles appear in *Psychological Abstracts.* Each monthly issue contains a Brief Subject Index and a Table of Contents. A semiannual *Index* is issued to help collate the large number of headings and specific references in the monthly issues. By using *Psychological Abstracts* one can obtain an overview of research completed during any given year and can then proceed directly to specific articles of interest.

Other useful sources for surveying research are *Psychological Bulletin* and *Annual Review of Psychology.* The *Bulletin* contains review articles on topics of contemporary interest which summarize, organize, and criticize the existing literature. You will probably receive useful insights on methodology, theory, and suggested follow-up research if you can locate a *Bulletin* article related to your area of interest. The *Annual Review* publishes approximately eight major reviews each year (such as in developmental psychology, memory, and audition). Review topics generally change yearly, so that within a three-year period it is likely that a general area of interest will have been summarized and analyzed.

Following the leads provided by the above-mentioned search aids, you can find original sources to uncover new data and theory as well as to check the accuracy of previously learned information. You then

**Box 6.1   Major Psychological Journals:
Summary Sources and Research Journals**

*Column A:
Search Aids*

Major Sources
Psychological Abstracts
Psychological Bulletin
Annual Review of
Psychology

Secondary Sources
Psychological Review
American Psychologist
Journal of Experimental
Psychology: General

*Column B:
Useful Research Journals*

Animal Learning
Journal of Experimental
Psychology: Animal Behavior
Processes
Journal of Comparative and
Physiological Psychology
Learning and Motivation

Human Learning
Journal of Experimental
Psychology: Human Learning
and Memory
Journal of Verbal Learning and
Verbal Behavior
Memory and Cognition
Cognitive Psychology

Perception
Journal of Experimental
Psychology: Human
Perception and Performance
Perception and Psychophysics
Perceptual and Motor Skills

Personality and Motivation
Journal of Personality and
Social Psychology
Journal of Experimental
Approaches to Personality

Social
Journal of Personality and
Social Psychology
Journal of Experimental Social
Psychology

begin the task of reducing, analyzing, and integrating all available information. Throughout your research you will want to continue to locate your study as precisely as possible within a historical perspective. From a general statement of the problem proceed to narrow and refine particular questions of concern. Use existing knowledge as a background against which you can develop the novel or critical features of your hypotheses and design. Clarify your design and variables so that a reader can understand in a general way the research strategy which will answer your questions. Remember: Specify the issue, why it is of importance, and how you propose to address it experimentally. Be concise, be precise, and be interesting. Later in this chapter we will return to a more detailed consideration of the mechanics of writing the introduction, such as correct citations and the use of proper tense.

Method

The descriptions provided in the method section should enable the reader to replicate your study. Generally, this section is broken down into several components: subjects, design, apparatus or materials, and procedure. However, if any single part is very brief (e.g., the apparatus consists only of a standard memory drum), then it should be omitted as a separate section and the essential information placed in another section.

Subjects. The number of subjects and their most salient, important characteristics are to be described in detail. For instance, if the population under study is composed of juniors and seniors from a particular college, then little additional information will be needed except the number of subjects, their sex distribution, and any special considerations about IQ or education. On the other hand, if you were studying retarded children, then you would certainly include the number, location of population, sex, age, mental age (or IQ), type of retardation, relevant motor or visual disabilities, years of institutionalization, grade level or reading capacity, and any other essential characteristics. Remember to describe the subject characteristics in sufficient detail so as to enable the reader to generalize from your sample to the appropriate population.

Often the method of obtaining the subjects—whether they volunteered or were paid—will affect the experimental outcome. Also, whether the subjects are highly trained for the task, have previous experimental participation in similar tasks, or are naive are important considerations which should be included in the subjects section. Finally, you should report measures of central tendency (means values) and variability (standard deviations) with respect to subject characteristics such as age and IQ.

Design. If your study includes a number of independent variables, each having various levels, then it is sometimes wise to refer the reader to the specific variables that make up the design. Mention not only a description of your variables, but also whether they represent within- or between-subjects manipulations. The design section is commonly omitted if either the independent variables are fully spelled out in the introduction or they are few in number.

Apparatus and/or materials. The apparatus section should describe either the type of apparatus (brand name) or, if it is not commercially available, its essential features and dimensions. The apparatus section should tell what the equipment does rather than how it was put together. Include key dimensions and functional operations instead of a picture or a diagram. If the to-be-presented materials are complex—such as the number and size of categorically related words in a free recall list of 30 items—then their specifications should be presented in a separate materials section.

Procedure. The best way to handle the procedure section is to place the reader in the position of the subject. Treat first things first, proceeding from the point where the subject begins the experiment to the point of final recorded behavior. The Procedure section should describe exactly what the subject was presented with and what he or she was asked to do. Generally, it is best to focus on the subject's activity rather than on the movements of the experimenter. For instance, in a reaction-time study it is assumed that the experimenter had to reset the clock after each trial. Such details as the order of events, the timing of events, the instructions to subjects (paraphrased rather than reported verbatim unless the instructions represent one of the independent variables), the type of response measurements, and the controlled events should all be reported in the procedure section. However, report only those details essential for replication. Be sure to avoid redundancies in the procedure section.

Results

The results section should include tables and/or figures to enlarge upon and summarize the text. Both the visual display of data, whether tabular or graphical, and the verbal presentation of statistical analyses are necessary. Keep in mind the fact that tables and figures are supplementary information to the text proper. The text should be able to stand alone without visual aids, but charts and graphs cannot be interpreted without reference to the text. In other words, tabular and graphical information must be coherently presented by means of a smooth, integrated, polished writing style. We will consider in some detail the preparation of visual displays in the last part of this chapter.

Students often find the results section of the research report the most difficult section to write. Our advice is to carefully read the results sections of several recently published articles before you outline in detail your own. Only then should you tackle the difficult task of presenting your summarized data and their analyses.

The results section generally begins with a verbal statement defining the contents of a key figure or table. The corresponding analyses of these data are then presented. Start with the highest order interaction of importance and proceed to the lowest level of the least important simple effect. Since you will at times have more than one dependent measure, be sure to present all of the analyses associated with the major response measure before proceeding to those of secondary interest.

Remember that the results section is a verbal statement of the outcome backed up by statistics that describe but do not explain what an insightful reader might see in the tables and graphs. The statistical tests support the verbal statements and describe the direction of the results. For instance, rather than saying, "Conditions A and B were different," you should report, "Condition B resulted in significantly faster reaction times than Condition A, t (30)=3.97, p <.05." In the latter sentence we have reported that: (1) A and B were significantly different, (2) B led to a superior level of performance, (3) statistics were employed to analyze the validity (significance) of the apparent difference and to allow the rejection of the null hypothesis at the .05 level of confidence.

Discussion

The purpose of the discussion section is to integrate the introduction and results sections. In the discussion you might: (1) Interpret the meaning of the results in terms of specific hypotheses. (2) Describe apparent discrepancies between your predictions and your results, or discrepancies between your results and the findings in the existing literature. (3) Point out sources of procedural inconsistencies within the existing literature which might have led to the discrepancies referred to above. (4) Suggest new research. All conclusions presented in the discussion section must be traceable in one way or another to the data in the results section. It is at times tempting for beginning experimenters to draw conclusions not actually supported by statistical analyses or to develop interpretations or theories far removed from their actual data. Such errors in interpretation should be scrupulously avoided. The beginning experimenter should also avoid the explanation of nonsignificant results and should be careful in interpreting results in direct opposition to a hypothesis. Finally, if you find that the only way to handle your results is to list a number of uncontrolled factors, any one of which might have caused your results, then you obviously need to redesign the experiment, exercising more careful methodological and procedural controls.

Abstract

The abstract represents the initial section of the research report. It should summarize the manipulated variables, major task and procedural features, results, and conclusions. We intentionally saved discussion of this first section until last in order to emphasize that, in practice, the writing of the abstract follows the completion of the main body of the report. Students sometimes make the mistake of trying to develop the abstract as the first order of business. Take the easy route and write the abstract last.

In the abstract section you are required to present the essential features of the design, the major variables, and the most important results and their meaning in a space of no more than 150 words. Conciseness, precision, and significance are the ingredients that characterize a successful abstract. Of all the information contained in a well-written abstract, the main conclusions are the most critical. Finally, do not overlook the fact that a good abstract, much like the title, is likely to induce the reader to pursue your report in greater depth since the abstract appears first in the published version of your article. Hence, you should construct the abstract with carefully chosen words, sentences, and transitional phrases.

AN APPLICATION OF WRITING PRINCIPLES

It is impossible to write your first research paper in a competent fashion without having read in advance, with much attention to detail, several published articles. Read through the sample research paper in Box 6.2 dealing with the effects of anxiety on short-term memory. Keep in mind the requirements and suggestions we have made in the preceding sections of this chapter. We will devote the immediately following paragraphs to a detailed discussion of the sample research paper.

Box 6.2　Sample Research Paper

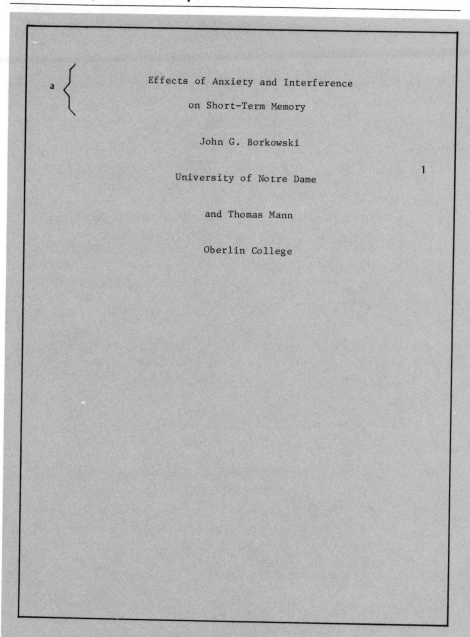

a

Effects of Anxiety and Interference

on Short-Term Memory

John G. Borkowski

University of Notre Dame

and Thomas Mann

Oberlin College

1

219

Abstract

Short-term recall for high- (HA) and low-anxious (LA)   2

subjects was compared using a "single-item" technique

designed to produce inter-item competition between

6 consecutive CCCCs and to evoke situational anxiety.

Results indicated that in the absence of specific, pro-

active interference (PI) there were no differences as a   3

function of anxiety level. As PI developed, the LA group

recalled significantly more items than the HA group.

However, the superiority of the LA group was not related

to the absolute amount of PI. Rehearsal activity (i.e.,

digit recitation) increased and STM decreased as PI de-

veloped. It was concluded that individual differences,   4

such as anxiety, influence the course of short-term

memory.

220

Introduction

Only a few studies have investigated the effects of motivation on short-term memory (STM). Kernoff, Weiner, and Morrison (1966) and Weiner (1966) found that when stimuli were associated with a monetary reward or shock, they were recalled significantly more often at retention intervals of 15 and 17 sec. than "neutral" stimuli. High-arousal words have been shown to be recalled more accurately than low-arousal words after long retention intervals (i.e., 24 hr.), but to result in poorer recall after short-term intervals (Kleinsmith & Kaplan, 1963; Walker & Tarte, 1963).

The purpose of the present study was to investigate the effects of motivation as defined by manifest anxiety, on STM. Specifically, this study attempted to determine the manner in which anxiety interacted with the development of proactive interference (PI) to influence the course of STM. Spence (1960) has used overt anxiety, as indexed by responses on the Taylor Manifest Anxiety Scale, to manipulate drive level in conditioning and verbal learning contexts. In general, high-anxious (HA) groups have demonstrated more rapid eyelid conditioning than low-anxious (LA) groups and also acquired "noncompetitive," paired-associate lists more efficiently than LA subjects. When competition characterized list construction (i.e., strong inter-pair associations), HA subjects required more trials to reach criterion than LA   8 subjects because of increased frustration associated with interfering response tendencies.

g { The present investigation employed a "single-item"   9 technique similar to that used by Keppel and Underwood (1962). The procedure as well as list construction were designed to generate potential interference and situational anxiety. In such a context, the recall of HA and LA groups was contrasted in the presence and absence of PI.

Method

Subjects. A total of 330 introductory psychology students at Oberlin College were given the Taylor Mani-

fest Anxiety Scale (Taylor, 1953). The mean score for
the entire sample was 17.4 with a standard deviation   10
of 7.5.

   The HA group (N = 25) had a mean anxiety score of
29.6 and the LA group (N = 25), 7.1. The groups were
matched in terms of sex and achievement as measured by
SAT scores. The mean verbal and quantitative score for
the HA group was 654, and for the LA group 660; the
difference between these means was not significant. The
matching procedure was used because previous data have
indicated that level of intelligence is related to potential susceptibility to interference effects in STM
(Borkowski, 1965). It should be noted that all subjects
seemed unaware of the basis for their selection when con-
tacted for the experiment proper some 2 mo. after responding to the anxiety scale.

   Procedure. A short period of counting activity (15
sec.) was included in the instructions. The main task
consisted of the presentation of six CCCCs on a Stowe
memory drum. The presentation duration for each CCCC was

j 3 sec., the retention intervals were 15 sec., and the recall periods 6 sec. During the retention intervals, re-

hearsal was controlled by instructing subjects to read

digits as rapidly as possible to the beat of a metronome

(3.6 beats/sec.). This rate was slightly faster than

their recitation abilities and hence was assumed to gen-

erate situational anxiety. In order to produce inter-

item interference, the specific materials (GPBH, XCHD,

k DLFM, MQWG, LWZS, BSJC) were constructed according to the

following rules: (a) one consonant from each item oc-

curred in a different position in the immediately suc-

ceeding item, and (b) one consonant was distributed in a

new position for one of the nonadjacent items. Order of

presentation was varied for each group to equate item

difficulty across the six presentation positions.

Results and Discussion

The proportion of letters correctly recalled (re-

sponses were scored as correct even if given in an order

l different from the order of presentation) as a function

of anxiety level and amount of prior interference is pre-

sented in Figure 1. An inspection of these data shows
that as PI increased, STM declined. Furthermore, in the
absence of specific PI (i.e., zero previous items) the
short-term recall for the HA group was not significantly
different from that for the LA group. However as PI developed, high anxiety resulted in a lower level of re-   12
call. The average superiority in recall over Items 2-6
for the LA subjects was 14%; since the differences in
retention between HA and LA groups remained relatively
constant as PI developed, the data were collapsed over
Items 2-6. The subsequent analysis showed that recall
for LA subjects was superior to that for HA, $t(48)$ =

Insert Figure 1 about here   13

3.03, $p < .01$. There were no significant differences in   14
the number of misplaced responses (i.e., an incorrect
letter which had been presented in a previous item) at
each level of PI for HA and LA groups. These results
suggest that, in the presence of specific interference,

the STM of HA individuals was inferior to that of LA

individuals when the two groups were matched in terms of

n { intellectual achievement. However, in the absence of PI,

there was no significant difference as a function of

anxiety level although recall for the HA group was

slightly superior to that for the LA group. Based on

Spence's (1960) results with competitive and noncompeti-

tive, paired-associate tasks, high anxiety might be ex-

pected to facilitate STM when inter-item competition is

minimal, when subjects are thoroughly adapted to the ex-

o { perimental task with extensive pretraining, or on the

initial item of any list where "specific" PI is minimal

or absent. With respect to the last alternative, the

high level of recall at zero PI (88%) might well have

masked the potential superiority of the HA group.

Analyses of counting activity showed no differences

between HA and LA groups at each of the presentation po-

sitions. However, at Position 1 the mean number of dig-

its recited was 36 compared to 41 digits during the last

p { retention interval than during the first, t(49) = 7.37,

p { p < .01, 49 of 50 subjects reciting more digits during the last interval. These results are interesting in light of Murdock's (1966) data which showed that as PI developed STM declined, but recall of the interpolated material improved. It appears that at least a portion of the decline in STM associated with the development of PI in the single-item technique is attributable to increased attention to the rehearsal task.

q { Evidence is accumulating showing that individual differences, such as anxiety and intelligence (cf. Borkowski, 1965), often interact with task-specific interference to influence the course of STM. 15

References

Borkowski, J. G. Interference effects in short-term memory as a function of level of intelligence. American Journal of Mental Deficiency, 1965, 70, 458-465.   16

Keppel, G., & Underwood, B. J. Proactive inhibition in short-term retention of single items. Journal of Verbal Learning and Verbal Behavior, 1962, 1, 153-161.

Kernoff, P., Weiner, B., & Morrison, M. Affect and short-term retention. Psychonomic Science, 1966, 4, 75-76.

Kleinsmith, L. J., & Kaplan, S. Paired associate learning as a function of arousal and interpolated activity. Journal of Experimental Psychology, 1963, 65, 190-193.

Murdock, B. B. Measurement of retention of interpolated activity in short-term memory. Journal of Verbal Learning and Verbal Behavior, 1966, 5, 469-472.

Spence, K. W. Behavior theory and learning. Englewood Cliffs: Prentice-Hall, 1960.   17

r

Taylor, J. A. A personality scale of manifest anxiety.
    Journal of Abnormal and Social Psychology, 1953, _48_,
    285-290.

Walker, E. L., & Tarte, R. D. Memory storage as a func-
    tion of arousal time with homogeneous and hetero-
    geneous lists. _Journal of Verbal Learning and Ver-
    bal Behavior_, 1963, _2_, 113-119.

Weiner, B. Motivation and memory. _Psychological Mono-
    graphs_, 1966, _80_ (18, Whole No. 626).

Journal of Experimental Psychology, 1968, _78_ (2),
    352-354.

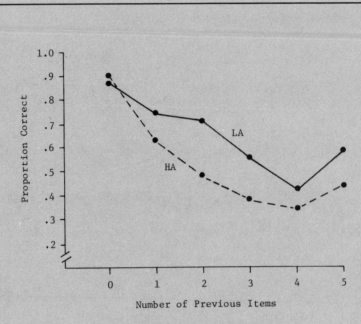

Figure 1. Correct recall as a function of anxiety and
proactive interference.

An Analysis of Writing Principles

We will now carefully examine the anxiety and memory article to reinforce your familiarity with the requirements of scientific writing. The following points represent commentary on the various sections of the paper and refer to the segments of the text identified alphabetically in the left-hand margin of Box 6.2.

Title   a. The title of this article related the independent variables (anxiety and interference) to the general behavior under study (short-term memory).

Abstract   b. In the first sentence of the abstract, the basic manipulations and some important details concerning the procedure were mentioned. That is, the two levels of anxiety, constituting the main subject variable, were related to recall performance in a short-term memory task. Both situational anxiety and inter-item competition developed across six memory trials, each consisting of a to-be-remembered CCCC unit. Since competition and situational stress were key aspects of the task situation, they were presented in the abstract.

                c. The most important results were emphasized first—namely, that no difference occurred in recall for HA and LA individuals in the absence of prior interference (i.e., in recalling the first unit in the list), but that the LA subjects recalled more than HA subjects as interference developed for CCCC units two through six. Another consequence of developing PI was an increase in digit recitation. This secondary result was mentioned since increased counting during the retention interval might have prevented rehearsal to a greater degree in the last few units in contrast to the first of the to-be-remembered units. Since the importance of this finding is not immediately obvious, it might have been omitted from the abstract section.

Introduction d. The beginning sentence of the introductory section stated in general terms the main theme or general hypothesis of the research: The relationship between motivation and memory. Furthermore, it implied that this was a relatively unresearched area of investigation.

e. Several examples were provided which showed pre-vious operational definitions of motivation as well as their effects on STM.

f. The specific purpose of this study—to examine the interaction of PI and anxiety in STM—was cited in the first two sentences of the second paragraph in order to contrast this type of motivational manipu-lation with those mentioned in the first paragraph. The remainder of the paragraph provided a descrip-tion of response-defined anxiety and how it influ-enced verbal learning when competition and non-competition characterize list construction.

g. The last paragraph of the introduction drew upon the findings cited in the prior paragraph (dealing with the importance of competition and interference) in determining the manner in which anxiety might influ-ence learning. The final paragraph mentioned that in this study the type of task to be used (i.e., the single-item technique) and the nature of task inter-ference were designed to generate situational anxiety. The reader was not informed at this point as to how the situational stress was induced. The reader was merely told in the last sentence that the recall of the two anxiety groups was compared at several levels of prior interference. Although no specific hypothesis was stated, the reader can infer, based on the results presented in the second paragraph, the main predic-tion: That HA subjects should recall less than LA subjects, especially under conditions of interference and stress.

Subjects   h. The subjects section described the type of population from which the sample was selected. It made concrete the designation of HA and LA subjects, cited the number of subjects per group, and mentioned two matching variables—sex and SAT scores.

i. The last sentence of the subjects section referred to the fact that a two-month period separated the ad-ministration of the Taylor Anxiety Scale from the STM session. Furthermore, it was noted that the subjects probably were naive in terms of realizing the reasons for their selection. A comment should have been included indicating whether the subjects were "experimentally naive," that is, whether they had participated in prior learning experiments.

Procedure   j. The second sentence of the procedure section described the conditions presented to each subject in the main task (i.e., the presentation and recall of the six CCCCs). The presentation rate and the retention and recall intervals were provided.

    k. The third through sixth sentences of the procedure section described the counting activity which occurred during the fifteen-second retention interval. The counting procedure was designed to prevent rehearsal and to generate situational anxiety. Rules for list construction were given in order to describe how list competition was generated and to allow the materials to be generated by another researcher.

Results   l. The first sentence of the results section was extremely important. It specified the response measure (i.e., proportion of letters correctly recalled even if given out of order from the original presentation). Also, this first sentence described the contents of Figure 1, where the overall data of the experiment were presented. Take special notice of the fact that the essential information of Figure 1 was referred to in the text proper as "proportion of letters correctly recalled . . . as a function of anxiety level and amount of PI."

    m. A summary of the difference between LA and HA recall averaged over items two through six was provided (14 percent). Next, this difference was analyzed by means of a *t* test. The results showed a superiority in recall favoring the LA subjects.

Discussion   n. Although the results and discussion sections were combined to save space, there is a point in the paper where the latter section begins. A new paragraph could have started with the first sentence of the discussion section—"These results suggest, etc." The meaning of the data in Figure 1 and a precise interpretation of the accompanying statistics were presented in the first part of the discussion.

    o. A subtle point was made in the last two sentences of this section related to the possible conditions under which HA subjects might recall more in a memory task than LA subjects. Essentially, several studies were proposed that could test whether situational stress (i.e., the proposed study dealing with extensive pretraining) or list competition (i.e., the proposed study dealing with the noncompetitive task) were the key factors contributing to the present results.

Results and Discussion

p. A final point related to both a secondary result and its interpretation focused on the statistical analysis of counting activity during the retention intervals for Item 1 versus Item 6. The interpretation implied that since more attention was given to counting following the presentation of Item 6, there was less effective rehearsal time for that item. Hence, a portion of the decline in STM with increased trials might be attributed to less active rehearsal for the later items.

Does this finding nullify the major conclusion that LA subjects recall more than HA subjects as PI develops? The answer was contained in the first sentence of the second-to-last paragraph. That is, there were no differences in counting activity for the two anxiety groups at each of the six retention intervals. Therefore, the HA-LA difference seemed due to increased susceptibility to PI on the part of the HA subjects rather than to counting-rehearsal differences.

Discussion

q. The final paragraph was a general statement referring the reader to a prior article on the interaction of PI and IQ. The argument here was that subject characteristics are important, although somewhat neglected, variables in memory research. In place of this general statement, the authors might have chosen to end the report by suggesting additional lines of research relating anxiety to memory functioning. For instance, does anxiety have its effect on STM in terms of encoding, storage, or retrieval processing?

Technical Aspects of Scientific Writing

You are now in a good position to profit from a thorough reading of the *Publication Manual of the American Psychological Association* (1974). Its suggestions and rules are of indispensable help in preparing a readable, accurate, and concise manuscript. Although there are a number of technical points to be mastered, you should now be able to understand and profit from them. You will find that much of the manual restates, refines, and supplements the information in this chapter.

To conclude our coverage of scientific communication, we will comment on the more important "rules of the game" specified in the *APA Manual*. Each rule we mention or suggestion we make is numbered and refers to an example in the anxiety and memory article. The numerical references are found in the right-hand margin of Box 6.2.

Abbreviations.   Abbreviations are used for most statistical terms and for common technical terms. However, the current trend is to use abbreviations sparingly. Most likely, the 1968 anxiety-memory article would be written by 1974 APA standards without abbreviations for high- and low-anxiety (HA and LA) and proactive interference (PI). The article would read more smoothly if these abbreviations were replaced by verbal descriptions. Abbreviations not in the *Webster's New Collegiate Dictionary* must be defined (2,3); however, frequently used abbreviations that appear as word entries in the dictionary, such as IQ or ESP, do not require further explanation. Statistical tests are always abbreviated when they appear with a specific statistical result (14). When the term experimenter or subject is used in the text, it is spelled out, never abbreviated (8). Units of measurement are expressed in the metric system. If they are accompanied by a number, they are abbreviated (11). Several cautionary comments are in order: *(a)* Never begin a sentence with an abbreviation, except in the abstract. *(b)* The use of too many abbreviations for technical terms makes for awkward reading and should be avoided. *(c)* Where they are necessary, compose abbreviations so that they are descriptive of the terms they denote (e.g., use LM and HM to denote a low and a high meaningful list of words rather than nondescript abbreviations such as W_1 and W_2).

Journal citations in the text.   The reason for listing references within the text is to allow the reader to locate a study in its published form. Hence, reference citations should be included whenever you draw upon the data, theory, or methodology set forth in a published article. This process is not only ethically sound, but also symbolic of the fact that science progresses only by mutual sharing. There are two general ways to cite the work of another psychologist: *(a)* Include his or her name in the context of a sentence, often as the subject of the sentence (5,7); *(b)* Include his or her name in parentheses at the end of a sentence (6). When referring to a particular page or pages, give the page numbers following the date of the reference. Always include page numbers when using direct quotes.

Journal citations in reference section.   Following the discussion section in the original manuscript is a page entitled "References" (see r). On this page you should list in alphabetical order all of the references cited in the body of the text. Consult the *APA Manual* for a detailed presentation of the rules of referencing. The two most frequent types of references are journal articles (16) and books (17). Be especially careful about the order of items to be listed in each citation as well as capitalization and punctuation.

Preparation of graphs.   Following are some guidelines you should use in preparing graphs: *(a)* Use 3:4 plots wherever possible (that is, the ordinate, or Y axis, should be shorter than the abscissa, or X axis). *(b)* Even when the figure is small, it should be drawn on $8^1/_2 \times 11$ paper. A figure for use in a journal article is then photographed, and glossy prints are made for submission to the journal editor. However, for most reports required in experimental psychology courses, it is sufficient to draw your figures on ordinary graph paper. *(c)* The dependent variable is to be placed on the Y axis, generally one independent variable on the X axis (often the *trials dimension* is placed on the X axis), and one or more independent variables in the body of the graph. *(d)* Each data point should be marked with an appropriate designation (e.g., a circle). This designation should remain consistent for a given level of a variable (e.g., circles are used for a low meaningfulness curve while triangles are used for a high meaningfulness curve). Differentiation between levels of a variable, or between several variables, is indicated by using different markings (e.g., open circles, closed circles, squares, triangles, etc.) or by connecting one condition with one type of line (solid) and a second with another (broken). *(e)* All lines should be made with a straightedge. *(f)* Bar graphs are used to represent a variable that is discrete rather than continuous. For instance, if the effects of three widely different drugs on schizophrenic hallucinations is the topic under study, the resulting data would be plotted on a bar graph since there is no continuous relationship which underlies the independent variable. If, however, three dosages of a single drug constitute the independent variable, then a line graph would be appropriate since here there is a continuous dimension along which the independent variable changes. If three or less mean scores are to be included, then you might dispense with a graph altogether and present the actual means in sentence form in the results section. Use a graph only to reduce the complexity which would otherwise be involved in presenting intricate data in the text. *(g)* The legend for each axis should be parallel to the respective axis. Also, each line within the body of a figure should be given an appropriate description in a legend. The legends for the lines within a figure consist of miniature lines and markings (circle, square, etc.) with verbal labels in the upper or lower right-hand corner. When only two functions appear in a graph, place each description close to the correct line and, perhaps, draw a short arrow from the description to the line (see the figure in the anxiety-memory article). *(h)* Each graph is given a figure caption which cites the relationship between the independent and dependent variables. All of the figure captions for graphs in the results section are placed on a "Figure Caption" page. *(i)* Show the approximate location of the figure in the text by providing a clear break in the typing (13).

Some basic stylistic requirements.   It is not uncommon for the beginning student to encounter difficulty in writing objectively and impersonally. Scientific writing generally uses the third person. However, greater latitude with respect to person has been provided in the 1974 *APA Manual.* Hence, it is now acceptable to say, "I used a single-item . . .," instead of (9).

Most of your manuscript will be written in the past tense (4, 10, 12). The exceptions to this rule include commonly accepted definitions, statements from a well-defined theory, explicitly stated hypotheses, and figure-table references (e.g., "Figure 1 contain*s* . . ."").

It should be obvious that a verb must agree in number with its subject. This point is made only because certain common psychological words (e.g., *data* and *criteria*) are often used in their plural form and, when used as the subject of a sentence, should be followed by the plural form of the verb.

Some basic mechanics of manuscript preparation.   Double-space your entire manuscript. The cover page contains four elements: title, author, affiliation, and abbreviated title. The first content page of the report is the abstract which is followed on a new page by the main sections of the text, from introduction to discussion. The title, authorship, and affiliation of the author(s) are placed above the introductory section (1) which, by the way, is labeled in our example only to clearly separate it from the abstract; it is not labeled in an actual manuscript. For journals that use blind reviewing (which include most APA journals), the authorship and affiliation must be omitted from the introductory page of the manuscript. The remaining sections of the body of the text are typed continuously. Following the discussion section are the reference pages, footnote page, tables (with title above each), figure caption page (listing titles for all graphs), and figures (each on a separate page).

The anxiety-memory article had two levels of heads. The main heads were centered while the second-level heads were indented paragraph heads. For longer articles, three levels of heads are frequently needed. In this case, use centered main heads, flush side heads, and indented paragraph heads. In multiple experiment reports where a series of experiments on the same general topic are interrelated, four levels of heads can be used. The editors of most major research journals encourage multiple experiment reports because they are systematic and integrative.

SUMMARY

Scientists must communicate with the society they serve. This lay communication requires literary, nontechnical writing skills. In addition, scientists must communicate with one another in order for their disciplines to grow and to mature. This communication with other scientists requires the ability to write more technical research reports. No matter who the intended audience, scientific manuscripts should be readable, accurate, and concise. Above all else a journal article must be accurate and must include sufficient detail so as to permit replication.

Research reports are composed of five major parts: abstract—which summarizes the subjects, design, procedures, results, and conclusions in 150 words or less; introduction—which provides the study's rationale, hypotheses, and some indication of the task, variables, and design; method—which contains enough detail about subject characteristics, apparatus, materials, design features, and procedures to allow for replication; results—which present basic data and accompanying statistical analyses; discussion—which contains final conclusions, interpretations, and suggested research. Don't forget that the title of the manuscript, telling something of your area of concern and the variables of interest, should be given careful consideration for it must attract potential readers. Be assured that by applying yourself diligently to the task of scientific writing you will become a more knowledgeable, skillful, and meticulous researcher.

We have tried to present as much information about scientific writing as you will need to develop your first manuscript. Careful reflection on the major points in this chapter and the *APA Manual* will be required before you begin writing. We also wish to make one final suggestion—read several published articles in an area related to your topic so that you can get a "feel" for good scientific writing. You will then be in a position to author your first scientific manuscript.

QUESTIONS

1. With what two communities does the scientist communicate? What are the general forms of these two types of communication?

2. What are the three requirements of good scientific writing? Describe why each is an important characteristic of a good scientific manuscript.
3. Why is the title of a paper important? What are the three basic forms a title may take?
4. What questions does the introduction section answer for a reader?
5. What are the important bibliographic sources available to the writer in gathering information relevant to the introduction section?
6. What are the main subsections in the method section? What characteristics of the subjects should be included? How much detail should be included in the procedure section?
7. What is usually contained in the first part of the results section? Which statistical analyses should be presented first? Last? What must the verbal statement accompanying a significant difference include? What is the basic form for presenting the results of a *t* test?
8. What should a discussion section accomplish? What should be avoided in this section of the scientific report?
9. What are the key features of an abstract?
10. How are journals and books cited in the body of the text? In the reference section?

Glossary: Research Tactics and Methodolog

ALPHA (α) The probability of occurrence of a Type I error in making a decision about the tenability of a null hypothesis.

ARRANGEMENT OF CONFOUNDING VARIABLES Refers to those variables related to the ordering and sequencing of events which can obscure the effects of the independent variable on the dependent variable.

BASELINE Refers to the steady, stable behavior shown by an organism prior to the institution of treatment in a single-subject design.

BEHAVIORISM A psychological school which argues that data should be both public and verifiable, and that observable aspects of behavior be used to develop laws and build theories.

BETA (β) Risk of making a Type II error which is determined by the number of subjects, the level of α, sample variability, the use of a one- or two-tailed test of significance, and the true nature of the distribution of mean differences.

BETWEEN-SUBJECTS DESIGN A research design in which each subject is presented with only *one* of several conditions in an experiment.

BIASED SAMPLE A sample in a hypothetical sampling distribution whose statistic (mean) is not the population parameter (mean) in question.

CONFOUNDING VARIABLE A variable, inadvertently introduced into an experiment, which makes a clear interpretation of the results difficult or impossible.

CONTROL Methods and procedures that eliminate or minimize the occurrence of unwanted variables. A controlled experiment is one in which the experimenter can unambiguously conclude that the manipulated variable did or did not have an effect on the dependent variable.

CORRELATION A research strategy concerned with the degree of relationship between two or more variables.

CORRELATION COEFFICIENT A statistic which shows the degree of relationship between two variables under investigation.

COUNTERBALANCING Method of control which evenly distributes carryover effects across the conditions of an experiment.

CUT-OUT FEATURES Real features or objects which require special conditions for their observation.

DEDUCTIVE THEORIZING Method of theory construction in which the logical movement is from the *general* level of theory formulation to the *particular* level of experimental research.

DEFINITION Statement about the use of words in the form "A if and only if B, C, etc." Definitions are a shorthand means of communicating so that unequivocal meaning is preserved while verbiage is held at a minimum.

DEPENDENT VARIABLE A response measure which reflects the effects of the independent variable.

DESCRIPTION Simplest research strategy, involving the act of observing and recording behavior as it occurs.

DOUBLE-BLIND An experimental procedure in which neither the subject nor the experimenter have prior knowledge of the specific condition being administered.

EMPIRICISM Philosophical method which asserts that factual, verifiable, sensory experiences are the foundation for observation.

ENVIRONMENTAL VARIABLE A situational confounding variable involving those aspects of the environment that can produce unwanted performance changes by covarying with the independent variable.

EXPERIMENT A set of rules that guide the arrangement and occurrence of certain events in a logical way so that sense-data can be used to formulate lawful relationships among those events.

EXPERIMENTAL HYPOTHESIS An explicit reformulation of the general research question which clarifies the relationship between the manipulated variables, the subjects, the procedures and materials, and the response measures used. The experimental hypothesis predicts that a systematic variation will occur between two observations or treatments.

EXPERIMENTER CONFOUNDING VARIABLE A situational confounding variable involving those cues emitted by the experimenter and detected by the subjects which subsequently influence their performance, either knowingly or unknowingly.

EXPLANATION Refers to use of concepts, laws, and theories to account for an experimental outcome or for a naturally occurring event. An explanation is testable only when facts that would falsify it are known and dismissed.

FACT In the most general sense, a stated observation conveying some sort of empirical knowledge about the world. Facts are the basis for theory construction and explanation.

F TEST A statistical test for comparing two or more means in an experiment. The *F test* is a ratio of the variance between groups (ms_b) divided by the variance within groups (ms_w).

FUNCTIONALISM A psychological school which is concerned with the purposes of mental events and the how and why of mental operations. Functionalism is the first native American system of psychological thought.

GESTALT A psychological school which emphasizes the immediate experience of the whole organism. Gestalt psychologists feel that the whole is more than the sum of its parts.

HIGHER-ORDER THEORY   The integration of a large number of simple laws and variables by the use of abstract concepts, processes, and principles.

INDEPENDENT VARIABLE   One of the variables to be manipulated in an experiment. There are three types of independent variables: situational, subject, and organismic.

INDUCTIVE THEORIZING   Method of theory construction in which the logical movement is from the specific experiment to a more general statement.

INSTRUCTION CONFOUNDING VARIABLE   A situational confounding variable involving those aspects of the instructions which result in misleading the subject, or otherwise affect performance in ways other than those produced by the manipulated variable.

INTERACTION   When the effects of one independent variable are different for each level of a second independent variable.

INTERVAL SCALE   A scale of measurement which not only provides for statements of greater than or less than, but also specifies how many units greater than or less than (e.g., IQ scale). The interval scale has the properties of order and additivity of numbers.

INTROSPECTION   Method used by early structural psychologists which required trained subjects to look into themselves and to reflect on changes in their conscious experiences and to faithfully report these changes to an experimenter who systematically related one subjective report to another in formulating R-R laws about the contents of the mind.

LATIN SQUARE   A procedure for distributing carry-over effects in a within-subjects design. Sequences of treatments are chosen in such a way so as to be representative of all treatment combinations, each treatment occupying a different location in each sequence and occurring only once in each ordinal position.

LAW   A statement of a systematic relationship between variables or concepts. An instance of one concept is always connected with an instance of another concept.

MAIN EFFECT   A comparison of overall means with data often collapsed across the levels of another variable.

MANIPULATION   Most powerful research strategy which involves the alteration of one or more independent variables. Manipulation is most useful for determining causal relationships.

MATCHING   A control procedure which is an explicit attempt to ensure that experimental and control groups are quantitatively similar on one or more measures at the outset of an experiment.

MINIATURE THEORIES   Small-scale theories that represent a compromise between higher-order theory and the semiatheoretical position. These theories are characterized by close adherence to data, minimal use of abstract concepts, and a tendency to restrict explanations to relatively circumscribed problem areas.

MIXED DESIGN   An experiment with at least two variables, one or more of which is a between-subjects variable and one or more a within-subjects variable.

MULTIPLE BASELINES A control procedure used in single-subject research. Different subjects can receive the same treatment(s) at different times or the same subject can receive the same treatment for different responses across time or settings.

NATURALISTIC OBSERVATION Descriptive strategy which requires observations and measurement of behavior as it occurs in its natural or normal state.

NOMINAL SCALE A scale in which numbers or other symbols are used merely to designate one object in a class from another (e.g., basketball jersey numbers).

NULL HYPOTHESIS A statement which maintains that any differences between two observations, groups, etc., are due to chance rather than systematic variation; the hypothesis of no "real" difference between sample means.

OBSERVATION LANGUAGE Words used to directly depict observable events. This language consists of terms that specify and identify, or indicate properties of objects, or describe relations between objects; it is the starting point for scientific communication.

OMEGA^2 Represents a measure of the proportion of the total variation in performances that can be accounted for by the experimental manipulation; helps establish *scientific significance.*

ONE-WITHIN, ONE-BETWEEN DESIGN A two-variable design in which one variable is between-subjects, the other within-subjects.

ONE-WITHIN, TWO-BETWEEN DESIGN A three-variable design in which two variables are between-subjects, the other within-subjects.

OPERATIONAL DEFINITIONS Definition in the "if-then" form which states the specific conditions for observation or measurement as well as the outcome which will be observed or measured after the conditions are imposed.

ORDINAL SCALE A scale in which assigned numbers indicate differences in magnitude (e.g., the order in which runners cross the finish line in a race).

PHENOMENOLOGY Psychological school which seeks to understand the world from the subject's point of view. In contrast to behaviorists, phenomenologists make use of subjective individual experience, introspective reports, and mental processes.

PLACEBO A control condition in which all features are identical to an experimental condition except for the key aspect of the experimental condition.

POPULATION Refers to a frequency distribution of all members of a particular class having one or more common characteristics.

POPULATION PARAMETER A measurement (e.g., mean) of some characteristic based on scores for an entire population.

RANDOM SAMPLE Sample chosen in such a way that every member of the parent population has an equal chance of being selected.

RANDOMIZATION A procedure which ensures that a sample is selected from a population so that each member's probability of selection is the same as the probability of selecting any other subject from the same population; hence, each and every member of the population is equally likely to be included in a random sample.

RATIO SCALE Scale of measurement that possesses all of the properties of nominal, ordinal, and interval scales with the additional property of an absolute zero as its point of origin (e.g., common physical measurements of weight and length).

RATIONALISM Philosophical school which asserts that every effect has a cause and that all causal sequences are located within the realm of nature, which can be analyzed and understood by reason alone.

RESPONSE RELIABILITY Refers to the consistency with which a behavior is detected.

RESPONSE SENSITIVITY The degree to which a response is reflective of the effects of the independent variable.

RESPONSE VALIDITY The degree to which a response represents what it is supposed to represent.

REVERSAL A single-subject control procedure in which a return to the conditions present during baseline are reintroduced following the treatment.

SAMPLE A subgroup of a population; a specific group upon which measurements are taken.

SAMPLING DISTRIBUTION A frequency distribution of an infinite number of sample means, usually hypothetical; its average value is equal to the population mean.

SAMPLING DISTRIBUTION OF MEAN DIFFERENCES A frequency distribution of mean differences (Y_E-Y_C) obtained from an infinite number of mean differences between samples; the average value of a sampling distribution of mean differences is zero.

SAMPLING ERROR A nonsystematic error between samples due to misrepresentations of population characteristics in the samples.

SCIENTIFIC THEORY A systematically related set of laws that provides a unified account of a limited range of phenomena; uses concepts, principles, and processes to achieve integration.

SIGNIFICANCE LEVEL Establishes limits beyond which obtaining a particular experimental outcome is unlikely due to chance factors alone.

SIMPLE EFFECT When an interaction is present, the analysis focuses on mean differences (e.g., A_1 vs. A_2) at each level of another variable (at B_1 and B_2).

SIMPLE RANDOMIZED DESIGN An experiment with two or more levels of a single variable; often one level is an experimental condition and the other is a control condition.

SITUATIONAL VARIABLES An independent variable which involves manipulation of some aspect of the physical environment, the task given to the subject, or the social situation.

STANDARD ERROR The standard deviation of the scores in a sampling distribution of means; calculated from the formula $\sigma_m = \sqrt{\dfrac{S^2}{n-1}}$, where S^2 is the variance of scores and n is the number of subjects.

STANDARD ERROR OF THE DIFFERENCE BETWEEN MEANS The standard deviation of the mean difference scores (e.g., $\overline{Y}_E - \overline{Y}_C$) in a sampling distribution of mean differences. Standard error is equal to the square root of the sum of the variances of the two sample means ($\sqrt{\sigma_1^2 + \sigma_2^2}$).

STAND-OUT FEATURES Features or objects of sensory experience which need no definition besides a list of their observable attributes.

STATISTICAL SIGNIFICANCE Difference between sample means which is not likely to happen by chance; specified in terms of the level of significance.

STATISTICS Scores (e.g., means or standard deviations) based on sample data; used to estimate the parameters of the parent population.

STRATIFIED SAMPLE Process of ensuring a representative sample by imposing certain restrictions on the composition of the sample.

STRUCTURALISM The first school of psychology, founded by Wilhelm Wundt; it attempted to reduce the mind into its basic elements and developed introspection as an experimental method.

SUBJECT CONFOUNDING VARIABLE Refers to the many individual differences among people which can obscure the effects of the independent variable on the dependent variable.

SUBJECT VARIABLE An independent variable reflecting some aspect of the subject's previous life experiences; subject variables are not easily manipulated and are usually confined to use with the R–R (correlational) strategy.

TASK VARIABLE A situational confounding variable involving any feature of the task, including its construction and method of presentation, which is not an explicit part of the manipulated variable and which affects the outcome of the experiment.

THEORY A statement which interrelates a large number of simple laws and their associated variables by way of abstract concepts, processes, or principles. Theory serves two major functions: (1) by integrating otherwise isolated laws, it contributes to the comprehensiveness of scientific knowledge; (2) it generates new testable hypotheses.

THREE-FACTOR DESIGN An experiment with three between-subjects variables. Three-factor and two-factor interactions are analyzed before turning to main or simple effects.

TREATMENT-BY-LEVELS DESIGN A two-variable design in which one of the variables serves as an equating or matching variable; the effects of the equating variable are negated when the variable of interest is assessed. In order for the matching (or levels) variable to be effective, it must be significantly correlated with the dependent measure.

TREATMENTS-BY-SUBJECTS DESIGN An experiment with one variable in which each subject receives all the levels of that variable. Individual differences are eliminated in the comparisons of the means in this design.

TREATMENT-BY-TREATMENT DESIGN A two-variable design in which the interaction and main or simple effects are of experimental interest; the simplest form is the 2 × 2 factorial design.

TRIPLE-ORDER INTERACTION   Interaction which occurs in a three-factor (ABC) design. A triple-order interaction implies that one or more two-factor interactions will likely be significant at one level of the third factor (e.g., AB is significant at C_1), while one or more two-factor interactions involving the same terms are not significant at another level of the same third factor (AB is nonsignificant at C_2); a triple-order interaction may also occur if the forms of two-factor interactions change radically across the levels of the third factor.

t **TEST**   A statistical test for contrasting the means for two conditions (often the experimental condition and control condition).

TWO-FACTOR, WITHIN-SUBJECTS DESIGN   An experiment in which two variables are manipulated and in which all levels of each variable are presented to each subject.

TYPE *I* ERROR   Error in judgment resulting from the rejection of the null hypothesis when it is, in fact, true.

TYPE *II* ERROR   Error in judgment resulting from acceptance of the null hypothesis when it is, in fact, false.

TYPE *G* ERROR   Extrinsic type of sampling error due to accidental occurrence of some environmental feature which influences the performance of an entire sample.

TYPE *R* ERROR   Intrinsic type of sampling error due to selection of a sample containing some relatively permanent feature which differentiates it from its parent population.

TYPE *S* ERROR   Type of sampling error due to inclusion of unrepresentative individuals in a sample.

UNBIASED SAMPLE   A sampling procedure in which no restrictions are placed on the possible inclusion of each subject of a population in a given sample; a statistic for an unbiased sample is, *on the average,* equal to the population parameter that it represents.

VARIABLE   Some feature of the world specified by at least two mutually exclusive scale values; any quantity or property that is manipulated, measured, or controlled in an experiment.

WITHIN-SUBJECTS DESIGN   Each subject is presented with all of the conditions in the experiment.

WÜRZBURG SCHOOL   A psychological school which emphasized acts and processes and used introspection as a method; a forerunner of Functionalism.

YOKED-CONTROL   Matching control procedure which exposes a control subject to those features of the treatment that have been previously determined by an experimental subject.

Part Two
Applications of Research Tactics

Psychophysics and Perception

7

Chapter

BY W. TOM BOURBON

Psychophysics in the form in which it appears here is a theory in the first stages of gestation. . . . It should be understood as a demonstration of a theory that still is in an elementary state.

(Fechner, 1860/1966, p. xvii)

It goes without saying that the range of these investigations will be broadened more and more the further they are developed. And so I look for the main harvest of our present investigations less in terms of what they have yielded so far than in what they promise to yield. The present report is nothing but a paltry beginning of a start.

(Fechner, 1860/1966, p. xxix)

No fairer destiny could be alloted to any physical theory, than that it should of itself point out the way to the introduction of a more comprehensive theory, in which it lives on as a limiting case.

(Einstein, 1961, p. 77)

PERCEPTION AND PSYCHOPHYSICS

Is it possible to measure events in the private world of subjective experience? If so, how? Those questions were part of the legacy psychology inherited from philosophy. In 1860, Gustav Fechner answered "yes" to the first question. In response to the second, he established the area of psychophysics, which contributed directly to the establishment of experimental psychology. Psychophysics is a basic area of research and theory in perception—the way or ways organisms obtain and use information about themselves and their environment. It is a diverse array of methods, theories, and models which precisely specify relationships between characteristics of stimuli and associated characteristics of the responses of organisms. Publication of Fechner's *Elements of Psychophysics* (1860) is often cited as the origin of psychophysics and of quantitative psychology.

Ideas That Influenced Fechner

As is frequently true of formal points of origin, Fechner's work had antecedents. We will briefly review three earlier lines of research and theory.

Reaction time.   *Reaction time* is the time that elapses between presentation of a stimulus to an observer and the occurrence of an associated response by that observer. According to Boring (1950), it was first investigated by astronomers trying to solve a basic problem in their area. Before the development of sophisticated timing devices, astronomical events were timed by observers using a difficult combination of clock-watching, telescope-viewing, counting, and estimation. In the 1820s, Bessell developed a simple mathematical procedure to calculate and correct for differences between the time judgments of various observers. His method, called the "personal equation," was one of the first attempts to quantify and analyze individual differences. It was hardly the last, however, for research on the personal equation and on reaction time has flourished. In 1868, for example, the physiologist Donders described procedures for estimating three varieties of reaction time. Imagining a task in which an observer must respond quickly to stimulus *A* with response *a,* to stimulus *B* with response *b,* and so on, while many stimulus-response pairs are presented in random sequence, Donders theorized that total reaction time to one of the stimuli is the sum of three factors: (1) *choice time* (the time required to choose the appropriate response); (2) *discrimination time* (the time required to discriminate between stimuli); and (3) *simple reaction time* (the time required to respond to a given stimulus when it is presented alone).

Donders' assumptions about the simple additivity of reaction times were incorrect. However, his attempts to isolate and to identify the components of a psychological process and to estimate relative durations of those components are similar to those of contemporary experimental psychologists. Reaction time is commonly used as a dependent variable in studies of psychological processes such as attention and performance (cf. Keele, 1973; Welford, 1976), cognition (cf. Neisser, 1976), and the structure of human memory (cf. Cofer, 1975).

Specific nerve energies.   Many early psychologists assumed that reaction times were the result of time required for activity to travel along nerves and through the brain. In 1850, Helmholtz used such reasoning to estimate the velocity of nerve impulses in humans (cf. Boring, 1950).

Speculation concerning relationships between psychological processes and physiology was supported by the *doctrine of specific nerve energies,* proposed by Johannes Müller in the 1830s. This doctrine stated that what we perceive is the activity of our nerves, not the presence of external events. The senses are assumed to allow external events to influence the state of our nerves, thereby influencing perception (cf. Boring, 1950; Sahakian, 1975). Müller also stated that, no matter what form of stimulus is applied to a nerve or sense organ, the resulting sensation will be of the same type. Thus, light shining into the eye, the gentle pressing of a fingertip against the eyelid, and the passing of weak electric current across the eyeballs all produce visual sensations. Light is the typical stimulus for seeing, but not the only one or the necessary one.

One logical extension of Müller's concepts occurs in contemporary efforts to develop visual prosthetic devices or "bionic eyes" (cf. Dobelle, Mladejovsky, Evans, & Girvin, 1976). Electrodes implanted in the visual cortex of individuals blinded by accidents are activated by signals originating in a television camera. Patients can discriminate shapes and read braille with the system.

Scaling subjective magnitude.   The problem of scaling subjective magnitude, of attaching numbers to perceptions in a way that meets agreement among different people, originated long before Fechner. Fechner (1860) cited Bernoulli, in the 1700s, and Laplace, in the early 1800s, for their discussions of perceived value and noted the problem of estimating stellar magnitudes. The ancient Greek scale of stellar magnitude was used in the 1860s. That scale provided six categories, from 1 (the brightest) to 6 (the dimmest), into which astronomers grouped all stars. Fechner cited several experimenters who had studied relationships between scale categories and intensities of the stars. He believed their research supported the theory of psychophysical scaling established by Ernst Weber, his professor and predecessor at the University of Leipzig. Weber's ideas played a dominant role in the work of Fechner, as we shall see later in this chapter.

Fechner: His Goals and Contributions

Fechner believed that psychological experience was associated with *inner psychophysics,* the flow of energy in the nervous system as a function of stimulus energy or of the process of thought. Currently, the term psychophysiology refers to such processes. He believed that inner psychophysics could not be measured directly, but that it could be inferred from *outer psychophysics,* the measurement of stimulus variables which correlate highly with specific psychological states or events.

Significance of Fechner.   Fechner had immediate impact on the emerging science of psychology. He provided the first formal and systematic statements of rigorous quantitative methods and theory in psychological research. He also brought to a focus centuries of thought on the concept of a threshold between perception and nonperception. As a result, he affected Sigmund Freud's concepts of the pleasure principle and of the threshold of consciousness (Ellenberger, 1970). Hermann Ebbinghaus, the pioneer in research on human learning and memory, derived his methods after reading *Elements of Psychophysics* (cf. Boring, 1950). William Stern, a student of Ebbinghaus who initiated studies of individual differences and developed the concept of the IQ, was also influenced strongly by Fechner's writing.

Much of Fechner's impact came about, however, because of the way other scientists and philosophers set about the task of supporting or challenging his ideas. Among them was Wilhelm Wundt, whose laboratory devoted considerable time to questions raised by Fechner.

Sensitivity and threshold.   Fechner attempted to measure the sensitivity of human observers to controlled and quantified stimuli. He described two types of sensitivity: (1) *absolute sensitivity,* defined operationally by the *absolute threshold* or the lowest detectable intensity of a stimulus; and (2) *differential sensitivity,* defined operationally by the *difference threshold* or the smallest detectable amount of change in a stimulus. Because the German term for threshold is *limen,* the absolute threshold is often called the *absolute limen* (AL) and the difference threshold, the *difference limen* (DL). Another common term for DL is *just-noticeable-difference* (jnd).

Concerning the nature of sensitivity, Fechner wrote:

> In so far as sensitivity is a variable, we should not seek a constant as its measure. We may, however, look for (1) its limits and (2) its mean values; we may also investigate (3) how its variations depend on conditions; finally we may seek (4) lawful relations that remain constant during variation. (Fechner, 1860/1966, p. 45)

Fechner considered sensitivity to be a variable quantity in inner psychophysics and inferred it from measurements of threshold in outer psychophysics. Because sensitivity varied, he assumed that estimates of threshold varied and that a large number of samples of the threshold were necessary. Fechner further assumed that the distribution of estimates was normal. His psychophysical methods are based on sampling techniques and on statistical concepts appropriate to normal distributions.

Experimental rigor.   Just as important as his work on sensitivity and thresholds were Fechner's statements on "general considerations and precautions" related to psychophysical research (Fechner, 1860/1966, pp. 66–73). He called for absolute rigor, consistency, and objectivity in such research. These qualities were to be applied to every phase of an experiment: planning and scheduling of experimental sessions and stimulus presentations; conducting experimental sessions; recording data; and analyzing results. Meticulous concern for detail was a hallmark of Fechner's research. He expected the same from all others.

MEASURING ABSOLUTE AND DIFFERENTIAL SENSITIVITY

The techniques Fechner described for measuring thresholds are the *method of limits,* the *method of constant stimuli,* and the *method of adjustment.* We will examine the first in detail and will briefly describe the other two.

Method of Limits

The method of limits is a simple procedure commonly used in laboratory and clinical settings. It provides quick, reliable estimates of thresholds.

Absolute sensitivity.   To measure the absolute threshold (AL) with the method of limits, the experimenter presents stimuli to the observer in an orderly sequence of discrete values. The observer responds to each trial with "yes" or "no," supposedly indicating presence or absence of a sensation. Two types of stimulus series are possible. The first is an *ascending series,* in which the first stimulus value is *below* threshold and elicits a "no." Each succeeding stimulus is *increased* by a constant amount over the one before until one elicits a "yes." The second is a *descending* series, in which the first stimulus value is *above* threshold and elicits a "yes." Each succeeding stimulus is *decreased* by a constant amount below the one before until one elicits a "no." The stimulus intensity at which the transition in responses occurs is an estimate of threshold. Using either ascending or descending series, or both, the experimenter obtains a large number of estimates. The AL is defined as the mean of the distribution of estimates.

Table 7.1 contains a portion of the data from a hypothetical experiment employing fifty ascending series. Figure 7.1 illustrates several ways of graphing the data from Table 7.1. Figure 7.1A shows the number of times a transition from "no" to "yes" occurred at each intensity and the probability of such a transition. The distribution is normal, as is typical of distributions composed of many estimates of the AL. The mean of the

Table 7.1   A portion of a table of hypothetical "method of limits" data for absolute threshold (AL) estimated with 50 ascending series.

Stimulus Intensity		10	11	12	13	14	15	16	17	18	19	20
Series	1	N	N	N	N	N	N	N	N	Y		
Numbers	2	N	N	N	N	N	N	N	Y			
	3	N	Y									
	48	N	N	N	N	N	N	N	N	N	Y	
	49	N	N	Y								
	50	N	N	N	N	N	Y					
Analyses	a	0	1	3	6	10	11	10	5	3	1	0
	b	.00	.02	.06	.12	.20	.22	.20	.10	.06	.02	.00
	c	0	1	4	10	20	31	41	46	49	50	50
	d	.00	.02	.08	.20	.40	.62	.82	.92	.98	1.00	1.00

Absolute Thresholds = Mean Estimate = 14.96
N = No; Y = Yes.
a = Number of times the change from N to Y occurred at a given intensity.
b = Probability that the change from N to Y occurred at a given intensity (obtained by dividing each value in row a by 50, the number of series).
c = Cumulative number of times the change from N to Y occurred at a given intensity or at a lower one (obtained by summing row a from the lowest intensity to each given intensity).
d = Cumulative probability that the change from N to Y occurred at a given intensity or at a lower one (obtained by summing row b from the lowest intensity to each given intensity).

distribution is the best estimate of the AL. Figure 7.1B shows the cumulative number of times the transition from "no" to "yes" occurred at a given intensity or at a lower one, and the cumulative probability of such transitions. The curve in the figure is an *ogive*, a *sigmoidal* curve, or a *psychophysical function*. It illustrates the concept that as stimulus intensity increases the probability of reaching the AL increases, from 0 to 1.0, over a range of transition. In our example, no estimates of threshold occurred at or below an intensity of 10, while 60 percent occurred at or below an intensity of 15, and 100 percent occurred at or below an intensity of 19. On a psychophysical function, the intensity associated with a cumulative probability of 0.5 is the best estimate of the AL. That estimate is the same as the mean of the distribution in Figure 7.1A.

Figure 7.1

Distribution of estimates of AL (A) and psychophysical function (B) derived from hypothetical data in Table 7.1. The axes labeled a, b, c, and d correspond to rows in Table 7.1.

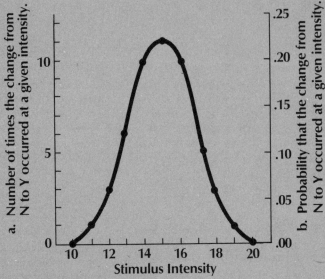

A. Distribution of estimates

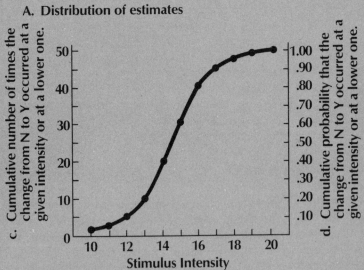

B. Psychophysical function

If we repeated our hypothetical experiment using descending series, the results would be similar, but the mean estimate of the AL probably would be lower than that obtained with ascending series. Such differences between ascending and descending series are fairly common. An experimenter who believes the differences represent errors of measurement often attributes them to *habituation or perseveration* by the observer. The observer is assumed to continue making the original response for a few trials after the stimulus passes threshold. An experimenter who believes the differences represent valid sensory experiences often attributes them to selective attention. Supposedly, in a descending series, the observer initially senses the stimulus quite clearly and is able to "follow" it to low intensities. In an ascending series, the observer does not recall the stimulus precisely and it must reach sufficient intensity to "capture" attention.

Whatever the assumption by the experimenter, differences between ascending and descending series may be controlled either by obtaining estimates of the AL using both methods, and using the mean of the two estimates or by alternating between ascending and descending series on successive series and using the mean estimate across all series. Another common control procedure in the method of limits is to begin successive series at different stimulus values. This procedure controls for errors of *anticipation,* which occur when the observer counts the number of trials and anticipates that the AL will be reached after a certain number of trials. Box 7.1 contains an example of the use of measures of the AL in assessing the effects of noise on hearing.

Differential sensitivity. Stimuli strong enough to exceed the AL are not always detected, but the stronger the stimulus, the more likely it is to be detected. Given two detectable stimuli, subjects can discriminate between them if the differences between them are great enough. Sensitivity to such differences is measured as a difference threshold (DL or jnd), the average amount by which stimuli must differ if they are to be told apart.

The method of limits is often used to estimate the DL. Two stimuli occur on each trial. They are the *standard stimulus* (St), identical on all trials, and the *comparison stimulus* (Co), which changes by discrete increments or decrements on successive trials. In an *ascending series,* the Co on the first trial is judged "lesser" in magnitude than the St. On successive trials, the experimenter increases the value of the Co by discrete steps until the subject reports it is "equal" to the St. Further increases in the Co produce more judgments of equality, until a value is reached which is reported as "greater" than the St. The value at which the Co is first reported "equal" to the St provides an estimate of the *lower difference threshold,* (L_L), while that at which the Co is first reported "greater" provides an estimate of the *upper difference threshold* (L_U).

Box 7.1   Noise and Auditory Thresholds

Absolute thresholds for hearing are measured routinely in large numbers of people. Normative data on auditory thresholds are available and international standards on average hearing levels are widely used. Noise interferes with hearing and causes increases in auditory thresholds. Ward, Glorig, and Sklar (1958) provide a detailed analysis of another effect of noise on hearing, Temporary Threshold Shift (TTS). TTS is defined as a change in auditory threshold as a result of exposure to sound. When at a rock concert or in the presence of noisy machinery, we shout to be heard over the interference; for a few minutes after the intense sound ends, we shout to overcome the effects of TTS.

Permanent Threshold Shift (PTS) may occur after brief exposure to extremely intense sound or after prolonged exposure to less severe sound. In 1966, Kryter, Ward, Miller, and Eldredge proposed the adoption of criteria defining the effects of noise on TTS and PTS and establishing limits on the amount of noise to which a person might be exposed with minimal risk of hearing loss. The Walsh-Healey Public Contracts Act of 1969 established such limits.

Cohen, Anticaglia, and Jones (1970) described many sources of "sociocusis," PTS induced by nonoccupational noise. They proposed establishing standards for nonoccupational noise exposure. Their list of potential sources of noise hazards resembles an advertisement from a utility company (power appliances and tools, lawnmowers, garbage disposals, food blenders, toys, washer-dryers, amplified rock music, and so on) or from a fuel company (chain saws, sport planes, snow mobiles, automobiles, public transportation, and so on). They even include the noise of children playing. The U. S. Noise Control Act of 1972 charges the Environmental Protection Agency with establishing standards for noise exposure in the general population (cf. Møller, 1975).

In a *descending series,* the Co on the first trial is judged "greater" than the St. Successive reductions in the Co produce first a transition from "greater" to "equal" and second, from "equal" to "lesser." Those transitions represent L_U and L_L respectively.

To estimate L_U and L_L, the experimenter presents many series of Co-St pairs. To control for errors of *habituation* and *perseveration,* or for errors of *anticipation,* the experimenter uses the same controls as those used to estimate the AL. Table 7.2 presents hypothetical data for an experiment to estimate DLs for brightness. The procedure for calculating

Table 7.2   Analysis of a hypothetical experiment to estimate the DL for brightness using descending series in the method of limits (B: Co brighter than St; E: Co equal to St; D: Co dimmer than St).

Stimulus Intensity	10	12	14	16	18	20	22	24	26	28	30	32
Trial 1				D	E	E	E	B	B	B		
2		D	E	E	E	E	B	B	B	B	B	
3			D	E	E	E	E	E	B			
4				D	E	E	E	B	B	B	B	B
5			D	E	E	E	E	B	B	B		
6				D	E	E	E	E	B	B	B	B
7		D	E	E	E	E	E	E	B	B		
8			D	E	E	E	E	E	E	B		
9			D	E	E	E	E	B	B			
10				D	E	E	E	E	B	B	B	

Upper Threshold	L_U = Mean of transitions from B to E =	23.0
Lower Threshold	L_L = Mean of transitions from E to D =	14.6
Interval of Uncertainty	IU = $L_U - L_L$ = 23.0 − 14.6 =	8.4
Difference Threshold	DL = ½(IU) = ½(8.4) =	4.2
Point of Subjective Equality	PSE = ½($L_U + L_L$) = ½(23.0 + 14.6) = ½(37.6) =	18.8

L_U and L_L is shown. Notice that the experimenter used descending series and began the series at various intensities of the Co.

The range of stimulus values between L_U and L_L is called the *interval of uncertainty* (IU). In that interval, the subject fails to discriminate between Co and St. The best estimate of the DL is defined as half the IU. The midpoint of the IU is called the point of subjective equality (PSE), the value of the Co which theoretically should appear exactly equal to the St. The procedures for calculating IU, DL, and PSE are shown in Table 7.2.

Procedures for estimating DLs involve presenting two stimuli on each trial. Fechner (1860/1966, pp. 73–77) described two types of *constant errors* (CE) which may arise due to the two stimuli occurring at different times (*time errors*) or at different places on the sensory receptor surface (*space errors*). *Time errors* may occur because of the duration of the interval between the two stimuli or because of the temporal order (Co-St or St-Co) in which they are presented. The observer may systematically pay closer attention to one interval than to the other or may recall one better than the other while responding. To control time errors, the experimenter counterbalances the order of presentation across series or across blocks of series, leaving enough time between the two stimuli for two distinct perceptions to occur.

Space errors may arise because the Co always occurs in one position while the St occurs in another. For example, if an observer is asked to compare the weight of a Co held in the left hand to the weight of the St held in the right, then the handedness of the subject may introduce constant errors into the judgments. Space errors might also occur for a subject asked to observe two meters on a control panel, a variable one on the left and a standard one on the right, during estimation of DLs for displacement of a needle on the meter; a tendency to prefer looking in one direction more than the other or greater visual acuity in one eye than in the other could be sources of error. The control for space errors is simple. The experimenter counterbalances the positions of the Co and the St across series or blocks of series.

Constant errors are not mistakes. They arise from carry-over effects of prior stimuli. Fechner (1860) described them as another aspect of sensitivity which may be measured and explained. Constant errors are indications of how the senses work, not of how they fail.

Method of Constant Stimuli

The method of constant stimuli may be used to estimate both the AL and the DL. The method derives its name from the use of the same small number of stimuli during the entire experiment.

Absolute threshold.   To estimate the AL with the method of constant stimuli, the experimenter selects several stimulus values. The weakest stimulus should be detected only occasionally, while the strongest should be detected nearly every time it occurs. Stimuli are presented in random order, one on each trial, and the observer responds "yes" or "no" to indicate detection or nondetection of the stimulus. The probability of a "yes," p(yes), is determined for each intensity and plotted as an ogive, similar to the one in Figure 7.1B. The intensity at which p(yes) = 0.5 is taken as the best estimate of absolute threshold. By presenting stimuli in random order, one averts the errors of habituation and anticipation found in the method of limits.

Difference threshold.   To estimate the DL with the method of constant stimuli, the experimenter selects a value of the St and several values of the Co. One value of the Co should equal the St, while the others should differ slightly from the St in either direction on the stimulus dimension being tested. On each trial, two stimuli occur and the subject judges whether the Co is less or more than the St. The value of the Co varies randomly on consecutive trials. Probabilities of responses "more" and "less" are calculated and plotted for each intensity of the Co. The intensity of the Co at which p(more) = p(less) = 0.5 is the PSE, the hypothetical intensity of the Co which should seem equal to the St. To control for constant errors in the method of constant stimuli, order of presentation and spatial position are counterbalanced across blocks of trials.

Method of Adjustment

The method of adjustment may be used to estimate both the AL and the DL. Its use for the latter is limited to stimuli which are continuously variable and which may be presented simultaneously as the St and the Co.

Absolute threshold.   To estimate AL, the experimenter sets the stimulus to an intensity far from threshold. The subject or observer adjusts the intensity until the stimulus is first detected or first not detected. The intensity at which the change occurs is an estimate of the AL. Such estimates should be normally distributed. The mean of the distribution is the best estimate of the AL.

The method of adjustment is used in clinical tests of auditory thresholds by the Békésy method (von Békésy, 1947). In that method, an observer presses a button when a test sound is heard, activating a motor which lowers intensity of the sound. When the sound is no longer heard, the button is released, reversing the motor and increasing intensity. The observer thus tracks intensity up and down across threshold. An automatic record is kept of changes in intensity of the sound. Békésy systems exist which automatically test large numbers of subjects simultaneously.

Differential threshold.   The method of adjustment is used more often to estimate the PSE than to estimate the DL. The observer adjusts the Co until it seems equal to the St. Both stimuli are presented simultaneously. Each setting of equality provides an estimate of the PSE. The mean of a large number of such estimates is the best estimate of the PSE, since the estimates tend to be normally distributed. Measures of dispersion of the estimates serve as estimates of DL: small dispersions indicate greater sensitivity to differences than do large dispersions.

The method of adjustment is frequently used to study the ability of subjects to match two stimuli on dimensions such as brightness or hue. Anyone who attempts to balance the intensities of speakers in a stereo system also uses a rough approximation of the method of adjustment. In all such uses, space errors must be controlled by counterbalancing positions of the Co and the St across trials or blocks of trials.

SCALING THE MAGNITUDE OF SENSATION

The methods used to estimate the AL and the DL allow only a partial analysis of sensory systems. They are intended to permit estimates of the limits of sensitivity of the senses. Threshold estimates are stated in terms of stimulus magnitudes, not in terms of attributes of sensation. Sensory attributes, labeled by terms such as loudness, painfulness, sweetness, and hue, are the contents of subjective experience. The description and analysis of such attributes is the goal of psychophysical scaling.

Concepts in Psychophysical Scaling

The ability of observers to discriminate between stimuli or sensations is basic to all other sensory experiences. It is the basis of our perception of an increase in loudness when we increase the intensity of a radio or stereo and of our perception of changes in pitch when a pianist plays a run from one end of the keyboard to the other. Psychophysical scaling provides ways to explore lawful relationships between the magnitudes of such perceptions and of the accompanying stimuli.

Discriminal dispersion.   Thurstone (1927) expanded Fechner's ideas in psychophysics. He developed a mathematical model of scaling and a method of scaling sensory attributes (cf. Corso, 1967; Green & Swets, 1966; Swets, 1973). The basic features of his model are shown in Figure 7.2. The distributions shown there were inferred from psychophysical

Figure 7.2

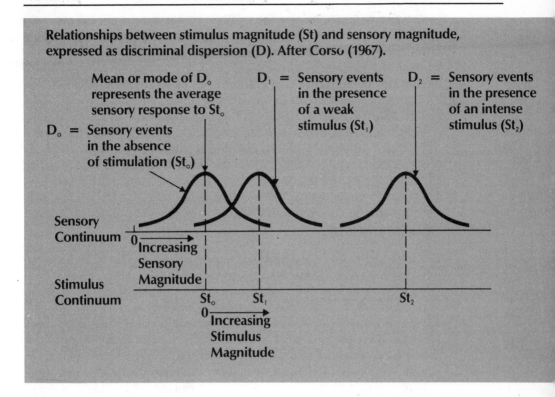

Relationships between stimulus magnitude (St) and sensory magnitude, expressed as discriminal dispersion (D). After Corso (1967).

data. Thurstone assumed that a stimulus produces a *discriminal process*, a response on a sensory continuum. The magnitude of the discriminal process varies directly with the magnitude of the stimulus. The discriminal process, or sensory magnitude, also fluctuates on successive presentations of a given stimulus, so that many presentations produce a normal distribution of *discriminal dispersion*. The mode of the discriminal dispersion is the best estimate of sensory magnitude associated with that stimulus value.

Thurstone assumed that observers are able to discriminate between different discriminal dispersions and to judge their relative magnitudes on the sensory continuum. The discriminability of any two dispersions is a function of the distance between their modes and of the degree of their overlap or confusability.

Prothetic and metathetic continua.   Stevens (1961, 1975) described two types of sensory continua: prothetic and metathetic (cf. Gescheider, 1976). *Prothetic continua* are those on which changes represent increases or decreases in the magnitude of a sensation. *Methathetic continua* are those on which changes represent shifts in the kind of sensation or the location of a sensation.

If the stimulus continuum in Figure 7.2 represents the *intensity* of a sound, substitution of one stimulus value for another on that continuum produces substitution of one discriminal dispersion for another on the sensory continuum of magnitude. We assume that neural elements which responded before the change continue to do so, but at a different rate. The result is perception of a change in loudness: a prothetic change.

If the stimulus dimension in Figure 7.2 represents the *frequency* of a sound, substitution of one stimulus value for another on that continuum produces substitution of one discriminal dispersion for another on the sensory continuum of pitch. We assume that some neural elements which were active before the change become inactive, while some which were inactive become active. The result is perception of a change in pitch, which involves a substitution of one subjective sound for another: a metathetic change.

Direct and indirect scaling.   Psychophysical scaling involves measurement of relationships between events on stimulus continua and events on sensory continua. *Direct* methods of scaling assume that observers can match dispersions on sensory continua to numbers on number scales and require observers to match differences and ratios between sensations with differences and ratios between numbers. For example, observers might be presented with a series of tones of various intensities. To each tone, they assign a number so that the relationships between the numbers directly reflect the relationships between the apparent loudnesses of the tones. The relationship between intensity and estimated magnitude can then be used to construct a psychophysical scale of loudness. *Indirect* methods assume that psychophysical scales may be constructed from estimates of the DL or of the discriminability of stimuli. For example, an experimenter might estimate the absolute threshold of a putrid odor. Beginning with that intensity, the experimenter could then estimate the increase in intensity required to produce a DL or perception of greater strength of the odor. From that intensity, the next DL could be estimated, and so on, right up to the strongest putrid sensation the subject is willing to tolerate. Based on the estimates of DL, relative to stimulus intensity, a psychophysical scale may be constructed (cf. Engen, 1972; Watson, 1973).

Sensory attributes and semantic labels.   Watson (1973) describes a basic issue in scaling, in fact, in all of psychology: the distinction between subjective experiences and the words used to describe them. Assume that a musically skilled observer perceives events on a sensory continuum of pitch. The observer may emit responses relating to that continuum. When we strike a piano key which causes a sound with a frequency of

440 vibrations per second (440 Hz) and ask, "What is that tone?" the observer says, "A."

The issue raised by Watson would be this: What is the "A"? It is not the sound, nor is it truly an attribute *of* the sound. Neither is it an attribute of the sensation of the observer. "A" is a culturally defined semantic response given by the observer when exposed to the stimulus. For purposes of convenience, we assume that semantic labels which are applied consistently to stimuli describe certain attributes of the stimuli, even though they do not.

How Psychophysical Scales Relate to Numerical Scales

In Chapter 3, we discussed the characteristics of four types of number scales along which variables might be distributed. They are nominal, ordinal, interval, and ratio scales. We will now consider examples of psychophysical scaling procedures relating to each of these number scales.

Nominal scales: Naming.   On a *nominal* scale, numbers or other symbols designate individual objects or classes of objects which are discriminated from other individuals or classes. Nominal scaling requires that the observer distinguish between discriminal dispersions on a sensory continuum and attach a distinctive semantic label or behavioral response to each of them. For example, the ability of preverbal infants to make discriminations between colors may be assessed by measuring the amount of time they look at comparison stimuli that differ in wavelength from a standard to which they are habituated (Bornstein, Kessen, & Weiskopf, 1976; Peeples & Teller, 1975).

Nominal scaling often involves recognition or naming in an *absolute-judgment* paradigm. Stimuli are presented one at a time and the observer is asked to identify each with an appropriate discriminative label. On many sensory continua, observers can successfully discriminate large numbers of stimuli when they occur simultaneously. When large numbers of stimuli occur individually, however, observers tend to use a small number of response categories, indicating that they recognize and label fewer differences when making absolute judgments (Miller, 1956).

Ordinal scales: Ranking.   On *ordinal* scales, numbers or other symbols are used to indicate that differences exist in the magnitudes of things. Ordinal scaling requires the observer to discriminate between dispersions on a sensory continuum and to rank-order differences in magnitude between them. In the method of *absolute judgments,* or *stimulus rating,* one stimulus occurs on each trial. The observer assigns to the stimulus an ordinal response, such as "small," "medium," or "large." Numerical values may be assigned to the response categories and may be analyzed by percentiles or by rank-order correlations (Stevens, 1975).

In the method of *paired comparisons* developed by Thurstone (1927), two stimuli occur on each trial. The observer determines which stimulus ranks higher or lower on the sensory continuum. Each stimulus must be paired with all others. All pairs may be presented to each observer, or each observer may receive only one pair. In the method of paired comparisons, counterbalancing must be used to control for time and space errors. Box 7.2 describes two experiments employing paired comparisons. The experiments reach different conclusions, because one controlled for time error while the other did not.

In the *ranking* method, an observer arranges stimuli along some sensory dimension in an order based on the amount of a given attribute they are perceived to possess. The entire stimulus array may be presented simultaneously. Rankings may be obtained on dimensions as diverse as the effectiveness of faculty in a university, the prestige of various professions, and the popularity of flavors of ice cream.

Data distributed on ordinal continua may be analyzed in only a few ways. Statistical procedures that assume more precise levels of measurement should be applied to ordinal data only with caution (Stevens, 1951, 1960, 1975). Failure to exercise such caution results in a psychological literature containing large amounts of statistically significant, but scientifically meaningless, clutter.

Interval scales: Categorizing.   On interval scales, numbers are applied to things so that differences between the numbers correspond to the magnitude and direction of perceived differences between the things. On such scales, any given difference between two numbers should correspond to that same difference between any other two, no matter where the numbers are located on the scale. For example, on a calendar, the difference between May 4 and May 5 is the same as that between April 14 and April 15, unless you pay federal income tax. Interval scaling requires the observer: (*a*) to discriminate between dispersions on a sensory continuum; (*b*) to perceive differences in magnitude between the dispersions; and (*c*) to identify or to produce equality of differences between dispersions.

In the method of *equisection,* the observer divides the sensory continuum into *equal sense distances.* Presented with two clearly discriminable stimuli, the observer identifies a third stimulus which is perceptually half-way between the first two. In an alternative method, the observer adjusts a third stimulus until it is equally distant from the first two. The mean of the distribution of values selected by the observer is taken as the estimate of the stimulus value which bisects the distance between the other two (cf. Engen, 1972).

In the method of *equal-appearing intervals,* the experimenter presents two stimuli (anchors) near the extremes of the range of stimuli to be scaled and identifies each with a whole number. The observer then

Box 7.2   Paired Comparisons in Studies of Time Perception

Psychologists use many methods to study the perception of time. Some use the method of paired comparisons, a procedure which may induce time-order effects as constant errors in perception. If paired comparisons are used to study the perception of *time,* then *time-order effects* must be controlled. Occasionally, they are not.

Ornstein (1969) studied relationships between the complexity of visual stimuli and their apparent durations. He used six irregular geometric patterns as stimuli. The patterns varied in complexity, the least complex having four sides and the most complex having nineteen sides. One figure, with ten sides, was the standard stimulus (St) and the other five were comparison stimuli (Co). Each subject saw two slides, one containing the St, followed by one containing a Co. Both slides lasted thirty seconds. Subjects marked a line on paper to indicate the apparent duration of each slide. Ornstein then calculated the ratio of the lines for the St and Co lines: if $\frac{Co}{St} = 1$, the perceived durations were equal; if $\frac{Co}{St}$ is greater than 1, the duration of the Co slide was perceived as longer; and if $\frac{Co}{St}$ is less than 1, the duration of the St slide was perceived as longer. All the ratios in the study were less than, but close to, 1, meaning that the second, Co, stimuli were consistently judged shorter in duration than the St. Because the least complex Co differed most from St in perceived duration, Ornstein concluded that the complexity of stimuli determined their perceived duration. In fact, the second stimulus consistently was judged shorter than the first, a clear demonstration of a time-order effect.

Farrar (1974) also studied relationships between stimulus complexity and perceived duration. She used patterns of five, ten, or forty sides. Each subject saw two different slides, with all possible orders and combinations of slides counterbalanced across subjects. Subjects decided which pattern seemed longest and wrote their response. Both slides lasted five seconds. Whatever the order of presentation or the complexity of the slides, the first was judged longest significantly more often than the second. The data of Ornstein (1969) and of Farrar (1974) are compatible with the hypothesis that visual stimulus complexity correlates with perceived duration, but that the time-order effect correlates even more highly.

compares each test stimulus to the memory of the anchors, decides how much it differs from them, and assigns to it a whole number which differs from those assigned to the anchors by the same magnitude as that by which the perceptions differ. The mean or median category to which each stimulus was assigned is calculated.

Category scales require many presentations of the test stimuli. The stimuli should not be perfectly discriminable. To obtain valid results, the experimenter should present more stimulus values than there are response categories. Stevens and Galanter (1957) and Stevens (1975) identify and suggest controls for biases which frequently occur in category scales.

Ratio scales: Estimating magnitude.   On ratio scales, numbers designate relationships between things that differ along a dimension which has the properties of order, distance, and a true zero point. On ratio scales, the ratios of scaled values must be kept constant through all numerical manipulations or calculations. Ratio scaling requires the observer to do all the things required for interval scaling. In addition, the observer must estimate or produce specific ratios between discriminal dispersions on a sensory continuum. In the method of *ratio production* or *fractionation*, the observer attends to a standard stimulus (St) and adjusts a continuously variable comparison stimulus (Co) until it is in some specified ratio to the St. The desired ratio may be a fraction, such as one half as great, or a multiple, such as twice as great. The method of *ratio estimation* is quite similar to ratio production, except that the observer responds to two stimuli by estimating the ratio between them (cf. Engen, 1972; Gescheider, 1976).

In the method of *magnitude estimation,* observers make direct numerical estimations of magnitudes of stimuli, or of dispersions on a sensory continuum. The strength of each dispersion is compared to that of a standard or *modulus* (Stevens, 1961, 1975). The experimenter may present the modulus and tell the observer it has a certain value. On test trials, other stimuli occur. The observer compares the sensation associated with each stimulus to that produced by the modulus and assigns a number which expresses the ratio between the two sensations. An alternative and commonly preferred procedure omits the experimenter-defined modulus and allows the observer to choose a modulus from among the stimuli presented. The order of stimulus values is varied between subjects. From ten to twenty stimuli occur in a session. Experimentally naive observers may be used. To produce a psychophysical function of sensory magnitude, one plots the average magnitude assigned by all observers as a function of values on the stimulus continuum. Functions have been obtained by magnitude estimation for a wide range of sensory continua including brightness, loudness, strength of odor, size of objects, and beauty (Stevens, 1975).

In the method of *magnitude production,* the complement of magnitude estimation, the observer adjusts a continuously variable stimulus until it is perceived in some requested ratio to a modulus. The two magnitude methods require similar controls and produce similar results.

The method of *cross-modality matching* completely avoids the use of numbers and the assumptions associated with them. The observer adjusts the magnitude of a Co in one sensory modality until it is perceived as equal to an St in another modality. This procedure is a variation on the psychophysical method of adjustment, differing in that the Co and the St are in different sensory modalities. An *equal-sensation function,* based on cross-modality points of subjective equality, is produced by plotting average values of the Co as a function of the St. Stevens (1961, 1975) reported many experiments in which observers matched their perceptions of the force of their handgrip (measured on a dynamometer) against various sensory continua.

Comparing Psychophysical "Laws"

So far, our discussion of psychophysical scaling has focused on basic methods for acquiring data. Now we will examine several attempts to describe lawful relationships in psychophysical data.

Weber's law.   In our discussion of differential thresholds, we examined several methods for estimating jnds. In the early 1800s, Ernst Weber measured jnds for lifted weights (Fechner, 1860/1966, pp. 114–116). He observed that, no matter what the weight of the standard, the amount of change needed to produce a jnd was approximately $1/18$ of the standard. Fechner and others elaborated Weber's data into *Weber's law,* also known as the *Weber fraction* or as *Weber's constant.* Weber's law is expressed in the equation:

$$\Delta I/I = k,$$

where I is the magnitude of a standard stimulus, ΔI is the change in magnitude needed to produce a jnd relative to I, and k is a constant. Weber's law states that, as stimulus magnitude (I) increases, the magnitude of change necessary to produce a jnd (ΔI) increases, but that $\Delta I/I$ is a constant.

Table 7.3 presents data from a series of estimations of jnds. Absolute threshold is 10 units of intensity. The values of ΔI were obtained empirically as dependent variables in estimates of jnd. Values of k were derived from estimates of jnd. In this example, $k = .33$ or $\Delta I = (\frac{1}{3})I$. Figure 7.3 presents two graphs of the data from Table 7.3. Weber's law, in the basic form presented here, is generally valid for a portion of many prothetic scales. The dashed lines in Figure 7.3 show the most commonly

Table 7.3   Analysis of hypothetical data for estimation of jnd, based on Weber's law ($\Delta I / I = k$).

Intensity of Standard Stimulus (I)	ΔI	k
10	3.30	0.33
50	16.50	0.33
100	33.00	0.33
150	49.50	0.33
200	66.00	0.33

observed type of deviation from Weber's law: typically, empirical values of ΔI are larger for weak stimuli than Weber's law predicts.

Fechner's law.   Fechner used the indirect procedure of analyzing data from measurements of jnds, expressed as units of stimulus magnitude, to derive a scale of subjective magnitude. His scale is expressed in the equation:

$$S = k \times \log I,$$

where S is subjective magnitude, the number of jnds above absolute threshold; $\log I$ is the logarithm to the base 10 of the stimulus magnitude; and k is a constant. Table 7.4 shows how a logarithmic sensory scale may be derived from the hypothetical data presented in Table 7.3. The derived values of ΔI in Table 7.4 fit on the function in Figure 7.3A. Figure 7.4 presents two ways of graphing the data from Table 7.4. The function in Figure 7.4B is a straight line. The linearity of this relationship

Table 7.4   Derivation of a sensory scale from measurements of DL. (Based on hypothetical data from Table 7.3.)

Number of jnds above Threshold	Stimulus Intensity (I)	$\Delta I = I \times k$ (k = 0.33)	jnd = I + ΔI	$\mathrm{Log_{10}}\ I$
0	10.00	3.33	13.33	1.00
1	13.33	4.39	17.69	1.12
2	17.69	5.84	23.53	1.25
3	23.53	7.76	31.29	1.37
4	31.29	10.33	41.26	1.50
5	41.62	13.73	55.35	1.62
6	55.35	18.27	73.50	1.74
7	73.50	24.25	97.75	1.87
8	97.75	32.26	130.01	1.99
9	130.01	42.90	172.91	2.11
10	172.91	57.06	232.08	2.24
11	232.08	76.59	308.67	2.37

Figure 7.3

Weber's Law. Graphs based on hypothetical data from Table 7.3.

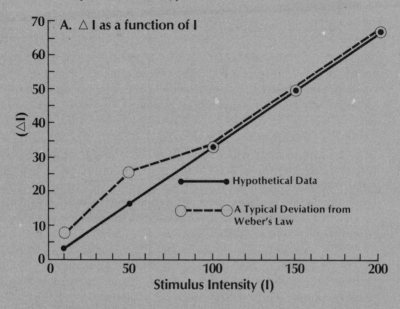

A. $\triangle$ I as a function of I

Hypothetical Data

A Typical Deviation from Weber's Law

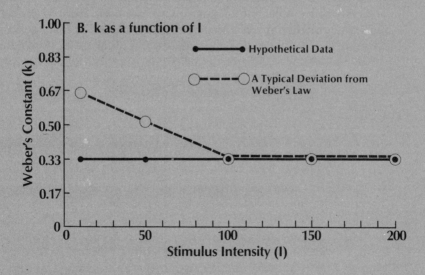

B. k as a function of I

Hypothetical Data

A Typical Deviation from Weber's Law

was the basis of Fechner's claim that sensation magnitude, estimated in terms of jnds, increases directly as a function of the logarithm of stimulus magnitude. However, the values of jnd in Figure 7.4 were *derived* from data in Table 7.3, where it was assumed that Weber's constant was in fact constant. It is not, especially for weak stimuli. To the extent that Weber's law lacks validity, Fechner's law lacks validity.

Stevens' law.   Stevens (1975, pp. 22–26) recalled events in 1953 when he concluded that observers could directly estimate the magnitudes of sensations. He expressed the relationship between estimated sensory magnitude and stimulus intensity in the equation:

$$S = k \times I^n,$$

where S is apparent sensory magnitude, I is stimulus intensity, n is an exponent characteristic of a given sensory continuum, and k is a constant which depends on the units of measurement on the stimulus scale. The equation indicates that sensory magnitude increases as a function of I raised to a power which is characteristic of the sensory modality and of stimulus parameters.

The research of Stevens on magnitude estimation represents a direct approach to scaling. Scale values of sensory magnitude as a function of stimulus magnitude are obtained directly from observers, not from statistical manipulations of data obtained in other contexts. Figure 7.5 presents data from magnitude estimation experiments by Stevens in which observers scaled apparent intensity of electric shock, apparent length of lines, and visual brightness. Similar results, obtained by many researchers using widely divergent stimulus materials—social, political, moral, esthetic, and commercial—were viewed by Stevens (1975) as support for his claim that the power law is a universal feature of human perception.

GESTALT PRINCIPLES AND INFORMATION THEORY

We have examined some of the methods and concepts of psychophysics that are basic to experimental psychology. Psychophysics represents a highly structured and reductionistic approach to the study of perception. Gestalt psychology arose in part as a reaction against the quantitative rigors of psychophysics. We briefly discussed Gestalt psychology in Chapter 2. We will now examine certain Gestalt tactics and concepts in more detail, especially as they relate to the structuring of perception. We will then review basic paradigms in information theory, a system which is more quantitative than Gestalt psychology but which also stresses the organization of perception.

Figure 7.4

Fechner's Law. Graphs based on hypothetical data from Table 7.4.

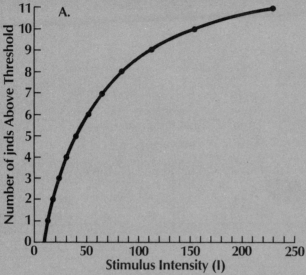

A. Number of jnds above threshold as a function of stimulus intensity (I). At threshold, I = 10.

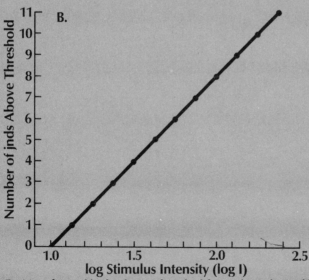

B. Number of jnds above threshold as a function of $\log_{10}$ Stimulus Intensity (log I). At threshold, log I = 1.0.

Figure 7.5

Psychological magnitudes of electric shock, length of lines, and brightness as functions of stimulus magnitude. A. Linear coordinates. B. Log-log coordinates. From Stevens (1961, p. 11).

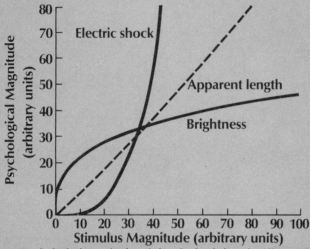

A. Psychological magnitudes of electric shock, length of line, and brightness, as functions of stimulus magnitude. In the power law, the exponent (n) for shock is 3.5; for length, 1.1; and for brightness, 0.33. On linear coordinates, $n = 1$ produces a straight line; $n > 1$ curves upward; and $n < 1$ curves downward.

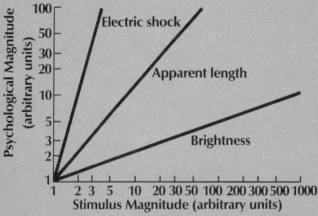

B. The same relations shown in A, but now plotted on logarithmic coordinates. All functions become linear and the slopes of the lines reflect the value of n: The greater the value of n, the steeper the slope.

Demonstrating Gestalt Principles

The hallmark of Gestalt psychology is the *experimentum crucis,* an immediately clear demonstration of a major principle or relationship. Boring (1950) states that Gestalt psychologists use diagrams as *experimenta crucis* to " . . . make a phenomonologist of the reader, letting him have at once the immediate experience which constitutes the evidence" (p. 602). For example, in answer to a request for a definition of movement aftereffects, a Gestalt psychologist might respond: "*If* you will stare at a rotating disc for two minutes, at which time you shift your gaze to the nose on your friend's face, *then* you will see a movement aftereffect." The definition is in terms of operations which yield directly observable consequences.

Gestalt theorists describe perception as an interaction between stimuli and mental processes, both of which are assumed to possess intrinsic organization and structure. The interaction is one in which stimuli influence an observer, but the nature of the influence and its associated perception is determined by innate characteristics of the observer. We will examine apparent movement and figural goodness as examples of Gestalt principles of organization.

Movement: Real and apparent.   Theories of movement perception must account for both real and apparent movement. Real movement is perceived when an object moves through the visual field of an observer at such a rate that transitions of the object from point to point are discerned. *Apparent movement* is perceived in two circumstances: the phi phenomenon and movement aftereffects. The *phi phenomenon* occurs when discrete stimuli, located at different places, follow one another in time at certain rates, but the observer perceives a single moving stimulus; if two lights several feet apart flash on and off alternately in a dark room, an observer will perceive a single light darting back and forth. *Movement aftereffects* occur when an observer, or an object seen by an observer, stops moving and the observer perceives movement in the opposite direction.

In perception of real movement, it is assumed that the object produces an image on the visual receptors of the observer and that the image moves across the receptor surface in a continuous path. Movement of the image causes activity in successive groups of neural elements in the visual system, producing a metathetic or qualitative change in perceived location. In the phi phenomenon, there is no uniform displacement of an image across the receptor surface. A stimulus at one place replaces one at a distant place.

In 1912, Wertheimer published a paper on the phi phenomenon, thereby initiating the field of Gestalt psychology. He used a toy stroboscope to produce shadows at two places on a screen in rapid succession, yet his subjects saw a single shadow which apparently moved smoothly from place to place on the screen. Wertheimer and his colleagues argued that the movement seen in the phi phenomenon is a "pure" perceptual experience, not an illusion, as was assumed by most others (Köhler, 1969). To bolster their argument, they relied on another demonstration, one related to aftereffects of seen movement. Box 7.3 describes simple procedures to induce movement aftereffects.

Wertheimer required his subjects to view apparent movement in one direction, in a version of the phi phenomenon. After alternation of the stimuli terminated, the observers reported movement aftereffects: a stationary stimulus appeared to move opposite to the direction of the earlier apparent movement. Gestalt theorists interpreted the results as direct evidence that apparent movement is not an illusion, but that it arises from perceptual organizing principles in the observer (Köhler, 1969).

Law of prägnanz: Good figures.   In German, the word *gestalt* means "form" or "shape." Gestalt theorists emphasized the total form or configuration of perception, rather than an analysis of its components. As described by Koffka (1935), the Gestalt law of *prägnanz,* or *good figure,* is the basic law of perceptual organization. It states that "psychological organization will always be as good as the prevailing conditions allow. In this definition the term good is undefined" (p. 110). In characteristic style, early Gestalt psychologists defined goodness of figures on the basis of demonstrations. Figure 7.6 illustrates some of the basic Gestalt factors in the organization of visual perceptual fields, based on concepts of Wertheimer (cf. Miller and Buckhout, 1973) and of Kanizsa (1976).

In Figure 7.6 the following principles are illustrated:

A. *Similarity:* we usually perceive things which are similar as belonging together. Therefore, in A, we tend to see alternating rows of light circles and dark spots.

B. *Proximity:* we usually perceive things which are close in space and time as belonging together. Therefore, in B, we tend to see two double rows of spots.

C. *Conflict* or *opposition:* when two basic principles of organization are in conflict or opposition, the resulting organizations are usually unstable. Therefore, in C, we may see three narrow rows, each composed of light and dark shapes; or we may tend to see two broad rows, one based on dark spots, the other on light circles. The organization may oscillate between these two.

D. 1. *Good Continuation:* we usually perceive partial or broken patterns as being extended along lines which produce continuous contours.

2. *Closure:* we usually perceive open or incomplete patterns as being closed or complete patterns if the resulting closure produces goodness, stability, balance, persistence, and symmetry. Therefore, in

Box 7.3 How to Induce Movement Aftereffects

Following the prolonged visual perception of real movement in a given direction, an observer perceives apparent visual movement in the opposite direction. Such aftereffects are easily produced. Detune the vertical hold on a television until the picture drifts slowly up or down, or place a record on a turntable set to the slowest speed possible. Look steadily at a single point on the screen or on the record label for about a minute, then stop the movement. The television screen or the record label will seem to move slowly in a direction opposite to that of the earlier real movement.

Gestalt theorists called such aftereffects "pure" perceptions or perceptions of pure movement, independent of any specific external stimuli. To see what they meant literally, repeat the demonstration you just performed. When the movement stops this time, immediately look away to a familiar object. You will see apparent movement in the part of your visual field which earlier was occupied by real movement. The movement aftereffect is obviously independent of the stimulus that induced it. It seems to originate in some property of the observer. Spinning in one direction until you are dizzy produces a similar effect, but visual stimuli are not the only ones involved.

Figure 7.6

Examples of selected Gestalt factors in perceptual organization. After Miller and Buckhout (1973) and Kanizsa (1976).

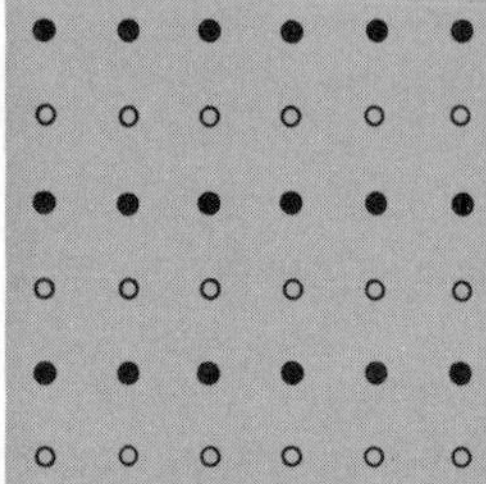

A. Similarity

B. Proximity

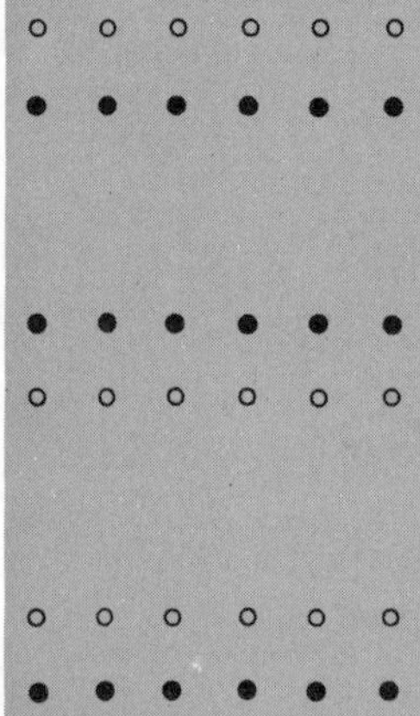

C. Similarity and proximity
   in conflict or opposition

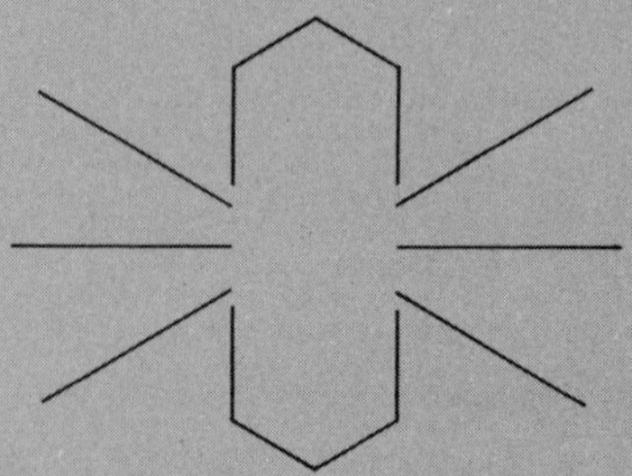

D. Combination of
   1. Good continuation
   2. Closure

D, we tend to perceive a continuous hexagonal surface, behind or beneath which three lines cross.

Quantifying Gestalt principles.   Many psychologists have attempted to quantify Gestalt principles. For example, Kolers (1963, 1964) examined the stimulus variables which produce real and apparent movement and concluded that, while observers are unable to distinguish between real and apparent movement, the two are mediated by neural processes which differ in some significant ways. Hochberg and Silverstein (1965) examined interactions between proximity and brightness in a pattern similar to Figure 7.6A. Intensity cues from the stimulus elements tended to produce a horizontal organization based on similarities in brightness. Hochberg and Silverstein did the equivalent of systematically reducing the distance between alternate columns in the figure. Eventually, a distance was reached which changed the perceptual organization from one based on brightness to one based on proximity, or from horizontal to vertical organization.

Research such as that of Kolers and of Hochberg and Silverstein quantifies some of the classic Gestalt demonstrations of perceptual organization and brings them within the paradigms of experimental psychophysics. However, some psychologists maintain that such quantification does nothing to *explain* the basic principles (cf. Prentice, 1959).

Measuring Information

Information theory developed as a way of conceptualizing and quantifying the process of communication. Developers of information theory were immediately concerned with finding ways to improve the transmission of messages over noisy channels (cf. Slepian, 1973). Much of the initial work on information theory occurred at Bell Telephone Laboratories, the major basic research facility of The American Telephone and Telegraph Company.

In the field of communication, information theory initiated a major revolution. It led to more precise quantification of the informational content of a message and of the fate of that information as the message passed through the components of a communication system. The theory also focused attention on the communication system itself, leading to new insights into the process of information handling. The developers of information theory, along with several mathematical psychologists, saw parallels between information transmission (in the strict sense) in an electronic system and information processing (in the general sense) in the behavior of organisms (cf. Attneave, 1959; Garner, 1962). Concepts and procedures derived from information theory were incorporated into every level of research and theory in psychology (cf. Buckley, 1968; Garner, 1974; Gibson, 1967; Neisser, 1976).

The involvement—even to the point of infatuation—of many psychologists with information theory quickly drew criticism. Cronbach (1955) attacked what he considered to be "non-rational" or unnecessary applications of information theory to psychology. Rapoport (1956) acknowledged the positive role information theory might play in psychology but seriously questioned the broad theoretical leaps he saw others making. In a more subdued and systematic fashion, information theory continues as a source of theory and of research in psychology. It has been a major factor in the development of the information processing model in psychology. We will therefore review some of the major concepts associated with the theory before we examine how they relate to an analysis of the Gestalt concept of good figure.

Information, uncertainty, and redundancy.   The quantification of information is a major feature of information theory. Information theorists define "information" in terms of "uncertainty." The technical meanings of information and uncertainty are close enough to their conventional meanings that we may illustrate them by analogy.

Assume that we meet in the corridor of a windowless building. You say, "It is raining outside." If I recently came inside, I already know what the weather is: I have no uncertainty about it, so your statement communicates no information about that topic. If I have been inside for several hours, I may not know what the weather is: I am uncertain about it, so your statement reduces my uncertainty by communicating information. In information-theoretic terms, the maximum amount of information that may be transmitted in a situation is determined by the amount of uncertainty which initially exists.

Our conversation might illustrate another important concept. Assuming that your first statement did eliminate my uncertainty about the weather, an additional comment from you, "It is really wet outside," is *redundant:* it provides more information than the minimum amount necessary to eliminate my uncertainty. Redundancy is neither good nor bad; it is simply a condition that may exist in communication.

For communication to occur between you, as the *source,* and me, as the *destination,* we must be *matched:* we must possess the appropriate vocal and auditory systems and must share both common knowledge and a common language. To the extent that we are not matched, or that environmental circumstances interfere with our conversation, information transmission is degraded. All factors that degrade communication or introduce error into communication are called *noise.*

Binary digits (bits).   The basic unit in information theory is a binary digit or *bit.* Conceptually, a binary event is one that may occur only in either of two ways. For example, a simple light switch on the wall is a binary device; normally it may only be either "on" or "off." The outcome of a coin toss is a binary event; ordinarily, the coin must land either "heads" or "tails." The outcome of a roll of a die is not a binary event, since there are six possible outcomes. However, the outcome of the roll of the die or of any other situation with several equally likely outcomes, may be expressed in terms of several binary units, or bits, of information.

Assume that, in full view of an experimental subject, we place a dollar under a box. We allow the subject to ask *binary* questions. The subject can keep the money after locating it. In our example, the subject has no uncertainty about the location, therefore no questions are necessary. In Table 7.5, the task confronting our subject when there is only one location is summarized in the column for n = 1 and in computational example *a*.

Now assume that, out of sight of the subject, we place the money under one of *two* boxes. The subject is permitted to ask only one binary question to locate the money. The obvious question is along the lines of, "Is it under the box on the left?" Whatever our answer, the subject knows the location of the money. The task confronting our subject when there are two boxes is summarized in Table 7.5 in the column for n = 2 and in computational example *b*.

If we now confront our subject with 64 boxes, only six binary question are needed to locate the money, so long as each question reduces the alternatives by half (e.g., "Is it under one of the 32 boxes on the right?").

Table 7.5   Calculation of the number of bits of information for a hypothetical choice task in which all categories are equally likely to be correct. ($H_i = \log_2 1/P_i$)

n	1	2	4	8	64	512
P_i	$\frac{1}{1}$	$\frac{1}{2}$	$\frac{1}{4}$	$\frac{1}{8}$	$\frac{1}{64}$	$\frac{1}{512}$
2^H	2^0	2^1	2^2	2^3	2^6	2^9
H^i	0	1	2	3	6	9
Bits	0	1	2	3	6	9

n = number of possible categories.
$P_i = 1/n$ = probability of any given category (i) being correct.
2^H = number of possible categories (*n*) expressed as a power of 2.
H_i = number of binary questions needed to identify the correct category ($H_i = \log_2 1/P_i$).
Bits = number of binary units of uncertainty (U) about which category is correct, which is identical to the number of binary units of information transmitted in locating the correct category.

Computational Examples:
a. If n = 1, then $H_1 = \log_2 \left(\frac{1}{\frac{1}{1}} \right) = \log_2 (1 \times \frac{1}{1}) = \log_2 1 = 0$
b. If n = 2, then $H_2 = \log_2 \left(\frac{1}{\frac{1}{2}} \right) = \log_2 (1 \times \frac{2}{1}) = \log_2 2 = 1$
c. If n = 64, then $H_{64} = \log_2 \left(\frac{1}{\frac{1}{64}} \right) = \log_2 (1 \times \frac{64}{1}) = \log_2 64 = 6$

In Table 7.5, the situation for 64 boxes is summarized in the column for $n = 64$ and in computational example c.

In all situations where events are equally likely to occur, doubling the number of events adds one bit of uncertainty, or of information. In situations where events are not equally likely to occur, uncertainty is less than maximal. If we roll a loaded die, the probability of one result is greater than that of the other five. The higher the probability of the biased result, the lower the uncertainty about the outcome. Computational procedures for determining information in any stimulus ensemble, even if events are not equally likely, are available from many sources (cf. Attneave, 1959; Coombs, Dawes, & Tversky, 1970; Corso, 1967; Garner, 1962; Keele, 1973; Miller, 1963; Snodgrass, 1975; Welford, 1976).

Information and human performance.   Information theory provides a way of looking at communication in terms of what might have been transmitted, as well as what was transmitted. It therefore allows comparisons between the amount of information in an array of potential stimuli and the amount of information in the discriminative responses to that array by an organism. In a classic paper, Miller (1956) applied information theory to the analysis of absolute judgments, the nominal scaling procedure which assesses the ability of an observer to identify or name consistently individual items out of an array of items. Miller concluded that observers can accurately name or identify only about seven stimuli which differ along a single dimension. Thus, while the amount of information presented to an observer may increase indefinitely, the limit on consistent discriminative responses is between 5 and 9 (between 2.32 bits and 3.17 bits). Simon (1974) describes procedures observers employ to group bits of information into organized "chunks," thereby increasing their capacity for information.

One of the first topics we considered in this chapter was reaction time, perhaps the first aspect of behavior to be studied experimentally. Many psychologists apply information analyses to studies of reaction time. Hick (1952) assumed that, in a choice reaction time paradigm, the observer gains information at a constant rate. In this paradigm, increases in the number of alternative stimuli that might occur and in the number of accompanying discriminative responses produce increases in reaction time. Hick demonstrated that for arrays in which each stimulus is equally likely to occur choice reaction time increases linearly as a function of the number of bits of stimulus uncertainty, a relationship known as "Hick's law." Recall that if one event in an array of possible events occurs with a much higher probability than the others, then the amount of uncertainty about the array is less than if the events are equally probable. Choice reaction times for such arrays are shorter than for equally probable arrays (cf. Keele, 1973; Welford, 1976).

Good figures and redundancy.   We now return to the Gestalt concept of the "goodness" of a figure. Information theory, which deals with quantifying the structure of arrays of information, provides concepts useful in attempting to answer the question of how one identifies figures as good or bad and explains the difference between them. Hochberg and McAlister (1953) and Hochberg and Brooks (1960) explained "goodness" in terms of "simplicity," concluding that as a figure becomes more simple the amount of information needed to specify or describe its organization decreases and its perceived goodness increases. Attneave (1954) described much of the information received by organisms as redundant: by sampling only a small portion of the sensory information available at a given time, organisms extract enough lawfully related information that they may generate lawfully related behaviors. He demonstrated that most of the information needed to specify or to reproduce outline drawings is concentrated at points where contour changes most abruptly. Thus, in a triangle, the three corners specify the figure, while the sides are redundant. Salapatek and Kessen (1966) and Karmel, Hoffman, and Fegy (1974) demonstrated that human neonates visually fixate and scan the information-rich transitions in figures rather than their redundant portions.

Attneave (1959) stated that "roughly speaking, organization and redundancy are the same" (p. 82). He suggested that figural goodness is equivalent to redundancy. Garner pursued that notion, and in 1974 he published a review of over a decade of personal research on figural organization. Figure 7.7 summarizes a portion of that research (Handel & Garner, 1966). After rotating each of the dot patterns in Figure 7.7 in 90° steps and reflecting each pattern as in a mirror image, they were divided into three subsets according to their informational redundancy:

Subset A: Patterns which produced only one alternative; they remained identical after all transformations (0 bits of uncertainty).

Subset B: Patterns which produced four alternatives (2 bits of uncertainty).

Subset C: Patterns which produced eight alternatives (3 bits of uncertainty).

In Figure 7.7, patterns that produce no alternatives form a highly redundant subset. One orientation of such a pattern specifies all other orientations, since they are identical. Mathematically, such patterns have zero bits of uncertainty. Behaviorally, observers have very little uncertainty about the subset to which such a pattern belongs. Patterns that produce eight alternatives form a subset low in redundancy and high in uncertainty. Mathematically, such patterns have three bits of uncertainty. Behaviorally, observers have considerable uncertainty about the subset to which such a pattern belongs. Patterns that produce four alternatives form a subset which is intermediate in redundancy and in uncertainty.

Subjects rated the patterns for "goodness" on a scale from 1 (very

Figure 7.7

Dot patterns used in an experiment on good figures and redundancy. The number below each pattern is the mean rating assigned by subjects, where 1 = "very good" and 7 = "very poor." After Handel and Garner (1966).

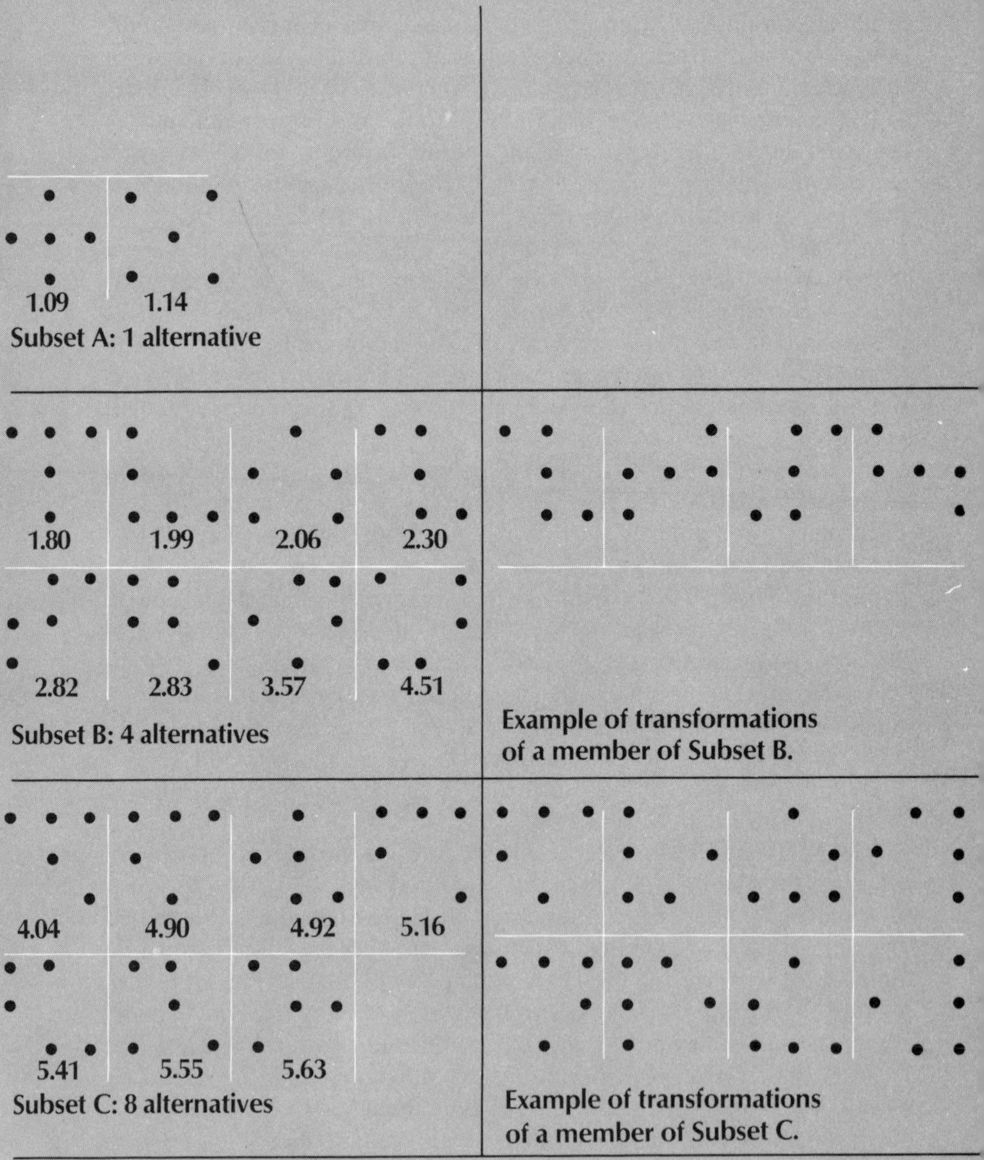

1.09   1.14
Subset A: 1 alternative

1.80   1.99   2.06   2.30

2.82   2.83   3.57   4.51

Subset B: 4 alternatives

Example of transformations
of a member of Subset B.

4.04   4.90   4.92   5.16

5.41   5.55   5.63

Subset C: 8 alternatives

Example of transformations
of a member of Subset C.

good) to 7 (very poor), where goodness was undefined. They produced the mean ratings shown under each pattern in Figure 7.7. The smaller the subset to which a pattern belongs, the higher its rated goodness. Handel and Garner reasoned that patterns in the smallest subset contained the least uncertainty about configuration. As a consequence of the low uncertainty, observers were able easily to identify such patterns and to assign them to a perceptual category. Such ease of identification and of categorization results in high ratings of pattern goodness. The reverse is true for patterns of high uncertainty. Their ambiguous structure leads to ambiguity and uncertainty on the part of the observer and to low ratings of pattern goodness. Garner (1974) summarized the situation in the comment that "Good patterns exist in small subsets and are thus very redundant" (p. 15).

In the work of Garner, we find an excellent example of the convergence of a rigorous system of quantification, information theory, and an intentionally nonquantitative system of speculation, Gestalt theory. The result is an enrichment of the body of knowledge in both fields.

THEORY OF SIGNAL DETECTABILITY: CONTINGENCIES AND DECISIONS

Classical psychophysics and Gestalt psychology began as philosophical and academic inquiries. In contrast to these two, information theory developed out of a practical desire to improve the efficiency of telephone communication, thereby reducing costs and increasing corporate profits. The theory of signal detectability also grew out of practical concerns. We will examine some of the inadequacies of classical psychophysics that provided the impetus to develop the theory of signal detectability (TSD). Then we will review the major assumptions and experimental paradigms of TSD.

Psychophysics in the Real World

Fechner developed classical psychophysics as a means of answering philosophical questions about how mental events relate to neural energy flow. From its lofty beginnings, psychophysics quickly affected the emerging field of psychological testing. The collection of normative data on sensory thresholds soon grew into the various standardized techniques for assessing visual and auditory acuity. As technology produced systems that placed increasing burdens on human operators, classical psychophysics provided methods to study the efficiency of those operators. During efforts to study the efficiency of radar operators, serious inadequacies of classical psychophysics became apparent and TSD developed (cf. Swets, Tanner, & Birdsall, 1961).

Probability of stimulus occurrence.   Classical paradigms for estimating thresholds present a stimulus on every trial. Occasionally, an experimenter omits a signal from a series in the method of limits or from a random sequence in the method of constant stimuli. Observers who respond "yes" on such a "catch trial" are instructed to be more careful. The experimenter then performs a statistical "correction for guessing" on their data (Swets, 1961; Swets, Tanner, & Birdsall, 1961).

In most situations confronting organisms, stimuli do not occur every time they might. The effects on threshold of varying the probability of occurrence of a stimulus are quite consistent: as the probability of a stimulus *decreases,* an observer's estimated AL for that stimulus *increases.* The reverse is also true (Green & Swets, 1966). Both theoretically and practically, it is undesirable for an estimate of absolute sensitivity to be influenced by changes in the probabilities of stimulus events.

Response contingencies.   In classical psychophysics, the observer is treated as a system with uniform characteristics and capabilities over time. The minor variability an observer shows is attributed to random influences which average out over large numbers of trials or sessions.

In reality, observers may be profoundly influenced by their setting and by the contingencies associated with their responses. Radar operators in combat zones, where their responses to small spots on cluttered radar screens may mean life or death for themselves and others, have lower thresholds for seeing targets than when they are assigned to stations far from combat. The rewards and punishments associated with detection performance influence classical estimates of sensitivity (cf. Galanter, 1974; Green & Swets, 1966; Snodgrass, 1975), an undesirable state of affairs.

Sensory capability and response proclivity.   Fechner assumed that his psychophysical procedures for estimating thresholds provided a measure of the sensitivity of an observer. There is a serious error in that assumption: estimates of threshold are based on the *behavior* of observers, not on their *sensations.* The responses analyzed by a psychophysicist are those of a person, not of an eye, an ear, or a brain center. Watson (1973) distinguished between sensory capability and response proclivity. *Sensory capability* is a true "limit of sensitivity and resolving power of sensory systems"; while *response proclivity* is a tendency to respond to certain sensory events in a consistent way (Watson, 1973, p. 278). It seems likely that classical measures of absolute thresholds are measures of response proclivity, rather than of sensory capability.

Sensation and Confusion

The theory of signal detectability (TSD) grew out of efforts to describe and predict more precisely the performance of human observers in detection tasks. Early detection theorists drew on sources in statistical decision theory and in psychometrics (cf. Egan & Clarke, 1966; Swets, 1973; Swets, Tanner, & Birdsall, 1961). We will see how concepts from those areas relate to the psychophysical procedures of TSD. We will emphasize the yes-no procedure and will briefly review the confidence rating and forced choice procedures.

Sensory continua. The "law of comparative judgment" (Thurstone, 1927) relied heavily on the concept of "discriminal dispersion." We defined that concept and used it extensively in our discussion of psychophysical scaling (see Figure 7.2). Green and Swets (1966) describe the major similarity between TSD and the law of comparative judgment as the assumption that:

> . . . by analyzing the subject's confusion . . . , one could relate a physical measure of stimulus intensity to a psychological scale value of inferred loudness. The unit of measurement is . . . arbitrary . . . and is directly related to the confusability of the stimulus. Ultimately, then, Thurstone's procedure rests on the two assumptions: (1) that similar stimuli tend to be confused and (2) that distance can be used to represent similarity. (p. 55)

Figure 7.8 presents two pairs of discriminal dispersons. In both pairs, the curve on the left represents a dispersion produced by nonsignal events and is called "noise" or *Nonsignal (n)*. The curve on the right represents a dispersion produced by the combination of the noise background with signals added and is called *Signal (s)*. In Figure 7.8A, the difference between the means, $\bar{X}(s)$ and $\bar{X}(n)$, is one standard deviation (one unit of z), while in Figure 7.8B, the difference is two standard deviations (two units of z). Assume that the sensory continuum in Figure 7.8 is one of loudness. Because the curves overlap on the sensory continuum, the observer is confused about which of the two conditions, Signal or Nonsignal, caused a given loudness sensation. The confusion is greater in Figure 7.8A than in Figure 7.8B. We will now see how the yes-no method in TSD can be used to analyze the responses of an observer to such confusion.

The Yes-No Method

In the yes-no method, the observer monitors a series of trials. On a given trial, either a Signal or a Nonsignal occurs. After each observation, the

Figure 7.8

Theoretical distributions of dispersion on a sensory continuum for the conditions Nonsignal (n) and Signal (s) for two different values of Signal intensity.

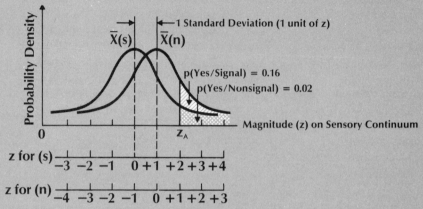

A. Distributions for weaker signal (d′ = 1.0).

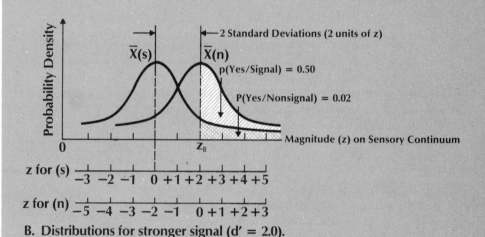

B. Distributions for stronger signal (d′ = 2.0).

observer responds "yes" or "no" to indicate a judgment that the Signal condition was present or absent. Table 7.6A presents the possible outcomes of responses in the yes-no paradigm; the four outcomes are the dependent variables from which measures of performance are derived. Table 7.6B is a *payoff matrix,* summarizing the combinations of *values* and *costs* which might apply to the outcomes in Table 7.6A. Values apply to correct responses, while costs apply to incorrect ones.

Assume that we present to an observer 100 Signal trials and 100 Nonsignal trials, in random order, and that the discriminal dispersions associated with each Signal and Nonsignal are represented in Figure 7.8A. The observer says "yes" after each trial containing an apparent Signal and "no" after apparent Nonsignals. The observer cannot tell the difference between Signal and Nonsignal, but can discriminate between

Table 7.6   Matrices associated with the Yes-No paradigm in TSD.

A. The Stimulus Response Matrix

		Responses	
		Yes	**No**
Stimulus Events	Signal (s)	HIT p(Yes/Signal)	MISS p(No/Signal)
	Nonsignal (n)	FALSE ALARM p(Yes/Nonsignal)	CORRECT REJECTION p(No/Nonsignal)

B. The Payoff Matrix

		Responses	
		Yes	**No**
Stimulus Events	Signal (s)	+ (Value of a Hit)	− (Cost of a Miss)
	Nonsignal (n)	− (Cost of a False Alarm)	+ (Value of a Correct Rejection)

loudnesses. The observer decides that any time the loudness on a trial is as loud as, or louder than, the point marked z_A on the continuum in Figure 7.8A, a "yes" response should be given. After presenting the 200 trials, we find that the response "yes" occurred 18 times: 16 times following Signal and 2 times following Nonsignal. We may calculate the following probabilities:

$$p(Yes/Signal) = \frac{16 \; Yesses \; to \; Signals}{100 \; Signal \; Trials} = 0.16, \; and$$

$$p(Yes/Nonsignal) = \frac{2 \; Yesses \; to \; Nonsignals}{100 \; Nonsignal \; Trials} = 0.02.$$

These probabilities are represented by the crosshatched areas in Figure 7.8A. We now have data concerning the confusability of the two sensory dispersions. From such data we may calculate measures of detectability and of criterion, or the willingness of the observer to respond "yes."

Measuring detectability (d'). Thurstone assumed the distance (d) between two discriminal dispersions was a measure of their confusability. In TSD, the distance is called d-prime (d') and is used as a measure of the detectability of the difference between the two dispersions or of the sensitivity of an observer. We may calculate d', based on the data from a yes-no experiment, by using the following equation:

$$d' = [z \; for \; p(Yes/Nonsignal)] - [z \; for \; p(Yes/Signal)]$$

where "z for p(Yes/Signal)" is the z-score or standard deviation, from a normal distribution, which is associated with the probability of saying "Yes" on signal trials, and "z for p(Yes/Nonsignal)" is the z-score associated with the probability of saying "Yes" on nonsignal trials. Box 7.4, an abbreviated version of a table of area under a normal curve, contains several probabilities and associated z-scores which may be used in calculating d'.

In our hypothetical experiments, we obtained the following results:

$$p(Yes/Signal) = 0.16, \; and$$
$$p(Yes/Nonsignal) = 0.02.$$

By locating the associated z-scores in Box 7.4 and by using the appropriate equation, we may calculate d' in the following way:

$$d' = (+2.0) - (+1.0) = +1.0.$$

The data from the hypothetical experiment are represented by Figure 7.8A, where the distance between the means $\overline{X}(s)$ and $\overline{X}(n)$ is one standard deviation, a distance corresponding to the calculated value of d'.

Box 7.4 Standard Scores (z) and Ordinates of the Normal Curve to use when Calculating d' and β. (An abbreviated Table of Area Under a Normal Curve as a Function of z)

Probability (p) of an event. such as p(Yes/Signal) or p(Yes/Nonsignal) (Equivalent to area under a normal curve beyond a given z.)	Standard Scores (z)	Ordinate (Height of a normal curve at a given value of z)
0.99	−2.5	0.018
0.98	−2.0	0.054
0.93	−1.5	0.130
0.84	−1.0	0.242
0.69	−0.5	˙0.352
0.50	0	0.399
0.31	+0.5	0.352
0.16	+1.0	0.242
0.07	+1.5	0.130
0.02	+2.0	0.054
0.01	+2.5	0.018

$$d' = [\text{z for p(Yes/Nonsignal)}] - [\text{z for p(Yes/Signal)}]$$

$$\beta = \frac{\text{ordinate for p(Yes/Signal)}}{\text{ordinate for p(Yes/Nonsignal)}}$$

Assume that in a second phase of our hypothetical experiment we increase the intensity of Signal relative to Nonsignal, producing the dispersions in Figure 7.8B. The observer chooses to say "yes" to loudness as great as, or greater than, z_B on the continuum in Figure 7.8B. After 200 trials, we find that the observer responded "yes" 52 times, producing the following probabilities:

$$p(Yes/Signal) = 0.50; \quad p(Yes/Nonsignal) = 0.02.$$

By locating the associated z-scores in Box 7.4 and by using the appropriate equation, we can calculate $d' = 2.0$, which corresponds to the distance, in standard deviations, between the means of Signal and Nonsignal in Figure 7.8B. The increase in Signal intensity in the second phase of our experiment produced a corresponding increase in the detectability of the Signal relative to the Nonsignal, a common occurrence.

Figure 7.9 presents the data from our two experiments plotted as functions of p(Yes/Signal) and p(Yes/Nonsignal). The curve passing through each data point represents an equal d' curve or relative operating characteristic (ROC) curve (cf. Swets, 1976). Notice that the higher the value of d', the more the ROC curve bellies toward the upper left of the probability space. ROC curves are discussed in the next section of this chapter.

Measuring criterion values: β and ROC's.   Each of the data points in Figure 7.9 is on a symmetrical ROC curve representing a different d'. In TSD, the position of a data point on an ROC curve represents a particular criterion value adopted by an observer and is called beta (β). In our example of loudness detection, β represents the position on the loudness continuum in Figure 7.8 above which the observer says, "Yes, a Signal occurred." To calculate β based on data from a yes-no experiment, we use the following equation:

$$\beta = \frac{\text{ordinate for p(Yes/Signal)}}{\text{ordinate for p(Yes/nonsignal)}}$$

where "ordinate" refers to the ordinate or height of a normal curve at the z-score associated with a given probability. Ordinate values are included in Box 7.4.

In the first phase of our hypothetical yes-no experiment, we obtained the following results:

$$p(Yes/Signal) = 0.16, \text{ and}$$
$$p(Yes/Nonsignal) = 0.02.$$

By consulting Box 7.4, we may obtain the following associated ordinate values:

$$\text{ordinate for p(Yes/Signal)} = 0.242, \text{ and}$$
$$\text{ordinate for p(Yes/Nonsignal)} = 0.054.$$

Figure 7.9

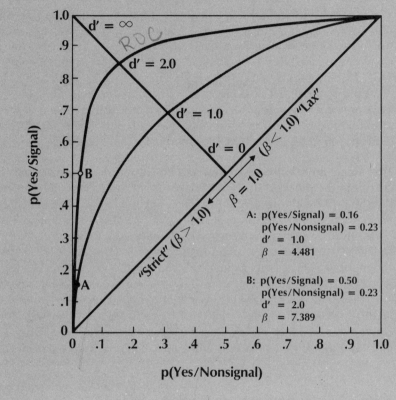

Relative operating characteristic (ROC) curves for data from two hypothetical yes-no experiments.

A: p(Yes/Signal) = 0.16
p(Yes/Nonsignal) = 0.23
d′ = 1.0
β = 4.481

B: p(Yes/Signal) = 0.50
p(Yes/Nonsignal) = 0.23
d′ = 2.0
β = 7.389

We may then calculate β in the following manner:

$$\beta = \frac{0.242}{0.054} = 4.481.$$

In the second phase of our yes-no experiment, we obtained the following results:

$$p(Yes/Signal) = 0.50 \text{ and}$$
$$p(Yes/Nonsignal) = 0.02.$$

Obtaining the associated ordinate values from Box 7.4, we may calculate β in the following manner:

$$\beta = \frac{0.399}{0.054} = 7.389.$$

The value of β in the second phase was higher than that in the first phase. The meaning of an increase in β will be discussed later in this chapter.

The observer is free to select a value of β at any point on the sensory continuum. For a given pair of dispersions, there is a single value of d'. The locus of all the values of β associated with a given d' is a specific ROC curve. Table 7.7 and Figure 7.9 summarize the possible positions where β may be located. Recall that threshold measures are sensitive to changes in probability of a stimulus and in response contingencies. In TSD, β (criterion) is sensitive to such changes, while d' (sensitivity) is not. One of the major advantages of TSD over threshold theory is that TSD provides two independent indices of performance, d' and β, while threshold theory provides only p(Yes). We will now examine influences of the payoff matrix and of the probability of signal occurrence on β.

How signal probability, p(s), influences β.   In threshold experiments, increases in the probability of a signal, p(s), lead to decreases in estimated threshold (AL); the reverse is also true. Such changes in estimated AL result from changes in the probability that an observer will say "yes," p(yes). Rather than saying threshold changes as a function of p(s), we should say p(yes) changes as a function of p(s). However, classical psychophysics has no way to distinguish a change in p(yes) from a change in sensitivity. Signal detection theory allows us to make that distinction.

Table 7.8 summarizes the results of a hypothetical yes-no experiment involving three phases in which payoffs for responses were held constant but in which p(s) increased in each successive phase. Using the table and the equations in Box 7.4, d' and β were calculated for p(Yes/

Table 7.7   Description of various values of β.

Position of β on the sensory continuum	Relationship of Ordinate Values	Values of β	Name applied to that range of β
1. At the point where Signal and Nonsignal Curves intersect	Ord.(Signal) = Ord.(Nonsignal)	$\beta = 1.0$	"Neutral" or "Moderate"
2. To the left of the point where Signal and Nonsignal intersect	Ord.(Signal) < Ord.(Nonsignal)	$\beta < 1.0$	"Lax"
3. To the right of the point where Signal and Nonsignal intersect	Ord.(Signal) > Ord.(Nonsignal)	$\beta > 1.0$	"Strict"

Table 7.8   Results of a hypothetical Yes-No experiment consisting of three phases in which payoffs were held constant, while the probability of a signal, p(s), varied.

Payoff Matrix:

		Responses	
Stimulus Events		Yes	No
s		+$1	−$1
n		−$1	+$1

Phase	p(s)	Data
A	.20	Yes No s .16 .84 n .02 .98 $d' = 1.0$ $\beta = 4.481$
B	.50	Yes No s .50 .50 n .16 .84 $d' = 1.0$ $\beta = 1.649$
C	.80	Yes No s .93 .07 n .69 .31 $d' = 1.0$ $\beta = 0.369$

Signal) and p(s). As p(s) increased, d' remained constant at 1.0, but β decreased. In the terminology of TSD, criterion went from "strict" to "moderate" to "lax." Figure 7.10 presents the data from this experiment as points A, B, and C for $d' = 1.0$. The other data in that figure will be described in later sections of this chapter.

In general, the influence of p(s) on β is as follows: When the Signal occurs infrequently, the observer demands a strong sensation before saying the Signal occurred; but when the Signal occurs frequently, the observer accepts weak sensations as indications of the Signal. Data from published research are very similar to those in our example in Table 7.8 and Figure 7.6 (cf. Galanter & Holman, 1967; Swets, Tanner, & Birdsall, 1961; Tanner, Swets, & Green, 1956; Linker, Moore, & Galanter, 1964).

Figure 7.10

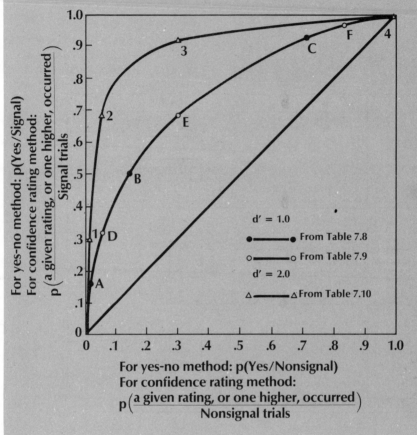

Relative operating characteristics (ROCs) based on data from hypothetical experiments described in Tables 7.8, 7.9, and 7.10.

How response contingencies influence β. In threshold experiments, increases in rewards for saying "yes" lead to decreases in AL while increases in punishments for saying "yes" lead to increases in AL. As was the case with changes in p(s), a change in response contingencies actually leads to changes in p(yes), not to changes in sensitivity. Again, classical psychophysical methods cannot distinguish between the two types of change; sensitivity and criterion are confounded in Fechnerian measurements. Detection theory, which provides independent measures of sensitivity and criterion, allows us to analyze the influences of contingencies, or payoffs, on β.

Table 7.9 presents data from a hypothetical yes-no experiment consisting of three phases in which p(s) was held constant but in which payoffs varied over three combinations. Payoffs in phase D favored saying "no" more than saying "yes"; in E, payoffs were equal for "yes" and "no"; and in F, payoffs favored "yes" more than "no." As payoffs changed, d' remained constant while β changed. The criterion went from "strict" to "moderate" to "lax." In such experiments, when payoffs favor "yes," observers accept weak sensations as Signal; but when payoffs favor "no," they demand strong sensations before saying "yes." The data from Table 7.9 are plotted in Figure 7.10 as points D, E, and F, for d' = 1.0. Published data from experiments in which payoffs vary are similar to those in our example. They indicate that subjects establish and change their criterion in a way which increases their long-term gains from the

Table 7.9   Results of a hypothetical Yes-No experiment consisting of three phases in which probabilities of Signal and Nonsignal were held constant but in which payoffs were varied.

Number of Signal trials (s) =   100, p(s) =   0.50
Number of Nonsignal trials (n) = 100, p(n) =   0.50
Number of trials =   200, p(s) + p(n) = 1.00

Phase	Payoffs	Data
D	Yes No s +$1 −$1 n −$2 +$2	Yes No s .31 .69 n .07 .93 d' = 1.0, β = 4.481
E	Yes No s +$1 −$1 n −$1 +$1	Yes No s .69 .31 n .31 .69 d' = 1.0, β = 1.000
F	Yes No s +$3 −$3 n −$1 +$1	Yes No s .98 .02 n .84 .16 d' = 1.0, β = 0.223

payoff matrix (cf. Galanter & Holman, 1967; Green & Swets, 1966; Swets, Tanner, & Birdsall, 1961).

Summary of yes-no method.   The yes-no method incorporates most of the basic assumptions of TSD. On a given trial, the observer is assumed to receive a sample sensory event drawn from one of two possible sensory dispersions. The observer is assumed (*a*) to calculate the likelihood that the sample came from either of the two dispersions, (*b*) to weigh the relative values and costs of accepting the hypotheses that the sample was from Signal or from Nonsignal, and (*c*) to respond in a manner that maximizes long-term positive gains.

Confidence Rating Method

To generate an ROC curve with the yes-no paradigm, an experimenter may vary stimulus probabilities or payoffs across experimental sessions. These experimental changes induce the observer to change criterion and produce data points at various positions on the ROC. This can be a time-consuming procedure. A more direct approach for producing an ROC curve is the confidence rating procedure. In this procedure, the observer uses several categories of response to indicate the uncertainty of decisions concerning Signal and Nonsignal events.

Data from an experiment in which an observer used four response categories to indicate the degree of subjective certainty that Signal or Nonsignal occurred are summarized in Table 7.10. The table shows the number of times and the probability that each rating was used for each of the stimulus conditions. The bottom row in each half of the table presents the probability that a given rating, or one higher, was used. For example, the observer used rating 3 or higher for 69 Signals but for only 7 Nonsignals while rating 2 or higher was applied to 93 Signals but to 31 Nonsignals.

The summed probabilities from the bottom rows of Table 7.10 are plotted in Figure 7.9 as points 1, 2, 3, and 4. Each data point represents a different criterion along the ROC curve. An estimate of d' may be obtained by using the z scores for the two summed probabilities associated with one of the rating categories. Using rating 2:

$$d' = (z \text{ for } .31) - (z \text{ for } .93) = (+0.5) - (-1.5) = 2.0.$$

The confidence rating procedure and the yes-no method tend to produce similar estimates of d' when used by the same observer (Egan, Schulman, & Greenberg, 1959; Swets, Tanner, & Birdsall, 1961; Watson, Rilling, & Bourbon, 1964). The agreement of estimates of d' between the two methods and the stability of d' as a measure of sensitivity are sources of satisfaction to many psychophysicists (cf. Green & Swets, 1966).

Table 7.10   Data from a hypothetical confidence rating experiment.

Rating Category		Certain Nonsignal	Possible Nonsignal	Possible Signal	Certain Signal
Rating Number		1	2	3	4
Signal	n	7	24	38	31
trials	p	.07	.24	.38	.31
(N = 100)	Σp	1.00	.93	.69	.31
Nonsignal	n	69	24	6	1
trials	p	.69	.24	.06	.01
(N = 100)	Σp	1.00	.31	.07	.01

N =   Number of trials.
n =   Number of times a given rating category was used.
p =   n/N, probability that a given rating category was used.
Σp =   the sum of all p's from category 4 down the scale to a given category. Σp represents the probability that the observer used a given category or one higher on the scale.

Forced-Choice Procedure

The forced-choice procedure allows estimates of sensitivity that are free from the effects of changes in criterion. On each trial, two observation intervals occur: one interval contains stimulus A; the other, stimulus B. The observer must report which interval contains the "correct" stimulus. The order of A and B varies randomly over a series of trials. Stimuli A and B might represent Signal and Nonsignal conditions. The possible outcomes of a two-interval forced-choice experiment are presented in Table 7.11.

The dependent variable in the forced-choice method is percent correct responses, P(c), a measure of sensitivity. Criterion, β, is not measured in the forced-choice paradigm; but observers may show a bias toward responding in one of two intervals. Watson (1973) discussed several ways to correct for such biases; the simplest procedure is to demonstrate to the observer the probabilities of stimuli occurring in the two intervals. Box 7.5 describes the implications of TSD for "subliminal perception," a concept which developed from incorrect interpretations of the classical model of sensitivity. Data from forced-choice experiments helped clarify the issue.

In addition to explaining subliminal perception, TSD has been applied to examining, or re-examining, many issues and problems in psychology. Frequently, the result of applying TSD to a traditional problem

Table 7.11   Matrix of possible outcomes in a two-interval forced-choice experiment.

	Responses	
	"Interval 1"	"Interval 2"
Interval 1	Correct 1/1	Incorrect 2/1
Interval 2	Incorrect 1/2	Correct 2/2

$$\text{Percent Correct} = \frac{\text{Number Correct } [(1/1) + (2/2)]}{\text{Total Number of Trials}}$$

is to modify earlier interpretations or theories. Detection theory has been applied to analyses of human learning and memory, psychopathology, decision making, obesity, animal learning, and speech communication (cf. Coombs, Dawes, & Tversky, 1970; Green & Swets, 1966; Snodgrass, 1975; Swets, 1973).

PSYCHOPHYSICS: IMPLICATIONS AND PROSPECTS

Research in psychophysics and perception continues to focus on basic issues of methods and of quantification. In psychophysical scaling, Stevens (1961) proposed to "honor Fechner and repeal his law." Savage (1970) proposed to "abandon the concept of psychological magnitude, thus abandoning both Stevens' law and Fechner's law, and any other law" of the psychophysical form (p. 408). Stevens (1975) considered the comments of Savage to represent a retreat from the concept of psychophysical measurement. At another level, Anderson (1974) challenged traditional scaling in general, and magnitude estimation in particular. Anderson considered the power law of Stevens to be inadequate and to represent no more than an exercise in fitting curves to data. Anderson proposed an algebraic model of *psychological* scaling which he considered to be more basic than *psychophysical* scaling.

Psychologists continue to use both Gestalt principles and measure of information in research on perception. Pomerantz (1977) examined relationships between the Gestalt concept of pattern goodness and the speed of encoding of visual information. A student of W. R. Garner, he used dot patterns differing in goodness as stimuli in a recognition task. He concluded that good patterns are retrieved from memory more rapidly than poor patterns, but that goodness is unrelated to the time

Box 7.5 TSD and "Subliminal Perception": Correcting a Misperception

On every trial in a two-interval, forced-choice paradigm, an observer attends to two intervals, decides which of the two contained a Signal and responds accordingly. In a masking problem, a signal occurs in a background of noise which may be easily confused with the signal. After a series of 100 trials in which the observer discriminates the correct interval 80 times [p(c) = 0.80], it is not unusual for the observer to report, "I only heard 5 or 6 of them that time." The statement contradicts the data, yet such reports are common (cf. Green & Swets, 1966). The results do not mean that the observer detected the stimuli subliminally, or "without awareness." In fact, the concept of *subliminal perception* (literally, "below threshold perception") rests upon a misunderstanding of the measurement of thresholds.

In 1860, Fechner defined absolute threshold (AL) as the stimulus intensity which an observer says is present 50 percent of the times it occurs. Obviously, for any threshold stimulus (liminal stimulus) there are weaker stimuli ("subliminal" stimuli) to which the observer will respond "yes" less than 50 percent of the times they occur. Ogives or psychophysical functions based on data from estimates of AL clearly present a range of stimuli which, by definition, are "subliminal," and which will be detected with predictable regularity. A psychophysical threshold is a *distribution* of stimulus values, the mean of which is arbitrarily chosen to represent the entire distribution.

In addition, an estimate of AL is an estimate of behavioral threshold, the stimulus intensity at which the observer *says* the stimulus is present. Response contingencies and the probability of stimulus occurrence exert strong influences on what observers say, or upon their response criterion. Under contingencies which discourage "yes" responses, observers produce high estimates of threshold. Later, under contingencies which encourage "yesses," the same observers may produce estimates that are lower and that appear to be subliminal when compared to the earlier estimates. Measures of sensitivity in TSD tend to be independent of factors that influence criterion, or the probability of saying yes, and thus are stable during changes in contingencies. Furthermore, the sensitivity of an observer estimated in a TSD paradigm is greater than that estimated by threshold paradigms. Thus, correct responses in a forced-choice paradigm are "subliminal" only in a semantic sense. Although debates concerning subliminal discrimination, or "discrimination without awareness," continue (cf. Brandeis & Lubow, 1975; Dawson, 1973), for the most part they are lacking in appreciation of basic psychophysics and detection theory.

Box 7.6   Gestalt Principles and Visual Detection

A common paradigm in studies of the detection of visual signals involves a target stimulus presented in an array of nontarget items. Detectability of the target generally decreases as a function of increased similarity between targets and nontargets and as a function of increases in the number of nontarget items. Attempts to explain such effects often invoke the concept of interactions between the neural pathways or channels carrying information about targets and nontargets (cf. Estes, 1972, 1974). In two related experiments, Banks and Prinzmetal (1976) and Prinzmetal and Banks (1977) challenged the "interactive channel" hypothesis as an explanation for visual detection phenomena. They examined effects on detection of the overall configurations formed by targets and nontargets. In both experiments, they concluded that Gestalt principles related to pattern goodness were of major importance.

Banks and Prinzmetal (1976) studied the detection of visual targets in a forced-choice paradigm. On each trial, one of a small number of possible targets occurred in an array of nontarget items and subjects indicated which of the targets occurred. Stimulus arrays remained on until the subject detected and identified the target. Reaction time, recorded from the onset of the stimulus array, and accuracy of identification were the dependent variables. In the conditions of greatest interest and significance, stimuli were presented in two types of arrays; type one, in which the target and the nontargets grouped together to form a "good figure" or pattern, such as a line of elements or the corners of an imaginary square, and type two, in which the target and the nontarget items did not group together, but formed separate perceptual groupings. In both types, the target was equally close to nontargets. There were more nontarget items in type-two arrays than in type-one arrays. Reaction times were significantly shorter for type-two arrays than for type-one arrays. Banks and Prinzmetal concluded that if a target and an array of nontargets group to form a good figure detection of the target is more difficult than if they do not group into a good figure.

Prinzmetal and Banks (1977) used a forced-choice paradigm similar to that of Banks and Prinzmetal (1976) to study the effects on detection of the Gestalt principle of good continuation. In one phase of the experiment, stimuli were presented briefly in arrays similar to those shown in

Figure 7.11. On a given trial, the target might be grouped in a line with most of the nontargets or to the side of the line of nontargets. When the target was not grouped in the line of nontargets, it was positioned to be closer, on the average, to nontargets than when it was in line with them. Reaction times for correct identifications of targets, measured from the onset of the array, were significantly shorter for targets out of line than for those in line with nontargets. Prinzmetal and Banks interpret their results as indicating that grouping of stimulus elements according to the Gestalt principle of good continuation occurs prior to the processing of differences between the targets and the nontargets in an array. Should the target be grouped with the nontargets, then additional time is required to locate it and respond to its presence.

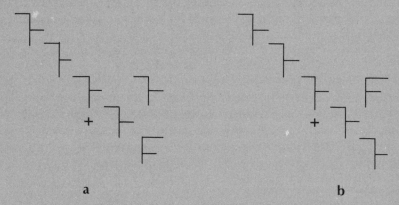

a   b

Figure 7.11 Examples of stimulus arrays used to test effects of overall stimulus configuration on the detectability of targets (F) presented with an array of nontargets (⊤). In array a, the target groups with the nontargets to form a line, while in array b, the target does not group with the nontargets. The small fixation cross is shown in its position relative to the arrays but was not visible during presentations of the arrays. From Prinzmetal and Banks (1977, p. 390).

required to encode information about the stimuli. Bower (1974) summarized research with infants concerning the influence of learning on the Gestalt principle of good continuation. Box 7.6 describes experiments that examined relationships between visual detection and the Gestalt principles of "good figure" and "good continuation."

Luce and Green (1974) summarized recent progress in signal detection theory. Their collaboration symbolizes one major development in TSD; Green participated in the early elaboration of TSD, while Luce advocated threshold concepts and the application of learning principles to psychophysics. Together, Luce and Green considered problems associated with measuring detection performance in settings where signals occur at random times and where there are no special cues to indicate when the observer should attend to the signal or should respond. Their research involved analyses of sequential effects in detection tasks. Luce and Green used response latency as an index of the time required to process stimulus material and to decide on a response; response latency increases as detection becomes more difficult. Box 7.7 describes a related study by Jesteadt, Luce, and Green (1977) which analyzes sequential effects in magnitude estimations of loudness.

During the first century of research on psychophysics and perception, basic experimental methods and tactics were developed. Recently, many of those tactics were combined, along with concepts from other areas of psychology, to form the information processing paradigm. Future research in psychophysics is likely to continue that trend. The classical Gestalt principles will continue to stimulate research employing methods and measures from information theory and TSD. All the major psychophysical methods will be used to analyze components of the information processing paradigm, from initial encoding and detection of stimuli to their interpretation at higher levels. Research concerning the development of perception in infants will begin to incorporate more methods from contemporary psychophysics, as will research concerning "states of consciousness." As a result, the quality of data and the meaningfulness of theory in both areas will be enhanced. Significant progress also should occur in establishing psychophysiological correlates of psychophysical processes; such correlates will be of value both to theoreticians and to applied psychologists.

This chapter began with quotes from Fechner concerning the early development of psychophysics and from Einstein concerning the evolutionary nature of scientific theory. Both statements seem appropriate to the material reviewed in this chapter. From its limited, academic origins, psychophysics grew rapidly into a major area of research and theory. In the process, psychophysics provided a paradigm for the emerging science of psychology. It continues to be a fertile research tactic for analyzing both new and old phenomena. In a science generally devoted to the analysis of behavioral responses and of their antecedent stimuli, psycho-

Box 7.7 Sequential Effects in Magnitude Estimation and Absolute Judgment of Loudness

Sequential effects frequently occur in psychophysical research. In studies concerning loudness, such effects would appear as increases or decreases in the apparent loudness of a given signal as a function of the apparent loudness of an earlier signal or as a function of the overt response made to an earlier signal. Ward and Lockhead (1971) described sequential effects in absolute judgments of loudness. They concluded that such effects extended over as many as five trials. Cross (1973) described similar effects for magnitude estimations of loudness.

In an experiment designed to analyze distributions of magnitude estimations of loudness, Jesteadt, Luce, and Green (1977) found it necessary first to determine the extent of sequential effects on such estimations. On each trial, they presented a 1000 Hz tone of 500 msec duration. There were 27 possible signals, ranging in intensity from 36–88 dB (SPL) in 2 dB steps. Observers were instructed to assign a number to each tone so that the ratio of the numbers was the same as the ratio of the loudnesses. Jesteadt, Luce, and Green found evidence of sequential effects in their data. However, after analyzing the data with a simple linear regression model, they concluded that the sequential effects extended only from one trial to the next, not over five trials. Furthermore, the magnitude of the effect varied inversely with the difference in intensity between successive stimuli. Jesteadt et al. concluded that earlier claims that sequential effects in magnitude estimation and absolute judgment persisted for five trials were based on compounding of the effects by inappropriate data analyses. Such a conclusion is significant, for severe and extended sequential effects would seriously limit the usefulness of the magnitude estimation paradigm.

physics is concerned with both in the most rigorous, quantitative sense. Perhaps for that reason, paradigm shifts in psychophysics tend to exert basic influences far beyond their immediate application. They often deal with the nature of knowledge itself.

SUMMARY

The work of Gustav Fechner marked the beginning of psychophysics and of experimental psychology. Fechner devised quantitative methods to study absolute and differential sensitivity and to construct scales relating stimulus magnitude to response magnitude. For over a century, his thinking dominated research and theory concerning sensation and perception. His methods also provided basic tactics for research in areas as diverse as learning, memory, personality structure, psychometrics and cognition. Now we know that his measure of sensitivity, the threshold, hopelessly confounds sensitivity with factors related to response bias and to response criterion. His assumptions concerning psychophysical scaling are also vulnerable to serious criticism. In spite of subsequent challenges and revisions to his methods, however, Fechner's contribution to psychology is enormous. He set the fledgling experimental science on a rigorously quantitative course and provided its first general paradigm and tactics.

Perception functions to provide awareness of the overall patterns and organizations in stimulus arrays, as well as to provide reductionistic analyses of individual stimulus events. Gestalt theory was an early attempt to stress the integrative, holistic aspects of perception. Gestalt theory relied heavily on demonstration as a basic tactic. More recently, information theory has provided quantitative methods for analyzing the structures of stimulus arrays and of associated patterns of responses. Both the generally descriptive concepts of Gestalt theory and the quantitatively precise tactics of information theory continue to play major roles in perceptual research and theory.

Major revisions have occurred in basic psychophysics. Signal detection theory provides independent measures of the sensitivity and response criteria of observers. Analyses of old phenomena and of new problems, using tactics based on TSD, form one basis of a major paradigm shift occurring in psychophysics. Another basis of that shift is found in the development of alternatives to Fechner's concepts of scaling. The method of direct magnitude estimation developed by Stevens differs radically from the methods of Fechner. Knowledge and use of methods and models derived from TSD and from direct psychophysical scaling are working their way into most areas of contemporary psychology.

Research tactics derived from psychophysical methods and concepts derived from psychophysical models are significant factors contributing to development of the information processing paradigm. Within that paradigm, basic psychophysical methods provide the means to isolate factors in stimulus-response associations which lead to strong inferences about various stages in information processing. Contemporary psychophysics attempts to deal with the ways in which response contingencies influence detection performance. In a major change from earlier thinking, decision processes are assumed to be major factors in psychophysical tasks.

QUESTIONS

1. Describe the three major psychophysical methods developed by Fechner. How may each be used to estimate absolute and differential thresholds? Why is it necessary to estimate thresholds, rather than to measure them precisely?

2. Define each of the following sources of "error" in psychophysics and describe control procedures for each: habituation, anticipation, time errors, and space errors.

3. Compare and contrast the following pairs of terms related to psychophysical scaling: (a) prothetic continua and metathetic continua, (b) direct and indirect scaling, and (c) sensory attributes and semantic labels.

4. Describe psychophysical scaling procedures related to each of the four major types of number scales.

5. Compare and contrast Weber's law, Fechner's law, and Stevens' law in psychophysics.

6. Distinguish between real movement, the phi phenomenon, and movement aftereffects. How were the latter two used by Gestalt psychologists?

7. What is the law of prägnanz or good figure? How does the concept of good figure relate to the concepts of information, uncertainty, and redundancy? How does the research of Handel and Garner contribute to understanding good figures?

8. What are the effects of (a) probability of occurrence of a stimulus and of (b) response contingencies on estimates of absolute threshold? How do those effects relate to Watson's distinction between sensory capability and response proclivity?

9. Describe the three major psychophysical procedures in the theory of signal detectability. Which ones may be used to produce ROC curves and how? What are d' and β and what factors influence their magnitudes? What are the advantages of TSD over classical psychophysics?

10. How do the tactics and concepts of psychophysical research relate to the information processing model in psychology?

Basic Processes In Learning: Concepts and Issues

8
Chapter

BY D. CHRIS ANDERSON

> Give me a dozen healthy infants, well-formed, and my own specified world to bring them up in and I'll guarantee to take any one at random and train him to become any type of specialist I might select—doctor, lawyer, artist, merchant, chief, and yes, even beggar-man and thief, regardless of his talents, penchants, tendencies, abilities, vocations, and race of his ancestors. I am going beyond my facts and I admit it, but so have the advocates of the contrary and they have been doing it for many thousands of years.
>
> (Watson, 1925)

This 1925 statement of Watson's, perhaps his most controversial, stands at the extreme nurture end of the nature-nurture controversy. It suggests great confidence in our potential to compile an exhaustive, understandable set of laws of learning and a technology of how to apply them. As it now turns out, over fifty years later, Watson's optimism has yet to be vindicated.

For one thing, Watson was overly selective in focusing only upon inheritance as the major alternative to learning in determining behavior. Many other classes of variables or processes that are not commonly viewed as sources of learning can affect performance. Developmental variables, such as those related to aging, tissue damage, and behavior changes due to strong physical exertion or to prolonged and repetitive stimulation, can all qualify as causal agents in producing changes in behavior. It is useful to know how to distinguish these alternative determinants of behavior from learned and inherited factors.

For another, there is much evidence that genetic variables can predictably affect the behavior of organisms, although it is not clear whether this is because there are one-to-one correlations between genes and the presence of specific behaviors or whether gene activity only indirectly influences behavioral ontogeny. Perhaps the most comprehensive statement summarizing current views is that of Moltz (1965) who concludes that: "the growth process, in establishing the general structural and functional plan of the nervous system, gradually becomes refined and elaborated through environmental interactions—[it is] a substrate, in other words, *that essentially determines the directions and limits of a response repertoire but not its details*" (italics added).

A third reason why Watson's statement was premature is that contemporary learning psychologists are probably less certain of their understanding of the nature of learning than was Watson. From this perspective, we will focus our attention upon the basic procedures and research paradigms that have been used by learning psychologists rather than upon any particular view as to what constitutes the "learning process."

THE DEFINITION OF LEARNING

Many psychologists believe that *practice* is a sufficient, if not necessary, condition for defining *learning*. A change in behavior that results from practice may more likely be taken as a reflection of learning than, say, as a reflection of maturation, habituation, or fatigue. Since practice can mean different things to different psychologists, a definition is needed.

Is Response Occurrence Necessary?

The operation that defines practice in most experiments entails repeated stimulus presentations and corresponding responses from the organism being trained. A controversy has arisen because of the problem of whether or not response occurrence is actually required as part of this definition. The reason for this controversy stems from a failure by many theorists to separate their theoretical conceptions about learning from an operational definition that distinguishes the concept from others (Rescorla & Holland, 1976).

The cognitive view.   The reason why the issue of responding, as part of a definition of practice, is so important is due to an ongoing theoretical controversy over what learning is all about. This controversy was first touched on in Chapter 1 in connection with our discussion of cognitive vs. S-R conceptions of behavior. The cognitive view of learning can be characterized in perceptual terms, the argument being that learning is essentially a matter of forming perceptions about significant environmental relationships. Practice thus boils down to perceiving, perhaps through repeated exposure, the importance of relationships among stimuli. This perception of significant relationships is the major antecedent for learning. Presumably, the key "responses" involved are those of "observing" or "attending" to those features of the world that are part of the important relationship. Some stimuli may receive more attention than others (Mackintosh, 1975), and stimulus importance may vary from species to species (Bolles, 1974), but any behavior other than that of observation is viewed as unnecessary for learning to occur. From this theoretical position, whatever is learned is a matter of central-state processing and reorganization, not a matter of repeated responding.

The S-R view.   The S-R interpretation of practice is that actual responding, along with stimulus occurrence, is required for learning. Learning is thus a matter of forming connections or associations between stimuli and behaviors, so-called S-R connections. Changes in the central state mediate these S-R connections, but these changes are only part of the learning process. The S-R view is that specific behaviors, not perceptual relationships, are actually learned. But the S-R view is not that new behaviors, foreign to an organism's repertoire, are learned; instead, new connections are formed between stimuli and an already existing but heretofore unconnected behavior.

Considerable research has dealt with the necessity of responding as a defining ingredient of practice. The general research strategy has been to restrict the opportunity to respond (Thistlethwaite, 1951) or to eliminate responding altogether during practice. Rats have been carried through mazes on toy carts, so that they could "see" but not "respond" in the presence of the maze stimuli, and then tested to determine if the experience reduced errors of maze performance (McNamara, Long, & Wike, 1956). The motor response system has been surgically or pharmacologically immobilized during practice so that the response to be learned could not occur, with testing for learning conducted upon the response system's regeneration (Beck & Doty, 1957). And subjects have been skeletally immobilized during the learning-practice phase by the drug d-tubocurarine, which immobilizes the skeletal but not the autonomic nervous system; tests for learning are then given upon recovery from the drug's effects (Solomon & Turner, 1962). In most cases, these experiments have shown behavioral changes during testing that could be taken as evidence for learning. However, in all cases the interpretation of central-state learning has been challenged by S-R theorists because of alleged methodological flaws. Basic arguments have taken several forms: (1) the response to be learned was insufficiently restricted and thus occurred in a repeated yet covert fashion; or (2) some other response, such as an autonomic reaction, was practiced and influenced the reaction under study during testing (cf. Hearst, 1975; Trapold & Overmier, 1972).

A compromise.   In spite of the conceptual differences between the cognitive and S-R positions on learning, there are some important similarities. One similarity is that both positions are associationistic in that, as a result of practice, a hypothetical connection of some sort is seen to result. They differ primarily upon what the association is between and how it is formed. Second, both entail probabilistic concepts of behavior in that the actual performance of what is learned is seen to depend upon many factors other than learning *per se*. Finally, neither view has been stated with such precision as to generate experiments that clearly predict differential outcomes. Presently, there is substantial similarity in the predictions that each generates about the effects of various manipulations on learning.

Is Reinforcement Necessary?

A second area of controversy is whether *reinforcement* should be a part of the definition of practice. Although the concept of reinforcement has been itself defined in many ways, it can be understood here as the presence during practice of a strong, behaviorally effective event. The procedures of many learning experiments frequently contain just such a stimulus event. For example, classical conditioning frequently involves the pairing of a relatively neutral stimulus with a much stronger, reflex-producing stimulus, the reinforcer. Similarly, the procedures of instrumental and operant learning also conclude with the presentation or removal of a strong, reflex-eliciting event (the reward or punisher) following the occurrence of a specified response. Many learning scientists consider the presence of "strong" stimuli as a sufficient, if not necessary, antecedent aspect of learning (Kimble, 1961, 1967). Yet there are a number of situations where no strong stimulus seems to have been part of antecedent practice but behavioral changes are nevertheless observed.

The Consequent Event: Behavior Change

Operational definitions must contain a consequent—a statement of what is being measured as the result of the antecedent events. The important question here is whether there is a particular kind of behavior change that can be taken as the unique result of practice. The answer is that there may be, but qualifications are needed. In general, many concede that a behavior change must be *relatively permanent,* or lasting, in order to qualify as learned. This position is in opposition to more short-lived changes in performance that typically characterize fatigue, adaptation, habituation, and satiation.

By what standards can a behavior change be judged to be relatively permanent? At a more complex level, by what operations can one say that behavior has changed, whether or not that change is relatively permanent? Consider the following as an illustration of some confusion that surrounds these aspects of the definition of learning. Having learned through practice to depress a lever with its forepaw for food, a rat does not continually engage in bar-pressing regardless of the circumstances. A specification of conditions other than pre-practice performance level is needed to know when and what to measure in connection with a "behavioral change." These conditions may include the following: that the animal is hungry, that a bar is present, that the animal is healthy, and so forth. In a sense, then, it can be argued that the animal has not learned an actual behavior change, but instead a *behavior-change potential.* Having repeatedly practiced bar-pressing, it has acquired a *relatively permanent potential* to bar-press in the future—given the right circumstances. It is in this connection that learning can be seen to be a dispositional concept. The subject has a disposition, a behavior potential, to bar-press when certain conditions are present. The behavior change of prime concern is designated by the fact that prior to practice these same conditions were not accompanied by the behavior under study. Box 8.1 reports a study which depicts learning as a behavior potential.

There remains the question of exactly how durable the behavior change must be in order to qualify as a reflection of learning. In terms of the phrase "relatively permanent," the question can be asked "relative to what?" Relative to performance changes that accompany fatigue? Habituation? Maturation? Or relative to any response changes that otherwise do not perseverate throughout the remaining life span of the organism? Again, just as was the case for the practice-response controversy, many have resorted to assumptions and theory as to what learning is in an attempt to answer this question. Unfortunately, much headway has yet to be made in achieving consensus on the precise temporal duration necessary to specify learning. Prominent learning theorists such as Guthrie (1935) and Estes (1959) have suggested that it should in theory be possible to eliminate learned responses on a single trial, while Pavlov (1927), Hull (1943), and Logan (1970) have reasoned that, once learned, the change in behavior potential remains throughout the life of the organism.

To summarize, learning generally can be defined as *a relatively durable behavior change that results from practice.* Table 8.1 presents this definition and specifies antecedent and consequent conditions and features of these conditions that represent issues or controversies.

Definitions and Theories of Learning

Any definition of learning will probably include a combination of specific conditions and theoretical preconceptions. In response to the question "what is learning," it would be safe to conclude that any answer

Box 8.1 Behavior Potential in a Cognitive-Oriented Experiment

To further illustrate the concept of *behavior potential,* consider the classic experiment of Tolman and Honzik (1930) in which three groups of rats were trained to learn a 14-unit T-maze. Doors separated each unit of the maze so that once a rat correctly traversed a segment, it could not retrace its path. For the first ten trials (one/day), one group was hungry and received food reward (Group HR) upon entrance to the goal area; the other two groups were hungry, but received no rewards. Figure 8.1 shows the performance of the three groups on initial trials and illustrates that the rewarded group exhibited more improvement in terms of a reduction in total errors than the two control groups. Following the initial trials, reward was given from trial 11 onward to one of the two non-rewarded groups (HNR-R) but not to the other (Group HNR). An immediate reduction in errors to the level of Group HR occurred for Group HNR-R, this improvement being maintained over further trials.

Because the performance change on Trial 11 for Group HNR-R to the level of Group HR occurred immediately, we could conclude that the maze training over the prior ten trials had produced equivalent learning for both groups. This learning can be seen as a behavior potential for the non-rewarded groups over the initial trials, not manifested because of the absence of an essential defining condition, namely, food. It can be deduced from this analysis that had Tolman and Honzik (1930) given food to Group HNR on trial 16 or so, these subjects would have shown an immediate performance change to the levels of the two rewarded groups; the special condition, food, was essential for revealing the behavior potential.

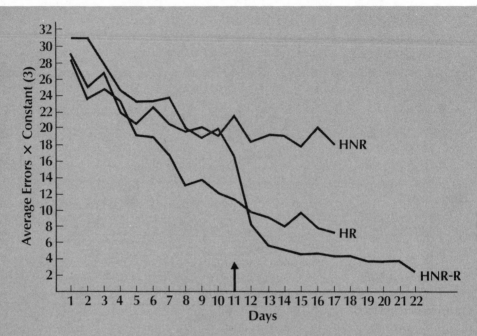

Figure 8.1 Error curves for Groups HR, HNR-R, and HNR. Group HR was given food reward at the end of a 14-unit T-maze on every trial (one trial/day) while Group HNR-R did not receive reward until trial 11. Group HNR never was given reward. After Tolman and Honzik (1930).

Table 8.1 **Summary of the antecedent and consequent conditions that define the term "learning," along with their associated controversies.**

ANTECEDENT CONDITION   CONSEQUENT CONDITION

LEARNING

1. And central-state,
   S-S associations?
2. And S-R associations?

PRACTICE   RELATIVELY PERMANENT
                                                CHANGE IN BEHAVIOR

1. And responding?   1. How permanent is permanent?
   a. Stimulus exposure plus   2. Change in behavior, or in
      observing responses?   behavior potential?
   b. Stimulus exposure plus
      repetitious responding?
2. And reinforcement?

given will largely depend upon whom one asks. A central-state, cognitive theorist may say that learning is a matter of forming predictions about the spacing and temporal nature of events, these predictions being the consequence of repeated exposures to the environment. In support of this definition, experimental results could be given that suggest that relatively permanent behavior changes occur even when organisms are prevented from responding during training or practice sessions. In contrast, an S-R theorist might state that an association between responses and their contiguous stimuli is formed. In support of this view, experiments could be marshalled that contradict those mentioned by the central-state theorist and support an S-R position (cf. Hull, 1952).

BASIC PARADIGMS IN LEARNING

Learning paradigms represent symbolized statements of the ingredients of a general procedure or experimental approach. We will discuss two basic paradigms that have been important to an understanding of basic processes in learning. The first is viewed by many as the most basic (Rescorla & Holland, 1976; Wagner, 1971) and is called *classical conditioning*. The second, although seen by some psychologists to consist of two separate approaches (Marx, 1969), can be subsumed under the heading *instrumental conditioning*. The reason that instrumental conditioning has sometimes been further subdivided is because of a procedural variation in which, for one "camp" of psychologists, learning trials are discrete events separated in time while, for another "camp," no such procedural separation is made. We will point to the unique contributions of each of these subdivisions. In the discussion of the basic learning paradigms that follows, prime consideration is given to the ingredients of the actual models involved and to some of the methodological problems and areas of controversy peculiar to each.

CLASSICAL CONDITIONING

Pavlov, the famous Russian physiologist, is credited with the discovery of psychology's most basic paradigm of learning, classical conditioning. The basic conditions necessary for classical conditioning, according to Pavlov (1927), are that a "neutral event" occur prior to, but overlap with the presentation of, a stronger, reflex-producing event. Pavlov's paradigm is nicely illustrated in Figure 8.2 by a diagram of classical eyelid conditioning procedure (Kimble, 1961). The uppermost line of each frame represents the onset (upward "deflection"), course, and offset (downward "deflection") of the "neutral" stimulus (a light). This stimulus is "neutral" in the sense that on initial trials it does not produce an eyeblink response. The offset of this stimulus coincides with the delivery of the "stronger, reflex-producing event," an airpuff to the cornea of the eye in this example. That the latter is "stronger" and "reflex-producing" is indexed by the second horizontal line in each frame of Figure 8.2. The pronounced downward deflection of the pen marks a strong, consistent eyeblink reflex in response to the airpuff. Note further in Figure 8.2 the *pairing arrangement* of these neutral and reflex-producing events so that the former occurs first and then temporally overlaps with the occurrence of the latter. This procedure fully meets the paradigm requirements of Pavlov's model of classical conditioning.

Pavlov's procedures can be further clarified by analyzing two important sets of defining operations; namely, the *choice* of appropriate stimuli, such as the light and the airpuff, and the *arrangement* of presentation of these events to the experimental subject, e.g., the presentation of the light so that it occurs first but overlaps with the airpuff. With regard to the operational specification of a neutral stimulus, Pavlov (1927) stated that "conditioned reflexes are quite readily formed to stimuli to which the animal is more or less indifferent at the outset, though strictly speaking, no stimulus within the animal's range of perception exists to which it would be absolutely indifferent . . . " (p. 29). Pavlov further indicated that a neutral stimulus was an event that was sufficiently strong to elicit an "investigatory reflex . . . a 'what is it?' response" as shown by a definite observing or orienting response by the subject to the event. But, to qualify as "neutral," the event should not be so strong as to consistently evoke a strong reflex, sometimes termed a *defensive reaction* (Sokolov, 1963), of its own. With respect to the nonneutral stimulus in the classical conditioning paradigm, Pavlov stated that its major defining property was its consistent elicitation of a strong, inborn reflex. Pavlov

Figure 8.2

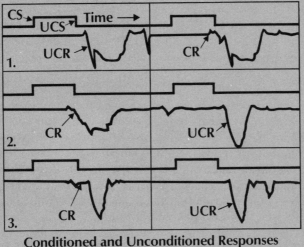

Conditioned and unconditioned responses in the same subjects on adjacent trials. The upper line in each panel designates the onset of a light CS (upward jog) and the airpuff UCS (downward jog) 0.5 sec later. The CR is distinguishable from the UCR in terms of latency. The CR precedes the onset of the UCS. From Kimble (1961, p. 55).

Conditioned and Unconditioned Responses
Adjacent Trials—Same Subjects

introduced terminology to characterize these two stimuli. He termed the *neutral stimulus* of the classical conditioning paradigm the *conditional stimulus,* and the *stronger stimulus,* because it consistently could elicit an inborn reflex, the *unconditioned stimulus.*

One of the measures that can be collected as a result of the application of the conditioning procedure is the reflex produced by the unconditioned stimulus (the UCS). This response to the unconditioned stimulus was termed by Pavlov the *unconditioned response* (UCR). Repeated pairings of the conditional stimulus (CS) with the unconditioned stimulus resulted in what Pavlov termed *conditioning.*

Measurement: Issues and Concepts

Classical techniques.   Using the procedures of Pavlov (1927), the *fact* of conditioning has been determined in two ways. First, if after repeated pairings of the CS with the UCS, an occasional presentation of the CS alone results in the appearance of a response that is similar to the unconditioned reflex, the possibility of conditioning is demonstrated. If the CS in Figure 8.2, a light, produces an eyeblink following extended light-airpuff pairings, conditioning may have occurred. This procedure can be termed the *UCS-omission* or "probe" procedure and was the method preferred by Pavlov. Given that several added stipulations are met, the response that is measured on these "probe" trials is designated the *conditioned response* (CR).

The second way of detecting conditioning has been to seek evidence of a CR during the period between the CS and UCS onsets, the *inter-stimulus interval* (ISI). This method of measurement is highlighted in Figure 8.2 in Frames 2, 3, and 4, where a modest but discernable portion of the eyeblink response occurs just prior to the onset of the UCS airpuff. This measurement procedure has been termed the *antedation method* since it clearly highlights the anticipatory nature of the CR. This measurement procedure capitalizes on the fact that, as the result of CS-UCS pairings, the CR appears to have "moved earlier" in time to occur prior to UCS onset. Actually, the "probe" procedure can also reveal this anticipatory aspect of the CR. This is done through a comparison of the latency from CS onset to CR onset with the ISI. If the former is shorter, then the CR has become antedated with regard to the UCS. Some psychologists believe the finding of CR antedation is the single most important indicator that conditioning has occurred (Kimble, 1961).

Both measurement procedures can also highlight another feature of the CR. While the CR is measured by both methods as part of the same response system as the unconditioned response (UCR), it differs from the UCR in terms of both temporal and topographical characteristics. Note in Figure 8.2 that the duration of the CR is shorter, the form is different, and the magnitude or strength of the response is considerably less than the UCR. For these reasons, the CR may be viewed as a *fractional* component of the UCR since, while part of the same response system, it is "diminished" in most respects. Pavlov concluded that when it has been demonstrated that the CS elicits a response it formerly did not, it has become a *conditioned stimulus*. Prior to conditioning the neutral event was designated as a conditional event but, as the result of pairings with the UCS, it became a conditioned stimulus. Often it is difficult to discern whether the measured response is due to CS-UCS pairings. Certain factors, such as those in Box 8.2, can produce "pseudo" CRs. Procedures must be developed to distinguish between actual and pseudo CRs.

Classical indices of conditioning.   The indices or dependent variables of conditioning include the response attributes of *latency, amplitude,* and *frequency.* For CR *latency,* the typical function that results from CS-UCS pairings shows decreases in latency, averaged over subjects, with increasing trial blocks. This change in performance describes an acquisition-of-CR or learning function. *Amplitude* of the CR has been measured in a

Responses can occur in the presence of or to the CS that are not the result of the conditioning procedure. Consider a study of classical eyelid conditioning in which age level was the manipulated variable (Braun & Geiselhart, 1959). Three groups, children, young adults, and older adults, were given identical CS-UCS conditioning procedures, the CS being an increase in the apparent brightness of a 6-cm circular disc upon which Ss were told to fixate, the UCS an 0.5-sec airpuff to the cornea of the eye (2.0 lb/sq in), and an ISI of 0.5 sec. The first eight 10-trial blocks involved CS-UCS pairings as *acquisition trials* and the last two blocks, CS-only presentations as *extinction trials*. The results, mean CR percentage by trial blocks for each group, are shown in Figure 8.3. The children and young adults showed apparent eyelid conditioning during acquisition with increases in mean CR percentages over trial blocks. In contrast, the older subjects did not. The two younger groups that conditioned showed typical extinction curves to the CS-only presentations.

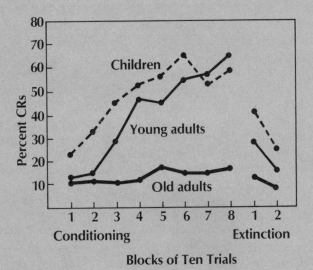

Figure 8.3　Mean percent conditioned eyelid responses for children, young, and elderly adult humans averaged for eight consecutive blocks of ten conditioning (acquisition) and two consecutive blocks of ten extinction trials. After Braun and Geiselhart (1959).

The issues here are not these age-related behavior differences in conditioning, but instead the various features of this study that highlight typical measurement concerns. For example, note that on the first block of trials all groups had an average of about 1.0 to 2.0 responses to the CS. Since the groups that eventually showed conditioning probably were not statistically different here from the older group that did not, it cannot be known whether or not these initial reactions qualify as "true" CRs.

If these responses are not CRs, what are they? Also, what about the responses of the older group who, while not showing conditioning, continued to show an above-zero response level throughout the study? In general, these initial reactions constitute what is termed *respondent level*, and can be viewed as nonassociative in nature. Nonassociative sources of responding in an eyelid conditioning study can include such factors as spontaneous blinking, voluntary eye closings, heightened responsiveness to any stimulation due to prior UCS presentations (termed *pseudoconditioning*), and changes in the reflexive activity of the CS itself (termed *sensitization*). While eyeblinking to the CS would not increase systematically over trials due to some of these factors (spontaneous closings), it might because of others, such as pseudoconditioning. Regardless of whether increases occur over trials, all these nonassociative sources of responding can obscure an accurate assessment of: (1) when the first CR occurs on early conditioning trials; or (2) how much responding on later trials is due to the actual conditioning procedure. Fortunately, certain of these nonassociative responses exhibit particular characteristics that allow a distinction to be made between them and a true CR.

Grant and Norris (1947) found that reflex-like eyeblinks to the CS, termed *alpha responses*, showed a different kind of latency distribution than did CRs. These authors devised a special scoring procedure that allowed separation of pseudo-CRs from actual CRs. Their scoring method took into account differences such as latency of the response from the onset of the CS (shorter latencies for the pseudo-CR), duration of the CR (longer for the pseudo-CR), and magnitude of the CR (larger for the pseudo-CR). Bonneau (1958) extended this procedure by showing that certain of these attributes changed over acquisition trials for "true" CRs but remained relatively unchanged for pseudo-CRs. The point to be made here is that certain methodological problems in classical conditioning can be handled by the use of special measurement procedures. The research of Grant and Norris (1947) and Bonneau (1958) illustrates how special scoring practices and conditions can be combined to minimize the unwanted and misleading contributions of irrelevant sources of responding in the conditioning process.

variety of ways, including assessments of number or strength, e.g., drops of saliva per trial or the amount of deflection in a polygraphic record (cf. Figure 8.2). In general, the amplitude measure is best for response systems that are continuous in nature. Mean CR amplitude usually increases as a function of trial blocks during acquisition training. The *frequency* or *percentage* CR measure is calculated by counting the number of times a CR has occurred for a given block of trials and expressing the result as a percentage value. If two CRs occurred for a particular block of ten trials, the score would be 20 percent. Mean CR percentages increase during acquisition training (cf. Braun & Geiselhart, 1959). Importantly, this measure can be quite misleading for response systems where there is an unusually high level of spontaneous responding, a high respondent level, prior to and during the early stages of conditioning. However, if an index of initial preconditioning response level can be obtained, it can be used as a correction factor.

Virtually all measures show a decline, longer latencies, decreased magnitudes, and/or attenuated percentages as a function of experimental extinction (cf. Braun & Geiselhart, 1959). *Extinction* occurs in classical conditioning when the UCS is omitted on all CS trials following a number of CS-UCS pairings.

Advantages and disadvantages. Consider first the advantages of the "probe" measurement technique. Along with the convenience of precise recording, this procedure allows for relatively uncontaminated measurement of the CR, undisturbed by any possible disruptions in responding by the UCR. This is a good technique, especially when the CR latency is quite "sluggish" (as often is the case for such autonomic responses as EKG and GSR) and the ISI is relatively short. Under these conditions, the CR may *blend* with the UCR, thus making accurate measurement difficult. Again, consider Figure 8.2 where even for the relatively rapid response of eyeblinking the ISI is so short and the CR so close to the UCR that there is probably some merging of both responses.

There are two main disadvantages of the "probe" procedure. First, an occasional UCS omission introduces the equivalent of a partial reinforcement procedure. If experimental interest is exclusively upon determining an acquisition function relating strength of CR to number of conditioning trials, this function would be contaminated by the occasional occurrence of CS-only trials when a "probe" procedure is used. Second, the use of a "probe" procedure introduces the possibility of a phenomenon called *perceptual disparity* (Grings, Dossett, & Honnard, 1959). This phenomenon is related to the general concept of "surprise" and rests upon the assumption that, following many CS-UCS pairings, unexpected omission of the UCS can introduce a strong novelty response that in many respects resembles a UCR. Clearly, a novelty response to UCS omission should not, strictly speaking, be taken as a CR. Nonetheless, this novelty reaction inflates the actual measure of the effects of the conditioning procedure.

Badia and Defran (1970) tested this possible artifact of the "probe" measurement procedure in a human conditioning experiment. As CSs and UCSs, they used moderately intense tones and lights. During the training phase of their study two basic groups of college students were given repeated pairings of these stimuli. Some subjects in each group received tone-light and others light-tone pairings as a counterbalancing precaution. The dependent variable was galvanic skin response (GSR), a relatively rapid, quickly habituable change in skin resistance that occurs as a response to most stimulus presentations. Since neither of the two stimuli was strong enough to qualify as UCSs, Badia and Defran (1970) found that the magnitude of the GSR decreased over pairings trials, thereby giving *no* evidence of classical conditioning.

A period of time followed during which *no* further pairings occurred. A test then was given, in which the CS was exposed to one group in a "probe-like" procedure and the usual tone-light (or light-tone) pairing was given to the other group. The GSR response for the CS-only group was much larger than for the pairings group. Badia and Defran (1970) concluded that the omission of a regularly-scheduled stimulus can induce an unconditioned perceptual disparity response. The omission of the UCS on a "probe" measurement trial may indeed be accompanied by a response to the CS. But the latter response may be little more than an unconditioned novelty reaction, a surprise UCR. No associative change may have occurred.

This discussion provides the background for understanding the two important advantages of the antedation measurement procedure. Although containing the major drawback that CR-UCR blending may occur, this method eliminates all interruptions in CS-UCS pairings. It therefore precludes inadvertent (1) partial reinforcement and (2) novelty effects. A disadvantage of the antedation procedure, along with the possibility of blending, is that accurate, precise measurements within a short ISI are sometimes difficult to achieve.

An alternative measurement procedure.   The use of either the probe or the antedation procedures can require extensive, elaborate, and expensive equipment. Experimenters should therefore be fully familiar with the characteristics of the response system that is involved, be able to construct and properly apply electrodes and use such sophisticated electronic devices as oscillographs and scopes, and be familiar with up-to-date computer-assisted recording techniques. However, even armed with this kind of information, experimenters can still encounter major difficulties in achieving a flawless implementation of their research. This has led to a search for less complicated measurement procedures in classical conditioning.

There is another reason for seeking alternate measurement procedures. This reason is highlighted by the work of Zener (1937) who, instead of recording only from a single response system during conditioning, also observed the entire organism. While finding evidence of salivary conditioning, Zener (1937) also noted much restless movement during the periods between CS-UCS pairings, directed movements toward the food mechanism when the CS came on, barking at the CS, tail wagging, and attention-like ear movements. It was as if the entire subject, not just the salivary glands, had become conditioned. No measurement techniques other than the subjective impressions of Zener (1937) were available to supply quantitative documentation for the notion of "whole-organism" classical conditioning. However, in 1941, Estes and Skinner introduced a procedure that yielded a general format that both provided quantitative documentation for the notion of whole-organism classical conditioning and served as the foundation for an alternative to the CS-CR measurement approach in classical conditioning. Their procedure involved placing a hungry rat in a small chamber (an operant chamber) where it was trained to press a lever for food pellet rewards. Once this response was established, the mechanism connecting the lever to the food-delivery system was scheduled so that bar-pressing produced food every four minutes. Conditioning sessions then were instituted for one hour, while the lever pressing food-delivery schedule remained in effect. A 3-min tone (the CS) was sounded and a brief, unavoidable electric shock was given through the chamber grid floor upon termination of each tone. Over sessions, the tone substantially diminished rate of lever pressing, a phenomenon termed *conditioned suppression.* Sidman (1960b), in repeating this procedure with monkeys, has provided a typical graph of the suppressing effect of such a tone CS upon responding. This is shown in Figure 8.4 as a disruption (horizontal pen tracing) in an ongoing cumulative record of lever pressing.

A wide number of variations in this basic procedure have followed from the early work of Estes and Skinner (1941). Major variations have included: (1) administering CS-UCS pairings in another chamber or with the lever removed and testing for CS effects with the lever present (termed an *off-the-baseline* conditioning procedure); and (2) exposure to CS-UCS pairings in one situation, followed by use of the CS to train a response that is not part of the subject's present behavioral repertoire in another setting (cf. Brown & Jacobs, 1949; McAllister & McAllister, 1965). In spite of these variations, all such procedures have several things in common: (1) the effectiveness of the CS is established through a pairings procedure with the UCS; (2) the test for the result of CS-UCS pairings is in terms of the effect of the CS upon some form of instrumental behavior, providing the general designation for this measurement procedure as a CS-IR method (Gormezano & Kehoe, 1975); (3) direct measurements of the UCR and CR are rarely taken although there

Figure 8.4

Results of an Estes-Skinner CS-IR response-suppression procedure. Bar-press responses are recorded cumulatively, with the pen automatically resetting to the base line after every 450 responses. The introduction of the CS is indicated by the slight oblique downward displacement of the pen at the first arrow. The shock UCS, which immediately follows termination of the CS, occurs at the point where the pen displacement is rectified, indicated by the second arrow. From Sidman (1960).

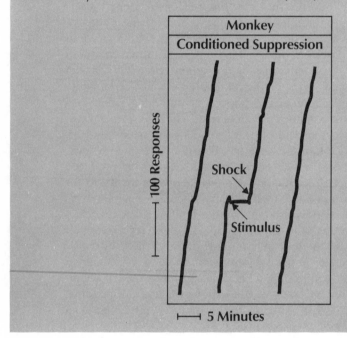

have been exceptions (cf. Ellison & Konorski, 1964, 1965; Shapiro, 1961, 1962; Williams, 1965; Wolf, 1963; Zener, 1937). The advantages of this approach are the ease of instrumentation and data collection, the relative versatility in ways to conduct such studies (a wide variety of test situations, response systems, and motivational conditions have been used with consistent results), and the apparent sensitivity to the effects of various CS-UCS pairings procedures.

Classical Conditioning: Definition Dilemmas

A number of features have gained consensus in definitions of a CS and a UCS. Box 8.4 summarizes these essential features, Pavlov's prescription

Box 8.3 A Measurement Controversy in Classical Conditioning

The advent of the Estes-Skinner (1941) measurement approach has sparked something akin to a "paradigm clash" (cf. Kuhn, 1970) in the field of classical conditioning. Some psychologists have argued that the information collected by this method is not relevant for generating laws about classical conditioning. For example, Gormezano and Kehoe (1975) assert that the only valid procedures in this regard are those that record a response during the CS that is from the same motor system that is activated by the UCS. These authors reasoned that a CS-CR measurement approach is the only way to specify with precision those stimuli that control the behavior being examined. They noted that the primary value of the classical conditioning procedure is that it affords a precise examination of stimulus control and behavior. It therefore makes little sense to adopt a measurement procedure that precludes any precise analysis in this regard. Since no direct UCR or CR measurement is taken with typical CS-IR procedures, no precise stimulus-response laws can be formulated about classical conditioning phenomena. In support of this, they indicated that the chain of events that can intervene between CS onset and changes in an instrumental response (such as lever-pressing) using the CS-IR procedure can be quite circuitous. There is a strong likelihood that observed behavior changes may only indirectly be due to the CR produced by the CS.

Whether the CS-IR approach ultimately becomes universally accepted as a proper measurement procedure will continue to depend upon how the results of its application compare with those of CS-CR procedures. But, it seems unlikely that results are comparable in all instances since the considerable movement that is afforded the subject during the ISI of a CS-IR measurement procedure probably makes the stimulus situation very different from CS-CR procedures. That this activity during the ISI may be an important determinant of what is learned during conditioning can be illustrated by several recent findings. For example, very short ISIs on the order of 0.5 sec tend to produce the strongest conditioning with CS-CR procedures. As shown in Figure 8.5, strong conditioning has rarely occurred when the ISI has been longer than 10 sec in such instances. Yet CS-IR procedures have often resulted in good conditioning for ISIs of from several minutes (cf. Estes & Skinner, 1941; Sidman, 1960b) to as long as several hours (cf. Revusky & Garcia, 1970). This discrepancy in ISI findings very likely has something to do with the fact that CS-CR procedures entail subject restraint and CS-IR procedures typically do not. The subjects' activity during the ISI of a CS-IR procedure undoubtedly brings them into contact with a large amount of extraneous stimulation, including that emanating from their own responses. This stimulation very likely becomes a functional part of the stimulus complex that is ultimately paired with the UCS. All this connected stimulation is absent in CS-CR procedures.

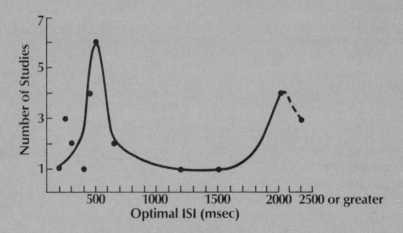

Figure 8.5   Curve of best fit summarizing 25 CS-CR studies to 1973 dealing with optimal interstimulus intervals. The number of studies reported are listed on the ordinate and the value of the optimal ISI for conditioning on the abscissa. In general, the shorter optimal ISIs were associated with responses involving skeletal and autonomic innervation and the longer ISIs with systems that were purely autonomic in nature.

A further illustration of the importance of responding during the ISI of a CS-IR procedure comes from some recent research illustrated by the initial work of Brown and Jenkins (1968). They first exposed pigeons to a briefly lighted (3 or 8 sec duration) key (the alleged CS) that, upon offset, was immediately followed by a 4 sec access to a tray of grain (the alleged UCS). These repeated CS-UCS pairings were accompanied by the emergence of behaviors that were not unlike those reported by Zener (1937) for his dogs. The birds first showed increased activity and postural orientations toward the lighted key, then began to approach it, and finally settled down to key-pecking even though this behavior had no effect upon grain delivery. Since the pigeons rather automatically seemed to "track" the sign that signalled food, this phenomenon has been designated *sign tracking* and/or *auto shaping* (Bilbrey & Winokur, 1973; Chao, 1972; Gamzu & Schwam, 1974; Wasserman, Franklin, & Hearst, 1974). In a recent follow-up study (Jenkins & Moore, 1973), the responses that developed to the key-CS were analyzed through high-speed photography. Analysis of the films revealed that the nature of the conditioned key responses resembled the *form* of those behaviors the pigeon normally made to the particular UCS that was used. If the UCS was grain, the key responses resembled grain-pecking behaviors; if the UCS was water, drinking-like movements occurred to the key (i.e., *the birds attempted to drink the key!*).

The point of this Box is that the evidence clearly suggests that CS-IR measurement techniques permit the occurrence of behaviors that simply cannot occur for the restrained subjects of a CS-CR procedure. The behaviors that can develop with a CS-IR procedure, along with the stimulation that may accompany them, represent uncontrolled portions of the classical conditioning procedure and, in support of Gormezano and Kehoe (1975), lend support to the view that precise stimulus-response conclusions cannot be drawn from this approach.

for how stimulus events should be arranged, and the methods of measurement that have been employed as part of the conditioning procedure. First, it seems unlikely that an exceedingly intense stimulus could function as a CS. For example, such a stimulus would produce a marked reflex of its own that very likely would obscure the detection of a CR as well as block the ocurrence of the unconditioned reflex that normally is produced by the UCS. Indeed, two strong reflex-producing stimuli, when paired with one another, most likely would result in a *reflex competition,* not in discernable conditioning. Razran (1957), in surveying the Russian conditioning literature, suggests that this does not mean that a less intense version of a normally strong stimulus cannot serve as a CS. For example, even though electric shock typically is regarded as a strong stimulus, a low-intensity shock could conceivably serve as a CS when paired with a stronger shock. Lockhart (1965) and Crowell (1974) have reported good conditioning in just such instances.

Second, for an event to qualify as a CS, it should be nonredundant with other stimuli when paired with the UCS. For the tone in an eyelid conditioning study to serve as a CS, no other stimulus should be paired with the airpuff at the same time. If a tone and a light were simultaneously paired with the airpuff, one would be redundant with the other. In general, the findings have been that if two neutral stimuli are employed, the one that (1) occurs first, (2) occurs earlier in the history of the conditioning sequence, or (3) is stronger seems to serve as the effective CS. The second stimulus apparently does not become part of the CS-UCS associative relationship (cf. Egger & Miller, 1962; Kamin, 1968, 1969; Razran, 1965; Wickens, 1965).

Third, for an event to become a CS, it should be novel to the situation at the beginning of the CS-UCS pairings sequence. By "novel" is meant that the CS should not have a history of presentations in the situation prior to its temporal pairing with the UCS. Lubow and Moore (1959) and Lubow (1973), using a CS-CR procedure, reported a decrement in the capacity of a stimulus to serve as a CS if it had been repeatedly presented alone prior to pairing with the UCS. Even more dramatic effects of CS pre-exposure in offsetting conditioning have been reported with CS-IR procedures (Carlton & Vogel, 1967; Crowell & Anderson, 1972).

Some Representative Phenomena

Aside from the phenomena of *acquisition, extinction,* and variations in the *ISI* (see Box 8.3), other effects worth noting are those of *CS and UCS intensity, intermittent UCS presentations, compound conditioning, generalization* and *conditioned discrimination,* and *higher-order conditioning* and

Box 8.4 Defining Conditions and Paradigm Ingredients in Classical Conditioning

Outlined in summary form herein are conditions that have been specified in general definitions of CSs and UCSs. Also included are the ingredients of the classical conditioning paradigm as presented by Pavlov (1927).

DEFINING CONDITIONS

Stimuli

Conditioned Stimulus (CS)
1. Must be above sensory threshold
2. Must be less intense than the UCS
3. Cannot have redundant signalling function
4. Should be novel to the conditioning situation

Unconditioned Stimulus (UCS)
1. Must be suprathreshold
2. Must consistently elicit a reflex response-UCR; i.e., non-habituable
3. Reflex-producing capacity should be experience-free, i.e., inborn

PARADIGM INGREDIENTS

Antecedent Conditions (Pairings operation)

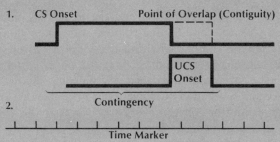

Consequent Conditions

1. CS-CR measurement procedures
   a. Measurement of CR on "probe" trials
   b. Measurement of CR during ISI
2. CS-IR measurement procedures
   a. CS-correlated change in a specified instrumental response

sensory preconditioning. Because of space limitation, only brief mention can be given to those topics.

CS and UCS intensity effects.   Variations in either CS or UCS intensity can produce two possible experimental outcomes. First, there is the outcome that is due to the motivational consequences of increased stimulus intensity. Second, an effect may occur because of a CS-UCS associative change. Immediate, short-lived CR changes typically are taken as due to a motivational effect while the more gradual development of a long-lasting CR change is taken as due to an associative influence. One's experimental procedure should therefore provide for measuring each of these effects. To assess motivational effects, a measure is needed during the actual conditioning procedure so that any abrupt CR increases that are correlated with respective CS or UCS intensity increases can be detected. The general finding here is that CR vigor is a positive function of increases in either CS or UCS intensity. For CS manipulations, this finding has been most consistent when the same subjects have been used at all of the intensity levels (Grice & Hunter, 1964) in a within-subjects design (cf. Chapter 6). In general, long-term behavioral changes have not been reported for CS-intensity manipulations (although see Crowell & Anderson, 1972), but have for UCS intensity (Anderson, Plant, & Paden, 1967; Sheafor & Gormezano, 1971, 1972; Spence, 1956; Spence, Haggard, & Ross, 1958a, 1958b).

Intermittent UCS presentation.   This procedure entails occasional omission of the UCS during CS-UCS acquisition trials. However, the effects on CR strength are not examined only during acquisition, but also during CS-only extinction trials. Unfortunately, the results have been equivocal for both the acquisition and the extinction phases of intermittent-UCS classical conditioning studies. Some show no difference or retarded learning in comparisons with the effect of continuous UCS occurrences in between-group studies of acquisition. Even more confusing has been the occurrence of all conceivable outcomes during extinction— no difference and less and greater resistance to extinction (less resistance to extinction means that fewer CS-only exposures are needed than for a control group to achieve zero CR response level).

These latter findings are at odds with the consistent finding of greater resistance to extinction for intermittently reinforced instrumental responses. However, there are certain procedural differences between classical and instrumental learning studies of intermittent reinforcement that, if equated, might assist in resolving these disparate results. In studies of classical conditioning, the total number of UCS presentations (*not* total number of trials) typically are equated for continuously and intermittently reinforced groups, whereas total number of trials (*not* total number of reinforcements) usually are equated in instrumental learning experiments. Another procedural complication is that in classical conditioning relatively simple responses (eyeblinks, GSRs, muscle flexions) located in close temporal proximity to the UCS-reinforcer are measured. The measures in instrumental studies typically are of more complicated series of responses, many of which are temporally quite distant from the reinforcer. Until these methodological differences are reconciled, comparisons of the effects of intermittent reinforcement will continue to produce confusing and disparate outcomes.

Compound conditioning.   While there are numerous variations on the basic compound-conditioning procedure (Kamin, 1969; Razran, 1965), it usually means the use of two or more neutral stimuli, presented in various combinations and permutations with each other, as a complex CS in CS-UCS pairing procedures. Two compound conditioning phenomena have been of special recent interest to U.S. psychologists; namely, *blocking* and *overshadowing* (each of these is related to stimulus redundancy). Blocking can be understood from the basic procedures of Kamin (1969), in which the UCS (an electric shock) is paired with one CS (CS_1), e. g., a light. This stimulus is then combined with another, e. g., a tone, to form a compound CS for further CS-UCS pairings. (The CSs are counterbalanced so that a tone is used first half the time, and then compounded with a light stimulus.) Using an Estes-Skinner type CS-IR bar-press suppression test, Kamin (1969) has shown that the initial CS (CS_1—the light, for example) will produce suppression but the additional stimulus (the tone), presented alone, will not. A control group that receives CS-UCS pairings with light alone half the time and tone alone the other half shows good suppression to either stimulus. Initial light-shock (or tone-shock) pairings thus "block" the tone (or light) from becoming an effective CS *only* if the tone (or light) occurs in combination with the light (or tone) during subsequent pairings with shock, i.e., only if the tone (or light) supplies redundant information about the shock-UCS.

 Overshadowing entails the use of a modestly intense stimulus, e.g., a 50 dB tone, and a stronger stimulus, e.g., a bright light, as a compound CS in a CS-UCS pairings procedure (again, stimulus order is reversed for half the subjects in a counterbalancing procedure). One stipulation is that each stimulus element, if used alone, be capable of becoming an effective CS. When combined into a compound CS that is paired with a UCS, e.g., shock, the stronger element alone will produce suppression in an Estes-Skinner type CS-IR suppression test, while the weaker element will not.

Blocking and a new conditioning theory.   The phenomena of blocking and overshadowing, along with several others, have suggested a new theory of classical conditioning to some psychologists (Kamin, 1969; Rescorla, 1974). Rescorla (1974) has argued from these data that *condi-*

tioning results from a comparison process in which the subject compares the memory of the UCS evoked by the CS with the actual UCS that is received. The degree of conditioning that occurs on any given trial is seen as a positive function of the disparity between this hypothetical *UCS memory* and the actual UCS. If the CS does not evoke any such memory, as would be the case on the initial acquisition trial, a CS-UCS pairing would result in substantial conditioning because of the large discrepancy between the memory (nonexistent) and the UCS. Later on, the CS would evoke a more substantial (less disparate) memory of the UCS, and further CS-UCS pairings would add little to the conditioning process. It is as if, in the presence of the CS, the UCS is *surprising* (cf. Kamin, 1969, p. 293) to the subject on early conditioning trials, while as conditioning proceeds, the CS supplies information that renders it less and less surprising.

By this view, *blocking* occurs because the original stimulus element, having been paired repeatedly with the UCS, evokes a nondisparate (unsurprising?) memory of the actual UCS when occurring in combination with the tone. Hence, little or no conditioning to the tone would occur. *Overshadowing* is accounted for by assuming primarily that the stronger CS element, perhaps because of its greater "salience" (attention value), becomes associated with the UCS more rapidly than the weaker component (Kamin, 1969, p. 288, has supplied evidence for this assumption). After a few initial $CS_{compound}$-UCS trials, the stronger component is seen to produce a nondisparate UCS memory in the presence of the weaker CS element: hence, "blocking" occurs to the latter. Overshadowing thereby can be seen as a special instance of blocking.

Generalization and discrimination.   Pavlov (1927) showed that, following CS-UCS pairings, other stimuli that were physically similar but not identical to the CS could elicit at least a partial CR. This phenomenon is termed *stimulus generalization.* It since has been shown that the strength of a generalized CR is a positive function of the degree of similarity between the test stimulus and the original CS. From these data, it can be inferred that conditioning probably never is to a single stimulus, but to a *class* of stimuli. The student is referred to good discussions of the many methodological issues that can be important in studies of stimulus generalization in Honig (1966), Mostofsky (1965), and Stebbins (1970).

Subjects can be trained not to respond to stimuli that are physically (and functionally) similar to the CS through a procedure termed *conditioned discrimination.* The basic operations here entail interspersed CS^+-UCS with CS^--only presentations. The CS^+ is the stimulus that is actually conditioned; the CS^- is the similar stimulus that is to be "discriminated." On initial trials, responses to both stimuli can be expected, but as trials continue, a differential performance will emerge in that fewer and fewer responses will occur to the CS^- while responding is maintained to the CS^+. The student is referred both to the preceding references and to a fine primer discussion by Riley (1968) on methodological issues relating to research on discrimination. Excellent recent chapters are also available by Nevins (Nevins & Reynolds, 1973), Rilling (1977), Mackintosh (1977), and Blough and Blough (1977).

Second-order conditioning and sensory preconditioning.   Second-order conditioning entails the use of an established CS (CS_1) as a UCS-like stimulus in pairings with another CS (CS_2). The sequence of operations includes, first, CS_1-UCS pairings to establish the effectiveness of CS_1 and, second, CS_2-CS_1 pairings to establish the effectiveness of CS_2. (Note that the fact of second-order conditioning is in direct contradiction to the assumption expressed in Box 8.4 that to qualify as a UCS a stimulus must elicit an inborn nonhabituable reflex. Pavlov was aware of this.)

Although the possibilities of second- and higher-orders of conditioning have been given much status in various learning theories, only recently have there been relatively well controlled studies supporting the existence of the former (Anderson, Plant, Johnson, & Vandever, 1967; Johnson & Anderson, 1969; McAllister & McAllister, 1964; Rizley & Rescorla, 1971). A major problem has been the failure of many studies to include proper control procedures so that potentially confounding sources of responding, not due to the actual higher-order associative process, can be ruled out (cf. Gormezano & Moore, 1969; Rescorla, 1977). However, the use of perhaps more sensitive measurement procedures, mostly of the CS-IR variety, seems to have alleviated the prior dearth of convincing, robust demonstrations of second-order conditioning. Indeed, Rescorla (1977) has gone so far as to argue that the second-order conditioning procedure well may be the test of choice for those instances where the presence of first-order conditioning is in doubt. One such example is the work of Garcia and his colleagues (cf. Revusky & Garcia, 1970) on intrinsic CS-UCS relationships where certain CS and UCS combinations do or do not seem to condition very well. The use of a CS_1 that appears ineffective on its own as a UCS-like stimulus in a second-order procedure may reveal conditioning effects much stronger than suspected.

Sensory preconditioning (SPC) is included in this section because the operations that define it are similar to those of second-order conditioning. The primary difference is that the CS_2-CS_1 pairings in SPC are conducted before rather than after CS_1-UCS pairings. A demonstration of CS_2 effectiveness with this procedure was at one time thought to be unequivocal support for the S-S, central-state interpretation of classical conditioning. This is because the connection between the CS_2 and the CR presumably could only be mediated by the perceptual CS_2-CS_1 relationship established prior to the formation of the CS_1-CR association produced by the conditioning procedure *per se*. Alternative S-R conceptions have recently made some comeback in this area (Coppock,

1958; Seidel, 1959; Tait, Marquis, Williams, Weinstein, & Suboski, 1969; although see Cousins, Zamble, Tait, & Suboski, 1971).

A major controversy.   Probably the most controversial issue in classical conditioning today centers around the pairings hypothesis of Pavlov (1927). The ingredients of this hypothesis are that (1) a forward-going CS-UCS contingency relationship and (2) CS-UCS contiguity are necessary for conditioning. Both assumptions have now come under serious attack. The exclusiveness of a forward CS-UCS temporal relationship as the only learning contingency has been assailed on several grounds, one being Pavlov's choice of an inopportune response system (salivation) for conditioning. The salivary system has a virtually zero respondent level at the outset of CS-UCS pairings. This system would thus be unable to reveal any kind of learning other than the excitatory conditioning shown by Pavlov in terms of increased responding (drops of saliva) over conditioning trials. Pavlov's response choice limited any demonstration of learning beyond what resulted from a forward CS-UCS arrangement; hence his conclusion that learning consisted of incremental excitatory associative changes. (In fairness, Pavlov believed that once learned, performance could be curbed through inhibitory processes. But inhibition could only develop after excitatory learning had occurred.)

In order to evaluate Pavlov's forward-contingency assertion, Rescorla and Lolordo (1965) used a CS-IR procedure in which response changes to the CS could occur in either an excitatory or an inhibitory direction. Among various sorts of pairings arrangements, some groups were given extensive forward CS-UCS pairings and others were given extensive backward UCS-CS pairings. When tested with their CS-IR procedure, the forward group showed excitatory learning, as Pavlov would probably have predicted. But, contrary to Pavlov, the backward-contingency group showed inhibitory learning. From these and many subsequent findings (most based on CS-IR procedures), Rescorla (1969a, 1972) concluded that both excitatory and inhibitory learning are possible and that the nature of this learning depends upon the particular CS/UCS contingency arrangement to which the subjects are exposed.

To understand this new use of the term "contingency," consider some of the various CS/UCS arrangements (each given to separate groups) that have been used in recent CS-IR experiments, as well as some of the consequent effects of the CS when presented during an ongoing instrumental performance. As shown in Box 8.5, the behavioral effects of the CSs used in CS-IR test procedures seem to be determined by their contingent signalling of predictive relationships regarding the UCS. If the CS routinely signals the occurrence of the UCS, it appears to develop excitatory properties. In contrast, if the CS predicts the nonoccurrence of the UCS, it seems to develop inhibitory effects.

Box 8.5 **The concept of "Contingency" and the *Kind* of Classical Conditioning**

Below are representative CS/UCS contingencies and respective CS effects using a variety of CS-IR test procedures. Testing approaches for assessing inhibitory contingencies include: (1) the *summation method* in which the inhibitory effect of a CS⁻ is measured in terms of the degree to which a CR that occurs to a CS⁺ is suppressed when both the CS⁺ and the CS⁻ occur as a compound; and (2) the *retardation method* in which a CS⁻ is rearranged as the CS⁺ in an excitatory CS-UCS relationship and the growth rate of the CR is compared with that in which the CS of a similar CS-UCS arrangement is initially neutral.

CS/UCS conditioning contingency		*CS-IR Test Effects*		*Representative Study*
1. Forward contingency	CS-UCS	CS	= excitatory	Rescorla & Lolordo, 1965
2. Backward contingency	UCS-CS	CS	= inhibitory	Moscovitch & Lolordo, 1968
3. Conditioned	CS_1-UCS	CS_1	= excitatory	Rescorla & Lolordo, 1965
discrimination	CS_2-only	CS_2	= inhibitory	
4. Explicitly	CS-only	CS	= inhibitory	Rescorla & Lolordo, 1965
unpaired	UCS-only			
5. Random pairings	CS; UCS	CS	= generally	Kremer & Kamin, 1971
			inhibitory	Kremer, 1971
				Benedict & Ayers, 1972
				Siegel & Domjan, 1971
6. Second-order	CS_1-UCS	CS_1	= excitatory	Rescorla & Lolordo, 1965
contingency *(extensive pairings)*	CS_2-CS_1	CS_2	= inhibitory	Herendeen & Anderson, 1968
7. Second-order	CS_1-UCS	CS_1	= excitatory	Herendeen & Anderson, 1968
contingency *(few pairings)*	CS_2-CS_1	CS_2	= excitatory	

Given that the nature of the learning process may vary in accord with the particular CS/UCS relationship involved, the role of contiguity between these two important stimulus events becomes very confusing indeed! Contiguity was seen by Pavlov as a critical ingredient in the development of the CR to the CS. Based upon this assumption, it was for many decades following Pavlov common practice to use a backward, UCS-CS, conditioning procedure for one group as a control for assessing the effects of a forward conditioning contingency. This is because the backward-conditioning procedure was believed to supply equivalent stimulation but presumably not the critical CS-UCS contingency thought necessary for learning. But, with the work of Rescorla and his colleagues, not only was the backward contingency rendered suspect as a proper control procedure for conditioning since it seemed to produce its own kind of learning, but the concept of stimulus contiguity no longer made much sense because both excitatory and inhibitory CS-related effects had been shown for CS/UCS relationships in which, during training, minutes sometimes intervened between the occurrences of either stimulus.

Some resolution to this confusion about the role of CS/UCS contiguity was supplied by another study (Rescorla, 1968) in which, using an Estes-Skinner CS-IR suppression-type procedure, the probability of UCS presentations was manipulated both between and during CS presentations for different groups. Rescorla measured the relative amount of bar-press suppression to the CS, calculated as the ratio of number of bar presses during the CS to the combined number of responses during and for a comparable period prior to the CS, as his dependent variable. As shown in Figure 8.6, three sets of probabilities were involved. For one (upper left graph of Figure 8.6), the probability of occurrence of a shock UCS *during* the CS was 0.4, and the probabilities of shock occurrence *between* trials for four different groups was either 0.0, 0.1, 0.2, or 0.4. Note that even though all groups were given the same number of CS-UCS pairings (4/10-trial block), the amount of suppression varied as a function of the change in proportion of unpaired UCSs. Suppression was greatest when the proportion was disparate in favor of CS occurrence (the 0.0 group). This basic finding was repeated for the remaining two probability sets where the probabilities of a UCS during the CS were 0.2 and 0.1.

Rescorla (1974) has noted that these data indicate a correlational-relativistic rather than a pairings interpretation of classical conditioning. In terms of this view, learning can be characterized as a central-state, organismic change that results from exposure to particular predictive relationships between the CS and the UCS. If the CS "predicts" the UCS in some manner, as defined by a particular experimenter-arranged contingency, it is presumably this predictive-correlational information that is learned. Forward, contiguous CS-UCS pairings represent but one of

Figure 8.6

Median suppression ratio for each group over the six test sessions. (Within each panel, all groups have the same probability of UCS during CS; the parameter in each panel is the probability of UCS in the absence of CS.)

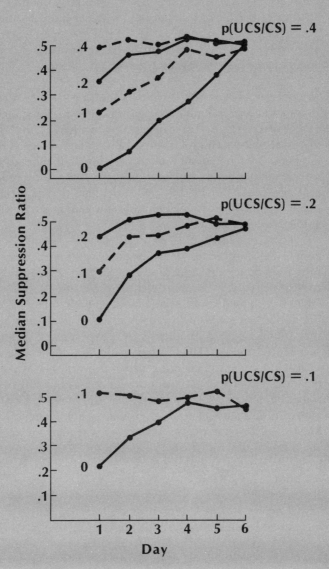

many ways in which a learning contingency can be arranged. Moreover, that CS/UCS pairings *per se* is not a necessary condition for learning seems to have been shown in Rescorla's (1968) study where, for an equivalent number of CS-UCS pairings, the predictability of the UCS was varied by the proportion of times that it occurred in the absence of the CS. The proportion varied from never presenting the UCS in the absence of the CS to presenting it the same proportion of the time in the absence of the CS as in its presence. When these two proportions were equal, the predictive value of the CS was seen to be zero—that is, no better prediction of the UCS occurred in the presence of the CS than in its absence—and no learning appeared to have resulted.

The concept of control.   Rescorla's challenge to Pavlov's hypothesis has created considerable methodological controversy over the issue of *proper control procedures for classical conditioning.* Ideally, to show conditioning experimentally, a control (comparison) group is needed that receives all but the critical ingredient thought essential to the formation of a learned association. Rescorla's formulation suggests that any predictive CS/UCS contingency can conceivably be learned and that an ideal control condition is one that involves comparable stimulation but in which there is no predictive value for the CS.

To accomplish the latter, Rescorla (1967) proposed a "truly" random CS/UCS procedure in which the programmed occurrence of the CS is entirely random in time (and space?) with regard to the UCS. To accomplish a "truly" random control procedure, a conditioning session might be subdivided into relatively small time frames of equal durations. The UCS then could be randomly assigned to a given number of these time frames equal in number of UCS exposures to that given to the experimental group(s). The CS then could be assigned in a similar manner such that all CS/UCS contingencies—forward, backward, simultaneous, unpaired, etc.—could and likely would occur randomly over an extended conditioning session. The alleged long-run result of this procedure is that an organism learns neither an excitatory nor an inhibitory association, but instead develops (learns?) no response tendency at all to the CS.

Empirically, the "truly" random procedure has not fared well. Organisms do seem to learn something about the CS, usually responding inhibitorily (cf. Benedict & Ayers, 1972; Kremer, 1971; Kremer & Kamin, 1971; Siegel & Domjan, 1971). Indeed, it is not clear logically why Rescorla's "truly" random procedure should be a control for learning *per se.* It seems clear from his prescription that Rescorla believes that a subject must have considerable experience with the CS and UCS in random sequences in order to learn CS/UCS independence. But "considerable experience" indicates that some sort of practice is needed for this independence perception to develop and, as noted in our introductory section, *practice* is a major antecedent defining operation of learning. Hence, at most, Rescorla's (1967) "truly" random procedure might serve as a control for the *kind* of learning that develops from exposure to various CS/UCS contingencies, but not for the *fact of learning per se.* Unfortunately, this section must be concluded on an unfinished note. At present, there appears to be little consensus on what constitutes a good control procedure for classical learning *per se,* especially since virtually *any* repetitious stimulation may result in some sort of relatively permanent behavioral effect.

INSTRUMENTAL LEARNING

If classical conditioning deals with the arrangement of stimuli as a way to understand the associative basis of behavior, instrumental learning deals with the arrangement of responses and their consequences for similar purposes. In classical conditioning, little attention is given to the functional effects of the CR except that it occurs. Learning is seen to result from pairings (or exposures to a contingent relationship) between stimuli, independent of the organism's simultaneous, previous, or later behavior. If a UCS is potent, in that it consistently produces a reflex, learning should occur automatically. However, everyday experience suggests that life is not simply the outcome of passive stimulus pairings superimposed upon ongoing daily activities. It may be better explained by the paradigm of instrumental learning which focuses upon the relationship of responses and their satisfying, annoying, and/or neutral consequences as a way of accounting for associative performance changes.

Thorndike (1898) stands in relation to the empirical beginnings of instrumental learning much as Pavlov does to those of classical conditioning. He began his research with an apparatus known as a "puzzle box." It consisted of a lever device in the floor, a door activated by displacement of the lever, and a bar framework at the front of the cage. By placing a food reward just outside the box, Thorndike could study the trial-by-trial behavior of a hungry cat as it learned to release itself from the box and obtain the food.

Thorndike observed that on initial trials the cat emitted many behaviors unrelated to the response that released the door. These irrelevant behaviors gradually disappeared over trials and were replaced with responses that more closely approximated the latch-displacement reaction. This reduction in unrelated behaviors was accompanied by shorter and shorter latencies before escape from the cage.

Thorndike's observation of a gradual but relatively lasting behavior change involved both different environmental circumstances and different measures than those of Pavlov, thus giving rise to a new paradigmatic view of learning, the instrumental paradigm. This new conceptualization of learning contains three major ingredients. The *first* is a motivated organism; the *second* is an event or condition in the environment which, as a consequence of a particular response, satisfies that motivation; the *third* is a precise way to determine whether or not the required response occurred.

Spence (1956) has since elaborated on these conditions, arguing that the response studied in instrumental learning situations ideally should be one that is initially unlikely. Thus, the initial responses that do occur should be those that do *not* lead to reward. Spence (1956) thus viewed the instrumental paradigm as a process of response reordering in an organism's behavioral hierarchy. This reordering occurs because the experimenter sets up a particular response-reward relationship so that a weaker response tendency comes to dominate initially stronger behaviors. The factors responsible for this reordering process constitute the focus of experimental research with this paradigm, and much attention has been given to Thorndike's statement that it comes about through motivated trial-and-error activity and the gradual reduction of dominant behaviors not followed by reward.

Relationship to Classical Conditioning

A major difference between Spence (1956) and Thorndike (1898) was that the latter assigned to the concept of reward the function of *strengthening new connections* between aspects of the environment and successful reactions. Spence accepted the same facts as Thorndike (namely, that rewards measurably strengthened performances), but he argued that performance changes did not reflect new central connections so much as rearrangement of already existing associative connections. These contrasting views underscore a major controversy that remains today. For those who have followed Thorndike, the instrumental paradigm stands beside classical conditioning as a second source of learning. Each paradigm produces its respective *kind* of learning (cf. Rescorla & Solomon, 1967, and Herrnstein, 1969, for thorough historical reviews of this position). For Spence and others, the instrumental paradigm is in part another way to study the operations and consequences of classical conditioning. They believe every instrumental learning situation contains the opportunity for classical conditioning to occur since environmental and other related stimuli must eventually be paired with the reward, itself a UCS-like event. This possibility of classical conditioning in instrumental situations formed the basis of Spence's response reordering view of instrumental performance. Since the initially weak rewarded response is the only one that produces pairings between the environment and the reward UCS, it is the only behavior among many others possible that is accompanied by the simultaneous presence of a CR. This CR was seen as a partial replica of the reward so that whenever the correct response occurred, it was in effect rewarded by the CR that also occurred. Spence thus gave classical conditioning major responsibility for the behavioral changes measured in instrumental learning situations. Mowrer (1960) has taken the most extreme position in this regard and adopted the view that *all* instrumental behavior is a by-product of classical conditioning.

Measurement: Issues and Problems

Measurement in instrumental learning has taken two quite different directions. One is exemplified by Thorndike's procedure, where learning is analyzed in terms of a trial-by-trial (trials) method in which a clear temporal separation is imposed between the end of one trial and the beginning of another, such as for Thorndike's puzzle-box study. Such features of the trials procedure as number of trials, intertrial interval (ITI), and so forth, are controlled by the scientist. The second approach, taken up in a later section, makes every effort to eliminate the trials aspect by giving the subject free and unimpeded access to the response device (manipulanda) within a prescribed time session. The subject thus can earn reward (or receive punishment) as frequently as its circumstances allow. In effect, the subject controls the intertrial spacings with this approach. This procedure is termed the *free-operant* method.

The trials and free operant approaches necessarily involve different response attributes in the measurement of learned behaviors. In the trials approach, these attributes include *response latency* (or the reciprocal, response speed), *number or proportion* of trials on which a full or a partial response occurs, number of *errors, trials to extinction,* and so on. The primary measure in free operant research is the *rate* of a response per unit time (usually per session). Another popular measure has been the elapsed times between all pairs of consecutive responses within a session, termed *interresponse times* (IRT). These IRTs are plotted into frequency distributions in order to examine their form and other characteristics (Morse, 1966).

There are several ways the trials approach has been applied. Early trials research involved the extensive use of various maze apparatuses (see Figure 8.7). Perhaps the most favored of these was the T-maze (Figure 8.7b). The T-maze was used so much because it simplified the experimental analysis of "choice" behavior through the elimination of all but a single "choice point." The right and left arms of the T-maze radiate at right angles from this choice point and lead to areas where food or some other reinforcing event can be hidden from the subject's sight. The standard procedure in T-maze studies is to include randomly in each block of trials free-selection (choice) trials and equalize the number of trials to each arm by forcing the choice in the rest of the trials. Thus each free choice to the left side is balanced by a forced choice to the right side

Figure 8.7

Representative apparatuses used for the study of instrumental and operant learning. SB = startbox, GB = goalbox. Panel (a) is a prototypical floorplan for a multiple T-maze with ten choice points. Panel (b) is the floorplan of the more simple T-maze. Panel (c) depicts a straight runway. Panel (d) is the cut-away view of the manipulandum in an operant conditioning chamber. From Marx (1969, p. 9).

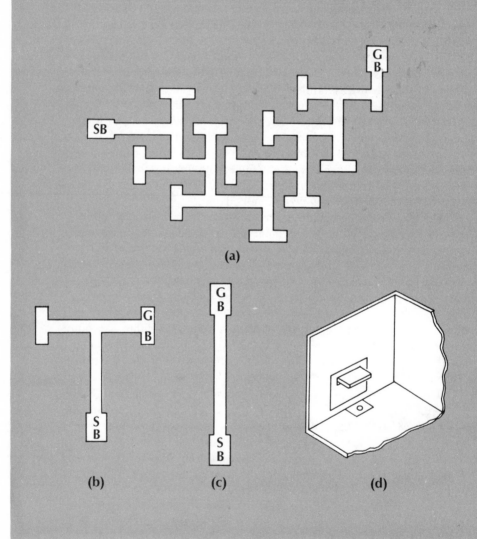

(a)

(b)   (c)   (d)

and vice versa. One measure of learning here is thus the percentage of correct responses per block of free-selection trials. Typically these percentages are averaged for a group of subjects and then plotted as a function of trial blocks (see Figure 8.8, Box 8.6).

A further simplification designed to make even less complex the study of instrumental behavior is elimination of choice points altogether. One apparatus adopted for this purpose has been the straight alley or runway (Figure 8.7c). The response measure most widely used here has been elapsed time to traverse some or all of the runway. Response sensing devices (photocells) placed at the exit of the alley start area, in parts of the runway, and at the entrance to the goal box and connected to respective elapsed time indicators permit response time measures to be collected from various apparatus subsections. Of these measures, one that is commonly reported is *start box time*. Another popular index is *running time*, collected for full alley performance and/or sometimes subdivided into performances for the beginning, middle, and last segments (see Box 8.6).

Major problems with response-time measures are that, when collected into distributions for purposes of calculating means and variances, they are often excessively variable and their distributions are highly skewed (non-normal). Both these problems prevent the proper application of advanced statistical analyses, thus prompting some psychologists to search for ways to transform these measures so that both variability and skewness are reduced. A common method has been to take the reciprocal of each running time measure prior to statistical treatment. Along with the two advantages of decreasing skewness and variability, a graph that depicts average reciprocal running time measures is somewhat easier to interpret than one of running times *per se*. As an example, we can consider the acquisition data of a six-foot alleyway running response. We can expect running times to be longer on early than on later training trials, so that, if plotted without transformation over blocks of trials, the graph would show a decreasing function as performance got better. A downward sloping curve depicting performance improvement is somewhat counterintuitive to many. However, for mean reciprocal running times (mean running speed), the graph of the same performance would show an increasing function. This can be understood by noting that the reciprocal of a very long running time of 20 sec in a six-foot alley, as would occur on early acquisition trials, is $\frac{1}{\frac{20\,\text{sec}}{6\,\text{ft}}}$, or 0.30 ft/sec. On later trials where a 1.25 sec time would not be unusual, and the reciprocal would be $\frac{1}{\frac{1.25\,\text{sec}}{6\,\text{ft}}}$, or 4.87 ft/sec. A graph of such reciprocal data seems intuitively easier to understand than one of untransformed running times. As in classical conditioning, instrumental performance times decrease (speeds increase) as a function of rewarded training (*acquisition*),

Box 8.6 Representative Acquisition Functions in Instrumental Learning

Figure 8.8 summarizes a factorial study of the combined effects of two reinforcement schedules and three amounts of reward on speed measures in the start, runway, and goal entrance of an alleyway apparatus. The performances of six groups of rats are depicted. The dashed and solid lines represent respective mean running speeds for groups given reward on 50 percent or 100 percent of the trials. The amount of reward was one (far left column), three (center column), or nine (far right column) food pellets. Running speeds are expressed as means of four trials, given on each of fifteen days. Figure 8.9 illustrates the results of a choice learning study using a simple T-maze. The data are expressed as the mean percent of the group that emitted a correct choice on acquisition trials (Clayton, 1969). Figure 8.10 depicts the acquisition of instrumental problem-solving behavior in which rhesus monkeys were exposed to different pairs of stimuli in different situations and could earn raisins for

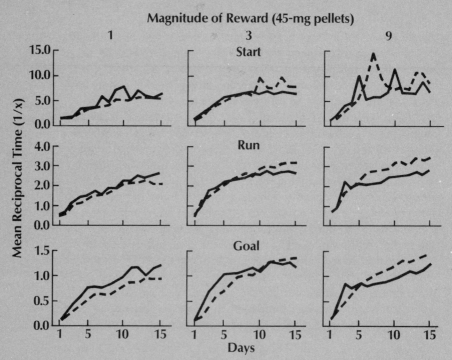

Figure 8.8 Acquisition of alley running, by segment (rows), for groups given partial (50 percent, dashed lines) or continuous (solid lines) food reward. Each column conforms to different reward magnitudes: one, three, and nine food pellets, respectively. From Hughes, Dunlap, and Dachowski (1974, p. 566).

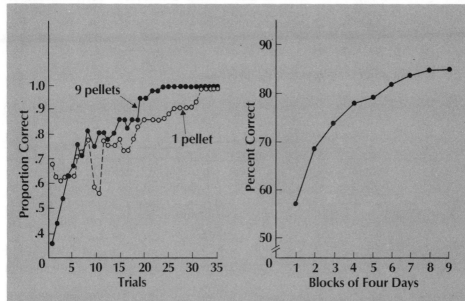

Figure 8.9 Proportion of subjects choosing the correct side of a T-maze. One group was trained with one pellet and the other with 9 pellets for the correct response. After Clayton (1969).

Figure 8.10 Discrimination learning by rhesus monkeys. Figure depicts the percent correct choices, averaged for blocks of four days, as a function of 36 days of practice. From Flagg (1974).

choosing the correct event. Forty trials per day were given over 36 days of training, and the data are expressed as percentage of correct responses, averaged by blocks of four days (Flagg, 1974).

Note for all these acquisition functions that the group curves are simple and negatively accelerated, and each shows a gradual increase in performance as a function of practice.

eventually leveling off without further change under otherwise constant reinforcement conditions (*performance asymptote*). Performance times increase (speeds decrease) over trials following removal of reward, thus defining *extinction* training.

Paradigms of Instrumental Learning

Whatever view one adopts about the role of classical conditioning in the study of instrumental learning, the general paradigms are indeed different for these two learning approaches. In classical conditioning, stimulus pairings occur independently of the behavior measured, while in instrumental learning, the stimulus environment is not paired with reward until the response occurs. Moreover, the natures of the responses under study are different. The CR is presumably a component of the UCR while the instrumental response is typically unrelated in almost every way to the reaction produced by the UCS-like reinforcer.

Given these basic differences between classical and instrumental procedures, a further distinction can be made within the instrumental paradigm based upon: (1) the nature of the consequence that is programmed to occur for a behavior; and (2) the kind of response-consequence contingency that is studied. Three major kinds of consequences—positive, neutral, and negative—have been studied with instrumental procedures. Positive consequences are defined as events, conditions, or situations that produce approach responses; negative consequences are those that result in withdrawal, escape, and/or avoidance reactions; neutral consequences produce neither approach nor withdrawal behaviors. Depending upon how these consequences are programmed, either an increase or a decrease in behavior may occur. When increased, the procedure is termed a *reinforcement paradigm;* when decreased, a *punishment paradigm.*

There are two kinds of reinforcement procedures. When a behavior increase results from application of a response-contingent positive consequence, it is called a *positive reinforcement paradigm.* When the response increase follows the response-contingent removal of a negative consequence, the paradigm is that of *negative reinforcement.* In both cases, the response under study must show an increase in probable reoccurrence to qualify as a reinforcement paradigm. For either of these reinforcement procedures, a particular stimulus may or may not be used as a signal that the response under study will be followed by a positive event or by withdrawal of a negative event. These stimuli, when used, are termed *discriminative stimuli.* Two variations in the negative reinforcement procedure have been studied extensively. One involves the removal of a primary negative event contingent upon the emission of a specified response, termed an *escape learning* procedure. The second entails termination of a stimulus when a specified response occurs to a stimulus that signals the occurrence of the primary negative event. This response also postpones the occurrence of the primary negative event as well, and the procedure is termed *avoidance learning.*

The second major instrumental learning paradigm, *punishment,* also can be subdivided depending upon how positive and negative events are arranged as behavioral consequences. If a decrease in behavior (behavioral suppression) results from presentation of a negative event, the procedure is called *positive punishment.* If behavior suppression instead follows removal of a positive event, the procedure is termed *negative punishment* (this is the same operation as experimental extinction).

Positive Reinforcement

Most psychologists agree that reinforcement is in some fundamental way important for understanding instrumental learning. There is, however, considerable controversy over its exact role. Probably the most neutral, and hence least disputed, stance on this issue is that if a reinforcer contingently follows a response, the probability of reoccurrence of that response will increase. This statement paraphrases what is termed the *empirical law of effect* (McGeoch & Irion, 1952; Postman, 1947). This law says that the strength of a response is determined by its effects, and it is empirical in that it contains no speculation as to how a reinforcer increases response probability. The law of effect contains no operations that define a reinforcer independent of its response-incrementing effects. Nonetheless, three factors are clear from this law. The first is that the positive reinforcement paradigm involves a contingency relationship between two events, a response (R) and a consequent stimulus (S), the term "contingency" being used here in much the same way as it was in our discussion of various CS/UCS relationships in classical conditioning. The second factor is that responses are seen to be affected by local or proximal consequences, not by events that are temporally, spatially, and/or situationally remote. The third factor is that the concept of reinforcement connotes response-produced stimulus change. In the case of positive reinforcement, the nature of that change is a response-correlated stimulus onset.

These three features of the law of effect have served to focus the research directions of students of instrumental learning. One such direction has been an experimental analysis of certain attributes of the reinforcer itself, probably the most researched of which have been the effects of variations in *amount.* Another direction has dealt with the effects of altering the interval between response termination and reward delivery, or of variations in *delay* of reward. Manipulations of the reinforcement schedule represent yet another way of examining the implications of the law of effect since they are directly concerned with the nature of the response-reinforcer contingency. These three directions will be taken up in order, and we will focus primarily upon the methodological aspects of each for understanding the basic instrumental learning process.

Amount.   There are numerous ways to vary amount. It can be manipulated in terms of the mass or volume of a substance, such as more or fewer grams of food or cubic centimeters of water for alley running, a lever press, etc. Amount can also be varied in terms of intensity (of rewarding electrical brain stimulation, or ESB) or concentration (of a sugar solution whose volume is held constant). Probably the most classic studies of amount are the experiments of Crespi (1942) and Zeaman (1949a). Both varied mass. In the latter study, seven groups of rats were given 18 alleyway trials per day for either 0.05, 0.2, 0.4, 0.6, 0.8, 1.6, or 2.4 g of cheese in the goalbox. Latency of leaving the start area and alley running times were the dependent variables. The larger food amounts were associated with shorter start latencies and faster alley running. More recently, increases in glucose or saccharin concentrations (Goodrich, 1960; Guttman, 1953; Kraeling, 1961; Rosen, 1966; Schrier, 1965; Young & Madsen, 1963) and in ESB intensity (Keesey, 1962, 1964) have, within limits, similarly been shown to increase response strength.

A major methodological concern with such studies is that variations in mass, volume, concentration, or intensity are usually accompanied by correlated changes in other aspects of the learning situation that may also influence performance. A variation in mass or volume is almost always accompanied by a variation in the amount of responding required for its consumption, i.e., by a variation in number of consummatory responses. Thus, more food means more chewing, more water means more swallowing, and so on. Other correlated effects of amount variations include differences in oropharyngeal stimulation, in levels of stomach loading, and in blood sugar and other internal chemical reactions. Any or all of these correlated changes can themselves be important determinants of performance.

Many experimental strategies have been introduced to evaluate separately some of these many potential sources of confounding. For example, a number of studies have assessed the contribution of the differences in consummatory responding that can occur with changes in amount. The general experimental strategy has been to vary consummatory behavior by subdividing the reward into smaller portions in order to increase chewing or swallowing, while holding the mass or volume of the food or water constant. This strategy has also been combined with the reverse manipulation of holding consummatory behavior constant while manipulating mass or volume. While this research has shown that either of these variations may be accompanied by correlated changes in performance strength, other uncontrolled factors have almost always been present to obscure clear interpretations. Indeed, it has not proven possible to separate and evaluate precisely all the variables that can confound amount manipulations, and the conclusion of Kling and Schrier (1971) may be noted here in this connection:

> ... the results indicate that in designs where each group receives but one condition of reinforcement, even quite large differences in amount of reinforcer may have little differential influence on behavior unless several other aspects of the situation are allowed to vary concomitantly. (p. 620)

Delay of reinforcement. Reinforcement is delayed when a period of time is inserted between completion of a designated instrumental response and the delivery of the reinforcer. The delay variable has been studied extensively in simple alleyway situations (Tarpy & Sawabini, 1974) where, following entrance into a goalbox, different groups have been given food following different elapsed durations (Logan, 1960, p. 46; Logan, Beier, & Ellis, 1955; Logan & Spanier, 1970). The effects of delay have also been investigated with a discrete-trial bar-press procedure where the bar is retracted between presses and food is given after a prescribed delay (Harker, 1956). Delay has also been evaluated in a variety of choice situations, the most widely used being the T-maze. The basic procedure here has been, for a correct left or right turn, to dispense the reward in the goal area after different delay intervals for each of several groups (Perkins, 1947). The general finding from all these procedures is that performance weakens as delay increases.

It has generally been assumed that if the passage of "pure" time and nothing else intervened between a response and a reinforcer, even very short delays would result in little or no learning (Spence, 1956). However, the concept of "pure" time is in practice probably little more than a theoretical fiction. Unauthorized, uncontrolled, and/or unobserved activity is likely to occur in any delay interval (Skinner, 1938, p. 73; Spence, 1956). These unauthorized behaviors will be more contiguous with the delayed reinforcer than the response under study and hence will inadvertently be strengthened over the latter. If the behaviors are similar in form to the response under study, then they can be expected to facilitate performance. This would in effect offset the behavior-debilitating effects of delay. However, if the behaviors are dissimilar, they may compete and hence impede the performance under study, thereby actually intensifying the degrading effects of delay. Several studies have tested this *interacting-response theory of delay* by employing procedures designed to minimize (Spence, 1956) or to increase (Grice, 1948) the occurrence of unauthorized incompatible behaviors during the response-

Box 8.7   Interacting Responses and Delay of Reward

Operant psychologists have developed a reinforcement procedure that encourages an organism to withhold a specific response, such as a bar press, for a specified period before finally emitting it. The subject is initially trained to emit the response at a high and stable rate. Reward is then withheld until the subject refrains from making the response for a short but constant period of time. The first response after this period is rewarded. This withholding-of-response training can be hastened by resetting the delay interval each time that the subject emits a premature response during the specified "dead" period. Once the subject learns to withhold behavior for this short period, the response-withholding time is increased and the entire training procedure is repeated, and so on, until the desired final response-withholding time is achieved. In effect, the subject is differentially rewarded for a much lower rate of responding than normally would occur, and this entire procedure is appropriately abbreviated a *DRL (differential reinforcement for low rates) reinforcement schedule.*

How does a subject learn to respond under such conditions of delayed reward? Laties, Weiss, and Weiss (1969) discovered that the presence of manipulable objects in the environment was correlated with more accurate response timing in this situation than was their absence. Further, when manipulable objects were not present, a rat timed the delay more accurately when it "filled" the dead interval with a stereotyped behavior such as "taking its tail in its mouth and nibbling on it" (Laties, Weiss, Clarke, & Reynolds, 1965). Analogously, human beings may repeatedly and covertly verbalize to themselves that reward is forthcoming in order to sustain behavior in the face of long delay intervals. This research provides a good illustration of how certain "mediating" responses may interact with and sometimes facilitate performance even when long delays between rewards and behavior are involved.

reward delay period. The major finding here has been that a reduction in opportunity for unauthorized behaviors during the delay results in shorter delay intervals that can sustain correct-response learning.

It turns out that the alleyway apparatus may not be well suited to an analysis of delay effects. While the alleyway has been a useful device to investigate the contribution of interacting responses, its use actually introduces another methodological problem. This problem can be understood by recalling from classical conditioning that situational stimuli, when paired with a reward-UCS, can come to produce CRs that are very similar to the UCR. These situational stimuli (the goalbox itself might be one) may in effect acquire many properties of the UCS, so that they can serve as a reward for behavior in their own right. Such stimuli have commonly been termed *secondary* or *conditioned reinforcers*. In alleyway studies, the stimuli of the goal area thus become, by virtue of repeated pairings with the reinforcer, conditioned reinforcers. It follows that in studies of delayed reward using runway apparatuses, any assessment of the "pure" effects of delay may be confounded by the concurrent behavior-maintaining presence of these secondary-reward goal cues.

A choice-learning situation can be used to nullify partly the contaminating effects of secondary reinforcement in delay studies. In principle, the choice-point stimuli of a T-maze should be no more nor less secondarily reinforcing whether a correct or an incorrect response is emitted. The ideal procedure would be to arrange the choice situation so that no particular spatial direction or other distinguishing feature of the environment is associated with reward, thereby eliminating all sources of conditioned reinforcement for both correct and incorrect behaviors. This procedure has been approximated (cf. Grice, 1948; Lett, 1973, 1974) but probably never fully implemented, and the data on the effects of delay in choice-learning situations remain confused. Some studies have shown that only very short delays of a few seconds can sustain effective learning (Grice, 1948) while others have shown that very long delays of several minutes (Lett, 1973, 1974) or even hours (Revusky & Garcia, 1970) may tolerate some learning.

Extinction, the ultimate delay. The extreme case of delay is when reward is omitted altogether for a reinforced response. This infinite delay eventually results in complete cessation of behavior; it is the basic operation for *experimental extinction*. Another way of viewing extinction is as a within-subjects procedure (D'Amato, 1969) in which the same subject is given consecutive experiences with two reward values, that used during training and zero. The question of interest then becomes whether the results of the latter operation are the same as when a subject is shifted from an immediate to a longer, but still finite, delay. This has been termed a delay-contrast procedure, and its results are discussed later.

Partial reinforcement. Most of the studies dealing with variations in amount and delay cited above involved reward for every response occurrence, termed a *continuous schedule of reinforcement* (abbreviated CRF). But in everyday life, most human responses are only occasionally followed by a reward. The question of what effect on behavior an intermittent reward procedure would have thus arises (see Box 8.6, Figure 8.8). We noted previously that the results of intermittent UCS presentations in classical conditioning are highly equivocal. Further, it seems intuitively reasonable in instrumental situations that a partial reward procedure on acquisition trials would be accompanied by weaker and more erratic performance than would a continuous-reward procedure. This is indeed the case, especially for the early and intermediate portions of acquisition training. Further, the higher the percentage of reinforced trials, the more performance strength and consistency resemble those of continuously rewarded subjects. However, when training is prolonged by increasing the number of trials, some studies have shown equal or even better terminal acquisition performances for partial- than for continuous-reward groups (Goodrich, 1959; Spear, Hill, & O'Sullivan, 1965). This latter finding, called an acquisition "crossover effect," has also been labeled the *partial reinforcement acquisition effect,* abbreviated PRAE.

A much more consistent effect of partial reinforcement (PRF) on instrumental behavior occurs for extinction training. To illustrate, consider Weinstock's (1954) study. Using one runway trial per day, he rewarded different groups of rats either on 17, 33, 50, 67, 83, or 100 percent of the trials (note that trials but *not* number of rewards were equated for each group). Weinstock (1954, 1958) reported an inverse relationship between resistance to extinction and the percentage of rewarded acquisition trials, with the 17 percent group taking more trials to reach extinction criterion than any other group. This study illustrates the highly-consistent *partial-reinforcement extinction effect,* abbreviated PREE.

Several variables have been found to interact with the PREE. For example, the more acquisition trials given, the larger the magnitude of the PREE. But a methodological note must be inserted here since increasing the number of training trials (much like increasing amount of reinforcement; cf. Sperling, 1965a, 1965b) seems to promote more rapid extinction for the 100 percent reward group; it does not much influence the extinction performance of PRF subjects. This is related to another methodological problem, touched upon earlier. Should PRF groups be given the same number of reward trials or of acquisition trials as CRF subjects? Clearly, one of these variables cannot be equated without the other differing across the two groups. But what about a three-group design in which for one PRF group the number of trials is equated with the CRF condition and for the other the number of rewards is equated? This design at least provides a basis for combining logic and empirical outcome in order to determine the respective effects of these two variables.

By separately comparing the performance of each PRF group with the CRF condition and with each other, it would be possible to deduce whether number of trials and/or number of rewards are important determinants of the PREE (Robbins, 1971).

Reinforcement contrast effects.   In most of the research summarized thus far, single reward conditions were assigned to separate groups; that is, we have focused on the results of separate-groups studies. However, special effects have sometimes been reported for variations in *amount, delay,* and *scheduling* of rewards within groups. These within-group phenomena are termed "reward contrast" effects, and the general experimental procedure has been to train the same group under one reward condition and then "shift" it to another when it reaches its performance asymptote. Actually, two basic procedures have been followed in "reward-contrast" studies. One is to give the different levels of the variable consecutively, i.e., to "shift" a group from one level to another. The second is to provide access to the different levels on a semi-concurrent basis. To illustrate the former, consider the classic "amount-shift" study of Zeaman (1949b). He first trained different groups of rats to run an alleyway for a small or a large amount of food. Each group was then shifted to the opposite amount for a few additional trials. One result of this reward shift was a relatively abrupt change in the performances of both groups. The switch from the small to the large reward produced a rapid decrease in startbox latencies, while the reverse shift resulted in a precipitous increase in the same measure. Spence (1956) thought these performance changes occurred too rapidly to be due to alterations in associative strength and attributed them to changes in motivational level; his view is now widely accepted (Logan, 1960). Zeaman (1949b) also found that an increase (or decrease) in amount of reward was accompanied by an increase (or decrease) in running speed to a level that was superior (or inferior) to the mean pre-shift running performance that was recorded under the original reward condition. Crespi (1942) called similar changes "elation" and "depression" effects but attempts to replicate the "elation," or *positive contrast effect,* have not met with consistent success (cf. Collier & Marx, 1959; Dunham & Kilps, 1969; pp. 118–119, text). However, several studies have duplicated the "depression," or *negative reward contrast effect* (cf. DiLollo & Beez, 1966; Ehrenfreund & Badia, 1962; Roberts, 1966; Spence, 1956). A similar procedure to that of Zeaman (1949a) has been used to study delay-shift (Harker, 1956; Sgro & Weinstock, 1963).

An example of a semi-concurrent reinforcement-contrast procedure comes from a within-subjects study of PRF by Amsel (1967). He gave the same subjects both CRF and PRF acquisition training and used a double-alleyway apparatus in which the same starting area was employed for both runways. One runway was painted white and the other black, and each could rapidly be interchanged in front of the start area. By pairing the respective runways with the different reinforcement conditions, e.g., counterbalanced so that half had black-CRF, white-PRF and half had black-PRF, white-CRF, the same subjects were concurrently trained on both schedules and learned to respond differentially to the CRF and PRF alleys. A control group received CRF in both alleys. When extinguished in the partially-rewarded alley, the PRF group showed the PREE relative to the CRF control subjects. When compared to the CRF group in the continuous-reward alley, the PRF group again showed a PREE-like effect, despite their previous CRF experience in this alley. That the CRF control group was a necessary part of the study was illustrated when extinction performances were compared for it and the PRF subjects in the continuously-rewarded alley. Had only the PRF group been tested in this alley, it would not have been possible to discern whether or not a PREE resulted since its performance was the same as in the partially-rewarded alley. But, when compared with the performance of the CRF group in the continuous-reward alley, the PRF group showed a PREE-like effect. In other words the extinction performance in the continuous-reward alley of a group that was given both CRF and PRF training was prolonged relative to a CRF-only group. Indeed, the performance of the PRF group was comparable to that which would have resulted from an exclusive history of PRF acquisition training in that alley.

Classical-instrumental interactions revisited. Explanations of the above-noted effects on instrumental performance of between-group variations in amount, delay, and schedules as well as of contrast effects based upon within-subjects designs have long included the concept of classical conditioning. Following our earlier discussion (p. 338) of Spence (1956), virtually all instrumental reward situations contain the elements of the classical conditioning paradigm. Presumably, CRs develop on early trials to the goal area stimuli that are contiguous with the reward-UCS. Then, as CR strength increases with further trials, partial CRs can be expected to generalize to alley stimuli near the goal because of the physical similarity of these cues to one another. Second-order conditioning may also come into play here because of the contiguous pairings of alley with goal-area cues. With even further trials, weak CRs may even generalize to the stimuli of the start area.

This basic notion of classical conditioning in discrete-trial instrumental learning situations was first emphasized by Clark Hull (1943) and later expanded upon by his follower, Spence (1956). Hull (1943) assigned secondary-reinforcement properties to hypothetical CRs in instrumental situations. He did so to account for the fact that most of the responses in any instrumental behavior sequence occur prior to any physical contact with the reward. That is, only goal-area responses, not the responses of leaving the start area and running down the alley, come in contact with reward. He saw the presence of a generalized CR in the start and other alley areas, because of its similarity to the actual eating-UCR from which it originated, as a covert source of conditioned reinforcement for initial and intermediate components of the instrumental running sequence. Conceived this way, classical conditioning provides a reward surrogate that covertly mediates the development and maintenance of instrumental performance. Hull (1943) labeled this hypothetical CR as r_g to denote that it was a fractional portion of the goal consummatory response, R_G. In S-R theory, a response *per se* cannot qualify as a reinforcer. Hull thus assigned this function to the stimulus aftereffects of r_g, namely s_g.

Spence (1956) introduced into this conceptual framework the notion that the r_g-s_g concept also can supply a source of motivation for the instrumental response. He argued that the more or less vigorous was r_g, the more or less drive level it contributed to performance. Since r_g was conceptually linked to R_G, the reward-produced UCR, Spence's (1956) notion is a reward-incentive theory of motivation. Spence used his r_g motivation conception to explain the effects of variations in reward amount and delay. Such manipulations were thought to affect the vigor of r_g, i.e., the more amount (or less delay), the stronger the r_g. The strength of an instrumental performance thus varied as a function of the motivation supplied by the current vigor of r_g. However, Brown and Farber (1968) have noted that it is illogical to view the conditioned component of an eating response, itself pacifying, as a source of arousal. Intuitively, it is more reasonable to assume that r_g itself should be relaxing and the stronger the r_g, the more relaxing. Brown and Farber summarize evidence supporting their views. However, in noting that instrumental performance indeed is invigorated by increases in amount and similar reward manipulations, they reasoned that commensurate increases in r_g in the absence of direct contact with food is analogous to increasing the anticipation for a desired object. But, under such circumstances, increased but unrewarded anticipation can be a strong source of frustration. It is thus this frustration that serves as a source of motivation, not r_g. Hence, increased r_g vigor due to increased amount or to decreased delay should be accompanied by increased frustration in the start and alley areas where food anticipation is high but no food is present.

Amsel (1958, 1962, 1972) has also injected the concept of frustration into classical conditioning conceptions of instrumental learning, primarily in regard to scheduling effects. He has argued that, following the development of a modest r_g-s_g response on early, continuous-reward trials (subjects are usually given enough initial CRF training to establish a response before they are placed on a PRF schedule in studies of partial reinforcement), the insertion of a nonrewarded trial introduces the element of frustration. This frustration reaction is seen as the equivalent of an unconditioned response, R_F, in such situations. Just as r_g can be conditioned to goal and alley cues as a component of R_G, so also can r_f be conditioned as a component of R_F.

However, r_f-s_f allegedly becomes strengthened and generalizes to the alleyway cues during PRF training in the context of two factors that counter its normally aversive and potentially disruptive effects on running. One factor is that an emerging r_f-s_f habit will occur in the presence of the reward given on rewarded trials, a condition that is seen to *countercondition* or neutralize its negative effects on performance. (Counterconditioning is a procedure whereby a negative stimulus is neutralized by pairing it in weak form with a stronger, positive stimulus. In continuing this pairings procedure, the intensity of the initially negative event is increased gradually over trials so that its disruptive effects are always offset by the appetitive effects of the positive stimulus.)

A second neutralizing factor is that r_f-s_f occurs and is further counterconditioned in the presence of r_g-s_g, itself stronger because of more rewarded than nonrewarded trials in the training procedure. The net effect of this alleged conditioning and neutralization of the negative effects of conditioned frustration, r_f-s_f, in a PRF situation is that the subject presumably learns to "persist" in running in the presence of such internal frustration stimuli. The explanation given by Amsel for a PREE, then, is that PRF subjects have learned to run in the presence of frustration such as is also produced by nonrewarded extinction trials, while CRF-trained subjects have not.

Frustration theory can also explain certain reinforcement contrast effects. For example, both downward amount-shift and short-to-long delay-shift procedures involve at least two factors that could degrade performance levels below those of subjects trained only to the smaller amount or to the longer delay. Shifts from a higher to a lower reward quantity (or from an immediate to a prolonged delay) are the equivalent of abruptly introducing the behaviorally disruptive effects of frustration, a factor that does not occur for unshifted subjects. Performances for the shifted subjects should thus decline below those of unshifted animals. Second, such shifts represent sudden environmental alterations from the original conditions of the training situation. As in classical conditioning, instrumental performances abruptly deteriorate as a function of degree of physical change from the stimulus conditions that prevail during learning. This type of performance change is attributable to *generalization decrement* and also would not occur for unshifted groups.

The status of the CR in instrumental learning research.   Any attempts to verify the role of classical conditioning in instrumental learning are plagued with conceptual and methodological difficulties. First, the classical-instrumental interaction theorists noted above have been equivocal on whether classical conditioning *actually* occurs in the instrumental learning situation. Instead, the classical-instrumental interaction notion has been proposed as but a conceptual model of how to understand the development, maintenance, and extinction of instrumental performance. The suggestion of this model for research thus was *not* to examine instrumental learning situations for the existence of CRs, but instead to determine if instrumental performances could be understood in terms of the laws of classical conditioning. The strategy of experimental analysis was to vary features of the instrumental paradigm as suggested by an understanding of the laws of classical conditioning. If changes in instrumental performance followed predictions based upon classical learning, then the latter would be upheld as a theoretical model of the former (cf. Chapter 1 on theory in science).

One experimental approach that has followed this conceptualization has been to introduce established CSs into the instrumental situation and to study their effects on the growth, maintenance, or extinction of instrumental responses. This approach conforms to the CS-IR procedure discussed in the section on classical conditioning (see 320 ff. and Box 8.3). Yet, while an external CS can influence instrumental behavior, this procedure unfortunately cannot illuminate whether or not that performance itself was established or is maintained by *covert* CS-CR learning.

A better test of the classical-instrumental interaction theory is a situation in which instrumental response training can be conducted devoid of the simultaneous possibility of classical conditioning. Miller and his colleagues (1969) attempted this by conducting instrumental training with autonomic (rather than skeletal) response systems normally thought susceptible only to classical conditioning (cf. Rescorla & Solomon, 1967) while paralyzing the skeletal musculature (with d-tubocurarine) so that alternative sources of responding could not occur during this autonomic training. These investigators rewarded (usually with ESB) increases and decreases in EKG, kidney secretion, peristaltic activity of the colon, and differential blood pressure. Control groups received equal numbers of rewards, but delivered noncontingently. Clear response changes for ESB reward were obtained in either direction for all of the measures. While these data indeed can be taken as indicating that instrumental learning may occur in the absence of concurrent classical conditioning, they have unfortunately been difficult to replicate by either Miller (Miller, 1973) or others (Whitman, Snyder, & Anderson, 1975).

A third strategy of investigating possible interactions between classical and instrumental learning has been to search for and measure directly possible CRs during the instrumental training procedure. Three main conditions should hold here for a classical conditioning interpretation of instrumental performance. First, the allegedly critical CR should develop and be manifest prior to emergence of the instrumental response. Second, elimination of the CR should produce a substantial deterioration in the instrumental performance. Third, instrumental performances should always be accompanied by an appropriate maintaining CR. The experimental literature to date shows that sometimes these conditions have been met and that other times no consistent or an opposite relationship between a CR and instrumental behaviors has been found (Rescorla & Solomon, 1967).

Negative Reinforcement

The two basic operations that define the negative reinforcement paradigm are those of *escape* and *avoidance learning*. Escape learning entails terminating an aversive event by emitting a specified response, the consequence being an increase in the future probable reoccurrence of that response. An example of escape learning would be termination of an electric shock, delivered through a grid floor, upon running down an alleyway into a goal box, followed by a faster running time on the following trial. Acquisition and extinction functions for escape learning parallel those for reward training. Avoidance learning is defined when response likelihood is increased for a behavior that terminates a signal for a painful stimulus as well as postpones the painful event itself. Shuttling from one side of a box to another to terminate a tone that has been paired with shock and to postpone the shock itself is an example of avoidance learning.

Variables and the methodology of escape learning.   The variable of *amount* is usually defined in terms of the degree of reduction in the physical intensity of a negative stimulus resulting from an instrumental response. Escape from cold or hot water of specified temperature levels, or from loud noises designated in terms of dB levels (Myers, 1965), or from electric shocks of given voltages, amperages, or wattages (cf. Campbell & Masterson, 1969; Campbell & Teghtsoonian, 1958) have been studied in this connection with similar results. Generally, the greater the resulting reduction in the physical intensity of the noxious stimulus, the greater the terminal speed of the escape response. Trapold and Fowler (1960), for instance, gave alleyway escape training to five groups of rats using shock levels of 120, 160, 240, 320, or 400 volts in a between-groups design. Running speeds into an uncharged goal box increased with voltage, the increase tapering off toward the higher voltages.

Delay in escape learning is defined by the time that elapses between response occurrence and termination of the negative event. Fowler and Trapold (1962) postponed shock reduction for different groups of rats for either 0, 1, 2, 4, 8, or 16 sec following entrance into an alley goal area. The greater the delay, the slower the terminal mean running performances. The effects of *amount* and *delay* seem to be the same for escape and for positive reinforcement learning paradigms. The general behavioral law here thus seems to be "the *more* and the *quicker* the delivery of the reinforcer, the better the performance."

Other variables of concern in escape learning have included *duration between trials* (intertrial interval, ITI) and *partial reinforcement*. Franchina (1969) reported that terminal escape times are faster when the time between trials is quite short (one minute), as opposed to quite long (24 hours). However, this finding held only for a CRF escape training procedure, i.e., shock given on each trial. On a PRF escape schedule in which nonshock trials occurred randomly 50 percent of the time, this ITI variation had little effect on performance.

An inherent methodological problem in PRF investigations of escape learning is that nonreinforced trials are difficult to implement. Since the reinforcement for an escape response is the response-correlated end of the aversive stimulus, it follows that nonreinforced trials should entail indefinite continuation of the aversive stimulus. This is an unreasonable procedure for both humane and procedural reasons. The aversive event *must* be terminated eventually. But this means that "unreinforced" trials are actually confounded with the operation of *delayed reinforcement*. This dilemma has been countered in many studies of PRF escape learning by simply omitting the negative stimulus altogether on nonreward acquisition trials. Unfortunately, this procedure introduces another potential source of confounding. For positive reinforcement studies of PRF, motivational level is established and maintained independently of reward conditions through relatively precise food- or water-deprivation regimens. But, omission of the reinforcer on nonreward trials in a negative reinforcement study of PRF also removes the primary source of motivation, i.e., the aversive stimulus. Two conditions thereby are manipulated with this procedure; namely, the PRF variable and the motivation level. The implication is that there seems no clear way to avoid confounding in the study of PRF effects in escape learning. However, see Box 8.8.

Avoidance learning.   Avoidance learning is actually a secondary rather than a primary negative reinforcement paradigm. This is because subjects must learn a response that terminates a stimulus which signals a primary aversive event, rather than terminates the aversive stimulus itself. The response also postpones delivery of the aversive stimulus and must increase in frequency to conform to a definition of instrumental avoidance learning.

A number of discrete-trial methods have been used to study avoidance learning (Herrnstein, 1969; Solomon & Brush, 1956). The more widely used have entailed variations of the Miller-Mowrer shuttlebox procedure (Miller, 1948). The shuttlebox is rectangular in shape, has a grid floor through which shock can be given, and is divided into two compartments separated either by a guillotine-type door, a hurdle de-

Box 8.8   Escape Learning, PRF, and Confounding

Bower (1960) combined the variables of *delay* and *intermittency* in an escape learning procedure in order to control partly some of the aforementioned problems of confounding. Four groups of rats were given 20 alleyway escape training trials in which 0, 5, 10, or 15 trials randomly were nonreinforced for different groups. Reinforced and nonreinforced trials were defined, respectively, as trials on which shock ended immediately or after a 20-sec delay upon entrance into the goal box. Asymptotic acquisition running speeds were slower for the PRF than for the CRF groups and were a negative monotonic function of reinforcement percentage. The test for a PREE entailed switching the 50 percent PRF and the CRF groups to 0 percent reward, i.e., every trial terminated with the 20-sec goal shock delay. In spite of equivalent motivation levels during extinction for these two groups, the CRF subjects showed rapid deterioration in mean running speeds compared to the 50 percent PRF group, which, interestingly, showed little change from their mean terminal acquisition performance (Figure 8.11). These data nicely parallel the PREE reported with positive reinforcement paradigms.

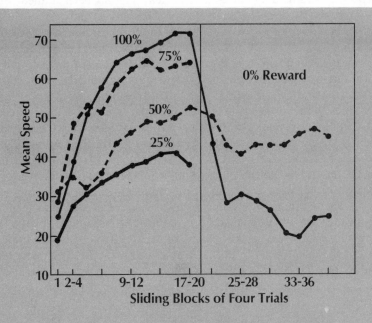

Figure 8.11 Escape learning under different percentages of reinforcement. Each curve depicts the performance (mean alley speed) of a different partial-reward condition. At the end of acquisition, the 100 percent and 50 percent groups were switched to 0 percent (zero reward) reward condition. From Bower (1960).

vice, or an archway through which the subject can shuttle. Either one- or two-way shuttle avoidance-response learning has been studied with this apparatus. By *one-way* is meant that the subject must learn to shuttle from one side of the box, e.g., side A, to the other, side B, in the same direction for each trial. (Half of the subjects are trained to shuttle from side A to side B and half from B to A in a counterbalanced procedure.) A typical one-way procedure involves presenting an initially neutral stimulus (the CS) and, if a shuttle does not occur within a specified period, introducing the primary aversive stimulus (such as electric shock, the UCS). Both the neutral and the aversive stimuli are then terminated by a shuttle response. An avoidance response is defined if shuttling occurs between CS- and UCS-onset; an escape response if shuttling occurs after UCS onset. Dependent variables have included latency to respond from CS onset, percent escapes, and/or avoidances per trial block, and so on.

There can be many uncontrolled sources of variation in one-way procedures. For instance, the subject must be transported by the experimenter from side B back to side A of the shuttle box on each trial. Aside from the inconvenience, this acts as a distraction to the subject because of extraneous handling, stimulation, exposure to apparatus noises, and so forth. These latter are extraexperimental, albeit random, and require many trials and subjects to be "averaged out." In part, the *two-way shuttle procedure* surmounts some of these problems since handling is averted throughout each training session. Here, shuttling in *both* directions (A to B *and* B to A) is required. This means that it must be possible to present the CS and UCS on either side of the shuttlebox. A trial is defined by CS onset on the side currently occupied by the subject. An avoidance is defined if shuttling occurs within the CS-UCS interval; otherwise the subject must shuttle to escape both stimuli. If no response occurs within a given period from UCS onset, both CS and UCS are terminated. A variable time period is programmed between trials to discourage temporal learning. *Temporal learning* is defined as responding to a fixed passage of time (rather than to the CS) to avoid the UCS; it will occur if a fixed interval of time intervenes between trials (Sidman, 1960a).

The response measures for the two-way procedure are the same as for the one-way method. We should, however, note that two-way shuttle learning entails repetitious shuttling into areas where shock was given on preceding trials. This is analogous to *avoidance-avoidance conflict* training (Miller, 1959) in that a choice must be made between two undesirable options. The subject can remain in the presence of the CS, where shock is imminent, or can shuttle to a place where shock has been given. This procedural anomaly has complicated precise experimental analyses of this learning phenomenon, including examinations of the effects of such variables as *amount, delay, intermittent reinforcement, intertrial interval,* and *CS-UCS interval.* (These latter variables produce quite different effects with the one-way procedure, [cf. Thios & Dunaway, 1964, 1969]).

To illustrate the effects of avoidance-avoidance conflict, consider how the administration of shock in both shuttle compartments complicates analyses of the effects of *amount*. In opposition to findings with one-way procedures, an inverse relationship between UCS intensity (amount) and avoidance performance has been the typical finding with the two-way procedure. The stronger the UCS intensity in a between-groups procedure: (1) the more escape trials before the emergence of an avoidance response; and (2) the fewer overall avoidance responses *per se* even after prolonged training (Cicala & Kremer, 1969; Kurtz & Shafer, 1967; Levine, 1966; Moyer & Korn, 1964; Thios, Lynch, & Lowe, 1966). McAllister, McAllister, and Douglas (1970) have nicely shown that these counterintuitive findings are due to shock administration on both sides of the shuttlebox in the two-way procedure. They demonstrated that for strong shock-UCS levels, unusually strong classical aversive conditioning occurs to both the CS *and* to the environmental cues of both sides of the shuttle apparatus. They further showed that either of these sources of stimulation alone was sufficient to produce immobilizing freezing responses for the rat, thus impairing (competing with) the development of shuttle behavior. A lower shock UCS during training did not produce as much freezing-immobilization to either the CS or the environment, thereby allowing for the more rapid emergence of consistency in shuttle behavior.

Another methodological issue (it applies to both one- and two-way procedures) also complicates the study of shuttlebox avoidance learning. The subject's response in avoidance experiments can have a far greater consequence than in most instrumental learning procedures. For example, an avoidance response produces, by virtue of the omission of the UCS, a *subject-imposed intermittent schedule of reinforcement*. Moreover, the exact *percentage* and *pattern* of UCS-reinforced trials are also subject-imposed. Finally, the *delay* of reinforcement (UCS offset) also is determined by the subject's response.

Method and theory in avoidance learning. The most controversial issue in avoidance learning deals with the two-factor theory mentioned in Box 8.9. Classical conditioning is invoked as *factor one* to establish the CS as an aversive substitute for the UCS. *Factor two* refers to the development, through trial-and-error activity, of an instrumental escape response from this secondary aversive stimulus. The subject is seen less as avoiding the UCS than as escaping the aversive CS.

The advantage of this theory is that it is a nonteleological account of what looks superficially like purposive avoidance behavior. The disadvantage of it is that it is confounded with an apparently more parsi-

Box 8.9   Reinforcement Delay in Avoidance Learning

The concept of delayed negative reinforcement is normally associated with delayed UCS termination. However, this concept must be modified for avoidance learning, where the CS comes to control responding. One view of the role of the CS in such procedures is that, because of classical-conditioning-like pairings with the shock-UCS on early escape trials, it also becomes aversive. The subject is seen, thereby, to learn an escape response from the CS. Thus, shock is not really avoided; instead, escape from the aversive CS is learned. Avoidance situations thus conceptualized entail a pair of escape responses, the first being escape from the UCS and the second being escape from the feared CS. This is the *two-factor theory* of avoidance learning (Mowrer, 1947). By this view, the concept of delay may be applied to both the CS and the UCS in avoidance-learning situations. Kamin (1956) did just that by giving two-way shuttle training to four groups of rats (the CS-UCS interval was 5 sec).

For the "normal" group, both CS and UCS were terminated immediately for escape responses and the CS immediately for an avoidance. For the "terminate-CS" group, the CS also was terminated for an avoidance, but shock nonetheless followed 5 sec after CS onset and continued until the subject again shuttled, i.e., escaped from shock. For the "avoid-UCS" group, the UCS could be avoided by shuttling during the CS-UCS interval, but CS offset was postponed for the remaining portion of the 5 sec CS-UCS interval. The "classical" group could escape the CS but not avoid the UCS and was given CS-UCS pairings for every trial. In this study, delay was thus defined in terms of both delayed UCS termination (the "terminate-CS" and "classical" groups) and delayed CS termination ("avoid-UCS" and "classical" groups). In both cases, delay impaired performance since, as seen in Figure 8.12, the "normal" group evinced both more avoidance responses and shorter response latencies than any of the other three. Not surprisingly, the "classical" group performed least well on these measures. The remaining groups performed indistinguishably from one another and intermediate to the other two. Kamin's (1956) interpretations of these data are complicated, and you are referred to his article and to Bolles, Stokes, and Younger (1966) for further expositions of the problems of delay in avoidance learning.

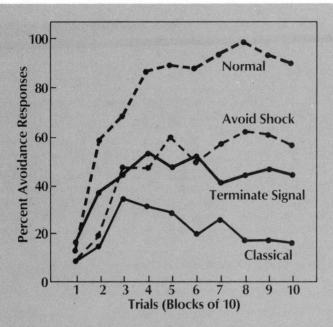

Figure 8.12 The two sources of reward for avoidance learning. Each curve depicts group percent avoidance responses in which an avoidance during the CS either avoided the UCS (avoid shock), terminated the CS (terminate signal), both avoided the UCS and terminated the CS (normal), or neither avoided the UCS nor terminated the CS (classical). From Kamin (1956).

Figure 8.13

Schematic of the procedure of Herrnstein and Hineline (1966). The tape advances every 2 sec. Deflections on the lines marked "post-shock" and "post-response" indicate when shocks would be given if the distribution was "in effect." The "distribution in effect" line depicts which of the latter two channels controls shock delivery. The responses and the shocks received are depicted on the last two lines. See text for further explanation. From Herrnstein and Hineline (1966).

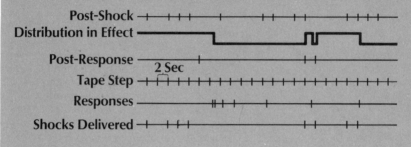

monious account of the same behavior (Herrnstein, 1969). Not only does an avoidance response terminate the CS in most procedures, but it also reduces the relative frequency of shock occurrence. A relative reduction in shock frequency, itself an apparent reward, is a more simple, unifactor account of avoidance learning than is a two-factor theory. Relative shock-frequency reduction, like food to a hungry subject, increases the probability of the response upon which it is contingent and thus meets the specifications of the empirical law of effect.

Herrnstein (1969) proposed a critical test of these two theories in which no possible warning CS was involved, but in which an avoidance response met with a reduction in the relative frequency of shocks. If the probability of avoidance behavior increased as a result, then the experiment could be taken as strongly supporting the more simple law-of-effect account of avoidance learning. The avoidance procedure proposed by Herrnstein to eliminate all CS-like warning signals (Herrnstein & Hineline, 1966) is illustrated in Figure 8.13. Each line is an event marker for the various possible stimulus arrangements or response occurrences in this procedure. The upper line, termed the post-shock distribution, depicts the rate at which brief shocks (0.3 sec, 0.8 mA), scheduled randomly across 2 sec time frames, are given unless an avoidance response (a bar-press) is made. Note that shocks can occur fairly frequently in this distribution (30 percent probability per 2 sec time unit). The third line is the second of the two shock-density distributions involved, the post-response distribution. If a bar-press response occurs while the subject is "in" the post-shock distribution, it automatically is switched to this post-response distribution. Note that the density of scheduled shocks in this latter distribution is much less (10 percent per 2 sec time unit) than for the post-shock distribution. The first shock received in the post-response distribution switches the subject back into the higher density distribution. The second line shows the distribution "in effect" at any given time. Line four depicts the 2 sec steps as the tape advances at 2 sec intervals. Line five shows the responses made. By visually correlating these responses with the first three lines, it can be seen that the first response "placed" the subject in the lower shock density distribution, the post-response distribution. Further responses were ineffective until a shock was received in this distribution, automatically placing the subject back into the post-shock distribution, and so on.

Herrnstein and Hineline (1966) used shock durations that were so short that a bar-press would always take longer to occur. Thus, actual *escape* learning was impossible. Since no external event signalled which shock distribution was "in effect," they argued that any avoidance learning must be due to the response-contingent reduction in relative shock frequency and not to escape learning from an aversive CS. Their learning curves for individual rats showed that, over thirty 2 hr sessions, most subjects showed gradually increasing rates of responding and decreasing post-shock response latencies.

Herrnstein (1969) concluded from these data that the subjects learned of the two shock density distributions and acquired a response that avoided the higher density. Most challenges to this conclusion have been based upon the views that: (1) Herrnstein and Hineline (1966) did not eliminate all the potential sources of CS-like warning signals (Crowell, 1973; Koehn, Anderson, Brown, & Crowell, 1973); (2) their subjects did not learn about two distributions of shocks but, more simply, that pressing leads to a longer average shock-free period (Crowell, 1973); and (3) their procedure actually was an escape-learning situation from closely packed shock-trains of stimulation. These challenges have emerged from the finding of no learning when the two density functions were changed so that shocks in the higher density, post-shock distribution were more widely spaced in time than in the Herrnstein and Hineline (1966) procedure and were commensurately even less dense in the post-response distribution (Koehn et al., 1973).

Punishment *is defined by the change in the response.*

Punishment is essentially the opposite of reinforcement. The major antecedent condition of punishment is presentation of an aversive stimulus (S) contingent upon the occurrence of an established behavior (R), i.e., an R-S contingency. The consequent condition is the suppression of that response. A clear methodological difference between the punishment and reinforcement paradigms is that the latter increases behaviors to above-zero levels while the former requires that responses initially be above zero in rate of occurrence so that their suppression can be studied. This means that punishment variables themselves are likely to be influenced by existing reinforcement conditions, including those involved in the initial training and in the maintenance of the response to be punished. An aversive stimulus (usually electric shock) will be more or less effective in suppressing behavior depending upon the level of food or water deprivation used to motivate the punished response, the nature of the schedule of reinforcement involved, the amount of the reward used, and so forth. Unfortunately, these factors often have not been held constant across studies of punishment, and results have often been conflicting.

Another methodological issue relates to the importance of the punishment contingency. Perhaps the best known early studies of punishment were reported by Estes (1944). He showed, among other things, that considerable response suppression may result simply from presenting the aversive stimulus in the same situation where the response also occurs. Considerable controversy has raged ever since as to whether any, some, or all response suppression occurs because of the allegedly essential R-S punishment contingency (Church, 1963). A number of studies have convincingly shown stronger suppression when aversive stimulation is response contingent than when it is not (Church, Wooton, & Matthews, 1970; Hoffman, 1969; Schuster & Rachlin, 1968). Interestingly, a recent growing literature shows that response-contingent aversive stimulation can also facilitate response occurrence under certain circumstances through "paradoxical punishment effects" (Boe & Church, 1968).

A final important issue in punishment has dealt with the degree of relative permanence in response suppression produced by a punisher. Estes' (1944) early research was again influential in establishing a persisting viewpoint on this issue. He showed that, whether a strong or a weak punisher was used, response suppression was not very lasting. However, this finding was probably the combined result of training procedures that established an unusually durable baseline response and of a narrow range of punishment intensities (Boe & Church, 1967).

Amount and delay. *Amount* in punishment studies conforms to the intensity of the punisher. Studies with rats and pigeons, using a wide variety of apparatuses, have shown that the magnitude of suppression produced by electric shock is a positive function of both shock intensity (Azrin, 1960; Boe & Church, 1967; Camp, Raymond, & Church, 1967; Church, Raymond, & Beauchamp, 1967) and punishment duration

Box 8.10   A Paradoxical Punishment Effect: Self-Punitive Behavior in the Rat

Brown, Martin, and Morrow (1964) gave 20 shock-escape acquisition trials in a six-foot alley (10 trials/day) to three groups of rats. Their start-box consisted of an upper and lower compartment. The subject was initially housed in the upper and exposed to an intermittent buzzer for about 10 sec. The compartment floor was then removed, dropping the subject onto an electrically-charged grid. The rat could learn to escape the shock and terminate the buzzer by running into a large, unshocked goal box. These trials were followed by five others in which descending shock intensities were given to the *extinction-only group* so that, from trial 26 thereafter, no further shock was presented. Sixty additional non-shock trials (10/day) were given, provided the rats continued to run. The *long-shock, extinction group* received the same treatment, except that the descending shocks were given in the startbox only. However, shock continued to be available in the alley throughout extinction testing. The *short-shock, extinction group* was treated the same as the long-shock subjects except that shock intensity was reduced to zero in both the start area and the first four feet of the alley by trial 26. Thereafter, shock was available only in the last two feet of the alley during the extinction trials. Figure 8.14 shows the mean running speeds for the first two feet of the alley for the three groups, averaged over blocks of ten extinction trials. These data show that the more punishment given during extinction, the greater the running speed. The *long-shock group* showed little tendency to stop running during extinction, while the *no-shock group* had virtually stopped running by the last trial block. The *short-shock group* performed intermediate between the other two.

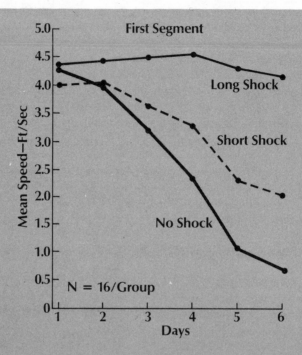

Figure 8.14 Extinction curves derived from measurements of runway speed in the first two-foot alley segment for groups that received either full alley but no startbox shock (long shock), shock in the last two feet of the alley (short shock), or no shock. From Brown, Martin, and Morrow (1964).

(Church et al., 1967). Degree of response suppression is negatively related to *delay* of punishment (Azrin, 1956; Baron, Kaufman, & Fazzini, 1969; Camp et al., 1967). This finding on delay further confirms the importance of the response-punishment contingency for producing maximum suppression.

Explanations of punishment effects have ranged from those that presume a disconnection in existing associations between the response and antecedent maintaining stimuli (i.e., a weakening of an S-R association due to the aversive stimulus) to those that involve the mechanism of classical conditioning. There are several good recent discussions on these positions (Campbell & Church, 1969; Dunham, 1971; Azrin & Holz, 1966; MacKintosh, 1974).

A Major Controversy in Instrumental Learning

As was the case for classical conditioning, there is much controversy over the respective roles of cognitive and S-R explanations of instrumental learning phenomena. One area where this controversy has most recently surfaced is with interference effects in avoidance learning. Consider a study by Seligman and Maier (1967) in which, using what they termed a "triadic design" (Maier & Seligman, 1976), two of their three groups of dogs were given physically identical shock treatments prior to shuttlebox avoidance training. One of these two treated groups (the escapable group) could terminate each shock of this treatment, while the other group (the inescapable group) was given the same shocks but could not escape them. A third group was not given shock treatment. All were given avoidance training 24 hours later. Table 8.2 shows, among other things, the mean latencies of shuttling, measured from CS onset, for each group.

The escapable and the non-shocked control groups performed the same and evinced significantly shorter response latencies and fewer failures to shuttle than the inescapable group. These data were explained in cognitive terms. The inescapable shock treatment was seen to produce a unique learning contingency of independence between responding and the shock stimulus. Presumably, dogs in this group cognitively grasped this response-shock relationship, learning thereby that "nothing I do matters" (Maier, Seligman, & Solomon, 1969, p. 326). This independence learning resulted in loss of incentive to respond to shock, thus explaining why the inescapable group did not shuttle during avoidance training. Presumably, the equivalently treated, escapable group showed no impairment because their shock treatment provided a response-shock dependency relationship, consistent with the cognition that "what I do matters." Seligman and Maier (1967) coined their account the "learned helplessness" hypothesis.

Table 8.2   Mean latency, percent subjects failing to escape, and mean number of escape failures in a two-way shuttlebox task for inescapably shock-treated, escapable shocked, and no-shock-treated dogs. From Seligman and Maier (1967).

Group	Mean Latency (in sec)	Percent Subjects Failing to Escape Shock on 9 or More of the 10 Trials	Mean Number Failures to Escape Shock*
Escape	27.00	0	2.63
Normal Control	25.93	12.5	2.25
"Yoked" Control	48.22	75	7.25

*Out of 10 trials

More generally, these authors (Seligman, Maier, & Solomon, 1971) conceive of learning in instrumental situations as the formation of response-reinforcer relationships, not S-R connections. The parallel between this view and cognitive, S-S conceptions of classical conditioning is obvious. Organisms are seen to learn predictions rather than responses in both cases, the major difference being that in instrumental learning, the prediction is based upon exposure to a particular response-reinforcer (R-S) rather than a neutral-nonneutral stimulus correlation.

The major rebuttal to this position has been on methodological grounds. Careful analyses of the experimental procedures of Seligman, Maier, and their colleagues reveal the possibility that their "triadic" design may encourage the development during shock treatments of quite different postural and other responses by the escapable and inescapable groups. An *interacting-response hypothesis* has thus been proposed as an alternative to their cognitive theory to account for interference effects in avoidance learning (Anderson, Crowell, Koehn, & Lupo, 1976; Black, 1977; Bracewell & Black, 1974; Lawry, Lupo, Kochevar, Hollis, Anderson, & Overmier, 1977; Levis, 1976). Rather than promoting independence cognitions, certain inescapable shock treatments are seen to produce postures that reduce pain and that, if transferred to the avoidance test situation, also compete with shuttling. In contrast, postures learned during escapable shock treatments, if generalized to the test situation, usually would be compatible with and thus not impair shuttling. Some aspects of the interacting-response theory have been confirmed (Anderson, Lupo, Cunningham, & Madden, 1974), although other complications have recently arisen for both theories (Lawry et al., 1977).

OPERANT LEARNING

A major difference between instrumental and operant approaches is in how responses are defined for each. Instead of giving consecutive trials to each of several subjects, operant psychologists use "sessions" within which large segments of a behavior are collected from individual subjects. Sessions can be from a few minutes in duration to, in some cases, several days. A prototypical operant situation consists of making a reinforcer, such as food or water (or a punisher), contingent upon the occurrence of some response, such as pecking a disc, pressing a bar, or pulling a chain. Motivation for such responses is maintained by food or water deprivation, and the subject is usually only intermittently reinforced so as to avoid satiation of the relevant need. In this manner, response emission can be maintained at a steady rate over long time periods.

Measurement Issues

The main measures in operant research are those of *rate*, i.e., number of responses per unit time, and of interresponse times (IRTs), i.e., distributions of elapsed times between all pairs of responses for a given experimental condition. Operant procedures thus depend upon the occurrence of *steady state* (Shimp, 1969) or *continuous behavior*, meaning that conditions are arranged to maximize continuity between responses that recurrently produce a reinforcer (or escape/avoid an aversive stimulus). Attainment of such behavioral continuity defines a *behavioral baseline*, and much early research in this area indeed focused upon analyses of procedures that produced stable performance baselines (cf. Ferster & Skinner, 1957; they report over 900 graphs, many that depict the astonishing behavioral regularity achievable with the operant methodology).

Once a steady state is achieved, learning variables can be introduced and their effects evaluated through any correlated changes from baseline that occur (cf. pp. 164 f, text). These changes usually can be detected visually as alterations in response rate in an ongoing cumulative record of behavior (cf. p. 167, text). It is often necessary in operant research to collect repetitious performances over many sessions from single subjects in order to document the effect of certain variables. One reason for this is that students of operant behavior often study the effects of complex reinforcement contingencies that, simply put, require extensive exposure to be discerned. The work of Herrnstein and Hineline (1966) on a unifactor study of avoidance learning (p. 364, text) is a good example of this. It took 30 two-hour sessions per subject to obtain discernible trends in behavior in this experiment.

Operant psychologists usually eschew the use of separate-groups experiments. They have thus taken a different approach to the concept of control than followed in most classical and instrumental experiments. The typical procedure in operant studies has been to expose the same subject to both the experimental and control conditions by repeatedly giving and withdrawing the experimental variable of interest. Correlated changes in the rate of behavior (to and from baseline) are taken as evidence of the effect of that variable. This procedure, termed a reversal design (p. 166, text), allows accumulation of a large amount of information on the influence of a variable with a minimum expenditure of subjects. *Reliability* also can be examined with a reversal procedure since it is reflected in the consistency with which treatment and baseline performances are duplicated upon repeated presentations and removals of the experimental variable. (Clearly, order of presentations must be random or follow a counterbalancing procedure.)

IRT distributions are plotted in order to reveal aspects of behavior that might otherwise be obscured by the rate measure. Certain complex intermittent reward schedules, while having similar effects on overall rate, nonetheless can produce distinctively different patterns of responding within sessions. Usually, IRTs are classified in terms of respective time intervals. This allows a determination of the relative frequency of short, intermediate, and relatively long IRTs that may develop for different schedules of reinforcement. Interestingly, the IRT distribution itself seems to be "shaped" by the particular reward-scheduling procedure being studied. Hence, the IRT can be viewed in the same way as any other response in that it may be learned, maintained, extinguished, and/or punished.

Schedules of Reinforcement

Although *amount, delay,* and so forth have been examined within the operant paradigm, the behavior patterns induced by the schedule of reinforcement in effect have often themselves become so firmly established as to have obscured the influence of these variables. Thus, scheduling variables that produce and maintain such behavior patterns instead have become the major focus of attention within this research approach. The following is a brief statement of the types and effects of various basic schedules and of some of the methodological concerns unique to the study of each.

By an *interval schedule* is meant that a reward (or a punisher) is made contingent upon the occurrence of a response following the passage of a specified period of time. For a *ratio schedule,* a reward (or punisher) is given for a specified number of responses. If a *fixed interval* of *time or* of *number* of responses is required between consecutive reinforcers, these schedules respectively are termed *fixed interval* (FI) or *fixed ratio* (FR) *schedules.* A *variable interval* (VI) *schedule* means that interreward durations vary randomly around a specified average inter-reward time. A VI 10 sec ($\pm$ 5 sec) schedule means that the average inter-reward time is 10 sec, but this value will vary randomly from reward to reward from a low of 5 sec to a high of 15 sec. A *variable ratio* (VR) *schedule* of 10, VR 10 ($\pm$ 5), means that an average of 10 responses is required to receive a reward. However, any given trial may require as few as 5 or as many as 15 responses for the reward. Each of these four kinds of schedules, FI, FR, VI, and VR, produce different effects on rate (and IRT distributions) of responding.

Ratio schedules. In general, ratio schedules produce and can sustain higher rates of behavior than interval-based schedules when number of rewards are equated for comparable time periods. When the response requirement is quite high on an FR schedule, however, *pauses* in responding often occur following each reward. By changing such a schedule to a VR procedure, such pauses are either reduced or eliminated altogether (Felton & Lyon, 1966; Ferster & Skinner, 1957). The phenomenon of post-reinforcement pauses on FR schedules has been the target for considerable experimental analysis.

One finding here is that the pause duration is a positive function of the response requirement on the FR schedule. Using water-satiated subjects, Premack, Schaeffer, and Hundt (1964) allowed rats to emit water-lick responses on different FR schedules, ranging from FR 10 to FR 500, to earn access to an activity wheel as the reward. The more responses between reinforcers, the longer the post-reinforcement pause. Felton and Lyon (1966) trained four hungry pigeons to peck a small disc for food on FR schedules of 25, 50, 75, 100, and 150. Order of schedule presentation was counterbalanced for each subject. With prolonged experience on each schedule in order to stabilize the patterns of behavior that evolved, durations of post-reinforcement pauses increased as a function of the magnitude of the ratio requirement. One pigeon, for instance, paused an average 120 sec on the FR 25, approximately 200 sec on the FR 50, 850 sec on the FR 75, 2600 sec on the FR 100, and approximately 5000 sec on the FR 150 schedule.

When responding resumes after a long pause, what about the pattern of behavior thereafter? The picture is not clear here. Ferster and Skinner (1957) found that response rate decreased slightly as the ratio requirement was increased, but Felton and Lyon (1966) showed that rate was relatively constant after pauses, no matter what the requirement. Noteworthy here is a potentially confounding variable in FR studies of post-reinforcement pauses. The force required to make a response may influence the experimental outcome in this regard. Mintz (1962) measured a precipitous decline in the response force exerted by subjects as responding was resumed after a post-reinforcement pause, this being followed by a progressive increase in force with further responding. The implication here is that the more difficult the manipulandum is to operate, the longer will be the post-reward pause and the lower the response rate once behavior is resumed.

Interval schedules   Interval schedules can maintain stable performance over prolonged periods but are typically unable to generate the high overall rates of responding reported for ratio schedules of comparable reinforcement densities. However, well trained subjects on an FI schedule show a behavior pattern similar to that of post-reinforcement pauses discussed for FR schedules. This unique response patterning shows up as a scallop-like profile in a cumulative record. One difference between these patterning effects on FR and FI schedules is that, for the latter, responding never quite ceases and only gradually picks up in rate just before each reward. Performance on FI schedules is thus best characterized as a *gradient of change* and is illustrated in Figure 8.15.

There is a feature of FI schedules that resembles Pavlovian temporal reward conditioning. A fixed passage of time can be construed as a CS-like event and is thus contiguously paired with a response-produced reinforcer, a UCS-like event. The analogy is imperfect since, unlike a strict Pavlovian procedure, the subject must respond on an FI schedule for the UCS to occur. Yet, the FI schedule is otherwise Pavlovian in paradigmatic outline. This similarity has suggested to some that the FI schedule may promote the development of fractional anticipatory goal

Figure 8.15

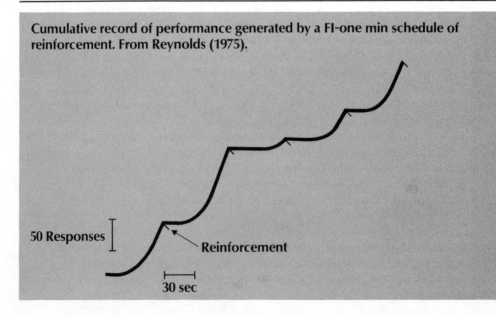

Cumulative record of performance generated by a FI-one min schedule of reinforcement. From Reynolds (1975).

50 Responses

Reinforcement

30 sec

responses much as envisioned for the r_g-s_g mechanism in instrumental alleyway training situations. Repeated pairings of the CS-like, fixed temporal interval with reward may result in the development of a consummatory CR. Given this possibility, the CR might then antedate to the temporal CS, thus occurring earlier and earlier in the interreward interval. This CR during the interreward interval could mediate the initiation of, as well as moderate, the gradual increase in responding that characterizes the scalloped FI behavior pattern. Alternatively, the FI schedule also introduces the equivalent of a fixed *delay of reward* procedure. Just as it was noted that instrumental learning is less disrupted by delay if the subject is provided with response opportunities during this interval, it seems possible that the FI scallop might similarly be determined by interacting responses that serendipitously develop during the interreward period.

Operant psychologists have analyzed FI schedules in terms of these two possibilities of temporal classical conditioning and delay-of-reward effects. If temporal conditioning is important, then the passage of time *per se,* the CS-like event, is a critical event for producing FI scalloping performances. If the delay factor is important, then the responses of the subject assume causal status in determining the scalloping. The respective roles of these concepts have been studied by disrupting the subject's behavior in some manner during various portions of the scalloping pattern (cf. Dews, 1962). If what the subject is doing at that time is critically important, disruption should alter the scalloping pattern. If time *per se* is all important, then disruption should exert little effect on the scallop. The general finding is that disruptions produce a transient effect upon some aspects of responding but basically do not interfere with the scalloping. The implication is that the FI scallop is at least partly mediated by Pavlovian temporal conditioning and not by delay-produced interacting responses.

A further analogy between FR and FI schedules is that the response pauses that occur for each can be eliminated by introducing variability (in number for ratio and in time for interval schedules) between successive rewards. As noted, both VR and VI schedules produce consistent, unchanging performance rates, although the rates are higher overall for the former than for the latter when rewards are equated. A methodological point here is that a VI schedule should be composed of an equal number of quite short, intermediate, and long intervals, randomly interposed between consecutive rewards in order to eliminate any possibility of temporal conditioning.

Another feature of the VI schedule is that it is the procedure of choice for maintaining great behavioral consistency over long periods of time. The reason for this is that a VI schedule allows the experimenter to hold constant the number of rewards dispensed to a subject over any specified time period, regardless of any other factors involved (such as how rapidly the subject responds). This control over reinforcement rate can be used to determine the rate that a subject satiates on the reinforcer. VI schedules are thus ideal for evaluating the effects of learning variables since they can produce highly durable baseline performances that can sensitively detect even slight behavior changes.

Schedules based on differential reinforcement procedures.   It is possible to speed up behavior by giving a reinforcer only when rate equals or exceeds a specified criterion. In effect, this is the equivalent of a *differential reinforcement procedure for high rates* (or short IRTs), abbreviated DRH. The opposite of the DRH procedure is possible simply by dispensing reward for low rates (or long IRTs). This procedure is termed *differential reinforcement for low rates* (DRL) (cf. Box 8.7).

Lane (1960) demonstrated that the same subject could master both a DRH and a DRL schedule of reinforcement in the same setting. He first trained hungry bantam chicks to emit a vocal "chirping" reaction on an FR 20 ("chirps") schedule to earn a 4-sec access to a wet-mash reward. Chirp rate increased from a baseline of 25 to approximately 112 chirps/min. Three different extinction procedures were given before placing the chirp response on an FI 2-min reward schedule, signalled by a green light. This was alternated with a DRL 2-min schedule, signalled by a red light in which food was given for the first chirp after two minutes had elapsed. High and low rates of chirping to the respective green and red stimuli were achieved within a one-hour session.

Complex schedules.   Lane's (1960) FI-DRL procedure uses a *complex schedule*, i.e., one in which one schedule alternates with another. There are numerous other ways that operant psychologists have combined schedules in order to illuminate how various reinforcement contingencies interact to control behavior. The following are but a sampling.

When each of two alternating schedules is accompanied by a distinctive stimulus (cf. Lane, 1960), the complex schedule is called a *multiple schedule*. The absence of a discriminative stimulus for the two schedule components defines a *mixed schedule*. More than one schedule can be programmed to operate simultaneously. To accomplish this, reward is given only when the requirements of both schedules or of either schedule have been satisfied. A *conjunctive schedule* is when the requirements of both must be met before reward is given. An *alternative schedule* is when the requirement of either must be met before reward is delivered. Different schedules can also be programmed simultaneously, each ascribed to a different manipulandum *(concurrent schedules)*, as in a chamber with two bars. Additional scheduling combinations and permutations have been discussed at length by Morse (1966).

Mixing schedules together allows an analysis of behavior that perhaps approximates everyday situations more closely than do other learning procedures thus far discussed. Everyday circumstances require ongoing adjustments to both concurrently and consecutively interacting reinforcement schedules. Moreover, these schedules may or may not be signalled by distinctive stimuli. For example, a child must learn to behave one way for a demanding parent in terms of one set of performance-reward contingencies and another way for the second parent who may be far more lenient. Similarly, a college student must learn to adjust his or her behavior in terms of performance-reward contingencies that vary from classroom to classroom and from classroom to living residence. But questions arise here: Does the reward contingency on one schedule affect behavior only for that schedule, or do contingencies somehow combine to affect performance across schedules? Are certain schedules more or less prone to the effects of other schedules? If schedules do influence one another, are there ways of minimizing these interactive effects?

Schedule interactions. This concern about interactions between the performances of a single subject on two levels of the same variable is not new to this chapter. The topics of within-subjects, negative contrast effects with variations in amount and delay and of within-subjects PRF-CRF comparisons are examples of just this sort of interaction. It thus should not be surprising to discover interaction effects when the same subject is exposed to two or more schedules of reinforcement. Two kinds of schedule interactions have been reported. The first is when performance on one schedule generalizes to and influences performance under another. This phenomenon is termed *blending;* it is illustrated by the fact that on a multiple FI-FR schedule the higher, consistent performance rate on the FR schedule generalizes to and obscures the typical "scalloping" that ordinarily occurs for the FI component. With extensive training, however, this generalization-interaction effect can be eliminated.

The other effect is the opposite of blending; it is illustrated by Reynolds' (1961a, 1961b) studies in which pigeons were trained to peck for food reward on a multiple VI-FR schedule. The discriminative stimuli for the subschedules were red and green key illuminations, respectively. The schedules rotated every three minutes and the VI component was always a VI 3-min. Following stable performances on both components (over many sessions), Reynolds introduced different FR values, including an FR 0 (extinction) value. In each case, performances were stablized before a new FR value was introduced, and the different FR schedules were rotated so as to nullify carry-over contamination effects.

Reynolds (1961a, 1961b) reported two major findings. First, consistent with other reports, the greater the response requirement on the FR component, the lower the rate of pecking on that schedule; e.g., as the FR was increased from an FR 75 to an FR 150, response rate decreased. Second, as the FR value was changed, pecking rate was affected on the constant VI 3-min schedule in a direction contrary to that expected from a schedule-blending effect. That is, as the FR value rose, pecking rate *increased* on the VI 3-min schedule.

This phenomenon, called *behavioral contrast,* may have been due to either of two covarying factors in Reynolds' (1961a, 1961b) research. First, the variations in response rate on the different FR components may somehow have affected performance on the VI schedule. For example, pigeons may have pecked so rapidly on low-requirement FR schedules that they were simply fatigued when the VI schedule was rotated; they may have "rested" during the latter periods. The reverse logic would apply for the high-requirement FR schedules. A second factor, however, was that as the FR value changed, so also did the *relative density of rewards* that were delivered during the VI component. That is, the fewer the number of rewards on the FR component, the higher the relative number on the VI schedule, and vice versa. Thus, the different pecking rates on the constant VI schedule could have been caused by inversely-correlated changes in response rate on the different FR components or by positively-correlated changes in relative reinforcement density on the VI schedule, or by both.

To unconfound these two variables, experiments were needed in which (1) response rates were varied on the non-VI schedule, holding reinforcement density constant for both components, and (2) reinforcement density was varied, holding responses constant for the non-VI schedules. If pecking rate on the VI component varied inversely with the *former* manipulation, then the response fatigue interpretation of behavioral contrast effects would be viable. If rate was unaffected, however, response fatigue could be ruled out. If rate on the constant VI schedule was found to be a positive function of reinforcement density with the *latter* manipulation, then a relative reinforcement density hypothesis would be tenable. If not, the response fatigue notion could be retained. Experiments designed along these lines have consistently supported the relative reinforcement density hypothesis (Bloomfield, 1967; Nevin, 1968; Reynolds, 1963; Zuriff, 1970). From a theoretical standpoint, this represents a direct assault on the law of effect. As discussed earlier (p. 345), a major implication of the law of effect is that responses are affected by their "local" consequences. Since the "local" reward contingency was constant on the VI component of Reynolds' procedure, a relative reinforcement density interpretation of his data means that performance on that schedule varied as a function of nonproximal reward contingencies in effect on another schedule.

A Major Controversy in Operant Learning

The relationship between the presumed strengthening and weakening effects of relative reinforcement density on performance has also been

Box 8.11 Concurrent Schedules, Relative Reinforcement Density, and Response Matching

Baum (1972) required a pigeon to live in the experimental situation and eat all its food on a two-key concurrent procedure. The two independent components associated with each key were VI schedules. Each time the pigeon switched keys, termed a changeover (it was free to do so at any time), a minimum time of 1.8 sec was inserted between its first peck on the new key and the subsequent reward. This latter procedural feature is called a *changeover delay* (COD). The pigeon was free to eat until satiation and could fulfill its normal food requirements by pecking exclusively on either alternative. Distributing its responses to both keys was unnecessary, yet it emitted thousands of responses on each key every day.

The most important finding here, however, resulted from Baum's (1972) occasional variation of the VI requirements of the schedule components. This, of course, resulted in commensurate changes in the relative reinforcement frequencies (densities) associated with each key. The pigeon "matched" the proportion of its pecks to the respective keys over the wide range of relative reinforcement densities that were used. That is, as relative reward density changed on a given key, the pigeon "tracked" this variation by a corresponding change in the proportion of responses it emitted on that key (termed *response matching*).

Baum (1974) repeated this study with 20 wild pigeons. He employed their natural habitat as the training situation. Using a modified operant key-pecking apparatus located in the attic of a frame house where the pigeons lived, he trained each to peck at two keys for access to grain. To limit access to one bird at a time, a very narrow perch was arranged in front of the keys (Baum nonetheless totalled the performances of the group to display his results). A COD was not used. Yet, over a wide range of different concurrent pairs of VI schedules, the proportion of pecks at each key "matched" the proportion of grain presentations available at each.

studied with continuous choice procedures. Such procedures are actually a form of concurrent schedule and differ importantly from the multiple-schedule technique of Reynolds (1961a) in that two alternative schedules of reinforcement *are available concurrently* and the animal can continually respond to one alternative or the other. There have been two concurrent scheduling methods. In one, Herrnstein (1961) used two spatially separated keys, each associated with different reinforcement schedules, between which pigeons could switch pecking back and forth. In another, Catania (1963a) programmed two schedules on the same key, each correlated with a different stimulus (key color). The subject could change schedules at any time simply by pecking at a second key. The first of these functionally equivalent methods is termed a two-key concurrent, and the second a changeover-key (CO) concurrent schedule. *In either case, if a reward becomes available on one schedule* (schedule A), *while the subject is responding on schedule B, the reinforcement on A is held until the animal switches and responds on the latter.* The measures in these situations include the number of responses and/or amount of time distributed to each alternative over an experimental session. These measures define schedule preference, i.e., the relative reward value of various reinforcement conditions.

As it turns out, properly conceived concurrent schedules have produced orderly relationships between rate measures of response strength and the reinforcement features of frequency, duration, and delay. The net result of most of this research shows a simple linear relationship between either relative response rates or time spent on respective keys and the relative frequency (Herrnstein, 1961), magnitude (Brownstein, 1971; Catania, 1963b), and immediacy of reinforcement (Chung & Herrnstein, 1967).

Implications of "response-matching" phenomena. Both response-matching and behavioral-contrast effects suggest relativistic rather than "localized" reward effects on behavior and, to many (Baum, 1973; Herrnstein, 1970; de Villiers, 1977), have forced a revision in traditional thinking about the law of effect (cf. p. 378). The rationale for this revision is perhaps nowhere better stated than by Nevin (1973a):

> The finding that behavior may be determined by a ratio of two average reinforcement frequencies raises some new problems, since it is difficult to understand how this ratio—a mathematical transformation of two numbers, each of which can only be defined over protracted time periods—can make contact with performance. An understanding of the processes through which responding comes under control of such remote specifications of its consequences is a major challenge for behavior theory. (p. 224)

Yet, a number of methodological issues must be resolved regarding response-matching and continuous-choice procedures before final acceptance of any revision in traditional thinking about reward effects.

Methodological issues.   Catania (1966) has noted that in simultaneous reinforcement procedures, it is essential that the two responses involved be made independent of one another. Otherwise, rapid alternation between schedules will occur, with responses on one becoming accidentally correlated with reward on the other. This could give rise to what Catania (1966) termed *concurrent superstitions.* A changeover delay (COD) is recommended in such studies (cf. Box 8.11) to eliminate these superstitions. By timing the COD from the first response after the changeover, a separation in time is ensured between a response on the "switched from" key and reinforcement on the changeover key. Catania and Cutts (1963) found a COD to be effective when the pair of schedules involved continued reward on one key and zero reward (extinction) on the other. Without a COD, response level was maintained above zero on the latter key (15 responses/min) over twelve one-hour sessions. With a COD, responding rapidly declined to zero level on the same key.

But, the need for a minimum COD duration is analogous to a punishment procedure (time-out from reward) for changeover behavior (Pliskoff, 1971). Resulting response-matching distributions could thus be byproducts of punished changeover responding and not of relative reinforcement densities. Indeed, Silberberg and Fantino (1970) found that response rates on both keys were equal during the COD period, but over-matched the overall frequency of reward prior to the COD. When these two rates were combined, the relative, response-reward matching function was obtained. When not combined, this function did not obtain. Clearly, the role of the COD and response-matching phenomena require further clarification.

Continuous choice situations also require a special schedule arrangement to prevent the subject spending all its time on the more favorable schedule. This arrangement has been to use dual VI schedules with the provision that a reward will remain available on the one not in effect until the changeover occurs. This dual VI procedure indeed encourages response distribution on both components. But, it effectively programs yet another unwanted reinforcement contingency; namely, the longer the interchangeover time, the higher the probability of reinforcement for the second response after the changeover (allowing for the COD). This procedural complication thereby introduces the added contingency of differential reinforcement for long interchangeover times that, alone, might produce response distributions similar to those reported in matching studies (Kuch & Platt, 1976; Shimp, 1975). Until clarified, any revision of the law of effect would be premature.

SUMMARY

This chapter was divided into four sections. The first concerned definitions and concepts in learning. It focused upon general methodological and conceptual issues dealing with the necessary and sufficient conditions traditionally invoked to depict learning. *Practice* was designated as the major antecedent condition. The two major issues raised in this connection were whether task-related responding and reinforcement were necessary aspects of practice. A *relatively permanent behavior change* was cited as the major consequent operation of learning. The issues raised here were whether this change should be specified as a behavior potential or as behavior *per se* and how permanent the behavior change should be to qualify as a reflection of learning. The question of what actually is learned was also discussed. A widely accepted viewpoint was that new responses are not learned; instead new connections or associations between antecedent stimuli and already existing behaviors are acquired. The major issue here revolved around what became connected to what: Stimuli to response, as in an S-R interpretation of learning? Or stimuli to stimuli, as in a central-state, S-S relational interpretation?

The final three sections dealt with the three basic paradigms that have served the experimental analysis of learning: classical, instrumental, and operant conditioning. *Classical conditioning* involves a CS, UCS, CR, UCR, and a pairing operation. One of two major measurement methods discussed was the Pavlovian CS-CR procedure in which the measured response is collected from the same motor system as the UCR. The second, CS-IR method entails assessment of CS effects on correlated changes produced in a specified instrumental response. Some of the advantages and problems associated with both CS-CR and CS-IR procedures were noted.

The CS was defined as a novel suprathreshold event less intense than the UCS (which should elicit a nonhabituable inborn reflex) and nonredundant with other stimuli. The major phenomena of the classical conditioning paradigm include CS and UCS intensity effects, intermittent UCS presentations, compound conditioning, blocking and overshadowing, generalization and discrimination, and second-order and sensory preconditioning. A major controversy in classical conditioning is whether or not Pavlov's CS-UCS "pairings" hypothesis is a necessary condition for learning. Rescorla's recent work was noted in this connection.

Instrumental and *operant research paradigms* differ operationally from classical conditioning in several ways. First, they require a response in order for a pairing to occur between antecedent stimulation and a consequent UCS-like event (the reward or punisher). Second, the measurement procedures are different for these two paradigm categories. The CS-CR measurement technique is directed at quantification of one or more attributes of a given reaction while instrumental-operant mea-surement procedures focus on the environmental effects on behavior, such as elapsed time in the instrumental and rate of manipulating a bar in the operant situation.

The primary differences between the instrumental and operant paradigms are that: (1) instrumental measurements are based upon dis-crete trial performances while operant psychologists collect behavior by sessions and/or experimental conditions; (2) measurements are accord-ingly time- or percentage-based for the former, but are expressed in terms of rate or interresponse-time (IRT) distributions for the latter; (3) groups and group averages along with experimental-control group re-search designs permeate the instrumental approach while single-subject, reversal- or multiple-baseline control procedures characterize the oper-ant approach; and (4) reinforcer parameters such as amount and delay have dominated the attention of instrumental learning researchers while reinforcement contingencies in the form of complex schedule effects have dominated the attention of operant learning scientists.

An ongoing analysis of the *law of effect* has focused the concerns of students of both paradigms. This law, that reinforcers increase (and pun-ishers decrease) the future probable recurrence of a behavior, has been the source of further paradigmatic subdivisions within the more general instrumental-operant framework. One primary subdivision is based upon the kind of response consequence studied, i.e., positive-appetitive vs. negative-aversive response outcomes. Each of these can be further characterized by how the consequent event is dispensed. Thus, the onset of a positive event, given a response, is called *positive reinforcement.* The end of an aversive event, given a reaction, is called *negative reinforce-ment.* The response-contingent onset of an aversive event is *positive pun-ishment,* and the response-correlated end of a positive one is *negative punishment* or extinction.

The variables of *amount, delay, extinction, scheduling,* and *contrast effects* and various methodological problems that attend each were dis-cussed in connection with these four subdivisions. In general, increases in amount, decreases in delay, and increases in reinforcement percentage correlate positively with performance increases, although special qual-ifications and methodological problems were noted for these findings on a paradigm-by-paradigm basis.

Virtually every instrumental paradigm allows classical conditioning. The concept of classical conditioning has thus been invoked to explain the effects of most reinforcement and punishment procedures on per-formance. Several conceptual and methodological approaches and prob-lems were noted in connection with using classical conditioning to ex-plain the development and maintenance of instrumental performance. Methodological approaches have included: (1) the manipulation in in-strumental situations of variables known to be potent within the classical paradigm; (2) evaluation of whether or not a correlation exists between the presence of critical CRs and instrumental performance; and (3) elimination of all opportunities for classical conditioning during instrumental training. The results of these research approaches have been equivocal.

One of the more widely researched of the negative reinforcement procedures has been the phenomenon of *avoidance learning*. A major methodological controversy in this area has been whether classical conditioning or a more parsimonious law-of-effect interpretation can account for the development of avoidance responses. The classical conditioning account is that subjects are conditioned to fear the signal for shock on early trials due to CS-UCS pairings and then, through trial-and-error activity, acquire a response that escapes that signal on later trials, thereby giving the appearance of shock avoidance. The law-of-effect interpretation is that an avoidance response is reinforced by a reduction in the relative frequency of shock exposure, an inevitable consequence of that behavior. Experiments designed to evaluate this issue were reviewed and critically analyzed.

Punishment was presented as the opposite side of the same coin as the reinforcement paradigm. Response-correlated increases in such variables as intensity (amount), delay, and intermittence generally result in, respectively, increased, decreased, and decreased suppression of that response. These effects were seen to interact partly with the reward conditions used to maintain the response. Three critical questions were examined in this paradigm: (1) whether a response-punisher contingency was more effective in suppressing behavior than response-uncorrelated presentations of the punisher; (2) how lasting was punishment-produced suppression; and (3) that punishment can sometimes facilitate rather than deter ongoing behavior.

A major controversy in instrumental learning dealt with contemporary cognitive interpretations of interference effects in avoidance learning. The learned-helplessness hypothesis was introduced in this connection, namely, that subjects can learn an independence relationship between their responses and inescapably delivered aversive stimulation that can transfer to and impair performance on an avoidance task. The implications of this hypothesis for a perceptual R-S theory of instrumental learning were discussed. An interacting-response hypothesis, evolved on the basis of possible methodological problems with the "triadic" learned-helplessness research design, was proposed as an alternative S-R view of instrumental learning.

Operant approaches have for the most part been concerned with the effects of reinforcement contingencies on behavior. Thus, the effects on performance of various reward and punishment schedules have been extensively examined. The performance effects of basic schedules based upon ratio or time requirements and upon predictable or unpredictable interreward values were listed. Most notable in these data were the development of pauses in responding on certain schedules and how IRT distribution had been useful in the analysis of these response-pause phenomena.

Two major interactive effects on performance of combining schedules were discussed. These were *blending* and *contrast effects*. Blending is the transfer of the behavioral effects of one schedule to the other so that performance on the latter is more like that on the former. Contrast effects produce performance change in a direction that is opposite from, and thus not attributable to, transfer-blending effects. In the initial research on contrast effects, the reinforcement requirement on one of two signalled components remained unchanged while the requirements on the other were varied from time to time. The use of concurrent VI schedules with a changeover delay (COD) has dominated the contemporary literature on the study of contrast effects.

It was the latter literature that provided the major controversy in operant research. Several studies using concurrent scheduling procedures were cited showing that pigeons distributed their responses on concurrent VI schedules in proportion to the relative density of rewards obtainable on each. This *response-matching* phenomenon has been taken as evidence that responding can be controlled by nonproximal reward contingencies, seemingly contrary to the traditional interpretation of the law of effect. However, such methodological considerations as the punishment-like nature of the COD and the fact that very special, dual-VI schedule components were required for response-matching concurrent procedures, require resolution before revision of this classical law can be taken seriously.

QUESTIONS

1. What is learning? What distinguishes learning from habituation? Maturation? Fatigue? Discuss the concepts of practice, reinforcement, and behavior potential as they relate to the definition of learning. Finally, compare and contrast S-R and S-S, central state conceptions of what learning is.

2. Discuss how classical conditioning is a learning paradigm. What are the essential ingredients of this paradigm? By what means can the fact of conditioning be determined? What are some of the sources of responding that might prevent a clear determination of conditioning? How can these sources be controlled?

3. What is a CS-CR measurement procedure? Discuss the two kinds noted in the text. What is a CS-IR measurement procedure? What are the advantages and limitations of either in the measurement of classical conditioning? Discuss some of the controversies that surround the use of each and how these relate to the methodology of one's experiment.

4. List and define all of the phenomena of classical conditioning noted in the text. Indicate some of the methodological problems that attend the study of each, and how these problems might be surmounted by the scientist.

5. Discuss how the concept "surprise" variously is used in the section on classical conditioning. Operationally define surprise. Discuss the implication of this term for a theory of how classical conditioning occurs. Finally, discuss the evidence that supports and that may contradict this theory.

6. Compare and contrast the paradigms of classical conditioning and instrumental learning. Discuss how the possibility of each may be present and operative within the other. Discuss some of the methods that have been used to study the possible contributions of classical conditioning to the development of instrumental responding.

7. What is the law of effect? Characterize the various ways in which it has been studied. Are there ways that this law might operate within the classical conditioning paradigm? If so, how? What sort of methodological safeguards might be taken to eliminate possible contributions of "effect" interpretations of classical conditioning?

8. Define the negative reinforcement procedures of escape and avoidance learning. How does the law of effect apply to each? Discuss some of the methodological problems that can attend a manipulation of delay, amount, and reward intermittency in avoidance learning studies. State the controversy that exists between a two-factor and a shock frequency reduction account of avoidance learning. What was Herrnstein and Hineline's research strategy to evaluate these two theories?

9. Compare and contrast the operant with the instrumental learning paradigms. What are the prime measurement procedures for the former? How do these measurement procedures relate to an analysis of reinforcement schedules? How could they be adapted to the study of learning within the instrumental paradigm?

10. How do the phenomena of behavioral contrast and response matching relate to each other? How have these latter effects influenced our contemporary views about the traditional law of effect? Are there any reservations to be made about possible modifications of this law in view of these phenomena? If so, upon what grounds?

Research Tactics in Complex Learning, Memory, and Cognition

9
Chapter

BY JOHN G. BORKOWSKI

Cognitive psychology's subject matter is people's mental states and processes. To expose these it used laboratory methods developed for the study of attention, memory, language, and perception, and especially the techniques of verbal learning experimentation. Its goal is to create generalized or nomothetic theory of human cognition. Its preferred form of theory is a complete specification, as in flow charts or computer programs, of the mental states and processes which occur between informational input and behavioral output.

(Butterfield & Dickerson, 1976, p. 107)

In this chapter we will discuss the major research paradigms used in the study of verbal learning, memory, and cognition. We will focus on the variety of tools the researcher of higher mental processes has at his or her disposal. We will describe how each research tool is used, its limitations and advantages, and its use in the analysis of selected issues and phenomena. Before beginning our main task, we will briefly consider how the processes of complex learning, memory, and cognition differ from the basic learning processes discussed in Chapter 8. We start with Hermann Ebbinghaus in the last part of the nineteenth century.

THE UNIQUENESS OF HUMAN MEMORY AND THOUGHT

Ebbinghaus: A Precursor of the Information Processing Model

Historically, verbal learning and memory research predates the classic work of Pavlov and Watson on basic learning processes. In the early 1880s, Hermann Ebbinghaus began his investigations into retention processes and, in 1885, published the first laboratory-based study of memory, *Uber das Gedachtnis*. Ebbinghaus's studies represented a departure from the standard research tactics of his period, dominated by the work of Wundt and his students (see Chapter 2, pp. 47–51). Wundt used introspection as a basic stratagem to analyze sensation and thought; his introspective technique required subjects to reflect on their mental contents of the moment and faithfully report all mental changes to the experimenter. In contrast to Wundt, Ebbinghaus was concerned with changes in external performance as they reflected the subject's ability to retain verbal information. He measured retention capacity in terms of performance on a recall test administered some time after original learning. Whereas sensation and feelings dominated the structural psychology of Wundt, learning and especially retention were the primary interests of Ebbinghaus.

In several respects, Ebbinghaus's research was a pioneering effort: (1) *Objective* measurement, in the form of relearning (or savings) scores, replaced the more *subjective* reports obtained with Wundt's introspective method. (2) Stimulus items—nonsense or nonmeaningful syllables—were scaled in order to provide standardized and reliable learning materials. (3) Statistics were used to assess the meaning of data and mathematical models were developed to explain how associations are formed in verbal learning tasks (cf. Ebbinghaus, 1885). Clearly, the more objective, precise, and reliable research tactics of Hermann Ebbinghaus stand in sharp contrast to those of his more famous contemporary, Wilhelm Wundt.

"Reinforcement" in Memory and Cognition Research

Just as there are important differences between the research tactics and interests of Wundt and Ebbinghaus, so too are there important differences between Ebbinghaus's work and that of Watson and Pavlov. Most of these differences remain with us today, distinguishing research tactics and theories in complex learning, memory, and thought from those in basic learning. Foremost among the differences is the status of *reinforcement* as an essential interpretative concept. In the preceding chapter, we presented the learning models of classical and instrumental conditioning. In both paradigms, reinforcement was central to understanding how basic learning processes operate. In contrast, our discussion of complex human processes will for the most part dispense with the term reinforcement.

In basic learning paradigms, rewards or reinforcers are effective because they strengthen the tendency for a response to occur at some future time. Rewards are closely tied to the motivational states of an organism that is often in a state of deprivation, discontentment, or need. However, in complex verbal learning and memory research paradigms, there is generally no clearly defined need state. The subject is neither deprived of food or water nor submitted to a noxious event. Subjects are merely asked to perceive and learn and, sometimes, remember verbal information. The experimenter, of course, must ensure through instructions and briefing procedures that the learner is willing to participate and is interested in performing the task at a level commensurate with his or her abilities.

Explicit reinforcements, in terms of the occurrence of experimenter-defined positive or negative events, are almost never clearly specified in verbal learning, memory, and cognition experiments. This is not to say, however, that a participant in these experiments receives no reinforcement. Most of the time correct responses and the satisfaction that accompanies the completion of a difficult task serve as personal rewards for the learner. We should point out that reinforcing events generally are neither manipulated by the experimenter nor are they the object of the investigations; usually reinforcers are not given exact specification or important status in memory and cognition research.

The Revolt Against Neobehaviorism

In the late 1950s, verbal learning and memory research broke loose from the bondage of rote learning paradigms and behavioristic, associationistic theory. The late 1950s witnessed a shift from the neobehavioristic orientation, in which verbal learning research was often designed to extend or test theories developed in basic research areas, often with animals, to a return to the positions first advocated by the functionalists and the Würzburg school of Külpe. These two early systems in the history of psychology shared a concern for the development of S-R laws, quite similar in fact to those in Watsonian behaviorism and later neobehaviorism. However, the functionalists and the members of the Würzburg school differed from the behaviorists in that the former advocated a view of the human organism as an active learning agent, capable of operating on and transforming verbal input. That is, they conceptualized each subject as adapting the experimenter's input to suit his or her idiosyncratic style of information processing. While the behaviorists focused almost exclusively on the objective, public behavior of the organism, emphasizing the importance of reinforcement, the functionalist and Würzburg schools chose not to ignore the mental or cognitive states that accompanied the observed learning of the subject.

Though the orientation of the new breed of verbal learning researchers in the late 1950s was consistent with the philosophy of the functionalists, several aspects of their work were original. Rather than attempting to minimize the importance of the learner's past habits by means of research tactics such as nonsense syllables, this new approach recognized the importance of verbal habits and strategies of the learner and tried to assess the influence of these habits on the experimental variables under investigation. In a sense, their research was more phenomenon oriented than theoretically oriented. What we wish to emphasize is not that theories were of no interest to them, but rather that they abandoned grandiose theory building, such as conducted by Hull and Tolman, in favor of miniature theories which were almost exclusively limited to the events under study (cf. Hilgard & Bower, 1975). Theory for the verbal learners was closely tied to the variables being analyzed, and it was isolated to circumscribed bits of behavior. This approach proved fruitful, and many important contributions in verbal learning, transfer, and retention were made by men such as Arthur Melton, Leo Postman, and Benton Underwood, who led the resurgence of interest in human learning research.

Information Feedback

The term *reinforcement* has been replaced in verbal learning research by the concept of *information feedback*. This concept refers to the flow of information from the experimenter to the subject. Information about correct and incorrect responses helps the learner modify his or her pattern of responding so as to achieve perfect performance. Perhaps an example will make the notion of information feedback more concrete. Assume a subject is to learn the association "key-horn" so that whenever "key" appears by itself, "horn," the correct association, can be reported. Suppose that after one presentation of the pair, the learner responds with "door" rather than "horn." The subject quickly recognizes the error as soon as "key-horn" is presented a second time by the experimenter. The subject then has the opportunity to form a more appropriate association and perhaps to unlearn the incorrect association ("key-door"), which was very likely strong in his or her verbal repertoire. The second pairing, or study trial, enables the learner to assess the incorrectness of the first response ("door") and to attempt to form the correct association ("key-horn").

Rather than conceptualizing the learner as experiencing a negatively or positively rewarding event, researchers in verbal learning generally prefer to think in terms of the *feedback value* of an event and to consider the learner as an active processor in an information feedback chain.

The Inadequacy of the Rote Learning Model

Researchers in complex learning place little value on the concept of reinforcement because the human organism rarely learns in rote associative

(S→R) fashion. Cognitive strategies or language habits almost always influence even the simplest form of verbal learning, transforming a seemingly elementary learning task into a higher-level, more complex form of learning. For instance, if we were to ask an eighth-grader to learn the association "key-horn," he or she might use an aid or crutch to help form the "key-horn" link (cf. Neimark, 1976). On one of the study trials, the child might imagine a key opening a suitcase containing a horn and then use this vivid image to help recall "horn" when presented with "key." Or a preposition, such as "in," might serve as a bridge between the to-be-learned words ("key-*in*-horn"). These examples represent higher forms of mental activity than are conveyed by the label *rote learning* and do not lend themselves easily to interpretations involving a reinforcement concept.

Complex forms of learning such as exhibited by our hypothetical eight-grader are accurately termed cognitive-structured learning. This type of learning occurs when a direct association between two events is enriched or replaced by some additional indirect association (cf. Wickelgren, 1972). The indirect association—perhaps a language association in the learner's verbal habit system—serves as a chain or bridge linking the to-be-learned events. It is because most verbal learning tasks involve cognitive-structured learning that we differentiate them from more basic forms of learning, such as classical and operant conditioning. In other words, as cognitive operations come to dominate our analyses of complex human learning tasks, the concept of reinforcement, and the research tactics common to basic learning phenomena, greatly diminish in necessity and utility.

THE ASSOCIATIONIST AND COGNITIVIST VIEWS

A Paradigmatic Revolution?

Segal and Lachman (1972) have argued that an "invisible" scientific revolution, of the type described by Kuhn (1970), is now underway in scientific psychology. This revolution constitutes a return to the philosophical framework of structuralism and functionalism and a departure from the neobehavioristic learning theories that for so long dominated the direction of psychological research. Where the neobehavioristic approach focused on learning principles and theories, the new research orientation emphasizes the structure and function of mental life, as reflected through language, memory, and information processing. It is a revolution not only of subject matter, but also of beliefs, concepts, analogies, and methodology.

Paradigm in the Kuhnian (1970) sense is not easy to define. Throughout most of this book, we have used the term to refer to a fixed or standard experimental tactic. This is not the sense in which Kuhn used the term, as in the phrase "paradigmatic revolution." In its more complex Kuhnian usage, *paradigm* refers to the role of research conventions in guiding progress, or lack of it, in any science. Such conventions as applied to a given paradigm come from the historical, intellectual systems which precede it; from metascientific ideas about the nature of events under study; from the specific subject matter to be researched and the manner in which it is to be researched (methodology); from the concepts and language to be used in theory construction; and, finally, from the types of models and analogies used to guide both research and theorizing (cf. Lachman, Butterfield, & Mistler-Lachman, in press).

Analyzed from the perspective of its research conventions, the cognitive or information-processing paradigm stands in sharp contrast to the neobehavioristic paradigm, upon which the associationistic position grew. As Lachman and his colleagues (in press) point out, its historical antecedents are neobehaviorism, which provided its basic scientific method; traditional verbal learning, which gave laboratory tools for researching learning as well as memory; human engineering, which lent the analogy of man as a decision maker and an information processor; computer science, which provided the analogy of man as a symbol manipulator as well as stimulated innovative computer simulation techniques; and linguistics, which advanced biological, evolutionary assumptions about the origins of mental events.

The information processing paradigm makes several metascientific assumptions about human beings and their mental structures and processing capacities: (1) mind itself is a "real" event acceptable for scientific study; (2) cognitive systems add to stimulus input and actively reconstruct the mind's view of reality; and (3) innate capabilities combine with experience to produce cognitive phenomena. It follows that the subject matter of information processing is the mental activity underlying problem solving and creativity, such as perception, memory, and language.

The information processing paradigm has borrowed its vocabulary from human engineering and computer science. Concepts like channel capacity, bits of information, input-output, storage-retrieval, and buffer are part of its more important models and theories. The analogy of the functioning mind to the operations of a computer program is commonly used. Finally, several new research techniques, using speed of responding as the key dependent variable, have been devised to help clarify the structures and processes lying behind the functioning mind (cf. Lachman et al., in press).

Clearly, new concepts and new research stratagems characterize the cognitive view. It is still too early to judge whether or not the impetus from information theory, mathematical psychology, computer simulation, and psycholinguistics has actually spawned psychology's newest paradigmatic revolution. Yet there is little doubt that change is in the wind. As Segal and Lachman (1972) conclude in their insightful commentary on what might be judged by history to be psychology's most important scientific revolution:

> With the demise of S-R behaviorism, research in the higher mental processes has flourished (cf. Neisser, 1967). We cannot at this time specify what the future of psychology will be; however, we see the near future containing many and varied approaches. As to our original problem, are we in the midst of a scientific revolution? If the controversies in psychology lead to continuing debate by the non-scientific educated elite and the concept of man is at stake, as we think it is, then in several years we will be able to say that a revolution took place. We can say with assurance that deep conceptual changes in psychology have already occurred. (p. 53)

An Eclectic Cognitive-Associative Position

The cognitivist's position, in its more moderate form, is not that associations are unimportant for a thorough understanding of verbal learning. Quite the contrary, it is nearly impossible to find a verbal learning, memory, or cognition task where some form of association is entirely absent. Obviously, the ease of forming associations between items is at the heart of many learning tasks. Also, memory and cognition paradigms force the learner to draw on old verbal habits and associations, or to store and retrieve new ones. Nevertheless, the act of association is generally made easier or more difficult by the strategies used by the learner to master or solve the to-be-learned task. Such cognitive or mental activity is often as experimentally interesting as the association process itself and, at times, is indispensable for a complete and parsimonious analysis.

What we must emphasize is that many verbal learning situations involve associative or rote learning in combination with cognitive learning or strategy utilization. It should not be surprising then to find researchers in verbal learning, memory, and cognition viewing the learner as active rather than passive, as forming associations as well as perceiving patterns and adopting strategies, as often transforming seemingly rote tasks into problem-solving puzzles.

We shall now examine several of the tactics used by researchers in the study of verbal learning, transfer, memory, cognition, and higher-order processes. As we proceed through an analysis of these tasks, you will notice that the newly developed research tactics of information processing lend themselves to an analysis of psychological events in terms of an integration of the cognitive and associative perspectives, with an emphasis on the former. Our view is that an eclectic position—based on principles which rely on information processing buttressed by association—is essential if we are to strive for, and eventually obtain, a complete analysis of complex human performance.

BASIC RESEARCH TECHNIQUES IN VERBAL LEARNING

Our knowledge of complex human learning and memory is closely tied to available research models and tactics as well as to our understanding of the learner's past habits, experiences, and specific associations (cf. Jung, 1968). We are convinced that, in order to research human memory and cognitive capacities, we must first have a working knowledge of the tools available to us, as well as hypotheses and theories about the mental life of the learner who must interface with these tasks and tools. In the remainder of this chapter we will discuss the standard tools and techniques used in verbal learning, memory, and cognition research.

The standard research tactics in verbal learning—serial, paired-associate (PA), and free-recall—have been used to provide answers to the following questions: (1) Why do some people learn faster than others? Is it because they study items longer, space their activity so that rest periods are interspersed with study periods, or use strategies or gimmicks (such as imagery) to make the learning task easier? (2) Why do some people organize material while they study, and what effect does organization have on the ease of learning? Is it because common features or characteristics among items in the list make active restructuring of a list possible? Is it because some learners have a tendency to organize even unrelated material? While these are only some of the questions addressed in serial, PA, and free-recall research, they provide some idea of the kinds of knowledge sought in typical verbal learning experiments.

Serial Learning

Ebbinghaus used *serial learning* in his work on learning and remembering lists of nonsense syllables. A series of items (RIV, LEK, SUB, etc.) was presented one at a time until Ebbinghaus, who was both experimenter and subject, was able to recite the entire list in correct order. Serial learning resembles the memorization of poetry in that verbal units are mastered in proper sequence.

For many years serial learning was to verbal learning what classical conditioning was to animal learning—the simplest, most elementary task available to the researcher. Serial learning was thought to be simple in the sense that an experimenter had some control over the learning situation. The quality and quantity of materials could be specified as well as presentation rates, intervals between successive trials, and other important factors. Furthermore, experimenters using a serial task felt they had control over the learning activity of their subjects. That is, subjects were expected to process the information by associating or hooking up each item to the preceding item, such that item A would be the stimulus for item B and, in turn, item B would elicit item C, and so forth. The stimulus for any response in a serial learning task was thought to be the immediately preceding item or items (e.g., sometimes items B and C might both serve to elicit item D).

If this were the whole story, then serial learning would indeed have represented a rather simple, analyzable learning task—one useful for a wide variety of research purposes in learning, memory, and cognition. It would be a "pure" research tool in the sense that it would be under the control of the experimenter and, with proper use, an appropriate technique for exploring how information is processed. But this is not the whole story; serial learning is more complex than we have indicated so far.

The actual or functional stimulus in a serial learning task is often *not* the preceding item in a list. Young (1962) has shown that an item's position in a list is sometimes the functional stimulus, that is, the stimulus actually used by the learner in forming a correct response. In order to understand the serial position hypothesis, assume that we have a five-item list consisting of items A, B, C, D, and E. If serial positions serve as the functional stimuli in list learning, then the respective stimuli and response units would be 1-A, 2-B, 3-C, 4-D, and 5-E rather than *-A, A-B, B-C, C-D, D-E, as would hold if the preceding item served as the functional stimulus for each successive response. A more detailed presentation of Young's (1962) experiment showing the importance of item position in serial list learning is presented in Box 9.1. It is interesting to note that Young used two serial tasks in his research strategy, the second task being used to document the formation of associations that developed during the first task.

Evidence has accumulated showing that the functional stimulus (the stimulus actually used by the subject) in serial learning varies as a function of an item's actual position in the list, with the items in terminal positions being more likely to be cued to position than middle items (Mueller, 1970). Also, the functional stimulus seems to vary from subject to subject depending upon past learning habits (cf. Shuell & Keppel, 1967), with both position *and* prior items being used as cues by many subjects (Posnansky, 1972). These facts have complicated our ability to predict and control how a subject goes about performing a serial task.

One problem of some consequence is that there are sizable intrasubject differences in serial learning (Battig, 1975). If a subject uses a combination of stimuli to recall responses (both item positions and preceding items) and if these functional stimuli change during the course of

Box 9.1　The Role of Serial Position in Serial List Learning

In Experiment III of Young's (1962) study of the importance of serial position as the functional stimulus in serial learning, a *transfer design* was used. That is, two lists were learned consecutively. The first allowed for position cues to develop, while the second served as a test condition. Both tasks required the subject to learn twelve-item serial lists. After learning the first list, the subjects were separated into one of two experimental conditions. In one, the even-numbered items of the first list occupied the *same ordinal position* in the second list, while the odd-numbered items occupied *different positions*. The other condition had the odd-numbered items in the same positions in the two lists, while the even-numbered items were varied.

It was hypothesized that if the items in the same positions were learned faster than items in different positions, then supportive evidence for the importance of position cues in serial learning would have been found. The role of the preceding item(s) was controlled in that both "same" and "different" items in list two were preceded by new items (e.g., if the order of list-one items was A, B, C, D, etc., then one possible order for list two might be F, B, H, D, etc. Here, even-numbered items [B and D] remained in the same positions in the two lists; however, both "same" and "different" [F and H] items were preceded by novel items in the second list).

It should be noted that the comparison of interest, "same" versus "different" items, represented a within-subjects contrast. That is, both types of items were learned by each subject; hence, within-subjects variability was eliminated from the comparison of the "same" and "different" items. In addition, the employment of two experimental conditions ensured that each of the twelve positions in the second list had "same" and "different" items an equal number of times. This procedure increased the generality of the results by permitting the serial position hypothesis to be tested over all twelve list positions.

Young (1962) found faster learning of the "same" items in comparison to "different" items during the presentation of list two. Since all items had been seen an equal number of times in list one, and hence were equally familiar, the superiority of "same" items was attributed to the fact that the *serial positions per se*, acquired during list one, served as functional stimuli during the serial learning of list two. It should be noted that these data do not rule out the possibility of *preceding items* serving as functional stimuli in serial learning. The design used by Young (1962) merely eliminated this hypothesis as a reasonable explanation for the differences found on the second task for same and different positioned items. A serial position hypothesis appears to be a viable explanation for some types of serial learning.

learning, then a supposedly uncomplicated tool is in actuality a complex, perhaps unanalyzable, research paradigm. Its use might confuse rather than clarify the phenomenon under study. One should not be surprised then to find that serial learning, the first paradigm used in the study of verbal learning, is not a preferred research tool, at least in its original form, in the contemporary study of memory and cognition.

Paired-Associate Learning

Since Calkins first introduced the technique in 1894, paired-associate (PA) learning has enjoyed widespread popularity. Paired-associate learning requires that a subject study a series of pairs (S-R units) connecting together the two members of each pair—the stimulus and the response—so that when the first member (S) is presented by the experimenter, the second (R) can be given. Calkins's technique has been used most extensively in verbal learning, transfer, long-term memory, and mediation research.

The unique feature of PA learning, in contrast to serial learning, is the explicit identification of the stimuli and responses as well as their physical separation. This means that the experimenter generally has greater control over the subject's functional stimuli during PA learning than serial learning. Furthermore, variables can be manipulated on either the stimulus side, the response side, or both during a PA task.

Commonly, a memory drum or slide projector is used to present a PA list. This allows for careful timing of study and test periods. For the sake of illustration, let's consider three pairs that might be embedded in a ten-pair list:"TIF-bright," "MEP-cup," and "HOV-pencil." Note that the list is characterized by nonsense units as the stimulus terms and common words as the response terms. The learner's job is to hook up each stimulus with its appropriate response. There are two standard methods of presenting PA lists—the *anticipation* method and the *study-test* (or *recall*) method (cf. Battig, 1972). The mode of presentation is different in each as is the way subjects go about learning.

The anticipation method. In the anticipation method, each pair presentation consists of two phases, a stimulus term shown alone and then the combined stimulus-response terms. During the first phase, called the *anticipation* phase, the subject is required to answer with a response before the onset of the second phase, in which the entire S-R unit is studied. For instance, the sequence of events employing the three pairs in our example would be: "TIF-?," "TIF-bright"; "MEP-?," "MEP-cup"; and "HOV-?," "HOV-pencil."

Obviously, it requires several trials for most learners to master an eight- or ten-item PA list, depending upon the difficulty of the material and the rate of presentation. The standard rate is 2:2 sec—2 sec being allowed for each anticipation interval and 2 sec for each study interval. The order of pair presentations is randomized on each trial so as to keep a learner from simply remembering the order of the response units and ignoring the stimulus units. Without randomization, the PA task would be transformed into a serial task. Randomization of pairs ensures that the learner will attend to all stimuli during the anticipation and the study intervals.

The study-test method.   Recently more attention has been focused on the second technique for presenting paired-associates—the study-test method. When learning with the study-test method, the subject sees all pairs presented one after another and then is tested individually on each stimulus unit. For example, the learner might see "TIF-bright," "MEP-cup," and "HOV-pencil" on one study trial, followed by "MEP-?," "HOV-?," and "TIF-?" on the subsequent test trial. Note that the act of studying is clearly separated from the act of testing as is not the case in the anticipation method. Also the order of test stimuli is different from the order of stimulus-response pairs on the previous study trial. Subsequent study and test trials would also have different, random orders.

Which of the two methods, study-test or anticipation, would you choose if you had to learn a PA task as rapidly as possible? On the surface of things, it might appear that the anticipation method is the better choice. This method gives immediate feedback as to the correctness or incorrectness of your responses immediately after you make each response. This immediate feedback, in turn, might help you strengthen correct associations and reform incorrect associations. In contrast, the study-test method forces you to wait until the next study trial, perhaps up to 20 sec, before receiving confirmation as to the correctness of any single response.

However, experiments comparing the two procedures show either no difference or that the study-test method is superior to the anticipation method (cf. Battig, 1972). The reason for the superiority of the study-test method seems due to the fact that there is less confusion when the study period is temporally removed from the recall period. This separation period allows for more effective study than occurs with the anticipation method, where the learner is constantly switching from recall to study phases during the presentation of the pairs. Assuming you wish to reduce variability as much as possible, you will find the study-test method a more appropriate research strategy in verbal learning experiments.

Component processes in paired-associate learning.   There are at least five different processes that operate during PA learning. The component processes are *forward associations, backward associations, contextual associations, response learning,* and *stimulus recognition.* Forward associations refer to the hookup of each stimulus with its appropriate response; they can be conceptualized as S→R type associations. Forward associations are the dominant process in PA learning.

Backward associations (R→S) refer to the links between response units and their appropriate stimuli. What this means is that during the course of normal PA learning in which S→R associations develop, most learners can also report some of the S units when tested by the presentation of the R units (R→S). Thus, many associations formed during PA learning are bidirectional (S⇄R). In fact, the principle of associative symmetry maintains that the strengths of the forward and backward associations are about the same (Asch, 1968). Although some research supports the associative symmetry hypothesis (e.g., Kanak & Neuner, 1970), other studies hold that asymmetry in the form of stronger forward associations is the more accurate interpretation (Asch & Ebenholtz, 1962; Wollen, Allison, & Lowry, 1969).

Contextual associations are the connections between nontask stimuli, such as objects in the experimental room, and specific responses in the to-be-learned list. Contextual, enviromental stimuli can serve as aids or cues for recalling the responses during a PA task. Although the exact operation of contextual associations in PA learning is not entirely known, it is probably safe to say that such associations are not nearly as important as forward and backward associations.

Response learning is the acquiring of response units in the list independently of their connection with specific stimuli. The importance of response learning as a separate, critical phase in PA learning was highlighted in 1959 by Underwood, Runquist, and Schulz. The details of their widely cited study are presented in Box 9.2. Their main contribution was the isolation and measurement of response learning independent of associative learning. This process analysis has aided our understanding of many issues in verbal learning and memory. For instance, Martin (1965) has used the two-stage, process-separation of PA learning to further our understanding of transfer phenomena. Kellas and Butterfield (1970) have shown that a major portion of the deficit of the mentally retarded on PA tasks can be attributed to inadequate response learning rather than to associative or hookup-phase deficits. This finding implies that if special attention is given to teaching responses to retarded children prior to commencing a PA task, a sizable learning deficit—a deficit once thought to be immutably linked to retardation—can be minimized.

The final process in PA learning is called stimulus recognition. Martin (1967) has shown that if learners do not make the same *perceptual* response to a stimulus on trial N + 1 as they made on an earlier trial, N, then they will probably be unable to treat the stimulus on trial N + 1 as the signal for the response they had previously learned to make to that stimulus. A correct response can occur only if the stimulus is recognized

Box 9.2 The Two-Phase Conception of Paired-Associate Learning

Underwood, Runquist, and Schulz (1959) conceptualized paired-associate learning as consisting of two phases or stages. In phase one, the *response learning* phase, the subject learns to form and report responses. If they are nonsense syllables, then the time spent on response learning should be considerably greater than if meaningful words occupied response positions. Phase one must occur before the second, or *associative phase* can occur. In the associative phase, the subject learns to attach responses to specific stimuli.

If paired-associate learning consists of two separate phases, then a number of hypotheses can be generated concerning the way in which specific independent variables might differentially effect the operation of each phase. Underwood and his colleagues chose to investigate response-term similarity. They formed paired-associate lists which had response terms similar (i.e., related in terms of their meanings to one another) or dissimilar. They then assigned seven groups to each list (with similar or dissimilar responses) and gave each group a different number of trials. One group had a full 15 trials; the other six were stopped after either 1, 2, 3, 5, 8, or 13 trials and subjects were asked to report all the responses they could remember. What was measured was essentially *ease of response learning as a function of response term similarity and learning trials.*

The results showed that the groups with less than 15 trials learned the highly similar responses better than the dissimilar ones. The response learning phase was thus aided by similarity among responses. In contrast, the 15-trial groups showed better learning of the list with dissimilar responses. Since their overall learning reflected both the response and associative phases, we can logically infer that the effects of high response-term similarity were detrimental to the associative process, presumably due to competing, incorrect associations (e.g., R_5 is given to S_3 because of the semantic or meaningful similarity between R_3 and R_5). Moreover, we can infer that the size of the negative effect on the associative phase due to response-term similarity is greater than its positive effect on the response learning phase. This is because overall paired-associate learning was impaired by the presence of high response-term similarity even though response learning was enhanced.

as the previous, and appropriate, occasion for that response. Further-more, given nonrecognition of any stimulus, the probability of a correct response will fall to chance level, irrespective of how many times the stimulus has been followed by a correct response on earlier test trials. Martin's (1967) data have given stimulus recognition a central position in our understanding of the component processes operating in PA learning.

Free Recall

One of the more popular tasks in contemporary research on verbal learn-ing and memory is the free recall paradigm. Its popularity stems from its structural simplicity and from the diversity of solution strategies it allows subjects. Free recall is simple—subjects are merely presented a string of words (e.g., 30). They are then asked to remember as many words as they can, in any desired order. Yet free recall is complex—subjects can orga-nize and reorganize the list of words on the basis of semantic features or their personal, idiosyncratic learning strategies. Free recall is very useful because a subject's output often tells us a great deal about input or or-ganizational processing.

Whereas serial learning requires the recall of items in a fixed order and PA learning requires responses to specific stimuli, the function of items in a free recall list is quite varied. Some or all items may serve as both stimuli and responses. Kausler (1974) states that the defining attri-bute of free recall is the permissiveness it allows between the order of in-put and the order of output.

Generally, the output order given by a subject is different from the input order presented by the experimenter and only rarely does recall re-flect a random reordering of input. Instead, output order is almost al-ways a product of primary or secondary organization (Tulving, 1968). *Primary organization* refers to consistent discrepancies between input and output orders which are independent of the learner's past familiarity with the input items. For instance, the tendency to recall the last or ter-minal items first during the recall period, the so-called *recency effect,* is an instance of primary organization (Tulving, 1968). *Secondary organiza-tion* occurs when the output order of items is governed either by seman-tic or phonetic relationships or by the learner's verbal strategies for deal-ing with the task's demands, based on his or her past familiarity with the words.

Primary organization.   There are two ways to present a free recall task, the single-trial method and the multiple-trial method. With the former, a single exposure to the material is followed by a recall period. Generally, a subject will first recall the last items with greatest accuracy (the recency effect), then the earliest items (the primacy effect); the middle items are recalled last and at the lowest level of accuracy. Figure 9.1 shows an idealized serial position curve for a 24-word list (Murdock, 1962). The striking recency and primacy effects seen in Figure 9.1 hold under wide variations in list length and presentation rates.

In multiple-trial free recall, the learner is given a number of alternating input-output sequences, each being defined as one trial. Generally, a different order of presentation is employed on each trial. In contrast to single-trial free recall experiments where the serial position curve shows great regularity, the primacy and recency effects are difficult to assess in multiple-trial experiments. Kausler (1974) provides a good account of this complex problem:

> The assessment problem rests in the fact that after the first trial the probability of recall for a given item is related both to its serial position during the preceding input phase *and* to the degree of learning for that item prior to that input phase. For example, items shifted from unfavorable (midlist) serial positions on Trial 1 to favorable (beginning or end) serial positions on Trial 2 may incur pronounced increments in their probabilities of recall as a consequence. How-

Figure 9.1

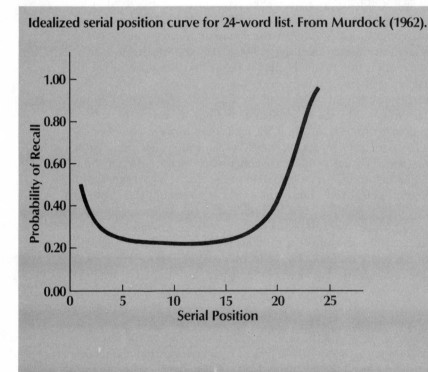

Idealized serial position curve for 24-word list. From Murdock (1962).

Box 9.3 Rehearsal and the PRNI Effect

Rundus (1974) designed a study to examine the interacting influences of rehearsal strategies, memory strength, and recall histories on the order of items recalled during free recall learning. In a session, subjects were shown three lists of thirty unrelated nouns at a presentation rate of five seconds per item. Overt rehearsal was monitored by asking subjects to *rehearse aloud* by reporting every word they were thinking about during the study period. Two minutes were given for written recall of all thirty words after each study trial, with three such study-test trials occurring for each list. A two-minute break was given after each of the three lists.

The first important finding by Rundus (1974) was that output ordering was directly related to memory strength, as defined by the amount of rehearsal activity. That is, the more actively a word was rehearsed, the more likely it would be given early in the output string. The only exception to this result was for the last two items, items 29 and 30, which were not actively rehearsed, but were nevertheless recalled first. This is presumably due to strong recency effects, which permit the final items in a list to be recalled first with little or no rehearsal needed.

Second, a PRNI effect was observed for newly recalled items on both trials 2 and 3. That is, items not recalled on trials 1 and 2 tended to be recalled first on the subsequent trial (trial 2 or 3). Third, the newly recalled items on trials 2 and 3 appeared early in recall because they were given extra rehearsal on the immediately preceding study trials. Rundus (1974) suggests that subjects adopt a strategy of giving additional attention, in terms of more active rehearsal, to those items which he or she has just failed.

It appears that items which are most easily retrieved, either because of favorable, terminal positions in the list or because they are emphasized during rehearsal because of previous failures, appear early in the recall sequence while less rehearsed items appear later. Rundus's (1974) results point up the need to monitor directly the strategies used by subjects during study periods if the process of organization is to be fully understood.

ever, in order to demonstrate primacy and/or recency effects on Trial 2, their probabilities must exceed those of the other items, that is, the items shifted from favorable to unfavorable serial positions. The latter items are likely to have degrees of learning at the onset of Trial 2 that are much greater than those for the new "primacy-recency" set of items, and their probabilities of recall may well match those of the newly favored items, despite their recent unfavorable serial input positions. The net effect is to make probability of recall an insensitive measure of primacy and recency beyond Trial 1. (p. 339)

What is of special interest in multiple-trial learning is the order of items during output rather than their recall probabilities. Brown and Thompson (1971) have shown that after the first trial the recency effect holds but not the primacy effect. Battig, Allen, and Jensen (1965) and Battig and Slaybaugh (1969) have shown a trend for the weakest items (those not previously given) to be recalled first and the strongest items (those previously correct) to be recalled last, especially on later trials. This effect has been referred to as the *priority of recall of newly learned items* (PRNI).

Battig et al. (1965) suggest that the PRNI effect could be due to increased attention paid to missed items during subsequent study periods or to a strategy which would report previously incorrect items first, before they were forgotten, and then would retrieve well learned items which presumably were more resistant to forgetting. The first possibility would reflect an input strategy, the second possibility an output strategy. Rundus (1974) has reported a set of interesting data supporting the input strategy hypothesis. His study, cited in Box 9.3, explains the PRNI effect in terms of a study strategy which allows learners to give additional rehearsal to some of the items which had not been recalled on the preceding test trial. The uniqueness of Rundus's (1974) experimental tactic is his use of overt rehearsal activity that enabled the direct monitoring of input strategies. The importance of this tactic is underscored by Belmont and Butterfield (1977) who cogently argue that direct measurement of learning strategies is essential if we are ever to gain a precise and meaningful appreciation of mental processing.

Secondary organization.   Tulving (1968) distinguished two types of secondary organization—clustering and subjective organization. *Clustering* occurs when the output order is determined principally by semantic or phonetic relations among items, while *subjective organization* is determined by the learner's own prior familiarity with the items in the list.

Clustering may be divided into two types—associative and categorical. *Associative clustering* depends on the subject's preexperimental verbal habits with word associations. If a list is formed on the basis of word association norms, such as Palermo and Jenkins's (1964), so as to include words and their primary associates (e.g., black-white), there is a tendency for pairs which had been separated during presentation to be recalled contiguously. Furthermore, the extent of associative clustering increases among items as associative strength increases (Jenkins, Mink, & Russell, 1958).

Categorical clustering is accomplished by selecting a list of items composed of words from several different taxonomical groups. The words are presented randomly to subjects for a series of study-test trials. Clustering occurs if more items from the same category are recalled next to one another than might be expected by chance. A classic study by Bousfield (1953) documented the phenomenon of categorical clustering by presenting a random list of 60 nouns composed of fifteen words from each of four taxonomic categories (animals, names, professions, and vegetables). Individual items were presented orally, one every three seconds, followed by a ten-minute recall period. The mean number of items recalled out of 60 possible was approximately 25, with a range of 12 to 36. Bousfield's measure of clustering, the repetition ratio (RR), was the number of within-category repetitions divided by the number of items recalled minus one. The mean RR value for 100 subjects was .45. This is to be contrasted with a chance value of .24, an estimate of RR which was obtained assuming no intentional organizational activity had taken place. Bousfield concluded that significant clustering had occurred. Other researchers have shown that categorical organization facilitates learning (Schuell, 1968).

One problem with the repetition ratio as a measure of clustering is that it does not take into account the number of categories represented in each subject's recall protocol (cf. Kausler, 1974). Most alternative measures of clustering use $N - K$ in the denominator instead of $N - 1$, where K is the number of categories represented in a subject's recall protocol and N is the number of items recalled.

We should point out that RR ratios, or any alternate measures of clustering, require a chance-expectancy baseline in order to ensure that the observed clustering is above the level of association found among categorized units when no organization is present. Chance levels can be established by conducting an artificial experiment to determine the chance level of clustering, as Bousfield (1953) did, or by developing mathematical formulae that can provide similar indices. Once chance level is determined, then a baseline is provided from which an accurate estimate of organization can be derived.

TYPICAL DEPENDENT VARIABLES IN VERBAL LEARNING

The preceding discussion on measures of clustering emphasizes the need to consider carefully the dependent measures used in verbal learning research. Some outcome variables are standard and can be usefully employed in most verbal learning and memory research. Others, though used quite frequently in past research and hence unquestioned by some researchers, ought to be used only with great caution.

Mean Correct Per Trial

Perhaps the most common measure in verbal learning research is the mean number of correct responses per acquisition trial. With this measure, all subjects are represented on all trials. For instance, if the scores for five subjects were averaged for each of ten trials (see Table 9.1), a function can be drawn relating the mean number of correct responses to the number of trials. The resulting performance curve is shown by the solid line in Figure 9.2.

At times, the mean total number of correct responses is reported in research articles. In our example, the mean total correct is 6.8. The problem with this measure, and an argument for the use of the mean correct per trial, is that the learners' performances across trials are camouflaged by the total correct measure. For instance, if we compared the performance of the subjects in Table 9.1 with that of five other hypothetical subjects receiving a different condition (whose trial by trial averages are shown by the dashed line in Figure 9.2), an interaction between the two treatments and the trials dimension would be obscured if we used only a measure of mean total correct performance in lieu of mean correct per trial. In short, trial by trial averages of correct responding yield a group performance curve which reflects more reliably changes in the acquisition process across time.

Trials-to-Criterion

A deceptively simple dependent measure, which has been widely used, is the number of trials needed to reach a specified criterion of learning. The most common criterion is the mastery of a list, usually to a level of 100

Table 9.1 Correct responses for five subjects on ten test trials.

Trials	1	2	3	4	5	6	7	8	9	10	
S_1	0	1	4	4	6	7	8	10	10	10	
S_2	3	5	7	7	7	7	8	9	9	10	
S_3	1	1	1	3	5	5	6	7	8	10	
S_4	4	5	8	8	9	10	10	10	10	10	
S_5	0	0	1	3	5	6	6	6	7	10	
Mean	1.6	2.4	4.2	5.0	6.4	7.0	7.6	8.4	8.8	10	6.8

Figure 9.2

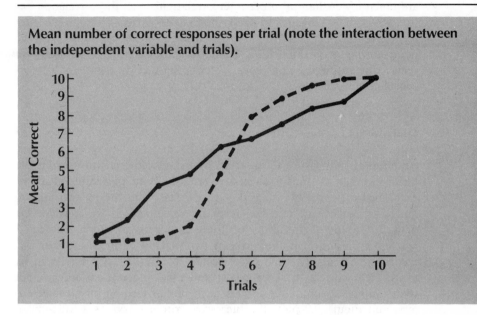

Mean number of correct responses per trial (note the interaction between the independent variable and trials).

percent correctness, although criteria such as two consecutive correct repetitions or 80 percent mastery of a list are sometimes used.

In our previous example in Table 9.1, the number of trials required to reach a criterion of one perfect recitation of the list for the five subjects is as follows: $S_1 = 8$, $S_2 = 10$, $S_3 = 10$, $S_4 = 6$, $S_5 = 10$. Hence the mean number of trials needed to reach a criterion of 100 percent mastery is 8.8 trials. There are at least two difficulties with measures of mean trials-to-criterion. The first is identical to the objection we raised above with respect to the measure of mean total correct. All interactions that occur prior to criterion are not detectable when we use a trials-to-criterion measure. For instance, the two conditions depicted in Figure 9.2 have somewhat similar mean trials-to-criterion measures (8.8 for the solid versus 8.0 for the dashed curve) yet have very different patterns of learning across trials. The learning patterns suggest that conditions interact with trials—an interaction not reflected in the trials-to-criterion measure.

A second problem with trials to a perfect criterion (e.g., 100 percent mastery) is that it is a by-product of the most difficult items in the list (Bahrick, 1967). Thus, time and energy spent on the one or two most difficult items in the list are disproportionately reflected in the trials-to-criterion measure at the expense of easier items (see pp. 109–111 for a discussion of this point). Bahrick (1967) has shown that the correlations between the number of trials needed to reach a criterion of one perfect recitation (100 percent) and all other criteria (e.g., 90, 80, or 70 percent) are much lower than all other intercorrelations (e.g., the correlation between 30 and 60 percent). In short, the trials-to-perfect-criterion measure for a given subject is not highly related to his or her learning at earlier points during acquisition trials. If a criterion measure is to be used that reflects the entire learning process, a criterion level of less than 100 percent should be chosen.

Trials-to-Successive-Criteria

An alternative measure to the trials to a single criterion measure is the mean number of trials-to-successive-criteria. With this latter measure, each level of learning is considered separately and the mean trials required to reach each criterion level are calculated. If we consider the data in Table 9.1 in terms of trials-to-successive-criteria, subject 1 reached the criterion of one correct in two trials; two, three, and four correct in three trials; five and six correct in five trials; seven correct in six trials; eight correct in seven trials; and nine and ten correct in eight trials. Table 9.2 summarizes the data in similar fashion for all five subjects and Figure 9.3 plots the successive-criteria curve as a function of trials (solid line). Note that the data in Table 9.2 represent not the number of correct responses per trial but rather the average number of trials needed to reach each successive criterion for the five subjects. You can easily see that subject four was a very fast learner, whereas subject five was the slowest learner in the group.

Several characteristics of the trials-to-successive-criteria measure become apparent in Figure 9.3. If a group of subjects learned the same material faster than our solid line group, their curve (A) would fall below the solid curve. Conversely, if another group experienced more difficulty in list learning than our group, their trials-to-successive-criteria curve (B) would be above that of our solid curve. Do not make the mistake of inferring that good performance is associated with the uppermost function

Table 9.2   Mean trials to successive criterion.

	Successive Criterion									
	1	2	3	4	5	6	7	8	9	10
1	2	3	3	3	5	5	6	7	8	8
2	1	1	1	2	2	3	3	7	8	10
3	1	4	4	5	5	7	8	9	10	10
4	1	1	1	1	2	3	3	3	5	6
5	3	4	4	5	5	6	9	10	10	10
Means	1.4	2.6	2.6	3.2	3.8	4.8	5.8	7.2	8.2	8.8

Figure 9.3

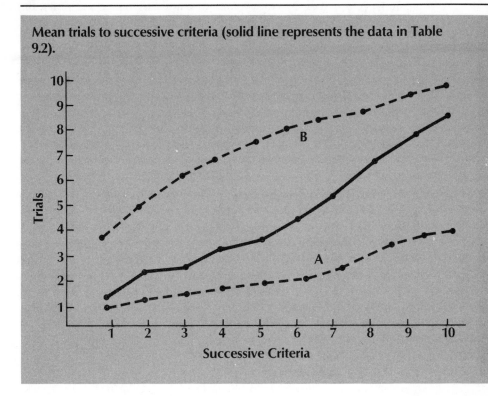

Mean trials to successive criteria (solid line represents the data in Table 9.2).

when viewing a trials-to-successive-criteria graph. With this caution in mind, you will find this measure useful as a way to chart the step-wise progress of a group of learners as they go about mastering a list.

Secondary Measures

In psychological research, more than one dependent variable is frequently used in a single study. Sometimes the secondary measure is used to document a process presumed responsible for the learning curve. Recall how Rundus (1974) related the number of overt rehearsals to the order of output in a free recall task. In other instances, secondary measures such as the type of errors or latencies serve as supports for the performance measure of primary interest.

Errors. Sometimes the types of errors made by learners are as illuminating as their correct responses. Omissions are generally the most frequent type of error occurring in list learning, especially if guessing has not been encouraged. Also certain subjects, like the institutionalized mentally retarded or the elderly, are more hesitant to give a response unless they are fairly certain of its correctness. High rates of omission errors are generally due to a tendency toward overcautiousness or to fear of failure.

Other common forms of errors are extralist and intralist intrusions. In the former, an item, usually a word from outside the list being learned, is incorrectly given by the subject. In the latter case, an incorrect item is given from within the list of possible correct responses but is mismatched or misplaced. An analysis of errors sometimes tells about the type of interference which makes the task difficult to learn.

Latency.   The time it takes for a response to occur (latency) can be a sensitive measure of performance. This is especially true if a decision or choice has to be made before the correct response can be given or if a detailed search of memory is required in order to retrieve information. For the most part, latencies have been useful in the analysis of sensation, perception, short-term memory, and decision-making phenomena. Latencies have proven to be of limited value, in contrast, in the analysis of traditional problems in verbal learning, transfer, and long-term memory. Latencies are more commonplace as dependent variables in information-processing research (cf. Lachman et al., in press).

A Problem with Averaging

We will close this section on the choice of dependent measures with a warning. Newell (1973) provides two injunctions for successful psychological experimentation: (1) Know the method (strategy) your subject is using to perform the experimental task, and (2) Never average over methods.

What are the implications of these golden rules of Newell for our choice of dependent measures in verbal learning research? The first injunction claims that we should know how our subject goes about performing our task. What method or strategy is selected by the learner to achieve a satisfactory level of task performance? Belmont and Butterfield (1977) tell us that we can know a subject's strategy only by monitoring and directly measuring his or her strategy as it is occurring. Rundus's (1974) counting of overt rehearsal activity is an example of direct strategy measurement.

Newell's (1973) second injunction urges us never to average over methods. He implies that if we know the strategy each subject is using to learn a task, we can compare strategies to test their similarity and effectiveness. If the methods are quite variable, we would be foolish to average data across subjects. Furthermore, Battig (1975) has shown that a single subject will often use different learning methods for different items in a list, or for the same item on different trials. If individual differences (either between or within subjects) in strategy usage occur, then averaging across items and/or trials is an inappropriate technique for reducing data for purposes of statistical analysis.

To sum up, averaging performance across subjects, or across items or trials for a single subject, is defensible only if we know that the methods used are consistent within and between subjects. Of course, this research maxim can only be applied if the subjects' strategies are known and measured independent of correct performance.

PARADIGMS IN TRANSFER AND LONG-TERM MEMORY

Most research designs that study the transfer of verbal information and its retention over relatively long periods of time (e.g., 24 hours or a week) have made use of *paired-associate* tasks. Some of the research designs in verbal transfer involve the learning of one list in order to make the learning of a second list easier or more difficult. Most experiments in retention involving paired-associate learning attempt to answer one or more of the following key questions: Why do we forget? Do bright people retain more than average people? Are some materials easier to remember than others? How can forgetting be minimized?

Although they possess certain unique theoretical and methodological aspects, transfer and retention share a common reliance on paired-associate learning. This research tactic allows for the generation of specific interfering or facilitating associations in the learning of consecutive lists. Such associations are at the heart of the analysis of transfer and retention phenomena.

Transfer of Training

Transfer refers to the way in which one learning experience influences a second learning experience. The direction of transfer can be either positive or negative. *Positive transfer* means that one learning experience facilitates a second, while *negative transfer* means that exposure to the first task in some way interferes with the learning of the second (Jung, 1968).

Transfer phenomena can be broadly divided along two lines—nonspecific and specific. *Nonspecific transfer* occurs when the transfer effect on the second task is unrelated to the associations developed in the first task, the transfer effect being simply a by-product of practice effects accumulated during the first task. In contrast, *specific transfer* refers to the fact that associations unique to the learning of the first task influence the associations developed in the second task.

Basic transfer designs. Assume that we give one group of learners list A followed by list B and wish to know if there are any transfer effects from A to B. Furthermore, to help decide whether the direction of transfer is positive or negative, a control group which receives only list B is included in the design. We hypothesize that the comparison of list B learning for experimental (A to B) and control (B only) groups might yield results in favor of the former, suggesting that the transfer was positive. Of course, if the control group learned list B faster than the experimental group, then the direction of transfer would be negative, or detrimental to second list learning.

The question now arises as to whether the transfer effects in our example, be they positive or negative, were due to specific or nonspecific sources. Does our design permit us to conclude in favor of one or the other? The answer is no. This is because we allowed both specific and nonspecific factors to vary in the sense that the experimental group had an opportunity for specific associations to develop during list A learning and also had more practice than the control group. Hence, any difference between the experimental and control groups during list B learning could be due to specific associations, nonspecific practice effects, or both. In fact, the negative effects from one of these factors could cancel the positive effects from another.

A more satisfactory experimental design, depicted in Table 9.3, allows for the separation of specific and nonspecific sources of transfer. Essentially, the experimental group learns list A, then list B. The single-list control group does nothing, then learns list B. A third group, a double-list control group, learns X, a list unrelated to list B but one which allows for practice and warm-up effects, and then learns list B. This design allows the effects on list B learning due to specific transfer (a comparison of the experimental and the double-list control groups) to be separated from the effects due to nonspecific transfer (a comparison of the double-list and single-list control groups). The implication is that if our experimental interest centers on specific forms of transfer, as is usually the case, we must employ a control group, such as the double-list control group, which provides adequate management of nonspecific sources of transfer.

Table 9.3   An experimental design for transfer.

Condition	Task 1	Task 2	Factors Transfer
Experimental	Learns A	Learns B	Transfer of specific factors from A to B & nonspecific factors
One-List Control	(rest)	Learns B	Nothing transferred
Two-List Control	Learns irrelevant list (X)	Learns B	Transfer of nonspecific factors only

Nonspecific transfer: Practice effects. Nonspecific transfer can be thought of as consisting of two components, one transitory and the other relatively permanent. The transitory component is called *warm-up* and occurs with all motor and verbal learning tasks. Perhaps the most striking example of warm-up effects is in athletic events where the participants engage in preliminary exercises and routines in order to benefit from the positive transfer of warm-up effects to the contest itself. The more lasting component is *learning-to-learn* which refers to the effects from practice that remain even after several days have elapsed.

It is rather surprising that so many undergraduate students fail to avail themselves of the powerful effects of warm-up and learning-to-learn in preparation for key examinations such as the GRE, Medical Boards, and Law Boards. This preparation could take the form of familiarizing oneself with the kinds of questions to be asked and the ways to proceed in answering them (e.g., reading passages upon which comprehension questions are based). Practice could take place over a period of days preceding the exam in order to develop learning-to-learn effects, with some brief warm-up being included on the day of the exam itself.

Specific transfer. In studying specific transfer effects, the most commonly used paradigms are the A-B, A'-B; A-B, A-C; A-B, C-B; A-B, A-B$_r$. In each case, associations developed during list 1 learning influence the ease or difficulty of list 2 learning. In A-B, A'-B, the responses of list 1 are identical in list 2, and while the stimuli are different, they are nevertheless similar (e.g., *pretty*-fox; *lovely*-fox). In A-B, A-C, the stimuli are identical and the responses different. In A-B, C-B, the responses are identical and the stimuli different. In A-B, A-B$_r$, the stimuli and responses are identical, but they have been re-paired in list 2 (e.g., if A$_1$-B$_1$, A$_2$-B$_2$, etc., symbolize several of the pairs in list 1, then corresponding pairs in list 2 might be A$_3$-B$_7$, A$_1$-B$_5$, A$_6$-B$_1$, etc.). In each of these paradigms the amount and direction of transfer is assessed by comparing the experimental paradigm to an appropriate control, A-B, C-D.

We should make three points concerning the A-B, C-D control condition. First, it controls for learning-to-learn and warm-up effects by allowing for their development during list 1 learning in the same ways as for any experimental condition (e.g., A-B, A-C). Second, no specific associations—similar to those in an experimental condition—are assumed to develop during list 1 learning which might influence list 2 learning. Third, the actual order of presentation is from C-D to A-B. That is, list 1, the first list seen, in this case is C-D, and list 2 is A-B. If we were to compare the A-B, A-C paradigm to its appropriate control condition (A-B, C-D), subjects in one group would be presented list A-C followed by A-B while another group of subjects would receive C-D followed by A-B. This permits the comparison of learning on identical second lists (A-B) when deciding whether significant positive or negative transfer has occurred. It is only by convention that we refer to transfer paradigms as A-B, C-D; A-B, A-C; A-B, A'-B; A-B, C-B; A-B, A-B$_r$, etc. The actual order of presentation is reversed in each instance.

From the five paradigms listed above, can you predict the order of results from best to worst on second list learning? Some predictions should be easy. For instance, most people would predict positive transfer in the A-B, A'-B paradigm, due to the fact that each A' stimulus would evoke an appropriate A link, which in turn could evoke and mediate the correct B response. Almost always A-B, A'-B leads to better second list learning than occurs in the standard A-B, C-D control condition. Another safe prediction is that sizable negative transfer should occur in the A-B, A-C paradigm. This prediction is based on the interference that appears during list 2 learning when many of the old stimuli (A) evoke their old responses (B) rather than their new, correct responses (C).

With respect to the A-B, A-B$_r$ and A-B, C-B paradigms, transfer predictions are less firm. In the former, you would probably predict negative transfer, but how much? More than in A-B, A-C? Why? In the latter, would you predict positive or negative transfer and why? The answers to these questions have been provided by Martin (1965) who has conceptualized specific transfer in terms of three sources: forward associations, backward associations, and response availability. Box 9.4 contains an illustration of Martin's analysis of specific transfer of training. His extension of the two-phase theory of paired-associate learning (cf. Underwood et al., 1959) has provided a framework for predicting positive and negative transfer in the A-B, C-B paradigm and for understanding why sizable negative transfer is usually found in the A-B, A-B$_r$ paradigm.

Long-Term Retention

Most research on long-term retention, defined as the recall of previously learned material over a time span generally greater than one hour, makes use of paired-associate tasks embedded in a transfer paradigm. One way to study losses in retention is to give a control group a test for recall immediately after acquiring a list and another group the same test some 24 or 48 hours later. The differences you would most likely observe—showing 60 to 90 percent forgetting in the latter group—reflect the fragile nature of the retention process over long time spans. The exact amount of forgetting depends on such factors as the level of original learning (with overlearning serving to forestall forgetting), the nature of the intervening task (with intervening activities similar to the learned task resulting in large losses), and the manner of testing recall.

Box 9.4 Bidirectional Associations and Response Availability in the A-B, C-B and A-B, A-B$_r$ Transfer Paradigms

Martin (1965) borrowed the two-phase conception of paired-associate learning (cf. Underwood et al., 1959) to increase our understanding of transfer of training. He reasoned that the processes of response learning and associative formation, both forward and backward, that occurred in first list learning were similar to the processes responsible for specific transfer effects in second list learning. He argued for an analysis of transfer in terms of whether the processes taking place in list one made similar activity in list two easier or more difficult. In the A-B, C-D or control paradigm, does the response learning of the B terms and the formation of A→B and B→A associations during list one learning have an influence on C-D learning? The answer is no. The specific associations, and the learning of the D responses, are unique to list two processing.

But what about the A-B, C-B and A-B, A-B$_r$ paradigms? In the former, response learning in list one makes response learning in list two easier. However, the backward associations (B→A) of list one are available to interfere with the development of forward associations (C→B) during list two learning. Under what conditions will positive transfer from response learning outweigh negative transfer from backward associations? The answer is tied to the actual level of meaningfulness (m) of the B units. If B terms are low in m, then positive transfer from prior response learning will be more influential than negative transfer due to interfering backward associations. Thus, a comparison of C-B learning to an appropriate control will show positive transfer. This is because the control group (A-B, C-D) will probably spend considerably more time in learning low m response units (D items) during list two, while the experimental group has already acquired its B terms.

In the A-B, A-B$_r$ paradigm, there is positive transfer of response learning since the same B terms are contained in both lists. Yet there is considerable negative transfer from both A→B and B→A associations during list two learning. These negative effects from forward and backward associations are very powerful and outweigh the beneficial effects from prior response learning. The net result is sizable negative transfer in A-B, A-B$_r$ when compared to an A-B, C-D control group. In addition, greater negative transfer generally occurs in the A-B, A-B$_r$ than in the A-B, A-C paradigm.

Methods of measuring retention.   There are four standard ways to measure the recall of a list of items after a long interval. Because of different sensitivities to amount of information in memory store, each yields a different index of retention. The *recall* measure is the most direct and commonly used measure of long-term memory (LTM). With this method, a learner is asked to report the contents of his or her memory either with no cues available or with only minimal cues. In a serial or free recall task, the test for long-term retention consists of unaided reports of everything that can be remembered from the original list. With paired-associate learning, minimal cues are given in the form of the stimuli used during the acquisition trials. The retention measure is the percentage of items correctly remembered.

A second method, often used in combination with the recall method to measure LTM, is called *relearning*. It was originated by Ebbinghaus and continues to be quite useful for measuring forgetting. Relearning requires the subject to study a list in the same manner as during original learning. For instance, if the study-test method was used during acquisition, then this method would be used during the retention test, with presumably the same criterion of learning. The relearning method is sometimes called the *savings method* because it is assumed that the learner will relearn the material at a faster rate than he or she had originally. The amount saved is calculated according to the following formula:

$$\text{SAVINGS} = 100\% \times \frac{\text{Number of OL trials} - \text{Number of RL trials}}{\text{Number of OL trials}}$$

In this formula OL refers to original learning and RL to relearning. If a subject originally acquired a list in 15 trials but required only 5 trials to relearn it, then the savings score would be $100\% \times \frac{15-5}{15}$ or $100\% \times \frac{2}{3}$ or 67%. In effect, relearning required 67% less effort the second time around.

A third way to measure LTM is by means of the *recognition* method. This measure does not require the learner to produce a response in the same way as in the recall and relearning methods. The subject merely chooses what he or she considers to be the correct response from a list of alternatives, usually four or five. This method is similar to a standard multiple-choice test, where the correct answer is surrounded by similar but incorrect alternatives. Of course, the degree of difficulty for any recognition task is the product of the number of alternative responses and their similarity to the correct response. With six alternative responses, all having high similarity to the correct response, the recognition method can be exceedingly difficult.

A final method, *reconstruction,* gives the learner disarranged responses (or stimuli and responses if the task involves paired-associates) and requires that the original list be reconstituted. In serial learning this would amount to rearranging the items to form the correct serial order.

In paired-associate learning, it would involve reforming the correct stimulus-response units. Reconstruction might be used when a tactic is needed to minimize the learner's reliance on the recall of specific stimuli and/or responses during the retention test and when interest is focused on associative formation.

The problem of controlling original learning. Differences in performance at the end of original learning are likely to be present on any later test for retention. In this case, retention differences do not reflect pure estimates of the amount lost during the retention interval, in that the estimates contain unwanted differences in acquisition levels. This methodological problem, referred to as the *control of degree of original learning*, has been addressed in considerable detail by Underwood (1964).

Let us consider an example to help clarify the issue. A well documented law in verbal learning relates level of meaningfulness in a serial task to ease of learning. High meaningfulness serial lists are learned more rapidly than low meaningfulness lists. What about the effects of meaningfulness on retention? Are high meaningfulness lists more easily retained than low meaningfulness lists? Intuition would probably cause you to respond yes. There is the "feeling" that highly meaningful material "stays with us longer."

One way to validate this intuition would be to present high and low meaningfulness lists to two groups of subjects for ten trials and to measure their recall and relearning scores one week later. We will assume that hypothetical results occurred similar to those shown in the lower panel of Figure 9.4. What could we conclude about the effects of meaningfulness on retention? Very little, since the differences at the end of the acquisition period confounded, or contaminated, actual retention differences. That is, differences on the first trial of the retention test may simply have represented acquisition differences which were apparent on trial 15.

A second way to handle this methodological problem would be to take each group, one receiving the high and the other the low meaningfulness list, to a common criterion of learning (e.g., one perfect recitation of the list). A test for retention, using recall and relearning techniques, would be given one week later. Hypothetical results are presented in the middle panel of Figure 9.4. With learning equated for degree of original learning (both groups learned to a 100 percent criterion), are retention differences due to meaningfulness now interpretable? Although the answer is less obvious than in the first example, it is still no. The reason is that the rates of learning for the high and low meaningfulness groups are different on the terminal acquisition trial. If one more acquisition trial had been given and if we had some way to measure overlearning (i.e., increases in learning after the 100 percent criterion was reached), then we might well see a superiority of the high meaningfulness group at the end of the acquisition trials. The problem then is

Figure 9.4

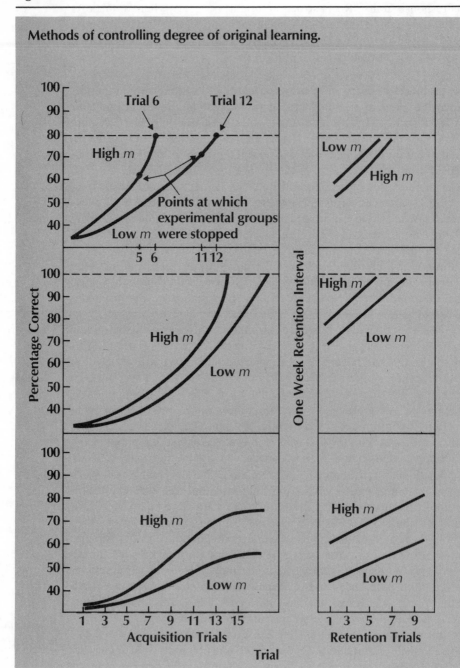

Methods of controlling degree of original learning.

that the first retention trial has a built-in bias, small but reliable, in favor of the group having the faster learning rate, in this case the high meaningfulness condition. This makes interpretations concerning pure retention effects difficult to formulate.

There are several satisfactory ways to overcome the problem of controlling the degree of original learning (cf. Underwood, 1964). One is to use two pilot groups in order to chart the rate of learning for the high and low meaningfulness conditions. Let us assume the pilot data are as shown in the top panel of Figure 9.4. We decide to choose a matching criterion less than 100 percent so as to avoid overlearning and the pitfalls associated with the learning of the most difficult items in the list. We decide on 8 of 10 correct responses, or 80 percent, as our criterion. We then observe that the high meaningfulness pilot group reached the 80 percent level in six trials on the average, while the low group took twelve trials. Furthermore, we realize that if we expose our subjects in the high group to five trials and subjects in the low group to eleven trials, their level of performance would be matched on their next trial. This trial is, in fact, the first trial of retention. Essentially, Underwood's (1964) procedure involves collecting pilot data and then giving N−1 trials to the subjects in the actual experiment, where N trials were required by pilot subjects to reach a specified criterion less than 100 percent.

There are several problems with this technique that explain why it has been used infrequently. It is very time consuming and, more important, there is usually considerable variability in the learning abilities of subjects in any one condition. This means that the average performance of pilot subjects may represent an inappropriate terminal stage of acquisition for 50 percent or more of the "real" subjects. Other possible methods to control for degree of original learning in studies of LTM are discussed by Underwood (1964). The fact that there is no single best method now available does not mean that the problem of controlling original learning can be ignored. It argues for methodological innovation in dealing with this problem in LTM research.

To illustrate the importance of this issue consider the results of Young, Saegert, and Linsley (1968) on the effects of meaningfulness on retention. Young et al. gave subjects either a high or low meaningfulness list for a single study trial; learning was less than 100 percent, with the best immediate recall occurring with the high meaningfulness material. Their tests for retention after 24 hours showed a surprising result. The best retention was by the group receiving the low meaningfulness list. In other words, if low and high meaningfulness lists are learned to about the same degree of original learning (less than 100 percent) better retention of the low meaningfulness material is likely to result. Why? Young et al. (1968) argued that highly meaningful items are more likely to be interfered with by items in the subject's verbal habit system. Since the learner brings this habit system to the laboratory, it is prior or proactive interference which is responsible for the fact that high meaningfulness material is more subject to forgetting than low meaningfulness material. The Young et al. (1968) study suggested that interference was necessary to explain a somewhat surprising result. We now will consider the standard paradigms used to study interference and forgetting.

Proactive and retroactive interference paradigms.   Most losses in LTM appear to be result of active interference rather than the mere passage of time. The designs used to test the interference theories of forgetting, summarized in Table 9.4, are referred to as the proactive (PI) and retroactive interference (RI) paradigms. Each is built on a transfer paradigm in which subjects learn two consecutive lists. However, our interest does not focus on second list learning as in transfer of training. Rather, our concern here is with the retention of either the first list (RI) or the second list (PI). With RI, the question is whether the second or interpolated list interferes or, perhaps, facilitates the retention of the first list. With PI, the question is whether the prior or first list interferes with or facilitates the retention of the second list. Of course, there is an appropriate control group in both cases. In the RI paradigm, the control group usually learns an irrelevant task during the intervening (second list) session. In the PI paradigm, the control group learns a "neutral" first list prior to the second list. The test for retention effects attributable to either PI or RI involves a comparison of each group's retention scores with those of the appropriate control group.

Most contemporary research on the interference theory of forgetting makes use of specific transfer paradigms like those discussed in the preceding section for generating interfering associations. A favorite RI paradigm is referred to as A-B, A-D, A-B. In this paradigm, the retention of A-B is tested after a period of time has elapsed following A-B and A-D learning. The issue is how and why A-D interferes with the recall of A-B. In order to answer these questions, Briggs (1954) used the standard RI

Table 9.4   Retroactive and proactive paradigms.

		Prior Learning	Original Learning	Intervening Learning	Retention
RI	Exp. Group		Learns list I	Learns list II	Test for list I
	Control Group		Learns list I	Learns un-related task	Test for list I
PI	Exp. Group	Learns list I	Learns list II		Test for list II
	Control Group	Learns un-related task	Learns list II		Test for list II

(A-B, A-D) paradigm, presenting lists of twelve paired-associates to a criterion of one perfect recitation for both list one and list two learning. The A-D list represented the standard negative transfer condition, in which the old A stimuli of list one were associated with new responses. Following A-D learning, subjects recalled the A-B lists after intervals of 10 minutes or 6, 24, 48, or 70 hours.

The feature of Briggs' design of greatest interest was his attempt to study the course of *unlearning* of A-B associations during second list (A-D) learning. On certain A-D test trials, a learner was shown a stimulus (A) and asked to give just one response (either B from list one or D from list two). This technique is called directed or *modified free recall* (MFR). The MFR trials were given after a subject had made 3, 6, 9, or 12 correct responses during A-D learning.

The MFR technique yielded evidence suggesting that first list associations (A-B) were being weakened or unlearned during second list learning (A-D). The problem was that the MFR test required only a single response for each A stimulus. Since subjects could give only one response per stimulus during second list recall, we do not know whether A-B associations were being unlearned, or simply that second list responses were momentarily dominant over first list responses. This latter interpretation implies not that A-B associations were unlearned, but merely that B responses were not as strong as D responses. It stands as an alternative interpretation to the unlearning hypothesis.

Barnes and Underwood (1959) did a follow-up study to that of Briggs (1954) in which they used a *modified, modified free recall* task (MMFR). Learners were asked to give both responses (B and D) to each A stimulus following various numbers of A-D trials in an A-B, A-D paradigm. Their procedure allowed for both the dominant and the non-dominant responses to emerge and hence was a much fairer test of the unlearning hypothesis. Figure 9.5 shows the recall of B and D responses on various trials of the A-D list. The results suggest that first list associations were extinguished or unlearned during second list learning in the RI paradigm. Further, as amount of second list learning increased, more RI occurred and was attributable to increased unlearning of first list responses. The net result was poor retention of the A-B list due to the unlearning of A-B associations during interpolated A-D learning.

Contrary to expectations, the evidence for the spontaneous recovery of unlearned, second list associations as a function of time since interpolated learning is weak (cf. Jung, 1968). Postman and his colleagues (1968, 1969) have shown that unless there is a high degree of first list learning, first list responses will not recover following second list learning. Postman argues that "recovery" reflects the dissipation of response set competition—the tendency developed during interpolated learning to suppress the responses from original learning. From this perspective, we might think of first list responses as *suppressed* rather than *extinguished,*

Figure 9.5

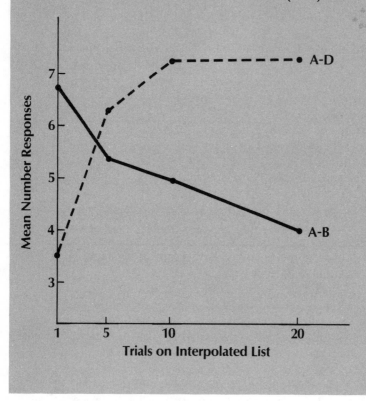

Frequency of responses from the first (A-B) and second lists (A-D) as a function of number of A-D trials when S is asked to recall the responses from both lists. From Barnes and Underwood (1959).

with spontaneous recovery as simply the elimination of the suppression. Kintsch (1970) states the revised formulation of Postman as follows:

> It seems that interference theory has come almost full circle: it started out with the notion that interference was produced by response competition; later, attention shifted more and more to unlearning as the basic mechanism of interference in transfer experiments; now Postman wants to reinstate response competition in the dominant role. However, response competition is back with a difference: 40 years ago, it was the competition between individual associations that was held responsible for interference; today, generalized response competition is thought to arise as a consequence of the inertia of the response selector mechanism. (pp. 60–61)

SHORT-TERM MEMORY PARADIGMS

The term "short-term memory" (STM) has been used in two rather different senses: (1) as a distinct psychological process, and (2) as a descriptive label for any experiment that involves brief retention intervals, generally less than 30 seconds (cf. Waugh & Norman, 1965). In the latter sense, STM stands in contrast to LTM, where longer periods of time, generally a matter of hours, define the retention interval. In the former sense, STM is often broken down into three component psychological processes: *immediate or sensory memory* (IM), *primary memory* (PM), and *secondary memory* (SM). While detailed theoretical discussions of these STM systems have been provided by Neisser (1967), Waugh and Norman (1965), Norman (1968), Atkinson and Shiffrin (1968), and others, our main concern in this section will be to survey the major research strategies used in the analysis of these component processes of STM.

Immediate Memory: Research Tactics

The main concern of IM research centers on how much information can be reported accurately following a single brief exposure. The IM component can be analyzed and discussed from the viewpoints of sensation, perception, or memory with equal justification. In fact, IM serves as a bridge between the formally distinct research areas of perception and memory, bringing these topics much closer together. Immediate memory has been categorized into iconic and echoic memory. *Iconic memory* refers to the registration of very brief visual information, while *echoic memory* refers to the registration of auditory information. Since our knowledge of iconic memory is more complete, we will consider only research tactics which focus on the registration and reporting of visually presented material over brief periods of time.

The Sperling technique. In 1960, George Sperling discovered that subjects could report back about 4.3 single letters when they were simultaneously and briefly presented. The device used to present the materials was a tachistoscope, which enabled Sperling to present the letter strings of various lengths (from 3 to 12) for periods of 50 to 500 milliseconds. An IM span of 4.3 correctly reported letters held regardless of string length or presentation duration. Since Sperling believed that the act of retrieving the letters may have limited the amount retained, he designed a partial report technique to overcome the forgetting associated with the time taken up by retrieval processing. In his procedure, three rows of four letters each were presented to the subject whose job was to recall one of the rows of letters on cue from the experimenter. Subjects were instructed which row to remember either .1 sec before the presentation period began, simultaneous with the presentation, or .15, .3, or 1.0 sec after presentation. Since the subject was unaware of which row would be cued for recall, Sperling assumed that he or she could do equally well independent of which specific row was designated for recall. This assumption led Sperling to multiply the number correct on any trial by three in order to get an unbiased estimate of the IM span, before retrieval processing obliterated a portion of that span.

Figure 9.6

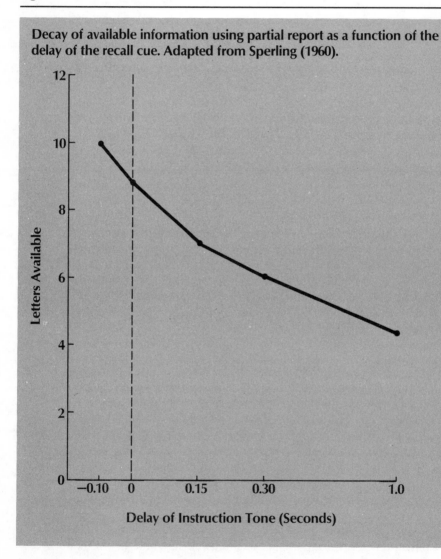

Decay of available information using partial report as a function of the delay of the recall cue. Adapted from Sperling (1960).

Span lengths, estimated from partial reports, are presented as a function of the delay in the onset of the recall cue in Figure 9.6. Apparently, more information was available to the subject than was demonstrated by uncued recall. About 9 items were available when partial reporting was requested, compared with 4.3 items in an uncued task. Also, the rate of forgetting was very fast. Within a second, span length had decreased to about 4.5 items, which was about the span length obtained with complete report instructions. In other words, it is the loss or decay of information within the first few hundred milliseconds after a presentation period ends that characterizes IM.

Sternberg's scanning technique.   Sternberg (1966) allowed subjects to view a series of randomly presented single digits. Two seconds later a target digit appeared, signalling the subjects to scan their memory and to recall whether they had seen the target digit or not. Subjects responded by pulling a lever to indicate whether they thought the target stimulus was "old" (i.e., was present in the string) or "new." The series varied in length from 1 to 6 digits, presented singly for 1.2 sec each.

Mean response latencies increased for both old and new responses as a direct function of the amount of information contained in a series. In the case of "new" target items, the subject had to scan the entire series in memory in order to eliminate each digit. In contrast, an exhaustive search was unnecessary if the subject identified an "old" item as the target digit; the search could be terminated if the subject so desired. However, the latencies for new and old responses were equivalent at each span length. It appeared to Sternberg (1966) that subjects scanned each series in a *serial* and an *exhaustive* manner, independent of whether they had responded to the target digit as old or new. An important feature of the Sternberg paradigm is the use of scanning time as the major dependent variable. This same variable is frequently used in contemporary cognitive research. The Sternberg research paradigm goes well beyond the boundaries of IM and borders closely on our next topic, primary memory.

Primary Memory: Research Tactics

Most theories of memory which postulate a limited capacity, short-term storage system invoke the concept of primary memory (cf. Waugh & Norman, 1965). The limited number of items carried in PM is referred to as its buffer. Craik (1971) has estimated that PM can hold about 2.5 to 3.5 items. Rehearsal or repetition of items in the buffer serves a dual purpose: maintaining items in PM and transferring information to a more permanent and stable store, secondary memory (SM). Generally, items in the PM buffer not rehearsed are displaced by other items. It is paradoxical that information in SM, if processed further with active rehearsal strategies, may permit retention for more than the very short time periods implied by the label STM, even as long as months or years.

Primary memory does not seem to be affected greatly by proactive interference (Murdock, 1968) and is minimally affected by rate of presentation. In contrast, these variables have quite the opposite effect on SM. Although words or other pronounceable units are apparently relevant units in PM, the particular characteristics of stored words—such as their concreteness-abstractness, semantic similarity, or frequency—make little difference on PM, while having a sizable effect on SM. In short, the PM-SM dichotomy is supported by considerable data showing PM to be unaffected by many variables which determine recall from SM. From another perspective, Glanzer and Cunitz (1966) have shown that the interpolation of a filled interval between the last item presented in a series and the test for recall greatly diminished PM but left SM unaffected. Let us now consider several types of STM tasks which have been used to isolate PM from SM.

The probe technique.   In 1965, Waugh and Norman reported a study in which they tested whether decay or interference produced losses in PM. They used lists of sixteen digits, always presented randomly. At the end of each list, the final digit had occurred once before in the series in position 3, 5, 7, 9, 11, 12, 13, or 14. The final digit was accompanied by a tone which signalled it as the probe digit. The subject used this probe to retrieve the digit which had *followed* it the first time the probe appeared in the list. For instance, in the series 7, 3, 12, 9, 1, 8, 14, 15, 11, 2, 5, 16, 6, 10, 13, 4, 5 (tone), the subject should respond to the probe (5) with the digit 16.

Lists were presented at rates of either 1 or 4 digits per second. Remember that the intent of this study was to analyze the respective effects of decay and interference on PM. If recall was poorer when the digits took four times as long to be presented (i.e., the 1 digit/sec presentation rate), the decay notion would be supported. If recall was independent of presentation rate, then the interference notion would receive support, provided, of course, that as the number of intervening items increased recall decreased. Results showed that recall was independent of presentation rate but dependent on the number of intervening items. Waugh and Norman's (1965) data tended to support an interference rather than a decay theory of PM.

Free recall and PM.   The fragile nature of PM can be seen in an innovative study by Craik (1970). Subjects received ten successive fifteen-word lists on each of four days, using the method of free recall. Each list was presented for only one study trial and then tested for unaided recall. However, before leaving each daily session, subjects were asked to recall

all the words they could remember from the ten lists presented on that day.

Craik (1970) argued that the strength of an item in the short-term storage (PM) should be unrelated to whether or not the item is transferred to the long-term store (SM). That is, he thought PM was a transient memory system from which three or four items might be retrieved with high accuracy at short retention intervals but that PM retrieval would not necessarily lead to transfer to SM. Craik's (1970) findings are presented in Figure 9.7. The top curve is the serial position curve for single-trial free recall averaged over forty lists. It shows the standard serial position effect with a very pronounced recency effect (PM) and a strong primacy effect (SM). The bottom curve shows average performance on the final test of each day. Note the loss of the pronounced recency effect. The lowest level of recall on the final test of each day was at position 15, the point at which recall had been the highest during standard single-trial, free recall learning. Craik labelled this dramatic reversal the *negative recency effect*. He also found that items recalled first

Figure 9.7

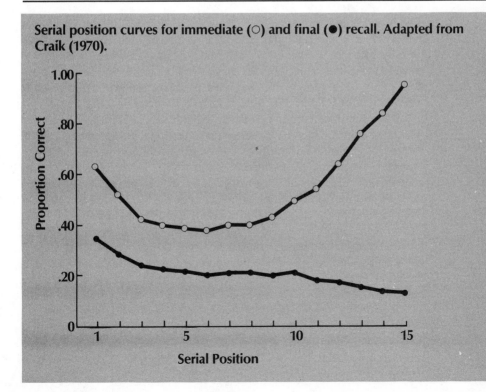

Serial position curves for immediate (○) and final (●) recall. Adapted from Craik (1970).

during single-trial learning were poorly recalled during the final test on each day. This finding seemed attributable to the fact that items recalled early are apparently quickly dropped from the PM buffer shortly after their recall. Craik's data suggest that words held in PM, a transient storage system, may be easily retrieved after a brief time period, but are unlikely to be transferred to a more permanent SM system unless actively rehearsed.

Secondary Memory and Other STM Tasks

In the preceding section we observed a number of studies suggesting that SM, the more permanent memory state, is "reached" only after an item has been attended to, perceived, and rehearsed. The free recall and probe tasks were shown to reflect the PM and SM components. We will now consider other STM tasks which allow us to study the effects of proactive interference on SM. Most of these tasks do not eliminate the PM component but rather permit extensive semantic encoding and active rehearsal—important processes in SM. It is these factors, together with the operation of proactive interference, which permit us to consider SM a unique memory state.

The Brown-Peterson technique.   Brown (1958) and Peterson and Peterson (1959) developed similar research procedures which have been used literally hundreds of times since the late 1950s to assess STM. We will consider in some detail the Petersons' now classic experiment. Essentially, they wanted to know how nonsense materials would be recalled after very short retention periods, from 0 to 18 sec in duration. Following the presentation of a three-consonant syllable (e.g., MLT), subjects were distracted from further rehearsal of that item by counting backwards by threes from a three-digit number until recall was requested at the end of the retention period. It was assumed that the counting task would prevent further rehearsal of the syllable and, because of its dissimilarity to the item, would result in minimal interference. A single trial consisted of the presentation of a syllable, a retention interval filled with counting, and a recall period. The next trial followed shortly thereafter. The retention intervals between presentation and recall were 3, 6, 9, 12, 15, or 18 sec, with the subject given no advance warning about the length of each retention interval. Subjects were tested eight times at each of the six retention intervals.

The major results of the Peterson and Peterson (1959) study are shown in Figure 9.8. This function presents the proportion of correct responses as a function of the length of the retention interval. Recall is most accurate after 3 sec and drops precipitously up to 12 sec, where an asymptotic level of responding is reached. The Petersons attributed this

Figure 9.8

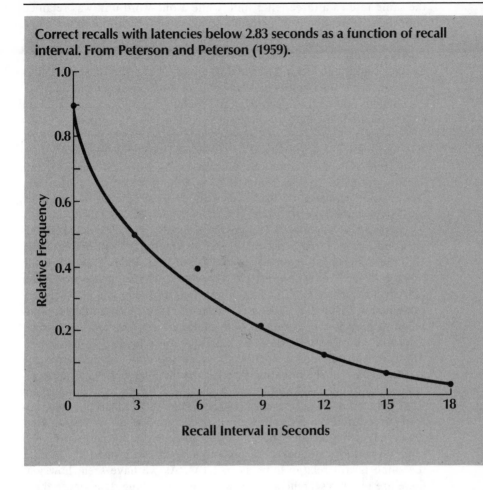

Correct recalls with latencies below 2.83 seconds as a function of recall interval. From Peterson and Peterson (1959).

dramatic loss in STM to decay, since, according to their interpretation of the data, there was no striking evidence for interference effects. To demonstrate this, they showed that recall performance at the 3 and 6 sec intervals was actually better during the last part of the experimental session than in the initial part. If proactive interference were present, then one would have expected recall on the final set of trials at any of the retention intervals to be poorer than recall on early trials. An early-late comparison of the 15 and 18 sec data showed identical recall levels at the beginning and end of the sessions. The Petersons interpreted these findings in favor of a decay position, with interference seemingly playing a minor role in STM.

If interference was not a factor in SM, what was it about the to-be-learned materials that determined the course of STM? Murdock (1961) demonstrated that a three-word (triad) presentation unit was forgotten at the same rate as a three-letter unit, while a one-word unit was retained almost perfectly (about 97 percent accuracy) up to retention intervals of 18 sec. Apparently, a three-letter unit and a word triad contain the same number of organizational units, or *chunks*. Thus, in addition to decay, another important factor determining the level of forgetting in a Peterson-type task is the number of chunks in the to-be-learned item.

Shortly thereafter, Keppel and Underwood (1962) and Melton (1963) pointed out that the Petersons' conclusion that proactive interference was not operating in their paradigm might have been premature. Their reasoning goes as follows: in a series of trials, interference does develop, but so do facilitating effects from practice such as warm-up and learning-to-learn. It is possible that the inhibitory effects from interference were cancelled by the positive effects from practice in the Petersons' 1959 study.

Using the single-item technique, Keppel and Underwood (1962) gave subjects six three-letter syllables at alternating rates of presentation. Half the subjects had retention intervals of 3, 18, 3, 18, 3, 18 sec while the other half had the reverse order. The results, in terms of the proportion of correct responses as a function of test trials and retention intervals, are presented in Figure 9.9. Tests trials, from 1 to 6, represented the manipulation of proactive interference, with minimal interference being associated with the first test trial and maximum interference with the last. There was an obvious interaction between the amount of interference and the length of the retention interval. At the 3 sec interval, the development of proactive interference had only a minor consequence on STM. In contrast, at the longer (18 sec) interval, STM declined as proactive interference increased. Keppel and Underwood (1962) and Melton (1963) concluded that there was little justification for postulating two separate memory systems since proactive interference in STM followed the same lawful relationships as in LTM. As we have seen, however, there are many researchers armed with equally telling data whose theories support multi-stage memory processing (cf. Atkinson & Shiffrin, 1968).

Release from proactive interference paradigm.   We have learned more about the nature of proactive interference in STM by studying its dissipation than from studying its accumulation. Wickens, Born, and Allen (1963) developed a STM research paradigm that has proven useful in the study of the *release from interference.* Two control groups were given either three-letter or three-digit units for ten trials. The retention intervals (11 sec each) were filled with a rehearsal-preventing, color-naming activity. There were six experimental groups who had 3, 6, or 9 trials on either letters or digits. Each group was then shifted to a new class of material to

Figure 9.9

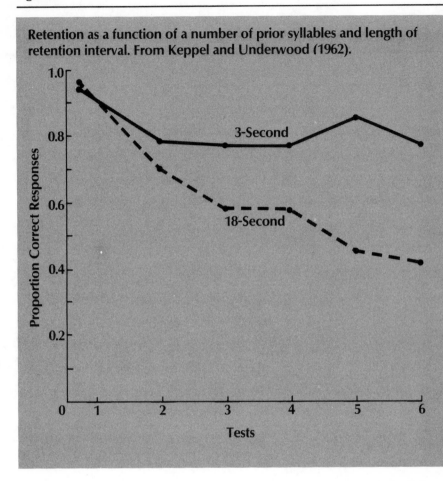

Retention as a function of a number of prior syllables and length of retention interval. From Keppel and Underwood (1962).

Figure 9.10

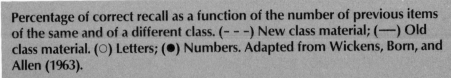

Percentage of correct recall as a function of the number of previous items of the same and of a different class. (- - -) New class material; (—) Old class material. (O) Letters; (●) Numbers. Adapted from Wickens, Born, and Allen (1963).

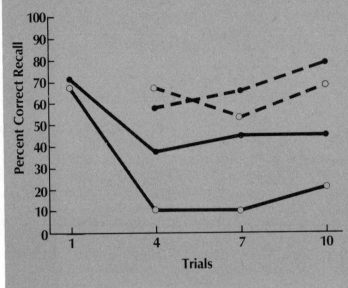

study. For instance, one experimental group had six trials with three-digit units and then saw a three-letter unit on trial 7. Another, of course, saw the letters first; this technique controlled for the possible confounding effect of type of material on the release phenomenon itself.

Release from interference can be seen in the data of Wickens et al. (1963), presented in Figure 9.10. The shift from one class of materials to another at trials 4, 7, and 10 was accompanied by a dramatic improvement in recall. In contrast, recall performance for control groups who studied the same type of material on all trials was much lower. A shift in the type of materials was related to a return to the level of retention which had occurred in the absence of any interference (i.e., recall on trial 1).

Apparently a stimulus is encoded into a specific category. If more stimuli are encoded into the same category, they will produce interference. If a new stimulus belonging to a different category is presented, the prior interference will not be related to recall of the newly categorized items. Loess (1967) has discovered that the same release phenomenon can be demonstrated with changes in the taxonomic classes of words (e.g., from three types of birds to three types of trees and vice versa). Also, Wickens and Clark (1968) showed that shifts on the semantic differential scale (cf. Osgood, 1952) also produced release from interference. For instance, after seeing three trials of "active" word triads (three-word units), a shift to a "passive" triad was accompanied by a dramatic improvement in recall.

Another way to demonstrate the release from interference effect is to lengthen the interval of time between successive trials in a Peterson-type task. Loess and Waugh (1967) found that proactive interference dissipated almost totally after an interval of two minutes had elapsed between trials, while Cody and Borkowski (1977) showed the same type of release effect with retarded adolescents.

Continuous presentation techniques in STM.   A great many continuous presentation techniques are used in the study of memory. In all cases a long series of items is presented. The subject is instructed to study each item as it appears but is not informed as to which item he will be instructed to recall. At the time of recall the experimenter may ask for one or all of the items; however, most techniques request only one item. These techniques have the advantage of preventing rehearsal of old material by requiring the observer to study new information continuously. They distract the observer "naturally" because he or she is engaged in an activity similar to the to-be-tested activity. In contrast, rehearsal activity in the Brown-Peterson paradigm is usually dissimilar to the to-be-remembered materials (e.g., counting backward or color-naming as rehearsal preventing tasks).

Earlier we presented the study of Waugh and Norman (1965) which made use of a digit-probe task. In their study, subjects were required to view a string of sixteen digits. The last, or probe digit, was a repetition of an earlier item. The subject's task was to recall the digit that followed the probe the first time it was shown. Notice that in this task there is no need to introduce a novel, rehearsal-preventing activity since all the retention intervals are continuously filled during the presentation of the string of items.

Another version of the continuous presentation technique was used by Schumsky and his associates in 1967. A series of five three-consonant syllables was presented. Following a short retention interval, which was filled to prevent rehearsal, the experimenter asked the subjects to recall either the first or the last item. Subjects, of course, had been instructed to study all units to the same degree and had no idea whether they would be required to recall one or all of the items. The study showed very good recall of the first item and much poorer recall of the last of the five items. It appeared that proactive interference was a more potent factor in producing forgetting in STM than retroactive interference, when a continuous presentation technique was used.

One additional point should be made concerning the relationship between research tactics and SM. Any task that involves active rehearsal is likely to implicate SM, since it is the rehearsal of information that determines the extent of SM registration. Furthermore, the verbal SM system depends to a great extent on *semantic encoding*. Research procedures that require subjects to focus on and rehearse to-be-learned materials in terms of their meaningful attributes are likely to tap SM processing. We shall see several examples of "deep" semantic encoding as we now consider some recently developed research paradigms in cognitive psychology.

RESEARCH TACTICS IN COGNITION

It is difficult to find contemporary learning, memory, and cognition research which relies exclusively on rote learning principles and theory. The reason is simple: adolescents and adults almost always fall back on their language habits, cognitive styles, and memorization strategies to master a task which the experimenter may believe requires only simple rote association formation. The area of cognition deals with strategic behaviors that a learner uses to solve a problem, be it a verbal learning task or a difficult conceptual puzzle.

The research tactics we will consider in this section allow us to view the subject in a more active processing role than has occurred in the paradigms we have already considered. The new image of the subject is that of an information processor, decision maker, mental executor, and symbol manipulator. These roles are played out in information processing research paradigms which analyze mediation, mnemonic activity, concept formation, executive decision making, metamemory, and levels of processing information.

Mediation Paradigms

In a general sense, a mediator can be represented by an implicit r→s association in the sequence of events, S→r→s→R. In contrast to rote verbal learning (S→R), mediated learning involves an implicit response (r), usually covert, to a stimulus event (S). In turn, the mediating response (r) elicits its own implicit stimulus (s) which leads directly to the terminal response (R). Most mediation paradigms fit the general S→r→s→R model, although many require a complex elaboration of the intervening, mediating r→s events (cf. Borkowski & Wanschura, 1974).

Jensen (1971) has listed eleven different tasks that have been used with varying degrees of frequency to study mediational processing. They range in diversity from discrimination learning and semantic generalization tasks, to natural language and three-stage learning paradigms. These tasks share a common theme in that they all invoke mediational concepts, intervening between stimulus and response events, when the to-be-learned task cannot be explained by reference to direct, rote associative processing. Of the eleven tasks listed by Jensen (1971), three-stage and natural language tasks seem to allow the highest degree of control over the experimenter-produced events antecedent to the mediational events (r→s). Because mediational activity in these two paradigms can be more easily controlled and manipulated than in other mediation paradigms, they offer more analytic power.

Three-stage mediation paradigms. The simplest multi-stage mediational research strategy is the chaining paradigm (cf. Horton & Kjeldergaard, 1961), in which three paired-associate lists (we will designate the lists as A-B, B-C, and A-C) are presented sequentially. The ease of learning the pairs (generally, word or picture associations) of the third list (A-C) is assumed to be related directly to mediational links developed in learning the two prior lists (A-B and B-C). That is, the occurrence of an A stimulus in stage III has a tendency to elicit B covertly and the occurrence of B tends to evoke C, the correct response (e.g., $A_7 \rightarrow B_7 \rightarrow C_7$). The presence of A-(B)-C mediational associations in the chaining paradigm can be inferred when the learning of the A-C list by the mediation group is superior to that for a non-mediation control group, which learns lists A-B, D-C, and A-C. In the control condition, laboratory-produced mediators are not available to aid A-C learning (e.g., A_7 leads to B_7 but B_7 does not evoke C_7); only the effects of warm-up and learning-to-learn are present.

Although the chaining paradigm has been used extensively in mediational research with adults and normal children (Goulet, 1968; Horton & Kjeldergaard, 1961; Jenkins, 1963), it has not always resulted in a facilitation of PA learning. It has, however, revealed a restricted set of conditions which seem to govern the presence of mediation in three-stage paradigms (cf. Schulz, 1972). The important factors responsible for producing mediated facilitation with normal adults are the following: (1) the (B) mediator must be highly learned and discriminably different, semantically or structurally, from the A and C terms so that it is readily available during stage III learning; (2) the association between A and C should be relatively difficult so as to encourage the use of the A→(B)→C strategy, but it should not lend itself to idiosyncratic, natural language mediators or to direct language associations; (3) the length of the test trial interval must be long enough to permit the "utilization" of mediators which the subject has available (Schulz & Weaver, 1968); test trial intervals of less than five seconds are not conducive to producing mediated facilitation (cf. Schulz & Lovelace, 1964); and (4) because mediation is an associative process (cf. Underwood, Runquist, & Schulz, 1959), it can be more clearly assessed if the role of response learning is minimized by using a recognition testing procedure; the use of multiple-choice test trials in A-C learning prevents a mediation chain from being discarded because of a failure to remember the terminal response (C). Schulz (1972) has shown that adherence to these four *boundary conditions* associated with list construction or procedural decisions in the chaining paradigm almost invariably leads to mediated facilitation of paired-associate learning with normal adults. For example, Schulz, Weaver, and Ginsberg (1965) found that if the A-C task was difficult, A-B and B-C mediators highly available, and recognition test trials used, facilitating effects occurred during A-C learning for the A-B, B-C, A-C group, when compared to A-C performance for a standard A-B, D-C, A-C control group.

Most of the early mediational research was incorporated into a rather simple associationist theory (cf. Jenkins, 1963; Schulz, Weaver, & Ginsberg, 1965). More recent research has led to a widening of the theoretical perspective in which research on three-stage mediational paradigms receives interpretation. For instance, Schulz (1972) likened the chaining paradigm to a simple form of problem solving in which A-C is the to-be-solved problem and A-B and B-C are previously acquired components which, when properly integrated and utilized, lead to rapid learning or problem solving. A more cognitive view seems necessary when one considers that stage III learning often occurs in the absence of A-C study trials. That is, if a subject is given only test trials during stage III, he or she is likely to demonstrate mediational facilitation of the A-C associations based solely on the presence of A-B and B-C links developed during the first two stages. Performance on the first A-C test trial is often considerably above chance level, even prior to the first opportunity to study stage III pairs.

Research on the strength of A-B and B-C associations, as they relate to mediational activity during A-C learning, does not fit well into an associationist framework. For instance, an increase in strength of A-B and B-C associations does not necessarily lead to the increased use of mediators (Schulz, 1972). In short, what appears to be emerging, at a theoretical level, is the real possibility that mediational activity in the chaining paradigm, as well as in more complex mediational paradigms, involves higher-order conceptual strategies. These strategies deal with the acquisition and employment of rules, as well as the formation of S-R bonds of an associationistic nature.

Natural language mediation paradigms. In contrast to laboratory-produced mediation models, natural-language mediation paradigms rely on word associations, phrases, sentences, and paragraphs as aids to learning. For instance, Jensen and Rohwer (1963) showed that children will learn the pair "shoe-clock" more rapidly if a short sentence "I threw the SHOE at the CLOCK" is given prior to the learning task. The sentence serves as a context in which to embed the stimulus and response units and provides a link in the form of a bizarre, vivid image.

Several techniques are available for use in the study of natural language mediation. For instance, Turnure, Buim, and Thurlow (1976) compared various types of mediational processing in normal and mildly retarded children as they learned paired-associate units. All children had mental ages of approximately 5 years, while the mean chronological ages were 5.3 and 7.5 years for the normal and retarded groups, respectively. The main interest in this study centered on an analysis of the *production deficiency hypothesis* as an explanation for the difficulties experienced by young normal children, and almost all retarded children, in mediational tasks (cf. Flavell, 1970; MacMillan, 1970). This hypothesis holds that certain individuals are not able to *produce* functional mediators spontaneously but are able to *use* ready-made, experimenter-generated mediators. Turnure et al. (1976) questioned the adequacy of the production deficiency hypothesis; instead, they preferred to conceptualize the mediational difficulties of young children as an *instructional deficiency.* They argued that few if any mediational tasks allow for spontaneity since some form of cue is almost always present during study or test trials.

The Turnure et al. (1976) study examined paired-associate learning for children given different sets of instructions on how to put the stimulus and response items of each pair together. Their research design was aimed at assessing whether specific forms of interrogatives would help normal and retarded children, often characterized as *production deficient,* to generate verbal responses which could then function as effective mediators in enhancing the acquisition and recall of paired-associates. Box 9.5 contains their procedure and results. The unique feature of the method was the use of the *questioning format* during the acquisition process to induce "deep" semantic processing (cf. Craik, 1973). We shall return shortly to the concept of *depth of processing* and the research strategies used to explore this phenomenon since it is an important new research tactic for understanding cognition and memory.

Mnemonic paradigms. A mnemonic is a highly practiced memory strategy which enables a person to store large amounts of information for relatively long periods of time. Consider the amazing mnemonic "tricks" of Harry Lorraine, the memory expert. Lorraine will meet each of over 200 guests upon their arrival to see the Johnny Carson show and will recall every one of their names, accurately and promptly, in the middle of the

Box 9.5 Production vs. Instructional Deficiencies in Children's Learning

Turnure et al. (1976) presented 60 retarded children and 36 normal children with 21 paired-associate pictures in one of six conditions: *Labelling, Sentence Repetition, Sentence Generation, Response to What, Response to Why A,* and *Response to Why B.* Each condition was preceded by a pretraining period to ensure that the experimental condition was fully understood. The experimental session consisted of one study trial during which each paired-associate unit was presented for 15 sec; then each stimulus picture was presented and the child was required to name the picture that "goes with it."

In the *Labelling* (or control) condition, subjects repeated the names of the items immediately after the experimenter ("soap-jacket"). In the *Sentence Repetition* condition, subjects repeated a relational sentence immediately after the tester ("The soap is hiding in the jacket"). In the *Sentence Generation* condition, the subject made up a sentence about the items ("Make up a sentence about the 'soap' and the 'jacket.' "). In the *Response to What* condition, the subject responded to a standard What-type question ("What is the soap doing under the jacket?"). In the *Response to Why A* condition, the subject responded to a standard Why question in which the auxiliary did not function as the main verb ("Why is the soap hiding in the jacket?"). In the *Response to Why B* question, the subject responded to a standard Why question in which the auxiliary functioned as the main verb ("Why *is* the soap in the jacket?"). Thus, the experimental design can be conceptualized as a 2 (normal and retarded subjects) × 6 (experimental conditions) factorial.

The data of Turnure et al. (1976) are presented in Figure 9.11. The only significant difference was the main effect of experimental conditions. Normal and retarded children performed at identical recall levels. Subanalyses of the conditions' effect showed that the three *questioning* groups were superior to the other three conditions, but not different from one another. Also, *Sentence Repetition* had better recall then *Labelling* and *Sentence Generation.*

The superiority of the interrogative methods over the other three conditions demonstrated that the *production deficiency hypothesis* was instructions-specific. Turnure and his colleagues suggest that children sometimes do not fully understand instructions or that "instructions inhibit their use of imagination or creative generative use of language." They argue that the interrogative prompting allowed the members of a pair to be integrated by a semantic or meaningful relationship. Such semantically based organization apparently functioned as an effective verbal mediator in enhancing the acquisition of the paired-associate units.

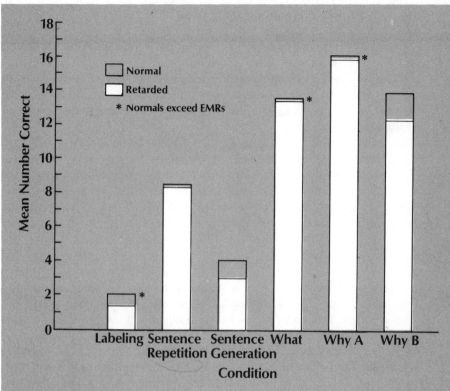

Figure 9.11 Recall as a function of the instructional format.

show, some two hours later. A highly effective mnemonic strategy, mental imagery, enables Harry Lorraine to accomplish this feat.

A favorite mnemonic is the *method of loci* which has been popular as a mnemonic aid to learning and memory processing since the time of the early Greeks (cf. Bower, 1970). The first step in using the method of loci is to imprint in memory a series of places (or loci). Next one creates vivid images, representing each of the to-be-learned items. Finally, one takes the items in order and *associates* them in memory *one by one* with *corresponding imaginary locations.* Bower (1970) describes the task of the mnemonist as follows:

> The associations are to be established by "mentally visualizing" the image of the items placed into the imaginary context of the locational snapshots. The same loci are used over and over for memorizing any new set of items. Without this feature—if an entire new set of loci had to be learned for each new list—the use of the method would be uneconomical. (p. 497)

The method of loci, as is true with most mnemonic devices, rests heavily on the process of imagination. Bower (1970) defines *imagination* as a mental process by which we manipulate and combine memory representations in a scene. Apparently, a constructed image can be stored in memory nearly as well as the actual memory for scenes people have witnessed. The importance of images is that learning proceeds much faster if the to-be-learned material readily evokes such images. They can serve as "pegs" upon which to associate or tie down the to-be-learned items in memory (cf. Paivio, 1969).

A recent report by Atkinson (1975) points out the important role that mnemonics can play in education. Atkinson calls his technique the *keyword method.* It is based on using two mediational links, one *acoustic* and one *imaginal,* to form each mnemonic association and can be easily applied to the learning of a foreign vocabulary. First, a foreign word is linked to the English keyword by similarity in *sounds;* then the keyword is linked to the English translation by an *imagery* link. Atkinson (1975) cites an example using the Spanish word for horse, "caballo" (pronounced "cob-eye-yo"). The pronounciation evokes the acoustic link "eye" (the middle syllable), which in turn leads to a mental image of a horse kicking a giant eye. In recall, a learner merely pronounces the Spanish word, "caballo"; the keyword "eye" comes to mind; a vivid image is evoked; the learner simply calls out "horse" after "viewing" the scene of a horse kicking an eye.

Using the keyword mnemonic method, learners comprehended about 25 percent more Russian vocabulary words immediately after acquisition and about 15 percent after a six week delay. Atkinson's (1975) research clearly demonstrates the usefulness of mnemonic devices in learning a foreign language, especially a more difficult one such as Russian.

Concept formation paradigms.   Bourne, Ekstrand, and Dominowski (1971) define a concept "as any describable regularity of real or imagined events or objects" (p. 177). When people learn about a concept, they acquire some understanding of a formerly unrecognized regularity. Generally, it is the regular attributes of a thing or event which give specification to its concept. Hence, learning about a concept implies learning about its defining attributes or relevant principles.

Attribute learning problems are a series of trials or experiences during which a learner acquires new information about a stimulus property or properties, while *principle learning problems* are opportunities to learn about a new relationship among known stimulus properties (cf. Bourne et al., 1971). For instance, learning to label a certain wave length on the electromagnetic spectrum as "red" and another as "green" would represent attribute learning, while learning that Daddy's car should always be stopped when "red" appears, whether it be a traffic light or a stop sign, would represent principle learning.

Two different research tactics can be used to study concept formation. They differ in whether the experimenter or the subject determines the set of events which occur across trials. In the *reception paradigm,* a single stimulus object is presented and the subject classifies the object by indicating its place within a set of possibilities. Following the subject's choice, feedback is given as to the correctness of the response. This sequence constitutes a trial; generally, multiple trials are presented in the reception paradigm. The number of trials to some errorless criterion (e.g., three consecutive errorless trials) is the most common dependent measure. The method of presentation can be *simultaneous* (all stimuli are laid before the subject and the experimenter directs attention to one) or *successive* (before a new stimulus is shown, the old one is removed). Since the simultaneous presentation method allows the subject to think about old stimuli and about the correctness of old responses, it generally results in faster concept learning (cf. Bourne et al., 1971).

In the *selection paradigm,* all stimuli are initially laid before the subject. The experimenter designates one of the stimuli as positive and asks the subject for an explanation or hypothesis. Next, the subject selects a stimulus, which the experimenter designates as positive or negative; the subject provides a reason for his choice. This process continues until the subject arrives at the correct answer. Although the selection pardigm generally leads to faster learning, the reception paradigm has been used more frequently in concept learning research (cf. Hunt, 1965).

"NEW LOOKS" IN MEMORY AND COGNITION RESEARCH

During the last decade, the neobehavioral-associationist model has proven particularly unsuccessful in its treatment of complex psychological processes such as language acquisition, reading, problem-solving, and creativity. To a large extent, the information processing research paradigm has arisen in the hope of shedding light on these important psychological processes. This model has as its cornerstone the analysis of the *functioning mind,* especially as mind gives meaning to words and events. In turn, the information processing paradigm has spawned its unique research tactics, which have widened the scope of its theories.

In closing this chapter, we will consider research designs in three areas of cognitive psychology: "depth of processing," constructive memory, and executive functioning and metamemory. We have placed these issues in a separate section. Although they bear on our earlier discussions, especially of free recall and memory, these issues also reflect the emergence of the information processing model as a new scientific paradigm. They represent a different style of experimentation in contemporary research, one associated directly with the information processing model. We will most surely witness further elaborations on these "new look" research tactics in the years ahead.

Depth of Processing

In 1972, Craik and Lockhart published a very influential article entitled, "Levels of processing: A framework for memory research." This article pointed out some difficulties with the multi-store memory models (cf. Atkinson & Shiffrin, 1968; Waugh & Norman, 1965), especially as they account for the capacity, coding, and forgetting characteristics of memory. Rather than postulate new stores to handle such difficulties, Craik and Lockhart (1972) focused on the *type* and *depth of encoding* to explain forgetting phenomena.

The "new look" in memory research stresses mental processing. The learner recalls primarily that which is actively encoded, in some meaningful way, during learning. Craik and Tulving (1975) contrasted the old and the new look in memory research and theory in the following way:

> In more traditional memory paradigms the major theoretical concepts were traces and associations; in both cases their main theoretical property was strength. In turn, the subject's performance in acquisition, retention, transfer, and retrieval was held to be a direct function of the strength of associations and their interrelations. The determinants of strength were also well known: study time, number of repetitions, recency, intentionality of the subject, preexperimental

associative strength between items, interference by associations involving identical or similar elements, and so on . . . [In the new para-
digm] the only thing that is manipulated is the mental activity of the
learner; yet, as the results show, memory performance is dramatically affected by these activities. (p. 292)

In the 1972 depth of processing model, "depth" implied a greater
degree of semantic-cognitive analysis on the part of the learner. A shallow "Type I" level of processing meant that an item is accessible in
primary memory, while a more permanent memory trace for that item is
not formed. "Type II" processing implied a deeper level of encoding,
where semantic features of the event are analyzed and stored. Memory
improves to the extent that more rehearsal time is devoted to Type II
processing. Finally, when attention is diverted from the to-be-remembered task, information is forgotten at a rate depending on its prior level
of processing.

The general research tactic used by Craik and Tulving (1975) made
use of *incidental learning* to operationalize depth of processing. Subjects
were told that the experiment concerned perception and that the speed
of their reactions was of primary interest. This was the *intentional* component of the experiment. On each trial a word was briefly exposed on a
tachistoscope for 200 msec. Prior to exposure of a word, a question was
posed by the experimenter about some characteristic of the word. The
question, and the subsequent answer, induced the subject to process the
word at one of several hierarchical levels of analysis. For instance, a
question about a word's physical characteristics was assumed to prompt
shallow, Type I processing ("Is the word printed in capital letters?"). A
second level of processing was induced by asking a question about the
word's rhyming features ("Does the word rhyme with SHOE?"). A semantic level of analysis, Type II, was achieved by asking either categorical questions ("Is the word the name of an article of clothing?") or
fill-in-the-sentence questions ("Would the word fit the sentence: 'He met
a____on the street.' "). At each level of analysis, half of the questions had
"yes" as the correct response and half had "no."

After hearing or reading a question, the subject looked into the
tachistoscope and, after the word appeared, immediately recorded his
answer by pressing a "yes" or "no" key. Processing time, defined from
the appearance of a word until the pressing of a "yes" or "no" key, was
recorded for each word. After a series of such judgments, the subject was
unexpectedly given a retention test for incidental learning of the words.
The retention test used either a free recall procedure, cued recall, or
recognition.

In one of the Craik and Tulving (1975) experiments, 60 words were
presented and 10 "yes" and 10 "no" questions were asked at each of
three levels of processing (upper- or lower-case letters; rhymes; fill-in-

Figure 9.12

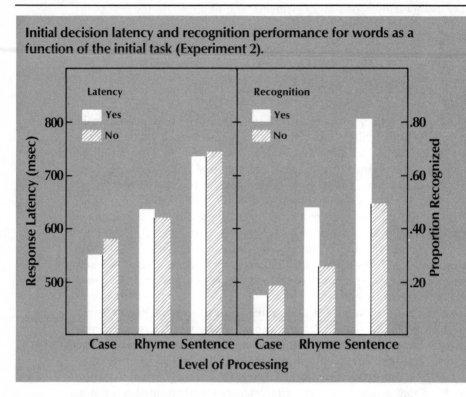

Initial decision latency and recognition performance for words as a function of the initial task (Experiment 2).

the-sentences). Following the 60 trials, subjects were given 180 words (the 60 old words and 120 irrelevant distractors) and told to check "old" words. The results, presented in Figure 9.12, showed that the type of encoding determined the response latency for a word, with Type II, semantic encoding requiring the longest processing time (left panel). At the same time, recognition increased with the degree of semantic encoding (right panel). Other studies by Craik and Tulving have led to the following conclusion: *Degree of stimulus elaboration,* rather than mere processing time, seems responsible for superior recall in the depth of processing model. Furthermore, spread of elaboration, rather than depth, may be a more accurate description of why subjects remember better in the Type II condition.

Constructive Memory and Comprehension

In 1932, Sir Frederic Bartlett published a book on remembering. In one of his tasks, subjects were required to repeat to each other a story called "The War of the Ghosts." As the tale passed from subject to subject, it became shorter and shorter and each successive version omitted more details. Bartlett's conclusion was that the acts of *interpreting* and *reconstructing* memory play important roles in remembering a story. Details drop out unless they are fitted into a familiar, organized framework. In similar fashion, a current theory of constructive memory assumes that linguistic information in a sentence or event is integrated with prior knowledge to construct semantic descriptions and increase comprehension (cf. Bransford, Barclay, & Franks, 1972).

Bransford and McCarrell (1974) report a study in which a listener's capacity to comprehend information was altered by varying the availability of information prerequisite to an adequate understanding of the message. Consider the following passage and try to recall it immediately after you read it:

> If the balloons popped the sound wouldn't be able to carry since everything would be too far away from the correct floor. A closed window would also prevent the sound from carrying, since most buildings tend to be well insulated. Since the whole operation depends upon a steady flow of electricity, a break in the middle of the wire would also cause problems. Of course, the fellow could shout, but the human voice is not loud enough to carry that far. An additional problem is that a string could break on the instrument. Then there could be no accompaniment to the message. It is clear that the best situation would involve less distance. Then there would be fewer potential problems. With face to face contact, the least number of things could go wrong. (p. 205)

No doubt your recall of this passage was extremely poor. However, if you could have seen the picture in Figure 9.13 *prior to* the passage, your recall would probably have been at least 100 percent more accurate. If the picture was given *after* the passage, recall would have been about the same as unaided recall. Apparently, the passage is given meaning insofar as it specifies events which could take place given the picture as a conceptual base. What these data imply is that a listener can have knowledge of words and sentences and yet be unable to understand messages. A prerequisite for comprehension is the capacity to activate an appropriate knowledge base of events in which sentences take on their meaning.

"Knowing About Knowing"

When we are confronted with a memory assignment, several different information processing subsystems need to be activated if we are to experience successful recall. The first subsystem consists of the structural processes responsible for perception and immediate memory. The sec-

Figure 9.13

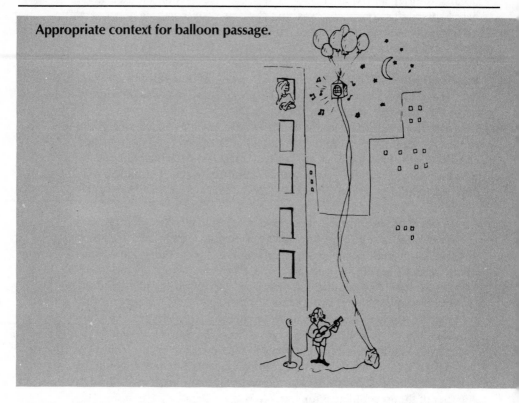

Appropriate context for balloon passage.

ond involves the voluntary control processes which the subject uses as strategies for accomplishing the memorization task (cf. Atkinson & Shiffrin, 1968). Active rehearsal, mental notes, or mnemonics constitute examples of this second memory system. Brown (1975) calls it "knowing how to know." The third subsystem, "knowing about knowing" refers to the learner's awareness of memory processing (Brown, 1975). Flavell (1971) refers to this process as *metamemory*. For example, learners use metamemory if they know when they can recall information and when they cannot, or when they are ready to recall and when they are not. In short, metamemory is thinking and knowing about when and why one should store and retrieve information.

Metamemory.   Flavell, Friedrichs, and Hoyt (1970) used two experimental tasks to assess a child's ability to predict his or her own memory span and to sense when a set of items had been studied sufficiently to guarantee perfect immediate recall. In their first experiment, four groups of children (nursery schoolers, kindergartners, second graders, and fourth graders) were asked to predict the size of their memory spans for objects; they were then tested on their actual memory span.

Starting at a span length of one, the experimenter asked the child if he or she could remember the object pictured on a strip of paper. The same procedure was repeated for strips of two, three, four, or more pictures until the child reported the span length was too long to recall accurately or until a series of ten pictures had been presented. Next, memory span was measured by having the child recall the series immediately after the experimenter had said the objects aloud. Recall was terminated when a given length was missed two times in a row.

The results of this experiment showed the following obtained and predicted memory spans: nursery age (3.50 vs. 7.21); kindergartners (3.61 vs. 7.97); second graders (4.36 vs. 6.00); fourth graders (5.50 vs. 6.14). Apparently, the young child's awareness of his or her memory capacity does not square well with actual ability. It is not until the fourth grade that most children have a realistic estimate of their memory spans for pictures, although a few four- and five-year-old children show very good correspondence between predicted and obtained span lengths. These data suggest a developmental increase in children's knowledge about memory capacity.

In a second experiment, Flavell et al. (1970) asked the children from the first study to name pictures of 33 common objects. The objects were mounted in windows on a large panel. Whenever the child pressed a button below a window, the object appeared and remained on as long as the button was pressed. The number of objects presented to the child was based on his actual memory span obtained during the first experiment. Each child was instructed to continue studying the pictures until he or she could remember the entire series. Three study and test trials were given, each with different pictures. The results indicated that there was a marked improvement from ages four to nine in the child's ability to "sense" when he or she had studied a series of items enough to recall them perfectly. Almost all the second and fourth graders could accurately assess their recall readiness, another measure of metamemory. Furthermore, these children showed active rehearsal strategies during the study periods. It is likely that metamemory—in the form of recall readiness—is more accurately appraised when the child is actively involved in studying and rehearsing the task.

An operational definition of the "executor."   The issue of "knowing how best to know," or executive functioning, has been addressed by Butterfield and Belmont (1977). They define this component of memory as follows:

> Executive functioning is exhibited when the subject spontaneously changes a control process or sequence of control processes as a reasonable response to an objective change in an information processing task. (p. 284)

In one of the experiments reported by Butterfield and Belmont (1977), 31 separate lists were presented to ten- and twelve-year-olds and to adults. Each list contained eight common words. Subjects were told to recall the last three words first and then the first five. If instructions were followed correctly, the recall order would be 6-7-8-1-2-3-4-5. This procedure is referred to as an *instructed output strategy*. No information was given on how to study or rehearse the items. A self-paced task, which yielded pause times at each of the eight positions during the presentation of a list, was chosen to allow direct monitoring of input (rehearsal) strategies. The process of *executive functioning* was indexed by observing *changes* in pause time patterns which corresponded to *changes* in task demands. These task changes were produced by the experimenter in the following way. Each list from trials 1 through 10 was unique, containing no repeated words. List 10 was repeated eight times, through trial 18. Unique lists were again seen from trial 19 to trial 26. Repeated lists occurred on trial 27 through trial 31 except that on trial 31 two new words were inserted in positions 4 and 5.

This experiment showed that the adults *stabilized* their *selected strategy* earlier than did the children, generally by trial 4. *Increasing pause times* for positions 1 to 5 signalled that a *cumulative rehearsal* type of strategy was adopted with the maximum study times occurring at the item position to be recalled last (item 5). Pause times were very brief for the final three items (6, 7, and 8), to be recalled first.

Upon the first repetition of a list (trial 11), the adults immediately revised their strategy by dropping all resemblances of cumulative rehearsal. Their study times for each of the eight items in the list were identical and very short. On trial 19, the adults quickly *reinstated* the cumulative rehearsal strategy used on trial 10 in order to learn a new, nonrepeated list. When a list was again repeated on trial 27, the cumulative strategy was again quickly discarded. On trial 31, when two words were repeated in positions 4 and 5, increased pause times occurred at position 5. This indicated that the adult subjects rehearsed the words at positions 4 *and* 5 during the study period for item 5.

In contrast to adults, the ten- and twelve-year-olds showed a somewhat different pattern of development in their executive functioning. The ten-year-olds took longer to "select" a strategy (e.g., about eight trials) while the twelve-year-olds took only about four trials on the average. That is, older children seem to be more rapid in their *strategy selection*. On the initial repetition of a list (trial 11), the twelve-year-olds began to revise their strategy, but little change was detected in the form of the strategy for ten-year-olds. By trial 13, strategy revision was complete for both groups. When a new list was inserted on trial 19, the *reinstatement* of the strategy took longer for the children than for the adults. The reinstatement process seemed to continue until trial 21 for the twelve-year-olds and trial 23 for the ten-year-olds. On trial 27, when a previous list was repeated, there was rapid abandonment of the cumulative rehearsal strategy. Finally, on trial 31 both groups of children responded to the repeated pairs (4 and 5) by increasing their pause times. However, they showed longer pause times at position 4 than they did on the previous trial, even greater than did the adults on trial 31. The pattern of pause times for positions 4 and 5 on trial 31 suggests that the children did not *recognize* and *evaluate* the demands of the task. They failed to realize that they could delay rehearsing the new fourth item until after seeing the fifth.

These data indicate some interesting similarities and differences in the development of executive functioning in ten- and twelve-year-olds and adults. Apparently, the monitoring functions of the "mental executor"—which include strategy selection, revision, reinstatement, and evaluation—develop with increasing age and experience (Butterfield & Belmont, 1977). The direction of future research in this area will probably be to assess whether instructional techniques can be constructed which allow children to acquire more mature forms of executive functioning. Most certainly, it will require a direct monitoring of cognitive activities as well as the direct measurement of recall accuracy.

SUMMARY

This chapter has presented the major research tactics and paradigms used in the study of complex learning, memory, and cognition. Emphasis was placed on paired-associate and serial learning, free recall, long- and short-term memory, mediation, and mnemonic research tactics. Serial learning requires the learner to master the ordering of a series of verbal units, while paired-associate learning requires that a response be "hooked-up" to its appropriate stimulus. Free recall, in which the learner recalls a string of words in any order, permits greater flexibility in the analysis of the organizational processes in memory. This organization can take the form of subjective organization of unrelated material or clustering of associated material in the list.

The manner in which one learning experience influences another is called transfer of training. The direction of transfer, positive or negative, is determined by comparing the performance of an experimental group (e.g., A-B, A-C), with that of an appropriate control group (A-B, C-D). Warm-up and learning-to-learn are controlled in the A-B, C-D paradigm. Perhaps the most important methodological point to remember in studying long-term memory is the control of degree of original learning by equating group performances at the end of the acquisition period, so as to assess "true" retention effects.

Short-term memory can be separated into three categories, differing in types of processing and, at times, in length of the retention interval: immediate memory, primary memory, and secondary memory. Secondary memory involves the study of rehearsal activity which leads to more permanent retention. Research tactics in cognition yield information on mediation, mnemonic processing, and concept formation. Finally, the "new look" in cognitive psychology—depth of processing, constructive memory, and metamemory and executive functioning—was shown to reflect recent changes in research interests and research strategies, with an emphasis on the direct measurement of what goes on as the mind functions in thinking and remembering. The emergence of the information processing model, with its emphasis on feedback rather than reinforcement, has placed research on memory and cognitive processes at the forefront of current experimental and theoretical analysis.

QUESTIONS

1. Contrast the importance of feedback versus the importance of reinforcement as useful concepts in information processing research.
2. Describe serial, paired-associate, and free recall learning. Contrast the types of associations developed in each task. Distinguish between clustering and subjective organization.
3. Transfer phenomena can be due to several sources. Describe these sources. Which sources should be controlled, and how can this control be carried out?
4. Describe the 2-factor theory of paired-associate learning. How did Martin extend this theory so as to increase our understanding of transfer of training?
5. Explain the major methodological problems associated with the study of long-term memory *vis-a-vis* methods of testing and control of original learning. How does research on long-term memory utilize transfer of training paradigms? What are PI and RI?
6. Describe various tactics used in the study of immediate memory, primary memory, and secondary memory. How can rehearsal activity in secondary memory be measured directly? Why is direct strategy measurement important?
7. What are the key differences and similarity between 3-stage mediational and mnemonic research paradigms? Which approach is now favored and why? In answering this last question be sure to consider the scientific paradigm guiding cognitive research.
8. What is "depth of processing"? How is it different from the Atkinson-Shiffrin model (see pp. 25–27)? How can Turnure's (1976) results on the use of an interrogative study strategy by young children be reconciled with the depth of processing model?
9. Distinguish between the concepts of metamemory and executive functioning. Are they related? If so, how? Cite one experiment related to each concept that demonstrates how the general form of the definition can be translated at the operational (or experimental) level.

Research Tactics in Social Psychology

10
Chapter

BY RICHARD J. SEBASTIAN

> ... toward the end of his life Comte was wrestling with a "true final
> science" which, if fully worked out, could only have been what we call
> psychology, even though Comte preferred to label it the science of *la
> morale positive*. ... he found himself driven to postulate a "true final
> science"—and ... his conception of that science parallels our present
> conception of modern psychology, especially social psychology. ... If it
> were possible to designate a single deliberate "founder" of social
> psychology as a science, we should have to nominate Comte for this honor.
>
> (Allport, 1968, pp. 6–7)

In a very real sense, each of us is a social psychologist. When we try to
understand or explain the behavior of one person in relation to another,
we face the same problems that social psychologists address in their research. And when we raise questions about the causes of aggression and
violence, the failure of bystanders to aid people in distress, and the effects of advertising on consumer attitudes, we do it again. In this chapter,
we will cover the techniques and methods used by social psychologists to
study the ways individuals are influenced by social events.

WHAT SOCIAL PSYCHOLOGY IS ALL ABOUT

Social psychology is a very broad area of inquiry. Why we like one another, how we form and maintain impressions of others, and when we
are most likely to go along with the opinions of others are only a few of
the topics studied by social psychologists. Recently, social psychologists
have become interested in the "naive psychologizing" of the ordinary
person, exploring systematically the ways people try to understand their
own and others' behavior. A concern with the individual's reactions to

social stimuli is the uniting theme for these diverse research interests. In general terms, *social psychology is the scientific study of social behavior.*

A fuller and more exact definition of social psychology has been provided by Gordon Allport (1968) who said it is "an attempt to understand and explain how the thought, feeling, and behavior of individuals are influenced by the actual, imagined, or implied presence of others" (p. 3). Several elements of this definition require additional elaboration. As a branch of general psychology, social psychology focuses on the reactions of *individuals.* It is concerned with many of the same psychological processes that capture the attention of psychologists in general—perception, motivation, and learning—yet it differs from general psychology in the examination of how these processes are affected by other persons or their symbols.

One of the oldest and most fundamental issues in social psychology is how the presence of other people can affect an individual's performance on a task. Do other individuals facilitate or improve a person's performance? Does he or she work faster and make fewer mistakes? Or is the individual's performance impaired? Does the nature of the task influence how the audience will affect individual performance? More simply, how does the actual presence of other people influence behavior?

Merely thinking about, or imagining, the presence of others and their reactions to our behavior affects how we respond. This concern of social psychology can be illustrated with several examples. When participants in an experiment are led to believe that their performance will later be evaluated by experts in the area, their performance is "facilitated" in comparison to that of subjects who have performed under identical circumstances but do not expect future evaluation (Henchy & Glass, 1968). Imagining the future reactions of these experts is sufficient to stimulate "better" performance. Similarly, when individuals are reminded of the important groups which they belong to and represent, they will modify their behavior substantially, even tolerating increases in pain (Buss & Portnoy, 1967). Again, imagining their fellow group members, and their standards or expectations for behavior, influences individuals to change in predictable ways. Other people need not be physically present to influence our behavior or for the issue itself to be a social psychological one.

The notion of implied presence is similar to that of imagined presence, but it more specifically "refers to the many activities the individual carries out because of his position (role) in a complex social structure and because of his membership in a cultural group" (Allport, 1968, p. 3). All of us occupy a number of specific positions in the social structure and because of these positions are expected to behave in a relatively narrowly specified fashion. This is so even when the other members of the social structure are not physically present. For example, because of your role as a student—your position in a social structure shared by your instructor—you presumably study and read your assignments even when your instructor is not present to oversee and directly influence your activity.

The implied presence of others also indicates that an individual's behavior is frequently influenced by human symbols. Such symbolic stimuli can be legitimately regarded as social. The various mass media (cultural symbols that pervade our lives) influence our actions. Social psychologists have devoted a great deal of attention to the effects of these symbolic social stimuli on our behavior. The recent extensive work on the effects of viewing film violence on the observer's subsequent aggression is a well-known example of this research direction (cf. Berkowitz, 1970).

The area of inquiry we call social psychology is broad, and its topics are diverse and numerous. In the next section one possible organization for the field of social psychology is presented. It divides the discipline in terms of general approaches to the study of human social behavior: the S-R and cognitive approaches.

THEORETICAL ORIENTATIONS TO SOCIAL PSYCHOLOGY

In the brief history of social psychology, several general theories of human social behavior have been proposed with the hopeful goal of encompassing and explaining a wide range of social phenomena. In contemporary experimental social psychology, however, there is comparatively less concern with these general theories; the field is now more accurately characterized by many relatively narrow theories which apply to specific topics or problems. But even though the field can be adequately described in this way, most contemporary research is still guided by one of two basic general theoretical *orientations*. These orientations can be called the stimulus-response (S-R) or behavioristic and the cognitive or phenomenological approaches.

The S-R, Behavioristic Orientation

Although they constitute a decided minority, some social psychologists prefer to examine at least some forms of human social behavior in terms of classical and instrumental (or operant) conditioning. These psychologists focus their examinations of social behavior on external stimulus and reinforcement control. They assume that "human behavior is subject to far greater control by environmental events than human awareness, and human vanity, typically assume" (Berkowitz, 1975, p. 80). With this orientation, analyses of social behavior involve the familiar concepts and language of basic learning processes, such as conditioned and unconditioned stimulus, discriminative stimulus, reinforcement, generalization, and extinction.

Implicit within this orientation are several assumptions about human nature. First, greater similarity between humans and other animals is assumed than in the cognitive orientation. This assumption is made insofar as principles derived from research on other animals are believed applicable to humans.

A second assumption is that behavior is under the control of external stimuli and reinforcements. This statement does not necessarily imply that individuals are unaware of the stimuli and reinforcements that influence their behavior. It only says that regardless of the individuals' awareness of these environmental events, they are important causes of their behavior. A stronger form of this assumption does, however, hold that environmental events occasionally affect behavior without awareness (cf. Rosenfeld & Baer, 1969). But even this strong assumption does not necessarily imply an absence of internal processes or a passive organism who fails to respond to stimuli in terms of their meaning. It simply means that once stimuli are interpreted or understood, the organism responds quickly without much thought or planning. The organism's habits, rather than its intellect, are emphasized as determinants of behavior.

A third assumption is that virtually all behavior is learned; innate determinants of behavior are relatively unimportant or, if important, are greatly modifiable by environmental events. Finally, the S-R orientation, like many other positions in psychology but more explicitly and emphatically than the others, assumes that human behavior is hedonistic or economic. That is, people seek out pleasure and avoid pain. They attempt to maximize rewards while minimizing their costs.

In summary, the S-R orientation sees humans as relatively similar to other animals, controlled by environmental events, sometimes without awareness, a product of their environment, and pleasure-seeking and pain-avoiding. Researchers having this orientation employ the methods and ideas of basic learning research when they study human social behavior. A couple of research examples within this tradition will demonstrate the use of learning paradigms in social contexts.

In a now classic study, Staats and Staats (1958) attempted to show that positive and negative attitudes toward national names and common names could be established through classical conditioning procedures. Conceptualizing attitudes as implicit responses with evaluative meaning (e.g., good or bad), Staats and Staats reasoned that names of nationalities repeatedly paired with words having previously established positive, neutral, or negative meaning should acquire similar evaluative meaning. The subjects, undergraduate students who were told they were participating in a verbal learning task, had stimuli presented to them in two ways—visually and aurally. In a first experiment, national names (e.g., "German," "Dutch," and "Swedish") were flashed on a screen in random order for five seconds each. Approximately one second after each name appeared, the experimenter said out loud the word with which the national name was paired. The experimenter asked the subjects to say the word aloud and to repeat it to themselves while they looked at the word on the screen. Each name was paired with eighteen different words; that is, there were eighteen conditioning trials. The national names "Swedish" and "Dutch" were always paired with words which had either previously established positive (e.g., "gift," "happy," "sacred") or negative (e.g., "bitter," "ugly," "failure") evaluative meanings. The other national names were paired with words which had no systematic meanings (e.g., "chair," "with," "twelve"). For one group of subjects, "Swedish" was always paired with positive words and "Dutch" was always paired with negative ones; this procedure was reversed for a second group. After the conditioning procedure, the subjects rated each word on a seven-point pleasant-unpleasant scale. The rating of the critical names "Dutch" and "Swedish" by the subjects in the two conditions indicated that these national names had indeed acquired the evaluative meaning of the words with which they had been paired. The national names served as conditioned stimuli and the previously determined positive, neutral, and negative words constituted higher order unconditioned stimuli. The results of a second experiment, in which first names (e.g., "Tom," "Bill") served as conditioned stimuli, provided further evidence for the efficacy of classical conditioning in the formation of attitudes. Basic learning procedures were demonstrated as relevant to the understanding of an important social phenomenon. Instrumental conditioning and the use of reinforcement are also very important to understanding many forms of social behavior. Box 10.1 contains an example of a study in which instrumental learning principles are shown to operate in a social context involving aggressive behavior.

The two studies above and in Box 10.1 illustrate the role of the S-R orientation in social psychology. Although this approach has not been as important in social psychology as the cognitive or phenomenological one, some social psychologists still prefer it, and important studies on the formation and change of attitudes, the acquisition of social behavior, and the determination of aggressive behavior have largely been guided by it.

The Cognitive, Phenomenological Orientation

In marked contrast to the relatively few social psychologists who work from a behavioristic orientation is the vast majority of social psychologists who operate from a cognitive or phenomenological perspective. Where the importance of external stimuli and reinforcements are em-

Box 10.1 Instrumental Conditioning and Aggression

Parke, Ewall, and Slaby (1972) trained male college students to select and repeat words which were either hostile, neutral, or helpful in meaning. On each of the training trials, a subject was presented with three words, one from each of the categories. When the subject selected the word appropriate to the condition to which he had been randomly assigned, the experimenter reinforced him by saying "correct." The criterion for successful training was twenty consecutive reinforced trials, and all but three subjects achieved this criterion. In a second phase of the experiment, all subjects were required to administer shocks to a second subject (actually a confederate of the experimenter) for the confederate's mistakes on a learning task. For each mistake, the subject was free to select one of ten levels of shock intensity and to control the length of the shock. While no shocks were actually administered by the subject, the intensity and duration of the supposed shocks on the ten critical trials (mistakes) served as the major dependent variables.

Did the previous verbal training affect the subjects' physical responses? Did reinforcement for verbal aggression produce more intense physical aggression? Put another way, did reinforcement of *verbal* responses generalize to *physical* ones? The results of this experiment and others (Loew, 1967; Slaby, 1974) unequivocally indicate that reinforcement of verbal aggressive responses leads to increased physical aggressive behavior. The subjects who had earlier been trained to say aggressive words delivered longer and more intense shocks than those trained to speak either neutral or helpful words. Furthermore, the subjects who were reinforced for verbalizing words presumably incompatible with aggression (i.e., helpful ones) were significantly less aggressive than those reinforced for speaking neutral words. The results of the Parke et al. (1972) study underscore the importance of basic instrumental learning procedures for some forms of human social behavior.

phasized by the behavioristically inclined, the cognitive social psychologist emphasizes the importance of internal processes and the role of understanding in explaining social behavior. From this perspective, people do not simply react to environmental events but instead attempt to achieve an understanding of their environment and their personal experiences. Their behavior is determined by beliefs, ideas, and interpretations of events.

The organism's need to understand the environment, including the internal psychological environment, is one of the central notions in the cognitive orientation to social psychology. People prefer to have their environments stable, predictable, and orderly—they prefer good organization. Poor organization and lack of understanding or uncertainty may cause anxiety and efforts to restore order. Despite individual differences in the tolerance for ambiguity and the search for novelty, people prefer to have their internal and external worlds well structured.

The five major tenets of the cognitive orientation in social psychology have been summarized by Shaw and Costanzo (1970). First, understanding complex behavior requires mentalistic concepts, such as perception, ideas, and expectancy. These central processes are necessary to conceptualize complex, meaningful behavior adequately. Second, the unit of analysis is molar rather than molecular in that behavior cannot be understood by analyzing molecular elements. As captured in the famous Gestalt dictum that the whole is greater than the sum of the parts, the cognitive social psychologist regards the organization or interrelationship of elements as more important than the individual elements. Third, the organization of behavior is the organism's active transformation of environmental stimulation. Fourth, mastery of the environment and the search for understanding, along with tension and its reduction, are important sources of learning and motivation. Finally, the cognitive orientation basically opposes the notion of reductionism and sees no necessary causal relationship between physiological and psychological events. Shaw and Costanzo (1970) summarize the cognitive orientation by stating that " . . . behavior is organized, that the organization is molar, and that the most important element in this organization is cognition" (p. 187).

If we compare the cognitive approach to the S-R approach, we can say that cognitive workers are more likely to see humans as unique in the animal kingdom because of their cognitive and linguistic (or rational) abilities. In addition, they see human behavior as being controlled less by external events than by internal processes and structures. Relatively little stress is placed on historical factors or past experience as a basis for understanding current behavior. The individual's understanding and his or her existing cognitive structures are mainly responsible for his or her current actions. However, rational behavior is not to be understood as equivalent to logical behavior; individuals frequently behave defensively and illogically. While all cognitive theorists agree that behavior is largely the result of learning, some do postulate the existence of innate factors as important determinants of human conduct. Furthermore, the processes and motives involved in learning are different from those found in the S-R orientation. A final assumption is that man, according to the cognitive perspective, is sometimes viewed as hedonistic or economic, but the emphasis on these motives is not as great as in the S-R orientation.

In cognitively oriented research, the important determinants of behavior are internal and cannot be directly observed. Yet the experimental social psychologist attempts to develop sensitive measures of these internal events or their products. Often these measures involve self-reports of beliefs and attitudes. A couple of experiments will provide a flavor of research in the cognitive tradition.

Most influential among the various *cognitive organization* or *consistency* theories is Leon Festinger's (1957) work on cognitive dissonance. The basic principle in Festinger's theory, as in the other consistency theories, is that "It is disturbing to have at one and the same time psychologically incompatible sets of knowledge and/or feelings about a given person, object, or situation, and this disturbance motivates attempts to reduce the cognitive inconsistency" (Berkowitz, 1972, p. 13).

Dissonance theory has been applied to situations in which a person is induced to make a statement opposed to his beliefs or attitudes; this is called *forced compliance.* In a classic experiment, Festinger and Carl-smith (1959) investigated the operation of cognitive dissonance in a forced compliance situation. In the first phase of the study, students were asked to perform two dull, monotonous tasks. For half an hour, each student was required to place twelve spools in a tray, empty it, and then refill it. For a second half-hour the subjects were required to turn each of 48 square pegs on a board a quarter-turn clockwise and then to return to the first peg and give it another quarter-turn, and so on. After completing these tasks, the subject was informed that there were two conditions in the experiment. In one condition, the one the subject had been in, the tasks were performed with no other introduction. In the second condition, however, the subjects were told that expectations were given about the experiment before the tasks were begun. The experimenter went on to explain that a student who worked for him talked to the subjects in this second condition and told them the experiment was a lot of fun and was exciting and interesting.

There were actually three experimental conditions in the study, and the treatments were introduced at this point. In the control condition, the subject was simply taken to another room and interviewed about the experiment. In the two incentive conditions, the experimenter informed the subjects that the person who worked for him couldn't make it today. The experimenter then asked the subject if he would be willing to talk to the next subject (actually an accomplice of the experimenter) and tell her how enjoyable and exciting the experiment was. In these latter two conditions the experimenter offered the subject either one or twenty dollars for his help. Next the subject was brought to a room where a girl was waiting and his conversation with her was tape recorded. Finally, the subjects in the incentive conditions were also interviewed about the experiment; among other things, they were asked to rate how interesting and enjoyable the tasks were on a scale ranging from −5 (extremely dull and boring) to +5 (extremely interesting and enjoyable). Essentially, the subjects in the incentive conditions were asked to lie about the experiment to another supposed subject and were offered either a small or a large sum of money for doing so. Presumably it would be psychologically discomforting, or dissonance-arousing, to tell a lie for minimal justification, whereas lying for twenty dollars would not be so upsetting. If this was the case, then the subjects who lied for one dollar should feel some "pressure" to restore psychological comfort or cognitive consistency. One way of restoring consistency would be to change attitudes about the experiment and report the experience as interesting and enjoyable. This is precisely what Festinger and Carlsmith found. The subjects paid one dollar for lying rated the experiment as significantly more interesting and enjoyable than either the twenty dollar incentive or the control subjects, with the latter two groups not differing from each other. Contrary to what might have been expected from a reinforcement explanation, it was found that greater attitude change was produced by the smaller reward. In this experiment, and many related ones, the person's cognitive organization, or lack of it, apparently impelled attitudinal changes.

The individual's desire for self-understanding and his or her use of others to gain it are the major themes of another line of work within the cognitive orientation. The major hypotheses of these *social comparison* processes for opinions and abilities were presented in an early and important paper by Festinger (1954) and were later extended to an individual's attempts to understand his own feelings in Schachter's (1959) famous work on fear and affiliation. The original experiment on this problem should exemplify these ideas.

In this simple experiment, women participants were exposed to one of two experimental variations. In the "high fear" condition, the women, who were run in groups of five to eight, were frightened by being told that they would be receiving painful but not permanently harmful electric shocks in the experiment. Present in the room was a formidable array of electrical equipment, none of which actually worked. In the "low fear" condition, the women were told they would be receiving mild electrical shocks which would merely cause a tickle or a tingle. At this point, the experimenter informed the participants in both conditions that there would be a ten-minute delay before the experiment began. The experimenter further explained that the women would have to wait elsewhere because the room they were presently in would be too crowded as preparations were being made. The women were told they could go either to individual waiting rooms with comfortable chairs and magazines or to classrooms where they could wait with some of the other women in the experiment. The women were then asked to indicate whether they preferred to wait alone or with others, or whether they had no preference. This rating served as one of the major dependent measures in the research, and shortly after it was taken the experiment was ended without any shocks actually being administered. Now, according to social comparison theory, the women in the "high fear" condition should have been more concerned than those in the "low fear" condition with understanding their feelings. For this reason as well as others, the frightened women should have been more motivated to wait with other participants and to increase their self-understanding by observing the reactions of these other women. The women in the "high fear" condition in fact showed a significantly stronger preference for affiliation. A great deal of subsequent work on this problem by Schachter and others has sharpened our understanding of the precise conditions of these social comparison processes for feelings, but the important point for the present is that under certain circumstances, especially novel and threatening ones, people seek out others to understand better their own reactions. The desire for understanding influences social behavior.

Theoretical vs. Problem Orientation and Grand vs. Mini-Theories

The development of grand theories of human social behavior is not a major concern of most contemporary social psychologists. Instead, they are more problem-oriented in their thinking and research; they develop "mini-theories" to describe, understand, predict, and control phenomena in a limited domain. Depending on the problem under scrutiny, the mini-theory may derive primarily from the S-R or the cognitive theoretical orientations. Thus the problem, along with the researcher's assumptions about human behavior, directs research to a greater extent than do specific deductions made from a more general theory of behavior.

Until a broader integration of the major theoretical perspectives can be achieved and the conflicting assumptions about human nature can be reconciled, it may be more desirable to have many mini-theories than to have a single grand theory. After all, human social behavior is exceedingly complex and cannot be adequately conceptualized or explained in all circumstances by principles one would propose from either major orientation exclusively. The assumptions made in both are valid, but only under particular circumstances; each orientation is useful in guiding its own research and interpreting behavior. At this point in the history of social psychology, eclecticism and mini-theories derived from either orientation would seem to serve the discipline well. In the remainder of this chapter the methods social psychologists use in examining and measuring social phenomena will be discussed, as will some of the problems they encounter.

RESEARCH TACTICS AND ATTITUDE MEASUREMENT

"The concept of attitude is probably the most distinctive and indispensable concept in contemporary American social psychology" (Allport, 1935, p. 798). Some writers have even defined social psychology as the scientific study of attitudes. It is unnecessary to agree with either of these statements to recognize the importance of attitudes in social psychology. Social psychologists from both theoretical orientations have over the years devoted a considerable amount of attention to attitude theory and measurement.

Despite the fact that everyone has some intuitive understanding of what an attitude is, defining this important concept has proven to be a difficult task for social psychologists. It is true today that no single definition will be agreed upon by all. In spite of this disagreement, most contemporary social psychologists would agree on the *evaluative character of attitudes.* The one aspect of attitudes that has been stressed is that they are fundamentally concerned with an individual's assessments of the "goodness" or "badness" of objects (Oskamp, 1977). Simply stated, "Attitudes are likes and dislikes" (Bem, 1970, p. 14). More formally, an *attitude* is an *evaluative response to an object.*

This simple definition of an attitude has at least two advantages over more complex ones. For one thing, this definition corresponds closely to the procedures frequently used in its assessment. For another, it is relatively nontheoretical, avoiding statements about the connections between cognitive, affective, and behavioral components of attitudes.

The goal of the research psychologist interested in attitudes is to develop ways by which these ordinarily unobservable, implicit responses may be made explicit and observable. Sensitive, reliable, and valid indicators or measures of attitudes must be constructed to make inferences about attitudes, and social psychologists have developed a vast number of such measures. Cook and Selltiz (1964) have divided attitude measurement procedures into five major categories: (1) measures in which inferences are drawn from self-reports of beliefs, feelings, or behaviors; (2) measures in which inferences are drawn from observations of overt behavior; (3) measures in which inferences are drawn from the individual's reactions to and interpretations of partially structured stimuli; (4) measures in which inferences are drawn from performance of "objective" tasks; and (5) measures in which inferences are drawn from physiological reactions to the attitudinal object or representations of it.

Self-Report Techniques

Of all the procedures used for measuring attitudes, those involving self-report are most common. The respondents are essentially asked to indicate what they think about, how they feel toward, or how they have behaved or would behave toward the attitude object or some representation of it. The assumption in this measurement approach is that there is a direct correspondence between people's attitudes toward an object and their verbal statements about it. To find out about attitudes toward an ethnic or racial group researchers might ask their subjects to indicate which traits, from a predetermined list, they believe are most characteristic of the group. Or they may be asked to indicate the degree to which they agree or disagree with a number of statements about the group. Finally, researchers may ask the subjects to indicate their willingness to have as a roommate a member of a particular ethnic or racial group. The most important and sophisticated self-report methods of attitude measurement are the Likert method of summated ratings, the Thurstone psychophysical approach, the Guttman scalogram analysis, and the semantic differential.

Likert's method of summated ratings.   Of the self-report methods, Likert's method is undoubtedly the most widely used. Respondents are asked to indicate the extent of their agreement-disagreement or approval-disapproval with a number of statements concerning the attitude object, generally by circling a number on a five- or seven-point scale. The subjects' responses to the various items are then summed to provide an overall index of the attitude. The following is an example of an item from a Likert scale:

All Negroes belong in one class and should be treated in about the same way.

Strongly Approve	Approve	Undecided	Disapprove	Strongly Disapprove
1	2	3	4	5

To develop a true Likert scale, an analysis of the suitability of each item for the scale must be conducted. Items not highly related to other items (not "tapping" the same attitude) or not discriminating between groups with extreme scores on the scale are discarded. Many agree-disagree scales used in attitude research are not true Likert scales in that they have not been item-analyzed. These scales are "Likert-like" or "Likert-type" scales.

Thurstone's psychophysical approach.   With Thurstone's attitude measurement technique, the initial step is to gather a large number of statements which express a full range of attitudes about an object, from very positive to very negative. The pool of statements is then given to groups of judges who are asked to sort them into eleven piles or categories along an attitude continuum ranging from very favorable to very unfavorable. The judges are asked not to consider their own attitudes toward the statements, but only to sort the items in such a manner that the distances between adjacent categories are equal. In other words, the items in pile two should be the same "distance" from those in pile three as those items are from items in pile four. Any items for which the judges show substantial disagreement in their sorting are discarded. Criteria are also established for excluding irrelevant items. The remaining items are assigned values that are the averages of the categories in which they had been placed. Examples of three items from a Thurstone scale and their corresponding scale values (higher numbers indicating a more favorable attitude) are the following:

Scale Value	Statement
0.8	The white race must be kept pure at all costs, even if the Negroes have to be killed off.
6.8	In 1000 years the Negro might become the white man's equal; then his social position might be equal to the white man's.
10.3	I believe that the Negro deserves the same social privileges as the white man.

A number of these items (usually around 20) without their scale values are then randomly ordered and given to respondents to assess their attitudes toward the issue or object. The respondents place a check mark by those statements with which they agree. An individual's attitude score is the mean or median of the scale values of the checked statements.

Guttman scalogram analysis.   In the Guttman self-report measurement scale, respondents are given a series of statements ordered in terms of their favorability along a single attitude dimension and asked to check all the items which are acceptable. The unidimensionality of the attitude scale is essential in this procedure; it is important that each of the items in this scale be related to one and the same attitude continuum. The items differ only in terms of their degree of favorability along the dimension.

In 1925, Bogardus developed a unidimensional scale of social distance. The respondents were given a list of racial or ethnic groups and asked to indicate whether they were willing to admit members of each of these groups to one or more classifications by placing a cross next to it. The original seven classifications were: (1) to close kinship by marriage; (2) to my club as personal chums; (3) to my street as neighbors; (4) to employment in my occupation in my country; (5) to citizenship in my country; (6) as visitors only to my country; and (7) would exclude from my country. Now, if the Bogardus scale was indeed unidimensional, then people who indicated that they would admit Armenians to their club as personal chums would also presumably indicate their willingness to admit these people to their street as neighbors and to employment in their occupation in their country. Agreement with a "stronger" or more favorable statement implies agreement with "weaker" or less favorable ones if the scale involves a single attitude dimension. Similarly, people with more favorable attitudes toward a particular ethnic group should agree to one or more of the more favorable statements along this continuum than people with less favorable attitudes.

In developing a Guttman-type scale the researcher administers it to groups of respondents, determines each individual's attitude (defined as his or her most extreme statement), and then looks for "errors" by examining each individual's response profile. An error occurs when a statement which is weaker than the respondent's score on the scale has not been checked. A scale is regarded as unidimensional as long as no more than 10 percent of the respondents' statements are coded as errors.

Osgood, Suci, and Tannenbaum's semantic differential. The connotative meaning of any concept or object for a respondent can be determined. Rather than asking individuals to agree or disagree with statements or to indicate degrees of agreement or disagreement, the *semantic differential* requires people to rate a single concept or object on a series of seven-point bipolar adjective scales. Some examples of the adjective pairs which anchor the opposite extremes of seven-point scales are: good-bad, pleasant-unpleasant, weak-strong, and passive-active. Extensive research with this measurement technique has revealed that there are three major dimensions of connotative meaning: evaluation (good-bad), potency (weak-strong), and activity (passive-active). Given an emphasis on the evaluative character of attitudes, the evaluative meaning of a concept should serve as a reasonable indicator of an individual's attitude. Osgood and his colleagues (1957) have reported that scores on this dimension are related to other assessments of attitudes. This measurement procedure was used in the earlier reported study by Staats and Staats (1958) and is commonly used in attitude research.

Some problems with self-report measures.   With self-report measures of attitudes, the intent of the measurement is generally quite clear to the respondent who can easily monitor and bias his responses. Consequently, results from self-report measures are often less than perfect reflections of people's true attitudes. Self-report measures are particularly susceptible to the influence of social desirability response sets. Rather than reporting true feelings or attitudes, people respond to the items in terms of how they feel most other people would respond, or in terms of what they think are the most appropriate or acceptable social responses. Response set and bias are likely to trouble self-report measurement because the intent of the measurement tactic is clear, because of the nature of the attitudes frequently assessed (e.g., racial prejudice), and because people prefer to appear intelligent, mature, and well adjusted. This concern, called *evaluation apprehension,* is a problem for almost all behavioral research and will be discussed more fully in the last section of this chapter. As applied to self-reports, evaluation apprehension suggests that respondents will give answers that make themselves look good, not ones that reveal their real feelings.

A number of controls have been proposed for reducing and minimizing the influence of response set. A straightforward approach would emphasize the importance of honesty in the preliminary instructions, stressing that the respondents should respond to the items with their initial reactions. The respondents may be informed that there are no right or wrong answers and that every answer is equally acceptable. The anonymity and confidentiality of responses may be stressed in the hope that this will facilitate truthful reporting. A less direct method of managing the problem of response set disguises the intent of the measure by embedding the critical attitude items in a larger questionnaire that contains innocuous distractor items. Still another method is to force the respondent to choose one of two attitude statements matched for their social desirability.

In addition to the social desirability response set, there are other biases that can affect the results from self-report measures. Where the social desirability response set necessitates a consideration of the content of the attitudinal items, the remaining two response sets do not. A positional response bias occurs when a respondent consistently marks a specific position on an attitude scale regardless of the content of the items. Two kinds of positional biases can be identified: people consistently indicate strong agreement or strong disagreement to all items or mark the neutral or undecided alternative. A technique for eliminating the latter problem is to use six-point attitude scales that do not have neutral points, thereby forcing either favorable or unfavorable responses to the statements. In order to detect the former, attitude statements can be worded in such a way that a positive attitude sometimes requires disagreement with a statement and at other times agreement. The operation of the response set can also be detected by alternating the meaning of the scale endpoints so that at times the seventh point indicates strong agreement and at other times it indicates strong disagreement. Once detected, the biased individual's data can be discarded since they are not valid indicators of true attitudes.

Behavioral Measurement

People's attitudes toward an object or event can be inferred from their behavior toward it. Put another way, their actions toward an object can be used as indicators of their attitude toward it. If they have a favorable or positive attitude toward the members of a racial or ethnic group or toward a particular individual, this should be reflected in any number of actions which they might direct toward these social stimuli. In contrast to a negative attitude, a positive attitude should lead them to approach the object, to seek out and desire contact with it, to aid it, and perhaps even to be reinforced by its presentation. As with self-report measures, the assumption with behavioral measures is that there is a direct correspondence between people's attitudes and their behavior.

A distinction between behavioral and behavioroid measures can be made. Whereas a true behavioral measure requires the subject to perform an overt action immediately, the behavioroid measure asks the subject to make a commitment to perform an action at a later time (cf. Aronson & Carlsmith, 1968). Both measures differ from self-report measures in that they have greater real-life consequences for the subject, with the behavioroid measure having slightly less immediate impact than the behavioral measure. Neither is used as frequently in social psychological research as self-reports because they are more difficult to obtain than paper-and-pencil measures. An example of a behavioral measure of attitudes is provided by DeFleur and Westie's (1958) famous work on white prejudice toward blacks, presented in Box 10.2.

A subject's willingness to spend a great deal of time escorting some visiting blacks around campus or the number of telephone calls a person voluntarily agrees to make for an experimenter are simple examples of behavioroid measures which have been used. In both cases, subjects commit themselves to action and its real-life consequences to a greater extent than they would by filling out a self-report measure.

Nonreactivity. Increased use of behavioral measures, especially unobtrusive or nonreactive measures, has been urged by Webb, Campbell, Schwartz, and Seechrest (1966). They criticize psychology's heavy reliance on self-report measurement techniques particularly because of their reactive nature—their susceptibility to subject bias. A number of other ways in which behavior can be measured without the individual's awareness and consequently without reactivity have been suggested. One class of unobtrusive measures that would permit inferences about attitudes involves the search for signs of wear and buildup in the environment which reflect its use by people. This kind of measurement is called *physical traces*—erosion and accretion. For instance, the popularity of exhibits at Chicago's Museum of Science and Industry can be inferred by the frequency with which the tiles around an exhibit need replacement. Tiles around the "hatching chicks" exhibit have to be replaced every six weeks, while those in other areas can go for years without replacement. Webb et al. (1966) suggest other general classes of environmental and archival data that are available for exploitation by the social psychologist who is interested in studying behavior nonreactively.

Box 10.2   A Behavioral Measure of Attitudes

The participants in DeFleur and Westie's (1958) research were shown a number of color slides depicting interracial pairs of men and women. Some of the slides portrayed a well-dressed, good-looking, young black man paired with a similarly groomed, attractive, young white woman. The other slides presented a white man with a black woman. The people in the photos were seated side by side and were looking at one another with pleasant expressions. Later the exeprimenter informed the participants that another set of slides was needed for further research and asked the subjects if they would be willing to pose with a black of the opposite sex for this purpose. A "standard photograph release statement" was then given to each subject, containing a graded series of uses to which the photo might be put: (1) laboratory experiments where it will be seen only by professional sociologists, (2) publication in a technical journal read only by professional sociologists; (3) presentation to a few dozen university students in a laboratory situation; (4) presentation to hundreds of university students as a teaching aid in sociology classes; (5) publication in the student newspaper as part of a publicity report on the research; (6) publication in the subject's home town newspaper as part of a publicity report on the research; and (7) use in a nation-wide publicity campaign advocating racial integration. Subjects were asked to sign their names below each use of the photograph to which they consented. The wider the use agreed to, the more favorable the subjects' attitude. Inasmuch as the subjects believed that their signatures obligated them to the releases, their responses were more immediately consequential than self-reports of attitudes toward blacks would have been. People commit themselves to action and its real-life consequences to a greater extent than they would in filling out a self-report scale.

Some problems with behavioral measures.   A problem with behavioral measures of attitudes is that behavior is multiply determined. The same behavior toward an object may be performed for many reasons, none of which may involve the person's attitude toward the object. Social psychologists have commonly assumed that attitudes and behaviors toward objects should be highly consistent and correlated. The fact of the matter is that attitudes and behaviors are often found to be only weakly, if at all, consistent (cf. Wicker, 1969). An individual's attitude is only one of several determinants of behavior, but all too often scientists and laymen alike have preferred to explain human conduct in terms of internal, individual characteristics while ignoring or underemphasizing the influence of current and future environmental events.

Although a thorough discussion of the attitude-behavior relationship is beyond the scope of this chapter, four general reasons for attitude-behavior inconsistency can be described. First, the individual's attitude may not be evoked by a "present" stimulus. An individual may dislike "whites" in general, but a good looking, attractive, young white might not be the "kind" of white person toward whom the attitude is felt. Second, competing motives and attitudes may be elicited along with the attitude of interest to the researcher; these other attitudes and motives may prevail and operate as functional social stimuli. A subject may really dislike all members of an ethnic group, including a particular individual, but he also may like to be photographed, and the favorable attitude toward being photographed may be stronger than the unfavorable one toward blacks and being seen with them. Third, extraneous environmental influences, especially the anticipation of rewards or punishments from others, may cause an individual to behave in a way which is inconsistent with his attitude. The subject's concern about the experimenter's evaluation of his emotional adjustment may cause him to agree to interact with members of a disliked group because the subject values the experimenter's opinion of him. Finally, it is virtually impossible to know a person's future plans. Even though an individual agrees to escort a visiting black around the campus and this is presumed to reflect a favorable attitude, the researcher has no way of knowing for certain how the subject will treat the visitor. Perhaps the subject believes that he or she can manifest a negative attitude more thoroughly by agreeing to be an escort and then mistreating the visitor.

Does this brief discussion of the problems of attitude-behavior inconsistency then indicate that attitudes should never be inferred from behavior? Does it mean that attitudes cannot be measured from observations of behavior? The answer is no. It should, however, alert one to problems inherent in this kind of measurement, to variables that need control, and to cautions in making inferences about attitudes from behavior. Behavior is determined by attitudes, but specific behaviors are influenced by specific attitudes toward specific objects as well as by other characteristics of the individual and his or her environment.

Projective Attitude Measures

Sometimes we do not directly ask respondents to evaluate or judge the attitude object. Instead, they describe a picture, tell a story, complete a sentence, or indicate how someone else would react to the situation. Inferences about individual attitudes can then be drawn from responses to such *projective tests*. The assumption is that the perception and interpretation of ambiguous stimuli reflect people's needs, motives, and attitudes. In filling in the contents of these relatively unstructured stimuli, people unwittingly reveal their own characteristics. An obvious advantage of projective techniques is that the purpose of the measurement is unclear to respondents. Response biases are presumably much less likely than with self-report techniques.

In one successful use of the projective technique, subjects described how people in a racially mixed group had come together. It was assumed that the subjects who attributed the gathering to chance or to work demands would be more prejudiced than those who said that the individuals had convened by their own choice. It was in fact found that the subjects who were more prejudiced as judged by an independent self-report assessment gave the former explanation to the projective test more often than those who were less prejudiced (Riddleberger & Motz, 1957).

Projective measures of attitudes suffer from a number of methodological problems. It is often difficult to get two observers to categorize consistently a subject's responses. In other words, the measurement's reliability may be low, so that no inferences about its validity can be drawn. Even if reliability is satisfactory, validity often remains suspect. People's responses to ambiguous stimuli may reflect their attitude or represent a variety of other internal dispositions such as their knowledge of social customs and stereotypes. Because of these basic problems with projective measures, they have not been frequently used as indicators of attitudes.

Performance on Objective Tasks

This type of attitude measurement is based on the assumption that systematic biases in people's responses on objective tasks are affected by attitudes. Subjects are not asked to indicate their attitudes toward an object, but rather to perform an objective task. For example, they might be asked to learn a written passage or a series of statements. The ease with which they learn the material or the amount of material remembered are assumed to be influenced by their attitudes.

Some early research on the influence of people's attitudes on the learning and forgetting of controversial material supported the notion that people were more likely to learn and remember material that was consistent rather than inconsistent with their attitudes (e.g., Levine &

Murphy, 1943). However, more recent research on attitudes and selective learning has failed to confirm these findings (Greenwald & Sakamura, 1967). One shortcoming of the earlier research was that the subjects' familiarity with the pro- and anti-attitudinal material was often overlooked. In the more recent studies the attributes of the attitude items themselves were more responsible for learning differences than were the subjects' attitudes. On the basis of this evidence, it does not appear that attitudes directly influence the learning and memory of material, although they may well influence people's exposure to material inconsistent with their attitudes and indirectly their knowledge of it (cf. Rhine, 1967).

In the sorting of items for the construction of Thurstone scales, judges are instructed to categorize the statements in terms of their favorability without regard to their own attitudes. Originally, it had been assumed that individuals could indeed do this; subsequent research has, however, indicated that the judges' own attitudes do influence their placement of the statements. This is true not only for judges with extreme attitudes (Hovland & Sherif, 1952) but also for those with more moderate positions (Zavalloni & Cook, 1965) at least for unfavorable and intermediate items. Thus, performance on this supposedly objective task can serve as an indicator of the judge's attitude. It should be noted that these results do not pose serious problems for attitude scale construction using the Thurstone method. The rank ordering of the items by groups of judges with very different attitudes toward the object of the statements is generally the same. Furthermore, while the differences between the placement of an item for two groups with extreme and opposite attitudes can be fairly great (two or more scale positions), one can avoid using individuals with such extreme attitudes in developing these scales. In short, this objective task can serve as an indirect measure of subjects' attitudes.

One final technique for assessing attitudes through performance on objective tasks has been reported by Jones and Cook (1975). These researchers have shown that racial attitudes influence the kind of social policies that are judged as effective in reducing racial inequality. Individuals with negative racial attitudes are more inclined to view favorably policies which aid self-improvement, while those with more favorable racial attitudes are more disposed to endorse policies which remove societal barriers. These findings suggest that this technique may hold promise as an indirect attitude assessment procedure.

To the extent that these indirect measures are presented as objective tasks rather than attitude measures, they are relatively nonreactive—free from the sources of bias which trouble self-report techniques. Nonetheless, their validity under many circumstances is dubious. On the one hand, it is by no means clear what the absence of systematic responding on these tasks means. Does this indicate that the respondent has no attitude toward the object, or that his attitude is neutral? On the other hand, it is by no means obvious that the only source of error on a so-called objective task is the individual's attitude. Insufficient information may just as readily produce systematic responses. People's behaviors are multiply determined, and systematic patterns of responding can reflect more than their attitudes. Nonetheless, several objective methods do seem to offer promise as indirect attitude measurement procedures.

Physiological Responses as Attitude Indicators

Physiological indicators of attitudes are at the opposite extreme from self-report measures—they are relatively free from response bias and conscious distortion. A number of physiological responses have been studied as possible indicators of a person's attitudes. They include galvanic skin response, heart rate, and pupillary changes. It is assumed that the magnitude of a physiological response to an attitude object is directly related to the intensity of the attitude toward the object. Even so, however, most physiological measures provide no information about the direction of an attitude. In other words, physiological responses can indicate whether an attitude is strong or weak, but not whether it is positive or negative. What is needed to advance research is a physiological measure which is bidirectional.

In 1965, the pupillary response was proposed as a bidirectional indicator of attitudes. Hess (1965) found that a person's pupils dilated in response to pleasant stimuli (e.g., pictures of female nudes for males) and constricted in response to aversive stimuli (pictures of sharks for female subjects). From these results, he suggested dilation indicates a positive attitude toward the stimuli, while constriction reflects a negative attitude. However, it now appears that the initial excitement generated by these findings may have been premature. The pupillary response has not been shown by other researchers to be bidirectional (e.g., Woodmansee, 1970; Brigham & Weissbach, 1970), although some still entertain the possibility that it may be (Oskamp, 1977). The pupillary response, like other physiological reactions, seems to serve as an index of arousal, interest, and attentiveness but is probably not a bidirectional indicator of attitudes.

Cook and his associates have been exploring one other response that might function as a bidirectional indicator of attitudes, the semantic generalization of conditioned autonomic responses, and have recently reported some success with this approach (Tognacci & Cook, 1975). First, subjects were classically conditioned to give autonomic responses to non-race-related statements previously judged as bad and to inhibit responses to other non-race-related statements previously judged as good. After conditioning, a test of generalization to race-related statements was conducted. The subjects were presented with statements which either favored or opposed integration. It was assumed that equalitarian (non-prejudiced) subjects would view the anti-integration statements as "bad" and show generalization of their conditioned responses to these stimuli. That is, the evaluative meaning (the attitude component) of these statements was the hypothesized basis for generalization. Prejudiced subjects, on the other hand, were expected to generalize their responses to the pro-integration or "bad" statements. The results showed that the technique was successful for the equalitarian subjects, but the predictions for the prejudiced subjects were not confirmed. Tognacci and Cook (1975) suggested that the prejudiced subjects were not extreme enough in their attitudes to categorize the pro-integration statements as uniformly bad, or as sufficiently bad to provide a basis for generalization. Whether this is true or not is an empirical matter. At present the conditioning technique can be viewed as a measure which holds promise as a bidirectional physiological indicator of attitudes.

A New Attitude Assessment Procedure: The Bogus Pipeline

One final attitude measurement procedure has recently been proposed but cannot readily be placed in the Cook-Selltiz classification. Concerned with the reactivity of self-report measures and the aforementioned problems in behavioral and physiological measures, Jones and Sigall (1971) presented what they hoped would be a new procedure for validly assessing attitudes. Their new procedure was "based on the simple assumption that no one wants to be second-guessed by a machine" (p. 349). This procedure, called the "bogus pipeline to the soul" because it purportedly assesses subjects' true feelings, involves three features: (1) the use of a device or instrument that supposedly measures one's true feelings about a person or issue; (2) some means of validating the machine in the subjects' eyes, i.e., convincing them that it can measure the direction and intensity of their true feelings; and (3) the measurement of the dependent variable or the prediction by the subjects of the machine's reading. If subjects in experiments do distort their responses because of concern about their social desirability, for example, then the pattern of results obtained under normal self-report conditions and bogus pipeline conditions should be different according to Jones and Sigall.

In a test of these ideas, Sigall and Page (1971) asked their white male college subjects to indicate how characteristic they thought each of twenty-two traits was of either Americans or Negroes (this is their wording which the subjects apparently understood). In addition, half the subjects in each of these conditions were led to believe that an independent and distortion-free physiological measure of their attitudes was being obtained (the bogus pipeline conditions) while the remaining half merely reported their responses under fairly standard conditions (self-report conditions). In the bogus pipeline conditions, the machine was validated for the subjects prior to the collection of the dependent variable by demonstrating that the machine could accurately report the subjects' responses to a questionnaire completed earlier (an accomplice of the experimenter, who had recorded these responses, presented them at the appropriate time via the machine). The subjects were then asked to predict the machine's measurement of their judgments of how characteristic the various traits were of either Americans or Negroes.

The different measurement procedures did in fact produce different patterns of responses. Under machine conditions, relative to standard ones, the subjects stated that unfavorable traits were more characteristic of Negroes (stupid, physically dirty, and lazy) and that favorable traits were more characteristic of Americans (honest, intelligent, and sensitive). For each of these characteristics, there was a significant interaction between rating procedure and group rated. Results similar to these have been obtained in other studies (e.g., Allen, 1975; Jones, Bell, & Aronson, 1972).

How should these results be interpreted? It could be, as Jones and Sigall (1971) suggested, that "bogus pipeline measures *operate like lie detection devices in facilitating scrupulously truthful reporting*" (p. 362). Whereas subjects don't ordinarily tell the truth, they do under these measurement conditions. There are, however, at least two other plausible interpretations. The first holds that subjects usually don't know their true feelings or, indeed, their feelings actually vacillate. However, because of their concerns about self-presentation, when they are asked to predict the meter readings, they prefer to be too harsh on themselves rather than too lenient. In other words, they would rather admit being a bigot and then be shown to be tolerant than vice versa. Thus, they are more unfavorable in their reactions to blacks under machine conditions than they normally are. The second alternative interpretation assumes that the procedure makes the affective component of attitudes more salient than the cognitive. The procedure may be asking people to predict their primitive affective responses over which they have little control. Although the subjects may not guide their behavior by these deep-seated feelings, they may believe in their existence and predict the machine's ratings on the basis of these impulses. Which of these interpretations, if any, is correct is unclear. The reader may be able to think of still other interpretations and is free to draw his or her own conclusions about the validity of the results from this procedure.

The bogus pipeline technique has drawn criticism from several writers for various reasons (Cherry, Byrne, & Mitchell, 1976; Ostrom, 1973). There is still no convincing evidence that it always provides a more accurate or sensitive measure of attitudes than other methods, it is impractical, and it involves more deception than other procedures. Nonetheless, the procedure is provocative and may yet prove to be a valid means of assessing attitudes.

Research on Attitudes: Some Conclusions

The study of attitudes—their measurement, formation, and change—continues to be a major concern of experimental social psychologists. Although the concept of an attitude can be simply defined, it is clear that *evaluative responses* to objects are related to a wide variety of other behaviors. The success of researchers in isolating multiple indicators of attitudes amply documents the importance of attitudes for understanding social behaviors. Evaluative responses to stimuli do assuredly influence behavior. Furthermore, the use of multiple indicators in making inferences about attitudes seems as valid today as it did when Cook and Selltiz (1964) wrote their highly influential article. Observations of the consistency and inconsistency among different measures of attitudes provide valuable information about behavior and point out the need continually to refine our methods for studying it. A vast amount of research on attitudes in social psychology has been concerned with theories of attitude formation, change, and resistance to change. We will conclude this section on attitudes with an example of a simple but amazingly robust phenomenon, the mere exposure effect. A study by Zajonc (1968), showing that the more often a stimulus is seen the more favorably it will be judged, is presented in Box 10.3.

RESEARCH ON AGGRESSION

Violence in the United States has risen to alarmingly high levels. Whether one considers assassination, group violence, or individual acts of violence, the decade of the 1960's was considerably more violent than the several decades preceding it and ranks among the most violent in our history. The United States is the clear leader among modern stable democratic nations in its rates of homicide, assault, rape, and robbery, and it is at least among the highest in incidence of group violence and assassination. (Final Report of the National Commission on the Causes and Prevention of Violence, 1969, p. xv)

In 1975, 20,510 murders were committed in the United States, and an estimated total of 1,026,280 violent crimes (murder, forcible rape, robbery, and aggravated assault) occurred (FBI Uniform Crime Reports, 1976). While the figure for murder actually represents a 2 percent decline from 1974, the murder rate has nevertheless increased by 21.5 percent

Box 10.3   Mere Exposure and the Enhancement of Attitudes

Does familiarity breed contempt? According to a hypothesis presented originally by Zajonc (1968), it most certainly does not. Zajonc believed that the more often people are exposed to a stimulus, the better they will like it. His sweeping yet simple hypothesis was "Mere repeated exposure of the individual to a stimulus is a sufficient condition for the enhancement of his attitude toward it." (p. 1) By mere exposure Zajonc meant that the stimulus needs only to be accessible to the individual's perception; a person need only look at a visual stimulus or hear an auditory one for the effect to occur.

In an experiment which supposedly dealt with the learning of a foreign language, subjects were exposed to twelve different Chinese-like characters. Six different exposure frequencies (0, 1, 2, 5, 10, and 25 exposures per character) were used during the first phase of the experiment; two characters were shown at each frequency. To control for the idiosyncratic effects of the individual stimuli themselves, the twelve characters were counterbalanced in six replications of the experiment. Each word appeared at each frequency for one of the six different groups of subjects. Seventy-two subjects were run, one at a time, with twelve subjects participating in each of the six replications. The stimuli were printed on 3 x 5 inch cards, and on each trial a card was shown to the subject for approximately two seconds. The subjects were instructed to pay close attention to the characters whenever they were exposed. Since there were two stimuli at each frequency, there was a total of 86 trials. After "frequency training," the subjects were told that the characters stood for adjectives and that their task was to guess their meaning. The experimenter said he realized how nearly impossible this was, and therefore would not require the subject to report the word meanings exactly. Instead, it would be sufficient if the subject indicated whether each character meant something good or something bad by rating it on a seven-point good-bad scale. These ratings were then made for the ten stimuli to which the subject had been exposed from 1 to 25 times, as well as for the two stimuli which the subject had not previously seen.

The results indicated a strong evaluative effect due to mere exposure. The more often a stimulus had been seen, the more favorably the subjects rated its meaning. This relationship was found for all but one of the individual stimuli. The results of this experiment, and another one using nonsense syllables, are shown in Figure 10.1. Note that as frequency of exposure increases, items are judged more positively. Other research recently reviewed by Harrison (1977) generally corroborates these findings. Within limits the mere repeated exposure to a stimulus leads to a more positive attitude toward the stimulus. In general, familiarity breeds liking.

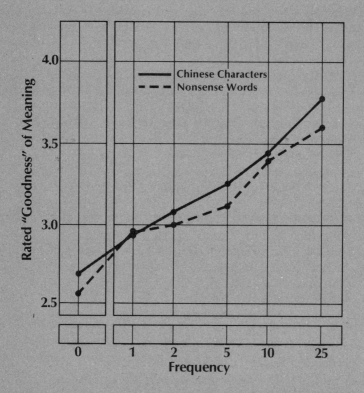

Figure 10.1 Average rated affective connotations of nonsense words and Chinese-like characters as a function of frequency of exposure. From Zajonc (1968).

from 1970, the end of the "violent decade" of the 1960s. For total violent crime, the 1975 figure represents percentage rate increases of 4.4 and 32.5 over 1974 and 1970 respectively. These observations make abundantly clear and concrete what each of us already knew—the United States is a violent society.

Since 1939, when five young Yale psychologists, Dollard, Doob, Miller, Mowrer, and Sears, published their seminal work *Frustration and Aggression,* psychologists have been interested in understanding the causes and control of aggression and violence. Ironically, the incredible violence and destruction of World War II temporarily interfered with research in this area as well as many others. However, shortly after the war, and especially during the late 1950s and early 1960s research on aggression expanded (Berkowitz, 1962; Buss, 1961).

It will undoubtedly come as no surprise to learn that definitional problems have troubled aggression research and theorizing. For our purposes, aggression will be defined as behavior intended to injure another person or to damage an object. A few features of this definition require further elaboration. For one thing, the essential characteristic of aggression is its physically and/or psychologically injurious nature. This point is important because aggression as the psychologist defines it must be carefully distinguished from other common uses of the term. For example, a salesman's "aggressive" behavior is by no means necessarily aggressive in an injurious sense; the salesman's behavior is quite probably influenced by different factors, motives, and processes, and his assertiveness should not be confused with aggression.

As problematic as the notion of *intent* is, it demands inclusion in an adequate definition of aggression. By including intent, accidental injury of another is justifiably excluded. The inclusion of intent also allows us to keep unsuccessful attempts to injure within the conceptual domain of aggression, a consequence which seems clearly appropriate.

Distinguishing intentional from accidental behaviors is difficult but not impossible. One way of inferring the intent of a behavior is to examine the influence of the consequences of a response on its subsequent occurrence. Do the response consequences act as reinforcers or punishers for the behavior? If the victim of aggression cries when attacked and this consequence increases the subsequent likelihood of his victimization by the same aggressor, then it is justifiable to infer that the aggressor has intended to do harm (cf. Patterson, Littman, & Bricker, 1967). Other features of the situation, especially antecedent events, can help strengthen the inference about the intent of behavior (Bandura, 1973; Buss, 1971).

While all aggression, as we have defined it, involves attempted or actual injury of a victim, most researchers agree that aggressive behavior has two major functions. The first of these, which has been called hostile, angry, or impulsive aggression, is primarily aimed at the injury of a victim. The main goal of the attack is plain—the infliction of harm—and anger is its major antecedent. In so-called personal instrumental aggression, injury is clearly intended but the attainment of noninjurious goals (money, approval, or prevention of future victimization) is the primary goal. Fighting to gain status in an adolescent gang, or the harm done by a mugger are common examples of personal instrumental aggressive acts.

Rule and Nesdale (1974) have presented a third major function of aggression—social instrumental. The main goal of harmful behavior is the achievement of consensually agreed upon, valued ends. The aggressive behavior of the soldier illustrates this function. By injuring and killing the enemy, the soldier is helping to achieve a societal goal—the preservation of a style of life. The parental punishment of children to inculcate societal values may also exemplify this form of aggression. Social-instrumental aggression is similar to what Sears (1961) earlier called prosocial aggression.

Analyzing aggressive behaviors into different classes is theoretically useful because they often involve different antecedents, intervening processes, and reinforcers. In the following discussion of aggression methodology, the distinction among the three kinds of aggression will be maintained. It will be seen that there are widely agreed upon operational definitions of aggression, despite the problems in definition at a more general, conceptual level. Although there is not always a simple or direct correspondence between definitions at the two levels, a working conceptual definition of aggression is required to guide theory, research, and measurement.

Paper-and-Pencil Measurement

Much of the original research on aggression involved paper-and-pencil or self-report measurement. As in attitude measurement, these procedures essentially ask subjects to describe their past, present, or projected feelings and behaviors. In some procedures, subjects might indicate how they behaved in the past in a situation similar to the one described, or to predict how they or others would respond in such a situation. Other measures ask people to evaluate others or their characteristics when these evaluations clearly have potentially injurious consequences. A final set of self-report measures requires subjects to indicate how well they like other persons or to evaluate them in some other manner, but these measures do not generally have direct injurious potential. As such, these responses are more accurately viewed as indices of hostility rather than aggression.

In one early study which tested a number of their ideas advanced in *Frustration and Aggression,* Doob and Sears (1939) used a procedure similar to the "reconstruction through retrospection" method. As the name suggests, this procedure asks respondents to look back and exam-

was supposedly another subject and they both were to fill out a personal question-
aire. The confederate acted according to a planned script either happy and fooling
around or angry followed by storming out of the room.

The mood of the subject was measured by a rating scale. The results
showed that the subjects who were misinformed about the reason for their arousal
state tended to feel the emotion and behave in ways appropriate to the situation
in which they were placed. Subjects who had been correctly informed did not tend
to experience the appropriate emotion. Subjects with no information gave intermediate results. (Schachter and Singer, 1962)

Experiment 1. Subjects were asked to estimate the length of lines. They were given one standard and three comparison lines. Control subjects who made their judgments by themselves were accurate 99% of the time.

In the experimental sessions, judgments were made by subjects in groups. Each session had only one actual subject in a group of seven to nine other people who had been coached to make their judgments differ from correct answer. The actual subject heard the judgments of all but one of these confederates before making his own decision.

The subjects were wrong a total of 33% of the time, however, they were consistent in their responses. Subjects who conformed to the majority early continued to do so throughout the session; those who did not conform disagreed repeatedly. (Asch, 1956)

Experiment 2. Two groups of kittens were raised in the dark except for 3 hours a day when the group P kittens were placed in little suspended cars which moved when the group A kittens, harnessed to the other side of the apparatus, moved about the experimental box. The P (passive) kitten's movement was restricted by the car, but it had the same amount of visual stimulation as the A (active) kitten.

When tested later on the visual cliff, the P kittens showed no evidence of depth perception, while the A kittens showed normal reactions. (Held & Hein, 1963)

Experiment 3. A state of physiological arousal was induced in male college students by injections of adrenaline. The subjects were told that they were receiving a vitamin compound.

One group of subjects was not told anything about the effects of the injection; another group were told the correct effects of the drug (increased heart

ine their past to see if they have had a particular experience. If they discover they have, they are then required to recall their own and possibly others' reactions in this situation. The Yale undergrads in the Doob and Sears study were asked to decide initially whether or not they had previously experienced sixteen different situations which other Yale students had earlier reported were common experiences for them. The participants then were asked to give four different responses to each of the situations they had experienced. These included an indication of which response alternatives best described their own reactions in the situation, ratings of which reactions would have brought the most satisfaction and the most unpleasant consequences or trouble, and a rating of essentially how badly they were frustrated. An example of one of the items from the questionnaire, the behavioral alternatives, and the frustration index is given in Table 10.1. Although the study provided substantial support for several hypotheses relating frustration to aggression, the procedures used have many methodological drawbacks.

The respondents may have trouble remembering whether they had the experience and, furthermore, how they behaved if they had. In addition to the problems which arise from "memory errors," this self-report procedure is susceptible to a number of problems involving conscious distortion of responses. The image of themselves people wish to present, together with their concern about the experimenter's evaluation of them, is a source of response contamination. Whether they wish to appear "tough" or meek will affect their responses, as will their assessment of how they think the experimenter evaluates these responses. These problems stem from concerns about self-presentation and evaluation apprehension. However, they are not the only sources of conscious distortion with this procedure. In some cases, respondents may try to "help" the ex-

Table 10.1   Sample item and response alternatives from the Doob and Sears (1939) study of frustration and aggression.

In a semi-formal group you heard a sneering comment about Yale which you felt was unjustified. You discovered that the speaker was a stranger whose appearance you disliked anyway.

— — — I made a slurring remark in return to put him in his place.
— — — I unobtrusively left the group.
— — — I was disgusted or felt resentful, but did not go to the trouble of challenging him.
— — — I ignored him and diplomatically turned the conversation to another topic.

How warmly did you feel toward Yale at the time?

After reading the item and deciding if they had experienced such a situation, the subjects checked which if any of the response options best described their own reaction(s). They then indicated which reactions would have brought the greatest satisfaction and which would have brought the most trouble by assigning each option a number from 1 to 4. For the final question, they checked which of four response options best described their own feelings. The options ranged from strong to weak.

perimenter by giving the kinds of responses they think the investigator desires, while in others they may try to harm the research by giving false answers (cf. Weber & Cook, 1972). Yet another possibility is that subjects themselves will "play psychologist" and attempt to predict how people in general will respond to the situation rather than giving their own reactions. Thus, this self-report technique, like others, is troubled by a number of validity problems.

These problems also exist in another type of self-report measurement which has been used in aggression research. Instead of recalling past behaviors, in this procedure subjects are required to indicate or predict how they would respond to a hypothetical situation. The research of Pastore (1952), Cohen (1955), and Rothaus and Worchel (1960), on the relative potency of arbitrary and nonarbitrary frustrations as determinants of aggression, used this procedure. For example, in Pastore's second study the subjects were given five arbitrary (unjustifiable) and five nonarbitrary (justifiable) frustrations and were asked to indicate which of four response alternatives most resembled their own reaction or what they imagined their own reaction would be. An example of an arbitrary frustration from this study is: "You're waiting on the right corner for a bus, and the driver intentionally passes you by." The nonarbitrary counterpart to this situation is: "You're waiting at the right corner for a bus. You notice it is a special on its way to the garage." The four response alternatives provided the subjects were:

a) I would feel hostile and show it in my behavior.
b) I would feel hostile and not show it in my behavior.
c) I would not feel any hostility.
d) I would try to do something about the situation without feeling hostile.

The research was successful in that the two types of frustrations produced a clear differentiation in responses, arbitrary resulting in more aggression than nonarbitrary. However, this measurement procedure has some of the same problems encountered by Doob and Sears (1939). If the subjects had previously experienced the hypothetical situation and were attempting to respond on the basis of a memory of the experience, the problems are identical to those mentioned previously. If, on the other hand, they were predicting how they would respond to the situation, never having previously experienced it, all the problems arising from conscious distortion would be present. Essentially, the problem concerns how accurate people are in predicting their own behavior. Each of us knows all to well how poor we are at predicting our reactions and how difficult it is to respond in terms of our ideals rather than in terms of the situation impinging on us. This inability to predict our own responses could not be more dramatically demonstrated than it was in Milgram's (1974) research on destructive obedience.

In Milgram's basic procedure, subjects were placed in a situation in which they either had to obey an experimenter's commands to hurt an innocent victim (actually an experimental accomplice), or defy the experimenter and follow the dictates of their conscience. Other subjects were asked to predict their own behavior in this obedience situation. *Every* person who was asked to predict his behavior in the obedience situation said he would defy the experimenter's commands to hurt an innocent victim. In fact, it was not uncommon to find 65 percent or more of the subjects showing full compliance to the experimenter's commands in the actual obedience situation. Once again, it should be noted that laymen and psychologists alike are all too inclined to explain and predict behavior in terms of internal characteristics, such as people's attitudes or values, while overlooking the power of situational factors as determinants of human conduct. In short, we should be extremely cautious in taking at face value people's predictions about their own behavior. What people say they will do and what they do are no doubt often remarkably different.

In a final class of self-report measures, subjects rate their liking of other participants or give their impressions of them (Berkowitz, 1960). A variation occurs when subjects are asked to evaluate someone's competence or other traits, thereby influencing the individual's future receipt of financial aid or his or her graduate career (Berkowitz, 1965; Zillman & Cantor, 1976). Responses which the subjects think can do real psychological or physical harm to the victim are potentially valid indices of aggression. When subjects communicate their liking for another or their appraisal of the other's personality directly to him or her, these responses are consequential and they appear to be valid indicators of intent to do harm. When responses are not communicated, they are better viewed as hostility than as aggression (Berkowitz & Knurek, 1969; Kaufman, 1965).

In some classic experiments on film violence and aggression, Berkowitz (1965) employed both verbal and physical measures of aggression. In the first of these experiments, the subjects were initially either angered or not by the critical experimenter who was presented as either a boxer or a speech major. Half the subjects who had been angered then viewed a violent boxing film while the remainder of the angered subjects viewed a neutral film about English canal boats. All the nonangered participants watched the boxing film. The subjects were then asked to fill out an evaluation of both the critical and the neutral experimenters for the Dean's office, ostensibly because the Dean wished "to assess students' reactions to the research that was being conducted on the campus" (p. 361). In a second experiment involving the same independent variables, the dependent measures of aggression were the number and duration of shocks the subjects supposedly administered to their partner (an experimental accomplice who was portrayed as either a boxer or a speech major) for his performance on a task. One important point of these studies is that the same results were obtained for the two measures of aggression. The verbal evaluation and the physical attack responded in the same way to the same experimental operations. The subjects who had been angered by the person portrayed as a boxer and who had seen the violent boxing film displayed the most intense verbal or physical aggression toward this individual. These outcomes increase our confidence in each of these measures as an index of aggression and in the conclusions drawn about the nature of the relationship between the independent variables and aggressive behavior. Also, these outcomes validate the conceptual definition of aggression that stimulated these operational definitions.

In summary, some of the self-report measures used in aggression research have yielded interesting and important findings. For some purposes, such as the study of violent crime, the "reconstruction through retrospection" method or other interview techniques may still be the only appropriate method (cf. Toch, 1969). For exploratory research, asking subjects to respond to hypothetical situations may also be an appropriate methodology. However, these procedures do have a number of problems associated with their use. More direct measures, whether they be self-report or verbal ones, like those described in this section, or physical indices, seem to be far superior indices of interpersonal aggression.

Behavioral Measurement of Aggression

In the 1960s, aggression researchers developed a number of direct measures of physical aggression that are still in use today. Invariably, the earlier measures involved the ostensible administration of electric shocks by the subject to another supposed subject who was actually an experimental accomplice. Depending on the particular procedure used, the quantitative index of aggression was the number, intensity, or duration of the shocks administered or some derived measure combining these separate measures. Since subjects were free to control these characteristics of the shock, the "more shock" they administered, the more intentionally injurious or aggressive their behavior was presumed to be. In using a shock measure, one requirement of the instructions is to provide subjects with a plausible experimental context for its use.

The evaluation of another subject's work on a creativity task is a commonly used rationale for allowing subjects to administer shocks (e.g., Berkowitz & LePage, 1967). After all the independent variables have been introduced, subjects are told they can now evaluate the quality of their partner's work. They are told that they can administer one to ten shocks, depending on their assessment of the work, by depressing a designated button or telegraph key. A similar procedure provides subjects with an opportunity to administer as many shocks as they wish for their evaluation of the creativity of their partner's associations to words (e.g.,

Konecni, 1975). This procedure again involves the use of a single button or bar which subjects depress to administer a shock. In both these procedures, the major index of aggression is the number of shocks delivered by subjects. The total or average duration of the shocks is also occasionally recorded. The operational definition of aggression involved in these procedures, the number of shocks administered by subjects as an evaluation of their partner's task performance, captures the essence of the conceptual definition. The response is physically injurious, and variations in its magnitude seem to reflect reasonably well variations in intent to do injury.

Without denying the importance of other procedures used in aggression research, those involving the Buss (1961) "aggression machine," or some modification of it, have clearly been the most numerous. This procedure generally involves a learning task, with the subject playing the role of a teacher or experimenter. The other person (a confederate) plays the role of learner. In some cases the actual experimenter arbitrarily assigns the participants their roles while in others a fixed lottery is conducted. In the latter case, both participants draw slips of paper from a bag. Both slips of paper have "experimenter" written on them, and the confederate merely indicates that he or she has drawn the "learner" role. This guarantees that the subject will administer the shocks.

Acting as the experimenter in the Buss procedure, the subject presents a predetermined series of stimuli to the learner and punishes his or her incorrect responses by administering electric shocks. In some cases, correct responses are also signalled or even reinforced. The "Buss machine" generally contains a row of ten numbered shock intensity buttons, which correspond to ten increasingly intense levels of shock. When the subject determines that an error has been made or is informed of a mistake by a light on the apparatus, he or she is free to deliver any one of the ten different shock intensities and to control its duration by holding the button down for as long as he or she wishes. Finally, in addition to the verbal information the subject is provided about the intensity of the shocks, he or she is also usually given sample shocks from at least two of the buttons on the apparatus.

In experiments using this procedure, the subject and the confederate are separated from one another by a partition or are actually in separate rooms. Located in the room with the confederate is a control panel from which the shock intensity data can be recorded. There are ten numbered lights on the panel corresponding to the ten shock intensity buttons on the subject's panel. The confederate records the intensity measure from these lights. A timer is connected to the apparatus in the control room and the duration of the shocks is recorded from it. A second timer is sometimes present to record yet another measure—the latency of the shock, or the time elapsed between the "error" signal to the subject and the administration of a shock.

The major indices of aggression are the average intensity and duration of shock administered by the subjects over several shock opportunity trials. A derived measure, the average of intensity times duration, has also been presented as a meaningful index of aggression (Hartmann, 1969). The data collected from the separate or derived measures are frequently collapsed into four or five blocks of trials, and the variations in level of aggressive behavior over trials can then be observed. It has been found that subjects frequently show a regular increase in the intensity of shocks they deliver over trials (cf. Baron, 1971; Buss, 1963; Zillman, 1971).

A wide range of questions concerning human aggression have been addressed using the "Buss machine." Research on the effects of film violence on the observer's subsequent aggression (e.g., Walters & Thomas, 1963), on the impact of a victim's suffering on the attacker's aggression (Baron, 1971), and on interracial aggression (Donnerstein & Donnerstein, 1976) are just a few of the problems which have been explored with this general procedure. Fortunately, the "Buss machine" shock measure of aggression and other similar machine-produced measures (e.g., noise instead of shock) have received substantial validation (Berkowitz, Parke, Leyens, & West, 1974; Shemberg, Leventhal, & Allman, 1968; Williams, Meyerson, Eron, & Semler, 1967; Wolfe & Baron, 1971). Essentially, these studies indicate that subjects classified as highly aggressive by some other means are most likely to administer high intensity shocks with the Buss machine. Counselor, peer, and social worker ratings of aggressiveness have been shown to be highly related to the laboratory measures of aggression. As would also be expected, violent prisoners have been found to be more aggressive in the Buss procedure than same-age college students (Wolfe & Baron, 1971). Collectively, these studies increase the confidence one has in the validity of this measure of aggressive behavior.

Although the Buss procedure seems to yield a valid measure of aggression, recent evidence has indicated that it may measure several kinds of aggression (Baron & Eggleston, 1972; Rule & Hewitt, 1971; Rule & Nesdale, 1974). It appears that both hostile and social-instrumental aggression are sometimes motivated in the Buss procedure. In other words, subjects have been shown to administer relatively intense shocks in this teacher-learner paradigm not only to hurt the learner, but also to help him. For example, in the Rule and Nesdale (1974) study, insulted subjects delivered more intense shocks when they thought the shocks would hinder rather than help the other person's learning. The opposite was found for noninsulted subjects; they punished the learner more when they thought the shocks would help rather than harm his or her performance.

To avoid or control these motivational problems in the Buss procedure, one of two steps can easily be taken. Hostile or so-called hurt instructions similar to those used by Rule and Nesdale can be used to minimize the subjects' belief that they can help learning by administering intense or long shocks. By means of these instructions, subjects are led to believe that longer and more intense shocks will not only hurt the learner physically but also probably interfere with his or her learning (e.g., Sebastian, in press). Controls may also involve changing the Buss procedure from a teacher-learner situation to a "stimulator-responder" situation (Baron, 1974). Subjects no longer administer shocks to another person for mistakes on a learning task. Instead, they are told the experimenter is interested in looking at the effects of shocks on physiological responding. The subject's partner will be the responder, and the subject will be the stimulator. Whenever a designated signal flashes, the subject is to administer a shock of any level he or she chooses. In this procedure the subject cannot easily aid the other individual by administering long or intense shocks.

One other procedure for measuring and examining physical aggression in the laboratory has been proposed by Taylor (1967). Subjects believe they are involved in a reaction time competition with another person. The supposed winner of each trial is allowed to give his or her partner a shock, usually from one of five intensity levels. Predetermined schedules of outcomes are mainly responsible for who "wins" on each trial. On each of the several trials the same series of events occurs: (1) a signal to set the degree of shock for the opponent; (2) a ready signal to press down on a telegraph key; (3) a response signal for the participants to release the key as quickly as possible; and (4) a light comes on to indicate the opponent's shock setting, as does a shock if the subject has "lost" the trial. If the subject wins the trial, he or she administers the shock previously set.

Although the Taylor procedure has not been used as frequently as the Buss procedure, it has been employed in research on alcohol and aggression (Gammon & Taylor, 1975), on control of aggression (Pisano & Taylor, 1971), and on the influence of observers on aggression (Borden, 1975). Because subjects can learn of their opponent's intentions without actually being attacked, it has been possible to demonstrate the importance of aggressive intent as a cause of aggression using this procedure (Epstein & Taylor, 1967).

Recently, because of concerns about the ethics of using shocks with human subjects, an increasing number of investigators have begun to use noise blasts rather than shocks as dependent measures of aggression (e.g., Berkowitz & Frodi, 1977; Konecni & Ebbesen, 1976). Inasmuch as the procedures and apparatus used with these measures are essentially the same as those used with shocks, this change should have little effect on the validity of the measurement or on the conclusions drawn from it.

It should also be mentioned that an interesting technique for measuring spontaneous verbal aggression has been proposed by Mosher,

Mortimer, and Grebel (1968). In this procedure, a naive subject and a confederate take turns working on a puzzle. While one participant solves the puzzle, the other is free to harass, distract, and criticize the partner and his or her performance. The subject always attempts the puzzle first so that different levels of verbal aggression can be introduced as independent variables. The subject's level of verbal aggression, the dependent variable, is tape recorded and later categorized on a ten point scale of verbal aggression by independent judges. This procedure has already been fruitfully employed by others (Parke, Berkowitz, Leyens, West, & Sebastian, 1977; West, Berkowitz, Sebastian, & Parke, 1976) and would appear promising as a tool for future research on verbal aggression.

Anger-Induction in Aggression Research

With the notable exception of Bandura (1973), most aggression researchers view anger as a very important determinant of aggression, and in most studies investigating other determinants of aggressive behavior, anger has also been systematically varied. Due to the importance of anger as an antecedent of aggression, a number of fairly standardized procedures for inducing anger in the laboratory have been developed.

Anger induction via shock. One procedure commonly used to induce anger involves the actual administration of electric shocks to subjects. In this technique, subjects are required to work on some creativity problem during the initial phase of the experiment. They are told that another subject (a confederate) will subsequently evaluate the quality of their solutions by giving them one to ten electric shocks. Regardless of their actual work, subjects who have been randomly assigned to the angered condition receive nine out of the possible ten shocks as their evaluation (e.g., Baron, 1971). Those in the nonangered condition receive the best possible evaluation, a single shock. In some experiments using this technique, the subjects in the angered and nonangered conditions also receive previously prepared written evaluations which are negative or positive and therefore consistent with the shock evaluation. This general procedure has usually proven to be highly effective in angering subjects. Because of its effectiveness, the procedure continues to be used even though it raises some ethical problems.

Researchers using this procedure take every precaution to ensure the safety of their subjects. The intensity of shocks typically used is not generally regarded as painful by the subjects. The apparatus used for generating the electricity is constructed so that it is impossible to administer a dangerous shock. Finally, the subjects are informed at the beginning of the experiment that shocks will be used, and without any penalty to them they are allowed to withdraw then or at any later time if they so desire.

In addition to its proven effectiveness as a means of angering subjects, the procedure seems to have one clear advantage over other procedures which do not use shocks for angering subjects but do use them as
a dependent measure. It helps validate the dependent measure. Having
received shocks themselves, subjects are far more likely to believe they
are actually administering shocks to another person when given this opportunity. The subjects' belief that they are delivering an aversive stimulus is critical for the measure's validity. Continued cautious and responsible use of the procedure seems justified.

Anger induction via insults.   An alternative method for angering subjects uses verbal insult. The experimenter or an accomplice, who is presented as another subject, disparage and criticize subjects and their personal characteristics (e.g., Berkowitz & Rawlings, 1963; Doob & Wood,
1972; Hartmann, 1969; Konecni & Doob, 1972). The procedure commonly used by Doob, Konecni, and their associates illustrates this kind
of anger-arousing procedure. Ostensibly, as a study of cognitive processes, the subject and the confederate are asked to solve seven seven-
letter anagrams in a short period of time. To learn more about the
thought processes involved, one of them, always the subject, is asked to
think aloud as he or she works on the problems and is therefore required
to wear a microphone, which is connected to a tape recorder, around his
or her neck. The real purpose for the microphone is to discourage the
subject from verbally retaliating against the confederate in the angered
condition.

In the angered condition, the confederate finishes his or her anagrams shortly after the experimenter leaves and then proceeds to insult
the subject. The confederate begins by saying, "Haven't you finished
yet?" and continues, "saying that the subject was slow, that anagrams
were easy to solve if one had any brains, and that everything about the
subject was somehow phoney. He commented on the subject's clothes,
wondered aloud how the subject managed to get into the university, said
he felt sure the subject had been getting poor grades, etc." (Konecni &
Doob, 1972, p. 383). The confederate's remarks are varied from subject
to subject so that he can pursue whatever seems to disturb the subject
most. In the nonangered condition, the confederate sits quietly throughout this period and does not disturb the subject.

This anger-arousing procedure has been shown to be very effective
in a number of experiments. Although it clearly poses no physical danger to the subject, like any other anger-arousing procedure it can potentially cause psychological harm. However, all anger-arousing procedures
must necessarily produce psychological injury. The obvious intention of
the experimenter is that the injury be short-lived and easily repaired
through a thorough and careful postexperimental debriefing should any
indication of injury still be evident. The opportunity to retaliate against
the provocateur later in the experiment in most cases probably provides

most subjects with their own opportunity to "even the score" and "heal their own wounds."

None of the anger-arousing procedures in aggression research seem to do any serious or long-lasting harm to the physical or psychological well-being of the participants. The experiences of subjects in a laboratory experiment on aggression are innocuous, as they should be, in comparison to most people's everyday experiences. If anything, the ethical guidelines which all conscientious researchers follow probably limit to some extent the advance in knowledge which could be achieved if there were some ethical way to study more extreme levels of anger arousal. Continued use of the methods described seems absolutely essential if our knowledge of the causes and control of aggression, presumably a consensually agreed upon goal, is to increase.

Internal and External Validity in Aggression Research

A primary goal of all psychological research is to make valid inferences about the causes of behavior. When a social psychologist studies aggression in the laboratory, his first and foremost concern is that his research be internally valid—that any differences in behavior due to the experimental conditions are unequivocally due to the treatments employed. "*Internal validity* is the basic minimum without which any experiment is uninterpretable" (Campbell & Stanley, 1963, p. 5). Only after the internal validity of an experiment has been established can the investigator be concerned about its external validity or generalizability to other situations, subject populations, and dependent variables. The apparent failure to appreciate fully these differences in the kinds of validity in experimental research seems to be at least partially responsible for the criticism of the laboratory research on the effects of film violence on observers' subsequent aggression.

Despite the volumes of research carried out on this problem and the basically similar results obtained from it (under specified circumstances viewing violent TV programs and films leads to aggression), some critics remain unconvinced (Howitt & Cumberbatch, 1975; Klapper, 1968; Singer, 1971). Virtually all the criticisms of this research have focused on external validity questions (cf. Liebert, Neale, & Davidson, 1973; Stein & Friedrich, 1975, for recent reviews of the findings). The questions concerning the generalizability of the laboratory findings to more "naturalistic" settings focus on four major issues: (1) the stimulus materials; (2) the persistence of the effects; (3) the frequency of exposure; and (4) the dependent measure. For each of these general categories, the materials and procedures used in laboratory research have been viewed as unrepresentative of real-life situations. Consequently, the results obtained from the laboratory research are also viewed as less than completely applicable to the naturalistic viewing context.

   To extend the generalizability of previous laboratory findings and to address some of these criticisms, Parke, Berkowitz, Leyens, West, and Sebastian (1977) carried out a series of field studies on film violence and aggression. Rather than using film excerpts or laboratory-produced stimulus materials, these investigators used five full-length commercially available films. They therefore avoided the objections that subjects in typical laboratory studies have limited exposure experience to unnaturalistic stimulus materials. The long-term and immediate effects of the film treatments were assessed by observing the behavior of their subjects for one hour after they viewed each film as well as during selected periods for the following three weeks. Finally, despite the fact that the dependent measures in laboratory research, including Bobo doll indices (Johnston, DeLuca, Murtaugh, & Diener, 1977; Walters & Brown, 1963), have essential validity, more naturalistic measures of aggression were employed in this research. Thus, in three separate studies, two in the United States and one in Belgium, these researchers examined the long- and short-term effects of viewing repeated exposures to naturalistic film violence on naturalistic indices of aggressive behavior. The first of the U.S. studies is presented in Box 10.4. The findings of Parke et al. (1977) substantiate the laboratory-derived conclusions that film violence increases aggressive behavior. Because of the materials and procedures employed they increase considerably the generalizability of past findings and the confidence placed in them.
   Field studies have addressed important questions concerning the external validity of previous research findings. They have also raised other important theoretical and methodological issues. However, they have done little to advance our understanding of the processes involved in the impact of film violence on the observer's aggression. It seems that theoretical advancement and increased understanding of problems is far better achieved in the "sterile, unrealistic" but better controlled laboratory experimental setting. The generalizability of research findings is a terribly important concern for all psychologists, and they are well advised to check occasionally for what is now popularly called the "ecological" validity of their results. It is worth repeating that concerns about external validity are secondary to those of internal validity. When the same results are obtained in different laboratories at different universities using different subjects, stimulus materials, and dependent measures, the generalizability of a result has already been documented to some extent.

Summary and Conclusions

In the past two decades in particular, social psychologists have devoted a considerable amount of attention to the laboratory investigation of the

Box 10.4   A Field Study of Aggression

The procedure of Parke et al. (1977) consisted of four major components. During an initial three-week baseline period, the subjects—inmates at a minimum security penal institution for juvenile offenders—were observed primarily for aggressive behavior. Pairs of trained observers recorded instances of aggressive behavior on three evenings for each of the three weeks during this first phase of the research. In all phases of the research, the same nonhierarchical, minimally inferential, time-sampling observational procedure was used. Ideally, each boy in each of the two cottages was observed for two 90-second periods on each evening. The observation code was nonhierarchical in that virtually none of the twelve behavior categories (e.g., interpersonal physical aggression, interpersonal verbal aggression, active social interaction) had priority over the others. The observational scheme involved minimal inference on the part of the observers because all categories were defined in terms of easily identified overt behaviors. Finally, the procedure was a time-sampling one in that every two minutes the observers were required to make observations of a different boy for three 30-second periods.

During the second phase of the research, the boys in one cottage saw five aggressive movies (e.g., *The Chase),* one each night of the week, Monday through Friday, while those in the other cottage saw five non-aggressive films (e.g., *Beach Blanket Bingo*). The assignment of cottages to the two treatments was random. The usual observations of the boys' behavior were made for one hour before and one hour after the movies were shown. During this movie treatment period, the boys were not allowed to watch any television.

The third phase of the research was a standard laboratory assessment of the boys' aggressive behavior on the Saturday following the movie week. In this first study, a modified Buss procedure was followed. The fourth and final phase entailed observing the boys in the same way they had been observed during the baseline period for three consecutive weeks after the movie treatment. The most important finding was that the boys who saw the aggressive movies were more aggressive than the control group. Consistent with other findings and theory (e.g., Berkowitz, 1975; Friedrich & Stein, 1973), there were indications that the initially more aggressive boys were most affected by the violent film portrayals.

causes and control of human aggression. Through their efforts, a number of fairly standard procedures for operationalizing independent and dependent variables have been developed. As a result, we now know much more about human aggression. It appears that if future decades are to be less violent than those of the recent past, research psychologists should be encouraged to continue ethical and systematic exploration of aggression in their laboratories.

RESEARCH ON SOCIAL INFLUENCE

Within a given society or group, individuals frequently display similar or even identical beliefs, attitudes, and behaviors. This uniformity frequently results from the influence of others who are present in the same situation, from earlier social influence and learning, or from the stimulus qualities of the environment. But not all uniformity of behavior is conformity. When individuals respond independently to common stimuli in a similar fashion because of the properties of the stimuli, they are not conforming to one another's behavior. Similarity of responding due to conventionality or to widely shared customs and norms is likewise not the same as conformity. Instead, most social psychologists view *conformity* as a change in *behavior produced by group pressure.* Because of the group's opposition to one person's views or behavior, the person modifies responses to bring them into greater agreement with the majority. This yielding to group pressure is the essence of conformity.

Group pressure may be active or passive. Other group members may attempt to persuade a deviant individual to change a belief. They may *actively* and directly communicate their opposing viewpoint and arguments against other views to the nonconformist. Alternatively, the other group members may simply express an opinion or judgment contrary to the individual's. The social pressure in this case is *passive* and is based on simple opposition.

What is the opposite of conformity? Is it nonconformity or independence? Actually, two types of nonconformity have been conceptually identified (Willis, 1963). On the one hand, an individual may completely disregard the opinions of others and base responses only on an assessment of the objective features of the situation. Disagreement by the individual with the group under these circumstances is viewed as independence. Alternatively, a person may fully consider the majority viewpoint and respond in opposition to it for any number of reasons. In this case, nonconformity is actually anticonformity. The individual's disagreement with the group is based on the group's position but is a reaction against it. Thus, there are at least three conceptually distinct modes of response available to an individual whose views are opposed by others: conformity, independence, and anticonformity. Although it is not always possible to classify nonconformity as either independence or anti-conformity, these responses are psychologically distinctive (Allen, 1965).

For several cultural, political, and historical reasons, social psychologists have in the past been interested mainly in examining the influence of a majority on a minority. However, despite the stability of many groups and societies, change does occur and minorities are often instrumental in producing change. Minorities also influence majorities, and this form of social influence has been the focus of some recent research by Moscovici and his colleagues (cf. Moscovici & Faucheux, 1972; Moscovici & Nemeth, 1974).

Majority Influence on the Minority

Asch's paradigm.   Asch's (1952, 1956) early and classic research on conformity and independence laid the groundwork for much subsequent research in this area. The basic procedure in this well-known research consisted of three essential features: (1) disagreement between a single individual and a group on a clear and simple matter of fact in the immediate environment; (2) an obviously erroneous group judgment of the facts which the individual could not help but judge correctly; and (3) public announcement of the judgments, thereby making the disagreement apparent to all. The single individual is thus confronted by a unanimously opposed majority. A more detailed account of the procedures and results from one of Asch's studies is presented in Box 10.5.

With some variations in this basic procedure, Asch has explored a number of other issues in conformity to and independence from group pressure. Some of the more noteworthy findings concern the conditions that sharply reduce the influence of the group on the individual. If one other person in a group of seven to nine gives correct judgments, the percentage of erroneous responses given by subjects is decreased to 13 percent or to about a third of what is found under unanimous majority opposition (Asch, 1952; Allen, 1975). Asch has also found that if the subject can express a judgment privately rather than publicly, the influence of the group is considerably weakened (Asch, 1956). The percentage of errors under these circumstances is once again approximately a third of that found under public responding in the face of unanimous majority opposition.

Although the data obtained by Asch from this procedure and the ideas he tested with it have proved highly influential, the procedure itself has a couple of practical shortcomings. First, only one subject at a time can participate in the Asch procedure. It is therefore a very time-consuming technique. Second, the procedure requires a great amount of "manpower" per subject. Six to eight confederates are required for each subject.

Box 10.5   The Asch Conformity Paradigm

In the basic Asch procedure one naive subject participated in an experimental session with six to eight accomplices. The experiment was presented to the group as a simple visual discrimination task. All participants were required to match the length of a standard line with one of three other lines. The critical standard lines were 3, 5, and 8 inches in length. One of the three comparison lines was equal in length to the standard; the remaining lines differed from the standard considerably, the differences ranging from .75 to 1.75 inches. The three comparison lines were numbered 1, 2, and 3, and on each trial the participants were asked to announce their judgment publicly by calling out the appropriate number. The order in which the judgments were made was determined by the participants' seating arrangement; this was always set up so that the naive subject was the second to last person to state his or her judgment.

In eighteen evenly spaced trials, nine comparisons were repeated twice each. The first two trials occurred without incident. The experimental accomplices announced obviously correct judgments. On the next comparison, however, the naive subject heard all the remaining participants make an obviously incorrect judgment. Specifically, the majority matched the 3-inch standard with the 3.75-inch comparison line. All told, the majority expressed incorrect judgments on twelve of the eighteen trials. For the remaining six trials, the majority matched the lines correctly. The major dependent variable in this procedure was the number or percentage of incorrect responses given by the naive subject. A total of 123 white male college students 17 to 25 years old participated in the experimental procedure described above. A comparable control group of 37 subjects also made the same judgments individually.

In the control group a total of 3 mistakes were made by the entire group on the 444 comparisons. In other words, less than 1 percent of the subjects' responses in this condition were errors, which highlights the ease with which the required judgments could be made accurately.

In striking contrast, 36.8 percent of the subjects' responses in the experimental condition were errors. All but 29 of the 123 experimental subjects made at least one error. The differences between the experimental and control conditions were highly significant. The unanimous majority opposition to the judgments of a single individual on a simple objective task produced a dramatic shift in the judgments of many individuals.

The Crutchfield paradigm.   In 1955 Crutchfield presented a procedure for studying conformity which overcame the shortcomings of the Asch paradigm. In this procedure, commonly used today, five naive subjects are seated in separate cubicles with open fronts allowing the participants to view slides displaying the stimuli to be judged. An electrical panel is located in the front of each subject's cubicle. Five rows (labelled A through E) of eleven lights are found on each subject's panel; each row corresponds to the supposed judgments given by one of the other subjects. On each panel there is also a series of eleven switches so that each participant can indicate a response on a particular task. After some preliminary trials, all five subjects are told they are person E, and they are thus required to respond last. The information provided subjects on their panels is not in fact the actual responses of the other participants. Rather, the information is controlled by the experimenter from an apparatus located behind the subjects. In this manner, each of the five subjects can be exposed to the same unanimous majority opposition. Other experimental variations can easily be introduced to explore other issues. The experimenter, of course, records the responses the subjects make after each trial. This technique allows the researcher to obtain data from at least five subjects at a time. It also does not require the assistance of any experimental accomplices. To run more subjects during a single session or to study the effects of larger groups, the apparatus and procedure are fairly easily modified.

Psychologically speaking, the Asch and Crutchfield procedures are similar in most important respects. They differ in one important way. The subject in the Asch procedure is in face-to-face contact with the other participants and communicates orally with them. In the Crutchfield procedure, the individuals are separated from one another, are somewhat anonymous, and communicate only indirectly. It might seem that the Asch situation is a more powerful social influence event than the Crutchfield, and comparisons of the two procedures have confirmed this (Krech, Crutchfield, & Ballachey, 1962). However, the difference in yielding found in the two procedures appears quantitative and not qualitative. Largely for practical purposes, the Crutchfield apparatus and procedure have been more commonly employed in recent studies of conformity (cf. Allen, 1965, 1975).

The situation of the subject in both procedures differs psychologically in several important respects from that found in more naturalistic settings. In neither procedure is the subject generally allowed to abstain from responding or to "leave the field," both common answers to social pressure. In fact, when subjects are given the opportunity to abstain *and* a social supporter previously abstains in the face of otherwise unanimous group opposition, the subjects do choose to abstain significantly more often than when they oppose a unanimous majority alone (Allen, 1975).

These procedures for investigating conformity also do not allow for interaction among the participants and discussion of the chosen alternatives and the rationales for their choices. The studies generally involve only passive social pressure. Although the absence of these features makes the situation different from many real-life ones, the exclusion of interaction and discussion does enhance experimental control. If interaction were allowed, the description, prediction, and explanation of the outcomes of the research would be considerably more difficult and complicated. Hence, most investigations of conformity have involved simple opposition rather than more active social influence.

Another feature of real-life conformity situations which is not represented in the typical laboratory study also relates to the kind of social influence involved. In the laboratory study the other participants, who oppose the subject, have relatively little control over resources important to the subject. The others are peers and strangers who have minimal ability to dispense rewards and punishments. In a real sense, the absence of this resource control appears to make the findings even more striking. Indeed, when the experimenter, a more authoritative individual with presumably greater resource control, corroborates the group's or the individual's judgments, the power of the group is strengthened or weakened, respectively (Krech, Crutchfield, & Ballachey, 1962). Other characteristics of naturalistic social pressure situations not typically found in laboratory studies include: (1) the choice of giving an indefinite or ambiguous response; (2) the opportunity to deliberate before making a choice or to gather additional information on which to base a judgment; and (3) prior familiarity or interaction among the participants.

The influence of these various features in the conformity paradigm is by no means unidirectional. Inclusion of these features would not, in other words, necessarily lessen the majority's influence on the minority. Some would instead enhance the majority effect. Furthermore, all these issues concern external validity, and as stated earlier, the researcher's first concern is with internal validity. These procedures have produced a sizable body of valid literature on the conditions of conformity to and independence from group pressure.

Minority Influence on a Majority

If majority views always prevailed, change would never occur. But any casual reading of history or simple observation of everyday life clearly indicates that change occurs, and that the process of change is frequently initiated by the minority. In the discipline of psychology, the change or revolution caused by Freud's ideas vividly illustrates the influence of a single man on an entire profession, despite the earlier vehement opposition to his ideas. A minority can obviously influence a majority.

Under what circumstances does the minority have its effect on the majority? Until recently, little attention had been given to this question. Hollander's (1958) work was the exception. He argued that an individual needed to acquire "idiosyncracy credits" or the right to deviate from the majority through earlier conformity to its standards or demonstrated competence. Minority influence is therefore the province of the relatively powerful. There is little doubt that the leader of a group, an individual who constitutes a numerical minority, can influence the majority. Limiting minority influence to these circumstances, however, would fail to include interesting and important instances of it.

Recently, a rather different conceptualization of minority influence has been offered (Moscovici & Faucheux, 1972; Moscovici & Nemeth, 1974). This view of minority influence, which is derived from a broader reconceptualization of social influence, emphasizes the importance of the *behavioral style* of the minority or "the orchestration and patterning of . . . behavior . . . " (Moscovici & Nemeth, 1974, p. 220). The particular characteristics of the minority's behavior which have received the most emphasis to date are the consistency, confidence, and firmness of the minority's style of responding. More precisely, the majority's *perception* of these behavioral qualities, even in the face of opposition, is viewed as critical for minority influence to occur. To illustrate the phenomenon of minority influence and the importance of the consistency of the minority's behavioral style, the research of Moscovici, Lage, and Naffrechoux (1969) is summarized in Box 10.6.

More traditional views of social influence emphasize the importance of people's dependence on others for information about reality and for approval or acceptance from others. In many instances of minority influence, it is apparent that the majority in no real sense depends on a single individual or on a small number of them in either of these ways. Moscovici, Nemeth, and their associates plausibly argue that these traditional views are generally inadequate for analyzing minority influence. In addition, their broader conceptualization of social influence emphasizes the role of conflict and conflict resolution rather than dependency. From this perspective, minority influence involves the actual creation of conflicts. while majority influence involves the resolution of conflict.

Other research on minority influence has indicated that the minority need not simply repeat its judgments constantly in order to be seen as consistent and influential. It is sufficient that the minority display a consistent pattern of responding, varying its judgments with other discernible stimulus modifications, to influence the majority judgments (Moscovici & Nemeth, 1974). When no established norms are present in a situation, the minority is also capable of influencing the majority in the establishment of norms by consistent responding (Moscovici & Nemeth, 1974). Work on this problem of minority influence is really only beginning. Understanding of the processes involved and of the critical characteristics of the minority's behavioral style is at present elementary. The

Box 10.6   The Consistent Minority's Influence on the Majority

The influence of a minority on the majority's response to an implicit but well established linguistic norm was investigated in the studies by Moscovici, Lage, & Naffrechoux (1969). Six female subjects—two experimental confederates and four naive subjects—participated in each experimental session. All viewed a series of 36 slides and indicated the color they saw on the slide. In fact, all the slides shown were the color "blue," although the intensity of the light was varied.

Before the judgment task began, each subject was tested for color blindness. This accomplished two goals. It allowed the experimenter to eliminate any naive subjects who might be color blind. It also enabled the researchers to demonstrate that the confederates had normal color vision. After some preliminary judgments, the participants then viewed the slides and indicated what color they saw. In the experimental condition, the two confederates gave "green" responses on each of the 36 trials. In the control condition no confederates were present and six naive subjects simply judged the same stimuli used in the experimental condition. The intra- and inter-individual consistency exhibited by the minority in the judgment of the stimuli therefore served as the major experimental variation.

In the control condition, one subject twice reported that she saw "green." All other subjects identified the stimulus as "blue" on every trial. The number of green responses for the control group was 0.25 percent. In the experimental condition, 8.42 percent of the responses given were "green," and the difference between the experimental and control groups was statistically significant. Thirty-two percent of the experimental subjects gave at least one "green" response. The minority of two had influenced the majority on a task for which a well established linguistic convention existed.

A second part of this experiment by Moscovici et al. provided further evidence for the minority's influence. After the group judgments had been made, each of the subjects was individually tested in a color discrimination task. The subject was presented with sixteen colored discs. Three of the discs were clearly blue, three were clearly green, and the remaining ten represented variations in the blue-green color range and were more ambiguous. For each stimulus the subject had to indicate whether the color was either blue or green. Intermediate (i.e., blue-green) judgments were not allowed. The subjects in the experimental group again differed significantly from those in the control condition in their use of the "green" response. An even more interesting finding was that the subjects who publicly had shown no evidence of influence in the first phase of the research were even more likely to give "green" responses during the second phase than were the 32 percent of the subjects who had earlier been influenced. It appears that those subjects who did not report "green" responses in the group setting had nonetheless been influenced by the minority. The minority not only affected the color-naming response but also apparently influenced the subjects' perceptual code, particularly for the ambiguous stimuli.

A final study carried out by Moscovici et al. highlighted the importance of consistency in responding for minority influence to occur. The same stimuli and procedures were used in this part of the research. However, the two confederates who constituted the minority did not respond consistently in this case. On 24 of the trials the confederates said they saw "green" while on the remaining 12 trials they gave "blue" responses. The minority did not influence the majority judgments under these conditions. Only 1.25 percent of the subjects' responses were "green." The consistency of responding by the minority is an important characteristic of its behavioral style if the majority is to be affected.

problem beckons future researchers and, more generally, focuses attention on an aspect of social influence which has been largely overlooked.

GENERAL METHODOLOGICAL PROBLEMS AND ISSUES IN SOCIAL PSYCHOLOGICAL RESEARCH

Behavioral research involving human subjects can be properly conceptualized as a social psychological problem. Because of the nature of the human organism and the interactive process between experimenter and subject, all behavioral research with humans is susceptible to some methodological problems. These difficulties are even more troublesome for research which is explicitly social psychological or which intimately involves social interaction.

Several of the more serious methodological problems stem from the simple fact that human behavior in the experimental situation can be due to factors other than the independent variables; they can be artifactual. Despite the hopes and assumptions of researchers, human subjects respond not only to the independent variables, but also to other supposedly irrelevant cues in the setting. These cues include those provided by a live experimenter, such as indications of what a socially desirable response would be, and more generalized expectations, feelings, and motives concerning behavior in this specialized setting. By virtue of their disciplinary concerns, social psychologists have been more sensitive to and interested in these various sources of artifact in behavioral research. Indeed, there is even a literature described as the social psychology of psychological research (cf. Miller, 1972).

Demand Characteristics

One kind of subject artifact in behavioral research, originally proposed by Orne (1962), stems from the so-called demand characteristics of the experimental setting. Based on the conceptualization of subjects' experimental performance as problem-solving behavior aimed at discovering the experimenter's true hypothesis, demand characteristics are broadly viewed as "the totality of cues which convey an experimental hypothesis to the subject . . ." (Orne, 1962, p. 779). "They include the scuttlebutt about the experiment, its setting, implicit and explicit instructions, the person of the experimenter, subtle cues provided by him, and, of particular importance, the experimental procedure itself" (Orne, 1969, p. 146). According to Orne, the subject in an experiment actively attempts to discover the experimenter's hypothesis, and the entire experimental context may contain cues which enable an individual to do so. This knowledge of the hypothesis then becomes an important determinant of the subject's behavior.

Despite the widespread attention which Orne's arguments have attracted and the proclivity of some researchers to interpret results in terms
of these ideas (cf. Page, 1969; Page & Scheidt, 1971), precisely how the
subject's behavior is typically affected by knowledge of the hypothesis is
by no means clear. That is, the specific way in which demand characteristics bias research outcomes is unknown (Kruglanski, 1975). Orne himself emphasized the subject's willingness to "help" the experimenter by
confirming the hypothesis, and he is most closely identified with the position which views the subject as cooperating with the experimenter in
research activity. He has, however, acknowledged other possible motivations. Under some circumstances, the subject may attempt to disconfirm
rather than verify the experimenter's hypothesis. In yet other circumstances the major concern of the subject may be to present himself or
herself in the most favorable possible light irrespective of the effects of
this behavior on the experimental hypothesis. A final possibility, not explicitly mentioned by Orne, is that the subject may attempt to behave in
an honest and genuine way in terms of the independent variables rather
than his or her knowledge of the hypothesis.

These different ways of responding, once the hypothesis has been
divined, correspond to the four different subject "roles" or motives which
subjects can adopt. These subject roles, each of which has been presented
as *the* typical one, are the good, negativistic, apprehensive, and faithful
roles (cf. Weber & Cook, 1972). The pattern of responses produced by all
the roles except the final one are biased and are therefore artifactual.

The evidence for these subject roles is usually indirect and, with one
exception, insubstantial (Kruglanski, 1975; Weber & Cook, 1972). According to Weber and Cook, the evidence for both the good and the
negativistic subject roles is confounded consistently with the subject's
concerns about being evaluated or with the apprehensive subject role.
The faithful subject role implies the absence of bias and consequently is
not a paramount concern (Weber & Cook, 1972). The only subject role
for which there is any compelling evidence is the apprehensive one. In
general, there does seem to be some tendency for subjects to behave in a
manner which makes them "look good." However, because of the flexibility involved in defining what the "best" response in a situation is, the
inference that this motivation "to look good" is present in the typical experiment is doubtful (Kruglanski, 1975).

To summarize, it seems that there is no typical motivation which
guides subjects' responses once they have discovered a hypothesis, with
the possible exception that they wish to appear healthy, intelligent, and
well-adjusted. Furthermore, the conditions which arouse these different
motivations are unspecified. Although the results of any single experiment can almost always be accounted for after the fact by some combination of hypothesis awareness with one of the subject roles, the
available knowledge about subject roles offers little support for these
contentions. In particular, the notion that subjects are compliant and

eager to help the experimenter has received little confirmation and seems mythical (Berkowitz, 1971). This seems especially true when the behavior being studied can be viewed as socially undesirable, such as behaving aggressively (Turner & Simons, 1974), and when behaving to confirm the experimenter's hypothesis conflicts with presenting oneself in a favorable way (Sigall, Aronson, & Van Hoose, 1970).

Even if there is no typical way of responding once a hypothesis has been discovered, it is still important to know if hypothesis awareness biases results regardless of the direction of the bias. To determine the effects of hypothesis awareness on research outcomes, a number of researchers have experimentally manipulated the disclosure of the hypothesis or have varied degrees of hypothesis awareness (e.g., Horowitz & Rothschild, 1970; Turner & Simons, 1974). In other studies the impact of subject sophistication upon experimental outcomes has been studied to determine if experienced subjects are more likely to figure out the true purpose of a study and bias their results relative to naive participants (e.g., Page, 1969; Page & Scheidt, 1971). Finally, to investigate the effects of hypothesis awareness on experimental bias, other researchers have relied on thorough postexperimental inquiries to probe for subjects' discovery of the true purpose of the experiment. The results produced by subjects who are classified as aware or unaware on the basis of these interviews are then examined for systematic differences purportedly due to bias (e.g., Page, 1969).

Of the three methods for exploring the effects of hypothesis awareness on experimental outcomes only the first provides evidence which itself is uncontaminated. The other two procedures have methodological problems themselves. For example, if sophisticated subjects are more likely to guess the hypothesis at the end of the experiment and behave according to it, it is unnecessary to conclude that their knowledge of the hypothesis mediated their earlier behavior. Other variables, such as their motivation to participate in the research and attention to the procedure, could account for the differences in their behavior from naive subjects (Kruglanski, 1975). Furthermore, two reviews of the literature on subject sophistication and experimental bias concluded that with the possible exception of conditioning studies there is no consistent evidence for the purported relationship (Kruglanski, 1975; Weber & Cook, 1972).

Classifying subjects as aware or unaware of the hypothesis on the basis of postexperimental interviews (probes) and then searching for systematic differences in the behavior of the subjects so classified is a procedure fraught with problems. The probes used could themselves produce awareness where none had earlier existed. It cannot easily be determined whether the subject's behavior produced the awareness or vice versa. Finally, probe analyses are basically correlational and therefore subject to the third variable problem (see p. 37, text). For example, subjects who condition easily and who report awareness of the hypothesis may be more intelligent than those who neither learn a relationship in the experiment nor report the hypothesis later. The evidence gleaned from this procedure for determining the effects of hypothesis awareness on experimental outcomes is highly questionable (Berkowitz, 1971; Kruglanski, 1975; Staats, 1969).

The direct experimental manipulation of the disclosure of the hypothesis or of the degree of hypothesis awareness indicates that subjects' performance is affected by knowledge of the hypothesis. Differential awareness of the hypothesis has produced more verbal conditioning, less conformity, and less aggression. The direction of the bias in these studies has been inconsistent but bias has nonetheless been frequently reported (Kruglanski, 1975; Weber & Cook, 1972). While these outcomes do not indicate how often or commonly subjects spontaneously discover the true hypothesis, they do indicate that efforts should be made to disguise the real hypothesis to eliminate bias. The subjects' awareness of the true hypothesis in an experiment can bias results, but the extent to which subjects guess the real hypothesis or are even motivated to do so seems to have been greatly exaggerated.

Evaluation Apprehension

The notion of evaluation apprehension was originally presented not so much as a pervasive artifact but rather as an alternative explanation for a more limited set of findings obtained in cognitive dissonance research. Rosenberg (1965), the concept's originator, thought the inverse incentive effect (the smaller the incentive for advocating an attitude not held, the greater the attitude change) frequently observed in dissonance studies (e.g., Cohen, 1962; Festinger & Carlsmith, 1959) might be more readily explained in terms of evaluation apprehension. His argument was that the results were due to the subjects' resistance to attitude change aroused by their suspicions about the experimenter's motives in the high incentive conditions rather than to dissonance processes. In a test of his hypothesis, Rosenberg was able to eliminate the inverse incentive effect and produce instead a direct reinforcement effect (more attitude change with greater incentives for arguing against one's own position). The more important of Rosenberg's contributions seem to be the introduction of the evaluation apprehension notion and the research and thinking stimulated by it.

According to Rosenberg (1969), evaluation apprehension for a subject is "an active anxiety-toned concern that he win a positive evaluation from the experimenter, or at least that he provide no grounds for a negative one" (p. 281). In presenting the notion, Rosenberg assumed "that the typical human subject approaches the typical psychological experiment with a preliminary expectation that the psychologist may undertake to evaluate his (the subject's) emotional adequacy, his mental health or lack of it" (p. 281). Rosenberg went on to argue that members of the general public, including introductory psychology students, learn to attribute special skills to psychologists in making these kinds of inferences. "Even when the subject is convinced that his adjustment is not being directly studied he is likely to think that the experimenter is nevertheless bound to be sensitive to any behavior that bespeaks poor adjustment or immaturity" (p. 281). Events that confirm these suspicions in the early phases of an experiment arouse evaluation apprehension. Rosenberg was mainly concerned about the arousal of evaluation apprehension through experimental procedures, especially the differential activation of this concern by the various treatments within a given experiment. Under the latter circumstances, evaluation apprehension would be a serious threat to the internal validity of an experiment. That is, if the various conditions in an experiment differ not only in terms of the manipulated variables but also in terms of the evaluation apprehension produced, the outcomes may be artifactual.

Rosenberg and others have conducted a large amount of research on evaluation apprehension and on what he has called cueing. Manipulations of this variable inform the subject of the kinds of responses usually made by well or poorly adjusted individuals. They indicate what the socially desirable responses in the situation are and may well activate concern about evaluation. For example, in one of Rosenberg's early studies the male and female subjects in one experimental condition were led to believe that past research had generally shown that psychologically mature and healthy people liked strangers better than others who were not as well adjusted (liking condition). The subjects in a second experimental condition were cued in the opposite direction; they were told disliking a stranger had generally been shown by past research to indicate psychological health and maturity (disliking condition). Before making any actual ratings, the subjects in both conditions were told that their own personalities were not being assessed; they were simply helping the experimenter standardize some stimuli for later research. The subjects then rated how well they liked twelve pictures of male faces on 21-point like-dislike scales. The subjects in a control group made these same ratings in the absence of any directional cueing and arousal of evaluation apprehension. The results for the female subjects were in exact accord with the predictions. The women in the liking condition rated the pictures more positively than those in the control condition, who in turn indicated greater attraction for the pictures than the subjects in the disliking condition. For the men, the difference between the two experimental conditions was significant and consistent with expectations. Similarly, the men in the liking condition indicated greater attraction for the stimuli than those in the control group. The only exception to the consistent pattern of findings occurred for the comparison between the control and disliking conditions for the men where no significant difference was found.

The results from this study and the others quite clearly indicate that subjects will generally perform in a fashion which supposedly indicates greater psychological health, intelligence, and maturity (cf. Kruglanski, 1975; Rosenberg, 1969; Weber & Cook, 1972). It appears that subjects are indeed motivated to "look good" and/or to make socially desirable responses. It therefore seems clear that to avoid bias researchers should avoid cueing subjects.

Rosenberg (1969) has argued that the cueing manipulation not only indicates what kind of a response is "good" but also arouses evaluation apprehension by confirming the subject's suspicions about the interests of psychologists in assessing mental health. To separate these two aspects of the cueing manipulation and to investigate the effects of different levels of evaluation apprehension on experimental performance, Rosenberg has conducted other research in which cueing and evaluation apprehension were independently varied. According to the evaluation apprehension notion, the subjects in the high evaluation apprehension conditions should be more responsive to the cueing manipulations than those in the low evaluation apprehension conditions. In other words, an interaction between the two variables is expected. For example, in one experiment (Rosenberg, 1969) subjects were again asked to make liking ratings of pictures, and they were assigned to one of the two previously described cueing conditions. In addition, in the high evaluation apprehension condition the experimenter expressed a strong interest in the experiment and psychology; he said he hoped to go into psychiatry. The subjects in the low evaluation apprehension condition worked with an experimenter who did not see the importance of the experiment; he was an engineering student and not particularly interested in psychology. The picture ratings of the high evaluation apprehension, liking condition subjects were significantly higher than those of their low evaluation apprehension counterparts. However, the ratings of the pictures did not differ for the high and low evaluation apprehension subjects in the disliking condition. Thus, this study provided only partial support for the expected interaction between evaluation apprehension and cueing.

Other research in which evaluation apprehension and cueing have been independently varied has yielded inconsistent results for the expected interaction. These inconsistencies have led Kruglanski (1975) to question the pervasiveness of the effects due to evaluation apprehension. Yet in some research on aggression, the manipulation of evaluation apprehension without any cueing manipulation has influenced the subjects' performances in the expected way (Turner & Simons, 1974). Subjects who thought the experimenter was interested in assessing personal adjustment were significantly less aggressive than those who were given no such information. If subjects assume that better adjusted people are less aggressive, and they probably do, then these results are consistent with the evaluation apprehension notion.

All in all, behavioral researchers seem well advised to guard against biases from evaluation apprehension. The findings from the cueing studies consistently demonstrate bias. Although Kruglanski (1975) does not believe these results unambiguously support an evaluation apprehension interpretation, he does admit that cueing manipulations suggest to subjects what the socially desirable or typical response would be. To the extent that social desirability concerns and evaluation apprehension produce similar responses from subjects, which certainly seems plausible, the issue is academic. Methodologically, the implications of the cueing research are the same regardless of the relevance of this research for evaluation apprehension *per se*. An experimenter should provide no information about what a socially desirable response would be.

Because of the flexibility of the evaluation apprehension notion, it can be overused and abused in accounting for virtually any set of results in *post hoc* fashion. Nevertheless, evaluation apprehension seems to have a better empirical foundation than other artifacts commonly discussed. It seems especially pertinent to investigations of behaviors, such as aggression and prejudice, for which there is some consensus as to what is socially desirable.

Experimenter Expectancy Effects

The notions of demand characteristics and evaluation apprehension focus on the subject as the source of contamination in behavioral research. But the experimenter can also be a source of bias. The experimenter, like the subject, is an active participant in the research process and brings to it expectations, feelings, and motives. Rosenthal (1963) originally proposed the experimenter expectancy effect as a possible source of bias. The basic idea of this experimenter artifact is that the experimenter unintentionally or intentionally influences the subjects' behavior to verify the research hypotheses. Somehow the experimenter "communicates" the research expectancies or hypotheses to the subjects so that they can confirm them. Results produced in this manner are, of course, artifactual. They are not due to the independent variables but rather to the influence of the experimenter on the subject.

The procedure for investigating this artifact is quite simple. One group of experimenters is given one specific, directional hypothesis or expectation concerning the results of the experiment. A second group is given the opposite expectation. It is then easy to determine if these different expectancies produce different experimental results. Experimenter expectancy effects have been found in laboratory research on animal and human learning, psychophysics, personality assessment, and person perception as well as in research in natural settings (Rosenthal, 1969).

The most commonly used procedure in studies of the experimenter expectancy effect involves the person perception task, as in the study of Rosenthal and Fode (1963) which initially demonstrated the effect. The experimenters in this study were ten advanced undergraduate and graduate psychology students enrolled in an experimental psychology course. Each experimenter was assigned a group of about twenty introductory psychology students as subjects. The task of the experimenters was to present to the subjects a series of ten photographs of people's faces. The subjects were required to rate the degree of successfulness of the face in the picture by assigning it a number from a 21-point scale. The scale ranged from −10, indicating extreme failure, to +10, corresponding to extreme success. The photos used had been previously judged to be, on the average, neutral on this dimension. All experimenters were given the same instructions on how to administer the task, and were also provided with identical instructions to read to the subjects. The purpose of the experimenter's participation was to see how well they could duplicate already established experimental results. Half the experimenters were led to believe that the subjects they were running should average a +5 rating, while the remainder thought their subjects should produce an average rating of −5. Each group of experimenters was, in other words, given an equally extreme but opposite expectancy as to what the established finding was. The dependent variable in the research was the rating of the photographs by the subjects. The experimenters expecting higher ratings in fact obtained significantly more successful judgments than those with the opposite expectation.

After reviewing more than 100 laboratory and field studies investigating this effect, Rosenthal (1969) concluded that "This unintended effect of the investigator's research hypothesis must be regarded as a potentially damaging artifact" (p. 269). While it is difficult to argue with this general conclusion, a number of other considerations must be kept in mind in evaluating the impact of this artifact on research. In the first place, the available evidence is inconsistent. Some studies demonstrate the bias in the expected direction, others show bias in the direction opposite that expected, and still others find no evidence of bias. Taking the evidence as a whole and using his own statistical criteria for evaluating it, Rosenthal thought the research convincing. Other reviewers, notably Barber and Silver (1968), have found the evidence far less compelling. At the time of their thorough and rigorous review of the literature, there were 31 pertinent studies. For a variety of statistical reasons, they classified nineteen of these studies as offering no clear-cut evidence for the experimenter bias effect while acknowledging that the remaining twelve studies apparently showed the effect. An especially significant overall conclusion was that "the experimenter bias effect appears to be more difficult to demonstrate and less pervasive than was implied in previous reviews . . ." (Barber & Silver, 1968, p. 23).

There are a number of good reasons for questioning the relevancy of the experimenter expectancy effect for the typical laboratory study. The studies that demonstrate the effect differ in important ways from more typical ones. Carlsmith, Ellsworth, and Aronson (1976) have presented several of these differences: (1) the typical experimenter expectancy experiment is a relatively simple two-condition study in which the experimenter's expectancy can be readily communicated; this is not true of most laboratory research, which often involves factorial designs; (2) the typical experimenter bias study involves repeated observations of the same subjects in a face-to-face setting; this situation provides a greater opportunity for subtle interpersonal influence processes to occur than many other studies do; and (3) in the usual experimenter expectancy study, each experimenter runs subjects in only one condition; this procedure is atypical of most laboratory research and again seems to encourage bias.

One final, bewildering aspect of the experimenter expectancy effect is that the process which mediates it is for all practical purposes unknown. Despite careful and numerous efforts to identify how the experimenter influences the subjects, the problem remains unsolved. Simple cheating (e.g., intentional false recording of the data) and operant conditioning (verbal or nonverbal reinforcement by the experimenter of the responses desired from the subject) explanations of the effect appear largely inadequate. Some evidence suggests that differential vocal emphasis of parts of the instructions by the experimenter may influence the results, but this evidence is far from conclusive. Rosenthal (1969) seems to prefer an explanation which states that the experimenters are subtly shaped by their subjects. When the subjects behave in accord with experimenter expectancies, they essentially reinforce the experimenter's pattern of unintentional cueing. Through such a reinforcement process, the experimenter learns how to elicit responses from the subject which are consistent with his hypotheses. This explanation is at best suggestive.

For the various reasons stated above, it appears that experimenter bias is not as worrisome a problem as has been suggested. However, because of its potential impact, experimenter bias needs to be taken seriously. There are a number of fairly simple procedures which can be followed to minimize its influence. Keeping the experimenter blind to one or more of the subjects' experimental conditions, using multiple experimenters each of whom is blind to at least one condition, tape recording instructions or in other ways automating experimental procedures, and running all conditions in an experiment simultaneously are some of the techniques that minimize the influence of experimenter bias (Carlsmith, Ellsworth, & Aronson, 1976).

Deception and Role-Playing

Deception is commonly, but *not* invariably, practiced on participants in social psychological research. Subjects are often not informed of the true purpose of an experiment but are instead provided with a fictitious purpose or "cover story." Experimental accomplices are often presented as other subjects. In some research the dependent measure is not actually what it appears to be (e.g., shock measures in aggression studies). In other procedures the experimenter or an accomplice provides subjects with false feedback about their performance on a task, possibly to arouse anger or lower temporarily their self-esteem.

The major reason for the use of deception is that many of the behaviors studied in social psychology are subject to conscious control and can therefore be modified in the service of other motives. It is not that the social psychologist is uninterested in these other motives if they are common determinants of behavior. However, it is the researcher's goal to understand the unconfounded influence of other presumed causes of behavior. If the intent of the experiment or measurement is clear, the responses of the subjects in a great many typical social psychology investigations can be due to a host of factors besides the independent variables. If systematic results were obtained in such an experiment, an outcome by no means certain, it would be virtually impossible to interpret them unambiguously. As a result, deception is used to minimize and control for extraneous causes of the behavior being studied and to encourage spontaneous responses to the independent variables. In short, deception is used to enhance internal validity.

Despite the essential function deception provides for social psychology, it has obvious shortcomings. For instance, at least two major ethical issues are raised by deception research. First, it constitutes an invasion of subjects' privacy in that they divulge information about themselves which they could not have fully agreed to reveal. Second, the deception violates subjects' rights to be told the truth about what will happen and be required in the research. No conscientious researcher glibly decides to violate the rights of subjects. Nonetheless, the social psychological researcher is obviously confronted with a moral dilemma. On the one hand, the researcher unquestionably values science *per se* and its application for the betterment of the human condition. The use of deception in research promotes these values. On the other hand, the scientist's other values about individual human rights are violated by deception.

This moral dilemma cannot be categorically and simply resolved. As in all other issues of this sort, we can propose only rough guidelines to the judgments involved in individual cases. At the very least, researchers must consider the ethical problems involved in all facets of their investigations, including the use of deception. They must be able to justify to themselves and, quite likely, to a human subjects' committee (a group of individuals now found at virtually all major research institutions; it determines whether a research project meets current ethical standards) that any psychological and/or physical harm done to subjects is minimal and outweighed by the potential importance of the research findings. In other words, researchers must conduct a cost/benefit analysis of the project.

Despite opposing viewpoints (e.g., Campbell, 1969), it seems that subjects in deception research should always be carefully debriefed after their participation. Experimenters should inform their subjects of the deceptions used and the reasons for their use. They should emphasize why deception is necessary while acknowledging that it makes them uneasy too. In order to prevent subjects from feeling further discomfort because they have not "seen through" the deception, experimenters should assure them that a great deal of effort was put into developing the experimental procedures. A careful, honest debriefing can alleviate much of the discomfort that may have been caused by deception. Indeed, subjects are frequently delighted to learn of the real purposes of the experiment, finding them far more interesting than the ostensible ones. Finally, in all cases, investigators should determine if there are other procedures available which would provide the same information and cause less harm (cf. Carlsmith, Ellsworth, & Aronson, 1976; Miller, 1972).

Is there a widely accepted, equally valid, alternative method for studying many of the problems of interest to social psychologists? A number of writers concerned about the ethical and methodological problems involved in deception research have suggested role-playing as a substitute (e.g., Brown, 1965; Forward, Canter, & Kirsch, 1976; Kelman, 1967). In this procedure, subjects pretend that they are participating in a fictitious study or adopt the role of an actual research participant (cf. Greenberg, 1967). The individuals then predict how they themselves or others would respond in this situation. This "as-if" or hypothetical research procedure supposedly avoids the major ethical problems involved in deception research. Although the participants are not necessarily told the researcher's real purposes, they are also not misinformed of those purposes. The subject-experimenter relationship is presumed to be "better" than the one in the usual deception experiment. In the role-playing procedure, the subject's help is actively solicited, and subject and experimenter are coparticipants in the research enterprise. The role-playing procedure may thus minimize some of the ethical problems in deception research although it is by no means clear that it altogether eliminates them. If, in fact, participants report their true responses to the hypothetical situations described without knowing the experimenter's hypotheses and the meaning which might therefore be attached to their behavior, it would seem that even in this procedure the subjects' right to privacy could be violated. They still might reveal something about themselves that they don't wish to make public.

A much more serious objection to role-playing as an alternative to deception has already been mentioned in the earlier discussion of hypothetical measures used in aggression research. What people say they will do is not equivalent to what they actually do.

> People are poor at predicting their behavior in reasonably familiar situations. . . . It must be much more difficult for them to predict their behavior in unusual, unique, unfamiliar situations. . . . They are only fallible humans who are for better or worse not very good at telling what they would do in a given situation unless they have just been in that very situation and not even very well then. (Freedman, 1969, p. 112)

People's behavioral ideals probably influence their predictions of behavior more than their actual behavior. Furthermore, the stimuli that govern people's responses to an imagined situation are not necessarily those to which they attend and which control behavior in the actual situation (Cooper, 1976). People's predictions about their own behavior are not substitutes for the behavior itself (cf. Cooper, 1976; Freedman, 1969; Miller, 1972).

Similarly, people's predictions about how other individuals will behave are also inadequate substitutes for actual behavior unless one is explicitly interested in the processes and variables responsible for this "naive psychologizing," as occurs in attirubtion research (cf. Harvey, Ickes, & Kidd, 1976). Even if a vast majority of the people questioned agree upon how others would behave in a situation, this can indicate nothing more than knowledge of clearly established norms for responding in these circumstances. In the absence of such norms, the responses may indicate nothing more than consensus and "Consensus is not truth" (Freedman, 1969, p. 111). Instead, "actual behavior is the only standard of truth" (Freedman, 1969, p. 110).

To conclude and summarize, a final quote from Freedman's (1969) vigorous and penetrating critique of role-playing seems most appropriate.

> Role playing is not a substitute for experimental research. It is totally unacceptable when used instead of experiments. . . . There is essentially one basis for these somewhat bold and uncompromising statements. The data from role playing are people's guesses as to how they would behave if they were in a particular situation; they are not data on how they would behave; and people's guesses as to future or hypothetical situations are not the stuff of which a science of human behavior is made. Role playing tells us what men think they would do. It does not tell us what men would actually do in the real situation. Despite all of its difficulties, experimental research is the foundation of the science of psychology and must remain so. (p. 114)

FUTURE DIRECTIONS IN SOCIAL PSYCHOLOGY

In the decade of the 1960s, cognitive dissonance theory and research virtually dominated social psychology. The successor to dissonance theory appears to be another "theory" from the cognitive orientation—attribution "theory." As indicated previously, attributional analyses are concerned with understanding how ordinary individuals explain the causes of their own and others' conduct. The seminal ideas for studying this "naive analysis" of human action were presented by Heider (1958). Influential refinements and extensions of these basic ideas were made by Jones and Davis (1965) and Kelly (1967). Although attributional analyses were not quickly adopted by many social psychologists, they now seem to have a firm foothold in the discipline. Attributional analyses have, in fact, become commonplace in the discussion of many standard social psychological topics, including attitude change, social influence, and aggression. For the immediate future, it appears that attribution theory and research will occupy the time and efforts of many social psychologists. The cognitive orientation will remain dominant.

The cognitive emphasis is also reflected in the development of information processing models for analyzing social phenomena. Leventhal (1974a, 1974b) has recently proposed such models to aid the understanding and further exploration of both emotions and attitudes. Bandura (1972) has proposed an information processing account of observational learning. Information processing analyses are fundamentally concerned with cognitive-perceptual processes and are exceptionally popular in much of contemporary psychology. Given the penchant of social psychologists for cognitive analyses, it seems reasonable to expect that information processing models will continue to be used by social psychologists.

Interestingly enough, some of the most recent theorizing in social psychology has integrated behavioristic or S-R notions into models that are decidedly cognitive. For example, Leventhal (1974b) emphasized the importance of spontaneous and involuntary reactions to stimuli, bodily feedback, and distinctive internal bodily stimuli in his model of emotional development, expression, and behavior. A number of his ideas are compatible with those a more behavioristically inclined researcher would use. Similarly, Bandura (1972, 1974) still discusses the influence of classical and operant conditioning in social learning while increasingly emphasizing cognitive factors in his theory and research. Finally, Rule (1977) has recently offered some preliminary ideas on the integration of classical conditioning and attributional notions in the analysis of aggression.

It can only be hoped that social psychologists will continue to strive to integrate cognitive and behavioristic analyses rather than succumb to theoretical dogmatism. Because of the problems studied and the usual laboratory context for their study, social psychologists may tend to over-estimate the importance of thought for everyday social behavior (Thorn-gate, 1976). The human organism may always be cognitive in the sense that it interprets or gives meaning to environmental stimulation, but it is not at all clear that the organism is always cognitive in the sense that its behavior is thoughtful, planful, and voluntary. Future research and theory on the circumstances giving rise to habitual or thoughtful behavior would be a valuable contribution to the discipline. Related to this point is the need for future research which explores the operation of attributional processes as mediators of social behavior. Attribution researchers have amply demonstrated that people *can* make complicated inferences about others' intentions, degree of responsibility, and dispositions. We can wonder, however, to what extent complicated causal inferences are involved in the mediation of actual harmful or helpful behavior. Do the attributions follow the behavior to justify or rationalize it? Or does the behavior flow from the attributions? Under what circumstances does one or the other process occur? How complex are the attributional processes usually employed by ordinary people?

Methodologically, social psychology has shown some movement away from laboratory experiments to field research and naturalistic observational strategies. These changes have been stimulated in part by concerns about the generalizability or "ecological validity" of laboratory findings and the social relevance of social psychology. Some writers have been unimpressed by these efforts and are critical of the attempts (or lack of attempts) by social psychologists to change and improve in their theoretical and methodological approaches (e.g., Helmreich, 1975; McGuire, 1973). But researchers interested in social phenomena *are* becoming methodologically more diversified and theoretically more sophisticated. Work is being done to remedy the discipline's problems. Furthermore, widespread movement away from laboratory experimentation may be seriously misguided. Different methodologies have different strengths and weaknesses and serve different needs. Exclusive reliance on any methodology, including laboratory experimentation, is ill-advised. The use of multiple methods and multiple measures, on the other hand, is highly recommended and can only increase our confidence in research outcomes and inform us where further theory and research is needed.

There has been a so-called crisis of confidence in social psychology (Elms, 1975). The heyday of social psychology, characterized by confidence, direction, and activity, is supposedly past, and confusion, despair, and lack of direction now characterize the discipline. Research findings are, in fact, at times hard to replicate; obtaining any significant outcomes is increasingly difficult; funds for research are drying up; important social problems are not finding ready solutions. However, research isn't easy and the problems wanting solution aren't simple ones.

But genuine progress has been made, and the process of discovery itself can be very gratifying. Social psychological research can be its own reward. Viewed properly, the crisis becomes a challenge and an incentive for future work.

SUMMARY

Social psychology, the scientific study of social behavior, is concerned with individuals' reactions to the actual, imagined, or implied presence of other people or their symbols. Two basic theoretical orientations guide the research strategies and thinking of social psychologists—the behavioristic or S-R and the cognitive or phenomenological. Social psychologists who operate from the behavioristic orientation stress external stimulus and reinforcement control of behavior and prefer to analyze human social conduct in terms of basic learning notions. Cognitively inclined researchers emphasize internal processes and structures and the individuals' understanding of events and personal experiences. Mentalistic concepts such as cognition, perception, and expectancy are used to understand behavior. Important research has been conducted by investigators from both orientations, and the assumptions made about human nature by each are undoubtedly valid under different specific circumstances. The cognitive orientation has, however, been far more influential in guiding and stimulating social psychological research.

Social psychologists have expended an enormous amount of energy in the study of attitudes. These implicit, evaluative responses toward objects are viewed as important determinants of various behaviors. This view is reflected in the variety of attitude measurement techniques which have been developed. These techniques can be grouped into five general classes: (1) self-report; (2) behavioral; (3) projective; (4) objective task performance; and (5) physiological. Self-report procedures, especially Likert-like scales, are most commonly used. Each class of procedures has problems associated with its use, but with the probable exception of projective measures, these different measurement approaches can provide valid information about attitudes.

Research on the causes and control of aggression has occupied many social psychologists. Developing valid measures of behavior intended to injure another person or to damage an object has been one research problem for investigators interested in aggression. Various paper-and-pencil or self-report measurement strategies have been used in aggression research. Methods of measuring direct physical aggression in the laboratory have also been developed. Procedures involving a modification of the Buss teacher-learner paradigm are most common; the subject supposedly is given an opportunity to administer aversive stimuli to another person for performance errors. Machine-produced measures of physical aggression have been validated in several studies. Other external validity questions about laboratory research on aggression have been raised and partially addressed by later work.

Groups often exert pressure on their members to conform to their views and expectations. Asch (1952) presented a paradigm for exploring conformity or a change in behavior produced by group pressure. A single naive subject participated with a group of experimental accomplices who unanimously opposed the individual's judgments. A more efficient procedure for examining the same problems of conformity to and independence from group pressure was later introduced by Crutchfield (1955). Five or more naive subjects can participate in a single session in the Crutchfield paradigm. Minorities also influence the majority, and research on this process has also been undertaken recently.

All behavioral research with human subjects is susceptible to a number of general methodological problems. Demand characteristics and evaluation apprehension are two commonly discussed subject artifacts. The evidence for the several motives which subjects in psychological research have been presumed to have is insubstantial with the exception of wanting to present themselves in a favorable manner. The subjects' knowledge of the research hypothesis has been shown to produce biased outcomes even though the direction of the bias is inconsistent. The experimenter bias or expectancy artifact does not appear to be as pervasive a problem as was once thought. Nonetheless, enough evidence for the artifact exists to justify precautions aimed at minimizing or eliminating its possibility.

Deception is frequently used to enhance the internal validity of social psychological research. Because of the ethical and methodological problems associated with deception research, role-playing has been offered as an alternative methodology. Role-playing, however, is a totally inadequate substitute for actual behavior. Consequently, social psychologists will necessarily continue to employ experimental methods involving deception. These researchers must simultaneously make every effort to protect the rights and welfare of their human subjects and to be certain that the benefits of research clearly outweigh its costs.

The cognitive proclivity of social psychologists will most likely persist in the future. It is currently reflected in their attraction toward attributional and information processing analyses of behavior. Some recent models of social phenomena have incorporated behavioristic and cognitive notions. Further integration of the ideas from these two orientations seems highly valuable to the discipline. The so-called crisis of confidence in social psychology should goad further theoretical and methodological advancement, not despair and confusion.

QUESTIONS

1. What is the uniting concern of the various topics studied by social psychologists? Explain and illustrate the notions of imagined and implied presence.
2. Compare and contrast the S-R/behavioristic and the cognitive/phenomenological orientations to social psychology in terms of the assumptions they make about the nature of man. What methodological implications result from these different orientations?
3. What are the five basic ways in which attitudes are measured? What are the strengths and weaknesses of these general categories of attitude measurement techniques?
4. Describe the four commonly used self-report measures of attitudes. Explain the difference between a true Likert attitude scale and a Likert-like scale.
5. Define aggression. Explain and illustrate the major functions which aggression is claimed to serve. How would you determine if, in fact, aggression serves these different functions?
6. What is the difference between behavioral and behavioroid measures of attitudes?
7. Describe the difference between measures of hostility and verbal aggression.
8. Define internal and external validity. Is one kind of validity more important than the other? Why?
9. What are the basic features of the Buss and Taylor procedures for studying physical aggression? Does either procedure seem to be a better way of studying physical aggression? Why or why not?
10. Describe the Asch and Crutchfield conformity paradigms. What are the advantages and disadvantages of each? What kind of group pressure is studied in these paradigms?
11. Describe the subject artifacts of demand characteristics and evaluation apprehension. What is the evidence for these artifacts?
12. Why is deception commonly employed in experimental social psychology? In your opinion, can role-playing serve as an adequate substitute for actual experimentation?
13. What are the important differences between typical laboratory experiments and those involved in the study of experimenter bias effects? What steps can be taken to guard against experimenter bias?

References

Adair, J. G. *The Human Subject*. Boston: Little, Brown, 1973.

Agassi, J. Sensationalism. *Mind*, 1966, *75*, 1–24.

Allen, B. P. Social distance and admiration reactions of "unprejudiced" whites. *Journal of Personality*, 1975, *43*, 709–726.

Allen, V. L. Situational factors in conformity. In L. Berkowitz (Ed.), *Advances in experimental social psychology* (Vol. 2). New York: Academic Press, 1965.

Allen, V. L. Social support for nonconformity. In L. Berkowitz (Ed.), *Advances in experimental social psychology* (Vol. 8). New York: Academic Press, 1975.

Allport, G. W. Attitudes. In C. Murchison (Ed.), *A handbook of social psychology* (Vol. 2). Worcester, Mass.: Clark University Press, 1935.

Allport, G. W. The historical background of modern social psychology. In G. Lindzey & E. Aronson (Eds.), *The handbook of social psychology* (2nd ed.; Vol. 1). Reading, Mass.: Addison-Wesley, 1968.

American Psychological Association. *Publication Manual* (2nd ed.). Washington, D.C.: American Psychological Association, 1974.

Amsel, A. The role of frustrative nonreward in noncontinuous reward situations. *Psychological Bulletin*, 1958, *55*, 102–119.

Amsel, A. Frustrative nonreward in partial reinforcement and discrimination learning: Some recent history and a theoretical extension. *Psychological Review*, 1962, *69*, 306–328.

Amsel, A. Partial reinforcement effects on vigor and persistence: Advances in frustration theory derived from a variety of within-subjects experiments. In K. W. Spence & J. R. Spence (Eds.), *The psychology of learning and motivation: Advances in research and theory* (Vol. 1). New York: Academic Press, 1967.

Amsel, A. Behavioral habituation, counterconditioning, and a general theory of persistence. In A. H. Black & W. F. Prokasy (Eds.), *Classical conditioning II: Current research and theory*. New York: Appleton-Century-Crofts, 1972.

Anderson, D. C., Crowell, C., Koehn, D., & Lupo, J. V. Different intensities of unsignalled inescapable shock treatments as determinants of non-shock-motivated open field behavior: A resolution of disparate results. *Physiology and Behavior*, 1976, *17*, 391–394.

Anderson, D. C., Lupo, J. V., Cunningham, C., & Madden, J. Variations in pretreatments as determinants of shuttlebox behavior and pain-elicited aggression. Paper presented at Psychonomic Society Meeting, Boston, November 1974.

Anderson, D. C., Plant, C., Johnson, D., & Vandever, J. Second-order aversive classical conditioning. *Canadian Journal of Psychology*, 1967, *21*, 120–131.

Anderson, D. C., Plant, C., & Paden, P. Conditioned suppression of a running response as related to competing responses, drive, and basal skin resistance level. *Journal of Comparative and Physiological Psychology*, 1967, *63*, 282–287.

Anderson, N. H. Algebraic models in perception. In E. C. Carterette & M. P. Friedman (Eds.), *Handbook of perception. Vol. II, Psychophysical judgment and measurement*. New York: Academic Press, 1974.

Aronson, E., & Carlsmith, J. M. Experimentation in social psychology. In G. Lindzey & E. Aronson (Eds.), *The handbook of social psychology* (2nd ed.; Vol. 2). Reading, Mass.: Addison-Wesley, 1968.

Asch, S. E. *Social psychology*. Englewood Cliffs, N.J.: Prentice-Hall, 1952.

Asch, S. E. Studies of independence and conformity: I. A minority of one against a unanimous majority. *Psychological Monographs*, 1956, *70*(9, Whole No. 416).

Asch, S. E. The doctrinal tyranny of associationism: Or what is wrong with rote learning. In T. R. Dixon & D. L. Horton (Eds.), *Verbal behavior and general behavior theory*. Englewood Cliffs, N.J.: Prentice-Hall, 1968.

Asch, S. E., & Ebenholtz, S. M. The principle of associative symmetry. *Proceedings of the American Philosophical Society*, 1962, *106*, 135–163.

Atkinson, R. C. Mnemotechnics in second-language learning. *American Psychologist,* 1975, *30,* 821–828.

Atkinson, R. C., & Shiffrin, R. M. Human memory: A proposed system and its control processes. In K. W. Spence & J. T. Spence (Eds.), *The psychology of learning and motivation: Advances in research and theory* (Vol. 2). New York: Academic Press, 1968.

Attneave, F. Some informational aspects of visual perception. *Psychological Review,* 1954, *61,* 183–193.

Attneave, F. *Applications of information theory to psychology.* New York: Holt, 1959.

Azrin, N. H. Some effects of two intermittent schedules of immediate and non-immediate punishment. *Journal of Psychology,* 1956, *42,* 3–21.

Arzin, N. H. Effects of punishment intensity during variable-interval reinforcement. *Journal of the Experimental Analysis of Behavior,* 1960, *3,* 123–142.

Azrin, N. H., & Holz, W. C. Punishment. In W. E. Honig (Ed.), *Operant behavior: Areas of research and application.* New York: Appleton-Century-Crofts, 1966.

Badia, P., & Defran, R. H. Orienting responses and GSR conditioning: A dilemma. *Psychological Review,* 1970, *77,* 171–181.

Bahrick, H. P. Retention curves: Facts or artifacts. *Psychological Bulletin,* 1964, *61,* 188–194.

Bahrick, H. P. Relearning and the measurement of retention. *Verbal Learning and Verbal Behavior,* 1967, *6,* 84–89.

Bandura, A. Modeling theory: Some traditions, trends, and disputes. In R. D. Parke (Ed.), *Recent trends in social learning theory.* New York: Academic Press, 1972.

Bandura, A. *Aggression: A social learning analysis.* Englewood Cliffs, N.J.: Prentice-Hall, 1973.

Banks, W. P., & Prinzemetal, W. Configurational effects in visual information processing. *Perception and Psychophysics,* 1976, *19,* 361–367.

Barber, T. X., & Silver, M. J. Fact, fiction, and the experimenter bias effect. *Psychological Bulletin Monograph Supplement,* 1968, *70,* 1–29.

Barnes, J. M., & Underwood, B. J. "Fate" of first-list associations in transfer theory. *Journal of Experimental Psychology,* 1959, *58,* 97–105.

Baron, A., Kaufman, A., & Fazzini, D. Density and delay of punishment of free operant avoidance. *Journal of the Experimental Analysis of Behavior,* 1969, *12,* 1029–1037.

Baron, R. A. Aggression as a function of magnitude of victim's pain cues, level of prior anger arousal, and aggressor-victim similarity. *Journal of Personality and Social Psychology,* 1971, *18,* 48–54.

Baron, R. A. Aggression as a function of victim's pain cues, level of prior anger arousal, and exposure to an aggressive model. *Journal of Personality and Social Psychology,* 1974, *29,* 117–124.

Baron, R. A., & Eggleston, R. J. Performance on the "aggression machine": Motivation to help or harm? *Psychonomic Science,* 1972, *26,* 321–322.

Bartlett, F. C. *Remembering: A study in experimental and social psychology.* Cambridge, England: Cambridge University Press, 1932.

Battig, W. F. *Paired-associate learning.* Morristown, N.J.: General Learning, 1972.

Battig, W. F. Within-individual differences in "cognitive" processes. In R. L. Solso (Ed.), *Information processing and cognition.* Hillsdale, N.J.: Lawrence Erlbaum Associates, 1975.

Battig, W. F., Allen, M., & Jensen, A. R. Priority of free recall of newly learned items. *Journal of Verbal Learning and Verbal Behavior,* 1965, *4,* 175–179.

Battig, W. F., & Slaybaugh, G. D. Evidence that priority of free recall of newly learned items is not a recency artifact. *Journal of Verbal Learning and Verbal Behavior,* 1969, *8,* 556–558.

Baum, W. M. Choice is a continuous procedure. *Psychonomic Science,* 1972, *28,* 263–265.

Baum, W. M. Choice in free-ranging pigeons. *Science,* 1974, *185,* 78–79.

Beck, E. C., & Doty, R. W. Conditioned flexion reflexes acquired during combined catalepsy and de-efferentiation. *Journal of Comparative and Physiological Psychology,* 1957, *50,* 211–216.

Békésy, G. von. A new audiometer. *Acta Otolaryngology,* 1947, *35,* 411–422.

Belmont, J. M., & Butterfield, E. C. The instructional approach to developmental cognitive research. In R. Kail & J. Hagen (Eds.), *Perspectives on the development of memory and cognition.* Hillsdale, N.J.: Lawrence Erlbaum Associates, 1977.

Bem, D. J. Self-perception: An alternative interpretation of cognitive dissonance phenomena. *Psychological Review,* 1967, *74,* 183–200.

Bem, D. J. *Beliefs, attitudes, and human affairs.* Belmont, Cal.: Brooks/Cole, 1970.

Benedict, J. O., & Ayres, J. B. Factors affecting conditioning in the truly random control procedure in the rat. *Journal of Comparative and Physiological Psychology,* 1972, *78,* 323–330.

Berkowitz, L. Repeated frustrations and expectations in hostility arousal. *Journal of Abnormal and Social Psychology,* 1960, *60,* 422–429.

Berkowitz, L. *Aggression: A social psychological analysis.* New York: McGraw-Hill, 1962.

Berkowitz, L. Some aspects of observed aggression. *Journal of Personality and Social Psychology,* 1965, *2,* 359–369.

Berkowitz, L. The contagion of violence: An S-R mediational analysis of some effects of observed aggression. In W. J. Arnold & M. M. Page (Eds.), *Nebraska Symposium on Motivation* (Vol. 18). Lincoln: University of Nebraska Press, 1970.

Berkowitz, L. The "weapons effect," demand characteristics, and the myth of the compliant subject. *Journal of Personality and Social Psychology,* 1971, *20,* 332–338.

Berkowitz, L. *Social psychology.* Glenview, Ill.: Scott, Foresman, 1972.

Berkowitz, L. *A survey of social psychology.* Hinsdale, Ill.: Dryden Press, 1975.

Berkowitz, L., & Frodi, A. Stimulus characteristics that can enhance or decrease aggression: Associations with prior positive or negative reinforcements for aggression. *Aggressive Behavior,* 1977, *3,* 1–15.

Berkowitz, L., & Knurek, D. A. Label-mediated hostility generalization. *Journal of Personality and Social Psychology,* 1969, *13,* 200–206.

Berkowitz, L., & LePage, A. Weapons as aggression-eliciting stimuli. *Journal of Personality and Social Psychology,* 1967, *7,* 202–207.

Berkowitz, L., Parke, R. D., Leyens, J., & West, S. The effects of justified and unjustified movie violence on aggression in juvenile delinquents. *Journal of Research in Crime and Delinquency,* 1974, *11,* 16–24.

Berkowitz, L., & Rawlings, E. Effects of film violence on inhibitions against subsequent aggression. *Journal of Abnormal and Social Psychology,* 1963, *66,* 405–412.

Bevan, W. The sound of the wind that's blowing. *American Psychologist,* 1976, *31,* 481–491.

Bilbrey, J., & Winokur, S. Controls for and constraints on auto-shaping. *Journal of the Experimental Analysis of Behavior,* 1973, *20,* 323–332.

Black, A. H. Comments on "Learned helplessness: Theory and evidence" by Maier and Seligman. *Journal of Experimental Psychology: General,* 1977, *106,* 41–43.

Blodgett, H. C., & McCutchan, K. Relative strength of place and response learning in the T maze. *Journal of Comparative and Physiological Psychology,* 1948, *41,* 17–24.

Blommers, P., & Lindquist, E. F. *Elementary statistical methods in psychology and education.* Boston: Houghton Mifflin, 1960.

Bloomfield, T. M. Behavioral contrast and relative reinforcement frequency in two multiple schedules. *Journal of the Experimental Analysis of Behavior,* 1967, *10,* 151–158.

Blough, D., & Blough, P. Animal psychophysics. In W. K. Honig & J. E. R. Staddon (Eds.), *Handbook of operant behavior.* Englewood Cliffs, N.J.: Prentice-Hall, 1977.

Boe, E. E., & Church, R. M. Permanent effects of punishment during extinction. *Journal of Comparative and Physiological Psychology,* 1967, *63,* 486–492.

Boe, E. E., & Church, R. M. *Punishment: Issues and experiments.* New York: Appleton-Century-Crofts, 1968.

Bogardus, E. S. Measuring social distance. *Journal of Applied Sociology*, 1925, *9*, 299–308.

Bolles, R. C. *Learning theory*. New York: Holt, Rinehart and Winston, 1974.

Bolles, R. C., Stokes, L. W., & Younger, M. S. Does CS termination reinforce avoidance behavior? *Journal of Comparative and Physiological Psychology*, 1966, *63*, 201–207.

Bonneau, C. A. The interstimulus interval and the latency of the conditioned eyelid response. *Journal of Experimental Psychology*, 1958, *56*, 464–472.

Borden, R. J. Witnessed aggression: Influence of an observer's sex and values on aggressive responding. *Journal of Personality and Social Psychology*, 1975, *31*, 567–573.

Boring, E. G. *A history of experimental psychology* (2nd ed.). New York: Appleton-Century-Crofts, 1950.

Borkowski, J. G., Levers, S., & Gruenenfelder, T. M. Transfer of mediational strategies in children: The role of activity and awareness during strategy acquisition. *Child Development*, 1976, *47*, 779–786.

Borkowski, J. G., & Wanschura, P. B. Mediational processes in the retarded. In N. R. Ellis (Ed.), *International review of research in mental retardation* (Vol. 7). New York: Academic Press, 1974.

Bornstein, M. H., Kessen, W., & Weiskopf, S. The categories of hue in infancy. *Science*, 1976, *191*, 201–202.

Bourne, L. E., Ekstrand, B. R., & Dominowski, R. L. *The psychology of thinking*. Englewood Cliffs, N.J.: Prentice-Hall, 1971.

Bousfield, W. A. The occurrence of clustering in the recall of randomly arranged associates. *Journal of General Psychology*, 1953, *49*, 229–240.

Bower, G. H. Partial and correlated reward in escape learning. *Journal of Experimental Psychology*, 1960, *59*, 126–130.

Bower, G. H. Analysis of a mnemonic device. *American Scientist*, 1970, *58*, 496–510.

Bower, T. G. R. *Development in infancy*. San Francisco: Freeman, 1974.

Bracewell, R. J., & Black, A. H. The effects of restraint and noncontingent preshock on subsequent escape learning in the rat. *Learning and Motivation*, 1974, *5*, 53–69.

Brandeis, R., & Lubow, R. E. Conditioning without awareness—again. *Bulletin of the Psychonomic Society*, 1975, *5*, 36–38.

Bransford, J. D., Barclay, J. R., & Franks, J. J. Sentence memory: A constructive versus interpretive approach. *Cognitive Psychology*, 1972, *3*, 193–209.

Bransford, J. D., & McCarrell, N. S. A sketch of a cognitive approach to comprehension: Some thoughts about understanding what it means to comprehend. In W. B. Weimer & D. S. Palermo (Eds.), *Cognition and the symbolic processes*. Hillsdale, N.J.: Lawrence Erlbaum Associates, 1974.

Braun, H. W., & Geiselhart, R. Age differences in the acquisition and extinction of the conditioned eyelid response. *Journal of Experimental Psychology*, 1959, *57*, 386–388.

Bridgman, P. W. *The way things are*. Cambridge, Mass.: Harvard University Press, 1959.

Briggs, G. E. Acquisition, extinction, and recovery functions in retroactive inhibition. *Journal of Experimental Psychology*, 1954, *47*, 285–293.

Brigham, J. C., & Weissbach, T. A. (Eds.). *Racial attitudes in America: Analyses and findings of social psychology*. New York: Harper & Row, 1972.

Broadbeck, M. Logic and scientific method in research on teaching. In N. L. Gage (Ed.), *Handbook of research on teaching*. New York: Rand McNally, 1963.

Brody, N., & Oppenheim, P. Tensions in psychology between the methods of behaviorism and phenomenology. *Psychological Review*, 1966, *73*, 295–305.

Brown, A. L. The development of memory: Knowing, knowing about knowing, and knowing how to know. In H. W. Reese (Ed.), *Advances in child development and behavior* (Vol. 10). New York: Academic Press, 1975.

Brown, C. W., & Ghiselli, E. E. *Scientific methods in psychology*. New York: McGraw-Hill, 1955.

Brown, J. Some tests of the decay theory of immediate memory. *Quarterly Journal of Experimental Psychology*, 1958, *10*, 12–21.

Brown, J. S., & Farber, I. E. Secondary motivational systems. *Annual Review of Psychology,* 1968, *19,* 99–134.

Brown, J. S., & Jacobs, A. The role of fear in the motivation and acquisition of responses. *Journal of Experimental Psychology,* 1949, *39,* 747–759.

Brown, J. S., Martin, R. C., & Morrow, M. W. Self-punitive behavior in the rat: Facilitative effects of punishment on resistance to extinction. *Journal of Comparative and Physiological Psychology,* 1964, *57,* 127–133.

Brown, P. L., & Jenkins, H. M. Auto-shaping of the pigeon's key-peck. *Journal of the Experimental Analysis of Behavior,* 1968, *11,* 1–8.

Brown, R. *Social psychology.* New York: Free Press, 1965.

Brown, S. C., & Thompson, C. P. Relationship between item strength and order of free recall. *Journal of Verbal Learning and Verbal Behavior,* 1971, *10,* 444–448.

Brownstein, A. J. Concurrent schedules of response-independent reinforcement: Duration of a reinforcing stimulus. *Journal of the Experimental Analysis of Behavior,* 1971, *15,* 211–214.

Bruning, J. L., & Kintz, B. L. *Computational handbook of statistics.* Glenview, Ill.: Scott, Foresman, 1977.

Buckley, W. (Ed.). *Modern systems research for the behavioral scientist: A sourcebook.* Chicago: Aldine, 1968.

Buss, A. H. *The psychology of aggression.* New York: Wiley, 1961.

Buss, A. H. Physical aggression in relation to different frustrations. *Journal of Abnormal and Social Psychology,* 1963, *67,* 1–7.

Buss, A. H. Aggression pays. In J. L. Singer (Ed.), *The control of aggression and violence: Cognitive and physiological factors.* New York: Academic Press, 1971.

Buss, A. H., & Portnoy, N. W. Pain tolerance and group identification. *Journal of Personality and Social Psychology,* 1967, *6,* 106–108.

Butterfield, E. C., & Belmont, J. M. Assessing and improving the executive cognitive functions of mentally retarded people. In I. Bailer & M. Sternlicht (Eds.), *The psychology of mental retardation: Issues and approaches.* New York: Psychological Dimensions, 1977.

Butterfield, E. C., & Dickerson, D. J. Cognitive theory and mental development. In N. R. Ellis (Ed.), *International review of research in mental retardation* (Vol. 8). New York: Academic Press, 1976.

Calkins, M. W. Association. *Psychological Review,* 1894, *1,* 476–483.

Camp, D. S., Raymond, G. A., & Church, R. M. Temporal relationship between response and punishment. *Journal of Experimental Psychology,* 1967, *74,* 114–123.

Campbell, B. A., & Church, R. M. *Punishment and aversive behavior.* New York: Appleton-Century-Crofts, 1969.

Campbell, B. A., & Masterson, F. A. Psychophysics of punishment. In B. A. Campbell & R. M. Church (Eds.), *Punishment and aversive behavior.* New York: Appleton-Century-Crofts, 1969.

Campbell, B. A., & Teghtsoonian, R. Electrical and behavioral effects of different types of shock stimuli on the rat. *Journal of Comparative and Physiological Psychology,* 1958, *51,* 185–192.

Campbell, D. T. Prospective: Artifact and control. In R. Rosenthal & R. L. Rosnow (Eds.), *Artifact in behavioral research.* New York: Academic Press, 1969.

Campbell, D. T., & Stanley, J. C. *Experimental and quasi-experimental designs for research.* Chicago: Rand McNally, 1963.

Carlsmith, J. M., Ellsworth, P. C., & Aronson, E. *Methods of research in social psychology.* Reading, Mass.: Addison-Wesley, 1976.

Carlton, P. L., & Vogel, J. R. Habituation and conditioning. *Journal of Comparative and Physiological Psychology,* 1967, *63,* 348–351.

Catania, A. C. Concurrent performances: A baseline for the study of reinforcement magnitude. *Journal of the Experimental Analysis of Behavior,* 1963, *6,* 299–300. (a)

Catania, A. C. Concurrent performances: Reinforcement interaction and response independence. *Journal of the Experimental Analysis of Behavior,* 1963, *6,* 253–263. (b)

Catania, A. C. Concurrent operants. In W. K. Honig (Ed.), *Operant behavior: Areas of research and application.* New York: Appleton-Century-Crofts, 1966.

Catania, A. C., & Cutts, D. Experimental control of superstitious responding in humans. *Journal of the Experimental Analysis of Behavior, 1963, 6,* 203-208.

Cattell, J. McK. A statistical study of American men of science. *Science, 1906, 24,* 658-665, 699-707, 737-742.

Cattell, R. B. Are IQ tests intelligent? *Psychology Today,* March 1968, pp. 56-62.

Cattell, R. B., & Eber, H. W. *The sixteen personality factor questionnaire.* Champaign, Ill.: Institute for Personality and Ability Testing, 1962.

Chao, E. T. Auto-shaping in the fish. Paper presented at the meeting of the Southeastern Psychological Association, Atlanta, April 1972.

Cherry, F., Byrne, D., & Mitchell, H. E. Clogs in the bogus pipeline: Demand characteristics and social desirability. *Journal of Research in Personality, 1976, 10,* 69-75.

Chung, S. H., & Herrnstein, R. J. Choice and delay of reinforcement. *Journal of the Experimental Analysis of Behavior, 1967, 10,* 67-74.

Church, R. M. The varied effects of punishment on behavior. *Psychological Review, 1963, 70,* 369-402.

Church, R. M. Systematic effect of random error in the yoked control design. *Psychological Bulletin, 1964, 62,* 122-131.

Church, R. M., Raymond, G. A., & Beauchamp, R. D. Response suppression as a function of intensity and duration of a punishment. *Journal of Comparative and Physiological Psychology, 1967, 63,* 39-44.

Church, R. M., Wooton, C. L., & Matthews, T. J. Discriminative punishment and the conditional emotional response. *Learning and Motivation, 1970, 1,* 1-17.

Cicala, G. A., & Kremer, E. The effects of shock intensity and d-amphetamine on avoidance learning. *Psychonomic Science, 1969, 14,* 41-42.

Clayton, K. N. Reward and reinforcement in selective learning: Considerations with respect to a mathematical model of learning. In J. T. Tapp (Ed.), *Reinforcement and behavior.* New York: Academic Press, 1969.

Cochran, W. G., & Cox, G. M. *Experimental designs.* New York: Wiley, 1957.

Cody, W. J., & Borkowski, J. G. Release from proactive interference in the short-term memory of the retarded. *American Journal of Mental Deficiency, 1977, 82,* 305-308.

Cofer, C. N. *The structure of human memory.* San Francisco: Freeman, 1976.

Cohen, A., Anticaglia, J., & Jones, H. H. "Sociocusis"—Hearing loss from non-occupational noise exposure. *Sound and Vibration, 1970, 4,* 12-20.

Cohen, A. R. Social norms, arbitrariness of frustration, and status of the agent of frustration in the frustration-aggression hypothesis. *Journal of Abnormal and Social Psychology, 1955, 51,* 222-226.

Cohen, A. R. An experiment on small rewards for discrepant compliance and attitude change. In J. W. Brehm & A. R. Cohen, *Explorations in cognitive dissonance.* New York: Wiley, 1962.

Collier, G., & Marx, M. H. Changes in performance as a function of shifts in the magnitude of reinforcement. *Journal of Experimental Psychology, 1959, 57,* 305-309.

Cook, S. W., & Selltiz, C. A. A multiple-indicator approach to attitude measurement. *Psychological Bulletin, 1964, 62,* 36-55.

Coombs, C. H., Dawes, R. M., & Tversky, A. *Mathematical psychology: An elementary introduction.* Englewood Cliffs, N.J.: Prentice-Hall, 1970.

Cooper, J. Deception and role playing: On telling the good guys from the bad guys. *American Psychologist, 1976, 31,* 605-610.

Coppock, W. J. Pre-extinction in sensory preconditioning. *Journal of Experimental Psychology, 1958, 55,* 213-219.

Corso, J. F. *The experimental psychology of sensory behavior.* New York: Holt, Rinehart and Winston, 1967.

Cousins, L. S., Zamble, E., Tait, R. W., & Suboski, M. S. Sensory preconditioning in curarized rats. *Journal of Comparative Physiological Psychology, 1971, 77,* 152-154.

Craik, F. I. M. The fate of primary memory items in free recall. *Journal of Verbal Learning and Verbal Behavior,* 1970, *9,* 143–148. (a)

Craik, F. I. M. Primary memory. *British Medical Bulletin,* 1970, *27,* 232–236. (b)

Craik, F. I. M. A "levels of analysis" view of memory. In P. Pliner, L. Krames, & T. M. Alloway (Eds.), *Communication and affect: Language and thought.* New York: Academic Press, 1973.

Craik, F. I. M., & Lockhart, R. S. Levels of processing: A framework for memory research. *Journal of Verbal Learning and Verbal Behavior,* 1972, *11,* 671–684.

Craik, F. I. M., & Tulving, E. Depth of processing and the retention of words in episodic memory. *Journal of Experimental Psychology: General,* 1975, *1,* 268–294.

Crespi, L. P. Quantitative variation of incentive and performance in the white rat. *American Journal of Psychology,* 1942, *55,* 467–517.

Crime in the United States–1975. Washington, D.C.: U.S. Government Printing Office, 1976.

Cronbach, L. J. On the non-rational application of information measures in psychology. In H. Quastler (Ed.), *Information theory in psychology.* New York: Free Press, 1955.

Cross, D. V. Sequential dependencies and regression in psychophysical judgments. *Perception and Psychophysics,* 1973, *14,* 547–552.

Crowell, C. R. The role of shock-induced emotionality in the reinforcing effects of response-contingent shock-rate reduction. Unpublished doctoral dissertation, University of Iowa, 1973.

Crowell, C. R. Conditioned-aversive aspects of electric shock. *Learning and Motivation,* 1974, *5,* 209–220.

Crowell, C. R., & Anderson, D. C. Variations in intensity, interstimulus interval, and interval between preconditioning CS exposures and conditioning with rats. *Journal of Comparative and Physiological Psychology,* 1972, *79,* 291–298.

Crutchfield, R. S. Conformity and character. *American Psychologist,* 1955, *10,* 191–198.

D'Amato, M. R. Part II: Instrumental conditioning. In M. H. Marx (Ed.), *Learning: Processes.* New York: Macmillan, 1969.

D'Amato, M. R. *Experimental psychology: Methodology, psychophysics, and learning.* New York: McGraw-Hill, 1970.

Darley, J. M., & Latane, B. Bystander intervention in emergencies: Diffusion of responsibility. *Journal of Personality and Social Psychology,* 1968, *8,* 377–383.

Darwin, C. *On the origin of species.* London: Murray, 1859.

Dawson, M. E. Can classical conditioning occur without contingency learning? A review and an evaluation. *Psychophysiology,* 1973, *10,* 82–86.

Deese, J. *Psychology as science and art.* New York: Harcourt Brace Jovanovich, 1972.

DeFleur, M. L., & Westie, F. R. Verbal attitudes and overt acts: An experiment on the salience of attitudes. *American Sociological Review,* 1958, *23,* 667–673.

de Villiers, P. Choice in concurrent schedules and a quantitative formulation of the law of effect. In W. K. Honig & J. E. R. Staddon (Eds.), *Handbook of operant behavior.* Englewood Cliffs, N.J.: Prentice-Hall, 1977.

Dews, P. B. The effect of multiple S^{Δ} periods on responding on a fixed-interval schedule. *Journal of the Experimental Analysis of Behavior,* 1962, *5,* 369–374.

DiLollo, V., & Beez, V. Negative contrast effect as a function of magnitude of reward decrement. *Psychonomic Science,* 1966, *5,* 99–100.

Dobelle, W. H., Mladejovsky, M. G., Evans, J. R., Roberts, T. S., & Girvin, J. P. Braille reading by a blind volunteer by visual cortex stimulation. *Nature,* 1976, *259,* 111–112.

Dodd, D. H., & Schultz, R. F. Computational procedures for estimating magnitude of effect for some analysis of variance designs. *Psychological Bulletin,* 1973, *79,* 391–395.

Dollard, J., Doob, L. W., Miller, N. E., Mowrer, O. H., & Sears, R. R. *Frustration and aggression.* New Haven, Conn.: Yale University Press, 1939.

Donnerstein, E., & Donnerstein, M. Research in the control of interracial aggression. In R. G. Geen & E. C. O'Neal (Eds.), *Perspectives on aggression.* New York: Academic Press, 1976.

Doob, A. N., & Wood, L. E. Catharsis and aggression: Effects of annoyance and retaliation on aggressive behavior. *Journal of Personality and Social Psychology,* 1972, *22,* 156–162.

Doob, L. W., & Sears, R. R. Factors determining substitute behavior and the overt expression of aggression. *Journal of Abnormal and Social Psychology,* 1939, *34,* 293–313.

Dunham, P. J. Punishment: Method and theory. *Psychological Review,* 1971, *78,* 58–70.

Dunham, P. J., & Kilps, B. Shifts in magnitude of reinforcement: Confounded factors or contrast effects? *Journal of Experimental Psychology,* 1969, *79,* 373–374.

Dunnette, M. D. Fads, fashions, and folderol in psychology. *American Psychologist,* 1966, *21,* 343–352.

Ebbinghaus, H. *Uber das gedachtnis: Untersuchungen zur experimentallen psychologie.* Leipzig: Duncker and Humbolt, 1885.

Edwards, A. L. *Experimental design in psychological research.* New York: Holt, Rinehart and Winston, 1972.

Egan, J. P., & Clarke, F. R. Psychophysics and signal detection. In J. B. Sidowski (Ed.), *Experimental methods and instrumentation in psychology.* New York: McGraw-Hill, 1966.

Egan, J. P., Schulman, A. J., & Greenburg, G. Z. Operating characteristics determined by binary decisions and by ratings. *Journal of The Acoustical Society of America,* 1959, *31,* 768–773.

Egger, M. C., & Miller, N. E. Secondary reinforcement in rats as a function of information value and reliability of the stimulus. *Journal of Experimental Psychology,* 1962, *64,* 97–104.

Ehrenfreund, C., & Badia, P. R. Response strength as a function of drive level and pre- and post-shift incentive magnitude. *Journal of Experimental Psychology,* 1962, *63,* 468–471.

Eibl-Eibesfeldt, I. *Ethology: The biology of behavior* (2nd ed.). New York: Holt, Rinehart and Winston, 1975.

Einstein, A. *Relativity: The special and the general theory.* New York: Crown Publishers, 1961.

Ekstrand, B. R. A note on measuring response learning during paired-associate learning. *Journal of Verbal Learning and Verbal Behavior,* 1966, *5,* 344–347.

Ellenberger, H. F. *The discovery of the unconscious.* New York: Basic Books, 1970.

Ellison, G. D., & Konorski, J. Separation of the salivary and motor responses in instrumental conditioning. *Science,* 1964, *146,* 1071–1072.

Ellison, G. D., & Konorski, J. An investigation of the relations between salivary and motor responses during instrumental performance. *Acta Biologiae Experimentalis Sinica,* 1965, *25,* 297–315.

Elms, A. C. The crisis of confidence in social psychology. *American Psychologist,* 1975, *30,* 967–976.

Engen, T. Psychophysics: I. Discrimination and detection. In J. W. Kling & L. A. Riggs (Eds.), *Woodworth and Schlosberg's experimental psychology* (3rd ed.). New York: Holt, Rinehart and Winston, 1972. (a)

Engen, T. Psychophysics: II. Scaling methods. In J. W. Kling & L. A. Riggs (Eds.), *Woodworth and Schlosberg's experimental psychology* (3rd ed.). New York: Holt, Rinehart and Winston, 1972. (b)

Epstein, S., & Taylor, S. P. Instigation to aggression as a function of degree of defeat and perceived aggressive intent of the opponent. *Journal of Personality,* 1967, *35,* 265–289.

Estes, W. K. An experimental study of punishment. *Psychological Monographs,* 1944, *57*(3, Whole No. 263).

Estes, W. K. The statistical approach to learning theory. In S. Koch (Ed.), *Psychology: A study of a science* (Vol. 2). New York: McGraw-Hill, 1959.

Estes, W. K. Interactions of signal and background variables in visual processing. *Perception and Psychophysics,* 1972, *12,* 278–286.

Estes, W. K. Redundancy of noise elements and signals in the visual detection of letters. *Perception and Psychophysics,* 1974, *16,* 53–60.

Estes, W. K., & Skinner, B. F. Some quantitative properties of anxiety. *Journal of Experimental Psychology,* 1941, *29,* 390–400.

Farrar, B. K. Developmental effects of stimulus complexity on duration experience. Unpublished master's thesis, Stephen F. Austin State University, Nacogdoches, Texas, 1974.

Fechner, G. T. [*Elements of psychophysics*] (H. E. Adler, Trans.; D. H. Howes & E. G. Boring, Eds.). New York: Holt, Rinehart and Winston, 1966. (Originally published, 1860.)

Feldt, L. S. A comparison of the precision of three experimental designs employing a concomitant variable. *Psychometrika*, 1958, *23*, 335.

Felton, M., & Lyon, C. O. The post-reinforcement pause. *Journal of Experimental Analysis of Behavior*, 1966, *9*, 131–134.

Ferster, C. B., & Skinner, B. F. *Schedules of reinforcement*. New York: Appleton-Century-Crofts, 1957.

Festinger, L. A theory of social comparison processes. *Human Relations*, 1954, *7*, 117–140.

Festinger, L. *A theory of cognitive dissonance*. Stanford: Stanford University Press, 1957.

Festinger, L., & Carlsmith, J. M. Cognitive consequences of forced compliance. *Journal of Abnormal and Social Psychology*, 1959, *58*, 203–210.

Feyerabend, P. K. Problems of empiricism, Part II. In R. G. Colodmy (Ed.), *The nature and function of scientific theories: Essays in contemporary science and philosophy*. Pittsburgh: University of Pittsburgh Press, 1970.

Final Report of the National Commission on the Causes and Prevention of Violence. Washington, D.C.: U.S. Government Printing Office, 1969.

Flagg, S. F. Learning of the insoluble conditional reaction problem by rhesus monkeys. *Animal Learning and Behavior*, 1974, *2*, 181–184.

Flavell, J. H. Developmental studies of mediated memory. In H. W. Reese (Ed.), *Advances in child development and behavior* (Vol. 5). New York: Academic Press, 1970.

Flavell, J. H. First discussant's comments: What is memory development the development of? *Human Development*, 1971, *14*, 272–278.

Flavell, J. H., Friedrichs, A. G., & Hoyt, J. D. Developmental changes in memorization processes. *Cognitive Psychology*, 1970, *1*, 324–340.

Fodor, J. A., Garrett, M. F., & Brill, S. L. Pi ka pu: The perception of speech sounds by prelinguistic infants. *Perception and Psychophysics*, 1975, *18*, 74–78.

Forward, J., Canter, R., & Kirsch, N. Role-enactment and deception methodologies: Alternative paradigms? *American Psychologist*, 1976, *31*, 595–604.

Fowler, H., & Trapold, M. A. Escape performance as a function of delay of reinforcement. *Journal of Experimental Psychology*, 1962, *63*, 464–467.

Franchina, J. J. Intertrial intervals and shock schedules in escape training. *Journal of Comparative and Physiological Psychology*, 1969, *67*, 510–515.

Freedman, J. L. Role playing: Psychology by consensus. *Journal of Personality and Social Psychology*, 1969, *13*, 107–114.

Friedrich, L. K., & Stein, A. H. Aggressive and prosocial television programs and the natural behavior of preschool children. *Monographs of the Society for Research in Child Development*, 1973, *38*(4, Serial No. 151).

Galanter, E. Psychological decision mechanisms and perception. In E. C. Cartette & M. P. Friedman (Eds.), *Handbook of perception. Vol. II, Psychophysical judgment and measurement*. New York: Academic Press, 1974.

Galanter, E., & Holman, G. L. Some invariances of the isosensitivity function and their implication for the utility of money. *Journal of Experimental Psychology*, 1967, *73*, 333–339.

Gamzu, E., & Schwam, E. Autoshaping and automaintenance of a key-press response in squirrel monkeys. *Journal of the Experimental Analysis of Behavior*, 1974, *21*, 361–371.

Garner, W. R. *Uncertainty and structure as psychological concepts*. New York: Wiley, 1962.

Garner, W.R. Good patterns have few alternatives. *American Scientist*, 1970, *58*, 34–42.

Garner, W. R. *The processing of information and structure*. New York: Wiley, 1974.

Gescheider, G. A. *Psychophysics: Method and theory*. New York: Wiley, 1976.

Gibson, E. J. *Principles of perceptual learning and development*. New York: Appleton-Century-Crofts, 1967.

Glanzer, M., & Cunitz, A. R. Two storage mechanisms in free recall. *Journal of Verbal Learning and Verbal Behavior,* 1966, *5,* 351-360.

Goodrich, K. P. Performance in different segments of an instrumental response chain as a function of reinforcement schedule. *Journal of Experimental Psychology,* 1959, *57,* 57-63.

Goodrich, K. P. Running speed and drinking rate as functions of sucrose concentration and amount of consummatory activity. *Journal of Comparative and Physiological Psychology,* 1960, *53,* 245-250.

Gormezano, I., & Kehoe, J. Classical conditioning: Some methodological-conceptual issues. In W. K. Estes (Ed.), *Handbook of learning and cognitive processes, Vol. 2: Conditioning and behavior theory.* Hillsdale, N.J.: Lawrence Erlbaum Associates, 1975.

Gormezano, I., & Moore, J. W. Part III: Classical conditioning. In M. Marx (Ed.), *Learning: Processes.* New York: Macmillan, 1969.

Goulet, L. R. Verbal learning in children: Implications for developmental research. *Psychological Bulletin,* 1968, *69,* 359-376.

Grant, D. A., & Norris, E. B. Eyelid conditioning as influenced by the presence of sensitized Beta-responses. *Journal of Experimental Psychology,* 1947, *37,* 423-433.

Green, D. M., & Swets, J. A. *Signal detection theory and psychophysics.* New York: Wiley, 1966.

Greenberg, M. S. Role playing: An alternative to deception? *Journal of Personality and Social Psychology,* 1967, *7,* 152-157.

Greenwald, A. G., & Sakumura, J. S. Attitude and selective learning: Where are the phenomena of yesteryear? *Journal of Personality and Social Psychology,* 1967, *7,* 387-397.

Grice, G. R. An experimental study of the gradient of reinforcement to delayed reward in visual discrimination learning. *Journal of Experimental Psychology,* 1948, *38,* 1-16.

Grice, G. R. Dependence of empirical laws upon the source of experimental variation. *Psychological Bulletin,* 1966, *66,* 488-493.

Grice, G. R., & Hunter, J. J. Stimulus intensity effects depend upon the type of experimental design. *Psychological Review,* 1964, *71,* 247-256.

Grings, W. W., Dossett, W. F., & Honnard, R. R. Conditioned GSR in perceptual disparity situations. *American Psychologist,* 1959, *14,* 393.

Guilford, J. P. *Psychometric methods.* New York: McGraw-Hill, 1954.

Guthrie, E. R. *The psychology of learning.* New York: Harper, 1935.

Guttman, L. A basis for scaling qualitative data. *American Sociological Review,* 1944, *9,* 139-150.

Guttman, N. Operant conditioning, extinction, and periodic reinforcement in relation to concentration of sucrose used as reinforcing agent. *Journal of Experimental Psychology,* 1953, *46,* 213-224.

Handel, S., & Garner, W. R. The structure of visual pattern associates and pattern goodness. *Perception and psychophysics,* 1966, *1,* 33-38.

Harker, G. S. Delay of reward and performance of an instrumental response. *Journal of Experimental Psychology,* 1956, *51,* 303-310.

Harrison, A. A. Mere exposure. In L. Berkowitz (Ed.), *Advances in experimental social psychology* (Vol. 10). New York: Academic Press, 1977.

Hartmann, D. P. Influence of symbolically modeled instrumental aggression and pain cues on aggressive behavior. *Journal of Personality and Social Psychology,* 1969, *11,* 280-288.

Harvey, J. H., Ickes, W. J., & Kidd, R. F. (Eds.). *New directions in attribution research* (Vol. 1). Hillsdale, N.J.: Lawrence Erlbaum Associates, 1976.

Hays, W. L. *Statistics for the social sciences.* New York: Holt, Rinehart and Winston, 1973.

Hearst, E. The classical-instrumental distinction: Reflexes, voluntary behavior, and categories of associative learning. In W. K. Estes (Ed.), *Handbook of learning and cognitive processes, Vol. 2: Conditioning and behavior theory.* Hillsdale, N.J.: Lawrence Erlbaum Associates, 1975.

Heider, F. *The psychology of interpersonal relations.* New York: Wiley, 1958.

Helmreich, R. Applied social psychology: The unfulfilled promise. *Personality and Social Psychology Bulletin,* 1975, *1,* 548-560.

Hempel, C. G. Fundamentals of concept formation in empirical science. *International Encyclopedia of Unified Science,* 1952.

Hempel, C. G. *Philosophy of natural science.* Englewood Cliffs, N.J.: Prentice-Hall, 1966.

Henchy, T., & Glass, D. C. Evaluation apprehension and the social facilitation of dominant and subordinate responses. *Journal of Personality and Social Psychology,* 1968, *10,* 446–454.

Herendeen, D., & Anderson, D. C. Dual effects of a second-order conditioned stimulus: Excitation and inhibition. *Psychonomic Science,* 1968, *13,* 15–16.

Herrnstein, R. J. Relative and absolute strength of response as a function of frequency of reinforcement. *Journal of the Experimental Analysis of Behavior,* 1961, *4,* 267–272.

Herrnstein, R. J. Method and theory in the study of avoidance. *Psychological Review,* 1969, *76,* 49–69.

Herrnstein, R. J. On the law of effect. *Journal of the Experimental Analysis of Behavior,* 1970, *13,* 243–266.

Herrnstein, R. J., & Hineline, P. N. Negative reinforcement as shock-frequency reduction. *Journal of the Experimental Analysis of Behavior,* 1966, *9,* 421–430.

Hess, E. H. Attitude and pupil size. *Scientific American,* 1965, *212,* 46–54.

Hick, W. E. On the rate of gain of information. *Quarterly Journal of Experimental Psychology,* 1952, *4,* 11–26.

Hilgard, E. R., & Bower, G. H. *Theories of learning* (4th ed.). Englewood Cliffs, N.J.: Prentice-Hall, 1975.

Hill, C. W., & Thune, L. E. Place and response learning in the white rat under simplified and mutually isolated conditions. *Journal of Experimental Psychology,* 1952, *43,* 289–297.

Hill, W. F. *Learning: A survey of psychological interpretations.* San Francisco: Chandler, 1963.

Hochberg, J., & Brooks, V. The psychophysics of form: Reversible-perspective drawings of spatial objects. *American Journal of Psychology,* 1960, *73,* 337–354.

Hochberg, J., & McAlister, E. A quantitative approach to figural "goodness." *Journal of Experimental Psychology,* 1953, *46,* 361–364.

Hochberg, J., & Silverstein, A. A quantitative index of stimulus similarity: Proximity vs. differences in brightness. *American Journal of Psychology,* 1956, *69,* 456–459.

Hoffman, H. S. Stimulus factors in conditioned suppression. In B. A. Campbell & R. M. Church (Eds.), *Punishment and aversive behavior.* New York: Appleton-Century-Crofts, 1969.

Holland, P. C., & Rescorla, R. A. Second-order conditioning with food unconditioned stimulus. *Journal of Comparative and Physiological Psychology,* 1975, *88,* 459–467.

Hollander, E. P. Conformity, status and idiosyncrasy credit. *Psychological Review,* 1958, *65,* 117–127.

Honig, W. K. *Operant behavior: Areas of research and application.* New York: Appleton-Century-Crofts, 1966.

Horowitz, I. A., & Rothschild, B. H. Conformity as a function of deception and role playing. *Journal of Personality and Social Psychology,* 1970, *14,* 224–226.

Horton, D. L., & Kjeldergaard, P. M. An experimental analysis of associative factors in mediated generalization. *Psychological Monographs,* 1961, *75*(11, Whole No. 515).

Hovland, C. I., & Sherif, M. Judgmental phenomena and scales of measurement: Item displacement in Thurstone scales. *Journal of Abnormal and Social Psychology,* 1952, *47,* 822–832.

Howitt, D., & Cumberbatch, G. *Mass media violence and society.* New York: Wiley, 1975.

Hughes, L. F., Dunlap, W. P., & Dachowski, L. Reward magnitude and partial reinforcement effects in a single runway. *Journal of Comparative and Physiological Psychology,* 1974, *87,* 563–570.

Hull, C. L. *Principles of behavior.* New York: Appleton-Century-Crofts, 1943.

Hull, C. L. *A behavior system.* New Haven: Yale University Press, 1952.

Hume, D. *A treatise on human nature*. London, 1739.

Hunt, E. Selection and reception conditions in grammar and concept learning. *Journal of Verbal Learning and Verbal Behavior*, 1965, *4*, 211–215.

The importance of being Ernest. *Notre Dame Magazine*, 1972, *1*(2), 41–45.

Janis, I. L. *Psychological stress: Psychoanalytic and behavioral studies of surgical patients*. New York: Wiley, 1958.

Janis, I. L. Group identification under conditions of external danger. In D. Cartwright & A. Zander (Eds.), *Group dynamics: Research and theory* (3rd ed.). New York: Harper & Row, 1968.

Jenkins, H. M., & Moore, B. R. The form of the auto-shaped response with food or water reinforcers. *Journal of the Experimental Analysis of Behavior*, 1973, *20*, 163–181.

Jenkins, J. J. Stimulus "fractionation" in paired-associate learning. *Psychological Reports*, 1963, *13*, 409–410.

Jenkins, J. J., Mink, W. D., & Russell, W. A. Association strength. *Psychological Reports*, 1958, *4*, 127–136.

Jensen, A. R. The role of verbal mediation in mental development. *Journal of Genetic Psychology*, 1971, *118*, 39–70.

Jensen, A. R., & Rohwer, W. D. Verbal mediation in paired-associate and serial learning. *Journal of Verbal Learning and Verbal Behavior*, 1963, *1*, 346–352.

Jesteadt, W., Luce, R. D., & Green, D. M. Sequential effects in judgments of loudness. *Journal of Experimental Psychology, Human Perception and Performance*, 1977, *3*, 92–104.

Johnson, D., & Anderson, D. C. Acquisition of a second-order classically conditioned response. *Canadian Journal of Psychology*, 1969, *23*, 174–183.

Johnston, A., DeLuca, D., Murtaugh, K., & Diener, E. Validation of a laboratory play measure of child aggression. *Child Development*, 1977, *48*, 324–327.

Jones, E. E., Bell, L., & Aronson, E. The reciprocation of attraction from similar and dissimilar others. In C. McClintock (Ed.), *Experimental social psychology*. New York: Holt, Rinehart and Winston, 1972.

Jones, E. E., & Davis, K. From acts to dispositions: The attribution process in person perception. In L. Berkowitz (Ed.), *Advances in experimental social psychology* (Vol. 2). New York: Academic Press, 1965.

Jones, E. E., & Sigall, H. The bogus pipeline: A new paradigm for measuring affect and attitude. *Psychological Bulletin*, 1971, *76*, 349–364.

Jones, S. H., & Cook, S. W. The influence of attitude on judgments of the effectiveness of alternative social policies. *Journal of Personality and Social Psychology*, 1975, *32*, 767–773.

Jung, J. *Verbal learning*. New York: Holt, Rinehart and Winston, 1968.

Kamin, L. J. The effects of termination of the CS and avoidance of the US on avoidance learning. *Journal of Comparative and Physiological Psychology*, 1956, *49*, 420–424.

Kamin, L. J. "Attention-like" processes in classical conditioning. In M. R. Jones (Ed.), *Miami Symposium on the Prediction of Behavior: Aversive Stimulation*. Miami: University of Miami Press, 1968.

Kamin, L. J. Predictability, surprise, attention and conditioning. In B. A. Campbell & R. M. Church (Eds.), *Punishment and aversive behavior*. New York: Appleton-Century-Crofts, 1969.

Kanak, N. J., & Neuner, S. D. Associative symmetry and item availability as a function of five methods of paired-associate acquisition. *Journal of Experimental Psychology*, 1970, *86*, 288–295.

Kanizsa, G. Subjective contours. *Scientific American*, 1976, *234*, 48–52.

Karmel, B. Z., Hoffman, R. F., & Fegy, M. J. Processing of contour information by human infants evidenced by pattern-dependent evoked potentials. *Child Development*, 1974, *45*, 39–48.

Kaufman, H. Definitions and methodology in the study of aggression. *Psychological Bulletin*, 1965, *64*, 351–364.

Kausler, D. H. *Psychology of verbal learning and memory*. New York: Academic Press, 1974.

Keele, S. W. *Attention and human performance.* Pacific Palisades, Cal.: Goodyear, 1973.

Keesey, R. E. The relation between pulse frequency, intensity, and duration and the rate of responding for intracranial stimulation. *Journal of Comparative and Physiological Psychology, 1962, 55,* 671–678.

Keesey, R. E. Duration of stimulation and the reward properties of hypothalamic stimulation. *Journal of Comparative and Physiological Psychology, 1964, 58,* 210–217.

Kellas, G., & Butterfield, E. C. Response familiarization and the paired-associate performance of non-institutionalized retarded and normal children. *American Journal of Mental Deficiency, 1970, 75,* 81–87.

Kelley, H. H. Attribution in social psychology. In D. Levine (Ed.), *Nebraska Symposium on Motivation* (Vol. 15). Lincoln: University of Nebraska Press, 1967.

Kelman, H. C. Human use of human subjects: The problem of deception in social psychological experiments. *Psychological Bulletin, 1967, 67,* 1–11.

Kennedy, B. A., & Miller, D. Persistent use of verbal rehearsal as a function of information about its value. *Child Development, 1976, 47,* 566–569.

Keppel, G., & Underwood, B. J. Proactive inhibition in short-term retention of single items. *Journal of Verbal Learning and Verbal Behavior, 1962, 1,* 153–161.

Kimble, G. A. (Ed.). *Hilgard and Marquis' conditioning and learning* (2nd ed.). New York: Appleton-Century-Crofts, 1961.

Kimble, G. A. The definition of learning and some useful distinctions. In G. A. Kimble (Ed.), *Foundations of conditioning and learning.* New York: Appleton-Century-Crofts, 1967.

Kintsch, W. *Learning, memory, and conceptual processes.* New York: Wiley, 1970.

Klapper, J. T. The impact of viewing "aggression": Studies and problems of extrapolation. In O. N. Larsen (Ed.), *Violence and the mass media.* New York: Harper & Row, 1968.

Kling, J. W., & Schrier, A. M. Positive reinforcement. In J. W. Kling & L. A. Riggs (Eds.), *Woodworth & Schlosberg's Experimental Psychology* (3rd ed.). New York: Holt, Rinehart and Winston, 1971.

Koehn, D. J., Anderson, D. C., Brown, J. S., & Crowell, C. Reconceptualization and extension of a unifactor account of avoidance learning. Paper presented at the 53rd Annual Western Psychological Association, Anaheim, Cal., April 1973.

Koffka, K. *The Principles of Gestalt psychology.* New York: Harcourt, Brace, and World, 1935.

Kohler, W. *Gestalt psychology.* New York: New American Library of World Literature, 1947.

Kohler, W. *The task of Gestalt psychology.* Princeton, N. J.: Princeton University Press, 1969.

Kolers, P. A. Some differences between real and apparent visual movement. *Vision Research, 1963, 3,* 191–206.

Kolers, P. A. The illusion of movement. *Scientific American, 1964, 211,* 98–105.

Konečni, V. J. Annoyance, type and duration of postannoyance activity, and aggression: The "cathartic" effect. *Journal of Experimental Psychology: General, 1975, 104,* 76–102.

Konečni, V. J., & Doob, A. N. Catharsis through displacement of aggression. *Journal of Personality and Social Psychology, 1972, 23,* 379–387.

Konečni, V. J., & Ebbesen, E. B. Disinhibition versus the cathartic effect: Artifact and substance. *Journal of Personality and Social Psychology, 1976, 34,* 352–365.

Kraeling, D. Analysis of amount of reward as a variable in learning. *Journal of Comparative and Physiological Psychology, 1961, 54,* 560–565.

Krech, D., Crutchfield, R. S., & Ballachey, E. L. *Individual in society: A textbook of social psychology.* New York: McGraw-Hill, 1962.

Kremer, E. F. Truly random and traditional control procedures in CER conditioning in the rat. *Journal of Comparative and Physiological Psychology, 1971, 76,* 441–448.

Kremer, E. F., & Kamin, L. J. The truly random control procedure: Associative or nonassociative effects in rats. *Journal of Comparative and Physiological Psychology, 1971, 74,* 203–210.

Kruglanski, A. W. The human subject in the psychology experiment: Fact and artifact. In L. Berkowitz (Ed.), *Advances in experimental social psychology* (Vol. 8). New York: Academic Press, 1975.

Kryter, K. D., Ward, W. D., Miller, J. D., & Eldredge, D. H. Hazardous exposure to intermittent and steady-state noise. *Journal of the Acoustical Society of America,* 1966, *39,* 451–464.

Kuch, D. O., & Platt, J. R. Reinforcement rate and interresponse time differentiation. *Journal of the Experimental Analysis of Behavior,* 1976, *26,* 471–486.

Kuhn, T. S. *The structure of scientific revolutions* (2nd ed.). Chicago: University of Chicago Press, 1970.

Kurtz, P. S., & Shafer, J. N. The interaction of UCS intensity and intertrial interval in avoidance learning. *Psychonomic Science,* 1967, *8,* 465–466.

Lachman, R., Butterfield, E. C., & Mistler-Lachman, J. *Cognitive psychology and information processing: An introduction.* Hillsdale, N.J.: Lawrence Erlbaum Associates, in press.

Lane, H. Control of vocal responding in chickens. *Science,* 1960, *132,* 37–38.

Laties, V. G., Weiss, B., Clark, R. L., & Reynolds, M. D. Overt "mediating" behavior during temporally spaced responding. *Journal of the Experimental Analysis of Behavior,* 1965, *8,* 107–116.

Laties, V. G., Weiss, B., & Weiss, A. B. Further observations on overt "mediating" behavior and the discrimination of time. *Journal of the Experimental Analysis of Behavior,* 1969, *12,* 43–57.

Lawry, J., Lupo, J. V., Kochevar, J., Hollis, K., Anderson, D. C., & Overmier, J. B. Interference with avoidance behavior is a function of qualitative properties of inescapable shocks but independent of species. *Animal Learning and Behavior,* in press.

Lett, B. T. Delayed reward learning: Disproof of the traditional theory. *Learning and Motivation,* 1973, *3,* 237–246.

Lett, B. T. Visual discrimination learning with a 1-min. delay of reward. *Learning and Motivation,* 1974, *5,* 174–181.

Leventhal, H. Attitudes: Their nature, growth, and change. In C. Nemeth (Ed.), *Social psychology: Classic and contemporary integrations.* Chicago: Rand McNally, 1974. (a)

Leventhal, H. Emotions: A basic problem for social psychology. In C. Nemeth (Ed.), *Social psychology: Classic and contemporary integrations.* Chicago: Rand McNally, 1974. (b)

Levine, J. M., & Murphy, G. The learning and forgetting of controversial material. *Journal of Abnormal and Social Psychology,* 1943, *38,* 507–517.

Levine, S. UCS intensity and avoidance learning. *Journal of Experimental Psychology,* 1966, *71,* 163–164.

Levis, D. J. Learned helplessness: A reply and an alternative S-R interpretation. *Journal of Experimental Pscyhology: General,* 1976, *105,* 47–65.

Liebert, R. M., Neale, J. M., & Davidson, E. S. *The early window: Effects of television on children and youth.* New York: Pergamon, 1973.

Likert, R. A technique for the measurement of attitudes. *Archives of Psychology,* 1932, No. 140.

Lindquist, E. F. *Design and analysis of experiments in psychology and education.* Boston: Houghton Mifflin, 1953.

Linker, E., Moore, M. E., & Galanter, E. Taste thresholds, detection models, and disparate results. *Journal of Experimental Psychology,* 1964, *67,* 59–66.

Lockhart, R. A. Dominance and contiguity as interactive determinants of GSR discrimination conditioning. Paper read at the meeting of the Psychonomic Society, Chicago, October 1965.

Loess, H. Short-term memory, word class and sequence of items. *Journal of Experimental Psychology,* 1967, *74,* 556–561.

Loess, H., & Waugh, N. C. Short-term memory and intertrial interval. *Journal of Verbal Learning and Verbal Behavior,* 1967, *6,* 455–460.

Loew, C. A. Acquisition of a hostile attitude and its relationship to aggressive behavior. *Journal of Personality and Social Psychology,* 1967, *5,* 335–341.

Logan, F. A. *Incentive: How the conditions of reinforcement affect the performance of rats.* New Haven: Yale University Press, 1960.

Logan, F. A. *Fundamentals of learning and motivation.* Dubuque, Iowa: William C. Brown, 1970.

Logan, F. A., Beier, E. M., & Ellis, R. A. Effect of varied reinforcement on speed of locomotion. *Journal of Experimental Psychology, 1955, 49,* 260–266.

Logan, F. A., & Spanier, D. Relative effect of delay of food and water reward. *Journal of Comparative and Physiological Psychology, 1970, 72,* 102–104.

Lubow, R. E. Latent inhibition. *Psychological Bulletin, 1973, 79,* 398–407.

Lubow, R. E., & Moore, A. U. Latent inhibition: The effect of non-reinforced pre-exposure to the conditional stimulus. *Journal of Comparative and Physiological Psychology, 1959, 52,* 416–419.

Luce, R. D., & Green, D. M. Detection, discrimination, and recognition. In E. C. Carterette & M. P. Friedman (Eds.), *Handbook of perception. Vol. II, Psychophysical judgment and measurement.* New York: Academic Press, 1974.

Luh, C. W. The conditions of retention. *Psychological Monographs, 1922, 31*(3, Whole No. 142).

Mackintosh, N. J. *The psychology of animal learning.* New York: Academic Press, 1974.

Mackintosh, N. J. A theory of attention: Variations in the associability of stimuli with reinforcement. *Psychological Review, 1975, 82,* 276–298.

Mackintosh, N. J. Stimulus control: Attentional factors. In W. K. Honig & J. E. R. Staddon (Eds.), *Handbook of operant behavior.* Englewood Cliffs, N.J.: Prentice-Hall, 1977.

MacMillan, D. L. Facilitative effect of verbal mediation on paired-associate learning by EMR children. *American Journal of Mental Deficiency, 1970, 74,* 611–615.

Madden, E. H. The philosophy of science in Gestalt theory. *Philsophy of Science, 1952, 19,* 228–239.

Maier, S. F., & Seligman, M. E. P. Learned helplessness: Theory and evidence. *Journal of Experimental Psychology: General, 1976, 105,* 3–46.

Maier, S. F., Seligman, M. E. P., & Solomon, R. L. Pavlovian fear conditioning and learned helplessness. In B. S. Campbell & R. M. Church (Eds.), *Punishment.* New York: Appleton-Century-Crofts, 1969.

Martin, E. Transfer of verbal paired associates. *Psychological Review, 1965, 72,* 327–343.

Martin, E. Relation between stimulus recognition and paired-associate learning. *Journal of Experimental Psychology, 1967, 74,* 500–505.

Marx, M. H. (Ed.). *Theories in contemporary psychology.* New York: Macmillan, 1963.

Marx, M. H. Learning Processes. In M. H. Marx (Ed.), *Learning: Processes.* London: Macmillan, 1969.

Marx, M. H., & Hillix, W. A. *Systems and theories in psychology* (2nd ed.). New York: McGraw-Hill, 1973.

McAllister, D. E., & McAllister, W. R. Second-order conditioning of fear. *Psychonomic Science, 1964, 1,* 383–384.

McAllister, W. R., & McAllister, D. E. Variables influencing the conditioning and the measurement of acquired fear. In W. F. Prokasy (Ed.), *Classical conditioning: A symposium.* New York: Appleton-Century-Crofts, 1965.

McAllister, W. R., & McAllister, D. E. The inverse relationship between shock intensity and shuttlebox avoidance learning in rats. *Journal of Comparative and Physiological Psychology, 1971, 74,* 426–433.

McGeoch, J. A., & Irion, A. L. *The psychology of human learning.* New York: David McKay, 1952.

McGuire, W. J. The yin and yang of progress in social psychology: Seven koan. *Journal of Personality and Social Psychology, 1973, 26,* 446–456.

McHose, J. H., Jacoby, L., & Meyer, P. A. Extinction as a function of number of reinfoced trials and squad composition. *Psychonomic Science, 1967, 9,* 401–402.

McHose, J. H., & Ludvigson, H. Role of reward magnitude and incomplete reduction of reward magnitude in the frustration effect. *Journal of Experimental Psychology, 1965, 70,* 490–495.

McNamara, H. J., Long, J. B., & Wike, E. L. Learning without response under two conditions of external cues. *Journal of Comparative and Physiological Psychology,* 1956, *49,* 477–480.

McNemar, Q. *Psychological statistics* (3rd ed.). New York: Wiley, 1962.

Melton, A. W. Implications of short-term memory for a general theory of memory. *Journal of Verbal Learning and Verbal Behavior,* 1963, *2,* 1–21.

Milgram, S. *Obedience to authority: An experimental view.* New York: Harper & Row, 1974.

Miller, A. G. Role playing: An alternative to deception? A review of the evidence. *American Psychologist,* 1972, *27,* 623–636. (a)

Miller, A. G. (Ed.). *The social psychology of psychological research.* New York: Free Press, 1972. (b)

Miller, G. A. The magic number seven, plus or minus two: Some limits on our capacity for processing information. *Psychological Review,* 1956, *63,* 81–97.

Miller, G. A. *Psychology: The science of mental life.* New York: Harper & Row, 1962.

Miller, G. A. What is information measurement? *American Psychologist,* 1963, *8,* 3–11.

Miller, G. A. Psychology as a means of promoting human welfare. *American Psychologist,* 1969, *24,* 1063–1075.

Miller, G. A. & Buckhout, R. *Psychology: The science of mental life* (2nd ed.). New York: Harper & Row, 1973.

Miller, N. E. Studies of fear as an acquirable drive. *Journal of Experimental Psychology,* 1948, *38,* 89–101.

Miller, N. E. Liberalization of basic S-R concepts: Extensions to conflict behavior, motivation, and social learning. In S. Koch (Ed.), *Psychology: A study of a science* (Vol. 2). New York: McGraw-Hill, 1959.

Miller, N. E. Learning of visceral and glandular responses. *Science,* 1969, *163,* 434–445.

Miller, N. E. Autonomic learning: Clinical and physiological implications. In M. Hammer, K. Salzinger, & S. Sutton (Eds.), *Psychopathology: Contributions from the social, behavioral, and biological sciences.* New York: Wiley, 1973.

Mintz, D. E. Force of response during ratio reinforcement. *Science,* 1962, *138,* 516–517.

Møller, A. R. Noise as a health hazard. *Ambio,* 1975, *4,* 6–13.

Moltz, H. Contemporary instinct theory and the fixed action pattern. *Psychological Review,* 1965, *72,* 27–47.

Morse, W. H. Intermittent reinforcement. In W. K. Honig (Ed.), *Operant behavior: Areas of research and application.* New York: Appleton-Century-Crofts, 1966.

Moscovici, S., & Faucheux, C. Social influence, conformity bias, and the study of active minorities. In L. Berkowitz (Ed.), *Advances in experimental social psychology* (Vol. 6). New York: Academic Press, 1972.

Moscovici, S., Lage, E., & Naffrechoux, M. Influence of a consistent minority on the responses of a majority in a color perception task. *Sociometry,* 1969, *32,* 365–379.

Moscovici, S., & Nemeth, C. Social influence II: Minority influence. In C. Nemeth (Ed.), *Social psychology: Classic and contemporary integrations.* Chicago: Rand McNally, 1974.

Moscovitch, A., & LoLordo, V. H. Role of safety in the Pavlovian backward fear conditioning procedure. *Journal of Comparative and Physiological Psychology,* 1968, *66,* 673–678.

Mosher, D. L., Mortimer, R. L., & Grebel, M. Verbal aggressive behavior in delinquent boys. *Journal of Abnormal Psychology,* 1968, *73,* 454–460.

Mostofsky, D. I. *Stimulus generalization.* Stanford, Cal.: Stanford University Press, 1965.

Mowrer, O. H. On the dual nature of learning—A reinterpretation of "conditioning" and "problem-solving." *Harvard Educational Review,* 1947, *17,* 102–148.

Mowrer, O. H. *Learning theory and behavior.* New York: Wiley, 1960.

Moyer, K. E., & Korn, J. H. Effect of UCS intensity on the acquisition and extinction of avoidance response. *Journal of Experimental Psychology,* 1964, *67,* 352–359.

Mueller, J. H. Response properties of the position indicant in serial learning. *Journal of Experimental Psychology*, 1970, *84*, 35-39.

Murch, G. M. *Visual and auditory perception*. Indianapolis: Bobbs-Merrill, 1973.

Murdock, B. B. The retention of individual items. *Journal of Experimental Psychology*, 1961, *62*, 618-625.

Murdock, B. B. The serial position effect of free recall. *Journal of Experimental Psychology*, 1962, *64*, 482-488.

Murdock, B. B. Serial order effects in short-term memory. *Journal of Experimental Psychology*, 1968, *76*, 1-15.

Myers, A. K. Instrumental escape conditioning to a low-intensity noise by rats. *Journal of Comparative and Physiological Psychology*, 1965, *60*, 82-87.

Natsoulas, T. Concerning introspective "knowledge." *Psychological Bulletin*, 1970, *73*, 89-111.

Neimark, E. D. The natural history of spontaneous mnemonic activities under conditions of minimal experimental constraint. In A. D. Pick (Ed.), *Minnesota Symposia on Child Psychology* (Vol. 10). Minneapolis: University of Minnesota Press, 1976.

Neisser, U. *Cognitive Psychology*. New York: Appleton-Century-Crofts, 1967.

Neisser, U. *Cognition and reality*. San Francisco: Freeman, 1976.

Nevin, J. A. Differential reinforcement and stimulus control of not responding. *Journal of the Experimental Analysis of Behavior*, 1968, *11*, 715-726.

Nevin, J. A. The maintenance of behavior. In J. A. Nevin & G. S. Reynolds (Eds.), *The study of behavior: Learning, motivation, emotion, and instinct*. Glenview, Ill.: Scott, Foresman, 1973. (a)

Nevin, J. A. Stimulus control. In J. A. Nevin & G. S. Reynolds (Eds.), *The study of behavior: Learning, motivation, emotion, and instinct*. Glenview, Ill.: Scott, Foresman, 1973. (b)

Newell, A. You can't play 20 questions with nature and win: Projective comments on the papers of this symposium. In W. Chase (Ed.), *Visual information processing*. New York: Academic Press, 1973.

Norman, D. A. Toward a theory of memory and attention. *Psychological Review*, 1968, *75*, 522-536.

Orne, M. T. On the social psychology of the psychological experiment: With particular reference to demand characteristics and their implications. *American Psychologist*, 1962, *17*, 776-783.

Orne, M. T. Demand characteristics and the concept of quasi-controls. In R. Rosenthal & R. L. Rosnow (Eds.), *Artifact in behavioral research*. New York: Academic Press, 1969.

Ornstein, R. E. *On the experience of time*. Harmondsworth, Middlesex, England: Penguin Books, 1969.

Osgood, C. E. The nature and measurement of meaning. *Psychological Bulletin*, 1952, *49*, 197-237.

Osgood, C. E., Suci, G. J., & Tannenbaum, P. H. *The measurement of meaning*. Urbana: University of Illinois Press, 1957.

Oskamp, S. *Attitudes and opinions*. Englewood Cliffs, N. J.: Prentice-Hall, 1977.

Ostrom, T. M. The bogus pipeline: A new *ignis factuus*. *Psychological Bulletin*, 1973, *79*, 252-259.

Page, M. M. Social psychology of a classical conditioning of attitudes experiment. *Journal of Personality and Social Psychology*, 1969, *11*, 177-186.

Page, M. M., & Scheidt, R. J. The elusive weapons effect: Demand awareness, evaluation apprehension, and slightly sophisticated subjects. *Journal of Personality and Social Psychology*, 1971, *20*, 304-318.

Paivio, A. Mental imagery in associative learning and memory. *Psychological Review*, 1969, *76*, 241-263.

Palermo, D. S., & Jenkins, J. J. *Word association norms*. Minneapolis: University of Minnesota Press, 1964.

Parke, R. D., Berkowitz, L., Leyens, J. P., West, S. G., & Sebastian, R. J. Some effects of violent and nonviolent movies on the behavior of juvenile delinquents. In L. Berkowitz (Ed.), *Advances in experimental social psychology* (Vol. 10). New York: Academic Press, 1977.

Parke, R. D., Ewall, W., & Slaby, R. G. Hostile and helpful verbalizations as regulators of nonverbal aggression. *Journal of Personality and Social Psychology,* 1972, *23,* 243–248.

Pastore, N. The role of arbitrariness in the frustration-aggression hypothesis. *Journal of Abnormal and Social Psychology,* 1952, *47,* 728–731.

Patterson, G. R., Littman, R. A., & Bricker, W. Assertive behavior in children: A step toward a theory of aggression. *Monographs of the Society for Research in Child Development,* 1967, *32*(5, Serial No. 113).

Pavlov, I. P. [*Conditioned reflexes*] (W. H. Anrep, trans.). London: Oxford University Press, 1927.

Pavlov, I. P. Experimental psychology and psychopathology in animals (1903). In I. P. Pavlov, *Lectures on conditioned reflexes.* New York: International Publishers, 1928.

Peeples, D. R., & Teller, D. Y. Color vision and brightness discrimination in two-month-old human infants. *Science,* 1975, *189,* 1102–1103.

Perkins, C. C., Jr. The relation of secondary reward to gradients of reinforcement. *Journal of Experimental Psychology,* 1947, *37,* 377–392.

Peterson, L. R., & Peterson, M. J. Short-term retention of individual verbal items. *Journal of Experimental Psychology,* 1959, *58,* 193–198.

Peterson, R. C., & Thurstone, L. L. *Motion pictures and the social attitudes of children.* New York: Macmillan, 1933.

Pisano, R., & Taylor, S. Reduction of physical aggression: The effects of four strategies. *Journal of Personality and Social Psychology,* 1971, *19,* 237–242.

Pliskoff, S. S. Effects of symmetrical and asymmetrical changeover delays on concurrent performances. *Journal of the Experimental Analysis of Behavior,* 1971, *16,* 249–256.

Pomerantz, J. R. Pattern goodness and speed of encoding. *Memory and Cognition,* 1977, *15,* 235–241.

Popper, K. R. *The logic of scientific discovery.* New York: Basic Books, 1959.

Posnansky, C. J. Probing for the functional stimuli in serial learning. *Journal of Experimental Psychology,* 1972, *96,* 184–193.

Postman, L. The history and present status of the law of effect. *Psychological Bulletin,* 1947, *44,* 489–563.

Postman, L., Stark, K., & Fraser, J. Temporal changes in interference. *Journal of Verbal Learning and Verbal Behavior,* 1968, *7,* 672–694.

Postman, L., Stark, K., & Henschel, D. Conditions of recovery after unlearning. *Journal of Experimental Psychology Monograph,* 1969, *82,* 1–24.

Premack, D., Schaeffer, W. W., & Hundt, A. Reinforcement of drinking by running: Effect of fixed ratio and reinforcement time. *Journal of the Experimental Analysis of Behavior,* 1964, *7,* 91–96.

Prentice, W. C. H. The systematic psychology of Wolfgang Kohler. In S. Koch (Ed.), *Psychology: A study of a science. Vol. 1, Sensory, perceptual and physiological formulations.* New York: McGraw-Hill, 1969.

Prinzemetal, W., & Banks, W. P. Good continuation affects visual detection. *Perception and Psychophysics,* 1977, *21,* 389–395.

Ramond, C. K. Performance in instrumental learning as a joint function of delay of reinforcement and time of deprivation. *Journal of Experimental Psychology,* 1954, *47,* 248–250.

Rapoport, A. The promise and pitfalls of information theory. *Behavioral Science,* 1956, *1,* 303–309.

Razran, G. The dominance-contiguity theory of the acquistion of classical conditioning. *Psychological Bulletin,* 1957, *54,* 1–46.

Razran, G. Empirical codifications and specific theoretical implications of compound-stimulus conditioning: Perception. In W. F. Prokasy (Ed.), *Classical conditioning: A symposium.* New York: Appleton-Century-Crofts, 1965.

Rescorla, R. A. Pavlovian conditioning and its proper control procedures. *Psychological Review,* 1967, *74,* 71–80.

Rescorla, R. A. Probability of shock in the presence and absence of CS in fear conditioning. *Journal of Comparative and Physiological Psychology,* 1968, *66,* 1–5.

Rescorla, R. A. Conditioned inhibition of fear resulting from negative CS-US contingencies. *Journal of Comparative Physiological Psychology*, 1969, 67, 504–509. (a)

Rescorla, R. A. Pavlovian conditioned inhibition. *Psychological Bulletin*, 1969, 72, 77–94. (b)

Rescorla, R. A. Second-order conditioning: Implications for theories of learning. In F. J. McGuigan & C. B. Lunsden (Eds.), *Contemporary approaches to conditioning and learning*. New York: Wiley, 1973.

Rescorla, R. A. A model of Pavlovian conditioning. In V. S. Rusinov (Ed.), *Mechanisms of formation and inhibition of conditional reflex*. Moscow: Academy of Science of the USSR, 1974.

Rescorla, R. A. Pavlovian second-order conditioning: Some implications for instrumental behavior. In H. Davis & H. Hurwitz (Eds.), *Pavlovian-operant interactions*. Hillsdale, N.J.: Lawrence Erlbaum Associates, 1977.

Rescorla, R. A., & Holland, P. C. Some behavioral approaches to the study of learning. In M. R. Rosenzweig & E. L. Bennett (Eds.), *Neural mechanisms of learning and memory*. Cambridge, Mass.: MIT Press, 1976.

Rescorla, R. A., & Lolordo, V. M. Inhibition of avoidance behavior. *Journal of Comparative and Physiological Psychology*, 1965, 59, 406–412.

Rescorla, R. A., & Solomon, R. L. Two process learning theory: Relationships between Pavlovian conditioning and instrumental learning. *Psychological Review*, 1967, 74, 151–182.

Rescorla, R. A., & Wagner, A. R. A theory of Pavlovian conditioning: Variations in the effectiveness of reinforcement and nonreinforcement. In A. H. Black & W. F. Prokasy (Eds.), *Classical conditioning II: Current research and theory*. New York: Appleton-Century-Crofts, 1972.

Revusky, S., & Garcia, J. Learned associations over long delays. In G. H. Bower (Ed.), *The Psychology of Learning and Motivation* (Vol. 4). New York: Academic Press, 1970.

Reynolds, G. S. An analysis of interactions in a multiple schedule. *Journal of the Experimental Analysis of Behavior*, 1961, 4, 107–117. (a)

Reynolds, G. S. Behavioral contrast. *Journal of the Experimental Analysis of Behavior*, 1961, 4, 57–71. (b)

Reynolds, G. S. Some limitations on behavioral contrast and induction during successive discrimination. *Journal of the Experimental Analysis of Behavior*, 1963, 6, 131–139.

Reynolds, G. S. *A primer of operant conditioning* (2nd ed.). Glenview, Ill.: Scott, Foresman, 1975.

Reynolds, G. S., & Limpo, A. J. On some causes of behavioral contrast. *Journal of the Experimental Analysis of Behavior*, 1968, 11, 543–547.

Reynolds, G. S., & McLeod, A. On the theory of interresponse-time reinforcement. In G. H. Bower (Ed.), *The psychology of learning and motivation* (Vol. 4). New York: Academic Press, 1970.

Rhine, R. J. The 1964 Presidential election and curves of information seeking and avoidance. *Journal of Personality and Social Psychology*, 1967, 5, 416–423.

Riddleberger, A. B., & Motz, A. B. Prejudice and perception. *American Journal of Sociology*, 1957, 62, 498–503.

Riley, D. R. *Discrimination learning*. Boston: Allyn & Bacon, 1968.

Rilling, M. Stimulus control and inhibitory processes. In W. K. Honig & J. E. R. Staddon (Eds.), *Handbook of operant behavior*. Englewood Cliffs, N.J.: Prentice-Hall, 1977.

Ritchie, B. F. Studies in spatial learning III: Two paths to the same location and two paths to two different locations. *Journal of Experimental Psychology*, 1947, 37, 25–38.

Rizley, R. C., & Rescorla, R. A. Associations in second-order conditioning and sensory preconditioning. *Journal of Comparative and Physiological Psychology*, 1971, 81, 1–11.

Robbins, D. Partial reinforcement: A selective review of the alleyway literature since 1960. *Psychological Bulletin*, 1971, 76, 415–431.

Roberts, W. A. The effects of shifts in magnitude of reward on runway performance in immature and adult rats. *Psychonomic Science*, 1966, *5*, 37–38.

Robinson, D. N. *An intellectual history of psychology*. New York: Collier Macmillan, 1976.

Rokeach, M. *The open and closed mind*. New York: Basic Books, 1960.

Rosen, A. J. Incentive-shift performance as a function of magnitude and number of sucrose rewards. *Journal of Comparative and Physiological Psychology*, 1965, *59*, 378–384.

Rosenberg, M. J. When dissonance fails: On eliminating evaluation apprehension from attitude measurement. *Journal of Personality and Social Psychology*, 1965, *1*, 28–42.

Rosenberg, M. J. The conditions and consequences of evaluation apprehension. In R. Rosenthal & R. L. Rosnow (Eds.), *Artifact in behavioral research*. New York: Academic Press, 1969.

Rosenfeld, H. M., & Baer, D. M. Unnoticed verbal conditioning of an aware experimenter by a more aware subject: The double agent effect. *Psychological Review*, 1969, *76*, 425–432.

Rosenthal, R. On the social psychology of the psychological experiment: The experimenter's hypothesis as unintended determinant of the experimental results. *American Scientist*, 1963, *51*, 268–283.

Rosenthal, R. *Experimenter effects in behavioral research*. New York: Appleton-Century-Crofts, 1966.

Rosenthal, R. Interpersonal expectations: Effects of the experimenter's hypothesis. In R. Rosenthal & R. L. Rosnow (Eds.), *Artifact in behavioral research*. New York: Academic Press, 1969.

Rosenthal, R., & Fode, K. L. Three experiments in experimenter bias. *Psychological Reports*, 1963, *12*, 491–511.

Rosenthal, R., & Rosnow, R. L. (Eds.). *Artifact in behavioral research*. New York: Academic Press, 1969.

Rosnow, R. L., & Rosenthal, R. Volunteer effects in behavioral research. *New directions in psychology*, 1970, *4*, 211–269.

Rothaus, P., & Worchel, P. The inhibition of aggression under nonarbitrary frustration. *Journal of Personality*, 1960, *28*, 108–117.

Rule, B. G. Classical conditioning and causal attributions in human aggression. Paper presented at the meeting of the Midwestern Psychological Association, Chicago, May 1977.

Rule, B. G., & Hewitt, L. S. Effects of thwarting on cardiac response and physical aggression. *Journal of Personality and Social Psychology*, 1971, *19*, 181–187.

Rule, B. G., & Nesdale, A. R. Differing functions of aggression. *Journal of Personality*, 1974, *42*, 467–481.

Rundus, D. Output order and rehearsal in multi-trial free recall. *Journal of Verbal Learning and Verbal Behavior*, 1974, *13*, 656–663.

Sahakian, W. S. *History and systems of psychology*. New York: Wiley, 1975.

Salapatek, P., & Kessen, W. Visual scanning of triangles by the human newborn. *Journal of Experimental Child Psychology*, 1966, *3*, 155–167.

Salapatek, P., & Kessen, W. Prolonged investigation of a plane geometric triangle by the human newborn. *Journal of Experimental Child Psychology*, 1973, *15*, 22–29.

Savage, C. W. *The measurement of sensation: A critique of perceptual psychophysics*. Berkeley: University of California Press, 1970.

Schachter, S. *The psychology of affiliation*. Stanford, Cal.: Stanford University Press, 1959.

Schaie, K. W. (Ed.). *Theory and methods of research on aging*. Morgantown: West Virginia University, 1968.

Schrier, A. M. Reinforcement variables and response rates of monkeys (Macaca mulatta). *Journal of Comparative and Physiological Psychology*, 1965, *59*, 378–384.

Schulz, R. W. Mediation. In C. P. Duncan, L. Sechrest, & A. W. Melton (Eds.), *Human memory: Festschrift in honor of Benton J. Underwood*. New York: Appleton-Century-Crofts, 1972.

Schulz, R. W., & Lovelace, E. A. Mediation in verbal paired-associate learning: The role of temporal factors. *Psychonomic Science,* 1964, *1,* 95-96.

Schulz, R. W., & Weaver, G. E. The A-B, B-C, A-C mediation paradigm: The effects of variation in A-C study- and test-interval lengths and strength of A-B or B-C. *Journal of Experimental Psychology,* 1968, *76,* 303-311.

Schulz, R. W., Weaver, G. E., & Ginsburg, S. Mediation with pseudomediation controlled: Chaining is not an artifact! *Psychonomic Science,* 1965, *2,* 169-170.

Schumsky, D. A., Grasha, A. F., Eimer, E. O., & Trinder, J. Intra-list interference in single trial short-term memory. *Psychonomic Science,* 1967, *9,* 545-546.

Schuster, R., & Rachlin, H. Indifference between punishment and free shock: Evidence for the negative law of effect. *Journal of the Experimental Analysis of Behavior,* 1968, *11,* 777-786.

Scott, W. A., & Wertheimer, M. *Introduction to psychological research.* New York: Wiley, 1962.

Sears, R. R. Relation of early socialization experiences to aggression in middle childhood. *Journal of Abnormal and Social Psychology,* 1961, *63,* 466-492.

Sebastian, R. J. Immediate and delayed effects of victim suffering on the attacker's aggression. *Journal of Research in Personality,* in press.

Segal, E. M., & Lachman, R. Complex behavior or higher mental process: Is there a paradigm shift? *American Psychologist,* 1972, *27,* 46-55.

Seidel, R. J. A review of sensory preconditioning. *Psychological Bulletin,* 1959, *56,* 58-73.

Seligman, M. E. P., & Maier, S. F. Failure to escape traumatic shock. *Journal of Experimental Psychology,* 1967, *74,* 1-9.

Sgro, J. A., & Weinstock, S. Effects of delay on subsequent running under immediate reinforcement. *Journal of Experimental Psychology,* 1963, *66,* 260-263.

Shapiro, M. M. Salivary conditioning in dogs during fixed-interval reinforcement contingent upon lever-pressing. *Journal of the Experimental Analysis of Behavior,* 1961, *4,* 361-364.

Shapiro, M. M. Temporal relationship between salivation and lever-pressing with differential reinforcement of low rates. *Journal of Comparative and Physiological Psychology,* 1962, *55,* 567-571.

Shaw, M. E., & Costanzo, P. R. *Theories of social psychology.* New York: McGraw-Hill, 1970.

Sheafor, P. J., & Gormezano, I. Effects of US magnitude on one-trial per day classical reward conditioning of the rabbit's jaw-movement response. *Proceedings of the Annual Convention of the American Psychological Association,* 1971, *6* (Pt. 1), 27-28.

Sheafor, P. J., & Gormezano, I. Conditioning of the rabbit's (Oryctolagus cuniculus) jaw-movement response: US magnitude effects on URs, CRs, and pseudo-CRs. *Journal of Comparative and Physiological Psychology,* 1972, *81,* 449-452.

Shemberg, K. M., Leventhal, D. B., & Allman, L. Aggression machine performance and rated aggression. *Journal of Experimental Research in Personality,* 1968, *3,* 117-119.

Shimp, C. P. Optimum behavior in free-operant experiments. *Psychological Review,* 1969, *76,* 97-112.

Shimp, C. P. Perspective on the behavioral unit: Choice behavior in animals. In W. K. Estes (Ed.), *Handbook of learning and cognitive processes* (Vol. 2). Hillsdale, N.J.: Lawrence Erlbaum Associates, 1975.

Shuell, T. J. Retroactive inhibition in free-recall learning of categorized lists. *Journal of Verbal Learning and Verbal Behavior,* 1968, *7,* 797-805.

Shuell, T. J., & Keppel, G. A further test of the chaining hypothesis of serial learning. *Journal of Verbal Learning and Verbal Behavior,* 1967, *6,* 439-445.

Sidman, M. Normal sources of pathological behavior. *Science,* 1960, *132,* 61-68. (a)

Sidman, M. *Tactics of scientific research: Evaluating experimental data in psychology.* New York: Basic Books, 1960. (b)

Siegel, S., & Domjan, M. Backward conditioning as an inhibitory procedure. *Learning and Motivation,* 1971, *2,* 1-11.

Sigall, H., Aronson, E., & Van Hoose, T. The cooperative subject: Myth or reality? *Journal of Experimental Social Psychology, 1970, 6,* 1-10.

Sigall, H., & Page, R. Current stereotypes: A little fading, a little faking. *Journal of Personality and Social Psychology, 1971, 18,* 247-255.

Silberberg, A., & Fantino, E. Choice, rate of reinforcement, and the changeover delay. *Journal of the Experimental Analysis of Behavior, 1970, 13,* 187-197.

Simon, H. A. How big is a chunk? *Science, 1974, 183,* 482-488.

Singer, J. L. The influence of violence portrayed in television or motion pictures upon overt aggressive behavior. In J. L. Singer (Ed.), *The control of aggression and violence: Cognitive and physiological factors.* New York: Academic Press, 1971.

Skinner, B. F. *The behavior of organisms: An experimental analysis.* New York: Appleton-Century-Crofts, 1938.

Skinner, B. F. Are theories of learning necessary? *Psychological Review, 1950, 57,* 193-216.

Slaby, R. G. Verbal regulation of aggression and altruism. In J. deWit & W. W. Hartup (Eds.), *Determinants and origins of aggressive behavior.* Hague: Mouton, 1974.

Slepian, D. (Ed.). *Key papers in the development of information theory.* New York: IEEE Press, 1973.

Snodgrass, J. G. Psychophysics. In B. Scharf (Ed.), *Experimental sensory psychology.* Glenview, Ill.: Scott, Foresman, 1975.

Sokolov, E. N. *Perception and the conditioned reflex.* New York: Pergamon Press, 1963.

Solomon, R. L., & Brush, E. S. Experimentally derived conceptions of anxiety and aversion. In M. R. Jones (Ed.), *Nebraska symposium on motivation* (Vol. 4). Lincoln, Nebraska: University of Nebraska Press, 1956.

Solomon, R. L., & Turner, L. H. Discriminative classical conditioning in dogs paralyzed by curare can later control discriminative avoidance responses in the normal state. *Psychological Review, 1962, 69,* 202-219.

Spear, N. E., Hill, W. F., & O'Sullivan, D. J. Acquisition and extinction after initial trials without reward. *Journal of Experimental Psychology, 1965, 69,* 25-29.

Spence, K. W. *Behavior theory and conditioning.* New Haven: Yale University Press, 1956.

Spence, K. W. The emphasis on basic functions. In M. H. Marx (Ed.), *Theories in contemporary psychology.* New York: Macmillan, 1963.

Spence, K. W., Haggard, D. F., & Ross, L. E. Intrasubject conditioning as a function of the intensity of the unconditioned stimulus. *Science, 1958, 128,* 774-775. (a)

Spence, K. W., Haggard, D. F., & Ross, L. E. UCS intensity and the associative (habit) strength of the eyelid CR. *Journal of Experimental Psychology, 1958, 55,* 404-411. (b)

Sperling, G. The information available in brief visual presentations. *Psychological Monographs, 1960, 74*(11, Whole No. 498).

Sperling, S. E. Reversal learning and resistance to extinction: A review of the rat literature. *Psychological Bulletin, 1965, 63,* 281-297. (a)

Sperling, S. E. Reversal learning and resistance to extinction: A supplementary report. *Psychological Bulletin, 1965, 64,* 310-312. (b)

Staats, A. W. Experimental demand characteristics and the classical conditioning of attitudes. *Journal of Personality and Social Psychology, 1969, 11,* 187-192.

Staats, A. W., & Staats, C. K. Attitudes established by classical conditioning. *Journal of Abnormal and Social Psychology, 1958, 57,* 37-40.

Stebbins, W. C. *Animal psychophysics: The design and conduct of sensory experiments.* New York: Appleton-Century-Crofts, 1970.

Stein, A. H., & Friedrich, L. K. Impact of television on children and youth. In E. M. Hetherington (Ed.), *Review of child development research* (Vol. 5). Chicago: University of Chicago Press, 1975.

Steinberg, D. D. Light sensed through receptors in the skin. *American Journal of Psychology, 1966, 79,* 324-328.

Sternberg, S. High-speed scanning in human memory. *Science, 1966, 153,* 652-654.

Stevens, S. S. Mathematics, measurement, and psychophysics. In S. S. Stevens (Ed.), *Handbook of experimental psychology*. New York: Wiley, 1951.

Stevens, S. S. Ratio scales, partition scales, and confusion scales. In H. Gulliksen & S. Messick (Eds.), *Psychological scaling: Theory and applications*. New York: Wiley, 1960.

Stevens, S. S. Psychophysics of sensory function. In W. A. Rosenblith (Ed.), *Sensory communication*. New York: Wiley, 1961. (a)

Stevens, S. S. To honor Fechner and repeal his law. *Science*, 1961, *133*, 80–86. (b)

Stevens, S. S. *Psychophysics: Introduction to its perceptual, neural and social prospects*. New York: Wiley, 1975.

Stevens, S. S., & Davis, H. *Hearing*. New York: Wiley, 1938.

Stevens, S. S., & Galanter, E. Ratio scales and category scales for a dozen perceptual continua. *Journal of Experimental Psychology*, 1957, *54*, 377–411.

Stevens, S. S., Volkmann, J., & Newman, E. B. A scale for the measurement of the psychological magnitude pitch. *Journal of the Acoustical Society of America*, 1937, *8*, 185–190.

Swets, J. A. Is there a sensory threshold? *Science*, 1961, *134*, 168–177.

Swets, J. A. (Ed.). *Signal detection and recognition by human observers: Contemporary readings*. New York: Wiley, 1964.

Swets, J. A. The relative operating characteristic in psychology. *Science*, 1973, *182*, 990–1000.

Swets, J. A., Tanner, W. P., & Birdsall, T. G. Decision processes in perception. *Psychological Review*, 1961, *68*, 301–340.

Tait, R. W., Marquis, H. A., Williams, R., Weinstein, L., & Suboski, M. D. Extinction of sensory preconditioning using CER training. *Journal of Comparative and Physiological Psychology*, 1969, *69*, 170–172.

Tanner, W. P., Swets, J. A., & Green, D. M. Some general properties of the hearing mechanism. University of Michigan: Electronic Defense Group, Technical Report No. 30, 1956. In J. A. Swets (Ed.), *Signal detection and recognition by human observers: Contemporary readings*. New York: Wiley, 1964.

Tarpy, R. M., & Sawabini, F. L. Reinforcement delay: A selective review of the last decade. *Psychological Bulletin*, 1974, *81*, 984–997.

Taylor, J. A. A personality scale of manifest anxiety. *Journal of Abnormal and Social Psychology*, 1953, *48*, 285–290.

Taylor, S. P. Aggressive behavior and physiological arousal as a function of provocation and the tendency to inhibit aggression. *Journal of Personality*, 1967, *35*, 297–310.

Taylor, S. P., & Gammon, C. B. Effects of type and dose of alcohol on human physical aggression. *Journal of Personality and Social Psychology*, 1975, *32*, 169–175.

Theios, J., & Dunaway, J. E. One-way versus shuttle avoidance conditioning. *Psychonomic Science*, 1964, *1*, 251–252.

Theios, J., Lynch, A. D., & Lowe, W. F., Jr. Differential effects of shock intensity on one-way and shuttle avoidance conditioning. *Journal of Experimental Psychology*, 1966, *72*, 294–299.

Thistlethwaite, D. A critical review of latent learning and related experiments. *Psychological Bulletin*, 1951, *48*, 97–129.

Thompson, R. F. The search for the engram. *American Psychologist*, 1976, *31*, 209–227.

Thompson, R. F., & Spencer, W. A. Habituation: A model phenomenon for the study of neuronal substrates of behavior. *Psychological Review*, 1966, *73*, 16–43.

Thonnard, F. J. *A short history of philosophy*. New York: Society of St. John the Evangelist, 1956.

Thorndike, E. L. Animal intelligence: An experimental study of the associative processes in animals. *Psychological Monographs*, 1898, *2*(4, Whole No. 8).

Thorngate, W. Must we always think before we act? *Personality and Social Psychology Bulletin*, 1976, *2*, 31–35.

Thune, L. E. The effect of different types of preliminary activities on subsequent learning of paired-associate material. *Journal of Experimental Psychology*, 1950, *40*, 423–428.

Thune, L. E. Warm-up effect as a function of level of practice in verbal learning. *Journal of Experimental Psychology*, 1951, *42*, 250–256.

Thurstone, L. L. A law of comparative judgment. *Psychological Review*, 1927, *34*, 273–286.

Thurstone, L. L. *Multiple-factor analysis*. Chicago: University of Chicago Press, 1947.

Thurstone, L. L., & Chave, E. J. *The measurement of attitude*. Chicago: University of Chicago Press, 1929.

Toch, H. H. *Violent men: An inquiry into the psychology of violence*. Chicago: Aldine, 1969.

Tognacci, L. N., & Cook, S. W. Conditioned autonomic responses as bidirectional indicators of racial attitude. *Journal of Personality and Social Psychology*, 1975, *31*, 137–144.

Tolman, E. C., & Honzik, C. H. Introduction and removal of reward and maze performance in rats. *University of California Publication in Psychology*, 1930, *4*, 257–275.

Tolman, E. C., Ritchie, B. F., & Kalish, D. Studies in spatial learning: I. Orientation and the short-cut. *Journal of Experimental Psychology*, 1946, *36*, 13–24. (a)

Tolman, E. C., Ritchie, B. F., & Kalish, D. Studies in spatial learning: II. Place learning versus response learning. *Journal of Experimental Psychology*, 1946, *36*, 221–229. (b)

Tolman, E. C., Ritchie, B. F., & Kalish, D. Studies in spatial learning: IV. The transfer of place learning to other starting paths. *Journal of Experimental Psychology*, 1947, *37*, 39–47. (a)

Tolman, E. C., Ritchie, B. F., & Kalish, D. Studies in spatial learning: V. Response learning versus place learning by the non-correction method. *Journal of Experimental Psychology*, 1947, *37*, 285–292. (b)

Torgerson, W. S. *Theory and methods of scaling*. New York: Wiley, 1958.

Trapold, M. A., & Fowler, H. Instrumental escape performance as a function of the intensity of noxious stimulation. *Journal of Experimental Psychology*, 1960, *60*, 323–326.

Trapold, M. A., & Overmier, J. B. The second learning process in instrumental learning. In A. H. Black & W. F. Prokasy (Eds.), *Classical conditioning II: Current research and theory*. New York: Appleton-Century-Crofts, 1972.

Tulving, E. When is recall higher than recognition? *Psychonomic Science*, 1968, *10*, 53–54.

Turner, C. W., & Simons, L. S. Effects of subject sophistication and evaluation apprehension on aggressive responses to weapons. *Journal of Personality and Social Psychology*, 1974, *30*, 341–348.

Turnure, J., Buium, N., & Thurlow, M. The effectiveness of interrogatives for promoting verbal elaboration productivity in young children. *Child Development*, 1976, *47*, 851–855.

Underwood, B. J. *Experimental psychology: An introduction*. New York: Appleton-Century-Crofts, 1949.

Underwood, B. J. *Psychological research*. New York: Appleton-Century-Crofts, 1957.

Underwood, B. J. Degree of learning and the measurement of forgetting. *Journal of Verbal Learning and Verbal Behavior*, 1964, *3*, 112–129.

Underwood, B. J. *Experimental Psychology* (2nd Ed.). New York: Appleton-Century-Crofts, 1966.

Underwood, B. J. Individual differences as a crucible in theory construction. *American Psychologist*, 1975, *30*, 128–134.

Underwood, B. J., Runquist, W. N., & Schulz, R. W. Response learning in paired-associate lists as a function of intralist similarity. *Journal of Experimental Psychology*, 1959, *58*, 70–78.

Underwood, B. J., & Shaughnessy, J. H. *Experimentation in psychology*. New York: Wiley, 1975.

Waddell, D., Gans, S., Kempner, P., & Williams, A. A comparison of place and response learning in very young rats. *Journal of Comparative and Physiological Psychology*, 1955, *48*, 375–377.

Wagner, A. R. Elementary associations. In H. H. Kendler & J. T. Spence (Eds.), *Essays in neobehaviorism: A memorial volume to Kenneth W. Spence.* New York: Appleton-Century-Crofts, 1971.

Walberg, H. J. Physics, femininity, and creativity. *Developmental Psychology,* 1969, *1,* 47–54.

Wallach, L., & Sprott, R. L. Inducing number conservation in children. *Child Development,* 1964, *35,* 1057–1071.

Walters, R. H., & Brown, M. Studies of reinforcement of aggression: III. Transfer of responses to an interpersonal situation. *Child Development,* 1963, *34,* 563–571.

Walters, R. H., & Thomas, E. L. Enhancement of punitiveness by visual and audio-visual displays. *Canadian Journal of Psychology,* 1963, *17,* 244–255.

Wanschura, P. B., & Borkowski, J. G. The development and transfer of mediational strategies by retarded children in paired-associate learning. *American Journal of Mental Deficiency,* 1974, *78,* 631–639.

Wanschura, P. B., & Borkowski, J. G. Long term transfer of a mediational strategy by moderately retarded children. *American Journal of Mental Deficiency,* 1975, *80,* 323–333.

Ward, L. M., & Lockhead, G. R. Response system processes in absolute judgment. *Perception and Psychophysics,* 1971, *9,* 73–78.

Ward, W. D., Glorig, A., & Sklar, D. L. Dependence of temporary threshold shift at 4kc on intensity and time. *Journal of the Acoustical Society of America,* 1958, *30,* 944–954.

Wasserman, E. A., Franklin, S., & Hearst, E. Pavlovian appetitive contingencies and approach vs. withdrawal to conditioned stimuli in pigeons. *Journal of Comparative and Physiological Psychology,* 1974, *86,* 616–627.

Watson, C. S. Psychophysics. In B. B. Wolman (Ed.), *Handbook of general psychology.* Englewood Cliffs, N.J.: Prentice-Hall, 1973.

Watson, C. S., Rilling, M. E., & Bourbon, W. T. Receiver-operating characteristics determined by a mechanical analog to the rating scale. *Journal of the Acoustical Society of America,* 1964, *36,* 283–288.

Watson, J. B. Psychology as the behaviorist views it. *Psychological Review,* 1913, *20,* 158–177.

Watson, J. B. *Behaviorism.* New York: Norton, 1925.

Waugh, N. C., & Norman, D. A. Primary memory. *Psychological Review,* 1965, *72,* 89–104.

Webb, E. J., Campbell, D. T., Schwartz, R. D., & Seechrest, L. *Unobtrusive measures: Nonreactive research in the social sciences.* Chicago: Rand McNally, 1966.

Weber, S. J., & Cook, T. D. Subject effects in laboratory research: An examination of subject roles, demand characteristics, and valid inferences. *Psychological Bulletin,* 1972, *77,* 273–295.

Weimer, W. B. Overview of a cognitive conspiracy: Reflections on this volume. In W. B. Weimer & D. S. Palermo (Eds.), *Cognition and the symbolic processes.* Hillsdale, N.J.: Lawrence Erlbaum Associates, 1975.

Weinstock, S. Resistance to extinction of a running response following partial reinforcement under widely spaced trials. *Journal of Comparative and Physiological Psychology,* 1954, *47,* 318–322.

Weinstock, S. Acquisition and extinction of a partially reinforced running response at a 24-hour intertrial interval. *Journal of Experimental Psychology,* 1958, *46,* 151–158.

Welford, T. A. *Skilled performance: Perceptual and motor skills.* Glenview, Ill.: Scott, Foresman, 1976.

West, S. G., Berkowitz, L., Sebastian, R. J., & Parke, R. D. The effects of viewing physical aggression on verbal aggression in delinquent girls. Paper presented at the meeting of the Eastern Psychological Association, New York, April 1976.

Weyl, H. *Philosophy of mathematics and natural science.* Princeton, N.J.: Princeton University Press, 1949.

Whitman, T., Snyder, C., & Anderson, D. C. Seven failures to control human heart rate with contingent reinforcement. Paper presented at Midwestern Psychological Association, Chicago, May 1974.

Wickelgren, W. A. Coding, retrieval, and dynamics of multitrace associative memory. In L. W. Gregg (Ed.), *Cognition in learning and memory.* New York: Wiley, 1972.

Wickens, D. D. Compound conditioning in humans and cats. In W. F. Prokasy (Ed.), *Classical conditioning: A symposium.* New York: Appleton-Century-Crofts, 1965.

Wickens, D. D., Born, D. G., & Allen, C. K. Proactive inhibition and item similarity in short-term memory. *Journal of Verbal Learning and Verbal Behavior,* 1963, *2,* 440-445.

Wickens, D. D., & Clark, S. E. Osgood dimensions as an encoding class in short-term memory. *Journal of Experimental Psychology,* 1968, *78,* 580-584.

Wicker, A. W. Attitudes versus actions: The relationship of verbal and overt behavioral responses to attitude objects. *Journal of Social Issues,* 1969, *25,* 41-78.

Williams, D. R. Classical conditioning and incentive motivation. In W. F. Prokasy (Ed.), *Classical conditioning: A symposium.* New York: Appleton-Century-Crofts, 1965.

Williams, J. F., Meyerson, L. J., Eron, L., & Semler, I. J. Peer-related aggression and aggressive responses elicited in an experimental situation. *Child Development,* 1967, *38,* 181-189.

Willis, R. H. Two dimensions of conformity-nonconformity. *Sociometry,* 1963, *26,* 499-513.

Wolf, K. Properties of multiple conditioned reflex type II activity. *Acta Biologiae Experimentalis Sinica,* 1963, *23,* 133-150.

Wolfe, B. M., & Baron, R. A. Laboratory aggression related to aggression in naturalistic social situations: Effects of an aggressive model on the behavior of college student and prison observers. *Psychonomic Science,* 1971, *24,* 193-194.

Wollen, K. A., Allison, T. S., & Lowry, D. H. Associative symmetry versus independent association. *Journal of Verbal Learning and Verbal Behavior,* 1969, *8,* 283-288.

Woodmansee, J. J. The pupil response as a measure of social attitudes. In G. F. Summers (Ed.), *Attitude measurement.* Chicago: Rand McNally, 1970.

Woodworth, R. S., & Schlosberg, H. *Experimental psychology* (Rev. ed.). New York: Holt, Rinehart and Winston, 1954.

Young, P. T., & Madsen, C. H., Jr. Individual isohedons in sucrose-sodium chloride and sucrose-saccharin gustatory areas. *Journal of Comparative and Physiological Psychology,* 1963, *56,* 903-909.

Young, R. K. Tests of three hypotheses about the effective stimulus in serial learning. *Journal of Experimental Psychology,* 1962, *63,* 307-313.

Young, R. K., Saegert, J., & Linsley, D. Retention as a function of meaningfulness. *Journal of Experimental Psychology,* 1968, *78,* 89-94.

Zajonc, R. B. Attitudinal effects of mere exposure. *Journal of Personality and Social Psychology Monograph Supplement,* 1968, *9,* 1-27.

Zavalloni, M., & Cook, S. W. Influence of judges' attitudes on ratings of favorableness of statements about a social group. *Journal of Personality and Social Psychology,* 1965, *1,* 43-54.

Zeaman, D. An application of the $_sE_r$ quantification procedure. *Psychological Review,* 1949, *56,* 341-350. (a)

Zeaman, D. Response latency as a function of the amount of reinforcement. *Journal of Experimental Psychology,* 1949, *39,* 466-483. (b)

Zener, K. The significance of behavior accompanying conditioned salivary secretion for theories of the conditioned response. *American Journal of Psychology,* 1937, *50,* 384-403.

Zillman, D. Excitation transfer in communication-mediated aggressive behavior. *Journal of Experimental Social Psychology,* 1971, *7,* 419-434.

Zillman, D., & Cantor, J. R. Effect of timing of information about mitigating circumstances on emotional responses to provocation and retaliatory behavior. *Journal of Experimental Social Psychology,* 1976, *12,* 38-55.

Zuriff, G. E. A comparison of variable-ratio and variable-interval schedules of reinforcement. *Journal of the Experimental Analysis of Behavior,* 1970, *13,* 369-374.

Name Index

Subject Index